Microsoft® Office 2000
MICROSOFT® CERTIFIED EDITION

Pamela R. Toliver

Yvonne Johnson

Philip A. Koneman
Colorado Christian University

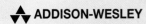 **ADDISON-WESLEY**

An imprint of Addison Wesley Longman, Inc.

Reading, Massachusetts • Menlo Park, California • New York • Harlow, England
Don Mills, Ontario • Sydney • Mexico City • Madrid • Amsterdam

Executive Editor: Michael Roche
Acquisitions Editor: Anita Devine
Project Manager: Deanna Storey
Assistant Editor: Holly Rioux
Senior Marketing Manager: Tom Ziolkowski
Production Services: Elm Street Publishing Services, Inc.
Composition and Art: Gillian Hall, The Aardvark Group
Cover Images: © 1999 PhotoDisc, Inc.
Cover and Interior Designer: Leslie Haimes
Design Supervisor: Regina Hagen
Manufacturing: Tim MacDonald

Addison-Wesley Publishing Company
One Jacob Way
Reading, MA 01867
http://www.prenhall.com/select

1 2 3 4 5 6 7 8 9 10-DOW-02010099

Dedication

To my wife, Tanya, and our children, Megan, Jonathan, and Andrew.
Thank you for supporting me during this project. —PAK

This book is dedicated to the memory of my mother-in-law, Juanita Hupp Toliver,
one of the most learned and well-read people I've ever known—except about computers.
May her experience surfing the Web have provided her insight into my world. —PT

This book is dedicated to the "real" Rachel Crawford,
an intelligent and energetic young woman who, like the fictional character in this book,
will make her mark on the world. —YJ

Individual Acknowledgments from Pamela R. Toliver

No work of this magnitude is ever the work only of the authors. Once again, I find myself
trying to remember all the people I'm supposed to thank as I try not to leave anyone out.

For John—my husband and best friend—my sounding board, my support—thanks for visiting me weekends in my office.

For my daughter Lori who worked with me to develop meaningful exercises, thanks.

For my friends who listened, thank you—it can't always have been easy.

Individual Acknowledgments from Yvonne Johnson

I would also like to thank my husband for putting up with me during some of the
stressful times and my sons for their insights into the "college" mind.

Preface

The SELECT Lab Series uses a class-tested, highly visual, project-based approach that teaches students through tasks that use step-by-step instructions. You will find extensive 4-color figures that guide learners through the basic skills and procedures necessary to demonstrate proficiency using each software application.

SELECT: Projects for Microsoft® Office 2000 introduces an all-new design with ample space for note taking. The easy-to-follow, clean presentation uses bold color and a unique design program that helps reduce distraction and keeps students focused and interested as they work. We have developed additional instructional features to further enhance the students' learning experience as well as provide the opportunity for those who want to go beyond the scope of the book to explore the features of Office 2000 on the Web. Each project concludes with a review section that includes a Summary, Key Terms and Operations, Study Questions (multiple choice, short answer, fill-in, and discussion), and two Hands-On Exercises. In addition, six On Your Own Exercises provide students the opportunity to practice and gain further experience with the material covered in the projects.

Microsoft Certification

The content of this text is driven by the Microsoft Office User Specialist (MOUS) guidelines, and the author has developed the material from the ground up to reflect these objectives. Everyone who masters the projects in this text will be prepared to take the core level exam in Microsoft® Office 2000. It is becoming more and more important in today's competitive job market to have the skills necessary to be productive with today's most widely used applications software. *SELECT: Projects for Microsoft® Office 2000* is designed with this purpose in mind.

Organization

Before launching into the application, *SELECT: Projects for Microsoft® Office 2000* familiarizes students with the operating system and some common elements of Microsoft® Office 2000 applications.

Introduction to Windows

This brief introduction to the operating system can be used with Windows 98, Windows 95, and Windows NT, all three of which support Microsoft® Office 2000. Students become familiar with the Office interface, use a mouse, get Help, and work with multiple programs before launching the software applications.

Common Elements

This all new section was created for *SELECT: Projects for Microsoft® Office 2000* to give students a basic overview of the elements common to the primary Office 2000 software applications. This two-project section introduces students to basic features such as launching and exiting applications, basic file management tasks such as saving and opening files, printing techniques, and common methods for working with text and graphics. This section can be used as a reference throughout the text as students work through the individual applications or included as part of the course overview.

Word 2000

Microsoft® Word 2000 features improved tools that simplify traditional word-processing tasks and adds an expanded menu of Web-related capabilities and e-mail integration. Six new projects in *SELECT: Projects for Microsoft® Word 2000* introduce students to features of Microsoft® Word 2000, focusing on the MOUS objectives needed to prepare students for the core certification exam.

Excel 2000

The new Microsoft® Excel 2000 spreadsheet tools can help you enter and manage your financial and numeric data more efficiently. New features include new date formatting options that address year 2000 concerns, see-through selection, list AutoFill, new cursors that provide visual cues, and improved chart formatting capabilities. Six new *SELECT: Projects for Microsoft® Excel 2000* teach students the certifiable skills and tasks that are important, both for business and for personal use. Students learn how to plan, design and format 3-dimensional workbook solutions.

Access 2000

Microsoft® Access 2000 has been streamlined from previous versions and provides new ways to integrate Access data with the Web. The six projects in this text show students how to use Access 2000 in a real world business scenario they can relate to. Coverage includes all of the objectives necessary for MOUS certification at the core level in Microsoft® Access 2000, as students create and relate tables, design queries, enhance data entry using forms, and publish Access data to the Web.

PowerPoint 2000

Whether you deliver your presentation online or on the Web, the new features in Microsoft® PowerPoint 2000 will make both development and delivery of your presentations much easier. Four visual projects in *SELECT: Projects for Microsoft® PowerPoint 2000* guide students through creating and enhancing presentations, slide show presentation, and master layout development. All core objectives of the MOUS core certification exam are covered in four projects that put students in the driver's seat as they design a store directory and then create a template for the regional offices.

Integrated Projects

Three integrated projects introduce students to the Microsoft® Office 2000 teamwork concept. Students work through step-by-step instructions designed to integrate files and data among Word, Excel, Access, and PowerPoint.

Overview of Internet Explorer 5

The Overview of Internet Explorer 5 introduces students to basic features that will enable them to get information from the Web.

Outlook 2000

The Outlook 2000 section includes information and instructions students need to know to pass the MOUS core level exam. Whether students cover this material in class or explore it on their own, this section is a valuable resource.

Features

 ## Running Case

The Selections, Inc. Department store is an all-new case for *SELECT: Projects for Microsoft® Office 2000*. As a **Running Case**, Selections, Inc. puts students in an environment they can relate to, both as students and as future professionals. Each project begins with a scenario that puts students in the department store where they perform tasks that relate to a particular area or division of the store. Students relate what they're doing in Excel 2000 to a real-world situation that helps prepare them for what they may encounter in the business world as professionals.

Challenge/Strategy/Setup

Once the student is familiar with the Running Case scenario for the project, the **Challenge** explains what they are actually going to do as they work through the tasks, and the **Strategy** summarizes a plan for achieving that goal. The **Setup** provides the settings necessary to ensure that the screen the student sees will match what is shown in the book.

Web Tip

This all-new feature for *SELECT: Projects for Microsoft® Office 2000* provides the student with links to helpful Web sites and tips for locating additional information about specific topics on the World Wide Web. ***Web Tips*** often relate to the Office 2000 suite, but include tips students can use in their everyday lives. Each project contains at least three ***Web Tips*** that encourage students to explore Web sites that relate to the tasks they are performing in the application, highlight professional organizations that enhance the material, or direct them to topics of interest on their own. Because the Web is constantly changing, some links referenced in ***Web Tips*** may become inactive during the course. All ***Web Tips*** links will be updated through the SELECT Web Site at http://www.prenhall.com/select.

Check Point

Check Points are placed at intervals throughout each project and provide review topics students can use to assess their skills or knowledge about related topics or about tasks previously covered.

Break Point

Each project in *SELECT: Projects for Microsoft® Office 2000* has been designed to take approximately one hour in the lab. Because students learn at different paces or may not have a full hour to complete a project, the ***Break Point*** feature appears at about the midpoint in each project and alerts students of a good stopping point if they need a break but want to continue the project later. ***Break Points*** take the guess work out of having to decide whether or not it's appropriate to stop and make it easier for students to start working on a project that they may not have time to complete.

Tips and Troubleshooting Boxes

These feature boxes, popular with both instructors and students, appear throughout the text and have been revised and updated for *SELECT: Projects for Microsoft® Office 2000*.

> **TIP** *Tip boxes* include material that may be useful but that is not required in the step-by-step task instructions.

> **TROUBLESHOOTING** *Troubleshooting boxes* alert students to problems they may encounter while using the applications and suggest possible causes for the problems along with potential solutions.

Modifying Worksheets and Workbooks

Now that you have created the Selections, Inc. Sales Summary workbook, you can modify it so that it is easier to use and provides more information. In this project you will enhance the functionality of the workbook by adding worksheets for additional sales regions, deleting worksheets you no longer need, and repositioning the worksheets in the workbook. In addition, you will move, copy, and delete data, and create formulas that share information among worksheets in the Sales Summary workbook.

Objectives

After completing this project, you will be able to:

➤ Open an Excel workbook
➤ Insert worksheets into a workbook
➤ Delete worksheets from a workbook
➤ Change the position of worksheets in a workbook
➤ Edit worksheets by copying and moving data
➤ Edit worksheets by revising data
➤ Enter additional text and number data into a workbook
➤ Create 3-D formulas that link information among worksheets

Running Case

Mr. Traylor is pleased with the progress you have made so far. He enthusiastically accepted your initial design, and now wants you to finish defining the structure of your workbook to include quarterly sales for the remaining sales regions, and a summary of sales for all regions.

EX-44

The **Introduction** sets the stage for the project and explains its purpose.

Clearly defined and measurable **Objectives** outline the skills covered.

The **Running Case** puts the student in the real-life environment of the Selections, Inc. department store.

The **Challenge** states the reasoning for the project.

The **Strategy** describes the plan for completing the project, which consists of tasks leading to the final product.

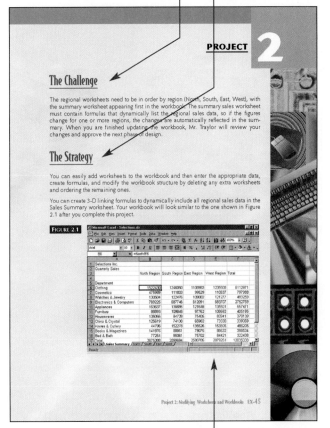

PROJECT 2

The Challenge

The regional worksheets need to be in order by region (North, South, East, West), with the summary worksheet appearing first in the workbook. The summary sales worksheet must contain formulas that dynamically list the regional sales data, so if the figures change for one or more regions, the changes are automatically reflected in the summary. When you are finished updating the workbook, Mr. Traylor will review your changes and approve the next phase of design.

The Strategy

You can easily add worksheets to the workbook and then enter the appropriate data, create formulas, and modify the workbook structure by deleting any extra worksheets and ordering the remaining ones.

You can create 3-D linking formulas to dynamically include all regional sales data in the Sales Summary worksheet. Your workbook will look similar to the one shown in Figure 2.1 after you complete this project.

FIGURE 2.1

Project 2: Modifying Worksheets and Workbooks   EX-45

EX-46

The Setup

Launch Microsoft Excel and make sure that you select the Excel settings listed in Table 2.1. This will ensure that your screen matches the illustrations and that the tasks in this project function as described.

Table 2.1

Location	Make these settings:
Office Shortcut Bar	Right-click the Office icon on the shortcut bar and click Exit.
Office Assistant	Hide the Assistant.
Tools, Customize	Click the Options tab and deselect the option to show recently used menu commands first. Deselect the option to display the Standard and Formatting toolbars on one row.
Tools, Options	Click the Edit tab and select Move selection after Enter.
View, Formula Bar	Display the formula bar.
View, Status Bar	Display the status bar.
View, Normal	View the workbook in Normal view.
Maximize	Maximize the application and workbook windows.

Opening a Workbook

Before you can modify your workbook, you must open it. To open an existing workbook you must specify the file name and location.

TASK 1:   To Open an Excel Workbook

1. Select Open from the File menu.

2. In the File Open dialog box, select drive A.

   TROUBLESHOOTING If you saved your workbook to another location at the conclusion of Project 1, select the appropriate drive letter.

3. Open the Selections folder by double-clicking it, highlight the *Selections.xls* file, and click Open, as shown in Figure 2.2. Depending on your settings, your screen may differ slightly.

The Setup tells the students exactly which settings should be chosen so their computer screens match the illustrations in the book.

An **illustration** shows the typical screen the student will see.

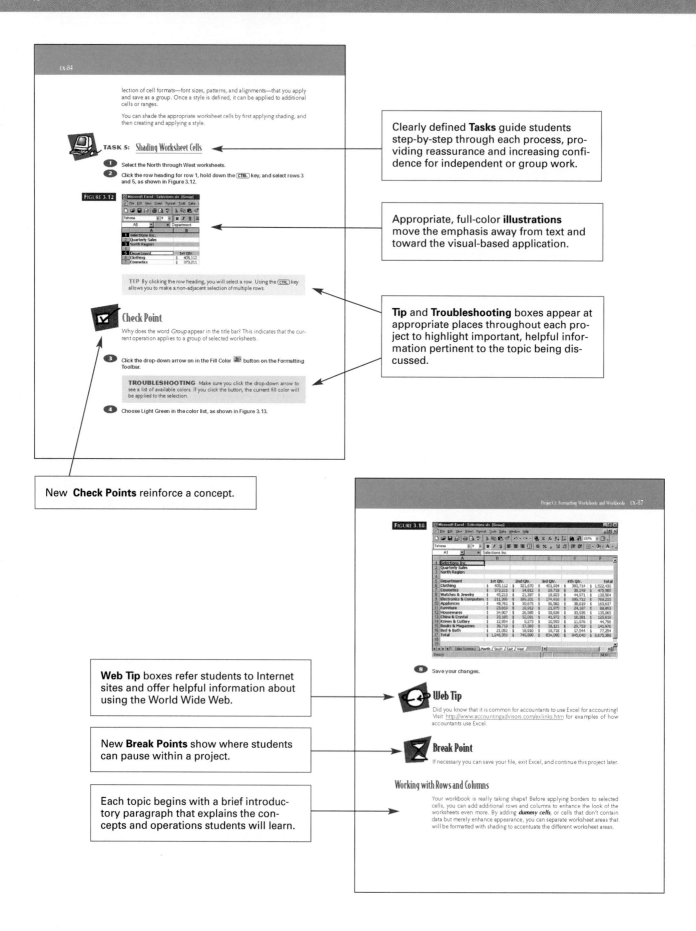

lection of cell formats—font sizes, patterns, and alignments—that you apply and save as a group. Once a style is defined, it can be applied to additional cells or ranges.

You can shade the appropriate worksheet cells by first applying shading, and then creating and applying a style.

TASK 5: Shading Worksheet Cells

1. Select the North through West worksheets.
2. Click the row heading for row 1, hold down the CTRL key, and select rows 3 and 5, as shown in Figure 3.12.

FIGURE 3.12

TIP By clicking the row heading, you will select a row. Using the CTRL key allows you to make a non-adjacent selection of multiple rows.

Check Point

Why does the word *Group* appear in the title bar? This indicates that the current operation applies to a group of selected worksheets.

3. Click the drop-down arrow on in the Fill Color button on the Formatting Toolbar.

TROUBLESHOOTING Make sure you click the drop-down arrow to see a list of available colors. If you click the button, the current fill color will be applied to the selection.

4. Choose Light Green in the color list, as shown in Figure 3.13.

Clearly defined **Tasks** guide students step-by-step through each process, providing reassurance and increasing confidence for independent or group work.

Appropriate, full-color **illustrations** move the emphasis away from text and toward the visual-based application.

Tip and **Troubleshooting** boxes appear at appropriate places throughout each project to highlight important, helpful information pertinent to the topic being discussed.

New **Check Points** reinforce a concept.

Project 3: Formatting Worksheets and Workbooks   EX-87

FIGURE 3.16

8. Save your changes.

Web Tip boxes refer students to Internet sites and offer helpful information about using the World Wide Web.

Web Tip

Did you know that it is common for accountants to use Excel for accounting? Visit http://www.accountingadvisors.com/exlinks.htm for examples of how accountants use Excel.

New **Break Points** show where students can pause within a project.

Break Point

If necessary you can save your file, exit Excel, and continue this project later.

Each topic begins with a brief introductory paragraph that explains the concepts and operations students will learn.

Working with Rows and Columns

Your workbook is really taking shape! Before applying borders to selected cells, you can add additional rows and columns to enhance the look of the worksheets even more. By adding *dummy cells*, or cells that don't contain data but merely enhance appearance, you can separate worksheet areas that will be formatted with shading to accentuate the different worksheet areas.

A **Summary** in bulleted-list format further reinforces the Objectives and the material presented in the project.

Key terms are boldface and italicized throughout each project, and then listed for handy review in the summary section at the end of the project.

Study questions bring the content of the project into focus again and allow for independent or group review of the material learned.

Project 3: Formatting Worksheets and Workbooks EX-97

Summary and Exercises

Summary

- You can easily apply formats to numbers to make them easier to interpret.
- Font formats include size, style, and weight.
- You can easily change the alignment of data in one or more cells.
- A style is a set of formats that are stored with a name.
- Once you create a style, you can apply it to other selections.
- You can insert, delete, and resize the rows and columns in a worksheet.
- You can format cells by applying borders and shading.
- You can use the Web Page Preview to see how a worksheet will display if exported to the Web.

Key Terms and Operations

Key Terms

Borders button	Font Size box
cell alignment	Format Painter
cell border	number formats
cell shading	Select All button
currency style	style
Font box	Universal Document Viewing

Operations

add borders to cells	insert columns
apply font formats	modify number formats
apply number formats	resize columns
apply styles	save worksheets as HTML
change cell alignment	shade worksheet cells
copy number formats	use Web Page Preview
create styles	

Study Questions

Multiple Choice

1. Which of the following is not considered a number format?
   a. percent
   b. altitude
   c. scientific notation
   d. currency

EX-100

3. How does inserting columns into a worksheet differ from inserting worksheets into a workbook?
4. What is Web Page Preview? How does a Web Page Preview differ from a Print Preview?
5. List three common number formats.

Hands-On Exercises

1. Indenting and Rotating Text

Excel supports indenting and rotating text as a method for formatting worksheet data to make it more visually appealing. In this exercise you will indent and rotate text in the Java Sales workbook.

1. Open the *Java Sales 4.xls* workbook.
2. Click the First Qtr worksheet tab to make it the active sheet.
3. Select cells B4:D4.
4. Select Cells from the Format menu.
5. Click the Alignment tab.
6. Change the Horizontal alignment to Center, and click the polygon next to 90 Degrees, as shown in Figure 3.32.

FIGURE 3.32

7. Click OK. Change the font format to bold for the selection.
8. Select cells A5:A8 and click the Increase Indent button on the Formatting toolbar, as shown in Figure 3.33.

In-depth **Hands-On Exercises** present tasks for building on the skills acquired in the project.

Six **On Your Own Exercises** are provided to invoke critical thinking and integration of project skills.

EX-102

FIGURE 3.35

5. Use the Format Painter to apply this format to the range A2:12.
6. Apply formats to the Sales Summary worksheet so that your worksheet appears like the one shown in Figure 3.36.

FIGURE 3.36

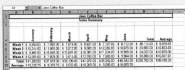

Formatted Sales Summary worksheet for the Java Coffee Bar

8. Save your workbook as *Java Sales 6.xls*.
9. Close the workbook.

On Your Own Exercises

 Web Tip

If you cannot obtain a copy of these files from your instructor, visit the SELECT Web site to download the necessary files: http://www.prenhall/select

1. Formatting the Websites Workbook

Open the *Financial Sites 2.xls* workbook you modified in Project 1. Edit the workbook so it contains borders and shading to accentuate the sites. Save your workbook to the Investments folder with the name *Financial Sites 3.xls*.

2. Formatting Your Class Schedule

Open the *Class Schedule By Day.xls* workbook you modified in Project 2. Apply any formats you deem appropriate to each worksheet in the workbook. Save the workbook as *Class Schedule By Day 2.xls*.

About the Authors

*SELECT: Projects for Microsoft® Office 200*0 is a collaborative effort among three experienced writers and educators: Philip A. Koneman, Pamela R. Toliver, and Yvonne Johnson. This combined effort draws from their diverse experience in higher education and corporate training. The goal of the authors and this text is to provide the user with a solid foundation in the core objectives required for the Microsoft Office User Specialist (MOUS) exam at the level of excellence in presentation that this unique author team is now widely known for.

Philip A. Koneman, Ph.D.

Philip Koneman has over ten years of experience in computers and education. He is an Associate Professor of Computer Information Systems at Colorado Christian University. He teaches many courses in computers, including Introduction to Computer Applications using Microsoft® Office.

Dr. Koneman has a broad professional portfolio that includes a variety of activities outside the university. In addition to being the lead author on *SELECT: Projects for Microsoft® Office 2000*, he is also the Series Consulting Editor for the entire SELECT Lab Series. He is the President of Instructional Design Consultants, Inc., a company that develops educational multimedia.

Dr. Koneman received his Ph.D. in instructional technology from the University of Colorado at Denver. His research interests include computer-based learning, the instructional design of educational testing and measurement, and ethical issues in computers and technology.

As a faculty member teaching Microsoft® Office to our incoming students, I am aware of the challenges we face in trying to adequately cover each application in the Office Suite. We have therefore designed SELECT: Projects for Microsoft® Office 2000 with faculty in mind, and utilize an approach that focuses upon covering the MOUS Certification Objectives for each Office application without overwhelming the learner with complexity. I know our approach works: I use it every semester!

Pamela R. Toliver

Pam Toliver has over fifteen years of experience teaching computers and computer applications in high schools, colleges, universities, and corporate classrooms. In addition to her teaching experience, she is a widely published author of texts for teachers, instructional manuals for corporations, and both high school and college textbooks.

Mrs. Toliver is an Expert level certified Microsoft Office User Specialist. She holds a bachelor's degree in business education from Southern Illinois University and a master's degree in Vocational Industrial and Technical Education from Louisiana State University.

Software training reaches beyond the classroom into all areas of the "real world." Interesting students in computer applications by incorporating case scenarios they can apply outside the classroom helps educators bridge the gap between education and work—a plus when students enter the job market.

Yvonne Johnson

Yvonne Johnson is currently the president of R and C Limited, a consulting firm that specializes in computer courseware development and computer training. She owned her own computer training center for twelve years and is an Expert level certified Microsoft Office User Specialist. Her technical expertise and knowledge of software is wide and varied. She has written over 20 computer books for major publishers, and she has practical experience in the fields of publishing, legal, public relations and marketing, corporate training, and higher education.

She received her bachelor's degree in education from the Centre College of Kentucky and did her master's work at the University of South Florida.

Supplements

Student Assessment Software   *SkillCheck Professional Plus for Microsoft® Office 2000* features fully interactive test items that allow students to answer questions by performing complete tasks in virtually any correct way the software allows. All of the essential software features are all fully simulated, so no additional software is required. In addition to independently validated tests that cover beginning, intermediate, and advanced skills, each SkillCheck Professional Plus system includes a database of more than 100 interactive questions for each Office application. The instructor has complete control over every important aspect of testing and reporting, allowing users to customize or create tests with ease and speed.

Companion Web Site   *SELECT: Projects for Microsoft® Office 2000* is accompanied by a Companion Web site. Interactive online study guides offer interactive quizzes, chat rooms, and much more to help students with the material covered in the text.

Instructor Supplements

Instructor's Resource CD-ROM   Instructors get extra support for this text from supplemental materials, including the Instructor's Resource CD-ROM with screen shots, diagrams, and tables from the text, and files that correspond to key figures in the book that can be used as electronic slides. Screen-by-screen steps in a project can be displayed in class or reviewed by students in the computer lab. The Instructor's Resource CD-ROM also includes the entire Instructor's Manual in Microsoft Word format, and Test Manager™, a computerized test bank designed to create printed tests, network tests, and self-assessment quizzes. Student data files and completed data files for Study Questions, Hands-On Exercises, and On Your Own Exercises are also on the Instructor's Resource CD-ROM.

Test Manager   Test Manager™ is a comprehensive suite of tools for testing and assessment. Test Manager™ allows educators to create and distribute tests for their courses, by printing and distributing through traditional methods or by on-line delivery via a Local Area Network (LAN) server. Four question formats are available: multiple choice, true/false, matching, and completion exercises. Answer keys and page references for test questions are provided.

Printed Supplements   The Instructor's Manual includes a test bank and transparency masters for each project in the student text, as well as Expanded Student Objectives, Answers to Study Questions, and Additional Assessment Techniques. The test bank contains two separate tests with answers and consists of multiple choice, true/false, and fill-in questions referenced to pages in the student text. Transparency masters illustrate key concepts and screen captures from the text.

Acknowledgments from the Authors

To Deanna Storey, Anita Devine, and Holly Rioux at Addison-Wesley: Thanks, Deanna, for going above and beyond the call of duty in making this work possible. You have truly been the best project manager any author could hope to work with. Thank you, Anita, for your insight, attention to detail, and great success in weaving our individual writing styles into a seamless whole. Thanks, Holly, for making sure our work meets each and every required certification objective. For getting this work into print, thanks to the Elm Street Publishing staff and especially to Michele Heinz; it has been a delight to work with you.

Acknowledgments

Addison-Wesley Publishing Company would like to thank the following reviewers for their valuable contributions to the *SELECT Lab Series*.

James Agnew
Northern Virginia CC

Joseph Aieta
Babson College

Dr. Muzaffar Ali
Bellarmine College

John Anderson
Northeastern State University

Tom Ashby
Oklahoma CC

Bob Barber
Lane CC

Gina Bowers
Harrisburg Area CC

Robert Caruso
Santa Rosa Junior College

Robert Chi
California State
Long Beach

Pat Coulter
Pennsylvania Technical
College

Jill Davis
State University of New
York at Stony Brook

Fredia Dillard
Samford University

George Dollar
Clearwater Christian
College

Peter Drexel
Plymouth State College

David Egle
University of Texas, Pan
American

Linda Ericksen
Lane CC

Jonathan Frank
Suffolk University

Rebecca Gatlin
University of Central
Arkansas

Patrick Gilbert
University of Hawaii

Maureen Greenbaum
Union County College

Sally Ann Hanson
Mercer County CC

Sunil Hazari
East Carolina University

Ric Heismann
Northern Virginia CC

Gloria Henderson
Victor Valley College

Bruce Herniter
University of Hartford

Rick Homkes
Purdue University

Lisa Jackson
Henderson CC

Cyntia Kachik
Santa Fe CC

Vincent Kayes
Mount St. Mary College

Bennett Kramer
Massasoit CC

Charles Lake
Faulkner State Junior
College

Ron Leake
Johnson County CC

Randy Marak
Hill College

Charles Mattox, Jr.
St. Mary's University

Jim McCullough
Porter and Chester
Institute

Gail Miles
Lenoir-Rhyne College

Steve Moore
University of South
Florida

Karen Mounce
Somerset CC

Anthony Nowakowski
Buffalo State College

Gloria Oman
Portland State University

John Passafiume
Clemson University

Leonard Presby
William Paterson College

Louis Pryor
Garland County CC

Michael Reilly
University of Denver

Dick Ricketts
Lane CC

Dennis Santomauro
Kean College of New
Jersey

Pamela Schmidt
Oakton CC

Gary Schubert
Alderson-Broaddus College

Mike Scroggins
Southwest Missouri State
University

T. Michael Smith
Austin CC

Cynthia Thompson
Carl Sandburg College

Marion Tucker
Northern Oklahoma College

JoAnn Weatherwax
Saddleback College

David Whitney
San Francisco State
University

James Wood
Tri-County Technical
College

Judy Wynekoop
University of Texas

Minnie Yen
University of Alaska,
Anchorage

Allen Zilbert
Long Island University

Contents

Overview of Windows

Overview of Windows

Windows is an ***operating system***, a special kind of computer program that performs three major functions. First, an operating system controls the actual ***hardware*** of the computer (the screen, the keyboard, the disk drives, and so on). Second, an operating system enables other software programs such as word processing or spreadsheet applications to run. Finally, an operating system determines how the user operates the computer and its programs or applications.

As an operating system, Windows and all other programs written to run under it provide ***graphics*** (or pictures) called ***icons*** to carry out commands and run programs. For this reason, Windows is referred to as a ***graphical user interface*** or GUI (pronounced gooey). You can use the keyboard or a device called a ***mouse*** to activate the icons.

This overview explains the basics of Windows so that you can begin using your computer quickly and easily. In general, the information in this chapter is applicable to Windows 95, Windows 98, and Windows NT 4.0.

Objectives

After completing this project, you will be able to:

➤ Identify the desktop elements

➤ Use a mouse

➤ Use the basic features of Windows

➤ Get help

➤ Work with multiple programs

➤ Exit Windows

Identifying the Desktop Elements

Because Windows is an operating system, it launches immediately when you turn on the computer. Depending on the way your computer is set up, you may have to type your user name and password to log on (to gain access to the program). After Windows launches, the working environment, called the ***desktop***, appears on the screen. Figure W.1 shows what a typical desktop might look like if you are using Windows 95, or the classic look of Windows 95 as the desktop style for Windows 98. If you are viewing the desktop as a Web page, the desktop may still look similar to Figure W.1, but the labels under the icons may be underlined. Table W.1 describes the icons that appear on the desktop.

FIGURE W.1

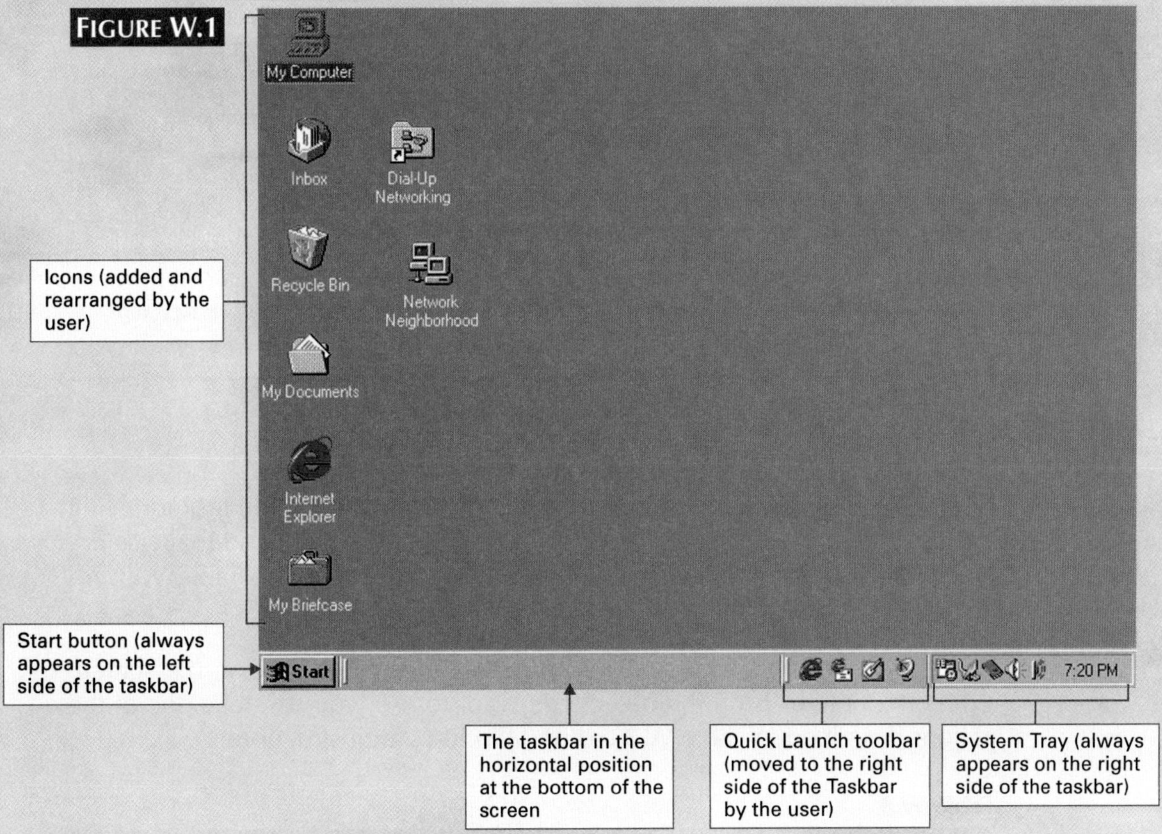

My Computer
Inbox
Dial-Up Networking
Recycle Bin
Network Neighborhood
My Documents
Internet Explorer
My Briefcase
Start
7:20 PM
Icons (added and rearranged by the user)
Start button (always appears on the left side of the taskbar)
The taskbar in the horizontal position at the bottom of the screen
Quick Launch toolbar (moved to the right side of the Taskbar by the user)
System Tray (always appears on the right side of the taskbar)

Table W.1

Icon	Description
My Computer	Enables you to organize your work and easily access your files and system folders.
Recycle Bin	Stores files that have been deleted from the hard disk. Files stored in the Recycle Bin can be restored to their original locations, if necessary.
Internet Explorer	Starts Internet Explorer, a program that browses the World Wide Web and provides access to other Internet services.
My Briefcase	Synchronizes files that are worked on using different computers.
Network	Accesses all the devices (drives, printers, and so on) on a network to **Neighborhood** which you've been granted access.

At the bottom of the desktop is the **_taskbar_**, used for displaying the Start menu, starting programs, checking the status of various software and hardware components (such as the date and time or the volume control), and switching between programs. Table W.2 describes the elements of the taskbar.

Table W.2

Taskbar Element	Description
Start button	Displays the Start menu, which has commands for launching programs, opening documents, finding documents, and so on.
Taskbar toolbars	Provide access to useful buttons. There are four taskbar toolbars available: the Quick Launch, Address, Links, and Desktop toolbars. Only the Quick Launch toolbar displays by default. It has buttons for launching Internet Explorer and other frequently used programs. It also has a Show Desktop button that you can use to quickly see the desktop without minimizing windows. You can display the other toolbars by right-clicking the taskbar and selecting a toolbar from the Toolbars menu.
System Tray	Contains icons for programs that are running in memory and displays the system time.

Using a Mouse

A pointing device such as a mouse is almost an indispensable tool for using Windows. Although you can use the keyboard to navigate and make selections, using a mouse is often more convenient and efficient. Table W.3 describes the actions that the mouse performs.

When you move the mouse on your desk, a pointer moves on the screen. When the pointer is on the object you want to use, you can take one of the actions described in Table W.3 to give Windows an instruction.

Table W.3

Action	Description
Point	Slide the mouse across a smooth surface (preferably a mouse pad) until the pointer on the screen is on the object.
Click	Press and release the left mouse button once.
Drag	Press and hold down the left mouse button while you move the mouse and then release the mouse button to complete the action.
Right-click	Press and release the right mouse button once. Right-clicking usually displays a shortcut menu.
Double-click	Press and release the left mouse button twice in rapid succession.

Windows interprets the instruction given by the mouse action based on the version of Windows or the desktop style that is used. For example, when you click the mouse once using Windows 95 or the classic Windows 95 style for Windows 98, Windows selects the item. If you double-click the mouse, Windows selects and executes. If you are viewing the desktop as a Web page, pointing is equivalent to clicking and clicking is equivalent to double-clicking.

> **TROUBLESHOOTING** The steps in the Tasks in this chapter assume that Windows 95 or the classic Windows 95 desktop style is in use. If you are using the Web page style desktop, you might want to deactivate it by right-clicking the desktop and choosing Active Desktop, View As Web Page.

TASK 1: To Use the Mouse

1 Point to the My Computer icon, press and hold down the left mouse button, and then drag the mouse across the desk. The icon moves.

> **TROUBLESHOOTING** If the icon appears to snap back to its original location, turn off the Auto Arrange command by right-clicking the desktop and choosing Arrange Icons, Auto Arrange.

2 Drag the My Computer icon back to its original location.

3 Right-click the icon. A shortcut menu opens.

FIGURE W.2

4 Click a blank space on the screen. The shortcut menu closes.

5 Double-click the My Computer icon. A window titled My Computer opens.

FIGURE W.3

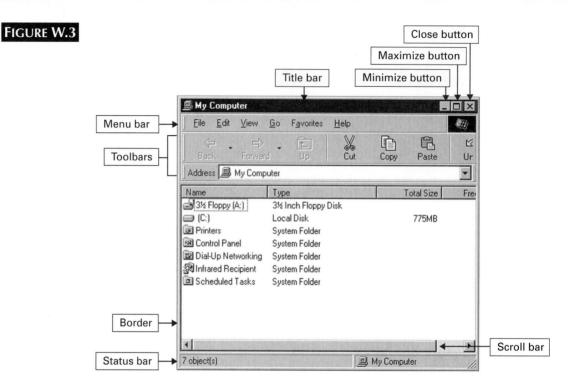

TIP Do not close this window, as you will manipulate it in the next task.

Using the Basic Features of Windows

The basic features of Windows are windows, menus, dialog boxes, and toolbars. These features are used in all programs that are written to run under Windows.

Using Windows

A *window* is one of the basic elements of the Windows operating system. All programs launched in Windows occupy a window. Figure W.3 shows the common elements of a window.

The *menu bar* displays options for performing *commands*. The *status bar* displays information such as menu descriptions and the size of files. The *borders* outline the boundaries of the window. The *scroll bars* let you see the entire contents. The *Close button*, the *maximize button* (which changes to a *Restore button*), and the *Minimize button* appear at the top right. Toolbars contain several specialized buttons. The *title bar* displays the application name.

TASK 2:   To Work with a Window

1 Click the Maximize ⬜ button if it is displayed. If it is not displayed, click the Restore 🔳 button, and then click the Maximize button. The Maximize button changes to a Restore button and the window occupies the entire screen.

2 Click the Minimize ➖ button. The My Computer window is no longer visible on the desktop. The taskbar now contains a My Computer button.

FIGURE W.4

3 Click the My Computer button on the taskbar. The window becomes the current application.

4 Click the Restore 🔳 button.

5 Point to the right border of the My Computer window until the pointer changes to a double-headed black arrow, and then drag the border to make the window as narrow as shown in Figure W.5.

6 Drag the bottom border up so the window matches the size shown in Figure W.5.

7 Click ⬜. The window occupies the entire screen.

8 Click 🔳. The window returns to its former size.

9 Click the Close ❌ button. The My Computer window closes.

FIGURE W.5

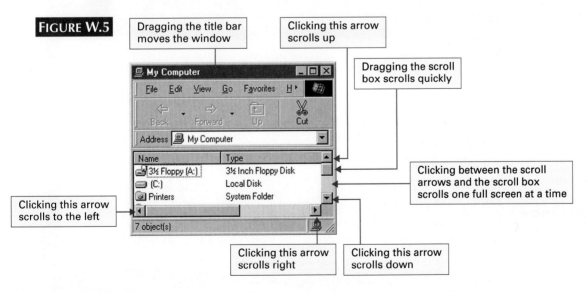

Dragging the title bar moves the window

Clicking this arrow scrolls up

Dragging the scroll box scrolls quickly

Clicking between the scroll arrows and the scroll box scrolls one full screen at a time

Clicking this arrow scrolls to the left

Clicking this arrow scrolls right

Clicking this arrow scrolls down

Using Menus and Toolbars

Almost every program, including Windows itself, uses various types of **menus** and **toolbars** to make commands accessible to the user. In most cases, you can perform the same command either by using the menus or by using a button on a toolbar.

> **TIP** Toolbar buttons and keyboard shortcuts are considered faster methods than menus for accomplishing common tasks.

Using Menus

Windows and Windows programs use several types of menus. One type of menu is the **drop-down menu**, appears when you make a selection from a menu bar. The menu bar in most programs appears at the top of the window under the title bar. Drop-down menus may also be referred to as **pop-up menus**. This term describes the way the menu displays when the menu bar is moved to the bottom of the screen. The Start menu in Windows is an example of a pop-up menu.

Figure W.6 shows a Word menu with many elements common to the menus used in other Windows programs. An option with an ellipsis displays a dialog box. Dimmed options are not available in the current circumstance.

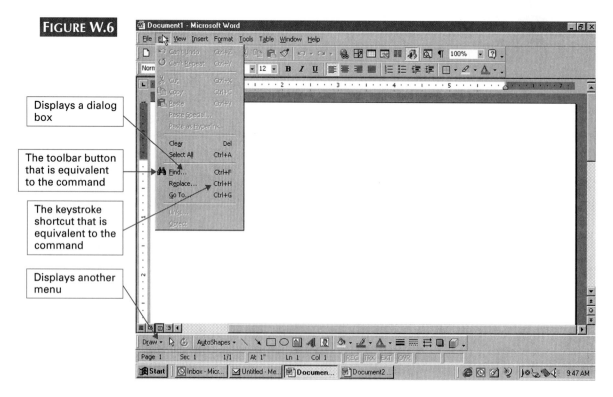

FIGURE W.6

Displays a dialog box

The toolbar button that is equivalent to the command

The keystroke shortcut that is equivalent to the command

Displays another menu

The shortcut menu that you saw in Task 1 is a ***context-sensitive menu***. This means that the menu displays only those options that are appropriate to the context, or current task. For example, in Task 1, when you right-clicked the My Computer icon, a shortcut menu opened with options that pertain only to My Computer. If you had right-clicked the Recycle Bin, a different shortcut menu would have opened. Shortcut menus are always displayed by right-clicking an object or an area of the screen.

You can select menu options, whether in a menu bar, a drop-down menu, or a shortcut menu, by clicking the option. If you prefer to use keystrokes, you can type the underlined letter for the option. To select an option from the menu bar, first press (ALT) to activate the menu bar and then type the under-lined letter of the option.

> **TIP** Because you can select menu commands in two ways, the steps with in-structions to select a menu command will use the word *choose* instead of dic-tating the method of selection.

Using Toolbars

Many programs have multiple toolbars. The buttons on a toolbar are usually related in some way, or the toolbar is a multipurpose toolbar, and the buttons are grouped by related functions.

To use a toolbar button, click the button; Windows takes an immediate ac-tion, depending on the button's function. Some toolbar buttons perform commands; others display drop-down lists or dialog boxes.

> **TIP** If you don't know what a button on the toolbar does, point to the button; a ***ToolTip***, a brief description of the button, appears near the button.

TASK 3: To Use Menus and Toolbars

1 Click the Start button, point to Programs, and click Windows Explorer. The Exploring window opens.

2 Choose View from the menu bar. The View drop-down menu appears.

3 Choose Large Icons if it is not already selected.

FIGURE W.7

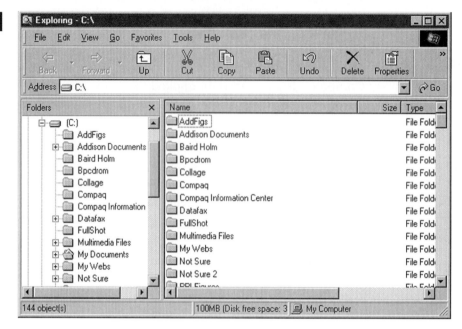

4 If the toolbar is not displayed, choose View Toolbars (in Windows 95) or View, Toolbars, Standard Buttons (in Windows 98).

5 Click the down arrow on the Views button and choose Details. The Details view appears. This can be the most helpful view when you are performing file maintenance because it displays the most information about a file.

6 Click ⊠.

Using Dialog Boxes

When many options are available for a single task, Windows conveniently groups the options in one place, called a ***dialog box***. Some functions have so many options that Windows divides them further into groups and places them on separate pages in the dialog box. Figure W.8 shows an example of a dialog box with three pages.

FIGURE W.8

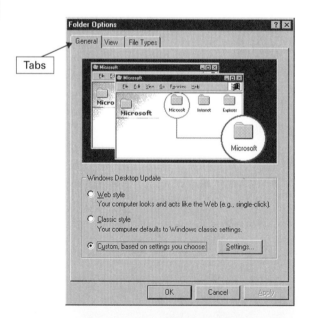

Working with Multiple Programs

The Windows **multitasking** feature allows you to launch multiple programs and switch back and forth between them. A button on the taskbar represents each open program, as each program is a specific task the user is accomplishing.

Check Point

When you run multiple applications, more than one program is running, but only one program is active at any given time.

TASK 4:   To Switch between Windows

① Click Start and point to Programs. The Programs menu appears.

② Point to Accessories and click Paint. Maximize the window if necessary.

FIGURE W.9

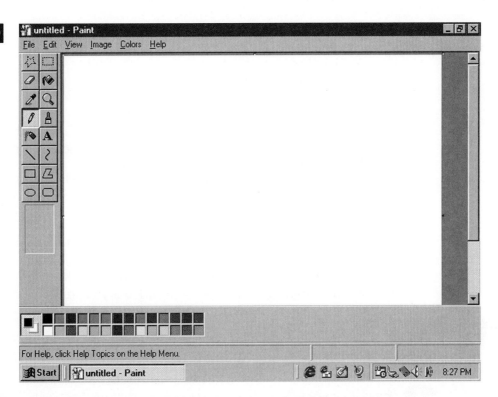

③ Choose File, Open, and select the Windows folder for Look in. Then double-click on any file name that has a *.bmp* extension. The file opens.

④ Click Start, point to Programs, point to Accessories, and click WordPad. The WordPad window opens.

⑤ Type **What do you think of this graphic?** and press (ENTER) twice.

6 Click on the Paint button on the taskbar. Windows switches to the Paint program.

7 Choose Edit, Select all. The graphic is selected.

8 Choose Edit, Copy. Windows copies the image to the Windows Clipboard.

9 Click the WordPad button on the taskbar. Windows switches to the WordPad program.

10 Choose Edit, Paste. The graphic file appears at the insertion point in the WordPad file.

11 Choose File, Save. The Save As dialog box opens.

12 Specify the drive and folder where you save your files in the Look in text box.

13 Type **My File** for File name and choose Save. The file is saved and the dialog box closes.

> **TIP** You also can use the keyboard shortcut (ALT) + (TAB) to switch between programs.

Getting Help

Instead of opening a Windows reference book, you can get help right at your computer using the Windows *Help* feature. Windows provides you with three methods of accessing help information: You can look up information in a table of contents; you can search for information in an index; or you can find a specific word or phrase in a database maintained by the Find feature.

Additionally, Windows provides context-sensitive help, called *What's This?* for the topic you are working on. This type of help is generally found in dialog boxes.

After you learn to use Help in Windows, you can use help in any Office 2000 application. The Help feature in Windows 98 is a little different from the Help feature in Windows 95. Perform Task 5 if you are using Windows 95 as your operating system; perform Task 6 if you are using Windows 98.

TASK 5: <u>To Use Help in Windows 95</u>

1 Click the Start button on the taskbar and click Help. The Help window opens.

2 Click the Contents tab if a different page is displayed. The Contents page appears.

3 Double-click Tips and Tricks, and then double-click For setting up the desktop efficiently. The topics on this subject appear.

4 Double-click Putting shortcuts on the desktop. The Help topic opens.

5 Choose Help Topics and then click the Index tab. The Index page of the Help feature appears.

6 Type **calculator**. The list scrolls to the first occurrence of the word calculator.

7 Double-click *starting*. The Help topic appears.

8 Choose Help Topics and then click the Find tab. The Find page of the Help feature appears.

9 Type **print** and click Find Now if necessary. A list of topics that contain the word *print* appears.

10 Double-click Changing printer settings. The Help topic appears.

11 Click the button in the first step. The Printers folder opens.

12 Select any printer that is listed (as instructed in the second step in the Help topic) and choose File, Properties (as instructed in the third step in the Help topic). The Properties dialog box opens.

13 Click the What's This button ⍰ as instructed in the Help Tips, and then click any option in the dialog box. A pop-up box with an explanation of the option appears.

14 Click the pop-up box to hide it and then close the Properties dialog box as well as the Help topic.

TASK 6: <u>To Use Help in Windows 98</u>

1 Click the Start button on the taskbar and click Help. The Help window opens.

2 Click the Contents tab if a different page is displayed. The Contents page appears.

3 Click Using Windows Accessories. The topic expands.

4 Click Calculator.

FIGURE W.10

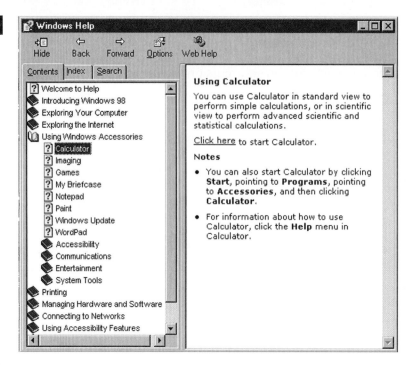

5 Click the Index tab, scroll the list, and double-click Active Desktop. The topic displays in the right pane.

6 Click the Search tab, type **print** in the text box and select List Topics. The topics display in the Topics list at the bottom of the dialog box.

7 Double-click To change printer settings. The topic appears in the right pane.

8 Click the Hide ⟨⟩ button on the toolbar. The left pane closes.

FIGURE W.11

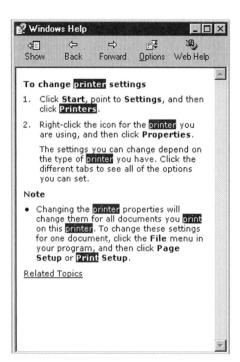

9 Click the Show ⟨⟩ button. The left pane appears again.

10 Click the Options 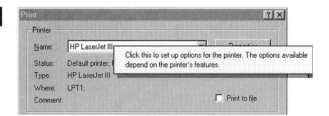 button. A drop-down menu appears.

11 Choose Print. The Print dialog box opens.

12 Click the What's This ? button. A question mark is attached to the mouse pointer.

13 Click the Properties button. An explanation appears.

FIGURE W.12

Print	? X
Printer	

Name: HP LaserJet III
Click this to set up options for the printer. The options available depend on the printer's features.
Status: Default printer;
Type: HP LaserJet III
Where: LPT1:
Comment: ☐ Print to file

14 Read the message and then click it. The message closes.

15 Click X in the Print dialog box.

16 Click X. The Help dialog box closes.

> **TIP** You can print any help article by right-clicking anywhere in the article and choosing Print Topic.

Exiting Windows

When you are ready to turn off the computer, you must exit Windows first. You should never turn off the computer without following the proper exit procedure because Windows has to do some utility tasks before it shuts down. Unlike most of us, Windows likes to put everything away when it's finished. When you shut down improperly, you can cause serious problems in Windows.

TASK 7: <u>To Exit Windows</u>

1 Click the Start button and then click Shut Down.

2 In Windows 95, choose Shut down the computer?, and then choose Yes. In Windows 98, choose Shut down, and then choose OK.

3 When the message "It's now safe to turn off your computer" appears, turn off the computer.

> **TROUBLESHOOTING** You may not see a message that says "It's now safe to turn off your computer." If you are using a computer in a lab, follow the shutdown procedures used by the lab. Instead of choosing Shut down (the computer) and turning off the computer, you may be instructed to choose Close all programs and log on as a different user and leave the computer on.

Summary

- Windows is an operating system with a graphical interface.
- The working environment is called the desktop.
- The Start menu has commands for launching programs and opening documents.
- The mouse gives instructions to Windows, which Windows interprets based on the interface that is in use.
- A window has a border, sizing buttons, a Close button, and other elements that are unique to a window.
- Menus and toolbars contain commands for performing procedures.
- Dialog boxes display options for commands.
- You can get help right at your computer using the Windows Help feature.
- You can copy, rename, move, delete, and restore files.
- The multitasking feature of Windows allows you to launch multiple programs and switch between them as you are working.
- You must exit Windows properly to allow Windows to perform its necessary functions.

Key Terms and Operations

Key Terms

command	My Briefcase
Close button	My Computer
context-sensitive menu	Network Neighborhood
desktop	operating system
dialog box	pop-up menu
drop-down menu	Recycle Bin
Graphical User Interface	Restore button
graphics	scroll bar
hardware	shortcut menu
Help	Start button
icons	status bar
Internet Explorer	taskbar
Maximize button	title bar
menu	toolbar
menu bar	ToolTip
Minimize button	What's This?
mouse	window
multitasking	window border

Operations

click	open a window
double-click	point
drag	right-click
exit Windows	switch between windows
launch a program	

Common Elements
In Office 2000

Basic Common Elements

O ne of the greatest advantages of using the ever-popular Microsoft Office suites is the number of features common to all programs that make up the office suite. Microsoft Office 2000 takes full advantage of many common elements. The increased number of common elements means that techniques you learn in one Office 2000 application can be used to accomplish the same task in other Office 2000 applications. This section introduces you to many of the features common to Office 2000 applications and describes some of the unique twists you'll find with these common features as you move from application to application in Microsoft Office 2000.

Objectives

After completing this project, you will be able to:

➤ Launch applications

➤ Perform basic file management tasks

➤ Use Help

➤ Select printers and print

➤ Exit applications

Launching Applications

Office 2000 offers a variety of techniques for launching applications. The procedure you use will depend on how Office 2000 is installed on your computer and your personal preference.

To launch Office 2000 applications, use one of the following procedures:
- Click Start, Programs, and then click the Office 2000 application you want to launch.

FIGURE 1.1

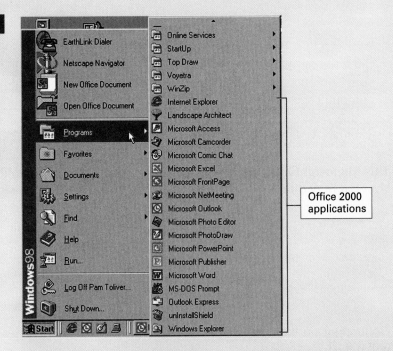

Office 2000 applications

TROUBLESHOOTING If shortcuts to the Office 2000 applications do not appear on your Programs list, click the arrow button at the bottom of the Programs list to scroll until the applications appear.

- Click Start, New Office Document, and then double-click the Blank file type that represents the application you want to launch. The application required to create the file launches. Blank files are identified by type on the General page of the dialog box. Design templates are grouped by type on additional pages of the dialog box.

FIGURE 1.2

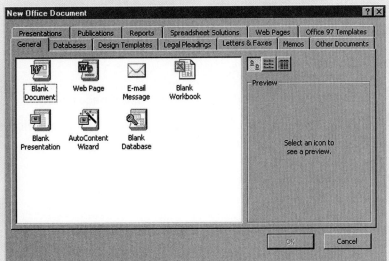

> **TIP** Office 2000 also offers a series of professionally designed file formats called ***templates*** that you can choose to create your file. Simply click the tab for the type of file you want to create, click a template name, and review the template preview.

- Double-click an application shortcut icon on the desktop.
- Click the application icon on the Microsoft Office Bar, if it is installed on your computer. The Microsoft Office Bar usually appears at the top of the computer screen when it is installed.

FIGURE 1.3

This Microsoft Office Bar has been customized to display application icons. Your bar may differ from the one shown here

> **TIP** You can also launch an Office 2000 application by selecting an Office file on the Start menu Documents list or by selecting the file in the Exploring or My Computer window. When you click a file shown on the Documents list, or double-click a filename in the Exploring or My Computer window, the application used to create the file launches and the file opens.

Depending on the application you launch, the item that appears on-screen will differ:

- Word and Excel display new files: Word displays a new blank document. Excel displays a new blank workbook template.
- Access and PowerPoint display dialog boxes that contains options for creating a new file or opening an existing file.

Because Word makes accessing and using all the common elements covered in this section easy, it was chosen as the application to introduce many of these features. The procedures for launching Word 2000 described here should be accessible from all computers on which Office 2000 is installed.

TASK 1:   Launching Microsoft Word 2000

1 Choose Start, Programs.

2 Scroll to the bottom of the Programs list, if necessary.

3 Click Microsoft Word. Screen elements common to all Microsoft Office 2000 applications are identified in Figure 1.4.

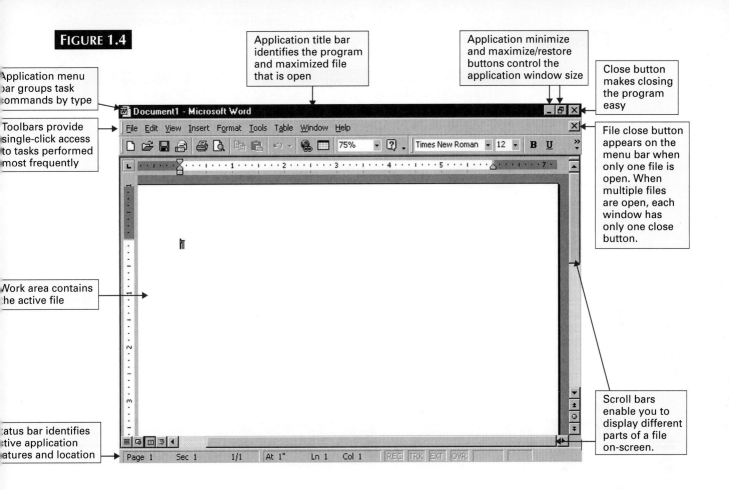

FIGURE 1.4

Application menu bar groups task commands by type

Application title bar identifies the program and maximized file that is open

Application minimize and maximize/restore buttons control the application window size

Close button makes closing the program easy

Toolbars provide single-click access to tasks performed most frequently

File close button appears on the menu bar when only one file is open. When multiple files are open, each window has only one close button.

Work area contains the active file

Status bar identifies active application features and location

Scroll bars enable you to display different parts of a file on-screen.

Performing Basic File Management Tasks

Basic file management tasks include opening files, creating new files, saving files, and editing file properties. The procedures for accomplishing these tasks are similar in all Office 2000 applications.

Opening Files

Office 2000 provides a number of different procedures that you can use to open an existing document, workbook, presentation, or database. The Open dialog box has been redesigned in Office 2000 and presents a Web-like look. To open a file:

- Choose File, Open.
- Click the Open 📂 button on the Standard toolbar.
- Press (CTRL) + O.
- Choose Start, Open Office Document.

Regardless of which of these four procedures you use, an Open dialog box similar to the one shown in Figure 1.5 appears. Features of the Open dialog box are described in Table 1.1.

FIGURE 1.5

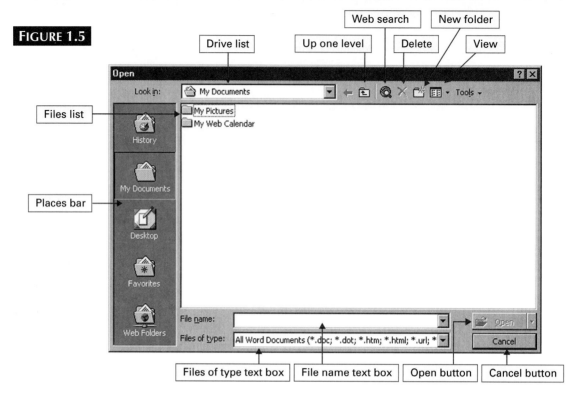

Table 1.1

Feature	Description
Drive list	identifies the current drive and/or folder
Up One Level button	accesses the "parent" folder when a folder is active or My Computer when a drive is active
Search theWeb button	launches Internet Explorer 5 or your default Web browser to the Microsoft Home, all in one page so that you can perform a search for the document to open
Delete button	removes the active document from the folder or drive
Create New Folder button	creates a new folder within the active drive or folder
View drop-down list	enables you to change the way files and folders are displayed in the dialog box and rearrange files
Tools drop-down list	contains commands often found on Open dialog box menus in other applications
Places Bar	contains folders and file storage locations so that you can open them quickly
File name text box text box	enables you to type the name of the document to locate or open
Files of type text box	identifies the types of files displayed
Files list	shows all folders and files in the active folder or on the active drive.
Open button	opens the selected (highlighted) file and contains a drop-down list that enables you to open a copy of the file, open the file in Read-Only mode, or open a Web document in a browser
Cancel button	closes the dialog box without opening a document

TIP A folder in Windows can contain files or additional folders.

TIP By default, if the file you want to open is one of the last four files opened on the computer you are using, the file name may appear at the bottom of the File menu. Click the file name to open the file. You can change the number of files that appear at the bottom of the File menu for any application using the Tools, Options command and then setting the number of files on the General page of the Options dialog box.

TIP You can also open one of the last fifteen files saved on the computer you're using by selecting the file name from the Start menu Documents list. In addition, you can open a file by double-clicking the file name in the Exploring or My Computer window. If the application used to create the file is not running, it launches when you open the file.

Web Tip

If you do not have a copy of the *Selections.doc* file on your student disk, you can download it from the SELECT Web site at
http://www.prenhall.com/select

TASK 2: Opening a Copy of a Document

1 Choose File, Open.

2 Open the folder or disk drive containing the *Selections.doc* file that you downloaded from the SELECT Web site, or follow the directions from your instructor to locate the file. The folder or disk drive name appears in the Look in text box.

3 Click the *Selections.doc* file. The file name appears highlighted.

4 Click the drop-down list arrow on the Open button.

FIGURE 1.6

5 Choose Open as Copy. Opening a copy of an existing document leaves the original intact so that you can use it later, if necessary.

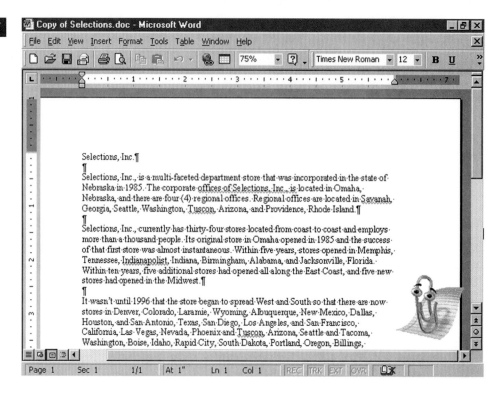

FIGURE 1.7

TIP Word underlines suspected spelling and grammar errors; Excel and Access do not.

TIP The settings active on your computer control the appearance of the document on your screen.

Creating New Files

As you discovered with opening files, Microsoft Office 2000 offers a variety of different techniques for performing tasks. A new document automatically appears when you launch Word, and a new blank workbook is created each time you launch Excel. As you explore all Office 2000 applications, you'll find that options for creating and opening files are presented when you launch PowerPoint and Access. To create a new file in any Office 2000 application after it is launched:

- Click the New ⬚ button on the Standard toolbar of any Office 2000 application. A new blank file automatically appears in Word and Excel. In Access, clicking the New button displays the New dialog box so that you can create a blank database, or a database using a template. In Power-Point, the New Slide dialog box opens so you can select a slide format for the first slide in the new presentation.

- Press (CTRL) + N. A new blank file automatically appears in Word, Excel, and PowerPoint. In Access, the New dialog box opens so that you can select the type of database you want to create. In PowerPoint, the New Slide dialog box opens so you can select a slide format for the first slide of the new presentation.

- Choose File, New. The New dialog box opens and displays a list of templates—professionally designed, preformatted file formats specific to the application you're using—that you can use to format your file.

The number of the new file on the title bar is incremented by 1. Another document button appears on the Windows taskbar.

> **TIP** You can also create a new Office 2000 document by choosing Start, New Office Document. A dialog box that contains a comprehensive listing of all Office 2000 templates grouped by type opens so that you can choose the type of document you want to create. After you choose the document type, the application required to create the file launches automatically, if it isn't already running.

Check Point

Create a new blank document in Word by clicking the New Blank Document □ button on the toolbar.

FIGURE 1.8

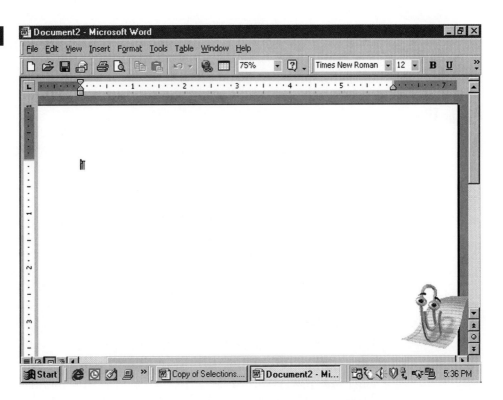

Switching among Open Files

Word, Excel, and PowerPoint enable you to open or create multiple files without closing files that are already open. These three applications place a file button on the Windows taskbar for each file you have open. To switch from one open file to another, you can:

- Click the Windows taskbar button for the open file you want to access.
- Press (CTRL) + (F6) to browse open files for the active application. Press (CTRL) + (SHIFT) + (F6) to move backward among open files.

> **TROUBLESHOOTING** This technique accesses open files for the active application only. Because each application and file you have open appears as a button on the taskbar, you can press (ALT) + (TAB) to move from one open application to another as well as from one open file to another.

- Choose the Window menu and then select the file you want to access from the bottom of the menu.

 Check Point

When you use multiple applications in Office, more than one program may be open, but only one is active. Similarly, when you open multiple documents, workbooks, or presentations, more than one can be open, but only one is active at any given time.

Closing Files

Office 2000 applications provide a variety of techniques for closing files. To close the active file:

- Click the file Close ☒ button at the right end of the menu bar.

> **TROUBLESHOOTING** In Word, the Close button appears on the menu bar only when one document is open. When multiple documents are open, click the Close button at the end of the title bar—Word stays open until all documents are closed.

- Right-click the Windows taskbar button for the file you want to close and choose Close.
- Choose File, Close.
- Press (CTRL) + (F4).
- Click the file control icon at the left end of the menu bar and choose Close.

> **TIP** Regardless of which procedure you use to close a file, if you have edited the file, the Office 2000 application will prompt you to save the file. Be sure to read the message carefully to determine your response and prevent unwanted loss of data.

Check Point

Before continuing with the rest of the features, use one of the close procedures identified to close the blank document you created earlier. After you close the file, the *Copy of Selections.doc* should appear.

Saving Files

Each new document you create, each copy of an existing document you open, and each document you edit all need to be saved. You'll find a number of different Save commands listed on the File menu of Office 2000 applications. Knowing the difference between the Save commands is important. Here's how they work:

Table 1.2

Command	Description
Save	Opens the Save As dialog box so that you can select a storage location for *new* files you create. The dialog box contains text boxes where you can type a file name and select a save format.
	Automatically overwrites previously saved files that you open and edit and saves existing files for which you opened a copy in the same folder of the same disk using the file name *Copy of xx*.
Save As	In Word, Excel, and PowerPoint, opens the Save As dialog box so that you can save changes to an already saved file and/or copies of existing files in a different storage location or using a different file name or file type.
	In Access, Save As allows you to export a specific database object only.
Save as Web Page	Opens the Save As dialog box, automatically activates Web Page (*.htm; *.html) as the Save as type, and adds a page title.

> **TIP** Because the procedure for saving Web pages differs among Office 2000 applications, procedures for saving Web pages are addressed in each application module.

To initiate the Save command, you can use one of the following techniques:

- Click the Save 🖫 button on the Standard toolbar.
- Press (CTRL) + S.
- Choose File, Save.

When you save a file, you may also want to create a new folder in which to store the file. You can create the folder "on the fly" using the Save As dialog box and prevent having to move the file later.

> **TIP** To access the Save As command, choose File, Save As.

TASK 3: <u>To Save a Copy of a File in a New Folder</u>

1 Click the title bar of the *Copy of Selections.doc* file to make it active, if necessary. Active windows usually have a darker title bar than inactive windows.

2 Choose File, Save As. The Save As dialog box opens.

3 Open the disk drive on which you want to create a new folder and click the Create New Folder ☐ button. The New Folder dialog box opens.

> **TROUBLESHOOTING** If you are creating a subfolder, open the main folder that will contain the subfolder.

4 Type your name in the Name text box and choose OK. The new folder appears in the Save in text box at the top of the Save As dialog box.

5 Choose Save. The new file named *Copy of Selections.doc* appears in the new folder, and the file name also appears in the title bar of the document.

Web Tip

You can save a Web page using the same basic save techniques used to save files in Office 2000 applications. Simply display the page or open the file you want to save and choose File, Save, select a folder to contain the file, type a file name for the file, and choose OK.

Changing File Properties

Properties, information about files, are automatically stored with each Office 2000 file you save. Properties are grouped into different categories and provide information such as the date on which the file was created, the date on which it was last edited, the author's name, the author's company, file size, and other application-specific information (such as number of words in a Word document). In addition, the Office 2000 application used to create the file automatically assigns a title for the file based on the file name assigned to the file. You can edit or add additional bits of information about the file and check existing information.

TASK 4:   Editing File Properties

1   Click the File menu. The File menu appears. Pause until additional commands appear.

> **TIP** Only menu commands used most frequently appear when a menu is initially displayed. After the menu is displayed for a few seconds, additional commands appear on the menu.

2   Choose Properties.

> **TIP** In Access, the command on the File menu is Database Properties.

FIGURE 1.9

Copy of Selections.doc Properties   ? ☒

| General | Summary | Statistics | Contents | Custom | ◄──── Information grouped by type

Title: Selections, Inc   ◄──── Document name

Subject:

Author: Author Name

Manager:

Company: School or Company Name|

Category:

Keywords:

Comments:

Hyperlink base:

Template: Normal.dot

☐ Save preview picture

OK   Cancel

3 Position the mouse pointer before the *S* in *Selections* in the Title: text box and click.

4 Type (**Your Name**)**'s Edits to**. The title now appears as (Your Name)'s Edits to Selections, Inc.

5 Choose OK.

 ## Check Point

Launch Microsoft Excel 2000 using the same launch procedures you used to launch Microsoft Word 2000.

 ## Break Point

If time is running short, save changes to the file. Then close Word. You can now power down your computer, if necessary, and continue this project later.

Using Help

In the Windows section, you learned how to use Windows Help and how to locate information about specific topics. Each Office 2000 application comes equipped with quite a variety of help features that will have you getting help from all over the world—right on your computer as you work!

Using the Office Assistant

The Office Assistant is a help feature that is growing in popularity. The Office Assistant is easy to use, is personably animated, and provides a focused list of help topics related to questions you "ask" the assistant. Depending on how the person using your computer left the Assistant, it may appear on-screen when you launch applications. When closed, the Assistant waits on the Standard toolbar and appears when you call it to look up information about topics for which you need help. After you start the Office Assistant in one application it remains on screen until you close it—even when you open another Office application. The information it provides when you ask it a question relates to the application that is active at the time you ask a question—regardless of what application was active when you started the Office Assistant.

TASK 5: To Use the Office Assistant

1 Click the Microsoft Help 🔲 button on the Standard toolbar. Clippit, the default Office Assistant, appears; it appears the same in all Office Applications. You can type questions or words related to the application, and Clippit will fetch a list of related topics. Light bulbs indicate hints and ideas that Clippit has. Notice that Excel is the active application in Figure 1.10.

FIGURE 1.10

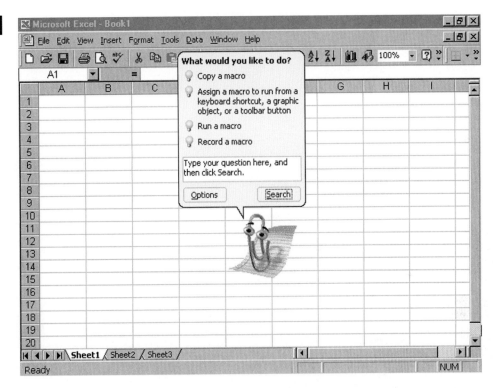

TIP The Office Assistant dialog box appears in different shapes and sizes, depending on how it was last used.

2 Type **How do I print a worksheet?** The Office Assistant takes notes as you type.

3 Click Search. Acting pleased with itself, Clippit displays topics related to printing worksheets.

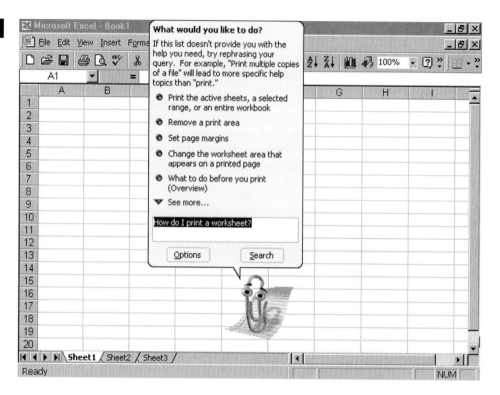

FIGURE 1.11

4 Click What to do before you print (Overview). The Excel window resizes to accommodate the Help window. The Microsoft Excel Help window displays a graphic button to access additional help. Clippit is watching what you are doing.

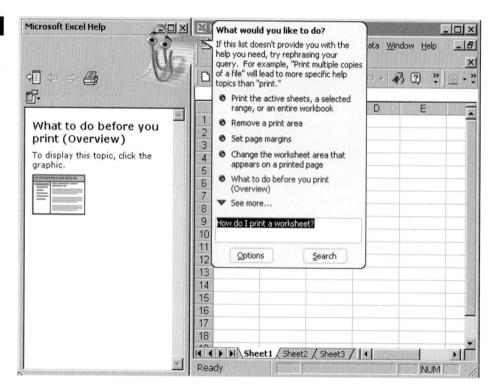

FIGURE 1.12

5 Click the graphic. The Microsoft Excel Help window enlarges and provides additional information.

> **TIP** As you work with Help, you'll discover that the format of information displayed after you select a topic varies. In some cases a list of step-by-step instructions appears in the Help window, while at other times another list of topics related to the topic you select will appear.

6 Close the Help window and then close the Help palette. The Excel window resizes to its original size.

7 Right-click Clippit. A shortcut menu opens.

FIGURE 1.13

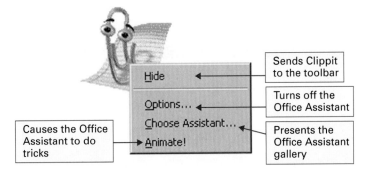

Causes the Office Assistant to do tricks

Sends Clippit to the toolbar

Turns off the Office Assistant

Presents the Office Assistant gallery

8 Choose Choose Assistant.

FIGURE 1.14

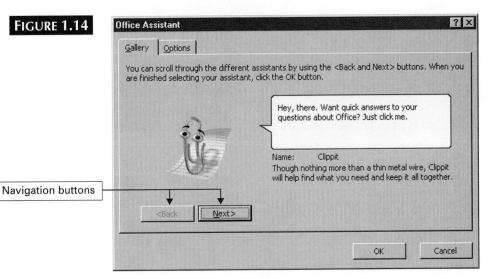

Navigation buttons

9 Click the navigation buttons to review additional assistants until you find one you like.

10 Choose OK.

Turning Off and On the Office Assistant

When the Office Assistant feature is active, it often offers unsolicited help that can become quite annoying. You can disable the feature in Office 2000 applications. After you turn off the Office Assistant, a Help window automatically opens when you click the Microsoft Help button.

TASK 6: <u>To Turn the Office Assistant Off and On</u>

1 Display the Office Assistant and right-click to display the shortcut menu.

2 Choose Options.

FIGURE 1.15

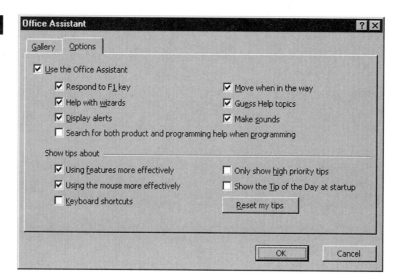

3 Clear the Use the Office Assistant checkbox. All other options are dimmed.

4 Choose OK. The Office Assistant closes.

5 Choose Help, Microsoft Excel Help, and then click the Answer Wizard tab, if necessary.

FIGURE 1.16

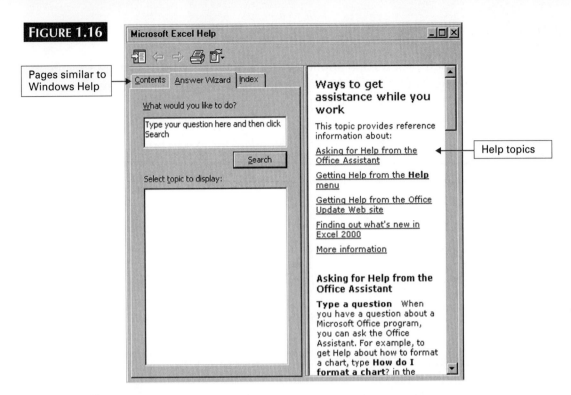

Pages similar to Windows Help

Help topics

6 Close the Help window.

7 Choose Help, Show the Office Assistant. The Office Assistant feature is reactivated so that clicking the Microsoft Help button will now call the Assistant.

8 Right-click the Office Assistant and choose Hide. The Office Assistant disappears and waits to be called again.

> **TROUBLESHOOTING** After you choose Hide several times, a dialog box will appear asking if you want to deactivate the Office Assistant. Read the options carefully and choose the option that best represents how you want to use the Office Assistant.

Web Tip

If you're connected to the Internet, you can access one of several Web sites maintained by Microsoft to provide up-to-the-minute help online. The Web provides information directly from Microsoft support team members as well as information and helpful hints from other Office users. To access the Microsoft Web site directly from an Office 2000 application, choose Help, Office on the Web. Your default Web browser launches and displays the Office 2000 Update page.

Selecting Printers and Printing

While each Office 2000 application has printing features that are specific to the application, printing basics are the same for all applications. There are three basic methods for printing documents:

• Choose File, Print to display the Print dialog box and set print options.
• Click the Print 🖨 button on the Standard toolbar to print the active file using default settings.
• Press (CTRL) + P to display the Print dialog box and set print options.

Before printing files, you must first select a printer.

Selecting Printers

By default, Office 2000 uses the default printer set up in Windows. You can change the printer selection to any printer that is installed on the computer. You can select the printer from the Print dialog box.

> **TROUBLESHOOTING** If the printer you want to use is not installed on your computer, check with your instructor or the lab assistant to obtain the necessary installation disks and information for the printer.

TASK 7: To Select a Printer

1 Switch to Word and choose File, Print.

FIGURE 1.17

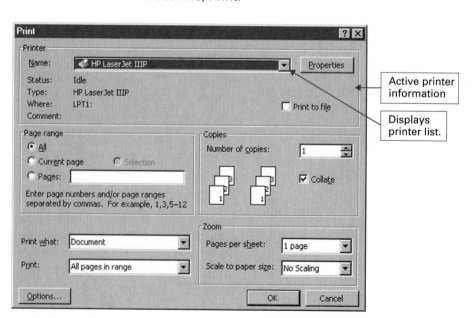

Active printer information

Displays printer list.

2 Click the Name drop-down list arrow. Note that fax setups are listed as printers.

FIGURE 1.18

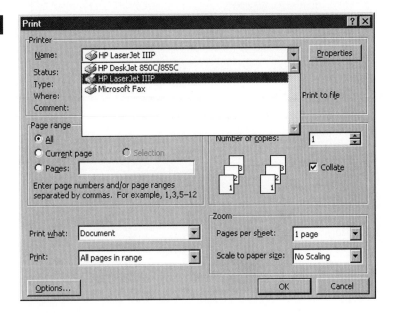

3 Select the desired printer.

4 Choose OK.

> **TIP** The selected printer appears in a Screen Tip when you point to the Print button on the Standard toolbar when the feature is activated.

Setting Print Options

Options displayed in the Print dialog box vary among Office applications. There are a number of options, however, that are similar in the Print dialog box of all applications. These are identified in Figure 1.19.

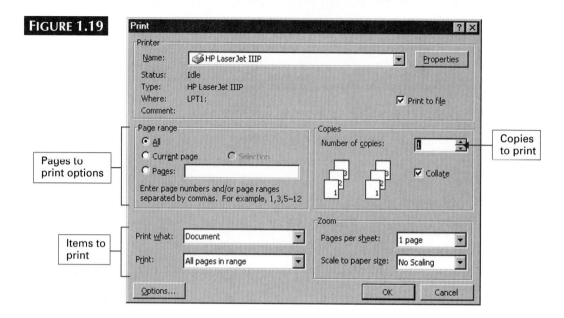

FIGURE 1.19

After you set the desired print options, all you have to do is choose OK to print the active file or other object you selected.

 **Web Tip**

You can print information from a Web site using the same basic procedures used to print an Office 2000 file. Display the page you want to print and choose File, Print from the Web browser menu.

Previewing Pages

Even though most applications display files in **WYSIWYG** (what you see is what you get) format, sometimes what you see on paper is not what you expected. It is always a good idea to preview pages of the file before sending the page to the printer to help prevent some of these surprises. Each Office 2000 application has some type of Print Preview feature that enables you to see what the file will look like when it's printed.

• For Word, Excel, and Access, display the preview by choosing File, Print Preview, or click the Print Preview button on the Standard toolbar.

- In PowerPoint, display each slide on-screen by choosing View, Slide Show, by pressing (F5), or by clicking the Slide Show 💻 button at the bottom of the presentation window.

Check Point

Print Preview toolbar buttons vary by application. Display the *Copy of Selections.doc* in Print Preview and use the Context Sensitive Help ▶? button to find out what each tool does.

When you're finished, close Print Preview, save, and close the document.

Exiting Applications

Before you exit Office 2000 applications, it's a good idea to save work that you want to keep and close files you have open. If you exit an application without saving changes to open files, the Office 2000 application prompts you to save changes to the file. Be sure to read these prompts carefully to ensure that you take the action you want to take and avoid unnecessary loss of data.

To exit Office 2000 applications, use one of the following procedures:

- Click the application Close ✖ button on the last open file in the application.
- Choose File, Exit. If multiple files are open in the application, all files close as you exit the application.
- Click the application control icon (for example 🔲) at the left end of the title bar, and choose Close.
- Press (ALT) + (F4).
- Right-click the application button on the Windows taskbar and choose Close.

Summary and Exercises

Summary

- The many common elements of Office 2000 allow you to use techniques learned in one application to accomplish the same task in other applications.
- Applications can be launched in a variety of common ways, based on your preference and how Office 2000 is installed on your computer.
- File management tasks include opening files, creating new files, saving files, and editing file properties.
- Documents can be opened as a copy or as read-only to ensure that your original remains intact.
- New documents can be created as blank files or by using a pre-designed template.
- Word, Excel, and PowerPoint enable you to open or create multiple files without closing files that are already open.
- When you elect to close a file that has been edited, regardless of which procedure you use, the application will prompt you to save the file.
- File properties are automatically stored with each file you save.
- Help is available by using the Office Assistant.
- Printing basics such as selecting a printer and setting print options are basically the same for all Office 2000 applications.

Key Terms

collate
Office Assistant
properties

save
templates
WYSIWYG

Study Questions

Multiple Choice

1. Which procedures for accomplishing tasks are basically same in all Office 2000 applications?
   a. presentation design
   b. file management
   c. data management
   d. toolbar options

2. Which of the following procedures is not an option to open an existing document, workbook, presentation, or database?
   a. choose Start, Open Office Document
   b. choose File, Open
   c. press (CTRL) + P
   d. click the Open button

3. To create a new file after an application is launched,
    a. press (CTRL) + N.
    b. click the New button on the Standard toolbar.
    c. choose File, New.
    d. all of the above.

4. Which are the three options for initiating commands in Office 2000?
    a. design buttons, keystrokes, and mouse options
    b. taskbar buttons, menu commands, and keystrokes
    c. menu commands, keystrokes, and design buttons
    d. both b and c

5. The programs that display new files automatically when you launch them are
    a. Access and Word.
    b. Excel and PowerPoint.
    c. Access and Excel.
    d. Word and Excel.

6. The Print Preview feature is the same in all Office 2000 applications except
    a. Word.
    b. Excel.
    c. Access.
    d. PowerPoint.

Fill in the Blank

1. _____ enables you to see what your printout will look like before you print it.

2. Click the _____ button to switch to a different open file.

3. _____ in the default Office Assistant.

4. The _____ appears down the left side of the Open and Save As dialog boxes.

5. When you want to leave the original file intact but want to use the file as a basis for a new file, you can open a(n) _____ of the original file and save it as a new file.

Short Answer

1. List three different ways you can launch an application.

2. Identify several different ways to exit an application.

3. The Word screen on one computer in the lab looks different from the Word screen on another computer in the lab. Explain the possible reasons why.

4. Regardless of the procedure you are using, what feature will help prevent unwanted loss of data, and when will this option be presented to you?

5. How can you turn off the Office Assistant?

For Discussion

1. Discuss the different ways to save a document, and explain when and why you might choose each particular option.

2. Briefly discuss when, how, and why you would use the Office Assistant.

Common Text and Art Elements

In the previous project, you learned some of the basic elements and features that all Office 2000 applications have in common. In this project, you learn some techniques for working with text in all applications, how to proof files, and how to insert pictures and change words into art work.

Objectives

After completing this project, you will be able to:

- ➤ Work with text
- ➤ Use proofing tools
- ➤ Add graphics to Office 2000 files
- ➤ Edit and format graphic objects

Setup

To ensure that your screen looks like those pictured in this project, you need to check some of the settings, as described in Table 2.1.

Table 2.1

Item	Action
Office Assistant	Hide the Assistant.
Toolbars	Reset default toolbars by choosing Tools, Customize, and then display the Toolbars page of the dialog box. Check the Standard and Formatting toolbars and the menu bar. Select each of these items individually and choose Reset. Choose OK to confirm each change. Click the Options tab and ensure that all Personalized Menus and Toolbars options are deselected. Then click the Reset my usage data button and choose Yes to restore menus. When all toolbars and the menu bar have been reset, choose Close.
View	Click the Print Layout View button at the bottom of the Word window.

Working with Text

Whether you're typing a letter in Word, entering values in an Excel worksheet, adding data to an Access table, or creating slides in Power-Point, you'll type and edit text using Office applications. Learning how to navigate, edit, enhance, format, align, and move and copy text now will make working with text in each module easier.

 Check Point

Open the *Copy of Selections.doc* you saved in the Basic Common Elements project and use it to practice the following techniques.

Navigating Text

Navigating text simply means moving from character to character, paragraph to paragraph, screen to screen, or page to page in text. You can use both the keyboard and the mouse to move the insertion point within a file. Mouse techniques common to all Office applications include using scroll bars to display different parts of a file or view and clicking to position the insertion point in the paragraph, cell, or field you want to edit.

Table 2.2 identifies keystrokes common to all Office 2000 applications for moving from place to place.

Table 2.2

Key	Action
←	Move left one character or column
→	Move right one character or column
↓	Move down one line or row
↑	Move up one line or row
PGUP	Move up one screen
PGDN	Move down one screen
HOME	Beginning of a line or row
END	End of a line or row
CTRL + END	End of a file
CTRL + HOME	Beginning of a file

TIP These keystrokes apply only to datasheets in Access.

TIP As you work with each application you'll discover additional keystrokes specific to that application. For example, in Excel, you'll learn to move from worksheet to worksheet in a workbook, in PowerPoint you'll learn to display presentation slides, and in Access, you learn to move among records in forms using the navigation controls.

Inserting, Deleting, and Typing Over Text

All Office 2000 applications are set with **Insert mode** active so that to insert text, you simply position the insertion point and start typing. Existing text moves over to make room for the new text. To replace existing text with new text, you can select text that you want to replace and type the new text.

TIP In Word, you can also switch to **Overtype mode** by pressing (INS) on the keyboard or by double-clicking the OVR area of the status bar to replace existing text as you type new text.

The position of the insertion point controls the technique to use to delete text:

- Position the insertion point immediately before the text you want to delete and press (DELETE) once for each character and space you want to delete.
- Position the insertion point immediately after the text you want to delete and press (BACKSPACE) once for each character and space you want to delete.

The easiest way to learn how to insert, type over, or delete text is by practicing navigation and selection techniques and seeing how they work.

Enhancing and Formatting Text

Word, Excel, and PowerPoint share common methods for changing the appearance of text. Special features enable you to enhance and format text by changing the text **font**—the way text characters are shaped and the text size—as well as text **attributes**—how text characters appear. Changes you make to text that has already been typed affect selected text only. However, you can "turn on" an enhancement or change font characteristics before typing text and then turn the enhancement off or change the font again when you are finished.

TIP In Access, these formatting methods apply only to datasheets.

TASK 1: ## To Enhance and Format Text

1 Open the *Copy of Selections.doc* file and select the title **Selections, Inc.** The text appears highlighted.

2 Click the Bold **B** button on the Formatting toolbar. In Figure 2.1, the Bold button is lighter and depressed. The title appears darker and remains selected.

FIGURE 2.1

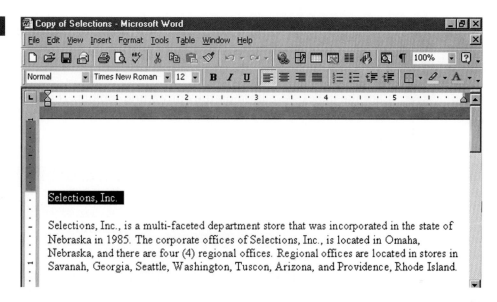

3 Click the Font drop-down list arrow. Font formats appear on the drop-down palette in alphabetical order by font name.

FIGURE 2.2

TIP Fonts listed are controlled, to some extent, by the printer you are connected to and the fonts installed on your computer. The fonts you see may be different from those shown here.

4 Choose Mead Bold. The selected text automatically reformats with the new font.

TROUBLESHOOTING If Mead Bold does not appear on your Font list, select a similar font or follow the direction of your instructor.

5 Click the Font Size drop-down list arrow. A list of numbers appears on a palette, with the current font size highlighted.

6 Select 24. The title appears much larger.

7 Click the Italics *I* button on the Formatting toolbar. The title appears slanted and the Italics button is lighter in color and depressed.

8 Choose Format, Font.

FIGURE 2.3

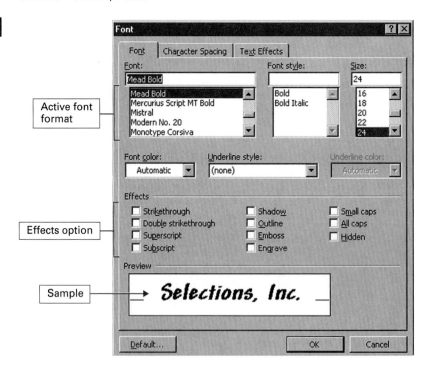

9 Click the Font color drop-down list arrow. A palette of colors appears.

10 Click Blue and choose OK. The title text is reformatted in blue print.

TIP You can also select a font color by clicking the Font Color drop-down list arrow on the Formatting toolbar.

11 Click the white space to the right of the title to deselect the title text.

Copying and Moving Text

Office 2000 offers three different techniques for moving and copying text:

- Click the Cut ✂, Copy 📋, or Paste 📋 button on the Standard toolbar.
- Choose Edit, Cut/Copy/Paste.
- Press (CTRL) + X for Cut, (CTRL) + C for Copy, or (CTRL) + V for Paste.

When you use the Cut command to move text or the Copy command to copy text, Office 2000 applications place the selected text or information on the Clipboard, where it stays until you paste it where you want it. While other Windows applications store only one snippet of information on the Clipboard, Office 2000 applications enable you to store multiple snippets of information on the Clipboard and then choose the snippet or snippets to place when you paste. The Office Clipboard is pictured in Figure 2.4.

FIGURE 2.4

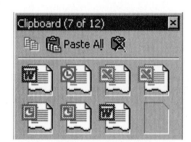

The icons identify the application from which the snippet was copied. You can paste all snippets at the current cursor location by clicking the Paste All button. You can click the snippet you want to insert and it automatically appears at the insertion point. Notice that the Office Clipboard can hold up to 12 items.

☑ Check Point

Use the techniques described for moving and copying text to adjust text in the *Copy of Selections.doc* so that it appears as shown in Figure 2.5. Then save changes to the document.

FIGURE 2.5

Copying Text Formats

Formatting text by applying enhancements, color, and font styles can be tedious—especially when you want to format text in several different locations and maintain consistency of format. You're in luck! Office 2000 applications are equipped with a Format Painter that's designed to help you copy text format and apply the format to additional text.

TASK 2: <u>To Copy Text Formats Using the Format Painter</u>

1 Select the formatted title text, *Selections, Inc.*

2 Click the Format Painter ☑ button on the Standard toolbar.

> **TIP** Double-click the Format Painter to apply the format to text in multiple places in a file or to text in other files. Positioning the insertion point in a word is usually sufficient to copy the text format, but when multiple fonts and character settings are contained in a paragraph or in a word, select the character that contains the format you want to copy.

FIGURE 2.6

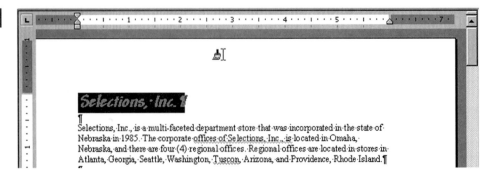

3 Scroll to the bottom of the document page until the *Regional Offices* text appears on the screen.

4 Click and drag the paintbrush across the text *Regional Offices*. The text is reformatted with the font and enhancements applied to the title, and the Format Painter is turned off.

> **TROUBLESHOOTING** If only a portion of the text is reformatted, select any formatted word, click the Format Painter again, and paint the additional characters.

Using Undo and Redo

The Undo feature in all Office 2000 applications reverses actions; the Redo feature restores actions that were reversed. Using Undo and Redo is quite simple. Office 2000 applications offer keyboard, mouse, and menu procedures, as shown in Table 2.3.

Table 2.3

Command	Procedures
Undo	Click the Undo button on the Standard toolbar.
	Choose Edit, Undo.
	Press CTRL + Z.
Redo	Click the Redo button on the Standard toolbar.
	Choose Edit, pause to display all commands, select Redo.
	Press CTRL + Y.

Each of these actions reverses the last action, but Office 2000 applications enable you to reverse numerous actions in succession. In addition, you can click the drop-down list arrow beside the Undo or Redo button and select the action you want to reverse. All actions down to and including the action you select will be reversed.

Aligning Text

Among the buttons you'll find on the Formatting toolbars in Word, Excel, and PowerPoint are buttons that control text alignment. You can use these alignment buttons on the Formatting toolbar to adjust the position of text in document paragraphs, table or worksheet cells, database forms, and presentation slides. You can also access alignment commands using the keyboard; menu commands for setting alignment vary among the applications. Table 2.4 identifies procedures for aligning text in Word, Excel, and PowerPoint.

Table 2.4

Command	Procedures
Align Left	Click the Align Left button. Press (CTRL) + L.
Center	Click the Center button. Press (CTRL) + E.
Align Right	Click the Align Right button. Press (CTRL) + R.
Justify	Click the Justify button. Press (CTRL) + J.

 Check Point

Use the procedures identified in Table 2.4 to align the document title on the right. Undo the action and center the title. Save changes to your work.

Using Proofing Tools

Proofing tools built into Office 2000 applications make it easy to locate text, replace text, and spell-check your files. There is also a tool that enables you to enter frequently mistyped text and have the Office application automatically correct your error! The procedures for using these tools are consistent among all Office 2000 applications.

Running the Spelling Checker

When you first opened the copy of *Selections.doc*, you saw red, wavy underlines below misspelled words in the document. Unless the spell-as-you-go feature is turned off, the Spell Check feature runs continuously as you work in Office 2000 applications. The Spell Check feature locates words that don't appear in the Office 2000 dictionary and highlights them for you so that you can determine whether they are correct or need to be changed.

> **TIP** Words that the Office application underlines as you work can be corrected quite easily. Simply point to the misspelled word and right-click. Office 2000 lists suggested spellings for the word not recognized. Choose the correct spelling of the word, choose Ignore All, or choose Add to add the word to the dictionary.

TASK 3: <u>To Spell Check a File</u>

1 Press (CTRL) + (HOME) and then click the Spelling 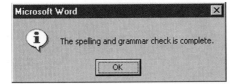 button on the Standard toolbar.

> **TIP** The button is named Spelling and Grammar in Word 2000.

FIGURE 2.7

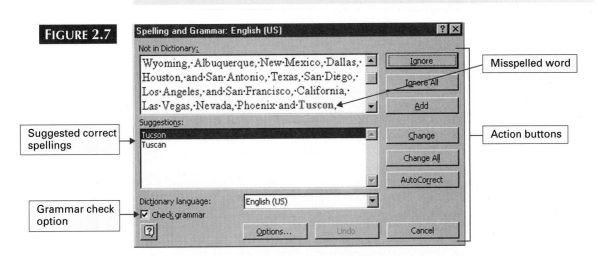

2 Choose Tucson in the Suggestions list and click Change. The correct spelling of the city Tucson replaces the misspelled word and the next error is highlighted.

3 Click Change to correct the grammar error.

4 Continue checking the file, correcting errors that appear, until Word tells you the spelling and grammar check is complete.

FIGURE 2.8

5 Choose OK and save changes to the file.

Finding and Replacing Text

The Find and Replace features enable you to locate text if it appears in a file and replace text with substitute text. These features are powerful tools for navigating and editing large files.

TASK 4: <u>To Find and Replace Text</u>

1 Choose Edit, Find.

> **TROUBLESHOOTING** In Access, the Find command is available only when an object is open. Find does not appear on the Edit menu when the database window is active.

2 Type **thirty-four** in the Find what text box and choose Find Next. The Office 2000 application highlights the first occurrence of the phrase.

FIGURE 2.9

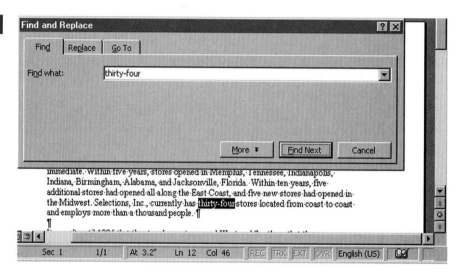

> **TROUBLESHOOTING** Word searches the document for the phrase beginning at the insertion point. As a result, you may find a different occurrence of the phrase.

3 Click the Replace tab. *Thirty-four* appears in the Find what text box.

4 Type **forty-four** in the Replace with text box and click Replace All. A message window tell you how many replacements were made.

5 Click OK, close the dialog box, and save your changes to the document.

Break Point

If necessary, you can save your file, exit the application, and continue this project later.

Adding Art in Office 2000

Adding art to Office 2000 files dresses them up and makes them more inviting. Each Office 2000 application offers such a variety of methods for adding art to your files that it's sometimes difficult to decide which feature you want to use. You can add clip art images, scanned images or picture files from other sources, WordArt, and manual drawings to files in all Office 2000 applications. Each art type has a complete set of tools that enable you to edit and manipulate the art object. As a result, we'll just whet your appetite with a few little tips and tricks and then let you explore features that you need most on your own.

Inserting Clip Art

All Office 2000 applications share a common Clip Gallery that contains a variety of different images you can add to your files. The first time you access the Clip Gallery, the Office 2000 application takes a few moments to build the gallery and then presents **thumbnails**—very small copies—of the images.

TASK 5: To Insert Clip Art

1 Create a new blank document in Word.

2 Choose Insert, Picture, Clip Art.

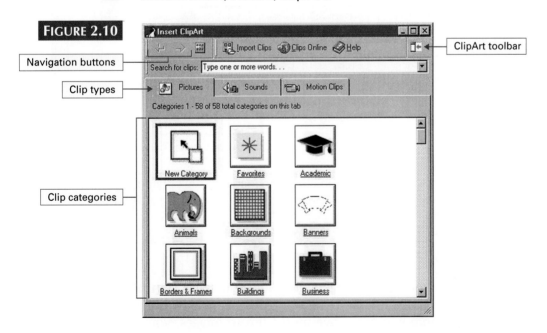

FIGURE 2.10

Navigation buttons

Clip types

Clip categories

ClipArt toolbar

TROUBLESHOOTING The clip categories may vary, depending on the categories that were installed during set up of PowerPoint 2000 and clips that have been downloaded from the Web.

 **Web Tip**

You can find additional clip art images on the Web by clicking the Clips Online button or go directly to the Microsoft Web site at http://cgl.microsoft.com/clipgallerylive. You'll be reminded about copyright laws governing clips found in the gallery and also be asked to accept a licensing agreement before you'll see any clips.

3 Scroll the list of categories and click Seasons. A list of season-related images displays.

4 Click an image that represents the current season.

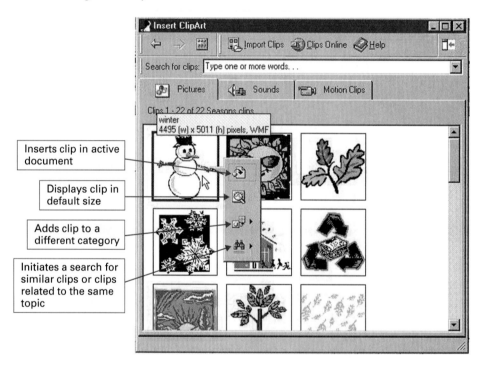

5 Choose Insert Clip and then close the Insert ClipArt dialog box. The image appears at the top of the new document and the insertion point is blinking to the right of the clip.

Moving and Sizing Clip Art Images

After you insert a Clip Art image into a file, you can size the image so that it fits the space you want it to occupy and move the image to position it more precisely. Before you can move most Clip Art images, you have to change the image layout settings.

TASK 6: <u>To Move and Size Clip Art Images</u>

1 Click the image.

FIGURE 2.12

Handles for sizing

> **TIP** The Picture toolbar often appears when a picture is selected. You can use tools on the toolbar to format your image.

2 Point to a corner handle and drag the handle to size the image. The pointer appears as a two-headed diagonal arrow when it's positioned on a corner handle.

> **TIP** To prevent the object size from becoming distorted, you can size an object's height and width together and maintain the object's proportion. Simply hold down the (SHIFT) key while you drag a corner handle.

3 Point to the center of the selected image and right-click. The shortcut menu appears.

4 Choose Format Picture. The Format Object dialog box opens.

5 Click the Layout tab. The In line with text option is active and limits the movement of the graphic, as shown in Figure 2.13.

FIGURE 2.13

6 Choose Square and then click Advanced.

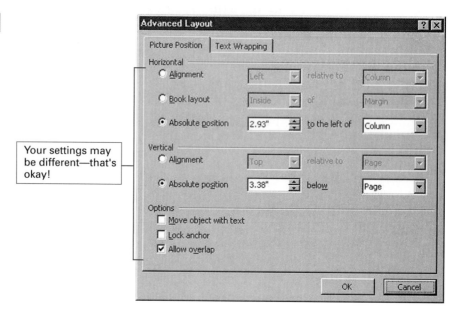

Your settings may be different—that's okay!

7 Clear the Move object with text option and choose OK twice. The image appears with white handles on all corners and sides.

8 Point to the center of the image, click, and drag it to a different location on the page. As you drag, the pointer appears as a four-headed arrow. You can drop the image anywhere on the document page and the text will flow to accommodate it.

9 Close the document without saving it.

Creating WordArt

WordArt is a feature that enables you to dress up your files by creating graphic text, shaping it on curves and flows. WordArt is easy to create and can be positioned in a file to fit the size and shape you need. You can use WordArt to create a letterhead for your Selections, Inc., stationery.

TASK 7: To Create WordArt

1 Click 🗋 to create a new blank document.

2 Choose Insert, Picture, WordArt. Each WordArt style is preformatted for shape, size, and color, as shown in Figure 2.15.

FIGURE 2.15

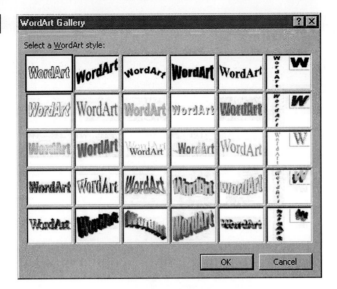

3 Double-click the shadowed vertical style in the lower right corner of the dialog box.

FIGURE 2.16

Your font may be different

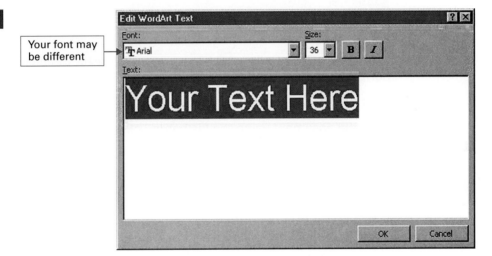

4 Type **Selections, Inc.**

5 Select Mead Bold from the Font drop-down list and choose OK.

> **TROUBLESHOOTING** If Mead Bold is not available on your computer, use a similar font or the font identified by your instructor.

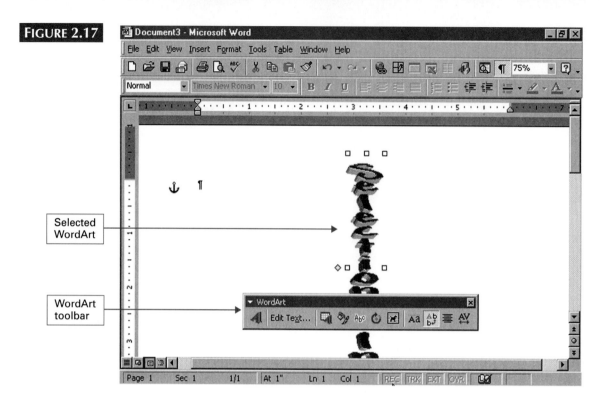

FIGURE 2.17

Selected WordArt

WordArt toolbar

6 Click the WordArt Gallery button on the WordArt toolbar, select a horizontal format, and choose OK.

7 Click a white area of the page to deselect the WordArt.

8 Save the document using the file name *Letterhead.doc*.

Creating and Manipulating Drawings

When you want to add shapes, lines, text boxes, and arrows to your Office 2000 files, you will find quite a sophisticated set of drawing tools that enable you to enhance your slides with original *freehand* creations. Even if you're no artist, you'll find the tools on the Drawing toolbar easy to use. Simply select the tool that represents the shape you want to draw, position the pointer where you want to start the drawing, and click and drag the pointer to the point where you want the shape to end. Then, while the shape is still selected, you can move, size, and edit the shape as needed.

TIP The Drawing Toolbar is not available in Access.

TASK 8: To Create and Manipulate Drawings

1 Click the Drawing button on the Standard toolbar. The Drawing toolbar appears as last positioned.

TROUBLESHOOTING If the Drawing button is hidden, click the More Buttons drop-down arrow at the end of the Standard toolbar, select Add or Remove Buttons, and click Drawing on the button list.

2 Dock the toolbar at the bottom of the window, if necessary.

3 Click the Rectangle ▭ button. The pointer appears as a large plus sign ✛ called a **crosshair**.

4 Position the crosshair just above and to the left of the WordArt object, and then click and drag diagonally to a position just below and to the right of the WordArt. The selected rectangle conforms to the shape and 3-D effect of the WordArt but hides the text.

5 Choose Draw, Order, Send to Back. The rectangle moves behind the WordArt and the text is visible.

FIGURE 2.18

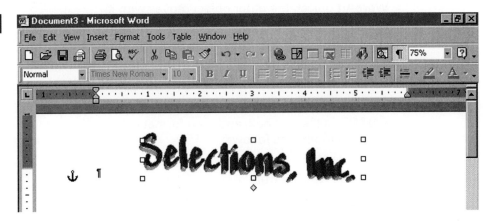

6 Click the Fill 🎨▾ button drop-down list arrow and select the color Indigo.

7 Click 🎨▾ again and select Fill Effects.

FIGURE 2.19

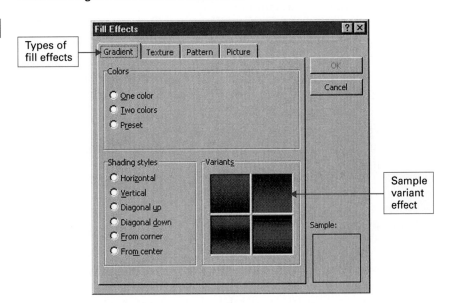

8 Set color, gradient, and texture options to customize your drawing, then choose OK.

9 Click the Select Objects ![cursor] button on the Drawing toolbar. Click and drag a dashed line around the WordArt object and rectangle. Both objects are selected.

FIGURE 2.20

10 Choose Draw, Group. One set of selection handles appears; the two objects are now considered one object so that when you move the rectangle or WordArt object, the other object moves with it.

11 Click the Text Box ![icon] button on the Drawing toolbar and drag the crosshair to create a narrow box at the bottom of the page. The style, color, and format of the previously set shape appears with the insertion point positioned at the left end of the textbox.

12 Type **1500 Woodmen Tower, 30th Floor, Omaha, Nebraska 68102** in the text box, and then format the text box using tools on the Drawing toolbar as follows:

- Choose No 3-D from the 3-D palette.
- Choose No Line from the Line Style dialog box.
- Choose No Fill from the Fill Color palette.
- Italicize and right-align text in the text box.
- Select a color for the text from the Font Color palette.

13 Click the Drawing ![icon] button to hide the Drawing toolbar and save your changes to the document.

Inserting, Sizing, and Positioning Image Files

As you continue to work with Office 2000 applications, you will begin to acquire images from a variety of sources—from the Internet, scanned images from friends and relatives, and from graphics collections you purchase. When you want to use one of these saved images in an Office 2000 file, you can simply insert it using basically the same techniques you used to insert a clip art image.

TASK 9: To Insert, Size, and Position File Images

1 Press (CTRL) + (HOME) to position the insertion point at the top of the document.

2 Choose Insert, Picture, From File. The Insert Picture dialog box opens.

3 Open the disk drive and folder containing the Selections, Inc., logo file you downloaded from the SELECT Web site.

 ## Web Tip

If you have not yet downloaded the file from the Web site, ask your instructor where to find the file.

4 Double-click *Selections Logo*. The logo appears on screen in a default format.

5 Size and position the logo so that it appears to the left of the Selections WordArt object.

> **TROUBLESHOOTING** You may need to adjust the logo settings to be able to position the graphic freely. Refer to the instructions found in "Moving and Sizing Clip Art Images" earlier in this project.

6 Save changes to the file and print a copy of your letterhead.

7 Close the document and exit Word.

 ## Web Tip

Interested in stories about famous people, places, and things? Explore the Entertainment area of http://www.geocities.com.

Summary and Exercises

Summary

- Navigating text allows you to move from character to character, paragraph to paragraph, screen to screen, or page to page.
- By selecting text, you can apply enhancements to text, change fonts, or move or copy text.
- Inserting and deleting text is the same in all Office 2000 applications, and Word allows you to switch to Overtype mode to replace text as you type.
- Enhancing and formatting text is made easy using the buttons on the Formatting toolbar.
- Text can be cut, copied, and moved within or among all Office 2000 applications.
- Office 2000 makes it easy to maintain text format consistency by using Format Painter.
- Using the Undo or Redo features enables you to reverse the last action, and you can reverse numerous and selected actions in Office 2000.
- Text can be aligned left or right, centered, or justified on the left and right.
- Proofing tools are used to locate text, replace text, and spell-check files.
- The AutoCorrect feature corrects commonly misspelled words and allows you to enter your own words to be automatically corrected.
- Clip art images, scanned images, WordArt, and manual drawings allow you to dress up files in all Office 2000 applications.
- The ClipArt Gallery contains graphics on a number of topics and allows you to search by topic for related images.
- A sophisticated set of drawing tools enable you to create original freehand art.
- When a shape or object is inserted, you can move, size, and edit the selected item as needed.

Key Terms

align	Insert mode	proofing
attributes	justify	Redo
crosshair	keyboard	Replace
Delete	mouse	Spelling Checker
Enhance	navigating	thumbnail
font	Overtype mode	Tools
Format	Page Down	Undo
freehand	Page Up	WordArt
Home	Paste	

Study Questions

Multiple Choice

1. Moving from character to character, paragraph to paragraph, screen to screen or page to page is called
   a. scrolling.
   b. skipping.
   c. navigating.
   d. keystroking.

2. You can change the appearance of text by changing the font, size, and
   a. art.
   b. attributes.
   c. paragraph.
   d. selection.

3. To move up one screen, the key that is used in all applications is
   a. (PRT SC).
   b. (↑).
   c. (CTRL) + (HOME).
   d. (PGUP).

4. Before you can move most ClipArt images, you must change which settings?
   a. Image Layout
   b. Graphic Format
   c. Image Size
   d. Format Object

5. To create a letterhead that arches over the top of a page, you would choose which feature?
   a. Headers
   b. ClipArt
   c. TextFont
   d. WordArt

6. Clearing which option restores free placement of a graphic?
   a. allow overlap
   b. lock anchor
   c. move object with text
   d. none of the above

7. To change the pattern of the inside of a rectangle in freehand drawing, select
   a. Line Color.
   b. Format Object.
   c. Fill Effects.
   d. Insert Text.

Short Answer

1. What must you do before you can apply, enhance, or change the text font or move or copy text?

2. List the three ways to delete text.

3. Which buttons can you use to reverse the last action or selected actions?

4. What are the first three steps of adding a ClipArt picture to a file?

5. If you would like the text to type over the graphic, which layout should you select?

6. Which feature would you use to draw a map with lines, arrows, and boxes?

7. What steps would you follow to insert a graphic from the Internet?

8. What are the three options you can choose from ClipArt?

9. What are the very small copies of images in the Clip Gallery called?

Fill in the Blank

1. You can use the keyboard or the _____ to move within a file.

2. _____ mode allows you to replace existing text as you type new text in Word.

3. Double-click the _____ button to copy a text format to multiple places.

4. Misspelled words are located and corrected using _____.

5. _____ is a feature that enables you to dress up files by creating graphic text.

6. Office 2000 applications share a common _____ that contains a variety of different images you can add to your files.

7. _____ appear on selected images, which allow you to resize or drag the object.

8. _____ buttons control the categories displayed and enable you to move back and forward among clips in the ClipArt Gallery.

For Discussion

1. Discuss several different ways of enhancing and formatting text.

2. Describe the steps you would follow to move and resize a ClipArt image.

Projects for
Microsoft
Word 2000

Introducing Word 2000

Word is the key program in the Office suite, with good reason. Almost every business, organization, or individual that uses a computer uses a word processing program. Word processing programs create all the traditional documents, such as reports, memos, letters, envelopes, and labels. The other programs in the Office suite, which are for more specialized work, may or may not be required, but Word is almost always required.

In Word 2000, you will find a large array of features for creating simple as well as complex documents. These features are easy to learn and easy to use, so you'll be creating great-looking documents in no time.

> **TIP** Word 2000 also extends the capabilities of word processing to include document creation in HTML (HyperText Markup Language), the format of documents that are used on the Internet as well as intranets, which are private networks used by companies and organizations for sharing documents.

Understanding the Document Cycle for Word Processing

Before you learn to use all the features of Word, it's important to understand the document cycle, that is, the processes you will use to create a document. These processes are not unique to Word, but are performed in any word processing program.

Listed here are the processes you would perform in a typical document cycle for a simple document—one that you would create in one sitting and save for future use.

1. Begin by creating a new document.
2. Type the text, editing and formatting the text as you go along.
3. While typing the text, save the document periodically.
4. After entering all the text, proof the document onscreen and make further edits and formatting changes.
5. When you are satisfied with the text, check the spelling and grammar.
6. Print the document and proof the hard copy.
7. Make additional edits and formatting changes if you find additional mistakes in the printed copy, and then print the final draft of the document.
8. Finally, save the file again and close it.
9. If the file is very important, make a backup copy of it.

If you examine these steps, you'll see that they follow a natural flow. Some processes, such as saving, editing, and printing, might be repeated several times in the flow; others, such as checking the spelling and grammar, might be performed only once.

Although a more complex document follows the same basic procedures, it might require additional procedures. For example, after creating the new document, you may have to change the paper size or orientation before you begin typing. Although you could make such a change at the end of the cycle, you would probably create more work for yourself by waiting so long. For example, if you changed the paper orientation from 8.5" × 11" to 11" × 8.5", all the tables in the document would have to be resized to span the new margins.

In the projects that follow, you will create documents using the natural flow of the document cycle. So while you are learning to use the features of Word, you will also be learning how to work in the context of real situations. This means, however, that the first few projects include quite a few features.

One advantage to using this real-world approach is that you will be able to produce a more complete document earlier in your learning experience. For example, you won't create a plain little document in the first project and then have to wait until the third project before you learn how to bold text.

Launching Word

There are several ways to launch Word. One of the most common procedures is listed here.

> **TIP** See Common Elements Project 1 for additional methods of starting Office 2000 programs.

TASK 1: ## To Launch Word

1 Click the Start button and point to Programs.

2 Choose Microsoft Word.

3 Choose Start Using Microsoft Word if the Office Assistant appears. The Word window opens as shown in Figure O.1, and Document1 appears in the document window. Because some screen elements can be hidden and the Word window can be customized in different ways, your screen may not look exactly like the one in the figure. For example, the two default toolbars, *Standard* and *Formatting*, may occupy only one line below the menu bar.

FIGURE O.1

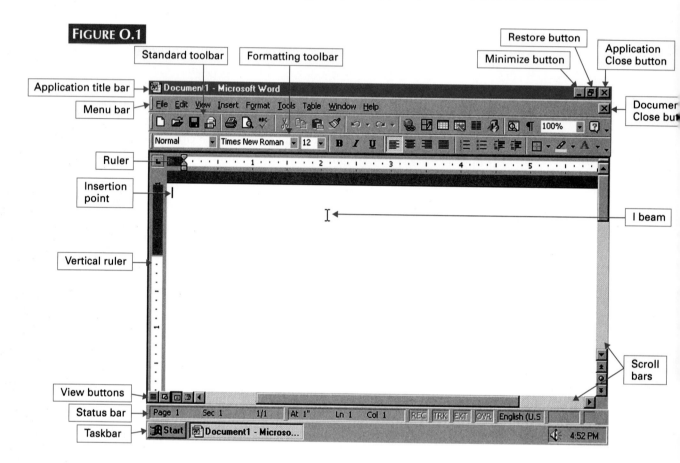

Identifying Window Elements

The Word window has many of the common elements of a typical window, such as a title bar, menu bar, and borders. It also has many elements that are unique to Word. Table O.1 describes the elements of Word.

Table O.1 Elements of the Word Window

Element	Description
Rulers	Word has two rulers—a horizontal ruler below the toolbar and a vertical ruler at the left edge of the screen. The horizontal ruler is simply referred to as the Ruler. It displays the settings for the margins, tabs, and indents, and it can be used to make these settings as well. The vertical ruler, used simply for a guide to the location on the page, appears only in the Print Layout view.
View buttons	The View buttons, located on the left side of the horizontal scroll bar, change the view of the document. They are, from left to right, Normal View, Web Layout View, Print Layout View, and Outline View.
Browse buttons	The Browse buttons, located at the bottom of the vertical scroll bar, include the following default buttons (from top to bottom): Previous Page, Select Browse Object, and Next Page. The Select Browse Object button displays a palette of objects that you can use to browse through a document, such as graphics and tables. If you select the Graphics object, the names of the Previous/Next Page buttons change to Previous/Next Graphic. Clicking the Next Graphic button moves the insertion point forward in the document to the next graphic.
I-beam	The I-beam is the name of the mouse cursor. To position the insertion point in text you must click the I-beam. In Word 2000, the new *Click-n-Type* feature also uses the I-beam to position the insertion point in blank areas of the document. When the I-beam moves through a blank area of the document, an icon connected to the I-beam displays the alignment that will be applied to text if you use Click-n-Type in that area.
Insertion point	The insertion point is a vertical blinking line that marks the typing position.

Identifying Indicators and Icons in the Status Bar

The status bar is a screen element found in every Office 2000 application. What appears in the status bar is unique to each application. The information that appears in the status bar in Word is different from the information that appears in the status bar in Excel. Figure O.2 shows a typical status bar in a Word document. Notice that some of the elements on the status bar (REC, TRK, EXT, and OVR) are dimmed, which indicates that the feature is not currently active. These elements are called *status indicators*. The REC indicator is active when a macro is being recorded; the TRK indicator is active when the Track Changes feature is on; the EXT indicator is active when Extend Selection mode is on; and the OVR indicator is active when Overstrike mode is on.

TIP Double-clicking an indicator turns the feature on or off.

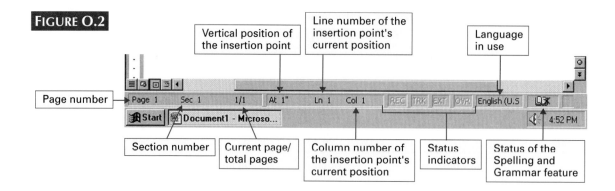

FIGURE O.2

TIP If the Spelling and Grammar icon in the status bar has an X on the page, Word has found spelling errors in the document.

Word uses two additional icons in the status bar when printing or saving in the background of a document. When Word is saving the current document, you will see a pulsating diskette. When printing, a printer icon appears with a number next to it that indicates the number of the page that it is currently printing.

Using Multiple Windows in Word

In all Office 2000 programs, you can open multiple files. Each file opens in its own window, called a ***document window***, and each window appears as a button on the taskbar. Of course, you can work in only one document window at a time, and the document window that you are working in is called the ***active window***. Clicking the document window button on the taskbar is the easiest way to select the window you want to work in, but you can select a document from the Window menu as well.

TIP In every Word document window, the names of the other Word documents that are open appear at the bottom of the Window menu. Clicking a document name in the Window menu makes that window active.

When only one document is open in Word, the Word window looks like the one in Figure O.1. Notice that there are two Close buttons—one in the application title bar and one in the menu bar. The Close button on the application title bar closes Word. The Close button on the menu bar closes the document. When additional Word windows are open, each window has only one Close button, which is in the application title bar. This button does not close Word; it closes the window for that document.

Closing a Document and Exiting Word

When you are finished with a document, you should close it to free memory in the computer. Likewise, when you are finished with Word, you should exit the program.

TASK 2:   To Close a Document and Exit Word

1 Click the appropriate Close ☒ button in the document window. If you have made changes in the document without saving the document, Word will ask whether you want to save the document.

2 Click the Close ☒ button in the application title bar.

Summary and Exercises

Summary

- Word has tools for creating traditional documents and documents used on the Internet and intranets.
- You can launch Word from the Programs menu.
- Word creates Document1 when it is launched.
- The Word window has common window elements as well as its own unique elements.
- Word opens separate windows for each document and displays a button in the taskbar for each window.
- When you are finished with a document you should close it, and when you are finished with Word you should exit the program.

Key Terms

active window	Ruler
Browse buttons	Standard toolbar
Click-n-Type	status indicators
document window	title bar
Formatting toolbar	toolbar
I-beam	vertical ruler
insertion point	View buttons
menu bar	

Study Questions

Multiple Choice

1. Which of the following is a false statement?
   a. The insertion point blinks.
   b. The insertion point marks the typing position.
   c. The insertion point is a vertical line.
   d. The insertion point can change shapes.

2. The Previous Page and Next Page Buttons change
   a. if you switch to the Normal view.
   b. when you select a different browse object.
   c. to Previous Screen and Next Screen if the document does not contain page breaks.
   d. when you choose Insert, Page Numbers.

3. The Select Browse Object button
   a. displays the Find dialog box.
   b. is located in the status bar.
   c. displays a palette of buttons.
   d. is located in the Standard toolbar.

4. If REC is dimmed in the status bar, it means that
   a. Receive mode is inactive.
   b. the macro recorder is not on.
   c. the Review/Edit/Comment toolbar is not displayed.
   d. the Recover Text feature is not active.

5. The I-beam
   a. displays the alignment that will be used for Click-n-Type.
   b. is another name for the insertion point.
   c. is a blinking vertical line that marks the typing position.
   d. is moved by the Up, Down, Left, and Right keys.

Short Answer

1. List the two default toolbars.
2. What is the name of the document that Word creates automatically when it is launched?
3. How do you activate a dimmed indicator on the status bar?
4. What is the purpose of the vertical ruler?
5. Where are the View buttons located?

Fill in the Blank

1. The _____ displays the settings for the margins, tabs, and indents.
2. The OVR indicator in the status bar stands for _____.
3. The vertical ruler appears only in _____ view.
4. The Spelling and Grammar status icon appears in the _____ bar.
5. The feature that allows you to type in blank areas of a document is _____.

For Discussion

1. Discuss Word's method of handling multiple open documents.
2. Using the document cycle, describe the process that you might go through to create a short term paper.

Creating a Document

In this project you will perform several of the procedures in the document cycle as described in the introductory chapter. Additionally, you will use a template to create a document.

Objectives

After completing this project, you will be able to:

➤ Change the view

➤ Enter text

➤ Edit text

➤ Preview a document

➤ Create an envelope

➤ Print a document

➤ Create a fax coversheet from a template

➤ Use Click-n-Type

➤ Create labels

Running Case

Matthew and Rachel, two recent college graduates, work in the Selections public relations department. After analyzing the customer base in the Fields and Home Page departments, they concluded that they are not reaching their college and career-oriented customers. As the result of many brainstorming sessions, they decided to start a promotion called College and Career Week. It will begin with a series of events to promote the Fields and Home Page departments and end with a Career Day to entice college recruits. Although their manager thought it was a fabulous idea, they will have to pitch it to Deborah Ritch and John Vicenti, the store owners.

The Challenge

Matthew will write the letter to the store owners explaining their ideas for the promotion. Before sending the letter, Matthew will fax a copy to Rachel. Rachel will create some labels for file folders to help organize the proposed project.

The Strategy

To create the letter you will:
- Use a file that already contains the letterhead.
- Create the envelope and labels using the Envelope and Labels tool.
- Create a fax using a Word template.

Figures 1.1a and 1.1b show the envelope and the first draft of the letter you will create, the fax that you will create to send to Rachel, and the file folder labels.

FIGURE 1.1a

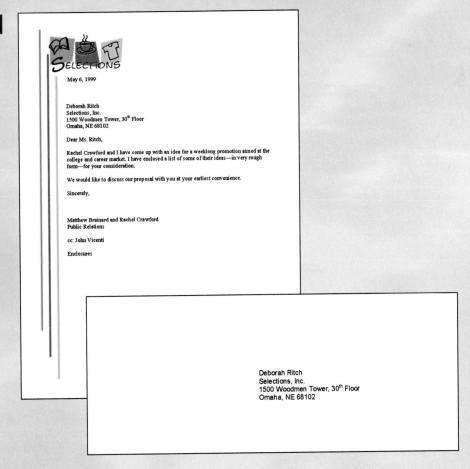

FIGURE 1.1b

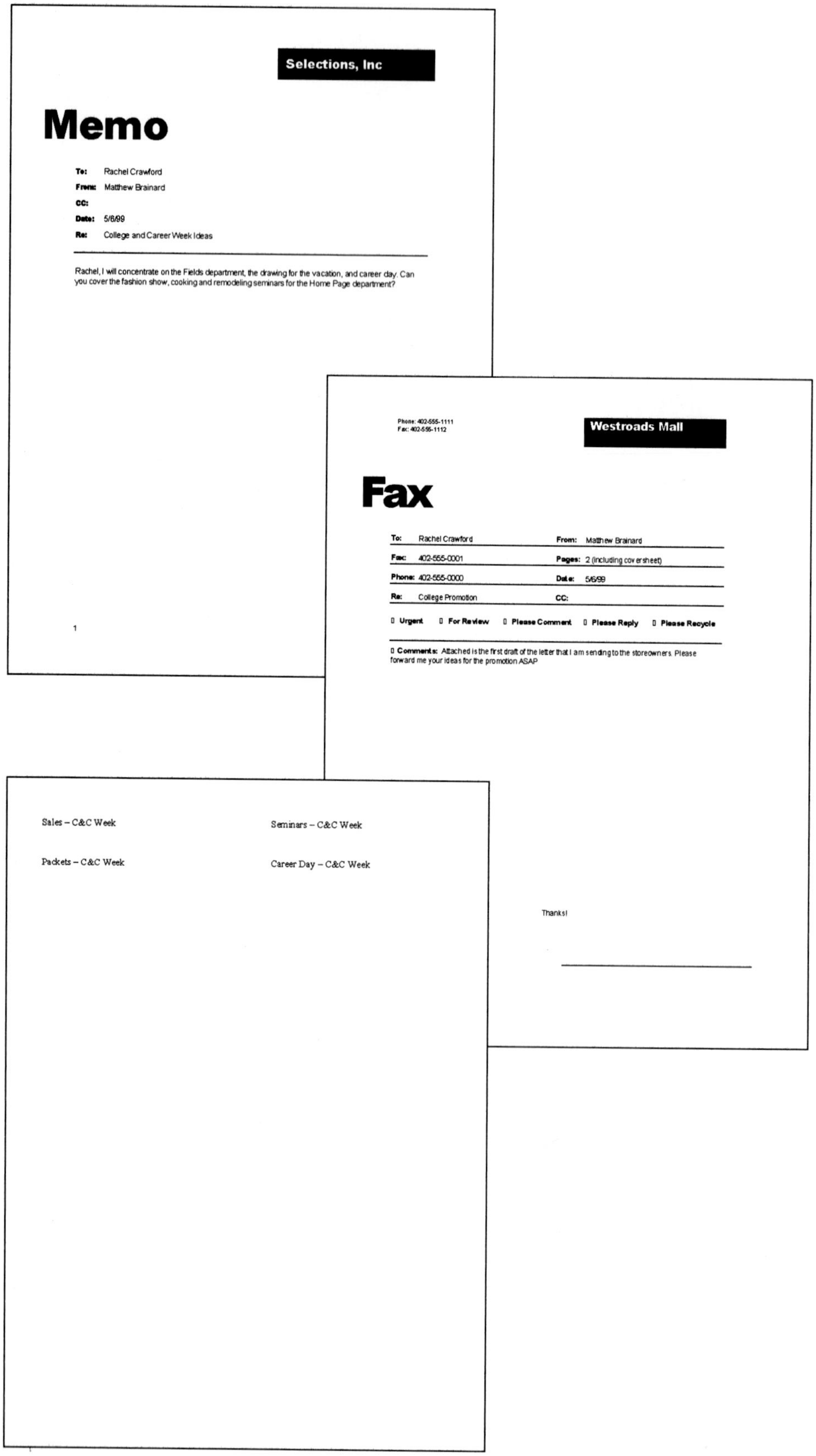

Selections, Inc

Memo

To: Rachel Crawford

From: Matthew Brainard

CC:

Date: 5/6/99

Re: College and Career Week Ideas

Rachel, I will concentrate on the Fields department, the drawing for the vacation, and career day. Can you cover the fashion show, cooking and remodeling seminars for the Home Page department?

1

Phone: 402-555-1111
Fax: 402-555-1112

Westroads Mall

Fax

To:	Rachel Crawford	**From:**	Matthew Brainard
Fax:	402-555-0001	**Pages:**	2 (including cover sheet)
Phone:	402-555-0000	**Date:**	5/6/99
Re:	College Promotion	**CC:**	

☐ **Urgent**   ☐ **For Review**   ☐ **Please Comment**   ☐ **Please Reply**   ☐ **Please Recycle**

☐ **Comments:** Attached is the first draft of the letter that I am sending to the storeowners. Please forward me your ideas for the promotion ASAP

Sales – C&C Week   Seminars – C&C Week

Packets – C&C Week   Career Day – C&C Week

Thanks!

The Setup

So that your screen will match the illustrations and the tasks in this project will function as described, make sure that the Word 2000 settings listed in Table 1.1 match those on your computer. Before checking these options, make sure that you have turned off the menu customization feature by choosing Tools, Customize, Options, and deselect the options Standard and Formatting toolbars share one row and Menus show recently used commands first.

Table 1.1: Word 2000 Settings

Location:	Make these settings:
View	Choose Ruler to ensure the ruler is activated.
View, Toolbars	Deselect all toolbars except Standard and Formatting. Then deselect any buttons that are selected in the Standard toolbar and set the Zoom to 100%.
Tools, AutoCorrect, AutoText	Deselect Show AutoComplete tip for AutoText and dates.
Tools, Options, Spelling & Grammar	Select all options in the dialog box except the following: Hide spelling errors in this document, Suggest from main dictionary only, Hide grammatical errors in this document, and Show readability statistics. Choose Standard for Writing style.

Changing the View

Word 2000 has four views for working with documents—Normal, Web Layout, Print Layout, and Outline. Each view has features that are useful in different situations. Table 1.2 describes the views and when to use them.

Table 1.2: Using Views

View	Description
Normal	Does not display unused white space on the page, including the margin space, headers and footers, or floating graphics. Use this view when you need to see the maximum possible amount of text on the screen.
Web Layout	Wraps all text to fit the width of the window. Use this view when you are working on a document that will be viewed onscreen or on the Web.
Print Layout	Displays margins and unused white space on the page, all graphics, and headers and footers, as well as a visual page break between pages. Use this view when you want to see how the page will look when it prints.
Outline	Displays the text of a document in outline form. Use this view for viewing and rearranging the structure of documents that contain headings and subheadings.

TASK 1: <u>To Change the View</u>

1 Launch Word by choosing Start, Programs, Microsoft Word. Document1 is created.

2 Click the Open 📂 button.

3 Navigate to your data directory by clicking the icon for the folder if it appears in the left pane or by selecting the drive from the Look in list and then, if necessary, by double-clicking the appropriate folder(s).

4 Click the document named *ColorLetterhead.doc.* The document is highlighted in the list.

FIGURE 1.2

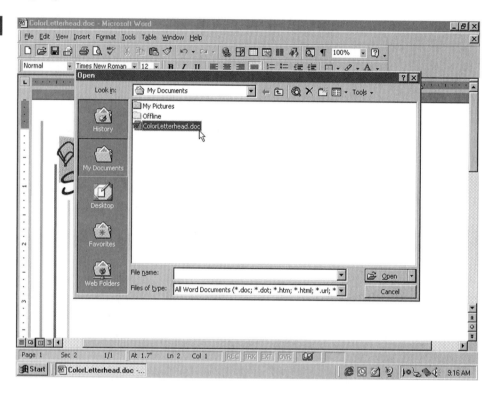

5 Click the Open drop-down list arrow and choose Open as Copy.

6 Press (CTRL) + (END). The insertion point moves to the end of the document.

7 Choose View.

FIGURE 1.3

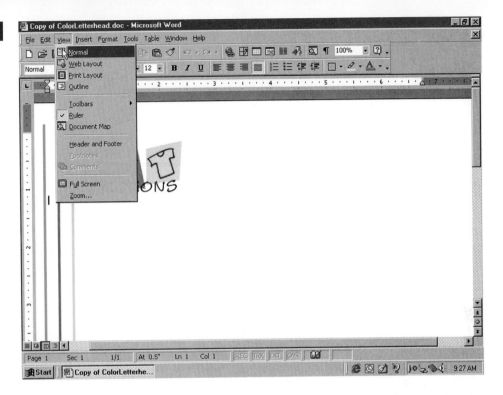

8 Choose Normal unless the option already has a checkmark beside it. The Normal View button appears depressed in the horizontal scroll bar and a hidden feature called a section break displays. You'll learn more about section breaks in Project 4.

9 Click the Print Layout View 📧 button in the horizontal scroll bar.

FIGURE 1.4

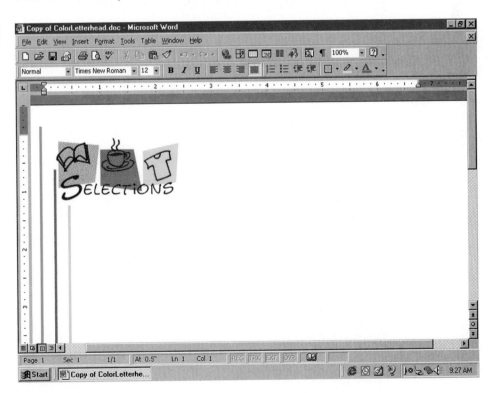

Checkpoint

Notice that the lines, which are drawing objects, do not appear in Normal view.

Entering Text

Instead of typing the complete letter you see in Figure 1.1a, you will type the letter in sections so that you can concentrate on individual features and commands. As you type, you will press the (ENTER) key only to end short lines, end paragraphs, or create blank lines. As you type text continuously, Word will **wrap** the text to fit within the preset left and right margins.

> **TIP** Word presets the left and right margins to 1.25 inches, and the top and bottom margins to 1 inch.

Inserting the Date

Although it is easy to type the date in a letter, Word provides a command that will insert the date for you. The command is really used more often to insert a **date code**, a date that automatically updates each time the file is opened. You can use the date code in a document that is revised and printed frequently to identify the date the version was printed.

TASK 2: To Insert the Date

 Choose Insert.

FIGURE 1.5

Insert
Break...
Page Numbers...
Date and Time...
AutoText ▶
Field...
Symbol...
Comment

Footnote...
Caption...
Cross-reference...
Index and Tables...

Picture ▶
Text Box
File...
Object...
Bookmark...
Hyperlink... Ctrl+K

2   Choose Date and Time.

FIGURE 1.6

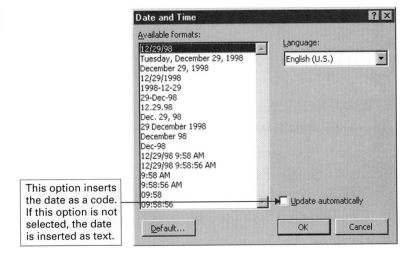

This option inserts the date as a code. If this option is not selected, the date is inserted as text.

3   Select the third format from the list shown.

FIGURE 1.7

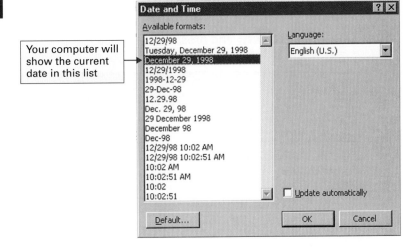

Your computer will show the current date in this list

TIP   If you want to use the same date format in all your documents, select Default and then select Yes.

4   Select Update Automatically.

TIP   Normally, you would not insert a date code in a letter because you would want the letter to reflect the date the letter was actually sent and not change every time you opened the file. In this case, the letter will not be sent out for several days, so when the letter is actually opened and printed for mailing, the date will be correct. If you keep the letter for future reference, you should delete the date code and type the date or insert it as text.

5 Select OK. The current date (if the date in the computer is accurate) appears in the document.

TASK 3: To Type the First Part of the Letter

1 Press (ENTER) four times after the date.

2 Type **Deborah Rich**.

3 Press (BACKSPACE) twice and then type **tch**. The (BACKSPACE) key erased two characters so you could retype the correct spelling of the name.

4 Press (ENTER). The insertion point moves to the next line.

5 Type the following lines, pressing (ENTER) after each line:

Selections, Inc.

1500 Woodman Tower, 30th Floor

Omaha, NE 68102

6 Press (ENTER) again to create a blank line between the address and the salutation.

7 Type **Dear Ms. Ritch:** and press (ENTER) twice.

FIGURE 1.8

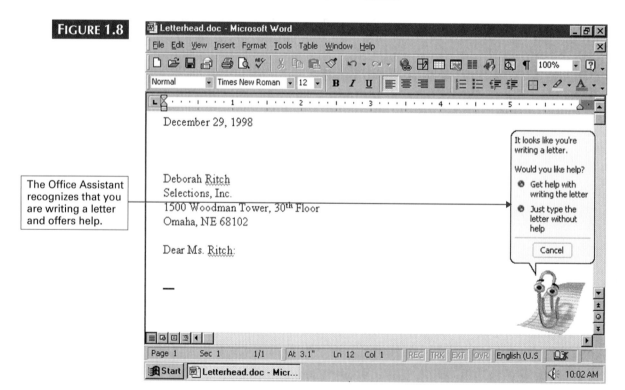

The Office Assistant recognizes that you are writing a letter and offers help.

8 Select Just type the letter without help. The Office Assistant closes.

TIP If the Office Assistant does not close, choose Help, Hide the Assistant.

9 Type the following:

Rachel Crawford and I have come up with an idea for a week-long promotion aimed at

10 Type the following (including the typo) and type a space after the period:

teh college and career market.

Word automatically corrects the typographical error because it is a default AutoCorrect entry.

11 Choose File, Save As; specify the drive and folder where you are keeping your work in the Save in text box; name the file *Promo Letter*; and select Save.

> **TIP** You might want to create folders on your data disk for each project in this book. To create a folder, click the Create New Folder ⬚ button in the Save As dialog box and specify the path and name of the folder.

> **TROUBLESHOOTING** If you find the Office Assistant annoying, you can turn it off by right-clicking the Office Assistant, choosing Options, and de-selecting Use the Office Assistant.

Inserting Symbols and Special Characters

The keyboard has a limited number of alphanumeric and punctuation characters it can produce. Other characters, such as Greek letters, mathematical symbols, and special symbols such as © and ® can be inserted by using the Symbol dialog box.

TASK 4: To Insert a Special Character

1 Type **I have enclosed a list of some of our ideas** and choose Insert, Symbol.

FIGURE 1.9

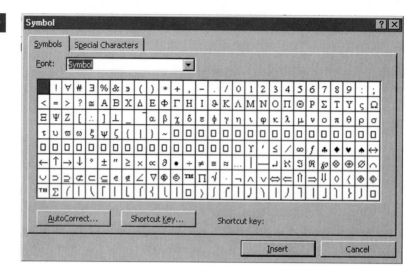

2 Click the Special Characters tab, if necessary.

FIGURE 1.10

Em dash is selected

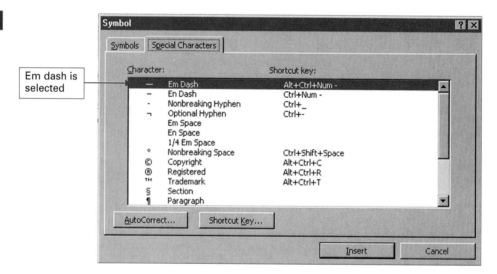

3 Select Insert. The character is inserted in the document, but the dialog box remains open.

4 Select Close.

TROUBLESHOOTING If you have a really long dash, you probably clicked Insert more than once. Just press (BACKSPACE) to erase.

5 Type **in very rough form**, insert another em dash, and then type **for your consideration.**

6 Press (ENTER) twice and type the following:

We would like to discuss our proposal with you at your earliest convenience.

7 Press (ENTER) twice; type **Sincerely,**; press (ENTER) four times; and type the following:

Matthew Brainard and Rachel Crawford
Public Relations

cc:

> **TIP** If Word automatically capitalizes the first letter *c*, the Capitalize first letter of sentences option is selected in the AutoCorrect dialog box.

8 Press (CTRL) + Z, if necessary. Word reverses the AutoCorrect.

9 Type **John Vicenti** and press (ENTER) twice.

> **TIP** This letter fits on one page. If you had been typing a letter that would not fit on one page, Word would have inserted a page break for you automatically when the text exceeded what would fit on the page.

Creating and Using AutoText Entries

Since you write a lot of letters, it would be nice to be able to press a few keys and get the *signature block* ("Sincerely," followed by four returns and your name) without having to type the same thing every time. The AutoText feature stores text, formatting, and even graphics, and recalls them on command. Watch how it works in this task.

TASK 5: To Create and Use an AutoText Entry

1 Select the signature block text from "Sincerely" through the department name, as shown in Figure 1.11.

> **TIP** Be sure to select all of the last line so the return at the end of the line will be included.

FIGURE 1.11

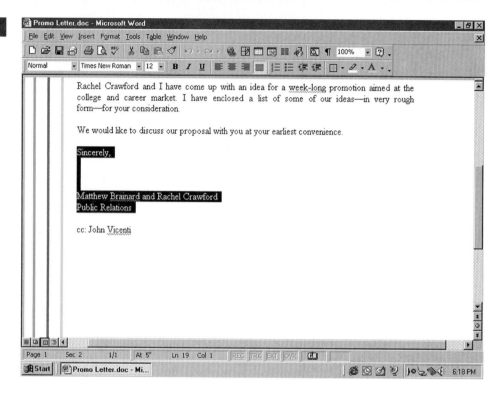

2 Press ⟨ALT⟩ + ⟨F3⟩.

FIGURE 1.12

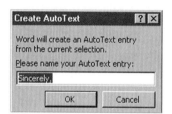

3 Type **sig block** and select OK.

> **TIP** Use short names or abbreviations for AutoText entries to cut down on your typing.

4 Press ⟨DEL⟩. The signature block is deleted.

5 Type **sig block** and press ⟨F3⟩. You can now use this signature block AutoText entry in any document.

> **TIP** AutoText is not case sensitive.

Using AutoComplete

The AutoComplete feature can complete some commonly used words such as the names of the days of the week and the names of the months. When

AutoComplete wants to complete a word or phrase for you, it displays a ScreenTip showing the word or phrase it will insert.

AutoComplete can also execute AutoText entries for you such as the one you created in the previous task. After you perform the steps in the next task, you may think that there is little to be gained by using AutoComplete as opposed to using the AutoText entry itself because both are executed by pressing a single keystroke. Think about it and see if you can determine the advantage of using AutoComplete.

TASK 6:   To Use AutoComplete

1 Choose Tools, AutoCorrect, AutoText. The AutoText page of the dialog box displays.

2 Select Show AutoComplete tip for AutoText and dates and select OK. The dialog box closes.

TROUBLESHOOTING You must select this option in the AutoCorrect dialog box before AutoCorrect will work with AutoText.

3 Delete the signature block and type **sig b**.

FIGURE 1.13

The AutoComplete tip displays the AutoText entry.

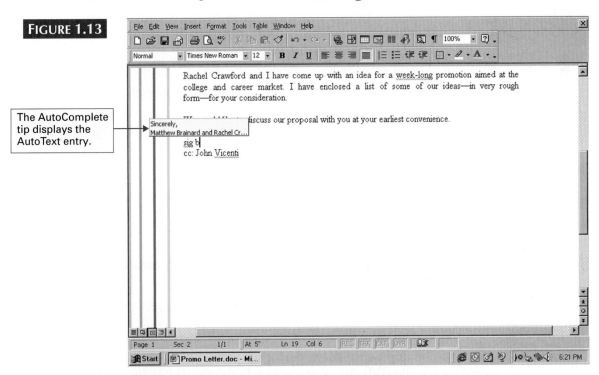

TIP AutoComplete is not case-sensitive.

4 Press (ENTER). The signature block appears.

> **TIP** If you don't want to use the AutoComplete tip, you can just keep typing when the AutoComplete tip appears and it will go away. For example, if you were typing the instruction, "Make sure the sig block is lined up with the left margin," you would just keep typing because you don't actually want the signature block.

Check Point

So, what is the advantage to using AutoComplete? You don't have to type the complete name of the AutoText entry. This allows you to give AutoText entries longer, more descriptive names.

Break Point

If necessary you can save your file, exit Word, and continue this project later.

Editing Text

At this point, you are ready to spell-check the document and proof the document on screen. To use basic editing and formatting skills, you will make a few changes to the document. Then you will check the spelling.

TASK 7: Making Changes in the Document

1 Launch Word and open *PromoLetter.doc*, if necessary. Press (CTRL) + (END). The insertion point moves to the end of the document.

2 Type **Enclosure** and press (ENTER).

3 At the end of the first body paragraph, select the word *consideration* and type **review**. Word replaces the text.

4 Click the Undo button. Word restores the original text.

5 Click the Redo button. Word changes the text back to *review* again.

6 Click the insertion point before the words *your earliest convenience* and press (INS). The OVR indicator appears in the status bar, indicating that Word is now in Overtype mode.

7 Type **some future date**, press (DEL) to delete the remainder of the word *convenience*, and press (INS) again.

8 Click the Undo drop-down list arrow.

FIGURE 1.14

9 Scroll to Typing "Review" and select it. Word reverses the edits you made to *consideration* and *your earliest convenience*.

10 Right-click the word *week-long* and select *weeklong*.

11 Save the document.

TASK 8: <u>Spell-Checking the Document</u>

1 Press (CTRL) + (HOME) and click the Spelling and Grammar button. The Spelling and Grammar dialog box opens. The first word it finds that is not in the dictionary is Ritch.

2 Select Ignore All. The spell checker displays the next word that is not in the dictionary or the next grammatical problem.

3 Respond appropriately to each word or grammatical problem and choose OK when the spell checker reports that it is finished.

> **TIP** See Common Elements Project 2, Common Text and Art Elements for more information on the Spell Checking feature.

Previewing a Document

Previewing a document is one of the frequently performed procedures in the document cycle outlined in "Introduction to Word 2000." Although Print Layout view displays the document as it will look when it prints, you may prefer to use the Print Preview feature, which allows you to see the complete page or as many as 24 pages on the screen at the same time. You can also edit and print in Print Preview mode and use all the menu options that are available to you in other views, except some of the options on the Window menu.

TASK 9: To Preview the Document

1 Click the Print Preview 🔍 button.

FIGURE 1.15

The default zoom is determined by the screen's resolution.

You can print from the Print Preview.

The Magnifier button is selected by default.

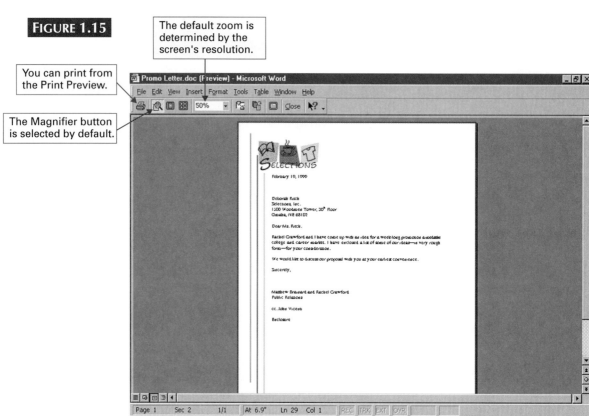

2 Click the inside address on the document. The Zoom changes to 100% and the pointer displays as a minus sign in the center of the magnifying glass.

> **TIP** Clicking the pointer when it looks like a magnifying glass with a minus sign in it returns the zoom to the default.

3 Click the Magnifier 🔍 button. Click before the *a* in *Woodman*.

4 Press ⌐DEL⌐ and type **e**. The spelling is corrected.

5 Click Close ⌐Close⌐. The Print Preview closes and the document screen appears.

Creating an Envelope

Now you need to create an envelope for the letter. If you create the envelope while the letter is open, you can use the Envelope and Label tool without having to type the address. The tool also inserts the return address automatically if you have previously specified a default return address.

> **TIP** It is not necessary to specify a return address if you will be printing on a preprinted envelope, one that already has the return address printed on it.

TASK 10: To Create an Envelope

1 Choose Tools, Envelopes and Labels. Click the Envelopes tab if necessary.

FIGURE 1.16

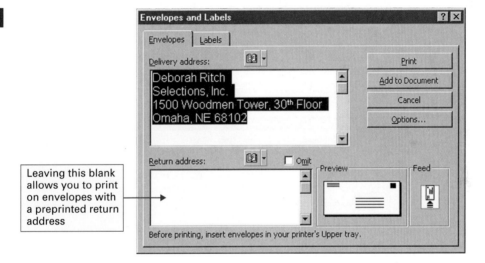

Leaving this blank allows you to print on envelopes with a preprinted return address

> **TIP** The default envelope size is a number 10 (business-size) envelope. To change the size, select Options, select the size you want, and select OK.

2 Select Add to Document. Word adds the envelope at the beginning of the document as page 0. The letter remains as page 1. Word automatically inserts a section break between the envelope and the letter because they have different page layouts, as shown in Figure 1.17. Remember, you'll learn more about section breaks in Project 4.

FIGURE 1.17

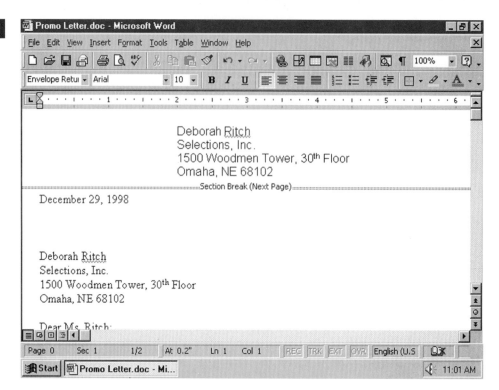

③ Click the Print Layout View 🔲 button and scroll to see the page break.

FIGURE 1.18

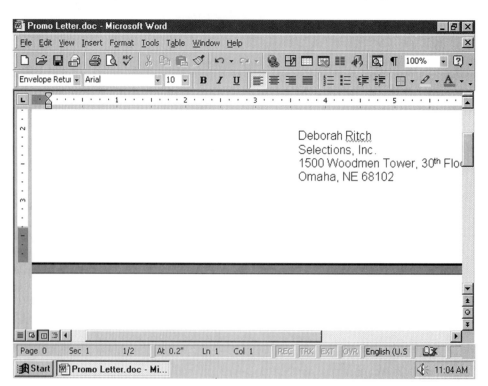

Printing a Document

At this point in the document cycle, it is a good idea to print the document. It seems that no matter how thoroughly you proof a document on the screen, you always miss something that jumps out at you when you print it.

In addition to the basic printing techniques described in Common Elements Project 1, Word has some additional printing capabilities. Table 1.3 explains the printing capabilities that are unique to Word.

Table 1.3: Additional Print Options in Word

Option	Description
Print what	In addition to the document, contains options for printing the properties of the document, a list of the comments inserted in a document, a list of styles used in the document, a list of AutoText entries in the template used by the document as well as the entries in the default template, and a list of keys assigned to functions.
Pages per sheet	Prints more than one page on a sheet of paper. Unless you have specified a custom paper size, however, the text is reduced to fit on the page. For example, if the paper size for the document is 8.5″ × 11″, and you print multiple pages on an 8.5″ × 11″ sheet of paper, the text will be reduced to fit all the pages on the sheet. On the other hand, if you specify a custom paper size of 5.5″ × 8.5″ in the Page Setup dialog box, you can print two pages on an 8.5″ × 11″ sheet of paper and the text will not be reduced.
Scale to paper size	Increases or decreases the font used in the document so that each page of the document will fit on a different size paper than the one specified in the Page Setup dialog box. For example, if you create a document to print on 8.5″ × 11″ paper, you can use this option to make the text of each page fit on A4-size paper (a smaller size paper used extensively in Europe).

TASK 11: To Print a Document

1 Choose File, Print.

FIGURE 1.19

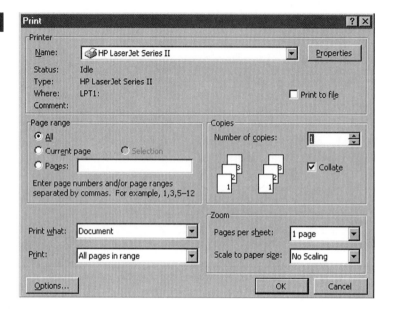

2 Type **1** in the Pages text box and select OK. The letter prints.

> **TIP** To print noncontiguous pages, enter the page numbers separated by commas. To print a range of pages, enter the page numbers separated by a hyphen. To print both noncontiguous pages and a range of pages, separate the noncontiguous pages from the ranges with commas—for example 1,3,6–10, 12.

3 Save and close the file.

Creating a Fax Cover Sheet from a Template

Now that the letter is completed, you must fax a copy of it to Rachel. To create the fax cover sheet, you will use a Word **template**, a file with a professionally designed format that may include its own menus and toolbars, boilerplate text, text entry fields, specific fonts, colors, graphics, backgrounds, and so on. Word provides templates for creating legal documents, letters, faxes, memos, miscellaneous documents (invoices, résumés, newsletters, press releases, reports, and so on) and Web pages.

> **TROUBLESHOOTING** Many templates must be installed on first use. If you do not have access to the installation CD or the installation files on the network, you will not be able to install the template if it has not already been installed.

TASK 12: To Create a Fax Cover Sheet from a Template

1 Choose File, New. Click the Letters & Faxes tab, if necessary.

FIGURE 1.20

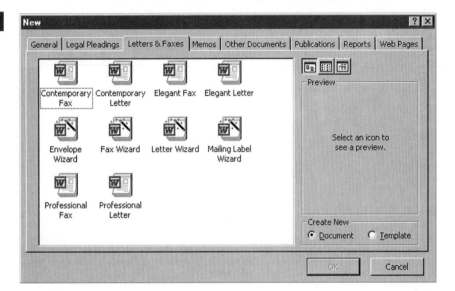

2 Select Professional Fax. If the template is installed, a preview of the template appears in the Preview area. If the template is not installed, the preview area displays an instruction to click OK to install the template and create a new file.

3 Select OK. The Professional Fax template appears, as shown in Figure 1.21.

> **TROUBLESHOOTING** If you are prompted to access the MS Office 2000 installation files, the Professional Fax template has not been installed. Ask your instructor for assistance with installing the template.

FIGURE 1.21

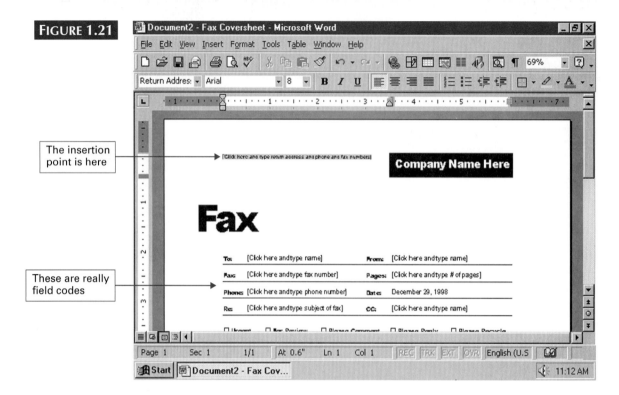

The insertion point is here

These are really field codes

4 If necessary, click the instruction that says "Click here and type return address . . ." and then type the following:

Phone: 402-555-1111

Fax: 402-555-1112

The field is replaced by the new information.

5 Click before the word *Company*, press (INS), type **Westroads Mall**, and press (INS) again. *Company Name* is replaced by *Westroads Mall*. Press (DEL) to delete the extra characters.

6 Fill in the information in the coversheet by clicking the appropriate instruction and typing the text as follows:

To:	**Rachel Crawford**	From:	**Matthew Brainard**
Fax:	**402-555-0001**	Pages:	**2 (including coversheet)**
Phone:	**402-555-0000**	Date:	Skip this field.
Re:	**College Promotion**	CC:	Click this field and press (DEL).

7 Select all the text after *Comments:* and type the following:

Attached is the first draft of the letter that I am sending to the store owners. Please forward me your ideas for the promotion ASAP.

TIP If you have a fax/modem that is configured properly, you can fax your documents directly from the computer.

Web Tip

New templates and other enhancements can be downloaded for free from the Microsoft Web site at http://www.microsoft.com. Look for links to Office products, updates, and downloads.

Using Click-n-Type

Click-n-Type is a new feature in Word 2000 that allows you to position the insertion point anywhere in the normal typing area of a document and start typing.

> **TIP** Click-n-Type automatically inserts tabs or returns as needed to position the insertion point.

Click-n-Type uses six typing areas called **zones** to determine the alignment that will be applied to text or objects inserted in that zone. The following diagram shows the zones, from the left to the right margin, and the appearance of the I-beam for each location. The I-beam changes to show the alignment that will be applied to the text if you type in the particular area.

Zone 1	Zone 2	Zone 3	Zone 4	Zone 5	Zone 6
left-aligned	left-aligned with a first line indent	left-aligned	centered	left-aligned	right-aligned
I≡	I≛	I≡	I	I≡	≡I

TASK 13: To Use Click-n-Type

1 Scroll to the bottom of the page and move the I-beam to the center of the document about an inch above the faint line on the right.

2 First try to click in the area. You can't.

3 Now, double-click and type **Thanks!**.

4 Print the file and then save it as *Fax*.

5 Keep this file open for the next task.

> **TIP** To deactivate Click-n-Type, choose Tools, Options, Edit; deselect Enable Click-n-Type, and select OK.

Creating Labels

Using the Envelopes and Labels feature in Word, the process of creating a label is almost as easy as creating an envelope. In this next task, you will create labels for organizing the project.

TASK 14: To Create a Label

1 Choose Tools, Envelopes and Labels, and click the Labels tab.

FIGURE 1.22

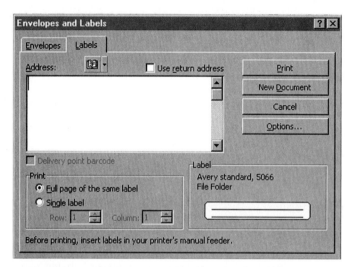

2 Select Options.

FIGURE 1.23

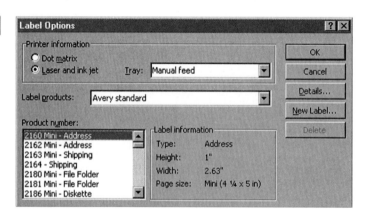

TIP In the Label Options dialog box, Word lists brands of label products that can be purchased at most office supply stores. The product number in the dialog box corresponds to the product number of the labels for purchase. Label information gives the label size and sheet size.

3 Select 5066 – File Folder from the Product number list and select OK.

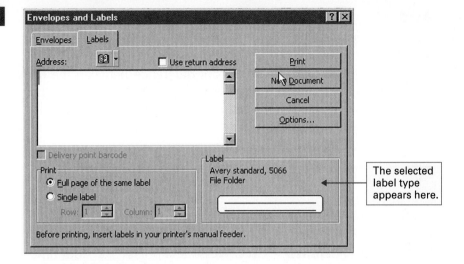

FIGURE 1.24

The selected label type appears here.

4 Select New Document.

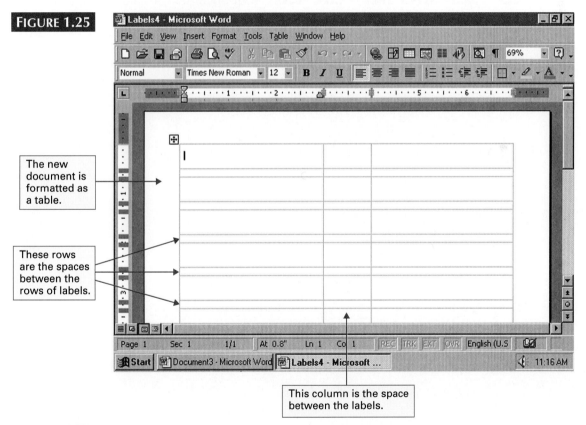

FIGURE 1.25

The new document is formatted as a table.

These rows are the spaces between the rows of labels.

This column is the space between the labels.

5 If your screen does not look like Figure 1.25, choose Table, Show Gridlines.

Check Point

Did you notice one significant difference between the options for creating labels and creating envelopes? On the Envelopes page, there is an option to add the envelope to the current document. On the Labels page, there is no such option. There is only an option to create a new document.

6 Type **Sales – C&C Week** and press (TAB) twice.

> **TIP** Create an AutoText entry for the text "C&C Week."

7 Type **Seminars – C&C Week** and press (TAB) four times.

8 Type **Packets – C&C Week** and press (TAB) twice.

9 Type **Career Day – C&C Week**. Your document should look like the one in Figure 1.1.

10 Save the file as *C&C Labels* and close the file.

11 Close the *Fax.doc* file.

Summary and Exercises

Summary

- Word provides four views for working with documents: Normal view, Web Layout view, Print Layout view, and Outline view.
- You can insert a date in various formats or insert a date code that automatically updates to the current date when the file is opened.
- You can insert special characters and symbols by using the Symbols dialog box.
- Word completes AutoText entries and some common words for you such as the names of the months and the names of the days.
- The Envelopes and Labels feature creates envelopes and label layouts automatically.
- Word provides many templates for creating and formatting documents.
- Click-n-Type is a new feature that allows you to type anywhere in a document.

Key Terms and Operations

Key Terms

AutoComplete	special character
AutoText entry	symbol
date code	template
Normal view	Web Layout view
Outline view	wrap
Print Layout view	zones
signature block	zoom

Operations

change the view	insert special characters
check spelling	insert symbols
create a document from a template	magnify a document
	preview a document
create a label	print a document
create an AutoText entry	redo an operation
create an envelope	undo an operation
enter text	use an AutoText entry
insert a date	use Click-n-Type
insert a date code	

Study Questions

Multiple Choice

1. Print Preview mode
   a. can show only one page at a time.
   b. can zoom to different magnifications.
   c. can display as many as 32 pages at once.
   d. appears automatically before you print a document.

2. A date code
   a. displays the same date each time the document is opened.
   b. displays the current date each time the document is opened.
   c. displays the date the document was last printed.
   d. displays the date the document was created.

3. The AutoComplete feature
   a. displays an AutoText entry in a screen tip.
   b. displays a frequently used word or phrase that you can select from a drop-down list.
   c. replaces AutoText entries automatically after you type them.
   d. cannot be disabled.

4. Which of the following keystrokes should not be performed when typing a document?
   a. Press (BACKSPACE) to erase the character to the left.
   b. Press (ENTER) at the end of every line.
   c. Press (ENTER) to create a blank line.
   d. Press (ENTER) to end a short line.

5. When you add an envelope to a document, the envelope is inserted
   a. after the active page.
   b. before the active page.
   c. as the last page.
   d. as the first page.

6. The default envelope size is number
   a. 9.
   b. 10.
   c. 11.
   d. 12.

7. Which of the following statements concerning Print Preview mode is false?
   a. Not all options on the Window menu are available.
   b. You cannot edit the document.
   c. You can print the document.
   d. You can view multiple pages at the same time.

8. You accidentally pressed a key that caused something unexpected to happen to the format of the document. What is the best action to take to correct the problem if you are not sure what you did?
   a. Close the file without saving it.
   b. Click the Undo button.
   c. Click the Redo button.
   d. Choose Tools, AutoCorrect.

9. How do you access a document template?
   a. Click the New button.
   b. Choose File, Open.
   c. Choose Tools, Templates and Add-Ins.
   d. Choose File, New.

10. Which of the following alignments is not used by Click-n-Type?
   a. left
   b. centered
   c. right
   d. justified

Short Answer

1. What is the difference between inserting a date and inserting a date code?

2. How do you insert a character that cannot be entered from the keyboard, such as the copyright symbol?

3. Can you edit a document in the Print Preview mode?

4. Which view wraps the text to fit on the screen?

5. If AutoComplete displays a phrase that you want to use, how do you use it?

6. What do you do if you do not want to use an AutoComplete phrase?

7. What determines the alignment that will be applied to text if you use Click-n-Type?

8. How do you position the I-beam when you want to use Click-n-Type?

9. How do you magnify the document in Print Preview?

10. How does Print Preview mode help the environment and save money too?

Fill in the Blank

1. To end a paragraph, press _____.

2. You can fax documents directly from your computer if you have a(n) _____.

3. Word's default left and right margins are _____ inch(es).

4. Word's default top and bottom margins are _____ inch(es).

5. Press _____ to move the insertion point to the end of the document.

6. In Print Preview, if the pointer looks like a magnifying glass and has a minus sign in the middle, the zoom is _____ %.

7. If a document has headings and subheadings, you can use _____ view to see its structure.

8. To insert a special character, choose Insert, _____.

9. To reverse an undo, click the _____ button.

10. To delete the character to the right of the insertion point, press _____.

For Discussion

1. Discuss the four views provided by Word and when they are used.

2. Describe the Click-n-Type feature.

3. Discuss the advantages of using a template to create documents.

4. Discuss the features of the Print Preview feature.

5. Discuss the additional print options that Word offers that are not available in the other Office 2000 applications.

Hands-On Exercises

1. Creating a Memo

So that Rachel and Matthew don't duplicate their efforts, Matthew is sending Rachel a memo as shown in Figure 1.26.

FIGURE 1.26

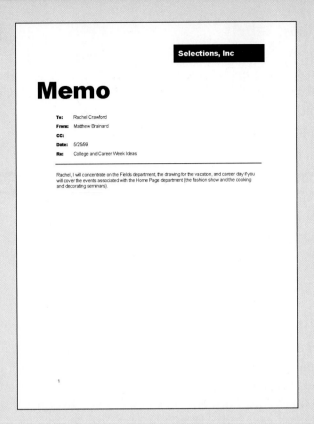

1. Create a new document using the Professional Memo template.

2. Select *Company Name Here* and type **Selections, Inc.**

3. Click the appropriate field codes and enter the following data:

   To: **Rachel Crawford**

   From: **Matthew Brainard**

   Re: **College and Career Week Ideas**

4. Click the field beside CC: and delete it.

5. Select the text below the horizontal line and type the following:

   Rachel, I will concentrate on the Fields department, the drawing for vacation, and career day if you will cover the events associated with the Home Page department (the fashion show and the cooking and decorating seminars).

6. Save the file as *Memo.doc*.

7. Send the file to your instructor as an attachment. Choose File, Send To, Mail Recipient (as Attachment). Address the e-mail and click the Send button.

8. Close the file.

2. Creating Mailing Labels

Rachel wants to form a volunteer advisory board made up of college students from colleges in the state. She intends to send a letter to the Dean of Students at each college asking for their cooperation and recommendations. You will create the mailing labels for the letters.

1. Open any document or create a new one.
2. Create a page of blank Avery 5160 address labels.
3. Search the Internet for the addresses of colleges and universities in Nebraska and type the addresses of at least ten of those that are closest to Omaha.
4. Save the file as *College Labels.doc* and close it.

On Your Own Exercises

1. Writing a Letter to a Friend

Using the Letter Wizard, create a letter to a friend. (Choose File, New, and click the Letters & Faxes tab. Double-click the Letter Wizard, choose Send one letter, and click OK. Then make selections or fill in information and click Next to continue. When finished, click Finish.) Add the proper spacing in the letter and then create and add an envelope to the document. Use Print Preview to view the letter and envelope. Save the file as *Letter1* and close it.

2. Writing a Letter to Another Friend

Open a copy of the letter you created in the previous exercise. Choose File, Save As; type **Letter2**; choose a different Save in location if you want to; and select Save. Edit the letter so it uses the name of another friend in both the inside address of the letter and the envelope. Insert additional text and delete text as appropriate. Save and close the file.

3. Creating Mailing Labels

Create a label document that has the mailing addresses of frequently used addresses. These might include addresses for your family and friends or billing addresses. Include duplicate labels for addresses that you mail to more than others. Save the document as *Frequent labels* and close it.

4. Creating AutoText Entries

Create a new document, enter text that you might use often and create AutoText entries for them. Suggested entries include your name, your address, a signature block with your name, your e-mail address, or your phone number.

5. Creating Your Own AutoCorrect Entries

Think of all the typographical errors you frequently make or words that you misspell and then choose Tools, AutoCorrect. Scroll the list of default AutoCorrect entries and see if yours are included. For any of the words on your list that are not included, type the incorrect word in the Replace: text box, type the correct work in the With text box, and select Add. When you've added all your entries, select OK.

6. Creating Your Own Quick Reference

Create a document that lists some of the shortcuts and tips that you need to remember. You can start by asking the Office Assistant to help you look for tips and keyboard shortcuts in the Help feature. To use the Office Assistant, press (F1) or choose Help, Show the Office Assistant, and click the character to display the "What would you like to do?" bubble. Type a question and select Search. Click the blue bullet of the topic you want to read or click See more to see more topics.

 **Web Tip**

After clicking See more, click None of the above, look for more help on the Web to see additional help on the Web.

Editing and Formatting a Document

I f you remember the document cycle discussed in "Introduction to Word 2000," you know that creating a document is just the beginning of your work. In this project you will polish your document by editing and formatting text and checking spelling and grammar.

Objectives

After completing this project, you will be able to:

➤ Insert a file

➤ Navigate through a document

➤ Browse for and delete objects

➤ Find and delete text

➤ Move text

➤ Find and replace text

➤ Format text

➤ Use writing and proofing tools

Running Case

Rachel and Matthew have both created documents that contain their ideas for College and Career Week. As you will see, the two documents are quite different in appearance. Rachel's document doesn't have much formatting, while Matthew's has lots of formatting and graphics. The two documents need to be combined into one cohesive report and enclosed with the letter to Deborah Ritch you prepared in Project 1.

The Challenge

It will be your job to combine the letter and the two documents from Rachel and Matthew. You will have to reconcile Rachel's and Matthew's different styles using editing and formatting techniques. Then you will check the documents' spelling and grammar before printing them.

The Strategy

You will begin by combining the files into one document by using the Insert command. Then you will use delete, rearrange, and format the text to create a professional looking report. Figures 2.1a and 2.1b show how you will combine the best features of both documents to produce the report.

FIGURE 2.1a

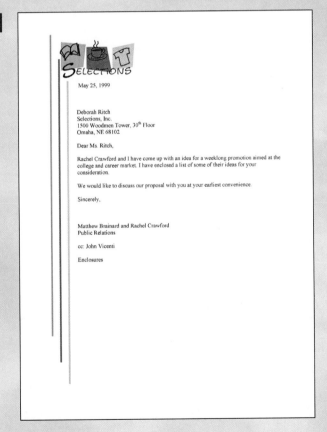

FIGURE 2.1b

College and Career Sales Promotion for Selections of Omaha

Advisory Board
Form a volunteer advisory board made up of local college students and young career people – there would obviously have to be some perks for volunteering like discounts on merchandise. Get their recommendation for the promotion and enlist their help in promoting it.

Career Day
Promote the store's management training program.
Distribute information on the company, its benefits, etc.
Make a live multimedia presentation or run a continuous video in a kiosk area.
Take resumes and do interviews.
Have recruiting personnel on hand to answer questions.

Drawing
Hold a drawing for prizes such as ski equipment and/or a ski trip. Let Peek-a-boo draw out the winning names.
To enter the drawing, have customers write their names/addresses on the back of discount coupons that they redeem when they purchase something. No limit to the number of entries – the more sales the better!

Money-Saving Discount Coupons
Print coupons to be included in a packet.
Use a different format for each type of coupon. For example, coupons for 10% off in the Fields department could look like tickets to a ball game.
Students must show their student IDs and register with their names and addresses to obtain the coupon packets.
Add names to our mailing list.

Sale in Fields Department
Feature world-famous skier Peek-a-boo Streak and his new line of skis.
If possible, get Streak to make a personal appearance.

Sale in Net-Works Department
Try to get several popular musical personalities/groups to appear for autographs and media sales. Suggested celebrities: Barf Crooks or Polly Darton for country and Industrial Nightmare or Steelica for rock.

Sale in Image Control Department
Fashion show. Members of the advisory board model clothes. Perhaps get someone like model Mindy Crawfish to host the show.

Sale in the Home Page Department
Seminars aimed at college kids, such as a dorm room makeover seminar and a cooking in the dorm room seminar. Get celebrities for these events.

Giveaways
T-Shirts with Selections logo.

Credit Card Applications
Set up booths throughout the store for applying for a Selections Credit Card.
Offer 10% off of the first credit card purchase.
Set up boots close to cash registers so sales clerks can refer buyers to the booth. (I've been in stores where the sales clerk tries to sign you up right at the register, but it's so annoying if you have to wait in line behind someone while they make an application!)

The Setup

So that your screen will match the illustrations and the tasks in this project will function as described, make sure that the Word 2000 settings listed in Table 2.1 match those on your computer.

Table 2.1: Word 2000 Settings

Location:	Make these settings:
View	Choose Ruler to ensure ruler is activated.
View, Toolbars	Deselect all toolbars except Standard and Formatting. Then deselect any buttons that are selected in the Standard toolbar and set the Zoom to 100%.
View, Options, Edit	Select Drag-and-drop text editing.
Tools, Customize, Options	Deselect Standard and Formatting toolbars share one row and deselect Menus show recently used commands first.
Tools, Options, Spelling & Grammar	Select all options in the dialog box except the following: Hide spelling errors in this document, Suggest from main dictionary only, Hide grammatical errors in this document, and Show readability statistics.
Help, Show Office Assistant	Right-click the Office Assistant and choose options, and Use the Office Assistant.

Inserting a File

You will begin with the letter written to Deborah Ritch and insert the two files from Rachel and Matthew. Inserting the file is easier than copying and pasting an entire file, especially if the file is lengthy.

TASK 1:   To Insert a Page Break and Insert a File

1 Open the *Promo Letter* file that you created in Project 1 and press (CTRL) + (END). The insertion point moves to the end of the document.

2 Press (CTRL) + (ENTER). A new blank page is created in the open document.

> **TIP** To delete a page break, display the document in Normal view so you can see the page break (a dashed line), click the page break, and press (DEL).

3 Choose Insert, File.

FIGURE 2.2

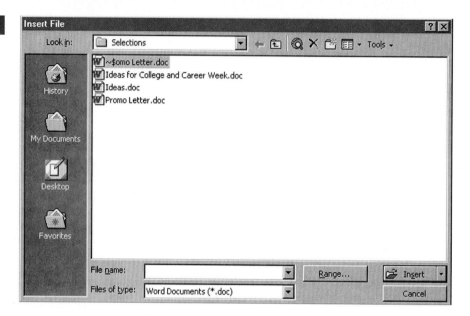

 4 From the Look in drop-down list, select the drive and folder where your files are stored. A list of files appears.

Web Tip

If you do not have a copy of the two files used in steps 4 and 6, you can download them from the SELECT Web site at http://www.prenhall.com/select.

5 Double-click *Ideas for College and Career Week.doc*. Matthew's file is inserted after the letter. The insertion point is located at the end of the file.

6 Insert Rachel's document, the *Ideas* file, at the end of the document. The document now has five pages. Check the status bar to confirm this.

 ## Check Point

How many sections does this document have? The status bar says the document has three sections.

Navigating through a Document

Being able to move around in a document quickly is key to editing efficiently. Word provides the following methods for navigating:

- keystrokes
- mouse techniques

- the Find command
- the Go To command
- the Browse objects

You will find that each method is best used in different situations.

Using the Mouse to Navigate

Moving around in the document with the mouse is easy. All you have to do is scroll with the vertical or horizontal scroll bar and then click the I-beam in the document. You can scroll the document up or down one line at a time by clicking the arrow buttons at the top or bottom of the vertical scroll bar. You can also scroll through large portions of the document by dragging the box in the vertical scroll bar. Additionally, you can click in the vertical scroll bar above or below the box to move back or forward one screen at a time. It is important to remember that when using the scroll bars, the insertion point does not move. You must click the I-beam to actually move the insertion point to a location that is visible on the screen.

Using Keystrokes to Navigate

Table 2.2 lists keystrokes you can use to move around in a document. When you use keystrokes to navigate, the insertion point actually moves. In the next task, you will use mouse and keyboard navigation techniques to look at the document so you can get an idea of how you need to edit and format the document.

> **TIP** Word remembers the position of the last three edits, which means that you can press (SHIFT) + (F5) three times to return to the last three edits.

TASK 2: ## To Navigate in a Document

1 Press (CTRL) + (HOME). The insertion point moves to the top of the document (the envelope).

2 Change the view to Print Layout, if necessary, and scroll to the second page of the document.

3 Click the I-beam before the word *Rachel* and then press (END). The insertion point moves to the end of the line.

4 Press (HOME). The insertion point moves to the beginning of the line.

5 Press (CTRL) + ⊙ three times. The insertion point moves forward three words.

6 Press (CTRL) + (↓) three times. The insertion point moves forward three paragraphs.

> **TIP** A paragraph ends with a paragraph return, so in word processing terms, even a blank line created by pressing (ENTER) is considered a paragraph.

7 In the vertical scroll bar, click below the box repeatedly to advance to the end of the document one screen at a time.

Check Point

What's the major difference between using the navigation keystrokes and using the scroll bar? The navigation keystrokes actually move the insertion point, but the scroll bars do not.

Table 2.2: Navigation Keystrokes

To move to the:	Press:
End of the document	(CTRL) + (END)
Beginning of the document	(CTRL) + (HOME)
Beginning of a line	(HOME)
End of a line	(END)
Next word	(CTRL) + (→)
Previous word	(CTRL) + (←)
Next paragraph	(CTRL) + (↓)
Previous paragraph	(CTRL) + (↑)
Top of the next page	(CTRL) + (PGDN)
Top of the previous page	(CTRL) + (PGUP)
Location of the insertion point when the document was last closed	(SHIFT) + (F5)
Position of the previous edit	(SHIFT) + (F5)

Browsing for and Deleting Objects

Matthew has too many graphics in his document; they wouldn't be appropriate in this particular document. The Browse Object feature is just the right navigation tool to find all the graphics so you can delete them.

The Select Browse Object button, located at the bottom of the vertical scroll bar, displays a palette from which you can select an object for browsing. The palette contains buttons for fields such as the date code field that you learned about in Project 1, endnotes, footnotes, comments, sections, pages, edits, headings, graphics, and tables. The Browse Object palette also contains buttons that open the Go To page and the Find page in the Find and Replace dialog box. The names of the Previous and Next buttons, located in the vertical scroll bar above and below the Select Browse Object button, reflect the browse object that you select. You can see the name of the button in a ScreenTip when you point to the button. For example, if you choose to browse tables, the buttons will be named Previous Table and Next Table when you move your pointer over the buttons.

> **TIP** Each time you open Word, the Browse Object defaults to the page object and the buttons are named Previous Page and Next Page.

In the next task, you will see how the Previous Page and Next Page buttons work and then browse the document for graphics so you can delete them.

TASK 3: To Browse for Objects

1 Click the Previous Page ⬆ button until you return to the top of the first page of the document, which is the envelope.

2 Click the Next Page ⬇ button. Page 2 displays the first page of the letter.

3 Click before the word *Rachel* to position the insertion point below the graphic in the letterhead, and then click the Select Browse Object ⊙ button.

FIGURE 2.3

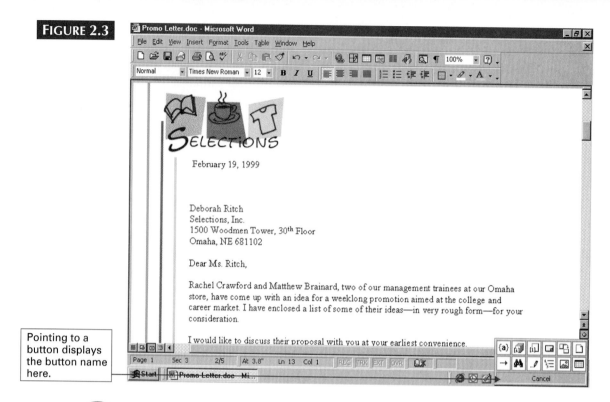

Pointing to a button displays the button name here.

4 Click the Browse Graphic 🖾 button. Three things happen: the insertion point automatically moves forward to the first graphic found, the arrows on the browse buttons change color from black to blue, and the names of the buttons change to Previous Graphic and Next Graphic.

FIGURE 2.4

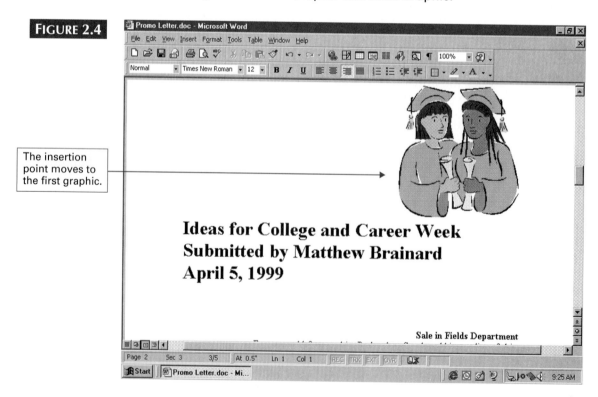

The insertion point moves to the first graphic.

5 Click the Next Graphic ⊻ button repeatedly until the insertion point will not advance.

6 Click the graphic to select it and then press ⟨DEL⟩. The graphic is deleted.

7 Use the Previous Graphic ⊼ button to go to the remaining graphics and delete them. Do not delete the Selections graphic in the letterhead.

> **TIP** After browsing by an object, you might want to reset the buttons manually by choosing Browse by Page.

Finding and Deleting Text

When editing or formatting text in a document, the Go To command and the Find command are two essential navigation tools that you will use repeatedly. The Go To command is used most often to go to a specific page number, but it also has options for going to footnotes, graphics, tables, and other items in a document. When you navigate with the Go To command, the insertion point moves to the desired page or to the specific item.

> **TIP** When using the Go To command, you can move the insertion point forward or backward by a number. For example, if you choose Footnote for Go to what and type **+2** in the Enter footnote number text box, the insertion point will move ahead two footnotes. When you close the Go To dialog box, you can use the Next and Previous Browse buttons to continue moving the insertion point forward or backward two footnotes at a time.

The Find command, which searches for specific text in the document, has an added bonus. It locates and also selects text so you can delete, copy, cut, or format text on the spot. If you need to select additional text, use the appropriate method as outlined in Table 2.3.

In the next task, you will use the Go To and Find commands to go to the locations in the document that require editing.

Table 2.3: Methods of Selecting Text

To Select:	With the mouse	With the keyboard
A word	Double-click the word.	Position the insertion point at the beginning of the word and press (SHIFT) + (CTRL) + (→).
A line	Click in the white area (called the *selection bar*) to the left of the line.	Position the insertion point at the beginning of the line and press (SHIFT) + (END).
A sentence	Click anywhere in the sentence while pressing (CTRL).	None
A paragraph	Triple-click anywhere in the paragraph.	Position the insertion point at the beginning of the paragraph and press (SHIFT) + (CTRL) + (↓).
An entire document	Click anywhere in the selection bar while pressing (CTRL).	Press (CTRL) + A.
A block of text	Drag the mouse pointer through the text.	Position the insertion point at the beginning of the block, and then press and hold down (SHIFT) as you press any combination of arrow keys to move to the end of the block.
A vertical block of text	Drag the mouse pointer through the text while pressing (ALT).	Click at the beginning of the block and press (CTRL) + (SHIFT) + (F8). Then use the arrow keys to extend the selection. Press (ESC) when finished.

TASK 4: <u>To Use the Go To and Find Commands</u>

1 Choose Edit, Go To.

FIGURE 2.5

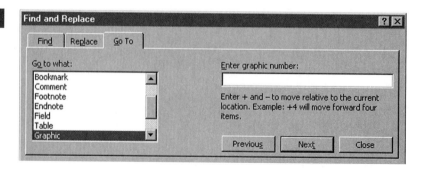

TIP Double-clicking the page number in the status bar, or pressing (F5), is a quick way to display the Go To page.

2 Select Line from the Go to what list box and type **+5** in the Enter line number: text box.

FIGURE 2.6

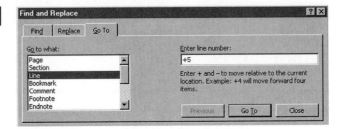

3 Select Go To and then select Close. The insertion point moves forward five lines.

4 Click the Next Find/Go to ⬇ button to move forward again, and then drag the I-beam over the text **—in very rough form—**, press (DEL), and insert the proper spacing. When you finish your edits, it won't look rough anymore.

5 Choose Edit, Find.

FIGURE 2.7

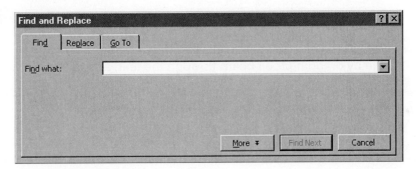

6 Type **Matthew** in the Find what text box, select Find Next, and then select Cancel. Word moves to the first occurrence of the name. This is not the one we want.

7 Click ⬇ .

FIGURE 2.8

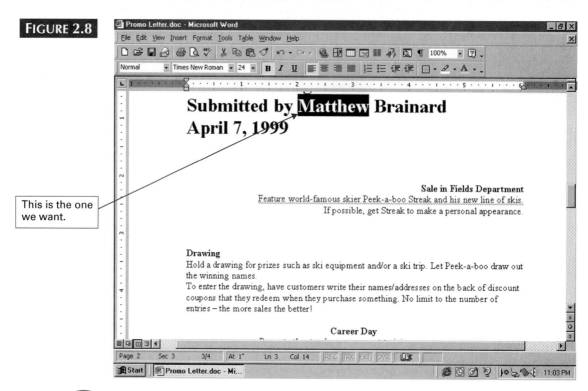

This is the one we want.

8 Select the complete line (including the paragraph marks) and the following line by dragging the I-beam through the text, and delete them both.

9 Use the Find command to locate the text that begins *Here are some of my ideas*.

10 Delete the entire line and the next one.

11 Make the revisions to Rachel's text that are shown in Figure 2.9.

FIGURE 2.9

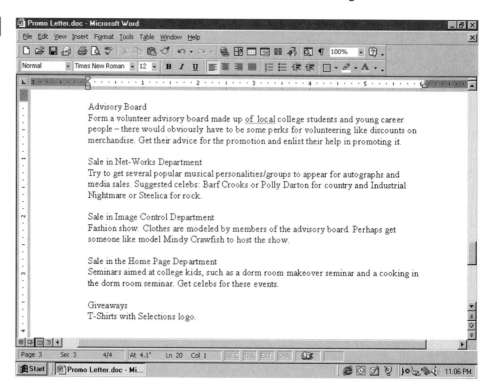

12 Save the document as *Promo Letter Revised*.

Moving Text

Word provides several different methods for moving text. You can use any of the following:

- Cut and Paste buttons.
- Cut and Paste commands on the Edit menu.
- Drag-and-drop method.

The Cut and Paste buttons and menu commands use the Windows Clipboard, which can hold only one item. The Office Clipboard can hold as many as 12 items.

Check Point

Do you remember what else you learned about the Office Clipboard in Common Elements Project 2? To display the Clipboard toolbar, choose View, Toolbars, Clipboard. To paste a single item at the position of the insertion point, click the item in the Clipboard. To paste all items at the position of the insertion point, click the Paste All button. By the way, if you cut or copy two objects in succession, the Office Clipboard appears automatically.

Using Cut and Paste

The Cut and Paste commands are handy tools for revising documents. You can move text in the same document or cut text from one document and paste it into another.

TASK 5: To Move Text with Cut and Paste

1 Press (CTRL) + F.

FIGURE 2.10

The last text you searched for is retained by the Find command.

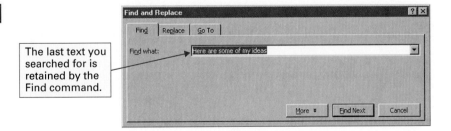

2 Type **format** and select More.

FIGURE 2.11

Finds only words that match the capitalization that you use in the Find what text box

Allows you to include a wild-card in the Find what text box, such as *info**

Finds homonyms for the word in the Find what text box, such as *their* and *there*

Finds forms of a word, such as *sell* and *sold*

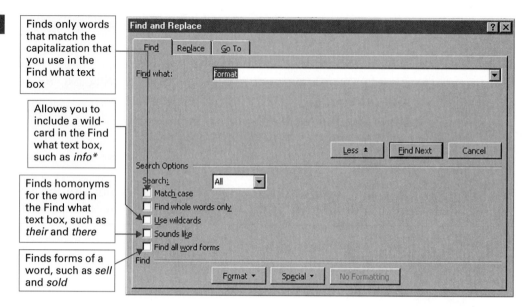

3 Select Find whole words only, click Find Next, and select Cancel. The dialog box closes and the word *format* is selected.

> **TIP** The settings in the Find and Replace dialog box are remembered.

Check Point

How would you continue searching for the same word if you closed the Find dialog box? You could use the Browse buttons.

4 Select the entire paragraph that contains the word.

FIGURE 2.12

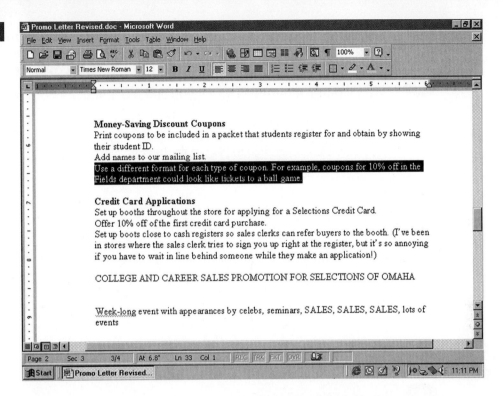

5 Click the Cut ✂ button, click the insertion point at the beginning of the first sentence in the topic, and click the Paste 📋 button. The text is moved.

FIGURE 2.13

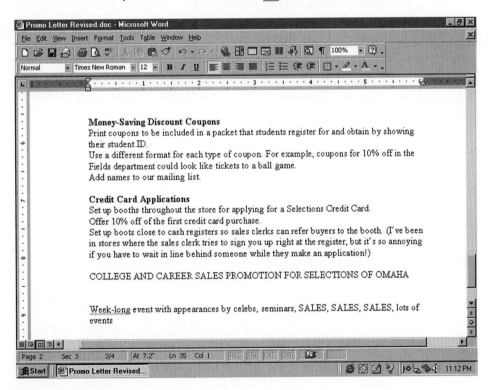

6 Cut the text *that students register for and obtain by showing their student ID*. (Do not include the period when you cut the text.)

7 Click before the text *Add names to our mailing list* and insert the text **Students must show their student IDs and register with their names and addresses to obtain the coupon packets.**

8 Insert a return after the text that you entered in the previous step.

> **TIP** To copy text, select the text, click the Copy button, position the insertion point, and click the Paste button.

Using Drag and Drop

When cutting and pasting in the same document, especially a very long document, you may find it useful to split the window and use the drag-and-drop technique.

TASK 6: To Drag and Drop Text

1 Switch to Normal view.

2 Point to the border above the vertical scroll bar until the mouse pointer changes to a double arrow.

FIGURE 2.14

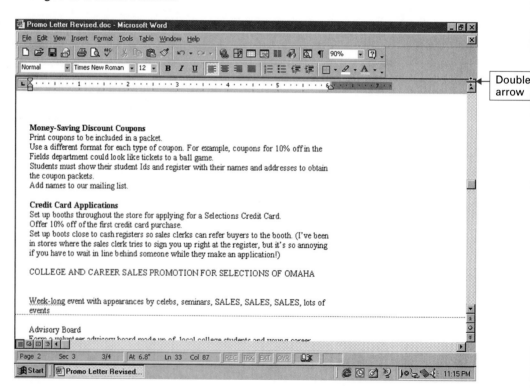

3 Double-click. The window splits.

4 Scroll the document in the top pane until you can see the title at the top of Matthew's document.

FIGURE 2.15

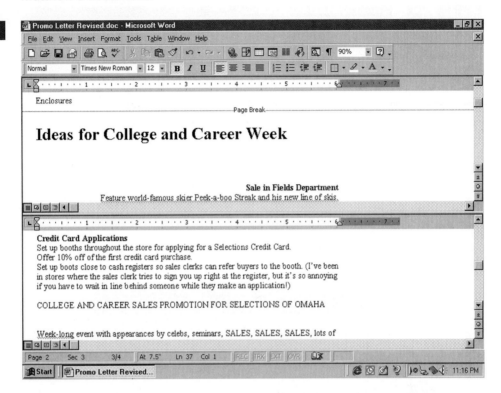

5 Scroll the document in the bottom pane until you can see the title at the top of Rachel's document.

FIGURE 2.16

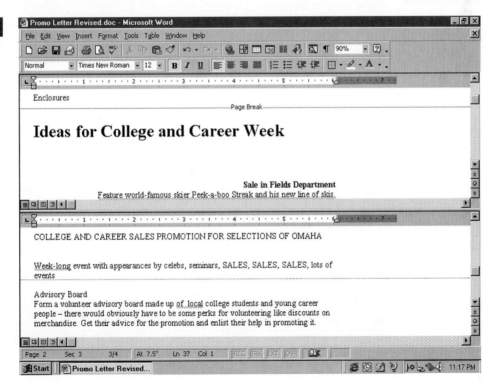

6 Select the text as shown in Figure 2.17.

FIGURE 2.17

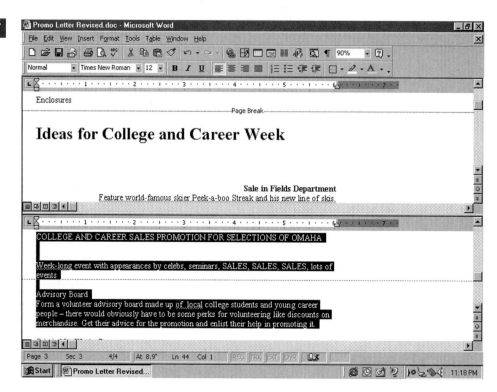

7 Drag the text into the top pane and drop it below Matthew's title.

FIGURE 2.18

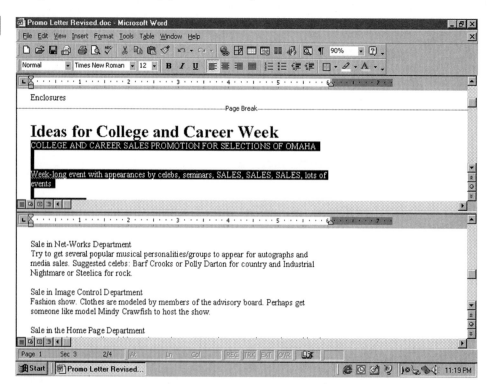

8 Delete Matthew's title and, if necessary, scroll down so you can see the space under the Advisory Board topic.

9 In the bottom pane, scroll up until you can see Matthew's topic on Career Day. Then select the topic and drag it into the top pane just under the Advisory Board topic.

FIGURE 2.19

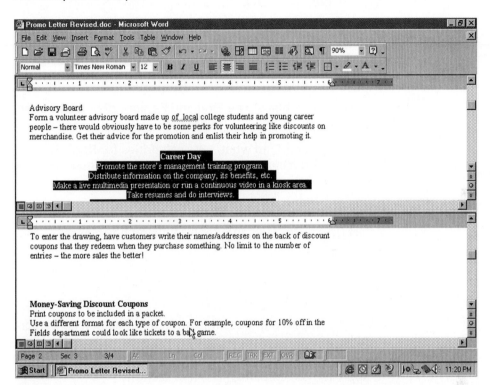

10 Point anywhere on the border that separates the two panes until the mouse becomes a double-headed arrow and double-click. The split is removed.

11 Make the necessary revisions so that the topics are arranged in this order with only one blank line between them:

- Advisory Board
- Career Day
- Drawing
- Money-Saving Discount Coupons
- Sale in Fields Department
- Sale in Net-Works Department
- Sale in Image Control Department
- Sale in Home Page Department
- Giveaways
- Credit Card Applications

12 Save the file.

Finding and Replacing Text

The Find and Replace command is another editing technique that can be very helpful if you need to make the same correction several times in the same document. In the next task, you will use this technique to change the word *celebs* to *celebrities*.

TASK 7: To Find and Replace Text

1 Choose Edit, Replace. The Find and Replace dialog box opens displaying the Replace page.

2 Type **celebs** for Find what, type celebrities for Replace with, select All for Search, and select Replace All. Word displays a message reporting how many changes were made.

3 Select OK. The message closes.

4 Select Close. The Find and Replace dialog box closes.

Formatting Text

Word provides techniques for formatting characters, paragraphs, and entire sections of a document. In this project you will apply formats to characters, the most basic kind of formatting in Word. In Projects 3 and 4, you will learn to apply formats to paragraphs and sections.

Character formats include bold, italic, underline, font, font size, color, special effects, and *case* (capitalization). You can use several different buttons in the Formatting toolbar to apply character formats. In this project you will change the default font, underline characters, add special effects to characters, and change the case of characters.

> **TIP** Here's a keyboard shortcut for changing the font size: Select the text and press (CTRL) + ([) to decrease the size one point or press (CTRL) + (]) to increase the size one point. This is a nice method to use because you can see the text size increasing and decreasing onscreen.

Setting the Font Defaults

Word uses a default font and a default font size. You can set these defaults to whatever is best for your use. Changing the font defaults changes the text of the document that you are in and all new documents created afterward.

TASK 8:   To Change the Font Defaults

1 Choose Format, Font.

FIGURE 2.20

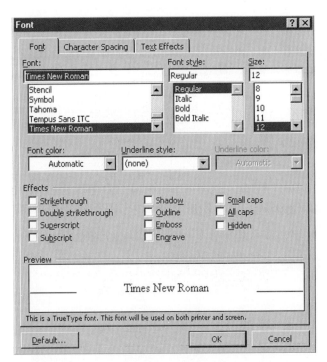

2 Select Tahoma from the Font list and select Default.

3 Select Yes.

FIGURE 2.21

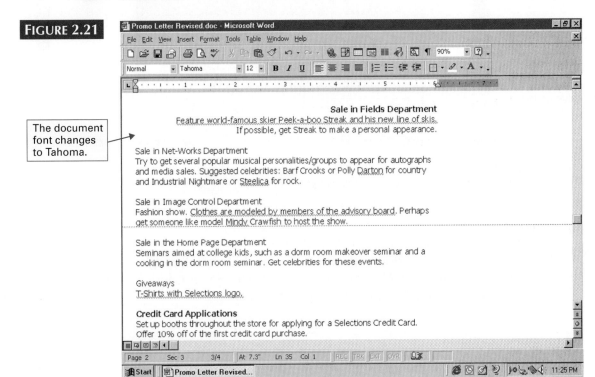

The document font changes to Tahoma.

Underlining Text

To apply a single underline to text, you can use the Underline button in the Formatting toolbar. To apply a different kind of underline, such as a double underline, dashed line, wavy line, or others, you must use the Font dialog box.

TASK 9: To Apply an Underline

1 Use the Find command to locate *Sale in Fields Department* or simply select it if you can readily see it.

2 Choose Format, Font. The Font dialog box displays.

3 Select the double underline from the Underline style drop-down list.

FIGURE 2.22

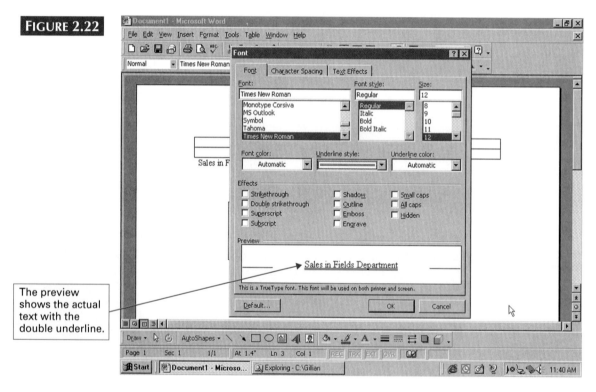

The preview shows the actual text with the double underline.

4 Select OK.

Applying Font Effects

Font effects include Strikethrough, Double Strikethrough, Superscript, Subscript, Shadow, Outline, Emboss, Engrave, Small Caps, All Caps, and Hidden. Figure 2.23 illustrates all these font effects.

TIP Hidden text appears on the screen as shown in Figure 2.23 only when the display of Hidden text is activated. Otherwise, it is invisible. Hidden text also does not print unless you specifically choose the option to print it.

FIGURE 2.23

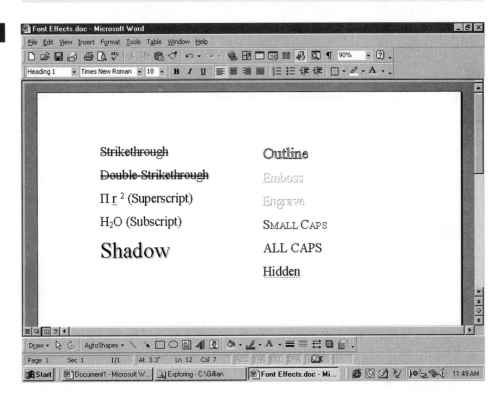

TASK 10: To Apply Font Effects to Text

1 The text that you underlined in the previous task should still be selected. If it's not, select it again.

2 Choose Format, Font. The Font dialog box displays.

3 Select Small Caps, select OK, and move the insertion point to remove the highlighting. The text appears as shown in Figure 2.24.

TIP Small caps look better with an underline than upper/lowercase because there are no descenders for the underline to overstrike. Look at the preview in Figure 2.22 to see how the underline cuts through the descender in the letter *p* in *Department*. Then look at the same text in Figure 2.24.

FIGURE 2.24

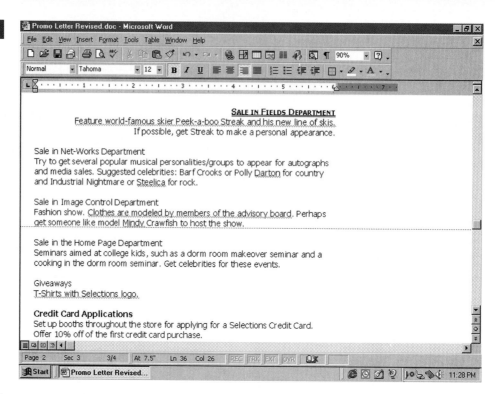

 4 Use the Find command to find *Credit Card Applications* and experiment with an underline and a font effect of your choice.

Changing Case

The Change Case command in Word has five options. Table 2.4 shows how each option would change the text *Sale in Fields Department.*

Table 2.4: Case Options

Case options	Example	Comment
Sentence case	Sale in Fields Department	Sentence case capitalizes the first character of the first word. No other characters are changed.
Lowercase	sale in fields department	Lowercase changes all characters to lowercase.
Uppercase	SALE IN FIELDS DEPARTMENT	Uppercase capitalizes all characters.
Title case	Sale In Fields Department	Title case capitalizes the first character of every word, even if the word is an article, preposition, or conjunction, which are not capitalized in titles.
Toggle case	sALE IN fIELDS dEPARTMENT	Toggle case reverses the capitalization of every character in every word. It is used to correct text that has been typed when Caps Lock was on by accident.

TASK 11: To Change the Case of Text

1 Choose Edit, Find. The Find and Replace dialog box opens.

2 Type **COLLEGE AND CAREER** in the Find what text box, select More if necessary, select Match case, select Find Next, and then close the dialog box.

3 Select all the text in the line.

FIGURE 2.25

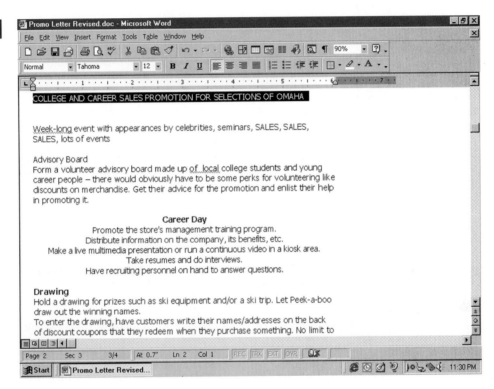

4 Choose Format, Change Case.

FIGURE 2.26

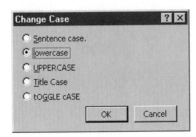

5 Select Title Case and select OK.

FIGURE 2.27

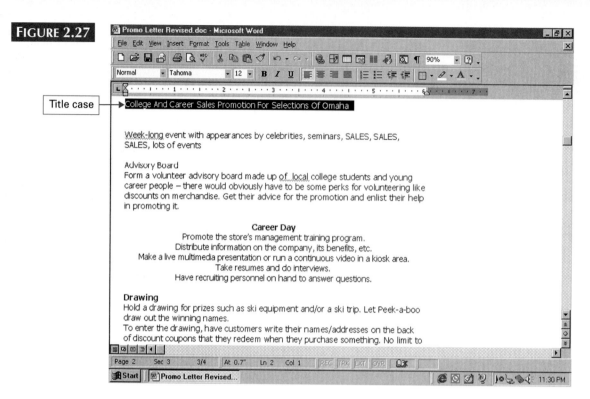

Title case

6 Change *and*, *for*, and *of* to lowercase.

7 Use the Find command to find *SALES, SALES, SALES*.

8 Press (SHIFT) + (F3) several times to cycle through the case options until the text is changed to title case.

> **TIP** The (SHIFT) + (F3) technique does not include Toggle Case.

9 Change the default font back to Times New Roman. All the text in the document changes from Tahoma to Times New Roman.

 Break Point

If necessary, you can save your file now, exit Word, and continue this project later.

Aligning Text

The Formatting toolbar contains buttons for aligning text on the left margin, centering text between the margins, aligning text on the right margin, and aligning text on the left and right margins (like a newspaper column).

> **TIP** The alignment buttons apply the alignment to the entire paragraph.

TASK 12: To Align Text

1 Launch Word and open the *Promo Letter Revised.doc*, if necessary. Use the Go To command to go to section 2 and then select all the text to the end of the document.

2 Click the Align Left ☰ button. All the text lines up at the left margin. The right margin is ragged; the text does not line up straight on the right margin.

> **TIP** When appropriate, use the Center ☰ , Align Right ☰ , and Justify ☰ buttons in the Formatting toolbar. The Center button centers selected paragraphs; the Align Right button aligns paragraphs on the right margin; and the Justify button aligns paragraph text on both the left and right margins (like a newspaper column).

3 Select the title *College and Career Sales Promotion for Selections of Omaha* at the top of the report, click the Bold **B** button, and then click the Center ☰ button. The text is bolded and centered—a fitting format for a title!

4 Scroll through the document, select each heading, and apply or remove formats, as necessary, so that each heading is bold and uses no special effects or underlines.

5 Delete any unnecessary blank lines and the text *Week-long event with appearances by celebrities, seminars, Sales, Sales, Sales.*

6 Save the document.

Highlighting Text

The Highlight ✐ button in the Formatting toolbar marks text with color just like a highlighting pen. It is used to call attention to text. The default highlight color is yellow, but a highlight prints as gray shading if you are using a black-and-white printer.

TASK 13: To Highlight Text

1 Click the Highlight ✐ button and drag the pointer through the text *at your earliest convenience* on the second page of the document. The text is highlighted with yellow and the I-beam has changed to a pen icon.

2 Press (ESC). The pointer changes back to an I-beam.

3 Click the drop-down arrow on the Highlight button. A menu appears.

4 Choose None and drag the pointer through the yellow highlight in the text. The highlight is removed.

5 Press (ESC). The pointer returns to an I-beam.

Using Writing and Proofing Tools

The writing and proofing tools help polish your documents and give them a professional look. The basic proofing tool is the Spelling and Grammar checker. This tool should be used in almost every document you create. The basic writing tools include the Thesaurus and the Hyphenation tool.

> **TIP** Word also provides an advanced writing tool that reports statistics such as word count and sentence complexity and scores the text on ease of readability and grade level.

You can check the spelling and grammar of a document at the same time by clicking the Spelling and Grammar button, but Word is constantly checking your spelling and your grammar as you type. You will see a pencil moving across the pages of the book in the spelling and grammar icon in the status toolbar. When Word finds a mistake in your document, the icon displays a red *X*. If no mistakes have been found, a red checkmark appears. To go to and correct a mistake, double-click the *X* in the Spelling and Grammar status icon. In the document itself, a spelling error is underlined with a wavy red line and a grammar error is underlined with a wavy green line.

> **TIP** Instead of checking grammar at the same time you perform a spell check, you may prefer to check grammar on an individual basis by right-clicking text that is underlined with a wavy green line and choosing a replacement.

The grammar checker looks for incorrect spacing and punctuation, incorrect verb tense, disagreement between the subject and the verb, sentence fragments, incorrect use of *that* and *which*, passive voice, and others. Sometimes the grammar checker questions things that are not incorrect and astounds you by suggesting changes that would be incorrect. You just have to choose Ignore for these.

> **TIP** You can customize the grammar checker by selecting the writing style and specific rules you want the grammar checker to use. To select the writing styles, choose Tools, Options, Spelling and Grammar. To select specific rules, select Settings on the Spelling and Grammar page.

Using the Thesaurus

The electronic Thesaurus in Word can suggest synonyms or antonyms for a word in a document and then automatically replace the selected word with the word you choose from the Thesaurus.

> **TIP** The Thesaurus must be installed on first use.

Web Tip

To improve your vocabulary, check Merriam-Webster Online at
http://www.m-w.com.

TASK 14: To Replace a Word Using the Thesaurus

1 Find and select the word *advice* and then choose Tools, Language, Thesaurus.

FIGURE 2.28

Displays different meanings for the word or phrase in the Looked Up text box

Selecting a meaning displays synonyms and sometimes antonyms in this box

Displays meaning for the selection, which can be in the Meanings list or the Replace with Synonyms list

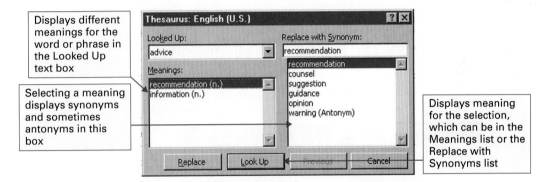

TIP   When using the Thesaurus to replace a single word, you can just click anywhere in the word instead of selecting it.

2 Select *opinion* in the Replace with Synonyms list and select Look Up. The Thesaurus looks for *opinion*.

FIGURE 2.29

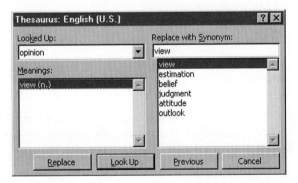

3 Select Previous. The Thesaurus looks up *advice* again.

4 Select Replace. The Thesaurus closes and replaces *advice* with *recommendation*.

Hyphenating a Document

Hyphenating a document makes the text next to the right margin less ragged by adding more characters to the end of a line when possible.

> **TIP** It is advisable to use hyphenation with justified text. Word justifies text by adding additional spaces in each line to force the text to extend to the right margin. The additional spaces added to the lines of text can be very noticeable on a page that contains nothing but text. The spaces create what is referred to as rivers of white that flow through the text. Hyphenating justified text can alleviate obvious rivers of white by forcing more text on a line and using less white space to justify the line.

TASK 15: To Hyphenate a Document

1 Choose Tools, Language, Hyphenation.

FIGURE 2.30

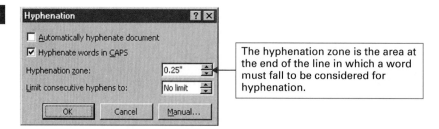

The hyphenation zone is the area at the end of the line in which a word must fall to be considered for hyphenation.

2 Select Automatically hyphenate document, select 3 for Limit consecutive hyphens to:, and select OK. Any eligible words that fall within the hyphenation zone are hyphenated.

> **TIP** You can lessen the number of hyphens by making the hyphenation zone wider. If after hyphenating, the right margin is still too ragged, make the hyphenation zone narrower.

3 Scroll through the document to see the hyphenated lines, and then open the Hyphenation dialog box, deselect Automatically hyphenate document, and select OK. Hyphenation is turned off.

4 Save the document and close it.

5 Optional: E-mail the finished file to your professor by opening the file and then choosing File, Send to, Mail Recipient (as Attachment). Fill out the address for the message, type a subject and a short message, and then send the file.

Summary and Exercises

Summary

- When a document is lengthy, it is easier to insert a file.
- You can use keystrokes or a mouse to move around in a document.
- Word inserts page breaks automatically when a page fills up, but you can insert a page break manually.
- You can browse forward or backward through a document moving from one object to another, such as from table to table.
- The Go To command and the Find command also move the insertion point to specific locations in the document.
- Word uses Times New Roman and 12 point for the font defaults.
- You can apply additional underlining styles and font effects from the Fonts dialog box.
- Word can change the case of text to sentence case, all uppercase, all lowercase, or title case, or it can toggle the case from uppercase to lowercase or vice versa.
- An easy way to move text in the same document is to split the window and drag the text across the split.
- Word is constantly checking your spelling and your grammar as you type.
- The thesaurus in Word looks up synonyms for words.
- Hyphenating a document makes the right margin less ragged.

Key Terms and Operations

Key Terms

case	Select Browse Object
Find command	selection bar
Go To command	thesaurus
Office Clipboard	title case
page break	toggle case

Operations

apply bold	hyphenate
change case	insert a file
check grammar	insert a page break
check spelling	paste text
cut text	underline
drag and drop	

Study Questions

Multiple Choice

1. By default, Word constantly checks
   a. for words that should be hyphenated.
   b. for spelling errors.
   c. for grammar errors.
   d. for spelling and grammar errors.

2. To insert a page break, press
   a. CTRL + SHIFT + ENTER.
   b. ALT +ENTER.
   c. CTRL + ALT + ENTER.
   d. CTRL + ENTER.

3. Rivers of white
   a. are caused by hyphenation.
   b. may appear in left-justified text.
   c. are caused by spaces that are added in lines of text.
   d. refer to text that looks washed-out when printed.

4. The button that splits the screen is located on the
   a. Formatting toolbar.
   b. horizontal scroll bar.
   c. vertical scroll bar.
   d. Standard toolbar.

5. The thesaurus displays
   a. only antonyms.
   b. only synonyms.
   c. only homonyms.
   d. synonyms and antonyms.

6. To move to the end of a document, press
   a. END.
   b. CTRL + END.
   c. ALT + END.
   d. CTRL + SHIFT + END.

7. When Word finds a misspelled word in a document, it marks a red X
   a. before the word.
   b. after the word.
   c. on the Spelling and Grammar status icon.
   d. beside the word in the Spelling and Grammar dialog box.

8. Which of the following does not move the insertion point?
   a. CTRL + HOME
   b. scrolling with the vertical scroll bar
   c. clicking the mouse
   d. SHIFT + F5

9. If the Grammar Checker makes too many erroneous suggestions, you might be able to improve its performance by
   a. choosing a different writing style and specifying the type of document.
   b. choosing a different writing style and selecting specific rules.
   c. checking spelling and grammar at the same time.
   d. right-clicking individual cases.

10. The Select Browse Object button is located on the
    a. Formatting toolbar.
    b. horizontal scroll bar.
    c. vertical scroll bar.
    d. Standard toolbar.

Short Answer

1. How do you move to the last revision?

2. When do the Browse buttons automatically reset to Next Page and Previous Page?

3. What happens if you double-click the page number in the status bar?

4. How can you quickly go to a spelling or grammar error?

5. How do you insert a file?

6. What is the hyphenation zone and how does it work?

7. How do you look up a synonym for a word?

8. How do you check grammar on a case-by-case basis?

9. Which option in the Find dialog box looks for homonyms?

10. When does Word insert a page break?

Fill in the Blank

1. Press (SHIFT) + _____ to change the case of selected text.

2. When you select an item from the Browse Object palette, the arrows on the browse buttons change from black to _____.

3. Press _____ to quickly display the Go To page.

4. To find all occurrences of *Ray* and skip all the occurrences of *ray*, choose _____ in the Find dialog box.

5. To go to the end of a line, press _____.

6. You can apply a double underline from the _____ dialog box.

7. Word uses Times New Roman and _____ point for the font defaults.

8. Navigation keystrokes move the _____, but the scroll bars do not.

9. A(n) _____ ends with a paragraph return.

10. Basic writing and proofing tools include the Thesaurus, the _____ tool, and the Spelling and Grammar checker.

For Discussion

1. Discuss the Select Browse Object feature, how it is used, and what effect it has on screen elements.

2. Compare and contrast moving the insertion point with keystrokes and with the mouse.

3. Discuss the options that you can use in the Find dialog box.

4. Compare the Go To command with the Select Browse Object palette.

5. Compare and contrast two ways of moving text in a document.

Hands-On Exercises

1. Checking Spelling and Grammar

The document you edited in this project needs to have the spelling and grammar checked.

1. Open the document *Promo Letter Revised.doc*.

2. Before checking the document, choose Tools, Options, and click the Spelling and Grammar tab. Choose the Formal Writing style. Select Settings and select Inside for Punctuation required with quotes. Select OK twice.

3. Scroll through the document and look for one occurrence of text that has a wavy green line. Right-click the text and choose an appropriate replacement.

4. Press (CTRL) + (HOME) to return to the top of the document in preparation for checking the spelling. (Word begins checking from the position of the insertion point.)

5. Click the Spelling and Grammar 🗹 button. Choose appropriate responses for spelling and grammar errors. Continue until the check is complete and then select OK.

6. Save the file as *Promo Letter Revised2.doc* and close the file.

2. Editing the Fashion Show Document

Rachel is formalizing her ideas on the fashion show that will be held during the College and Career Week promotion. In this exercise you will edit the document she has started on the subject and then proof and polish it. Figure 2.31 shows the final version of the document.

FIGURE 2.31

Fashion Show

Key Employees
Dave Martin, Manager of Image Control
George Holmes, Manager of Styles
Rick Putnam, Manager of Transition Threads
Soo Lee, Manager of Active Wear
John Brady, Manager of Headers & Footers
Nonie Betz, Manager of Jewelry
Marge Jones, Manager of Inter-Faces
Andrew Cyphers, Manager of The Main Board
Joy Quinn, Production/Advertising
Winston Robichaud, Manager of Nibbles & Bytes
Angie Stover, Manager of Java
James West, Manager of Pack and Go

Assignments
Dave Martin: Coordinate with managers in Image Control. Set up the runway and seating in the Image Control department.

George Holmes: Select three ensembles for men and four for women. Ensembles should be casual, business attire, and formal.

Rick Putnam: Select six ensembles each for young adult men and wome should include two which are suitable for lounging in the dorm, four wh for wearing to class, two which are "dressy," and one that would be suit dance.

Soo Lee: Select six sporting outfits. These can be unisex or mixed.

John Brady: Coordinate with Geroge Holmes, Rick Putnam, and Soo Le least three hats and all shoes and boots.

Nonie Betz: Coordinate with George Holmes, Rick Putnam, and Soo Le jewelry for appropriate ensembles.

Marge Jones: Select cosmeticians to do the make-up for the models. Sel to do a live makeover at the end of the fashion show.

Andrew Cyphers: Coordinate with Soo Lee to supply sports equipment for models to carry (skateboards, ice skates, snowboards, ski poles, etc.)

Joy Quinn: Prepare and print a brochure for the show that lists all items in the show, the department in which the items can be found, and the prices.

Winston Robichaud: Prepare hors d'oeuvre and set up tables in Image Control for the food the day of the show.

Angie Stover: Set up tables for coffee and sodas. Set up display and sale table for our special grinds.

1. Open *Fashion Show.doc*.

2. Change the case of *FASHION SHOW* to title case and make the text bold. Change the color of the text to blue.

3. Apply the outline font effect to the title and use the keyboard shortcut to increase the size of the font until it looks about as large as the title in Figure 2.31.

4. Make the headings *Key Staff* and *Assignments* bold, blue, and 16 point. (*Hint*: Use the (F4) key to repeat the last action.)

5. Find *h'ors deuvres* and look it up in the Thesaurus. Either correct the spelling or replace it with a synonym. Select the word *Staff* in the first heading and replace it with an appropriate synonym.

6. Add the following assignment after John Brady's assignment by copying the appropriate text that appears in John Brady's assignment and typing the remainder of the text.

   Nonie Betz: Coordinate with George Holmes, Rick Putnam, and Soo Lee in selecting jewelry for appropriate ensembles.

7. Change the order of the names listed at the top of the document to the order in which the names appear in the Assignments section. List James West last. (Hint: It will be easier to do this if you split the screen.)

8. Spell-check and grammar-check the document. (*Hints:* (1) Most proper names appear at least twice in the document. You might want to choose Ignore All when the spelling checker finds names that are not in its dictionary. (2) You may need to consult a grammar textbook for the proper use of *which* and *that.*)

9. Change the writing style to Formal. Check the document again for spelling and grammar and see if any additional errors are found.

10. Insert a page break so that more text appears on the second page.

11. Preview the file and then print it. Save the file as *Fashion Show Formatted.doc* and close the file.

On Your Own Exercises

1. Editing the Ski Trip Document

Matthew has created a document that explains the drawing that will be held for the Ski Trip. Open *Ski Trip.doc* and search the Web using keywords such as *ski resort, skiing,* and *skiing vacation.* Using the information that you find, add at least three more suggestions to the file. Write your descriptions in a similar manner to the ones that are included in the file. Check the spelling and grammar. Save the file as *Ski Trip Revised.doc* and close the file.

2. Browsing through Documents

Open the document named *Grand Resort.doc.* Using the Select Browse Object, browse the document by headings, then browse by table, and finally browse by graphics. View the document map. Close the file when finished.

3. Using the Office Clipboard

Open the *Grand Resort.doc* file. Copy the first paragraph, copy the first graphic, and then copy the first table. The Office Clipboard should appear automatically. Create a new document. Point to the first object in the toolbar and read the ToolTip. Paste the first object, paste the second object, paste the third object, and then paste all objects at once. Clear the Office Clipboard. Close all files without saving.

4. Creating a Report on Your Ideal Vacation Spot

Create a document that describes your ideal vacation spot. You might want to take a cue from the Grand Resort document for content or do a little research on the Internet. Use different fonts and font effects to format the text. Cut text and move it around. Use the Thesaurus and other writing tools, such as the Spelling and Grammar checker, to polish the document. Save the file as *Ideal Vacation Spot.doc.*

5. Improving Your Work

Open a document that contains a paper you have written for any class. Print the document as is. Use the Thesaurus, the Spelling and Grammar checker, and the Hyphenation tool to improve the paper. Print the revised document.

6. Grading Readability

Use the Help feature to learn more about the Readability feature and how to use it. Open one of your documents that contains a paper you have written for class and grade its readability. Type the readability statistics at the bottom of the paper and print it. See if you can improve the readability score by revising the document. Use the Spelling and Grammar checker to help you improve the writing style. Print the revised version (including the new readability scores). Be sure to save your document.

Creating a Brochure

Word recognizes three levels of formatting—character, paragraph, and section. In previous projects, you learned techniques for formatting at the character level. In this project you will focus on the techniques for formatting at the paragraph level. Before you begin formatting the paragraphs, you will define the page setup options and create columns.

Objectives

After completing this project, you will be able to:

➤ Define the page setup

➤ Create and revise columns

➤ Apply direct formatting to paragraphs

➤ Create bulleted and numbered lists

➤ Find and replace formatting

➤ Apply, create, and modify styles

Running Case

The College and Career Week promotion was a big hit with the store managers. Plans for the event are in full swing. Rachel and Matthew have come up with all the details on the "Remodeling Your Dorm Room on a Budget" seminar that will be given during the promotion. Now they must format the information into a handout that can be distributed.

The Challenge

After looking at the information, you decide that the best format is a trifold brochure that can be printed on 8.5″-by-11″ paper.

The Strategy

You will use page formats to set the page orientation to landscape (11″ wide by 8.5″ high) and create three columns in the document to accommodate the trifold for the brochure. To make your work easier, you will create paragraph styles to format the text and apply direct formatting when creating a style would be unnecessary. Figure 3.1 shows the front and back of the brochure.

FIGURE 3.1

Remodeling Your Dorm Room on a Budget

A Seminar Brought to You by the Home Page at Selections

Date	Time
2/14	5:00 pm
2/15	3:00 pm
2/16	7:00 pm
2/17	8:00 pm
2/18	3:00 pm
2/19	9:00 am
2/19	1:00 pm
2/19	4:00pm

Should I Attend?

If the answer to any one of the following questions is yes, then you NEED to attend!

☐ Do you require a fireman's ladder to get to the stuff that is stacked to the top of the ceiling?

☐ Is there a bed somewhere in the room, but you're not sure where?

☐ Does a drawing of Brad Pitt emerge if you connect the dots for the nail holes in your wall?

☐ Have you been served with a search warrant by the Committee to Investigate the Disappearance of your Last "Clean Enough" Pair of Socks?

☐ Are you failing your classes because the TV, stereo, VCR, Sega 2000, and microwave don't leave enough room on your desk to study?

☐ Are so many slats missing on your window blind that the sunlight wakes you up before noon every day?

☐ Would your mother have a coronary if she came to visit you before you had a chance to bribe the clean freak on the hall to let you "borrow" the room for the day so you can pretend it's your room?

How Much Will It Set Me Back?

It's Free!

In fact we'll actually pay you to attend. The first 20 arrivals at each seminar will receive a coupon for a free liter of Coke.®

What's in It for Me?

In this entertaining and highly educational seminar, you'll learn how to:

• make a futon out of two months of dirty laundry and duct tape

• recycle all those drink cans and pizza boxes piled up in the corner into a sturdy and attractive bookcase

• make room-darkening window treatments from your roommate's bedspread and plastic garbage bags

• disguise ugly walls with Interstate signs borrowed from the Department of Transportation

How Do I Sign Up?

Follow these easy steps to register for the seminar:

1. Take a photograph of your room. (If you don't have a camera, you can draw us a picture.)

2. Fill out the form below.

3. Cut the form out or tear it out since you obviously can't find any scissors in your room or you wouldn't be registering for the seminar in the first place.

4. Send the form and your picture in an envelope with a stamp on it to Selections, 1500 Woodmen Tower, 30th Floor, Omaha, NE 68102.

Name _____

Address _____

Phone # _____

Preferred Seminar Date _____

Alternate Seminar Date(s) _____

Space is limited to 20 people in each seminar. We will make exceptions, however, for extreme cases as determined by the pictures submitted. Pictures will be judged by an impartial panel of interior designers and our janitorial staff. In case of a tie, the registration with the earliest marked postmark will be awarded the seat in the seminar. All decisions by the judges are final.

The Setup

So that your screen will match the illustrations and the tasks in this project will function as described, make sure that the Word 2000 settings listed in Table 3.1 match those on your computer.

Table 3.1: Word 2000 Settings

Location:	Make these settings:
View	Choose Ruler to ensure ruler is turned on.
View, Toolbars	Deselect all toolbars except Standard and Formatting and deselect any buttons that are selected in the Standard toolbar and set the Zoom to 100%.
Tools, Customize, Options	Deselect Standard and Formatting toolbars share one row and deselect Menus show recently used commands first.
Tools, AutoCorrect, AutoFormat As You Type	Deselect all options under Apply as you type and Automatically as you type. Select all options under Replace as you type.
Tools, Options, Spelling & Grammar	Select all options in the dialog box except the following: Hide spelling errors in this document, Suggest from main dictionary only, Hide grammatical errors in this document, and Show readability statistics.
Help, Show Office Assistant	Right-click the Office Assistant and choose Option. Deselect Use the Office Assistant.

Defining the Page Setup

The settings that determine the setup of a page include the following:

- margins (the amount of white space at the top, bottom, and sides of the paper)
- page size
- orientation (the direction in which text prints on the page)
- paper source (the location in the printer from which the paper will come for the printing of the first page and for the following pages)
- layout options such as line numbers, vertical alignment on the page, and others

TASK 1: To Define the Page Setup

1 Open *Remodel.doc.*

Web Tip

If you do not have a copy of this file, you can download it from the SELECT Web site at http://www.prenhall.com/select.

2 Choose File, Page Setup, and click the Margins tab if the Margins page is not displayed automatically.

FIGURE 3.2

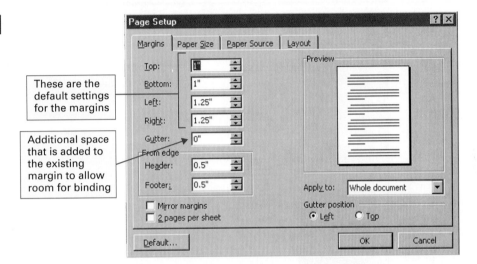

These are the default settings for the margins

Additional space that is added to the existing margin to allow room for binding

3 Change the top, bottom, left, and right margins to 0.5 and click the Paper Size tab.

FIGURE 3.3

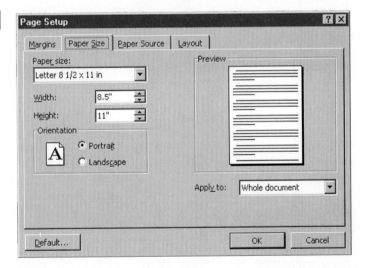

4 Select Landscape and choose OK. The dialog box closes.

5 Insert the graphic *Remodel.wmf* above the phrase *A Seminar Brought to You by the Home Page at Selections* on the first page.

> **TIP** To insert the graphic, click the insertion point where you want the graphic on the page and choose Insert, Picture, From File. Select the graphic and select Insert.

6 Click 🔍.

FIGURE 3.4

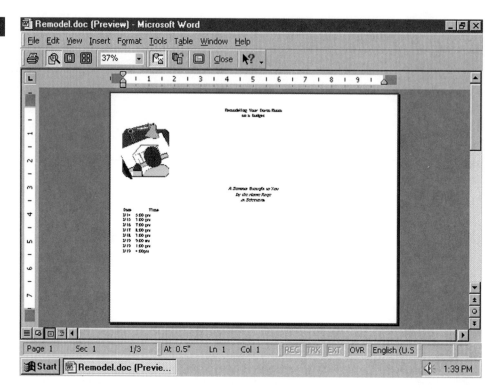

7 Click Close in the toolbar.

8 Switch to Print Layout view if a different view is currently activated.

9 Go to page 2.

> **TIP** You might like to know about one page format that you won't be using in this brochure. It's the page border. Check it out by choosing Format, Borders and Shading, Page Borders. Don't miss the Art options.

 Check Point

What page orientation default does Word use? It is called Portrait, and it orients the page layout to 8.5" wide and 11" long.

Creating and Revising Columns

In Word, you can create two kinds of columns—***newspaper columns***, which wrap from the bottom of one column to the top of the next, and ***parallel columns***, which are created with tables. In this project, you will create and revise newspaper-style columns.

> **TIP** Column settings are section formats; therefore, if you want to change the number of columns used, you must insert a section break between the sets of columns. For example, if you want to use two columns, followed by three columns, you must insert a section break after the two-column format.

Creating Columns

Word can create columns of equal width or different widths with or without a vertical line between the columns.

TASK 2: To Format the Page with Equal-Width Columns

1 Click the Columns ▦ button.

FIGURE 3.5

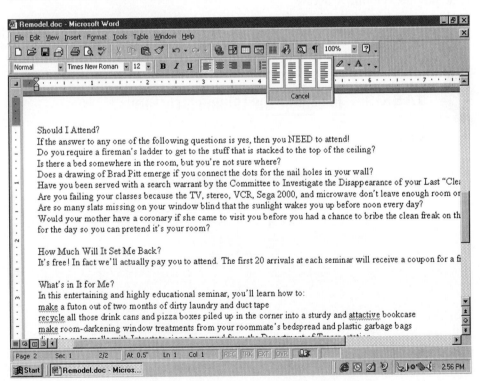

2 Click the second column. Word applies a two-column format.

FIGURE 3.6

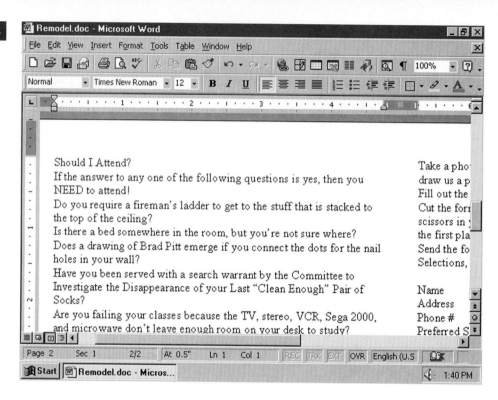

Should I Attend?

If the answer to any one of the following questions is yes, then you NEED to attend!

Do you require a fireman's ladder to get to the stuff that is stacked to the top of the ceiling?

Is there a bed somewhere in the room, but you're not sure where?

Does a drawing of Brad Pitt emerge if you connect the dots for the nail holes in your wall?

Have you been served with a search warrant by the Committee to Investigate the Disappearance of your Last "Clean Enough" Pair of Socks?

Are you failing your classes because the TV, stereo, VCR, Sega 2000, and microwave don't leave enough room on your desk to study?

Take a pho
draw us a p
Fill out the
Cut the forr
scissors in
the first pla
Send the fo
Selections,

Name
Address
Phone #
Preferred S

Changing the Column Structure

You can change the structure of columns by changing the width or the number of columns.

TASK 3: **To Change the Column Structure**

1 Choose Format, Columns.

FIGURE 3.7

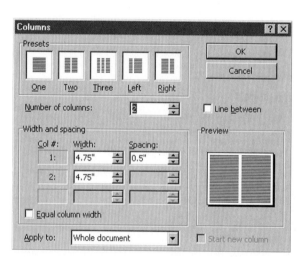

2 Select Three for Presets and notice that the columns are equal width; deselect Equal column width, so you can change the spacing values for the first two columns to 1.

TIP The spacing between columns is sometimes referred to as the gutter.

3 Select Line between and Equal column width and then select OK.

FIGURE 3.8

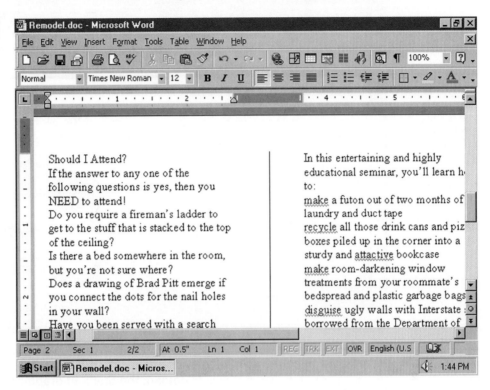

Inserting Column Breaks

If you want the text in one column to go to the next column, you must insert a ***column break***.

TASK 4: To Insert Column Breaks

1 Go to the top of page 1 and choose Insert, Break.

FIGURE 3.9

2 Select Column break and select OK.

FIGURE 3.10

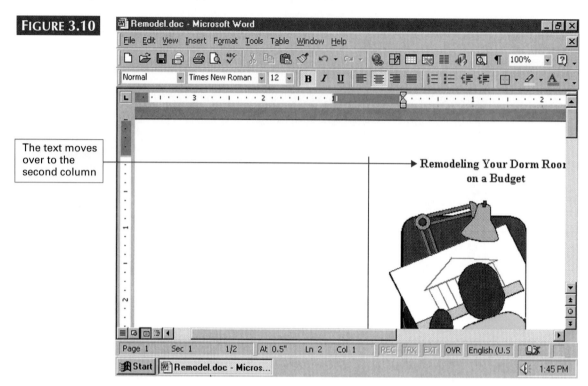

The text moves over to the second column

3 Insert another column break at the same location. The text moves over to the third column. When this is tri-folded, the title and graphic will be on the front of the brochure.

4 Insert a column break before the text *How Much Will It Set Me Back?* and another before the text *How Do I Sign Up?* The text following each column break moves to the top of the next column.

Applying Formatting to Paragraphs

Now that you have set up the page and created the columns, you'll turn your attention to formatting the paragraphs in the brochure. All the paragraphs in the document are currently formatted with the ***Normal style***. You can change the appearance of the paragraphs by modifying the Normal style, applying a different style, or applying formatting directly to the paragraph. First you will apply formatting directly to selected paragraphs; then, later in this project, you will modify styles and apply styles to format paragraphs.

Paragraph formats that you can apply directly include tabs, alignment, indentations, and spacing. When you apply direct formatting to a paragraph, the formats apply only to that paragraph. The formats can be carried forward to the next paragraph by pressing (ENTER) anywhere in the paragraph or at the end of the paragraph. For example, if you apply center alignment to a paragraph and press (ENTER) at the end of the paragraph, the next paragraph will also be centered.

TIP To apply the same formatting directly to nonconsecutive paragraphs, apply the desired format to the first paragraph, and then click in each subsequent paragraph and press **F4**.

Setting Tabs

When you want text to align in a particular way at a specific location on a line, you can use a ***tab stop***, which is set on the ruler. When you press the **TAB** key, the insertion point moves to the column on the line that aligns with the tab stop on the ruler. When you type, the text aligns on the tab. Table 3.2 describes the different types of tab stops available in Word.

Table 3.2: Types of Tab Stops

Type	Symbol	Description
Left	**L**	Aligns text on the left.
Center	**⊥**	Centers text on the tab.
Right	**⅃**	Aligns text on the right.
Decimal	**⊥:**	Aligns text on the decimal.
Bar	**⎮**	Inserts a vertical bar at the tab stop (used for drawing vertical lines). The bar tab inserts a bar automatically. It is not necessary to tab to the bar tab stop unless the bar tab stop is set beyond where the line ends.
Leader		Inserts characters (usually periods) before the text. Leaders can be added to all types of tabs except the bar tab. (Commonly used before the page numbers in a table of contents.)

Check Point

Remember the Click-n-Type feature in Project 1? When you use it to type in zones 3 and 5 of a blank area, a left tab is automatically set on the ruler at those locations.

Figure 3.14 shows the five different tab symbols on the ruler and the way text lines up on each. By default, Word sets a left tab on the ruler every half-inch, but no symbols appear on the ruler for default tabs. When a user tab is set, the default tabs to the left are disabled. For example, if you set a left tab at 2 inches, the default tabs at .5", 1", and 1.5" are disabled.

TIP When working with tabs and indents, you might find it helpful to display the nonprinting characters by clicking the Show/Hide ¶ ¶ button so you can see where the (TAB) key has been pressed. The nonprinting character for a tab is an arrow that points to the right.

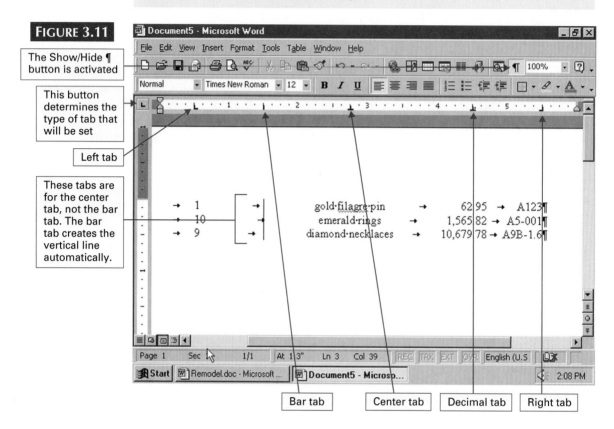

FIGURE 3.11

The Show/Hide ¶ button is activated

This button determines the type of tab that will be set

Left tab

These tabs are for the center tab, not the bar tab. The bar tab creates the vertical line automatically.

Bar tab   Center tab   Decimal tab   Right tab

In this task you will set a right tab with and without a leader character.

TASK 5: <u>To Set Right Tabs and Tabs with Leaders</u>

1 Select the paragraphs for the dates and times on the first page, as shown in Figure 3.12.

FIGURE 3.12

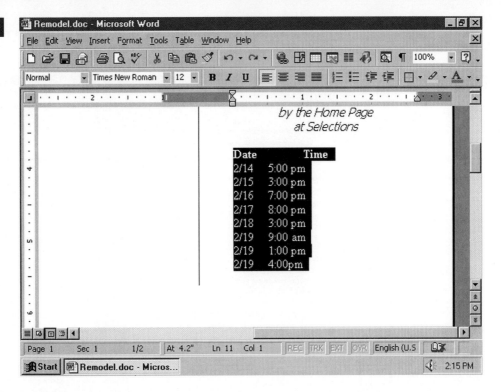

2 Click the Tab button until it displays a right tab and then point to the 2.5-inch mark on the ruler and click.

FIGURE 3.13

Notice that something is wrong here

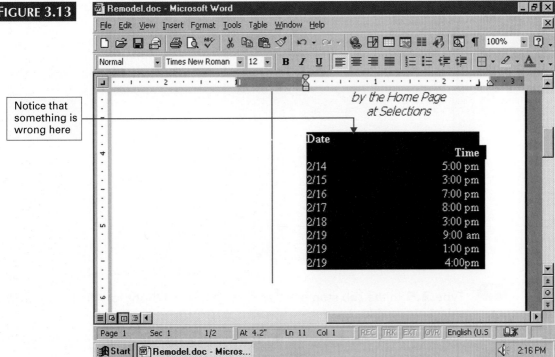

3 Click ¶ and notice that there are two tab characters before the word *Time*.

4 Delete one of the tabs and click ¶ again.

5 Select the paragraphs in the registration form in the third column of the second page, as shown in Figure 3.14.

FIGURE 3.14

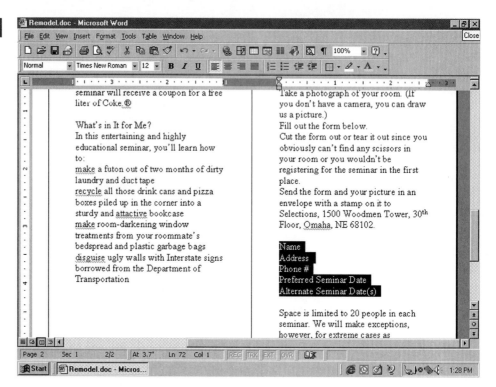

6 Choose Format, Tabs.

FIGURE 3.15

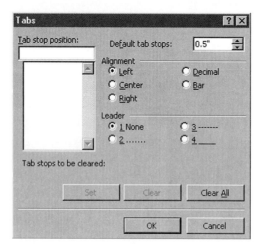

7 Type **2.5** in the Tab stop position text box, select Right for Alignment, and select option 4 for Leader.

8 Select Set and select OK. The Ruler displays a right tab at the 4-inch mark.

9 Click the insertion point after *Name* and press TAB. A line is created because the underline character was selected as the tab leader.

10 Click the insertion point at the end of the text on each line of the form and press TAB to complete the form.

FIGURE 3.16

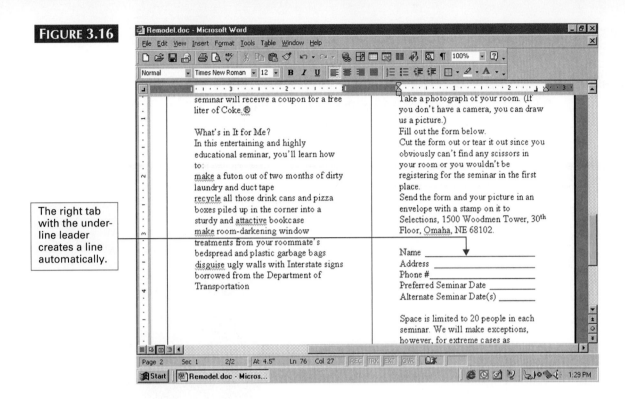

The right tab with the under-line leader creates a line automatically.

Setting Indents

You can format paragraphs with several types of indents—a *first line indent*, a *left indent*, a *right indent*, and a *hanging indent*. Figure 3.17 shows examples of each type of indent.

TIP The left and right indents are generally used in combination.

FIGURE 3.17

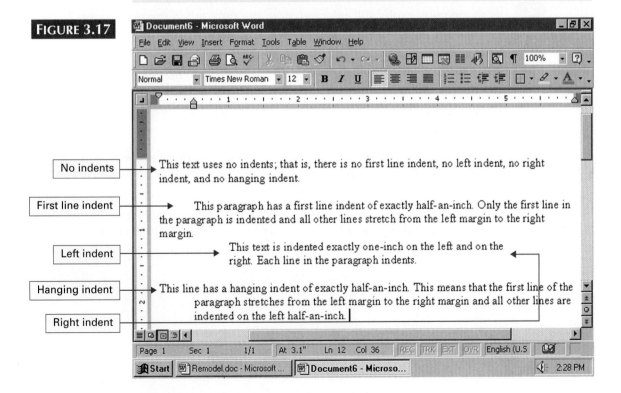

No indents

First line indent

Left indent

Hanging indent

Right indent

TASK 6: To Set Indents

1 Select the paragraphs at the bottom of page 1 (see Figure 3.18) and click the Increase Indent button. The text moves to the right, as shown in Figure 3.18.

FIGURE 3.18

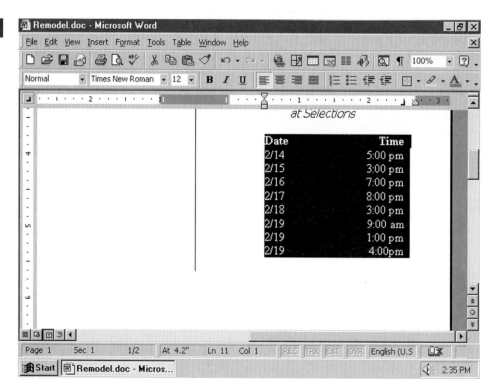

2 With the paragraphs still selected, drag the right tab in the ruler to the 2-inch mark. The times move to the left.

3 At the top of page 2, click anywhere in the sentence that begins *If the answer to any one of the following* and choose Format, Paragraph. The Paragraph dialog box displays.

4 Select First line from the Special drop-down list, type **.25** for By, and select OK. The first line of the paragraph indents.

5 At the top of the second column, click the insertion point anywhere in the sentence that begins *It's free!* and press (F4). Word sets the first line indent of the paragraph to .25 inches.

6 Using (F4) again, indent the first line of the paragraph that begins *In this entertaining and highly* in the second column and the paragraph that begins *Follow these easy steps to register* in the third column.

> **TIP** When using Click-n-Type to insert text in the second zone, the first-line indent is automatically applied to the paragraph.

Setting Paragraph and Line Spacing

Paragraph spacing adds space above or below a paragraph; ***line spacing*** adds space between the lines in the paragraph. By default, a paragraph has no space above it or below it, and the lines are single-spaced. Paragraph spacing is measured in points (12 points equal a line and there are 72 points in an inch). Line spacing includes single, double, and 1.5. Additionally, line spacing can be set to an exact measurement, a minimum measurement, and a multiple measurement.

TASK 7:   To Set Paragraph Spacing

1 Select the five paragraphs in the third column that make up the registration form. (Name, Address, Phone #, Preferred Seminar Date, and Alternate Seminar Date.)

2 Choose Format, Paragraph.

FIGURE 3.19

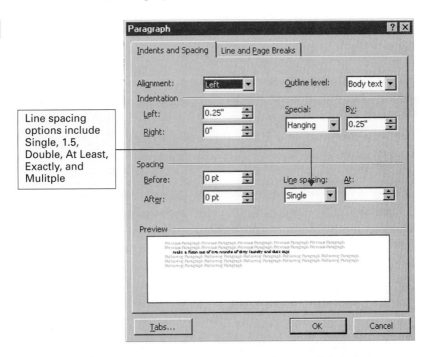

Line spacing options include Single, 1.5, Double, At Least, Exactly, and Mulitple

3 Type **6** for After and select OK. The paragraph spacing increases.

4 Click in the first paragraph at the top of page 1 (the brochure title) and set the paragraph spacing before the paragraph to 66 points.

Break Point

If necessary you can save your file as *Remodel Revised.doc*, exit Word, and continue this project later.

Creating Bulleted and Numbered Lists

To draw attention to paragraphs in a list, you can bullet the list or number it. A **bullet** is a symbol (usually a filled circle) that precedes the text in the list. Bulleted and numbered lists generally use a **hanging indent**, in which the second and subsequent lines of a paragraph are indented more than the first line of a paragraph. You don't have to know how to set a hanging indent because the Bullets button and the Numbering button do it for you.

> **TIP** Items in a list that have no particular order should be bulleted instead numbered.

TASK 8: To Create Bulleted and Numbered Lists

1 Launch Word and open *Remodel Revised.doc*, if necessary.

2 Use the Find command to find the text *make a futon out of . . . .*

3 Select the paragraphs as shown in Figure 3.20 and click the Bullets button.

FIGURE 3.20

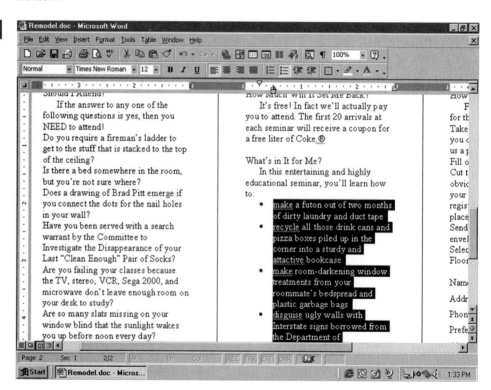

> **TIP** If you want a different-shaped bullet, choose Format, Bullets and Numbering, Bullets, select a different bullet, and select OK.

4 Following the same process, apply bullets to the paragraphs after the text *If the answer to any one of the following question is yes, then you NEED to attend!*

5 Click ⬚ until the bullets are flush left. The bulleted paragraphs move to the left margin.

6 Select the paragraphs under the Heading, Should I Attend in the first column as shown in Figure 3.21 and click ⬚. Decrease the indent so the bullets are on the left margin.

FIGURE 3.21

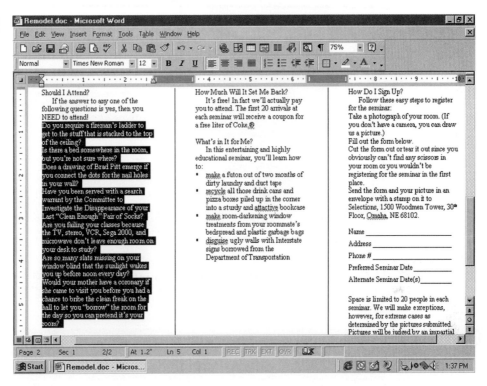

7 With the paragraphs still selected, choose Format, Bullets and Numbering.

FIGURE 3.22

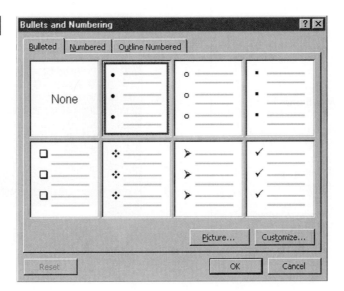

8 Select the checkmark bullets and select OK.

FIGURE 3.23

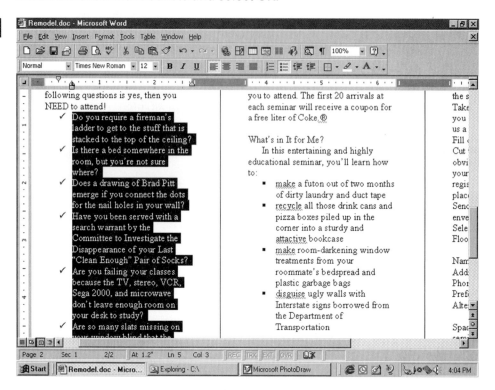

9 Find the text *Follow these easy steps to register* and select the paragraphs immediately below the text (as shown in Figure 3.24). Click the Numbering ≣ button.

FIGURE 3.24

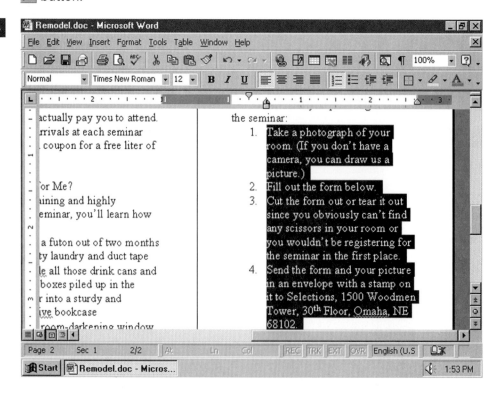

10 Set the paragraph spacing for all bulleted and numbered paragraphs to 6 points for After. (Hint: Use F4 after you set the first set of paragraphs.)

Finding and Replacing Formatting

In Project 2, you learned how to find and replace text. In the next task you will learn how to use the Find and Replace command to replace formatting. On the cover of the brochure, the font of the text *A Seminar Brought to You by Home Page at Selections* is Tahoma. All of the text in the brochure should be Times New Roman. To change all text that might be using the Tahoma font, you will use the Find and Replace command.

TASK 9:   To Find a Font and Replace It with Another Font

1 Press (CTRL) + (HOME) and then choose Edit, Replace. The Find and Replace dialog box opens to display the Replace page.

2 Delete any text that appears in the Find what and Replace with text boxes and then click in the Find what text box.

3 Select More, if necessary, and then select Format, Font, Tahoma, OK.

4 Press (TAB). The insertion point moves to the Replace with text box.

5 Select Format, Font, Times New Roman, OK.

FIGURE 3.25

Leaving the Find what and Replace with text boxes blank allows Word to replace all the *Tahoma* text with the same text in Times New Roman.

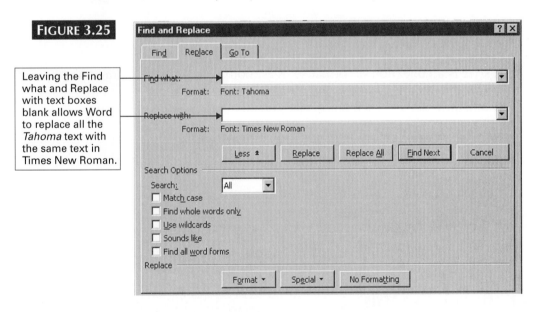

6 Select All in the Search list box, if necessary, and then select Replace All. Word reports that the Tahoma font is replaced by Times New Roman in five locations.

7 Select OK.

> **TIP** The Questions style uses Tahoma, but the Find and Replace command did not change the style, only the text formatted with the style.

8 Select No Formatting while the insertion point is in the Replace with text box, press (SHIFT) + (TAB), and select No Formatting while the insertion point is in the Find what text box. The formatting settings are removed.

9 Select Close. The Find and Replace dialog box closes.

10 Delete the text *It's free!* at the top of the second column and insert the WordArt as shown in Figure 3.1. You'll have to insert returns to make room for the art.

> **TIP** To insert WordArt, display the Drawing toolbar and click the Insert WordArt ◀ button. Select the style shown in Figure 3.1 and select OK. Type **It's Free** and select OK.

 ## Web Tip

Would you like to create your own brochure, a business card, or a Christmas card? Check out the PaperDirect Web site at http://www.paperdirect.com for a huge selection of pre-designed papers, including letterhead, brochures, business cards, labels, invitations, holiday designs, and other helpful ready-made paper products.

Applying, Creating, and Modifying Styles

A *style* is a collection of format settings, both character and paragraph, that are grouped together and given a name. When you apply a style to a paragraph, the text of the paragraph takes on all the formatting stored in the style.

Normal is the default style that Word applies to all text in a new document. This style uses the font defaults, single spacing, with no indents.

> **TIP** If you use styles to format paragraphs, you can make changes to multiple paragraphs by changing the style that is applied to them. If you use direct formatting, you have to change every paragraph individually.

 TASK 10: To Apply a Style

1 Click anywhere in the last paragraph on page 2 and choose Format, Style.

FIGURE 3.26

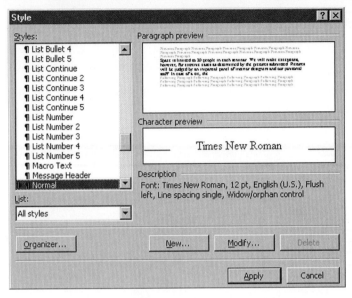

2 Select Comment Text from the Styles: list and select Apply.

> **TROUBLESHOOTING** If you do not see the style Comment Text in the Styles list, choose All Styles for List.

TASK 11: To Create a Style

1 Click anywhere in the first line on page 2 (*Should I Attend?*) and choose Format, Style, New.

FIGURE 3.27

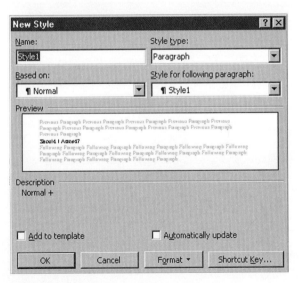

2 Type **Questions** for the Name and select Normal for the Style for Following Paragraph.

3 Select Format, Font. The Font dialog box displays.

4 Select Tahoma for the Font and Bold for the Font style and select OK. The New Style dialog box displays.

5 Select Format, Paragraph. The Paragraph dialog box displays.

6 Type **3** for After and select OK. The New Style dialog box displays.

7 Choose Format, Border.

FIGURE 3.28

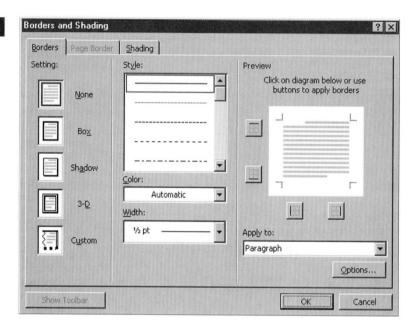

8 Select 1 pt from the Width drop-down list and click the bottom border on the Preview.

FIGURE 3.29

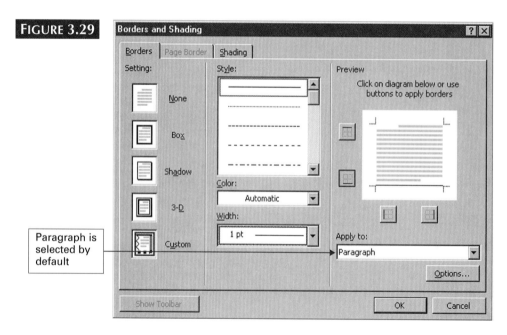

Paragraph is selected by default

9 Select Options.

FIGURE 3.30

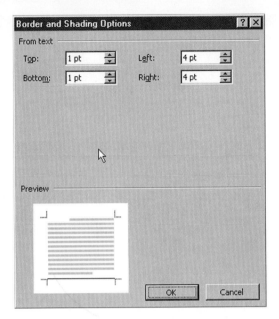

10 Type **2** for Bottom and select OK. The Borders and Shading dialog box displays.

11 Select OK. The New Style dialog box displays.

12 Select OK and select Apply. The new font is applied to the paragraph.

Check Point

Remember in Project 2 that underlining didn't look good because it cut through the descenders (the part of a character that extends below the baseline, as in the letters *j* and *y*)? By using a ***border*** instead of an underline, you have the option of specifying a distance from the text to the line so the line will not cut through the descenders.

13 Click in the paragraph *How Much Will It Set Me Back* at the top of the second column and press F4. The Question style is applied.

14 Click in the paragraph *What's in It for Me* and click the down arrow on the Style button in the Formatting toolbar.

FIGURE 3.31

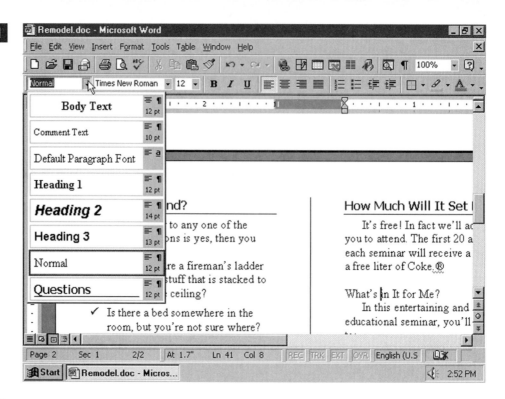

15 Select Questions. The style is applied to the paragraph.

16 Use the method of your choice to apply the Question style to the *How Do I Sign Up* paragraph at the top of the third column.

TIP If you have created a style in one document that you want to use in a different document, you can copy the style easily by copying a paragraph formatted with the style (or just the paragraph mark) and pasting it into the desired document.

TASK 12: To Create a Style by Example

1 Click anywhere in the paragraph that begins *If the answer to any one of the following* at the top of the first column and choose Format, Paragraph. The Paragraph dialog box displays.

2 Type **12** for After and select OK. The space is added below the paragraph.

3 Click in the Style text box in the Formatting toolbar. The Normal style is selected.

4 Type **Intro** and press (ENTER). A new style is created based on the formatting of the current paragraph.

5 Apply the new style to the paragraph that begins *In this entertaining and highly educational seminar* in the second column and to the paragraph that begins *Follow these easy steps* in the third column.

TASK 13: <u>To Modify a Style</u>

1 Press (CTRL) + (END) and choose Format, Style. The Style dialog box displays and the Comment Text style is selected in the Styles list.

2 Select Modify.

FIGURE 3.32

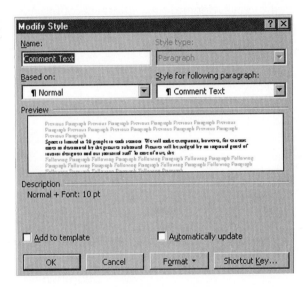

3 Select Format, Font; select 8 for Font size and select OK. The Modify Style dialog box displays.

4 Select OK and select Close. The text in the last paragraph, which is formatted with the Comment Text style, changes to 8 point.

5 Save the file as *Remodel Revised.doc* and close it.

Summary and Exercises

Summary

- Page setup options include margins, page size, page orientation, paper source, line numbers, and vertical alignment.
- The text in newspaper columns flows from the bottom of one column to the top of the next.
- Paragraph formats include tabs, alignment, indentations, line spacing, and spacing before and after the paragraph.
- Tabs align text in specific ways, depending on the type of tab.
- Word provides the Numbering button and the Bullets button for quickly creating simple numbered or bulleted lists.
- The Find and Replace command can find and replace formatting as well as characters.
- A style is a collection of character and paragraph formats.

Key Terms and Operations

Key Terms

bar tab	margin
border	newspaper columns
bullet	Normal style
bulleted list	numbered list
center tab	orientation
column	page setup
column break	paper size
decimal tab	paper source
first line indent	paragraph spacing
hanging indent	parallel columns
landscape	portrait
leader	right indent
left indent	right tab
left tab	style
line spacing	tab stop

Operations

apply a border	create columns
apply a style	find and replace formatting
apply direct formatting to a	indent
paragraph	modify a style
create a bulleted list	set margins
create a numbered list	set tabs
create a style	

Study Questions

Multiple Choice

1. When you modify a style,
   a. the format changes aren't reflected in the paragraphs that already use the style.
   b. the format changes are reflected in the paragraphs that already use the style.
   c. you must give the style a new name.
   d. you must reapply the style to paragraphs that already use the style.

2. You can create newspaper columns of unequal width
   a. by clicking the Columns button.
   b. by choosing Format, Columns.
   c. by clicking the Insert Tables button.
   d. by dragging the column guidelines.

3. To repeat the last typing or operation, press
   a. (F3).
   b. (F4).
   c. (F5).
   d. (F6).

4. If you use Click-n-Type, in what zones are left tab stops automatically set on the ruler?
   a. 1 and 3
   b. 2 and 4
   c. 3 and 5
   d. 4 and 6

5. Instead of applying formats directly to selected paragraphs, you can
   a. choose Format, Paragraph.
   b. choose Format, Font.
   c. click appropriate buttons on the Formatting toolbar.
   d. apply styles.

6. What is the default top margin?
   a. 1"
   b. 1.25"
   c. .5"
   d. 1.5"

7. How would you define the "Gutter" option as used in the Page Setup dialog box?
   a. The space between columns.
   b. The space above or below a paragraph.
   c. Additional space added to margins for the purpose of binding.
   d. Additional space on the screen on the left and right of the text.

8. How many points are in an inch?
   a. 12
   b. 48
   c. 72
   d. 96

9. Tab stops are used to align text
   a. on a specific character.
   b. at a specific location.
   c. instead of default tabs.
   d. on an indention.

10. When a style is applied to a paragraph,
    a. the name of the style appears in the selection bar.
    b. the paragraph takes on the formatting of the style.
    c. the paragraph can't be edited.
    d. the formatting of the paragraph can't be changed.

Short Answer

1. List at least three line spacing options available.

2. What is a bullet?

3. Where is the Tab selector button located?

4. How do you apply a style?

5. When is it better to bullet a list than to number it?

6. How do you create a style by example?

7. What is the difference between paragraph spacing and line spacing?

8. How do you add a line that is not an underline under a heading?

9. How do you change the style of a bullet?

10. How does the Show/Hide ¶ button help when you are using tabs?

Fill in the Blank

1. In Word, you can create two kinds of columns—newspaper columns and _____ columns.

2. A column _____ causes text in one column to move to the top of the next column.

3. Word uses a(n) _____ indent in a numbered list formatted with the Numbering button.

4. Space before a paragraph is measured in _____.

5. A _____ is a collection of character and paragraph formats.

6. If you press (ENTER) at the end of a centered paragraph, the next paragraph will be _____.

7. Instead of using the undersline feature, you can use a(n) _____ to draw a line under text.

8. The _____ tab creates a vertical line.

9. You set top and bottom margins in the _____ dialog box.

10. Click the _____ button in the Find and Replace dialog box to see additional options.

For Discussion

1. Describe some scenarios in which you would use the Find and Replace command to replace one type of formatting with another type of formatting.

2. Discuss the advantage of using styles to format paragraphs.

3. Discuss the advantage of using space before or space after a paragraph instead of adding space by pressing (ENTER).

4. Compare the two methods of setting tabs.

5. List and briefly describe at least four features provided by Word that automate the formatting process.

Hands-On Exercises

1. Formatting the Career Day Brochure

Matthew is designing the Career Day informational brochure that will go in the student packets. In this exercise, you will format the brochure as shown in Figure 3.33.

FIGURE 3.33

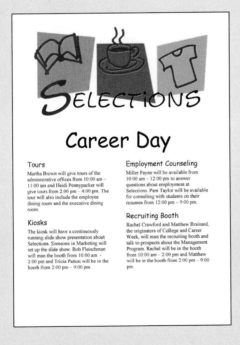

1. Open *Career Day.doc*.

2. Insert the graphic *Selections.gif* above the title and resize the graphic if necessary. (*Hint:* To allow the graphic to move freely, select the graphic, choose Format, Picture, Layout, and select Square.)

3. Select the title, center it, and choose Format, Font. Select Comic Sans MS, 48 point. Select the Character Spacing tab. Select Expanded for Spacing: and specify 4 points for By.

4. Create a new style named Activities, based on the Heading 1 style, that uses Comic Sans MS regular (not bold). Apply the style to *Tours*, *Kiosks*, *Employment Counseling*, and *Recruiting Booth*.

5. Select all the text from *Tours* to the end of the document and make it two columns. (*Note*: When you select the text, the title and graphic are not included.)

6. Insert a column break before *Employment Counseling*.

7. Print the file or preview it.

8. Save the file as *Career Day Formatted.doc* and close it.

2. Formatting the Cooking Seminar Brochure

In this exercise, you will format the brochure as shown in Figure 3.34.

FIGURE 3.34

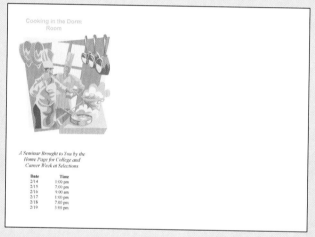

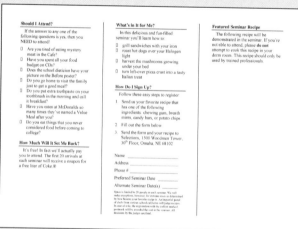

1. Open *Cooking Seminar.doc*.

2. Set the top, bottom, left, and right margins to .5" and change the page orientation to Landscape.

3. Format the page with three equal columns. Change the column spacing for the first two columns to 1 inch.

4. Open *Remodel Revised.doc*. Select the paragraph on the first page with the headings *Date* and *Time*. Click the Format Painter button. Switch to the *Cooking Seminar.doc* window and select the same text on the first page. The format is copied. Using the same procedure, copy the format of the first paragraph under the heading in *Remodel Revised.doc* and apply it to all the date/time paragraphs in the *Cooking Seminar.doc* window.

5. In *Remodel Revised.doc*, copy the paragraph mark after the text *Should I Attend?* at the top of the first column on page 2 and close the document. Select the paragraph mark after *Should I Attend?* and paste.

6. Apply the Question style to *How Much Will It Set Me Back?, What's in It for Me?, How Do I Sign Up?*, and *Featured Seminar Recipe.*

7. Apply the default style, Body Text First Indent, to the first paragraph under each heading (formatted with the Question style).

8. Bullet the paragraphs under the heading *Should I Attend?* and decrease the indent as shown in Figure 3.34.

9. Bullet the paragraphs under the heading *What's in It for Me?* and decrease the indent as shown in Figure 3.34.

10. Number the steps under *How Do I Sign Up?* and decrease the indent as shown in Figure 3.34.

11. Insert a column break before *What's in It for Me?* and *Featured Seminar Recipe.*

12. Log on to the Internet and go to the HGTV Web site at http://www.hgtv.com, or to the Food Network Web site at http://www.foodtv.com. Find an appropriate recipe to include in the third column of the brochure. Type and format the recipe appropriately.

13. Save the file as *Cooking Seminar Formatted.doc* and close it.

On Your Own Exercises

1. Creating a Template for Research Papers

When writing research papers, it is likely that you have been told to follow the guidelines set forth by a style manual such as the *MLA Handbook for Writers of Research Papers* or the *Chicago Manual of Style*.

 **Web Tip**

The MLA format for documenting sources from the World Wide Web is illustrated at http://www.mla.org/main_stl.htm#spaces.

Refer to the style guidelines that you are required to use and create a document that uses the prescribed formats. Set the appropriate margins, modify the default Normal or Body Text style so that it uses the proper font, font size, line spacing, indentation, and paragraph spacing. Modify the default Footnote, Header, and Footer styles so that they use the proper font, font size, line spacing, indentation, and paragraph spacing. Create pages with sample text for the required elements, such as a title page and bibliography. Save the document as a template by selecting Document Template (*.dot) in the Save as type: list box in the Save As dialog box. To use the template when you want to write a new paper, choose File, New. Select the template from the General page and choose OK.

2. Designing and Printing Gift Certificates

Create at least four gift certificates for your friends and family. The certificates can say something like, "This certificate entitles the bearer to one free car wash by <your name>." Use a custom paper size of 4.25" by 5.5" and print four pages per sheet. Experiment with different page borders and create appropriate styles for the text.

3. Designing and Printing Your Own Greeting Cards

Create your own greeting cards to send to your friends and family. Specify a page size of 8.5" by 5.5" and create two columns. Create a style for the text of the card.

 **Web Tip**

Check out the animated greeting cards at http://www.bluemountain.com for ideas.

4. Designing and Printing a Party Invitation

You're having a party. First decide on a theme for the party, and then be creative and design a unique invitation that illustrates the theme.

TIP If you can't find anything better to do at your party, use the suggested activity in the next exercise to create some party games.

5. Creating Word Puzzles with Graphics

Create a file and type the title *Word Puzzles* at the top. Using Word ClipArt or graphics you find on the Web, create at least three pictorial word puzzles, such as: In 1998 this state elected a retired Navy Seal as governor.

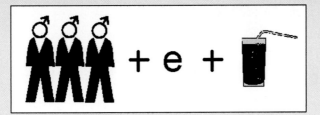

You might have to do a little research in Help on the topic of wrapping to get the graphics positioned correctly. Insert a footnote that has the answers in a very small font size. Save the puzzles in a file cleverly named as *Puzzles.doc*. By the way, the answer to the example puzzle is Minnesota. Can you name the governor? It's Jesse "The Body" Ventura, who now likes to be called Jesse "The Brain" Ventura.

6. Making Signs

Using page borders, styles, and graphics, make a variety of signs for the door of your room, such as Do Not Disturb, Donations are Tax Deductible, Don't Feed the Animals, Men Working, Women Working, and I'd Rather Be Surfing (Fishing, Ski-Diving, and so on).

Working with Multipage Documents

Multipage documents often require what might be considered more advanced formatting, such as section breaks, headers, and footers—formatting that is more complex than character or paragraph formatting. Longer documents may require additional navigation techniques. In this project you will learn techniques for working with longer documents and some features, such as outlines and footnotes, that are frequently associated with longer documents.

Objectives

After completing this project, you will be able to:

➤ Create a title page

➤ Create sections

➤ Create an outline

➤ Create and modify headers and footers

➤ Create footnotes

➤ Use the Document Map to navigate

➤ Print specific pages

Running Case

Matthew has electronic files for all of the events and details concerning College and Career Week. He wants to put all the files into one document and organize them into a professional-looking report that will be printed on both sides of the paper and bound.

The Challenge

It is your responsibility to make sure that the formats in the document are ready for printing, the pages are numbered correctly, and all the documents are inserted in the right place.

The Strategy

You will begin by creating a title page, followed by an outline that will serve as an executive overview of what is in the file. Then you will insert the various files following the outline. So that you can start page numbering with the first page of the outline, you will have to insert a section break after the title page. To number the outline, you will begin using lowercase roman numerals and then start numbering the actual report pages with arabic numbers (starting with one). You will also have to insert a section break after the outline. Figure 4.1a and 4.1b show the first few pages of the report.

FIGURE 4.1a

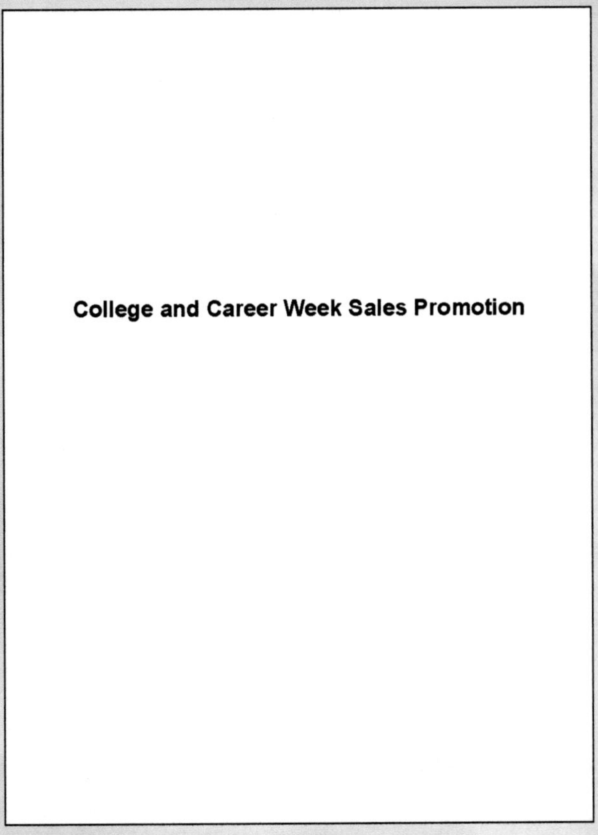

College and Career Week Sales Promotion

FIGURE 4.1b

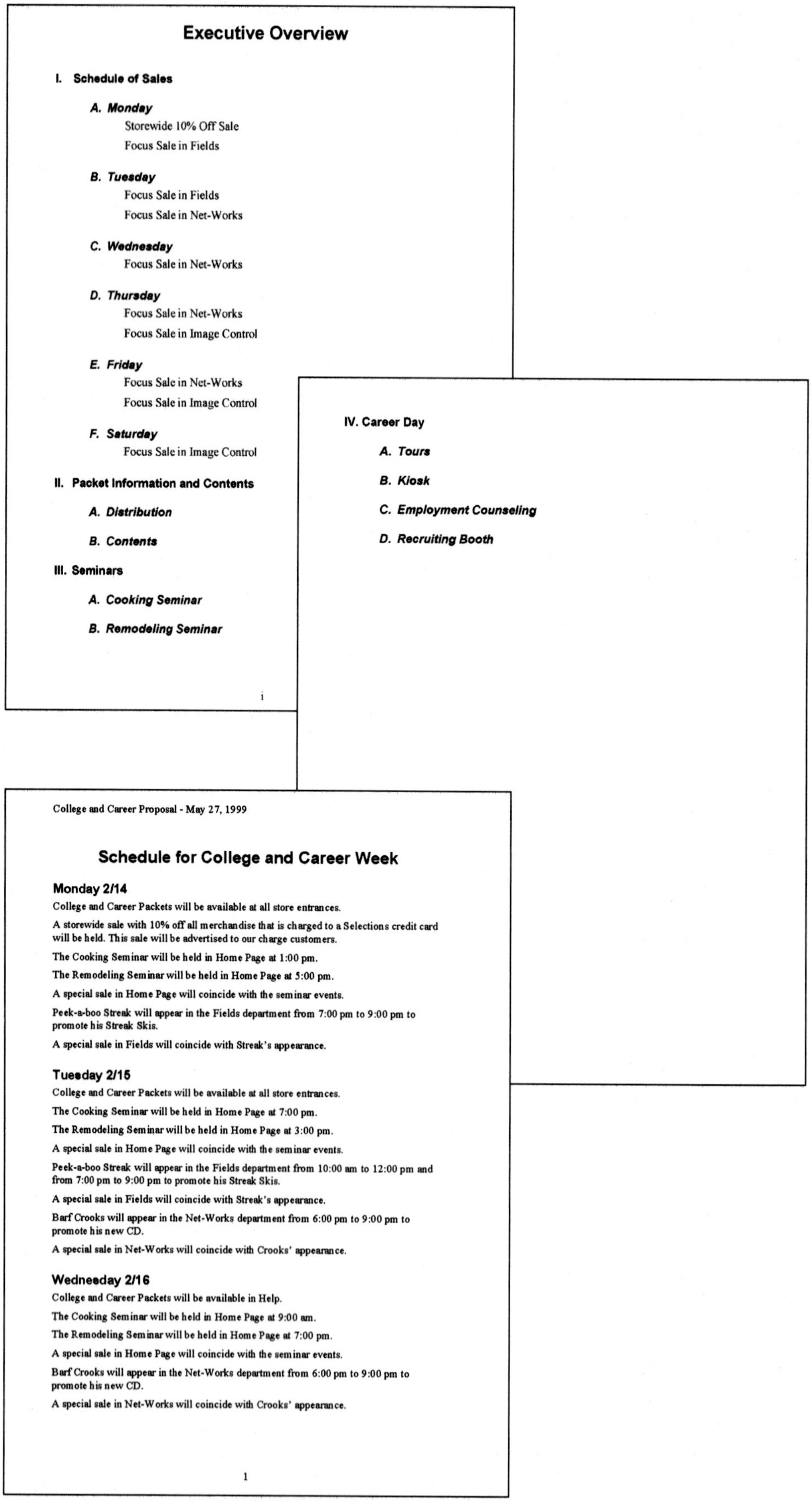

Executive Overview

I. **Schedule of Sales**

   A. Monday

   Storewide 10% Off Sale
   Focus Sale in Fields

   B. Tuesday

   Focus Sale in Fields
   Focus Sale in Net-Works

   C. Wednesday

   Focus Sale in Net-Works

   D. Thursday

   Focus Sale in Net-Works
   Focus Sale in Image Control

   E. Friday

   Focus Sale in Net-Works
   Focus Sale in Image Control

   F. Saturday

   Focus Sale in Image Control

II. **Packet Information and Contents**

   A. Distribution

   B. Contents

III. **Seminars**

   A. Cooking Seminar

   B. Remodeling Seminar

i

IV. **Career Day**

   A. Tours

   B. Kiosk

   C. Employment Counseling

   D. Recruiting Booth

College and Career Proposal - May 27, 1999

Schedule for College and Career Week

Monday 2/14

College and Career Packets will be available at all store entrances.

A storewide sale with 10% off all merchandise that is charged to a Selections credit card will be held. This sale will be advertised to our charge customers.

The Cooking Seminar will be held in Home Page at 1:00 pm.

The Remodeling Seminar will be held in Home Page at 5:00 pm.

A special sale in Home Page will coincide with the seminar events.

Peek-a-boo Streak will appear in the Fields department from 7:00 pm to 9:00 pm to promote his Streak Skis.

A special sale in Fields will coincide with Streak's appearance.

Tuesday 2/15

College and Career Packets will be available at all store entrances.

The Cooking Seminar will be held in Home Page at 7:00 pm.

The Remodeling Seminar will be held in Home Page at 3:00 pm.

A special sale in Home Page will coincide with the seminar events.

Peek-a-boo Streak will appear in the Fields department from 10:00 am to 12:00 pm and from 7:00 pm to 9:00 pm to promote his Streak Skis.

A special sale in Fields will coincide with Streak's appearance.

Barf Crooks will appear in the Net-Works department from 6:00 pm to 9:00 pm to promote his new CD.

A special sale in Net-Works will coincide with Crooks' appearance.

Wednesday 2/16

College and Career Packets will be available in Help.

The Cooking Seminar will be held in Home Page at 9:00 am.

The Remodeling Seminar will be held in Home Page at 7:00 pm.

A special sale in Home Page will coincide with the seminar events.

Barf Crooks will appear in the Net-Works department from 6:00 pm to 9:00 pm to promote his new CD.

A special sale in Net-Works will coincide with Crooks' appearance.

1

The Setup

So that your screen will match the illustrations and the tasks in this project will function as described, make sure that the Word 2000 settings listed in Table 4.1 match those on your computer.

Table 4.1: Word 2000 Settings

Location:	Make these settings:
View	Choose Ruler to ensure rule is activated.
View, Toolbars	Deselect all toolbars except Standard and Formatting. Then deselect any buttons that are selected in the Standard toolbar and set the Zoom to 100%.
Tools, Customize, Options	Deselect Standard and Formatting toolbars share one row and Menus show recently used commands first.
Tools, Options, Spelling & Grammar	Select all options in the dialog box *except* the following: Hide spelling errors in this document, Suggest from main dictionary only, Hide grammatical errors in this document, and Show readability statistics.
Help, Show Office Assistant	Right-click the Office Assistant and choose Options. Deselect Use the Office Assistant.

Creating a Title Page

The text of a title page is generally centered on the page vertically. Instead of pressing (ENTER) until you think you have reached the vertical center of the page, you can simply select a layout option that automatically centers text on the page.

TASK 1:   To Create a Title Page

1. Create a new document and switch to Print Layout view if necessary.

2. Type **College and Career Week Sales Promotion**, and press (ENTER).

3. Apply the Title style to the text; then select the text and change the font size to 18 point.

4. In the Formatting toolbar click in the Style box and press (ENTER). Word displays the Modify Style dialog box, as shown in Figure 4.2, because it knows you are reapplying the same style, but the style has been changed.

FIGURE 4.2

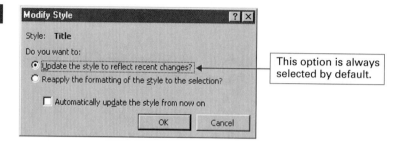

5 Select OK. The font size of the style changes to 18 points.

6 Choose File, Page Setup, and click the Layout tab.

FIGURE 4.3

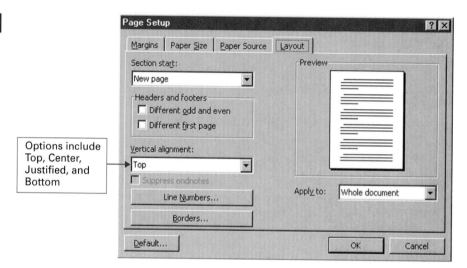

7 From the Vertical alignment drop-down list, select Center and select OK. The title moves to the vertical center of the page.

8 Press (CTRL) + (END) and insert a page break.

Creating Sections

Section breaks divide a page or a document into independent parts. A continuous section break divides a page into sections and allows each section to have different left and right margins and a different number of columns.

The other types of section breaks (next page, even page, and odd page) divide the document into sections by using page breaks. Table 4.2 describes section break options, as shown in Figure 4.30.

Table 4.2

Section Break	Description
Next page	Breaks the page and starts the new section on the next page
Continuous	Starts the new section on the same page
Odd page or Even page	Starts the new section on the next odd-numbered or even-numbered page

When one of these section breaks is inserted, each section can have a different page setup. Each section can have a different paper size, different orientation, different vertical alignment, different margins, and different headers and footers.

In the next task you will insert a section break after the title page so that you can change the vertical alignment for the next section.

> **TIP** The continuous section break is the only section break that does not insert a page break.

TASK 2:   To Insert a Section Break

 Choose Insert, Break, and select Next Page.

FIGURE 4.4

2 Select OK. Word creates a new page.

3 Switch to Normal view and scroll up with the vertical scroll bar to see the section break, as shown in Figure 4.5. A blank page after the title page ensures that the first page of text will start on a right hand page.

FIGURE 4.5

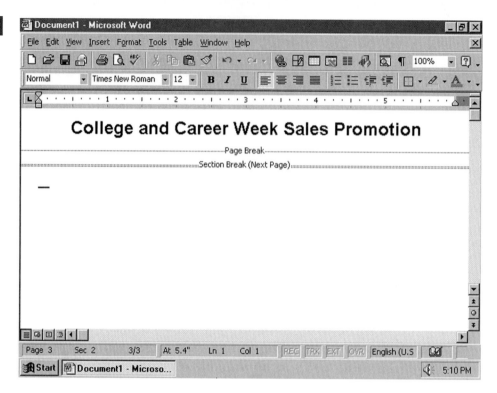

| Document1 - Microsoft Word |

File Edit View Insert Format Tools Table Window Help

Normal ▼ Times New Roman ▼ 12 ▼ **B** *I* U

College and Career Week Sales Promotion
·······························Page Break·······························
·······························Section Break (Next Page)·······························

—

Page 3   Sec 2   3/3   At 5.4"   Ln 1   Col 1   REC TRK EXT OVR English (U.S

Start Document1 - Microso...   5:10 PM

4 Switch back to Print Layout view and choose File, Page Setup. The Page Setup dialog box displays the Layout page because it was the last page used in the dialog box.

5 Select Top for Vertical alignment; under Apply to:, verify that This section is selected; and select OK. The insertion point moves to the top of the page.

Creating an Outline

The *outline numbering* feature in Word numbers each topic for you automatically. It also renumbers the topics if you add additional topics or delete topics. Several default outline numbering styles are available, and you can create your own style.

 **Web Tip**

Did you know that the Microsoft Support Web site maintains a Knowledge-Base of more than 150,000 help articles? To learn more about outline numbering, go to http://www.microsoft.com and click Support. Navigate to the KnowledgeBase and search for the phrase "outline numbering."

TASK 3: To Create an Outline

1 Type **Executive Overview** and press (ENTER) twice. Then apply the Title style to the text.

2 Press (CTRL) + (END), choose Format, Bullets and Numbering, and select the Outline Numbered tab. The Outline Numbered page appears.

3 Select the style that uses I. A. 1. for the headings, as shown in Figure 4.6.

FIGURE 4.6

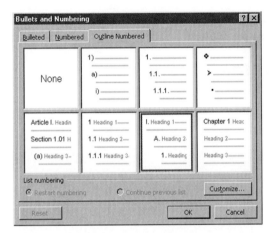

4 Select OK. The roman numeral I appears in the document.

5 Switch to Outline view. The Outline toolbar appears, as shown in Figure 4.7.

FIGURE 4.7

The Outline toolbar

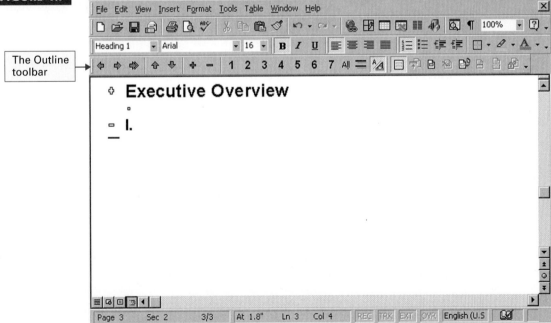

> **TROUBLESHOOTING** If your screen doesn't match Figure 4.7, click the Show Formatting ⬛ button.

6 Type **Schedule of Sales**, press (ENTER), and then press (TAB), as shown in Figure 4.8.

FIGURE 4.8

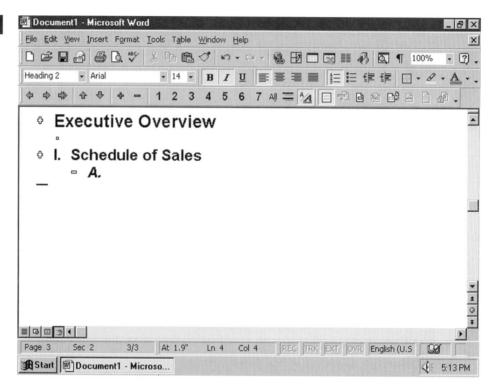

7 Type **Monday** and press (ENTER). Notice that Word is creating the heading levels based on the tab position.

8 Repeat step 7 five times, substituting the remaining days of the week through Saturday, as shown in Figure 4.9. (Be sure to press (ENTER) after typing Saturday.)

FIGURE 4.9

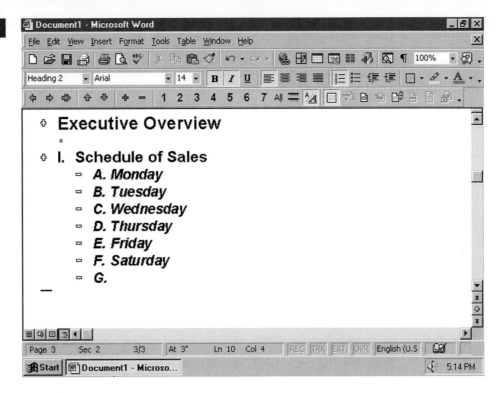

9 Press (SHIFT) + (TAB). The insertion point moves to the left margin and the G changes to II. This is called promoting a heading. You also can use the Promote button instead of pressing (SHIFT) + (TAB).

10 Click the Show Formatting ⅍ button to deactivate formatting.

11 Type **Packet Information and Content** and press (ENTER).

12 Type **Seminars** and press (ENTER).

13 Type **Career Day**, press (ENTER), and press (BACKSPACE). The outline number is erased on the new line.

14 Switch to Normal view.

FIGURE 4.10

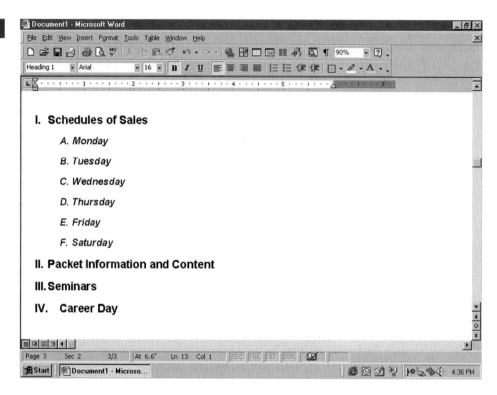

I. **Schedules of Sales**

    A. Monday

    B. Tuesday

    C. Wednesday

    D. Thursday

    E. Friday

    F. Saturday

II. **Packet Information and Content**

III.**Seminars**

IV. **Career Day**

TASK 4: To Create Body Text, Headings, and Subheadings

1 Switch to Outline view, click the insertion point after the *y* in *Monday*, and press (ENTER).

2 Click the Demote to Body Text ⇨ button and type **Storewide 10% Off Sale**. Text that is demoted to body text is not a heading in the outline.

3 Click the insertion point after *Tuesday*, press (ENTER), demote the heading to body text, and type **Focus Sale in Fields**.

4 Finish typing the body text and subheadings shown in Figure 4.1.

5 Click the Show Heading 1 **1** button. The ouline collapses, showing only the headings at the first level, as shown in Figure 4.11.

FIGURE 4.11

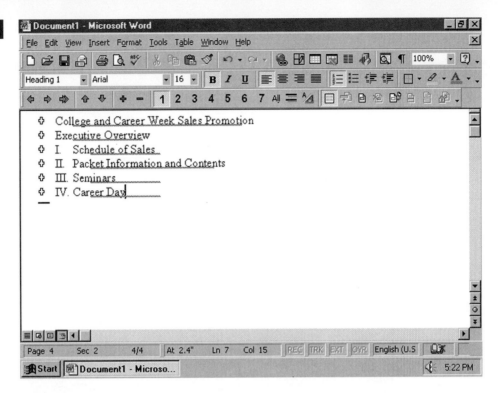

6 Click anywhere in the heading *Schedule of Sales* and click the Expand ⊞ button. Only that heading displays its subheadings, but it doesn't display the body text.

7 Click the All ⁿ button. All headings, subheadings, and body text appear.

8 With the insertion point still in the *Schedule of Sales* heading, click the Collapse ⊟ button. Word hides the subtopics under the heading.

FIGURE 4.12

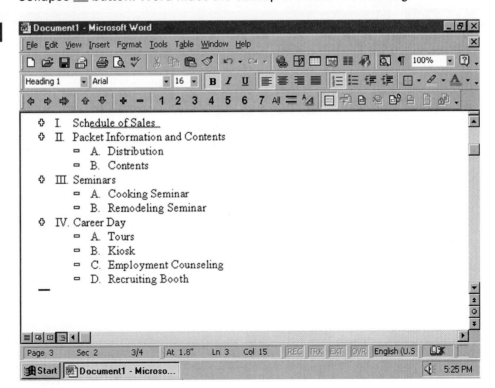

9 Click ▬ again. All subheadings for this topic collapse.

FIGURE 4.13

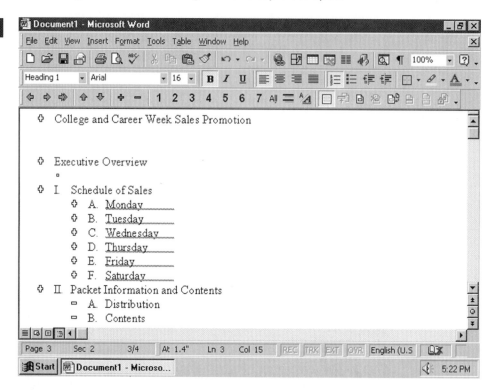

10 Click the Print Layout View 🔲 button. The full document appears in Page Layout view, as shown in Figure 4.14. Notice that the paragraphs are not indented as you would expect. You can enhance the appearance of the outline by modifying the styles.

FIGURE 4.14

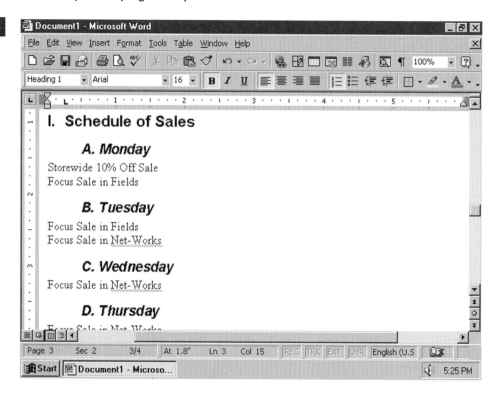

Check Point

Remember how to use the Find and Replace command to replace formatting? You can put this command to good use in the next step.

11 Change Heading 1 to 12 points and remove the Keep with next paragraph format. Change Heading 2 to 12 points. Apply the Block Text style to all body text, which currently uses the Normal style.

FIGURE 4.15

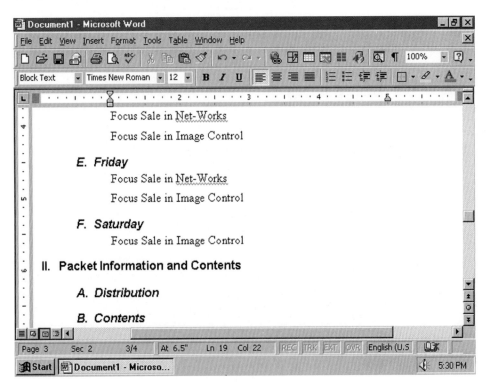

12 Insert a page break before the Career Day heading.

TASK 5:   To Create the Next Section

1 Press (CTRL) + (END) to go to the end of the file. Press (ENTER) if the insertion point is not positioned at the beginning of a new line, and insert a next page section break.

2 Insert the following files in this document and separate each file with a page break:

Schedule.doc

Packet.doc

Seminars.doc

Career Day.doc

TIP If you do not have copies of these files, you can download them from the SELECT Web site at http://www.prenhall.com/select.

Check Point

Do you remember the steps you learned in Project 2 for inserting a file? Choose Insert, File.

 Save the file as *Promo Proposal*.

Break Point

If necessary, you can close your file, exit Word, and continue this project later.

Creating and Modifying Headers and Footers

A **header** is text that prints at the top of every page in a section. A **footer** is text that prints at the bottom of every page in a section. The header prints within the default 1-inch top margin, $\frac{1}{2}$ inch from the top edge of the paper. The footer prints in the default 1-inch bottom margin, $\frac{1}{2}$ inch from the bottom edge of the paper.

Creating Headers and Footers

Every document contains a blank header and footer space. To create a header or a footer you open the header or footer space and enter text. By default, the header and footer space both have a center tab and a right tab.

Each time you open the header or footer space, the Header and Footer toolbar displays automatically. This toolbar has buttons for inserting text, buttons for formatting, and buttons for navigating.

TASK 6: <u>To Create Headers and Footers</u>

Launch Word and open the Promo Proposal.doc, if necessary. Click anywhere on the first page and choose View, Header and Footer. The Header and Footer toolbar appears, as shown in Figure 4.16. The header space always opens first.

FIGURE 4.16

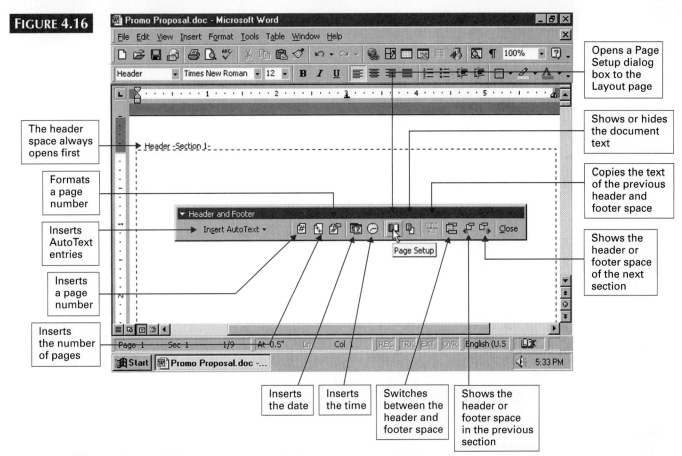

The header space always opens first

Formats a page number

Inserts AutoText entries

Inserts a page number

Inserts the number of pages

Opens a Page Setup dialog box to the Layout page

Shows or hides the document text

Copies the text of the previous header and footer space

Shows the header or footer space of the next section

Inserts the date

Inserts the time

Switches between the header and footer space

Shows the header or footer space in the previous section

2 Click the Page Setup button.

FIGURE 4.17

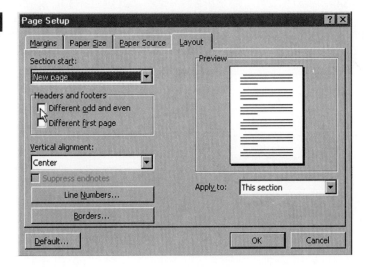

3 To create headers and footers that have different text on alternating page, select Different Odd and Even and select OK.

FIGURE 4.18

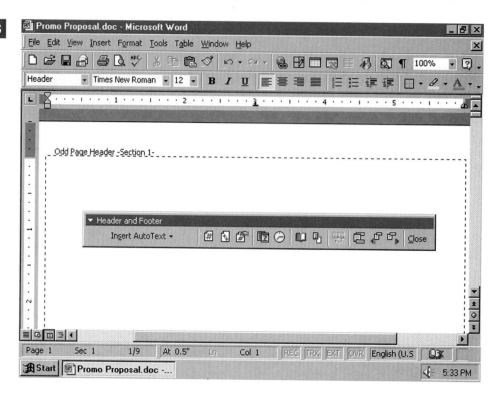

4 Click the Show Next 🖫 button twice. Word moves ahead to the header for section 2.

FIGURE 4.19

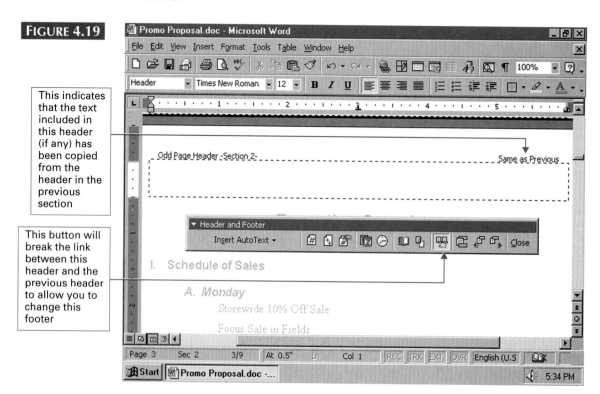

This indicates that the text included in this header (if any) has been copied from the header in the previous section

This button will break the link between this header and the previous header to allow you to change this footer

5 Click the Same as Previous ⬚ button. The link between this header and the header in section 1 is broken.

6 Click the Switch Between Header and Footer ⬚ button.

FIGURE 4.20

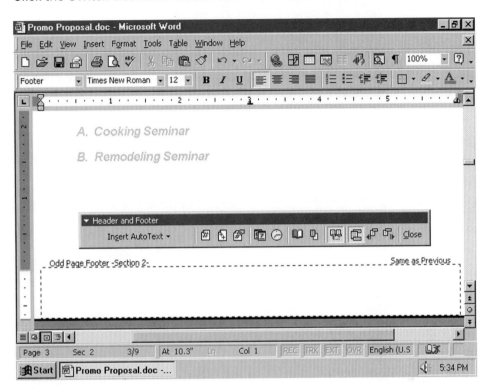

7 Click ⬚. The link between this footer and the footer in section 1 is broken.

8 Leave this footer open for the next task.

Inserting and Formatting Page Numbers

Page numbers in headers or footers can be formatted to use different number formats or include text.

TASK 7: To Insert and Format Page Numbers

1 The insertion point should still be positioned in the footer for section 2. Press (TAB) and click the Insert Page Number ⬚ button. The page number is centered in the footer.

2 Click the Format Page Number ⬚ button.

FIGURE 4.21

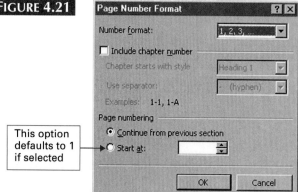

This option defaults to 1 if selected

3 Select i, ii, iii from the Number format drop-down list, select Start at, and select OK.

FIGURE 4.22

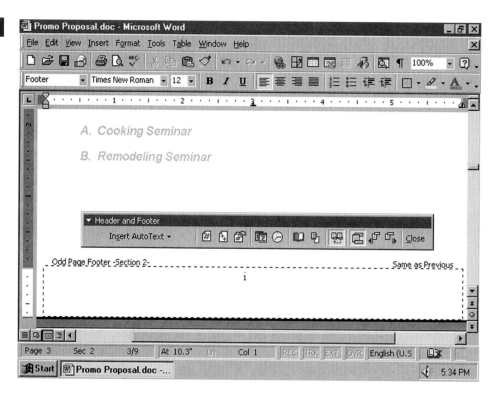

4 Click the Show Next button. The Even Page footer space opens, as shown in Figure 4.23.

FIGURE 4.23

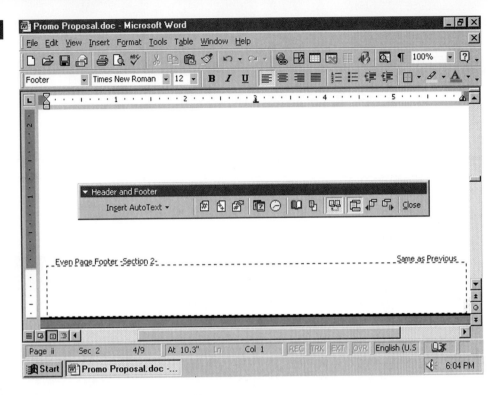

5 Click the Same as Previous ▦ button.

6 Press ⟨TAB⟩ and click ▦ . The roman numeral ii is inserted in the center of the footer.

7 Click ▣ , and then click ▦ .

8 Click ▦ , click ▦ , and then type **College and Career Proposal**.

FIGURE 4.24

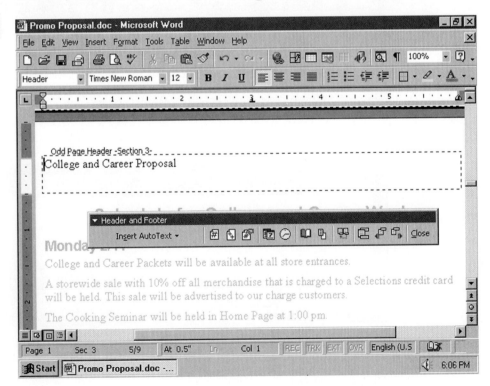

9 Click 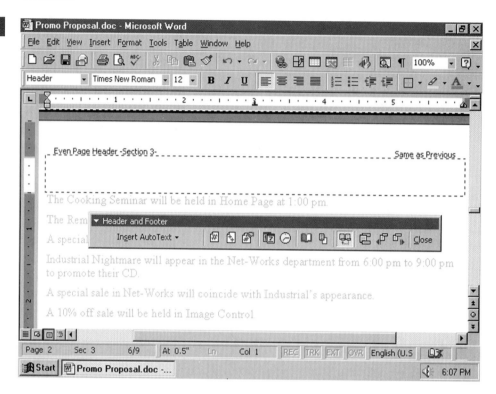.

FIGURE 4.25

10 Click , press (TAB) twice, and type **College and Career Proposal**.

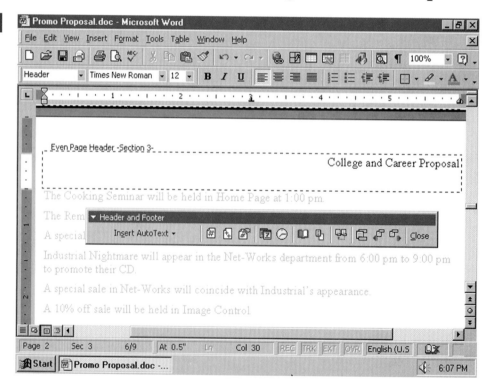

FIGURE 4.26

11 Click and click . The Even Page footer for section 3 displays.

12 Click the Show Previous 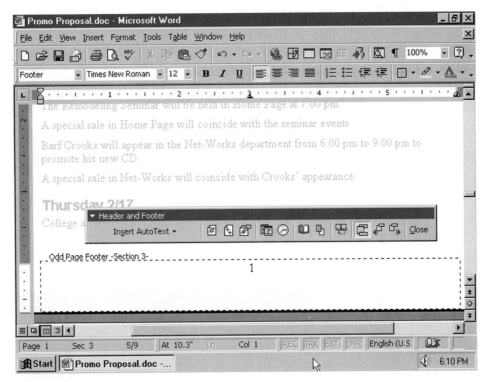 button and click 🔲.

13 Click 🔲 , select Start at, and select OK. The number 1 appears in the footer space, as shown in Figure 4.27.

FIGURE 4.27

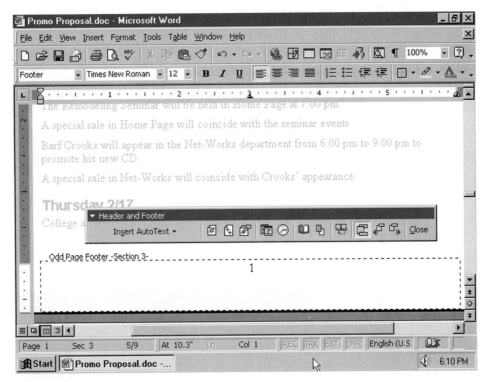

14 Click Close on the Header and Footer toolbar. The footer closes.

> **TIP** After you have broken the link with the previous header or footer, if you click the Same as Previous button again, Word asks if you want to delete this header and connect to the header in the previous section. If you select Yes, the text of the current header will be deleted and the text of the previous header will be inserted. To reverse this, click the Undo button in the Standard toolbar and the header space will close, restoring the original text in the header.

15 Ensure that Print Layout is the current view and scroll through the complete document. The headers and footers display as dimmed text in the Print Layout view.

Modifying Headers and Footers

You can modify a header or footer at any time by choosing View, Header and Footer. However, if the header or footer is visible, you can double-click the header or footer space to open it.

TASK 8: <u>To Modify a Header</u>

1 Go to page 5 and double-click anywhere in the header area. The header space opens.

2 Position the insertion point at the end of the text, type a space, a hyphen, and a space, and click the Insert Date 📅 button.

FIGURE 4.28

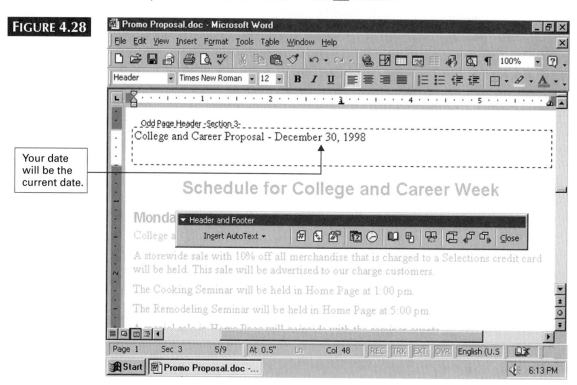

Your date will be the current date.

3 Add the date to the Even Page header at the beginning of the text and include the hyphen with a space on both sides.

4 Click Close on the Header and Footer toolbar. The header space closes.

Creating Footnotes

A **footnote** is a comment or reference that appears at the bottom of the page. The reference in the text to which the footnote applies is generally shown as a raised number. The associated footnote displays the corresponding number. When you create a footnote, Word automatically numbers the footnote in the text and provides sufficient space at the bottom of the page for the footnote.

You can jump around and insert footnotes in any order on any page, and Word will number or renumber them consecutively throughout the document.

You can create multiple footnotes on the same page. If you group the footnotes together at the end of the document, they are called **endnotes**.

When you insert a footnote in Normal view, a footnote space opens. When you insert a footnote in Print Layout view, the insertion point moves to the bottom of page where the footnote text actually appears. In the following task, you will use both methods.

> **TIP** Most academic style guidelines (including MLA and APA) recommend limited use of footnotes and endnotes because they can be distracting for the reader. Proper use of notes would include comments that evaluate or recommend a bibliographic source and explanatory notes that would seem digressive if included in the main text but might be interesting to readers.
>
> According to the MLA guidelines, notes should use consecutive superscript arabic numbers in the text. The notes themselves should be listed on a separate page under the title of *Notes*. Each note should be double-spaced, begin on a new line, and be numbered consecutively with superscript arabic numbers.

TASK 9: To Create a Footnote

1 Ensure that the document is in Print Layout view. Find the phrase *slide show presentation*, position the insertion point after the word *presentation*, and choose Insert, Footnote.

FIGURE 4.29

The numbering format is selected by default

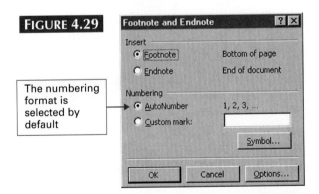

> **TIP** The Options button makes other numbering formats available, including upper- and lowercase letters, upper- and lowercase roman numerals, and special symbols.

2 Select OK. The insertion point moves to the bottom of the page.

FIGURE 4.30

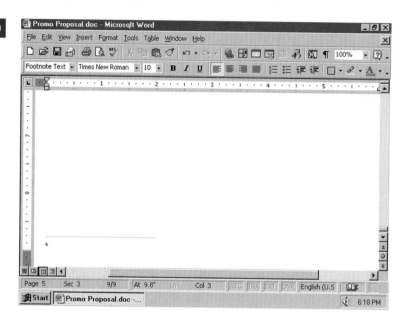

3 Type **Marketing will be responsible for creating this slide show**.

4 Click anywhere in the document. The insertion point returns to the previous typing position.

5 Switch to Normal view, and position the insertion point after the period that follows the word *t-shirt*.

6 Choose Insert, Footnote, and select OK.

7 Type **T-shirts will have the Selections logo on the back.** and click Close. The insertion point returns to the previous typing position automatically.

FIGURE 4.31

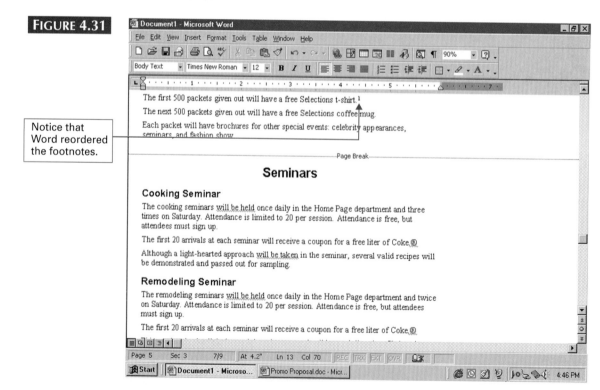

Notice that Word reordered the footnotes.

Using the Document Map to Navigate

The **Document Map** is a feature that lists all the document headings, similar to an outline, in a pane on the left. The headings are linked to the document so that you can click a heading and go directly to the text in the document.

TASK 10: To Navigate with the Document Map

1 Click the Document Map button.

FIGURE 4.32

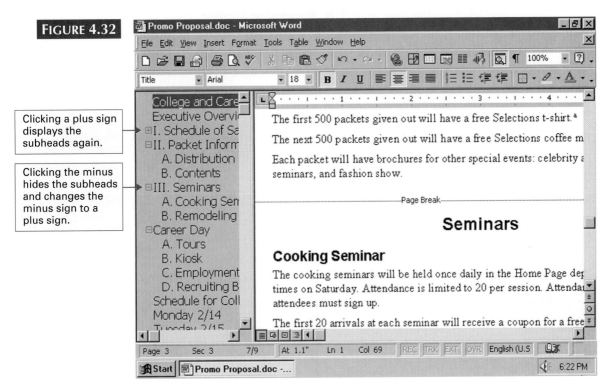

Clicking a plus sign displays the subheads again.

Clicking the minus hides the subheads and changes the minus sign to a plus sign.

2 Click *Distribution* in the left pane.

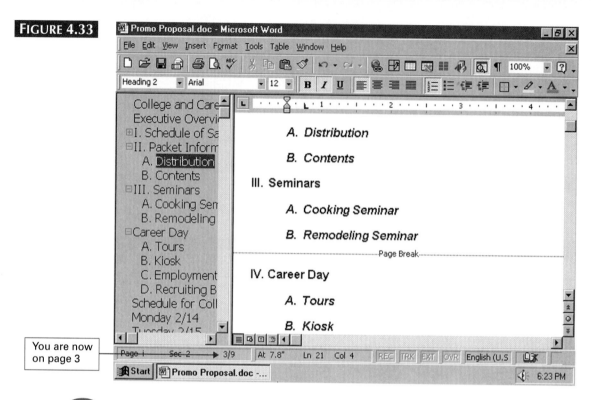

FIGURE 4.33

You are now on page 3

3 Click the minus sign beside *Seminars* in the left pane. The headings under the topic collapse.

4 Click the plus sign beside the same heading. The heading expands to show the subheadings.

5 Scroll in the left pane and click *Kiosk*. You are now on page 9.

6 Click [icon]. The document returns to the original view.

> **TIP** When you drag the box in the vertical scroll bar, you can see the page number and the headings on the page. This works whether you are using the Document Map or not.

Printing Specific Pages

It is easy to print an entire document. You just click the Print button. If you want to print specific pages in a document, you must use the Print dialog box, accessed by choosing File, Print. Table 4.3 lists the format that should be used in the Pages: text box of the Print dialog box for printing sections and pages in sections.

> **TIP** You can move the insertion point to a single page you want to print and choose Current page in the Print dialog box.

Table 4.3: Printing Specific Sections and Pages in Sections

To Print:	Example	Type:
Entire section	All the pages in section 1	s1
Range of sections	All pages in section 1 and section 2	s1-s2
Noncontiguous sections	All pages in section 1 and section 3	s1, s3
Specific page in a section	Page 1 in section 2	p1s2
Range of pages in the same section	Pages 1-4 in section 2	p1s2-p4s2
Noncontiguous pages in the same section	Pages 1, 3 and 5 in section 2	p1s2, p3s2, p5s2
Range of pages that span contiguous sections	Page 2 in section 2 through page 2 in section 3	p2s2-p2s3
Noncontiguous pages in sections	Page 1 in section 2 and page 2 in section 3	p1s2, p2s3

Summary and Exercises

Summary

- Word can position text on the page at the top, the center, or the bottom.
- Section breaks divide a page or a document into independent parts that can have different page setups.
- The outline feature in Word numbers and renumbers each outline topic for you automatically.
- A header is text that prints at the top of every page in a section, and a footer is text that prints at the bottom of every page in a section.
- Each time you open the header or footer space, the Header and Footer toolbar displays automatically.
- When you create a footnote, Word automatically numbers the footnote in the text and provides sufficient space at the bottom of the page for the footnote.
- The Document Map is a feature that can be used to navigate a document that has headings.
- When printing pages in a document that has sections, you may have to specify the section number with the page number in the Print dialog box.

Key Terms and Operations

Key Terms

Document Map
endnote
footer
footnote

header
outline numbering
section break

Operations

collapse an outline topic
create a footnote
create a header or footer
demote an outline topic
expand an outline topic
format a page number
insert a date

insert a page number
modify a header or footer
print pages in a section
promote an outline topic
switch between header and
    footer

Study Questions

Multiple Choice

1. Which of the following statements is true?
   a. A footnote is automatically renumbered if you insert another footnote.
   b. A footnote is automatically renumbered if you insert another footnote before it.
   c. A footnoe displays a subscripted number.
   d. A footnote doesn't appear in Page Layout view.

2. The Document Map
   a. is an outline.
   b. lists all the document headings in a pane on the right.
   c. displays headings that are linked to the document.
   d. displays all the headers, footers, footnotes, and other objects that aren't actually part of the body of the text.

3. Which of the following statements is true?
   a. A section break always inserts a page break.
   b. A section break allows you to use a different page orientation for different pages in the same document.
   c. A section break is another name for a page break.
   d. A section break must be applied to even or odd pages.

4. "Same as Previous" indicates that
   a. the section break will be like the one before it.
   b. the footnote will be like the one before it.
   c. the page break will be like the one before it.
   d. the header will be like the one before it.

5. The vertical alignment option is located on the
   a. Line and Page Breaks page of the Paragraph dialog box.
   b. Indents and Spacing page of the Paragraph dialog box.
   c. Layout page of the Page Setup dialog box.
   d. Margins page of the Page Setup dialog box.

6. Which view shows headers and footers?
   a. Normal
   b. Print Layout
   c. Outline
   d. Web

7. How do you promote a heading in an outline?
   a. Press TAB
   b. Press CTRL + TAB
   c. Press ALT + TAB
   d. Press SHIFT + TAB

8. How do you demote a heading in an outline?
   a. Press TAB
   b. Press CTRL + TAB
   c. Press ALT + TAB
   d. Press SHIFT + TAB

9. To turn off the formatting in Outline view,
   a. click the Show Formatting button.
   b. click the Hide Formatting button.
   c. click the Show/Hide button.
   d. choose View, Normal.

10. If you want the first page of a document to have portrait orientation and the next page to have landscape orientation, you must
   a. insert a page break.
   b. create two different documents.
   c. insert a section break.
   d. insert a footer.

Short Answer

1. What elements can be inserted automatically in a header or a footer?
2. How do you collapse a heading in the Document Map?
3. What's the difference between footnotes and endnotes?
4. Which section break does not carry a page break with it?
5. What would you type in the Pages: text box in the Print dialog box to print all the pages in section 5?
6. What would you type in the Pages: text box in the Print dialog box to print the first two pages in section 5?
7. What is body text in an outline?
8. How do you format a page number in a header or footer?
9. How do you collapse a heading in an outline?
10. How do you display the Document Map?

Fill in the Blank

1. Outline number styles are located on the Outline _____ page of the Bullets and Numbering dialog box.
2. When typing an outline, use _____ view.
3. The _____ section break divides a page into separate parts.
4. You can click a heading in the left pane in Document Map and go to the heading in the right pane because the headings are _____.
5. The number style I. A. 1. is a typical _____ numbering style.
6. A header is text that prints at the top of every page in a(n) _____
7. You can modify a header or footer by choosing _____, Header and Footer.
8. The Document Map is a feature that lists all the document _____ in a pane on the left.
9. When you drag the box in the _____ scroll bar, you can see the page number on the page.
10. The text on a title page is generally _____.

For Discussion

1. Discuss the advantages of inserting section breaks.

2. Discuss the benefits of using Word to create a long document with footnotes instead of typing it on a typewriter.

3. Explain why it is better to create headers and footers than to simply type what you want at the top or bottom of every page.

4. Discuss the methods of navigating in a long document.

5. Explain why you never really create a header or footer.

Hands-On Exercises

1. Creating an Itinerary

Rachel is putting together an itinerary for each of the celebrities that will be coming in for College and Career Week. Because each itinerary will be slightly different, Rachel will create a generic itinerary with markers that she can search for and replace with the specific information for each celebrity. The marker she will use is three slashes (///).

1. Create a new document and type **Itinerary for ///**. Apply the Title style to the text. Insert a Next Page section break.

2. Type **Flight Schedule** and apply the Title style to the text. Type the following text using tabs to create the columns.

Leaving	At	On Flight #	Arriving	At
///	///:///	///	Omaha	///:///

3. Insert a page break. Type **Schedule of Appearances** and apply the Title style.

4. Type the following text:

Date	Time	Department	Contact
///	///	///	///
///	///	///	///

5. Insert a page break and type **Hotel and Transportation Information**. Apply the title style and then type the following text under the title:

A limousine will pick you up at the airport when you arrive and take you to your hotel. You will be staying at the DoubleTree downtown. Your room has been reserved and prepaid. While you are in Omaha your host will be ///. Your host will be responsible for your transportation to and from the store for your appearances. If you have any questions or needs, you can contact your host anytime at this number: ///.

6. Insert a footnote after the slashes for the phone number that says **This is a cellular phone number**.

7. Insert a page break and type **Things to Do in Omaha**. Apply the Title style.

8. Search the Internet for some interesting things to do in Omaha and list them on this page.

9. Create headers and footers for odd and even pages. Starting on the second page, type **Itinerary** in the header on the left margin for even pages and type **Itinerary** in the header on the right margin for odd pages.

10. Insert a page number centered in the footer. Include the page number on every page except the first page.

11. Use the Document Map feature to move through the document.

12. Save the file as *Itinerary.doc* and close it.

2. Creating an Outline

Matthew is busy planning for the sale event in the Fields department. Figure 4.34 shows the outline that he is using to help him decide what should go on sale.

1. Create a new document and choose the outline numbering style shown in Figure 4.34.

2. Switch to Outline view, turn off the formatting, and type the text shown in the figure.

3. Switch to Print Layout view and then switch back to Outline view.

4. Print the document.

5. Save the document as *Fields Sale.doc* and close it.

FIGURE 4.34

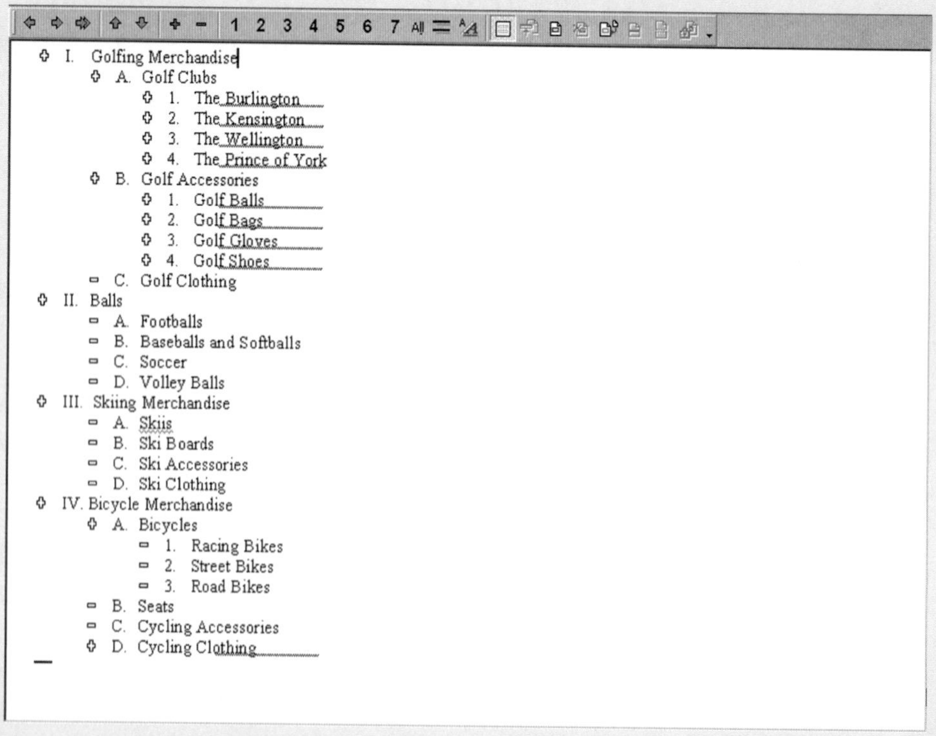

I. Golfing Merchandise
  A. Golf Clubs
    1. The Burlington
    2. The Kensington
    3. The Wellington
    4. The Prince of York
  B. Golf Accessories
    1. Golf Balls
    2. Golf Bags
    3. Golf Gloves
    4. Golf Shoes
  C. Golf Clothing
II. Balls
  A. Footballs
  B. Baseballs and Softballs
  C. Soccer
  D. Volley Balls
III. Skiing Merchandise
  A. Skiis
  B. Ski Boards
  C. Ski Accessories
  D. Ski Clothing
IV. Bicycle Merchandise
  A. Bicycles
    1. Racing Bikes
    2. Street Bikes
    3. Road Bikes
  B. Seats
  C. Cycling Accessories
  D. Cycling Clothing

On Your Own Exercises

1. Writing an Outline for a Long-Range Plan

Refer to the MLA guidelines (or the guidelines prescribed by your school) and create an outline that describes the activities and plans you have for your college years, your first five years after you get out of college, the next five years, and then the next five years. Include your personal and career goals, salary goals, savings goals, investment goals, and so on. Save the document as *Long Range Plan.doc*. Then close the document and try to stick to it!

2. Editing the Long-Range Plan

Now that you have an outline, let's flesh out the plan. Open the *Long Range Plan* document and switch to Print Layout view. Add a title page. Then add text to each of the outline headings until the document is at least three pages long. Format the paper according to the MLA (or other) guidelines. Use the Document Map to navigate in the document. Save the file as *Long Range Plan2.doc* and close the document.

3. Adding Headers and Footers

Open the *Long Range Plan2* document and add headers and footers to the paper. Print the file. Save the file as *Long Range Plan3.doc* and close it.

4. Adding Footnotes

Open the *Long Range Plan3* document and add several footnotes. Then add another footnote after the first footnote. Edit the text of at least one of the footnotes. Move a sentence that contains a footnote reference to a new location in the document and notice how the footnote numbers adjust. Move the sentence back again. Save the file with as *Long Range Plan 4.doc* and close the file.

5. Including a Bibliography

Open the *Long Range Plan4* document and add a bibliography using the MLA (or other) guidelines to format the works cited. Save the file as *Long Range Plan5.doc* and close it.

6. Creating a Proposal

Imagine that you are going into business for yourself. Create a short proposal to give to the bank asking for a small-business loan to get you started. The proposal should include a title page, a short outline that lists what you need to start the business, and a short report that explains how much money you need, how much money you anticipate making annually, and when and how you expect to be able to pay back the loan. Create appropriate headers and footers. Save the file as *Proposal.doc*.

Creating Tables

The table feature in Word is a great tool for organizing data. Tables can be used to type columns of data instead of setting tabs or used to create parallel columns. You can even create tables inside tables, position tables side by side, and wrap text around tables.

Objectives

After completing this project, you will be able to:

➤ Insert a table

➤ Move around in a table and enter text

➤ Modify the structure of a table

➤ Set table properties

➤ Use borders and shading

➤ Save a document as a Web page

➤ Draw a table

➤ Create a hyperlink

➤ Convert text to and from a table

Running Case

With so many people and activities to coordinate for College and Career Week, the job of managing the project is becoming complex. Rachel and Matthew have decided that it would be a good idea to create a master schedule and post it on the company's intranet. That way the employees who are involved can keep up with the schedule of events more easily. To keep employees informed about all upcoming events at the store, Matthew wants to create a Coming Events page for the intranet as well.

The Challenge

You will create both the master schedule and the Coming Events page in two formats: Word and HTML.

The Strategy

Since the master schedule for College and Career Week is going to be more work, you will tackle it first. Begin by creating a table for the schedule, and then create a file that lists the coming events at the store. Since Word is an HTML editor, you will create both documents in Word and save them. Then you will save them once again in HTML format. So that users can navigate between the two Web pages, you will create a hyperlink between the Coming Events page and the master schedule. Figure 5.1 shows the master schedule in HTML format and Figure 5.2 shows the Coming Events page in HTML format.

FIGURE 5.1

College and Career Events

February 14 - 19			Westroads Mall
Dates	**Event**	**Location**	**Comments**
2/14-2/19	Cooking Seminar	Home Page	20 per seminar
2/14-2/19	Remodeling Seminar	Home Page	20 per seminar - led by Christopher Pole, interior designer from HGTV
2/19	Career Day	Main floor and entrance from mall	Tables and booths will be set up and operated by store personnel
2/19	Drawing for Ski Trip	Main floor at main entrance	Person to draw names TBD
2/14-2/15	Appearance by Peek-a-boo Streak	Fields	Special pricing on Streak skis
2/15-2/16	Appearance by Barf Crooks	Net-Works	Special pricing on Crooks' new CD
2/17-2/18	Appearance by Industrial Nightmare	Net-Works	Special pricing on Industrial's new CD
2/19	Fashion Show	Image Control	Hosted by model Mindy Crawfish
2/14-2/15	Sporting Goods Sale	Fields	10%, 15%, and 20% off selected merchandise
2/17-2/19	Clothing Sale	Image Control	10% off everything in the department
2/15-2/18	Tapes and CDs Sale	Net-Works	15% off tapes 10% off CDs

FIGURE 5.2

Coming Events

Trick'r'Treat

Santa and His Elves

Pilgrim's Progress

New Year's Day Sale

College and Career

The Setup

So that your screen will match the illustrations and tasks in this project will function as described, make sure that the Word 2000 settings listed in Table 5.1 match those on your computer.

Table 5.1: Word 2000 Settings

Location:	Make these settings:
View	Choose Ruler to ensure the ruler is activated.
View, Toolbars	Deselect all toolbars except Standard and Formatting. Then deselect any buttons that are selected in the Standard toolbar and set the Zoom to 100%.
Tools, Customize, Options	Deselect Standard and Formatting toolbars share one row and Menus show recently used commands first.
Tools, Options, Spelling & Grammar	Select all options in the dialog box except the following: Hide spelling errors in this document, Suggest from main dictionary only, Hide grammatical errors in this document, and Show readability statistics.
Help, Show Office Assistant	Right-click the Office Assistant and choose Options. Deselect Use the Office Assistant.

Inserting a Table

A **table** contains **columns** and **rows** (like a spreadsheet). The intersection of a column and a row is called a **cell**. Word 2000 provides three methods for creating a table. You can insert a blank table, convert existing text to a table, or draw a table freehand.

TASK 1: To Insert a Table

1 Create a new file.

2 Choose Table, Insert Table. The Insert Table dialog box appears, as shown in Figure 5.3.

FIGURE 5.3

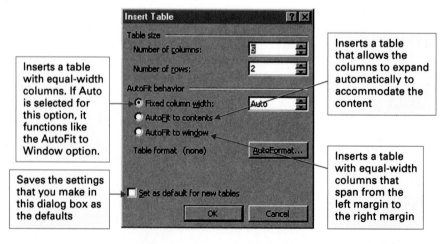

3 Type 4 for Number of columns, 8 for Number of rows, and select AutoFit to contents. Click OK.

TIP Use the Tables and Borders toolbar when you are working with tables. The toolbar appears automatically when you create a table by drawing it. To display the toolbar when inserting a table or converting text to a table, choose View, Toolbars, Tables and Borders.

Moving Around in a Table and Entering Text

The easiest way to go to a particular cell in a table is to click in the cell, but when you are entering data in blank cells it is more efficient to move around with the keyboard techniques described in Table 5.2.

Table 5.2: Navigating Empty Cells in a Table

To go to:	Press:
The next cell	TAB or →
The previous cell	SHIFT + TAB or ←
The next row	↓
The previous row	↑

TROUBLESHOOTING The navigation techniques in Table 5.2 work only when the cells do not contain data. When a cell contains data, pressing TAB and SHIFT + TAB moves the insertion point to the next and previous cells, but it also selects the text. Pressing → moves to the next cell only when the insertion point is positioned after the last character in the current cell. Pressing ↓ moves to the next row only if the insertion point is positioned in the last line of the text in the current cell.

TASK 2: To Enter Data in a Table

1 Type **Event** in the first cell, press TAB, and then type **Location**.

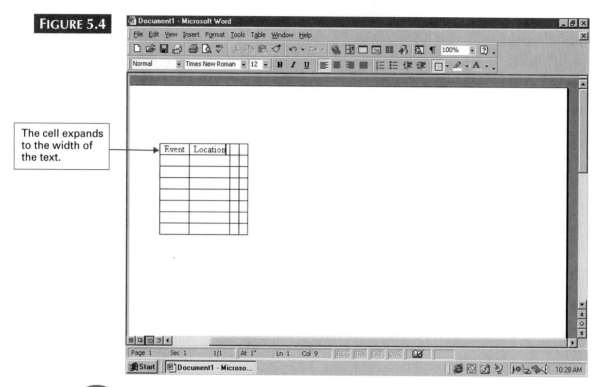

FIGURE 5.4

The cell expands to the width of the text.

2 Continue pressing `TAB` to move to each blank cell and type the data that follows starting with the third heading (Time).

TROUBLESHOOTING Notice that you have not created enough rows in the table for the data. Don't worry about it! When you get to the last cell in the last row and press `TAB`, Word will add a row for you.

Event	Location	Time	Comments
Cooking Seminar	Home Page	varies	20 per seminar
Remodeling Seminar	Home Page	varies	20 per seminar—led by Christopher Pole, interior designer from HGTV
Career Day	Main floor and entrance from mall	all day	Tables and booths will be set up and operated by store personnel
Appearance by Peek-a-boo Streak	Fields	10:00 – 12:00	Special pricing on Streak Skis

Event	Location	Time	Comments
Appearance by Barf Crooks	Net-Works	10:00 - 12:00	Special pricing on Crooks' new CD
Appearance by Industrial Nightmare	Net-Works	12:00 - 2:00	Special pricing on Industrial's new CD
Fashion Show	Image Control	afternoon	Hosted by model Mindy Crawfish
Clothing Sale	Image Control	all day	10% off everything in the department
Tapes and CDs Sale	Net-Works	all day	15% off tapes 10% off CDs
Sporting Goods Sale	Fields	all day	10%, 15%, and 20% off selected merchandise
Cosmetics Sale	Inter-Faces	all day	Contact cosmetic reps first

3 Click in any cell in the first row and choose Table, Heading Rows Repeat. This row will now repeat at the top of each page if the table spans more than one page. You can specify any number of rows at the top of a table as heading rows.

Web Tip

Did you know that you can copy a table from a Web page? Simply drag the insertion point through the text and press CTRL + C. When you paste the text in Word, the table structure is retained.

> **TIP** If you want to convert text that is typed as tabbed columns into a table, select the text and choose Table, Convert, Text to Table and then select OK. Word automatically counts the number of columns based on the number of tabs in a line, so you should delete any extra tabs between columns so there is only one tab between each column of text. To convert a table to tabulated text, select the entire table and choose Table, Convert, Table to Text and then select OK.

Modifying the Structure of a Table

As you enter data in a table you may find it will be necessary to change the original structure of the table. You may need to add more rows or columns to insert additional data, delete unwanted rows or columns, or change the height or width of rows or columns.

Inserting and Deleting Rows and Columns

When you delete a row or column, the row or column and all the data in the cells is removed from the table. Before inserting or deleting a single row or column, it is necessary only to click in a cell. Before inserting or deleting multiple rows or columns, you must first select the rows and columns as described in Table 5.3.

Table 5.3: Row and Column Selection Techniques

To select:	Use this technique:
A row	Point to the row in the selection bar and click. OR Point to the lower-left corner of a cell in the row until the pointer changes to a slanted black arrow and double-click.
Contiguous rows	Click and drag the pointer in the selection bar next to the desired rows.
A column	Point to the top border of the column until the pointer turns to a black arrow and then click.
Contiguous columns	Point to the top border of the first column until the pointer turns to a black arrow and then click and drag across the other columns.

TASK 3: ### To Insert and Delete Rows and Columns

1 Click in any cell in the row for Career Day. The row is selected even though it is not highlighted.

2 Choose Table, Insert, Rows Below. Word inserts a blank row.

3 Type the following data in the new row:

Drawing for Ski Trip	**Main floor at main entrance**	**9:00 pm**	**Person to draw names TBD**

4 Select the last row and press (DEL). Word deletes the text in the cells but leaves the row.

5 Choose Table, Delete, Rows. Word removes the row from the table.

6 Point to the top border of the column for Time until the pointer changes to a black arrow and then click. The column is highlighted.

7 Choose Table, Delete, Columns. Word removes the column from the table.

8 Click anywhere in the first column and choose Table, Insert, Columns to the Right. Word inserts a column to the right of the first column.

9 Type **Dates** as the heading in the first cell of the new column.

FIGURE 5.5

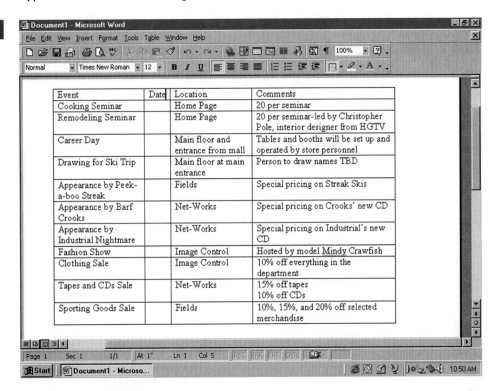

10 Type the data in the new column as follows.

Event	Dates
Cooking Seminar	2/14-2/19
Remodeling Seminar	2/14-2/19
Career Day	2/19
Drawing for Ski Trip	2/19
Appearance by Peek-a-boo Streak	2/14-2/15
Appearance by Barf Crooks	2/15-2/16
Appearance by Industrial Nightmare	2/17-2/18
Fashion Show	2/19
Clothing Sale	2/17-2/19
Tape and CDs Sale	2/15-2/18
Sporting Goods Sale	2/14-2/15

Moving Columns and Rows

One of the advantages of using a table to organize columnar data is the ease with which you can move columns and rows.

TASK 4: To Move a Column and a Row

1 Select the Date column and click ✂. The column is removed from the table.

2 Click in the first cell of the first column and click 📋.

FIGURE 5.6

The Date column moves here.

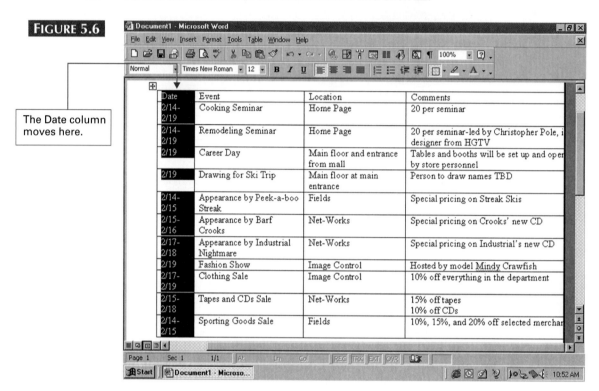

3 Select the row for the Sporting Goods Sale and click ✂. The row is removed from the table.

4 Click in the first cell in the row for the Clothing Sale and click 📋. The row is inserted in the table, but the last cell doesn't line up correctly. This is due to the fact that the columns adjust their widths according to the content. The row will fix itself when you do the next task.

> **TIP** If you intend to do a lot of cutting and pasting in a table, it might be better to create a table that uses fixed column widths.

Check Point

If you intend to do a lot of cutting and pasting in a table, which AutoFit behavior option should you choose when you insert the table? The fixed column widths would be best.

Changing the Height and Width of Rows and Columns

By default, the height of a row is determined by the size of the font used in the row. The height automatically changes to accommodate the size, but you can set the height of a row manually if you want to change the appearance of the row. Column widths change automatically to accommodate the width of the text that you type if you have AutoFit to contents activated; otherwise, you must adjust the width of the columns manually.

TASK 5:   <u>To Change the Height or Width of Rows or Columns</u>

1 Point to the bottom border of the first row until the pointer changes to a double-headed arrow.

FIGURE 5.7

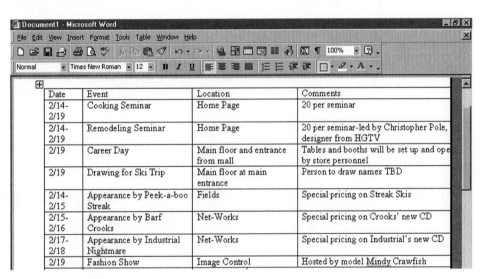

Date	Event	Location	Comments
2/14-2/19	Cooking Seminar	Home Page	20 per seminar
2/14-2/19	Remodeling Seminar	Home Page	20 per seminar-led by Christopher Pole, designer from HGTV
2/19	Career Day	Main floor and entrance from mall	Tables and booths will be set up and ope by store personnel
2/19	Drawing for Ski Trip	Main floor at main entrance	Person to draw names TBD
2/14-2/15	Appearance by Peek-a-boo Streak	Fields	Special pricing on Streak Skis
2/15-2/16	Appearance by Barf Crooks	Net-Works	Special pricing on Crooks' new CD
2/17-2/18	Appearance by Industrial Nightmare	Net-Works	Special pricing on Industrial's new CD
2/19	Fashion Show	Image Control	Hosted by model Mindy Crawfish

2 Drag the border down until it is about twice its original height.

FIGURE 5.8

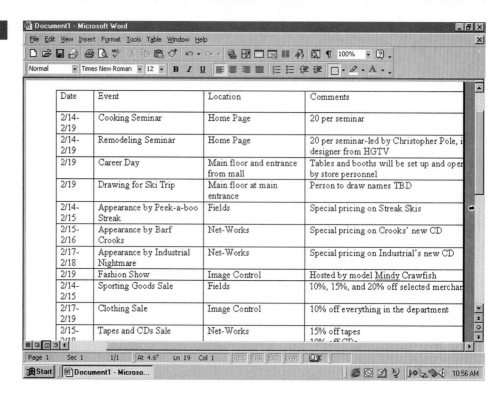

3 Point to the right border of the first column until the pointer changes to a double-headed arrow ◄|► and then drag the border to the right about ½ inch.

FIGURE 5.9

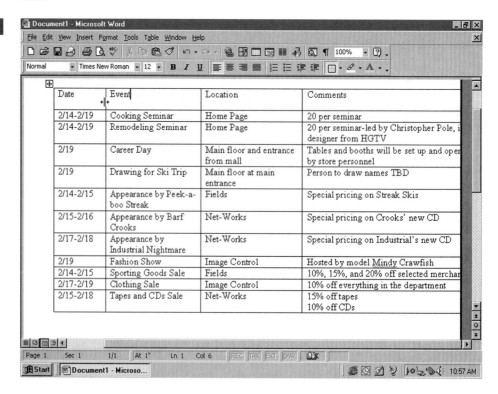

Splitting and Merging Cells

As you have probably noticed, all the cells in each column are the same width and all the cells in each row are the same height. If you need cells with different widths and heights, you can split cells or merge cells as appropriate. For example, you might want to merge several cells to create a column heading that spans over several smaller columns.

TASK 6:   To Split and Merge Cells

1 Select the first row in the table and insert a row above it. The new row is selected and has the same width as the first row.

2 Choose Table, Merge Cells. The row becomes one cell.

3 Type **College and Career Events** in the merged row and click ≣. The text is centered in the row.

4 Insert a new row below the first row. The new row has merged cells like the first row.

5 Choose Table, Split Cells.

FIGURE 5.10

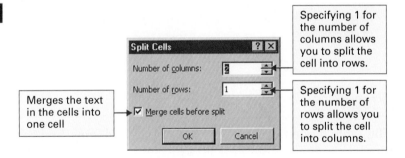

6 Select OK. The row divides into two cells.

7 Type **February 14-19** in the first cell and **Westroads Mall** in the second cell.

FIGURE 5.11

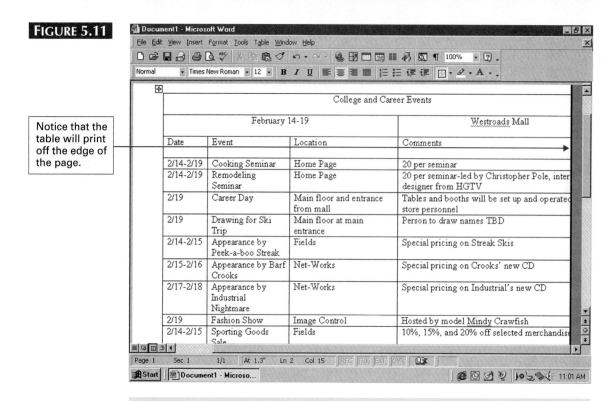

Notice that the table will print off the edge of the page.

TROUBLESHOOTING After splitting or merging cells, it is not always possible to select a column or row in a table. You may have to select a group of cells instead.

Setting Table Properties

The Table properties define the table, rows, columns, and cells in the table.

 TASK 7: To Set Table Properties

1 Choose Table, Table Properties.

FIGURE 5.12

2 Select Center and select OK. The table lines up in the center of the margins.

3 Point to the icon outside the upper-left corner of the table and click it when the pointer changes to a four-headed arrow. The entire table is selected.

TIP You can drag the table to a new location with the four-headed arrow icon. If you drag the table into an area of text, the text will wrap around the table automatically. You also can drag a table beside another table so the two are side by side.

4 Choose Table, Table Properties, and select the Row tab.

FIGURE 5.13

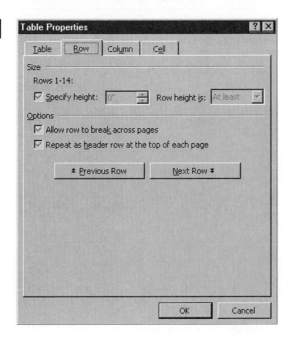

5 Deselect Allow row to break across pages by clicking it twice. By deselecting this option, you keep the contents of a row from being split by a page break.

6 Select the Cell tab.

FIGURE 5.14

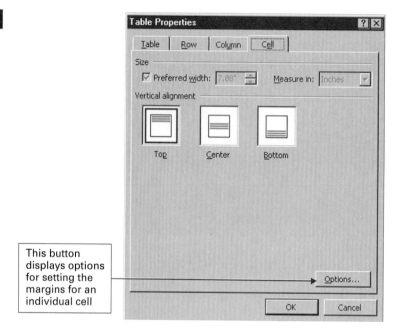

This button displays options for setting the margins for an individual cell

7 Select Center, select OK, and then click in the first cell.

FIGURE 5.15

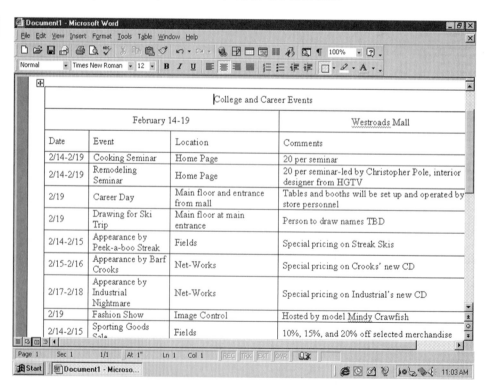

8 Make the Event column about a ½ inch wider.

9 Save the document as *CC Schedule.doc*.

Break Point

If necessary, you can exit Word and continue this project later.

Using Borders and Shading

By default, Word tables have ***borders*** around all cells. Removing or changing borders to different styles or colors, or adding ***shading*** to cells, can emphasize data in your tables.

> **TIP** If you remove all the borders, you will see gray lines on the screen called gridlines. These lines help you work in the table, but they do not print. If you want to hide the gridlines, choose Table, Hide Gridlines.

TASK 8:   To Change the Borders and Add Shading

1 If necessary, launch Word and open *CC Schedule.doc*. Select the first row and choose Format, Borders and Shading. Click the Borders tab, if necessary.

FIGURE 5.16

The Preview area displays the location and style of borders.

You can add or delete borders by clicking the diagram.

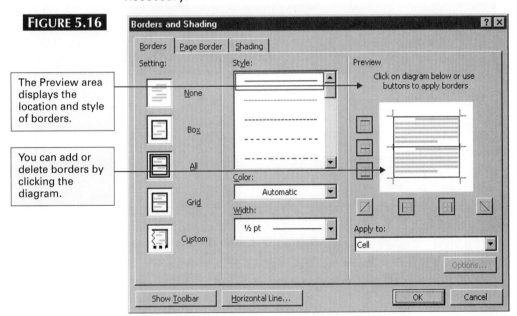

2 Under Setting, select None and select OK.

FIGURE 5.17

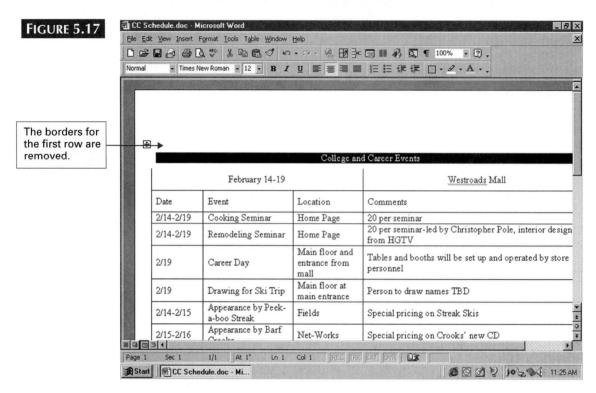

The borders for the first row are removed.

3 Select the second row, choose Format, Borders and Shading, and click the left, middle, and right borders in the Preview. The borders are removed in the Preview, indicating that they will be removed for the selected row.

4 Select OK.

FIGURE 5.18

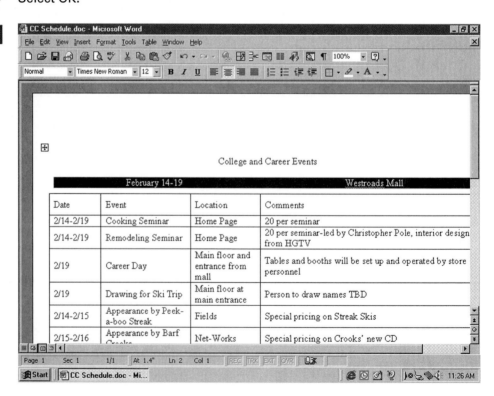

TIP Instead of using the menu commands to apply borders and shading, you can use the Tables and Borders toolbar.

5 Select the third row, starting with the entry *Dates*. Then choose Format, Borders and Shading, and select the Shading tab, as shown in Figure 5.19.

FIGURE 5.19

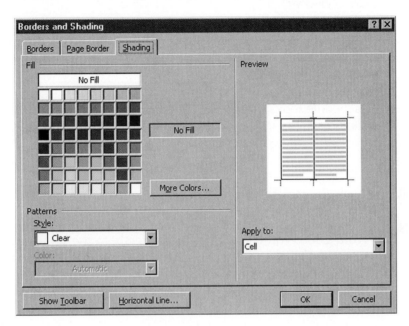

6 Select a light yellow and select OK. Click in the first cell of the row.

FIGURE 5.20

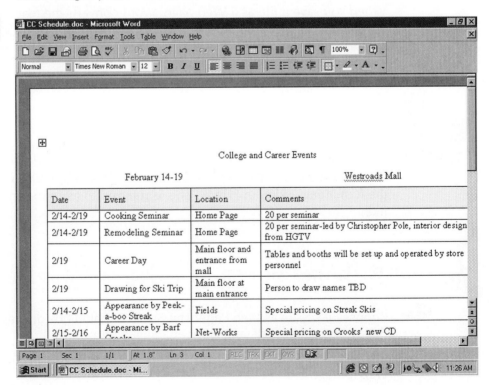

7 Select the row of column headings and click .

8 Save the file.

> **TIP** The Table, AutoFormat command adds borders and shading to a table automatically.

Saving a Document as a Web Page

The schedule looks great so far, but this information also needs to be posted on the Selections Web site on the Internet. If you want to post a page you have created in Word on a Web site, you must save the file as a Web page.

 Web Tip

In Word 2000, you can post a page directly to the Web server as easily as saving a file to the hard disk. Simply click the Web Folders button in the Save As dialog box and select the Web folder. Note, however, that the Web administrator must assign access rights to you before you can save to a Web folder.

When you save a file as a Web page, Word converts the features of the document to the new format and saves the file in the HTML (Hypertext Markup Language) format. After you save a file as a Web page, Word switches to its role as a Web page editing program.

 Web Tip

After converting a Word document to HTML format, Word 2000 also has the ability to convert HTML format back to Word format without losing any of the formatting added in HTML. This is referred to as *round-tripping* a document.

 TASK 9: <u>To Save a Document as a Web Page and Edit the Document</u>

1 Choose File, Save as Web Page. The Save As dialog box displays and the Save as type option defaults to Web Page (*.htm; *.html).

2 Change the path to your drive or folder and select Save. The file is saved in Web format.

3 Choose Format, Theme. The Theme dialog box appears, as shown in Figure 5.21. When you select a theme for a page, Word applies coordinated colors, backgrounds, and graphics to the page.

FIGURE 5.21

4 Select Blends and select OK. Click in any cell.

FIGURE 5.22

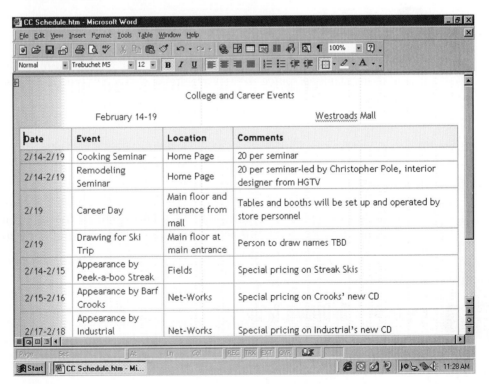

5 Choose File, Web Page Preview. The document appears as a Web page in Internet Explorer, as shown in Figure 5.23. (Maximize the page, if necessary.)

FIGURE 5.23

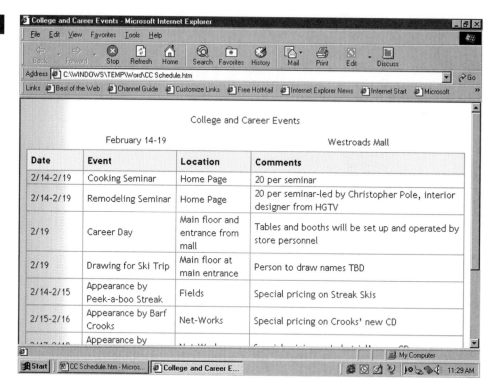

6 Close Internet Explorer and then save the file and close it.

> **TIP** Although Word is an adequate HTML editor, you may want to use the outstanding Office 2000 Web editor and Web site management program FrontPage 2000.

Drawing a Table

In some cases, depending on the final design of the table, it makes more sense to draw a table than to insert one. This is particularly true if the table has many different-sized cells.

TASK 10: To Draw a Table

1 Create a new file and choose Table, Draw Table.

FIGURE 5.24

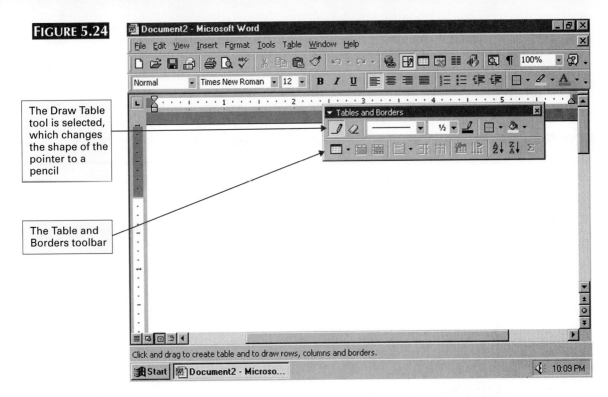

The Draw Table tool is selected, which changes the shape of the pointer to a pencil

The Table and Borders toolbar

2 Drag a rectangle in the middle of the screen by pointing to the location for the upper-left corner and dragging the pointer to the location for the lower-right corner. When you release the mouse button the outside border of the table is created.

FIGURE 5.25

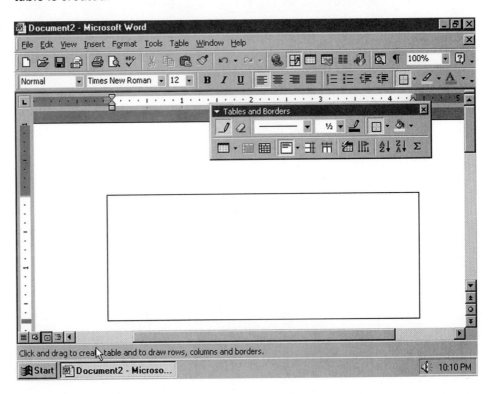

TIP You can press (CTRL) as you drag the table to allow the text in the area to wrap around the table.

3 Draw a horizontal line and then two vertical lines, as shown in Figure 5.26.

FIGURE 5.26

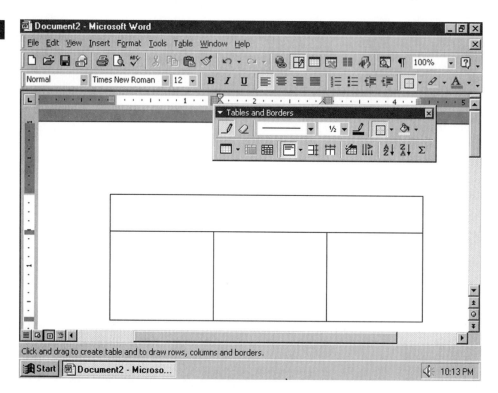

4 Click the drop-down arrow in the Line Style ⬚ tool and select the double wavy line.

5 Click the Border Color 🖉 button and select red.

6 Drag the pointer over the border for the first row and add additional borders, as shown in Figure 5.27.

FIGURE 5.27

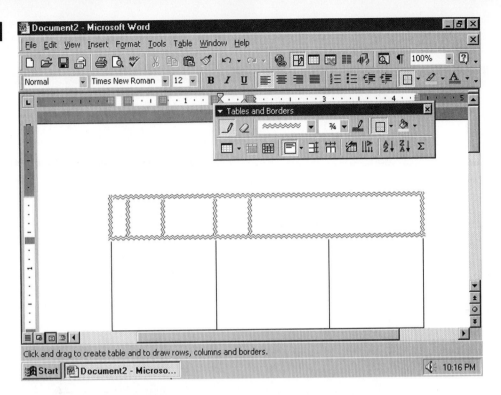

Click and drag to create table and to draw rows, columns and borders.

7 Click the Draw Table ✐ button. The pointer changes back to an arrow.

8 Select the cells on the left side of the first row and click the Distribute Columns Evenly ⊞ button.

FIGURE 5.28

The columns are now equal in width.

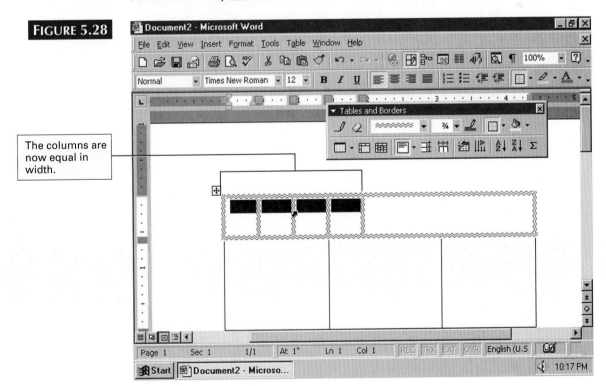

9 Type the text shown in Figure 5.29 and apply Heading 1 to *Coming Events*.

FIGURE 5.29

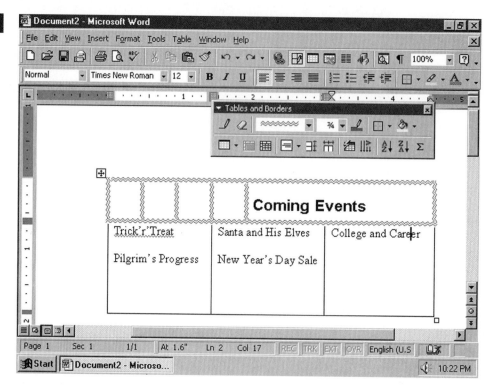

10 Click in the middle cell on the second row, click the arrow on the alignment button, and click the Align Center button.

11 Click in the last cell on the second row, click the arrow on the alignment button, and click the Align Center Right button.

12 Point anywhere in the table. A square sizing handle appears at the lower right corner of the table.

13 Point to the sizing handle. The pointer changes to a double-headed arrow.

14 Drag the table larger or smaller to match the size of the table in Figure 5.30.

FIGURE 5.30

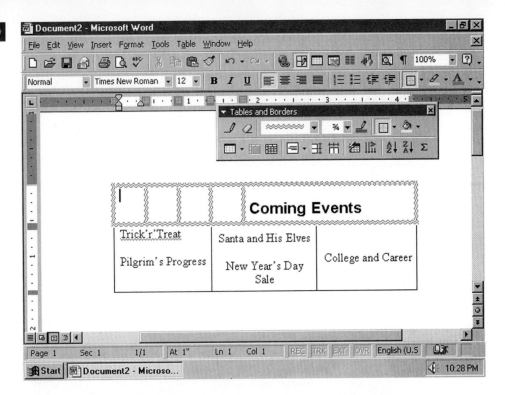

15 Save the file on your drive or in your folder as *Coming Events.doc*.

16 Save the file in the same location, with the same name, but this time, save it as a Web page. Word uses the same name and adds a different extension.

FIGURE 5.31

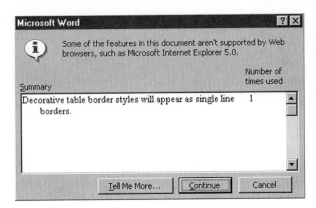

17 Select Continue.

18 Apply the Blends theme.

 **Web Tip**

Using a table in a Web page allows you to place text and graphics next to each other on the page.

Creating a Hyperlink

Now that you have created the master schedule and highlights as Web pages, you need to connect them using a *hyperlink*. A hyperlink, or a link, as it is sometimes referred to on the Web, is text or a graphic that, when clicked, jumps to another location on the same page or takes you to a different page. In Word, you can create hyperlinks that jump to other places in the same document, to other Word documents, to other Office 2000 documents, or to Web sites.

> **TIP** You can create a hyperlink in a regular Word document or a document that has been saved as a Web page.

TASK 11: To Create a Hyperlink

1 Select the text *College and Career* and click the Insert Hyperlink button.

FIGURE 5.32

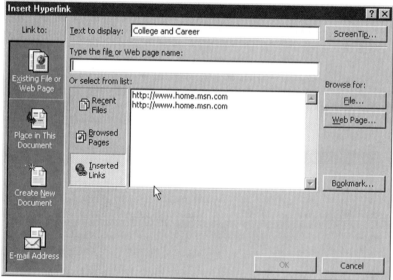

2 Select File, locate and select your *CC Schedule.htm* file, select OK, and then select OK in the Insert Hyperlink dialog box. The text is formatted in a different color and underlined to show that it is a hyperlink.

3 Save the current file and then preview the file by choosing File, Web Page Preview. Internet Explorer displays the file.

4 Point to the hyperlink and then click it. The *CC Schedule.htm* file opens.

> **TIP** Sometimes it is difficult to recognize a hyperlink on a Web page. When you point to a hyperlink (whether the hyperlink is text or a graphic), the pointer changes to a hand with a pointing finger.

5 Close Internet Explorer. The *Coming Events.htm* file reappears in Word.

6 Close the file and close the Tables and Borders toolbar.

Summary and Exercises

Summary

- You can insert or draw tables in Word 2000.
- Additionally, you can convert tabbed text to a table and vice versa.
- You can use a table instead of tabs to create columnar text and you can use a table to create parallel columns of text.
- You can change the structure of a table by adding and deleting columns and rows, splitting and merging cells, changing the height of rows, and changing the width of columns.
- You can apply borders and shading to tables.
- Word can save a file in HTML format, the format used on the Web.
- A hyperlink, when clicked, allows you to quickly go to another location in the same document, a new document, or a Web page.

Key Terms and Operations

Key Terms

border
cell
column

hyperlink
row
shading
table

Operations

change column width
change row height
convert a table to text
convert text to a table
create a hyperlink
delete a column
delete a row
draw a table
insert a column

insert a row
insert a table
merge a cell
move a column
move a row
preview a Web page
save as a Web page
split a cell

Study Questions

Multiple Choice

1. When you delete a row,
   a. the row is deleted but the data is not deleted.
   b. the row and any data in the row are deleted.
   c. the data in the row is deleted.
   d. the row is deleted and replaced with a blank one.

2. To move a column,
   a. use the Cut and Paste commands.
   b. use the Move command.
   c. drag the column.
   d. choose Table, Insert Column.

3. When you insert a row, it has
   a. the characteristics of the row above it.
   b. default characteristics.
   c. the characteristics of the row below it.
   d. the characteristics of the selected row.

4. One way to change the width of a column is
   a. to drag the left border of the column.
   b. to drag the right border of the column.
   c. to select the column and then drag the left border of the column.
   d. to select the column and then drag the right border of the column.

5. When inserting a column,
   a. you can insert the column to the left or right of the selected column.
   b. you must first highlight the entire column.
   c. the column is inserted to the right of the selected column by default.
   d. the column is inserted to the left of the selected column by default.

6. When selecting a column, the pointer changes to
   a. a slanted black arrow.
   b. a white arrow pointing down.
   c. a black arrow pointing down.
   d. a double-headed black arrow.

7. To move to the next cell in a table, press
   a. ⌈TAB⌉.
   b. ⌈CTRL⌉ + ⌈TAB⌉.
   c. ⌈↓⌉.
   d. ⌈PGDN⌉.

8. A table heading
   a. must be the first row in a table.
   b. can be any row in a table.
   c. can be only the first three rows in a table.
   d. repeats at the top of each page.

9. For columnar text to convert to a table properly,
   a. there should be only one tab between each column.
   b. there must be data in each column on each row.
   c. the text in each column must be left aligned.
   d. the columns must be equal width.

10. A hyperlink jumps to
    a. another hyperlink.
    b. a Web page only.
    c. another location.
    d. another Office 2000 document only.

Short Answer

1. What does HTML stand for?
2. What two elements make up a table?
3. What keystroke moves to the previous cell?
4. How do you center a table?
5. What program previews a Web page?
6. How do you keep a table row from breaking across a page break?
7. How do you add shading to cells in a table?
8. How do you change the borders of a table?
9. How do you draw a table?
10. When does the Tables and Borders toolbar appear automatically?

Fill in the Blank

1. The intersection of a column and a row is a(n) _____.
2. Press the _____ key in the last cell in a table to create a new row.
3. The height of a row is determined by the size of the _____ used in the row.
4. The _____ to Contents feature causes the columns to adjust their widths automatically.
5. The gray lines that look like borders but do not print are called _____.
6. The _____ command can add borders and shading to a table automatically.
7. Press _____ as you draw a table to make the text in the area of a table wrap around the table.
8. Use the Table _____ dialog box to keep a row from being broken by a page break.
9. Choose Table, _____ to create a row that repeats at the top of every page if the table spans more than one page.
10. To convert columnar text to a table, delete the excess _____ between the text.

For Discussion

1. Discuss the advantage of drawing a complex table as opposed to using the Table, Insert Table command.
2. Discuss various ways you could use hyperlinks in the same document.
3. Discuss the possible reasons you might add borders and shading to tables.
4. Discuss the reasons you might convert columnar text to a table.
5. Discuss the reasons you might include a table on a Web page.

Hands-On Exercises

1. Creating a Flight Schedule

You have four celebrities flying in for College and Career Week. In this exercise you will make a table that contains the flight schedules for each person. Figure 5.33 shows the table.

FIGURE 5.33

Celebrity Flight Schedule

Name	From	Number of Tickets	Arrival Date	Return Date	Airline	Flight #	Time Flight Leaves	Time Flight Arrives	Price
Mindy Crawfish	Chicago, IL	2	2/18	2/20					
Peek-a-boo Streak	Denver, CO	2	2/13	2/16					
Barf Crooks	Nashville, TN	2	2/14	2/17					
Industrial Nightmare	Los Angeles, CA	8	2/16	2/19					
Christopher Pole	New York, NY	2	2/13	2/20					

1. Create a new file and change the orientation to Landscape.

2. Type **Celebrity Flight Schedule** as the title, center it, and apply the Heading 1 style.

4. Insert a table with nine columns and six rows and select Fixed column width.

5. Enter the data shown in Figure 5.33.

6. Using a travel service on the Internet, such as Expedia, find round-trip first-class flights for each person and fill in the table with the appropriate information. If possible, schedule nonstop flights. If this is not possible, you may have to split some cells to enter more information.

7. Select the first row and choose Format, Text Direction. Select the option to turn the text sideways, and select OK.

8. Adjust the column widths and the alignments of text so your table matches the table in the figure.

9. Save the file as *Celebrity Flight Schedule.doc* and close it.

2. Creating a Newsletter

The store manager wants you to create a one page, two-column Newsletter to post on the company's intranet as a source of information about the upcoming College and Career Week. You will use a table as the structure for the newsletter and save the file as a Web page. Figure 5.34 shows the finished product.

FIGURE 5.34

College and Career Week Bulletin

College and Career Week Kicks Off

The week of February 14ᵗʰ through February 19ᵗʰ kicks off the first-ever College and Career Week at Selections. Plans for the special promotion are coming together nicely. All the celebrities have been lined up and the department managers are working hard on their sales events.

This special week was the brainchild of two of our newest management trainees, Rachel Crawford and Matthew Brainard. Rachel and Matthew both graduated from the University of Nebraska and were recruited by our college recruitment program. Their fresh and adventurous ideas reflect the entrepreneurial spirit of Selections.

Celebrity Luncheons

Selections will be hosting luncheons on February 14ᵗʰ, 16ᵗʰ, and 18ᵗʰ just to give our employees and their families a chance to meet and mingle with the celebrities that will be participating in College and Career Week. Feel free to bring your cameras and autograph books. All luncheons will be held in the executive dining room.

Selections to Give Away a Ski Vacation

To top off College and Career Week, Selections is giving away a ski vacation. The drawing for the vacation at Grand Resort will be held on the last night of the event.

Grand Resort is a favorite spot of Rachel Crawford (pictured above with her boyfriend at the Grand Resort). The resort is nestled in the Targhee National Forest at 8,000 feet in the high country of the Tetons, just 24 miles east of Jackson, Wyoming. Famous for its consistently superb snow conditions, this family-oriented resort has three mountains and 3,000 skiable acres.

Snowboarders are welcome on all trails. Four chairlifts and a surface lift serve Grand Mountain. Trails range from intermediate to advanced-intermediate. Cat Mountain is reserved for snowcat powder skiing and Western Flyer Mountain has 1,500 skiable acres, 2,800 feet of vertical, and unsurpassed scenery. Additionally, the resort has 20 miles of groomed cross-country trails.

1. Create a new document and save it as *Newsletter.doc*.

2. Set 1-inch margins for the top, bottom, left, and right.

3. Insert a table that is three columns by two rows. (Select Fixed column width when inserting the table.)

4. Drag the height of the second row to the bottom margin on the page.

5. Set the following column widths: first column 3.2 inches, second column .1 inches, and third column 3.2 inches.

6. Remove all borders. (Make sure the gridlines appear.)

7. Merge the cells in the first row and then insert a row after the first row.

8. Type **College and Career Week Bulletin** in the first row. Center the text and make it bold. Use the Tahoma font in 26 points.

9. Make the height of the third row 8 inches.

10. Draw a text box in the first cell in the third row the size of the cell. Copy the text box. Click in a table cell (not in the existing text box) and paste. Move the second text box to the third cell in the third row. Link the two text boxes by selecting the first text box, clicking the Create Text Box Link ⊚ button in the Text Box toolbar, and clicking the second text box. (*Note*: This will allow the text to flow from the first text box into the second text box.)

11. Remove the borders from each text box by selecting the text box, choosing Format, Text Box, Colors and Lines, selecting No Line for Line Color, and selecting OK.

12. Click in the first text box and type the following:

College and Career Week Kicks Off

The week of February 14th through February 19th kicks off the first-ever College and Career Week at Selections. Plans for the special promotion are coming together nicely. All the celebrities have been lined up, and the department managers are working hard on their sales events.

This special week was the brainchild of two of our newest management trainees, Rachel Crawford and Matthew Brainard. Rachel and Matthew both graduated from the University of Nebraska and were recruited by our college recruitment program. Their fresh and adventurous ideas reflect the entrepreneurial spirit of Selections.

Celebrity Luncheons

Selections will be hosting luncheons on February 14th, 16th, and 18th just to give our employees and their families a chance to meet and mingle with the celebrities that will be participating in College and Career Week. Feel free to bring your cameras and autograph books. All luncheons will be held in the executive dining room.

13. Press (ENTER) and choose Insert, File; select the file named *Newsletter Insert.doc*; and select Insert.

14. Apply the Heading 1 style to *College and Career Week Kicks Off* and *Celebrity Luncheons*. Apply the Body Text First Indent style to the paragraphs under these headings.

15. Insert an appropriate picture from the Food & Dining ClipArt category above the *Celebrity Luncheon* heading and size the graphic appropriately.

16. Insert the file named *RachelSki.jpg* above the Selections to Give Away a Ski Vacation heading. Size the graphic appropriately.

17. Display the Drawing toolbar and draw a rectangle with a 1-point line around the text of the newsletter, as shown in the figure. Send the rectangle behind the text by choosing Draw, Order, Send Behind text.

18. Save the file and close it.

On Your Own Exercises

1. Creating a Class Schedule

Create a table with a column for each day of the week. Fill in the rows in the table with the schedule of your classes and labs. Save the file as *Class Schedule.doc*.

2. Creating a List of Professors

Create a table that lists the name, building, floor, room numbers, and phone number for each of your professors, your advisor, and other key people at your school. Save the file as *Professors.doc*.

3. Creating a Calendar

Create a calendar for any month. Be creative with borders and shading. Insert appropriate clip art in the cells for holidays or special days, such as your birthday. Include the names of assignments and papers that are due during the month and create a hyperlink for these assignments to the *Professors.doc* document created in the previous exercise. Print the calendar. Save the file as *Calendar.doc*.

4. Creating a TV Schedule

Even though you spend a lot of time working on the assignments for this class, you probably take time out to watch *Friends* on Thursday nights. Am I right? Well, everyone has to have a little R & R, so create a table that lists the names, days, times, and channels of your favorite TV shows. Format the table appropriately, merge and split cells as necessary, and use borders and shading. Save the file as *TV Schedule.doc*.

5. Creating a List of the Items You Collect

What do you collect? CDs? Videos? Baseball cards? Matches from your favorite places? Books? Create a document and write at least two paragraphs that describe your collection, why you collect the items, how long you've been collecting them, and so on. Create a table that lists your collectibles and the pertinent information about each item. Format the table appropriately and use borders and shading. Experiment with the format of the document by moving the table into the text so that the text wraps around the table. Save the file as *Collection.doc*.

6. Creating Your Own Web Page

Create a document in Word and insert a table with at least two columns and three rows. Merge the cells in the first row and type a title for your Web page. Apply a theme to the page and save it as an HTML document with the name *My Web Page.html*. Enter appropriate text in the remaining cells and insert a scanned photograph of yourself in one of the cells. Save the file and close it.

Merging Documents

You can generate customized forms, documents, letters, envelopes, and mailing labels using lists of data in Word's **Mail Merging** feature. You can create a form letter and use it over and over again with a list of names and addresses and use the same list to create envelopes and labels. Although the mail merge feature is used most often with form letters, it can be used for any kind of form that uses the same text with the same type of variable information. For example, you could create an information sheet for employees that lists the employee's name, department, phone number, salary, employment date, and so on.

Objectives

After completing this project, you will be able to:

➤ Create the main document

➤ Create the data source document

➤ Merge the documents

➤ Merge data sources with envelopes and labels

Running Case

Anne Newton, head of personnel, received over a hundred promising résumés for the management program as a result of the recruiting done on Career Day during the recent College and Career Week promotion. You have been asked to send responses to the applicants. Ms. Newton has given you examples of two standard responses that she wants you to use. One response letter asks the recruit to call for an interview appointment, and the other response letter tells the recruit that the submitted résumé is being kept on file for consideration at a later date. Ms. Newton has indicated which response each recruit should receive.

The Challenge

You realize that the most efficient way of completing this task is to use mail merge in Word. You will create the list of data, called the ***data source document***, that contains the names and addresses of the college recruits. Additionally, you will create one of the letters as the form letter, which is called the ***main document***.

The Strategy

When setting up the data source document, you will include a column in the table with the heading "ResponseType." Applicants coded with ResponseType 1 will receive the letter asking for an interview. Applicants coded with ResponseType 2 will receive that letter that says the résumé will be kept on file. You will use this field to select the records when it is time to merge.

When setting up the main document, you will allow room at the top for the letter to print on the Selections preprinted stationery.

Figure 6.1 shows a sample of the letter that has been merged with a recruit's name. Since you are not sure whether Ms. Newton wants to use envelopes or mailing labels, you will create both and wait to see which one you should print.

FIGURE 6.1

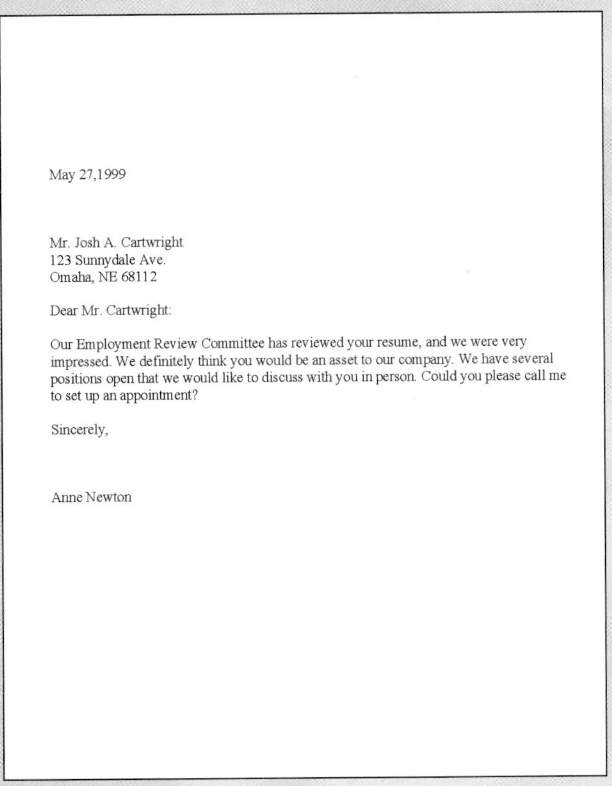

May 27,1999

Mr. Josh A. Cartwright
123 Sunnydale Ave.
Omaha, NE 68112

Dear Mr. Cartwright:

Our Employment Review Committee has reviewed your resume, and we were very impressed. We definitely think you would be an asset to our company. We have several positions open that we would like to discuss with you in person. Could you please call me to set up an appointment?

Sincerely,

Anne Newton

The Setup

So that your screen will match the illustrations and the tasks in this project will function as described, make sure that the Word 2000 settings listed in Table 6.1 match those on your computer.

Table 6.1: Word 2000 Settings

Location:	Make these settings:
View	Choose Ruler to ensure the ruler is activated.
View, Toolbars	Deselect all toolbars except Standard and Formatting and deselect any buttons that are selected in the Standard toolbar and set the Zoom to 100%.
Tools, Customize, Options	Deselect Standard and Formatting toolbars share one row. Deselect Menus show recently used commands first.
Tools, Options, Spelling & Grammar	Select all options in the dialog box except the following: Hide spelling errors in this document, Suggest from main dictionary only, Hide grammatical errors in this document, and Show readability statistics.
Help, Show Office Assistant	Right-click the Office Assistant and choose Option. Deselect Use the Office Assistant.

Creating the Main Document

The main document contains the text that will be merged with the variables in the data source document. You can create either the main document or the data source document first.

> **TIP** If you create the main document first, you have to insert the fields after you have created the data source document and associated it with the main document.

TASK 1: To Create the Main Document

1 Create a new document and type or insert the date, and then press (ENTER) nine times to leave room for the fields that will make up the inside address.

2 Type **Dear** followed by a space and a colon.

3 Press (ENTER) twice.

4 Type the text of the letter as follows:

Our Employment Review Committee has reviewed your resume, and we were very impressed. We definitely think you would be an asset to our company. We have several positions open that we would like to discuss with you in person. Could you please call me to set up an appointment?

Sincerely,

Anne Newton

5 Save the file as *Recruiting Response 1* in the location you are using for your work.

Creating the Data Source Document

The data source document contains the names, addresses, and other variable information that will be inserted in the main document. The variable information is listed in *fields*, which are categories, such as first name, last name, and address. All the fields that pertain to one item make up a *record*. For example, the first name, last name, and address fields would make up a record for a person.

Word assists you in creating the data source document in two ways: First, it provides a list of commonly used fields that you can use as is or modify. Second, it creates a data entry form so you can enter all the information for each record. The data source document is really just a table with the field names listed in the top row of the table.

> **TIP** You will not see the table unless you open the data source document as you would a regular file.

TASK 2: To Create the Data Source Document

1 Choose Tools, Mail Merge.

2 Select Create, Form Letters, Active Window. The **Mail Merge Helper** dialog box appears, as shown in Figure 6.2. Word confirms that you have selected *Form Letter* for your merge type and *Recruiting Response 1* as the main document.

FIGURE 6.2

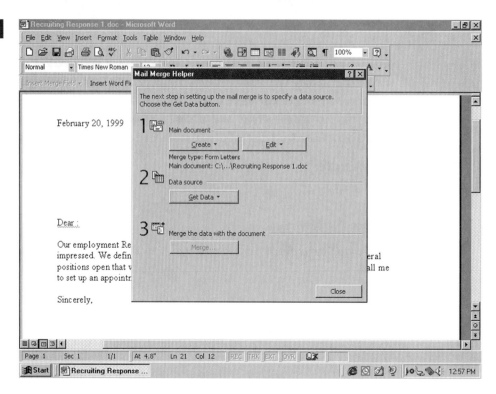

3 Select Get Data, Create data source. The Create Data Source dialog box appears, as shown in Figure 6.3. The Field names in header row: list box contains commonly used fields to give you a quick start in creating the data source document.

FIGURE 6.3

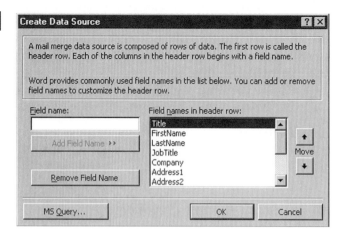

TIP All field names must be one word.

4 Next you will delete the fields you will not be using. From the Field names in header row list box select JobTitle, then select Remove Field Name.

FIGURE 6.4

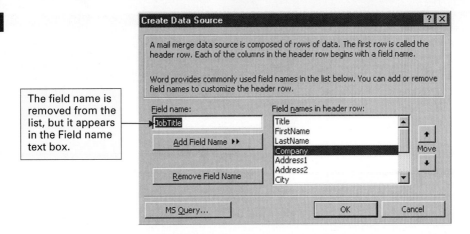

The field name is removed from the list, but it appears in the Field name text box.

> **TIP** You might wonder why the removed field name appears in the Field name text box after it is removed from the list. Actually, it's a way to allow you to undo the delete. If you remove a field by mistake, you can immediately select Add Field Name to add it back to the list. The field will go to the end of the list instead of taking its original place in the list.

5 Following the same process, remove the fields Company, Country, HomePhone, and WorkPhone.

FIGURE 6.5

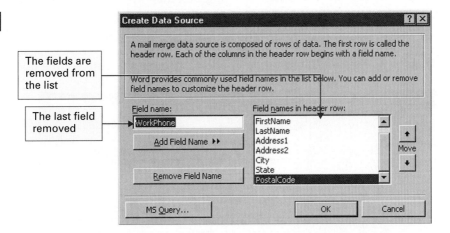

The fields are removed from the list

The last field removed

> **TIP** If you're in a hurry, you don't have to remove the fields you know you won't use. The mail merge will not be adversely affected if the data source document has fields that are not included in the main document. If you have to enter quite a few names, you will save time in the long run if you delete unwanted fields so you don't have to keep skipping them when you add each record.

6 Type **ResponseType** in the Field name text box and select Add Field Name.

FIGURE 6.6

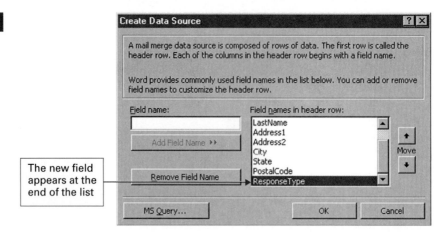

The new field appears at the end of the list

> **TIP** When you enter the actual data for the records, it is helpful to have the fields listed in a logical order, so you might have to move fields around in the list.

7 Add another new field named *Middlel* and then click the ⬆ button (above the word *Move*) until the field moves up above LastName in the list. The field moves up one position with every click of the ⬆ button.

8 Select OK. The Save As dialog box displays.

9 Type **Recruit List** in the File name text box, specify the appropriate Save in location, and select Save.

10 Select Edit Data Source to add records to the data source document.

FIGURE 6.7

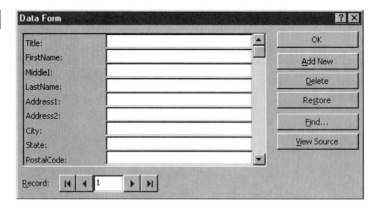

11 Next to Title, type **Mr.** and press (ENTER). The text appears in the Title text box, and the insertion point moves to the next text box.

> **TIP** The (TAB) key also advances the insertion point to the next field.

12 Type **Josh** and press (ENTER), type **A.** and press (ENTER), and then type **Cartwright** and press (ENTER). The text appears in each text box, and the insertion point is blinking in the Address1 text box.

13 Finish typing the address for the first record using this information:

Address1:   **123 Sunnydale Ave.**

Address2:

City: **Omaha**

State: **NE**

PostalCode: **68112**

ResponseType: **1**

> **TIP** When you press (ENTER) in the last text box, a new, blank form appears automatically for the next record.

14 Continue typing the following records:

Title: **Ms.**

FirstName: **Jennifer**

MiddleI: **B.**

LastName: **Eton**

Address1:   **Winston Estates**

Address2:   **3717 Sawyer Rd.**

City: **Omaha**

State: **NE**

PostalCode: **68109**

ResponseType: **2**

> **TIP** If you close the data form accidentally by selecting OK, click the Edit Data Source ✏️ ⌄ button and select Add New to continue entering records.

15 Add your own name to the list and give yourself a 1 in the ResponseType field. I think you deserve an interview!

16 Select OK. The blank main document appears with the Mail Merge toolbar.

FIGURE 6.8

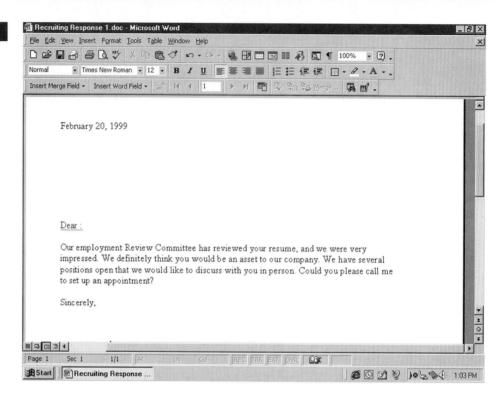

TIP At this point, the structure of the data source document (the field names) has been saved. The data that you entered has not been saved. Word prompts you to save the data source document later in the process.

 **Web Tip**

If you need a zip code for an address, go to the United States Postal Service Web site at http://www.usps.gov/ncsc.

 TASK 3: To Insert the Merge Fields

1. Position the insertion point four lines below the date at the top of the letter. This is the position where the inside address fields should be inserted.

2. Click Insert Merge Field on the Mail Merge toolbar. A list of the fields in the data source document drops down.

3. Select Title.

FIGURE 6.9

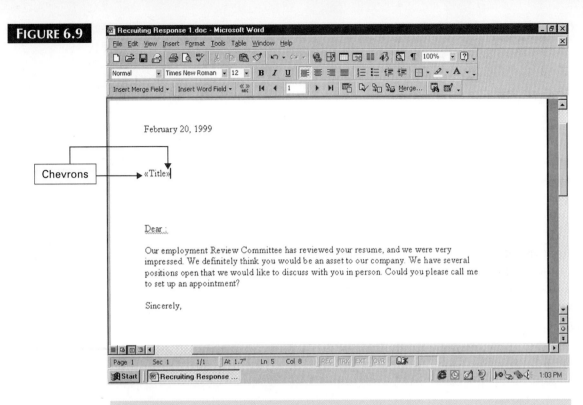

TROUBLESHOOTING Although you could easily type the field names enclosed in chevrons, it wouldn't work because it would not be a **_Merge Field code_**. Click anywhere inside the text <<Title>> and press (SHIFT) + (F9) to see the actual code. Press (SHIFT) + (F9) again to hide the code. Now press (END) to move the insertion point back into position so you can continue.

4 To complete the first line of the inside address, type a space, click Insert Merge Field, and select FirstName. Type a space, click Insert Merge Field, and select MiddleI. Type a space, click Insert Merge Field, and select LastName.

FIGURE 6.10

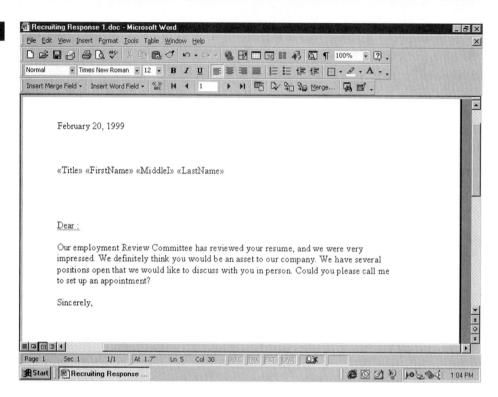

5 Press ⊕, click Insert Merge Field, and select Address1. The code is inserted.

6 Press ⊕, insert the Address2 field on this line, and press ⊕ again.

7 Insert the City field and type a comma after it followed by a space. Then insert the State field, type a space, and insert the PostalCode field.

FIGURE 6.11

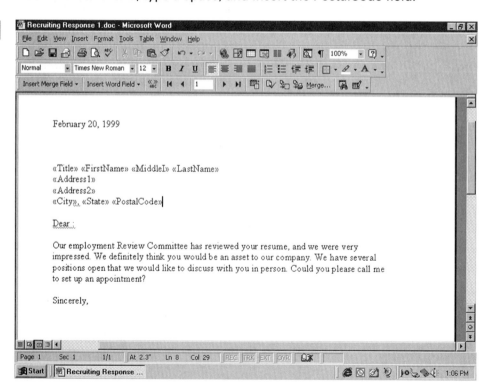

8 Move the insertion point before the colon on the salutation line and insert the Title and Last Name fields with the proper spacing.

TASK 4:   To Preview the Merged Data

1 Click the View Merged Data button. Real data appears instead of the merge field codes.

FIGURE 6.12

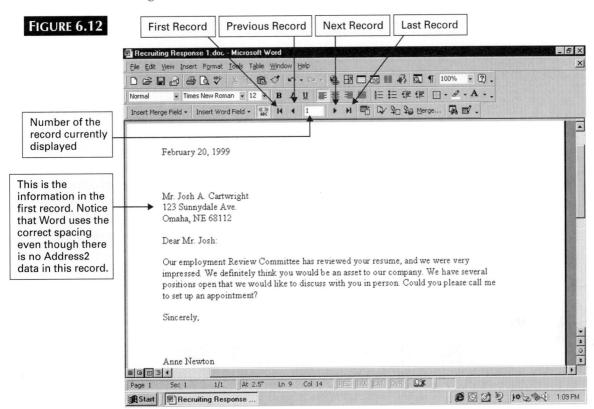

First Record   Previous Record   Next Record   Last Record

Number of the record currently displayed

This is the information in the first record. Notice that Word uses the correct spacing even though there is no Address2 data in this record.

February 20, 1999

Mr. Josh A. Cartwright
123 Sunnydale Ave.
Omaha, NE 68112

Dear Mr. Josh:

Our employment Review Committee has reviewed your resume, and we were very impressed. We definitely think you would be an asset to our company. We have several positions open that we would like to discuss with you in person. Could you please call me to set up an appointment?

Sincerely,

Anne Newton

2 Click the Next Record ▶ button. The data in the second record appears.

3 Click ▶ again and then click the First Record ◄ button. The data in the first record appears.

4 Click button. The merge field codes appear.

> **TIP** If you see an error in the real data, you can edit the data source document by clicking the Edit Data Source ▦ ▾ button.

5 Click 🖫.

6 Click ✕. Word asks if you want to save the data source document.

7 Select Yes. Word saves the *Recruiting List* file (the data source document) and closes the *Recruiting Response 1* file.

Check Point

Remember that the first time you saved the data source document, only the field names were saved, not the data.

Break Point

If necessary, you can exit Word and continue this project later.

Merging the Documents

When you merge the main document with the data source document, Word matches the field names in the main document with the field names in the data source document and inserts the appropriate data. Unless you specify records by creating a **query option**, Word merges all the records in the data source document with the main document. A query option specifies the criteria by which Word selects the records for merging. In the next task you will merge all the records with the Recruiting Response 1 letter; then in the next task you will specify a query option so you can merge only the records that Ms. Newton indicated should get the letter.

TASK 5: ## To Merge All the Records in the Data Source Document with the Main Document

1 Launch Word and open *Recruiting Response 1.doc*, if necessary. Click the Merge to New Document ⊞ button. Word creates a new document. A Next Page section break separates each letter.

> **TIP** If you don't want to create a new document, click the Merge to Printer ⊞ button instead and the documents will be printed.

2 Add the following postscript at the end of the letter addressed to yourself:

P.S.--We have an immediate opening for an applicant with credentials such as yours.

3 Save the file as *Merged Letters* and close the file. The main document appears.

TASK 6: To Merge Selected Records with the Main Document

1 Click the Mail Merge Helper ![icon] button. The Mail Merge Helper dialog box appears.

2 Select Query Options.

3 From the Field: drop-down list, select ResponseType and type **1** in the Compare to: text box, as shown in Figure 6.15. These choices build a query statement that says the ResponseType field must be equal to 1 for the record to be selected.

FIGURE 6.13

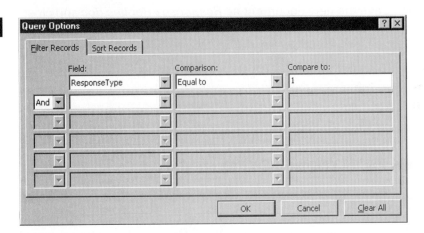

4 Select OK.

FIGURE 6.14

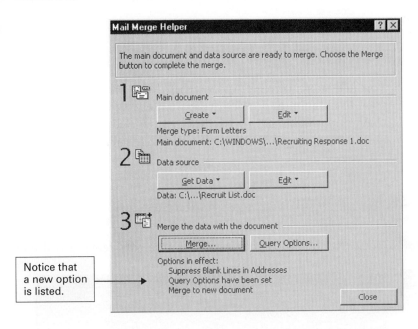

Notice that a new option is listed.

5 Select Merge. When a query option has been set, and All is selected under Records to be merged, Word retrieves all records that meet the query criteria.

FIGURE 6.15

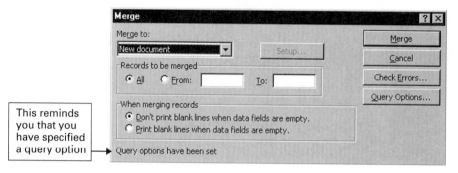

This reminds you that you have specified a query option → Query options have been set

6 Select Merge. Word merges the records to a new document.

7 Save the new document as *Response1 Replies.doc* and close it. The main document appears.

> **TIP** Once you set Query Options, Word remembers them and uses them in subsequent merges.

 TASK 7: To Remove Selection Criteria

1 Click 🖳 .

2 Select Query Options. The Query Options dialog box appears.

3 Select Clear All, and select OK. The Mail Merge Helper dialog box appears.

Merging Data Sources with Envelopes and Labels

You can merge envelopes or labels with the same data source document used to create the form letter. To merge with an envelope, you create a new main document that is set up as an envelope; to merge with labels, you create a new main document that is set up as labels.

 TASK 8: To Merge Envelopes with a Data Source

1 In the Mail Merge Helper dialog box, select Create, Envelopes.

FIGURE 6.16

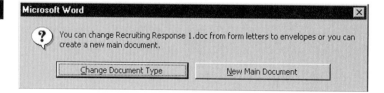

2 Select New Main Document. Word creates a new document.

3 Select Get Data, Open Data Source. The Open Data Source dialog box opens.

4 Select *Recruit List.doc* and select Open. This message appears: "Word needs to set up your main document. Choose the Set Up Main Document button to finish setting up your main document."

5 Select Set Up Main Document. The Envelope Options dialog box opens.

6 Select OK to select size 10 envelopes, which is the standard business envelope.

FIGURE 6.17

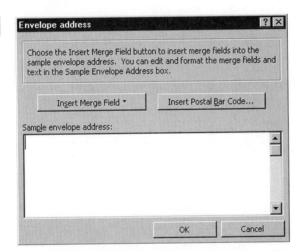

7 Select Insert Merge Field and select Title. The field is inserted.

8 Continue inserting fields to create the address, as shown in Figure 6.22.

FIGURE 6.18

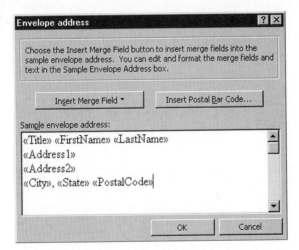

9 Select OK and close the Mail Merge Helper dialog box. The envelope appears with the merge field codes. The insertion point is located in the upper-left corner where you could type a return address, if needed.

10 Click . The envelope displays the first name and address from the data source document.

11 Save the file as *Recruiting Envelopes.doc* and close the file. The *Recruiting Response 1.doc* file appears.

TASK 9: To Merge Labels with a Data Source

1 Click 🖳. The Mail Merge Helper dialog box appears.

2 Select Create, Mailing Labels, New Main Document.

3 Select Get Data, Open Data Source; open *Recruit List.doc*; and select Set Up Main Document.

FIGURE 6.19

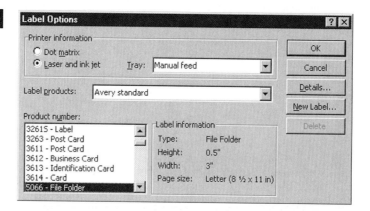

> **TIP** In the Label Options dialog box, Word lists brands of label products that can be purchased at most office supply stores. The product number in the dialog box corresponds to the product number of the labels for purchase. Label information gives the label size and sheet size.

4 Select 5160 – Address from the Product number list box, select appropriate printer options, and select OK.

5 Insert the fields using the same technique you used to create the address on the envelope and select OK.

FIGURE 6.20

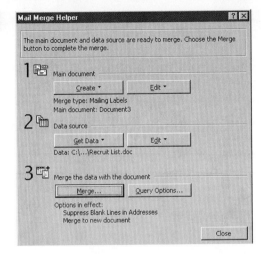

6 Close the Mail Merge Helper dialog box.

FIGURE 6.21

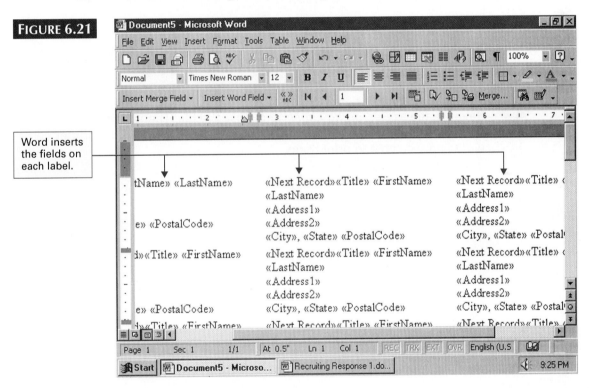

Word inserts the fields on each label.

7 Click [icon].

FIGURE 6.22

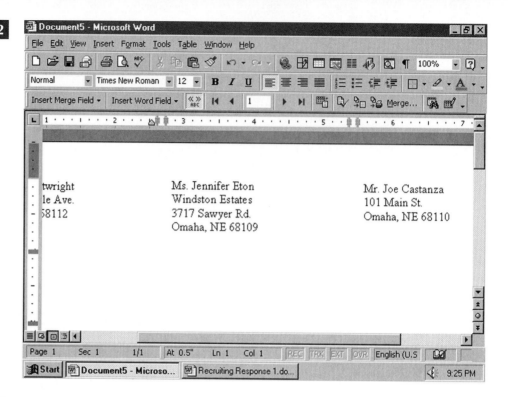

8 Save the file as *Recruiting Labels* and close the file. Then close the *Recruiting Response 1* document. If you had label sheets in the printer you would now be able to print them.

Summary and Exercises

Summary

- Mail merging is a process that generates customized form letters, envelopes, and labels.
- The main document merges with a data source document to create the customized forms.
- The main document contains the text and the mail merge fields.
- The main document can be any Word document, label, or envelope.
- The data source document contains the records.
- The Mail Merge Helper guides you through the complete merging process.
- You can merge to the printer or to a document.
- A data source document can be used with multiple main documents.
- You can select the records you want to merge by using the query feature.

Key Terms and Operations

Key Terms

data source document
field
Mail Merge Helper
main document

merge field code
query option
record

Operations

create a data source document
create a main document
merge to a document

merge to the printer
select records for merging
view merged data

Study Questions

Multiple Choice

1. A category of information is called
   a. a record.
   b. a field.
   c. a chevron.
   d. merged data.

2. To preview the data before merging, click the
   a. Mail Merge Helper button.
   b. Print Preview button.
   c. View Merged Data button.
   d. Check for Errors button.

3. To insert a merge field code in a form letter,
   a. type the field name enclosed in the proper punctuation.
   b. select the field name from the Insert Merge Field drop-down list.
   c. copy the field name from the data source document.
   d. copy the field name from the main document.

4. The document that contains the repetitive text is called
   a. the main document.
   b. the form document.
   c. the data source document.
   d. the secondary document.

5. The document that contains the variable information is called the
   a. the main document.
   b. the form document.
   c. the data source document.
   d. the secondary document.

6. A merge field code is enclosed in
   a. chevrons.
   b. quotes.
   c. square brackets.
   d. braces.

7. To see the actual merge field code,
   a. press F9.
   b. press SHIFT + F9.
   c. click the Show/Hide button.
   d. click the Mail Merge Helper button.

8. A field name
   a. must be enclosed in quotes.
   b. must not contain numbers.
   c. must be capitalized.
   d. must be one word.

9. The data source document is really formatted
   a. as the data entry form.
   b. in the main document.
   c. as a table.
   d. by the Mail Merge Helper.

10. To edit the data source document,
    a. open the file.
    b. click the Edit data source button.
    c. Both A and B.
    d. None of the above.

Short Answer

1. In what two ways does Word assist you in creating the data source document?

2. What can you do if you accidentally close the data form before you have added all the new records?

3. What is a query option?

4. How do you create an envelope for merging?

5. How do you create labels for merging?

6. How do you merge to a document?

7. What is a merge field code?

8. How do you view merged data?

9. Which document in the mail merge contains the records?

10. Can a main document be associated with multiple data source documents?

Fill in the Blank

1. Each category of information, such as first name or last name, is called a(n) _____.

2. Word inserts appropriate data in a form letter by matching the _____.

3. By default, Word merges _____ records.

4. All the fields that pertain to one person make up a(n) _____.

5. Each letter in a merged document is separated by a Next Page _____.

6. To print only the fourth page of a merged document, enter _____. for Pages in the Print dialog box.

7. To merge selected records, select _____ Options.

8. Once you set Query Options, Word uses them in _____ merges.

9. To create the main document in the open file, select _____ Window.

10. To create the main document in a new file, select New Main _____.

For Discussion

1. Explain the process of producing form letters with the mail merge feature.

2. Discuss the advantage of using mail merge instead of creating individual letters and list several circumstances in which you might use a mail merge.

3. Discuss the situations in which you might merge to a document instead of merging directly to a printer.

4. Explain the functions of the Mail Merge Helper.

5. Describe the process of inserting mail merge fields in a form letter and explain how the proper spacing is achieved.

Hands-On Exercises

1. Creating and Merging Recruiting Response 2

Now it's time to create the second letter, the one that says the résumé is being kept on file for later consideration.

1. Open a copy of the document named *Recruiting Response 1.doc*. This file is already associated with the correct data source. Save the file as *Recruiting Response 2.doc*.

2. Replace the last two sentences in the body paragraph with the following: **We do not have any positions open at the present time that would be suitable for you. We will keep your resume on file for consideration should an opening occur in the future. Thank you for interviewing with Selections.**

3. Save the file and merge it with the records that have a 2 in the ResponseType field. Merge the records to a new document. Save the new document as *Response2.doc*.

4. Save and close all files.

2. Creating a Form Letter for the College Recruiter

The college recruiter, Pat Bowles, would like you to find some new recruiting possibilities and create a recruiting letter to send to the new locations. Figure 6.27 shows the main document merged with a record.

FIGURE 6.23

March 1, 2000

Dean of Students
Mulberry College of Business
123 Main St.
Biloxi, NE 68201

Dear Dean of Students,

The Selections department store offers a very fine management-training program for eligible graduates. I have enclosed a brochure outlining our program and projected compensation rates.

I would be available to set up interviews on your campus on April 15. If you would be interested in having me come to the campus on that date, please contact me at our offices in Omaha. We are seeking students in their last year of study who are pursuing a degree in marketing or business.

Sincerely,

Pat Bowles
College Recruiting Director

Enclosures

1. Search the Web for colleges and universities that offer a marketing degree and search for business schools.

2. Create a data source document with the names and addresses of the schools you find. Include a field for the name of the dean of students, a salutation field, and a possible date to visit the campus. If it is not possible to find the name of the dean or an appropriate contact person, type **Dean of Students** for the name of the dean and the salutation field. Type different dates for the possible interview date.

3. Create a merge letter with the text shown in Figure 6.23. Save the file as *New Schools Merge.doc*.

4. Merge the letter with the data source and merge the records to a new file.

5. Save the merged letters as *New Schools.doc*.

6. Create a main document that is an envelope and merge it with the data source document. Merge the records to a new document and save the file as *New Schools Envelopes.doc*.

7. Save and close all files.

On Your Own Exercises

1. Creating a Personal Data Source

Create a data source file that contains the names and addresses of family and friends. Instead of using the Mail Merge Helper to create the data source, create a new file and insert a table. Type the field names in the first row, such as FirstName, LastName, Salutation, Address, and so on. Save the file as *My Personal Data*.

2. Creating a Personal Mail Merge Letter

Create a new document and type a letter that you can send to your family and friends. Use the Mail Merge Helper to select the data source you created in the previous exercise and then insert the merge fields. Save the file as *My Merge Letter.doc*. Merge the letter to a document so you can add additional comments to specific letters.

3. Creating Personal Envelopes

Create a main document that is an envelope. Associate the document with your personal data source file and insert the merge fields. Save the files as *My Merge Envelope*. Merge the envelopes with the data source and save the merge as a document named *My Envelopes.doc*.

4. Creating Personal Labels

Create a main document that is a mailing label. Associate the document with your personal data source file and insert the merge fields. Save the file as *My Merge Labels.doc*. Merge the labels with the data source and save the merge as a document named *My Labels*.

5. Reviewing Restaurants

You've been asked to create a restaurant guide for students at your school. You assignment is to eat at all the local restaurants (for free, of course) and then compile your findings. Create a data source document for the restaurants in your area. Include fields for the following: the name of the restaurant, address, proximity to your school, type of food, price range, service, and your overall grade for the restaurant. (Include your own additional categories, if desired.) Enter the data for the fields and grade each restaurant using a 4-point scale with 4 as the best grade and 1 as the worst grade. Save the file as *Restaurant Reviews.doc.*

6. Creating a Report

Create a file and name it *Restaurant Review Report.doc.* Make the document a main document and choose Catalog for the type of main document. (When creating a catalog, Word merges the records one after another without inserting a page break between them.) Associate the main document with the *Restaurant Reviews.doc* data source. Insert the merge fields in the report at the appropriate locations and save the file. Merge the records to a new document and then add the text that you want to include as an introduction. Save the new document as *Reports.doc.* Figure 6.24 should give you an idea of the report you can create. Note that you cannot include the introduction in the main document because it would be repeated for each record.

FIGURE 6.24

Restaurant Guide

As a new student, you may be wondering, Where are the best places to eat around here? This area has many restaurants that you may want to try when you re off campus, but instead of finding out about them the hard way, let a seasoned restaurant-veteran be your guide.

About the reviewer: *Your Name,* a college student at *Name of Your School,* is a frequent patron of the local restaurants and is imminently qualified to review them.

< Insert the name of the restaurant field>
<Insert the address field>

Proximity to School: *<insert field>*
Cuisine: *<insert field>*
Price Range: *<insert field>*
Service: *<insert field>*
Overall Grade: *<insert field>*

Projects for Microsoft Excel 2000

Introducing Excel 2000

While a graduate student in a finance class at Harvard in 1978, Dan Bricklin watched his professor "run the numbers." As the class explored different corporate investment scenarios, the professor would continually erase and replace columns of numbers on the chalkboard at the front of the room. Dan envisioned a computer program that would re-calculate numbers automatically, greatly decreasing the time required to explore financial models. With the help of MIT student Bob Frankston, Dan developed VisiCalc, the first electronic spreadsheet.

Today's electronic spreadsheets have revolutionized the use of personal computers for per-forming calculations. Electronic spreadsheet applications such as Microsoft Excel have many powerful features, but all spreadsheets are based upon the relatively simple concept of storing text and numbers in a two-dimensional grid.

Excel is especially useful for answering **"what if?"** questions by changing numbers to exam-ine alternative scenarios. You may want to know, for example, how the monthly payment on a loan will differ if the term is 5 years and the interest rate is 7 percent, versus a loan with a term of 4 years at 7 percent. By constructing a simple worksheet in Excel, you can quickly answer this question.

Objectives

After completing this project, you will be able to:

➤ Describe electronic spreadsheets and explain what they are used for

➤ Define common spreadsheet concepts

➤ Explain what steps are required to build an electronic workbook

➤ Launch Microsoft Excel

➤ Identify the Excel user interface

➤ Close a workbook and exit Excel

Worksheets and Workbooks

The first electronic spreadsheet applications worked with only one two-dimensional worksheet grid at a time. Think of an accountant who keeps financial ledgers on separate ledger sheets. If this accountant were to develop an electronic version of each ledger sheet, a separate electronic file would be required to store each ledger. As electronic spreadsheet software has evolved to incorporate new features, working with multiple worksheets is now commonplace.

In Excel, each ledger sheet can be represented electronically in a separate *worksheet*. An Excel file, called a *workbook*, contains one or more worksheets, and you can link data from one worksheet in a workbook to other worksheets in the same workbook. Thus, Excel allows you to create three-dimensional solutions.

As with the other Office 2000 applications, you can create a worksheet by entering data into a blank workbook, or by using one of Excel's many templates. A *template* is a special workbook file containing specific data—such as headings, initial values, and other supporting information—that you can use to create workbooks.

Where Data Resides and What Kind of Data Worksheets Contain

When you use Excel it is important that you identify where data resides in an Excel workbook, and what kind of data Excel contains. For simplicity, let us refer to these concepts as the where and the what. When you first launch Excel, you may notice that the screen looks different than the other Office applications such as Word. In Word, you create documents. In Excel, you create workbooks, which are composed of one or more worksheets.

Where Data Resides in a Worksheet

You create an Excel worksheet by entering data into the worksheet's two-dimensional grid. The horizontal and vertical dimensions of each worksheet each have a name. *Columns* are the vertical worksheet dimension, and are designated by a letter, which appears at the top of the column. *Rows* represent the horizontal dimension. Each row is designated by a number, which appears to the left of the row.

The intersection of a column and a row is a *cell*, which is identified by an *address*. For example, the cell at the intersection of column C and row 20 has the address C20. The data you enter into a worksheet is al-

ways entered into a specific cell. Each Excel worksheet contains 256 columns and 65,536 rows, for a total of over 16 million cells (16,777,216)! As you can see, each worksheet is a very large two-dimensional grid.

What Kind of Data Excel Worksheets Contain

You create an Excel worksheet by entering data into specific cells. The kind of data you enter into a cell depends upon whether the entry will act as a label, as a number used in a calculation, or as an expression that will perform a calculation. *Text* is any combination of numbers, spaces, and nonnumeric characters. You normally enter text as a *label* that describes the data within the worksheet. Regardless of what you enter, text will be stored as data in a cell.

Numbers in Excel are the values you will use to perform calculations. A number can contain only the following characters:

$$0\ 1\ 2\ 3\ 4\ 5\ 6\ 7\ 8\ 9 + - (\ )\ ,\ /\ \$ \% . E e$$

Excel ignores leading plus signs (+) and treats a single period as a decimal. All other combinations of numbers and nonnumeric characters are treated as text. You can also enter dates and times in Excel by typing a number, a character such as /, -, or :. Excel treats all date and time entries as numbers, which can be used in calculations.

A *formula* is a sequence of values, cell references, names, functions, or operators in a cell that produces a new value from existing values. A formula always begins with an equal sign (=). Formulas often contain *functions*, which are predefined formulas that perform calculations by using specific values, called arguments, in a particular order, or structure. Where you enter data in Excel and the kind of data workbooks contain are listed in Figure O.1. Your screen may not appear as shown, depending on your settings.

Planning Excel Workbooks for Timely, Useful, and Accurate Information

Planning and designing electronic workbooks is deceptively simple: The data displayed in a workbook is only as good as the structure of the worksheet, which will usually contain formulas that calculate results and link information. To maintain *data integrity*, or consistently accurate results, consider following a simple seven-step design process to minimize the risk of introducing errors into your workbooks, thereby insuring timely, relevant, and useful information. This process is shown in Figure O.2.

Determine the Workbook's Purpose

Since electronic worksheets consist of a matrix (a matrix is a two-dimensional representation of data) of cells that can contain text, numbers, formulas, and functions, you should carefully determine the workbook's scope and purpose. In addition to performing simple and complex calculations, electronic worksheets can be used as databases to sort and filter data. Before de-

FIGURE O.1

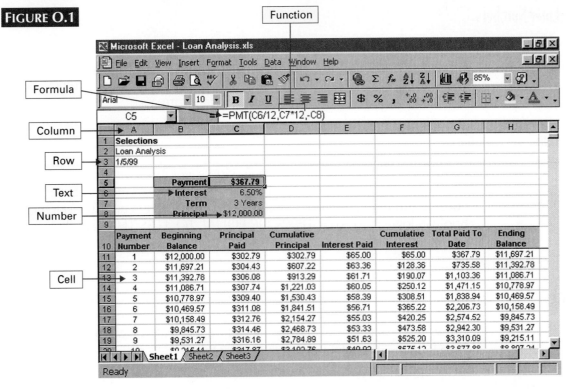

FIGURE O.2

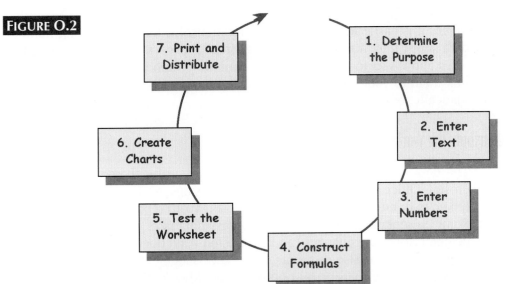

Seven steps for producing timely, relevant, and useful information in electronic workbooks

signing a worksheet, the user should have a clear idea of what task the worksheet is to accomplish.

Enter Text

Text entries provide the basic structure of an electronic worksheet. The labels give meaning to the numbers residing in the worksheet's cells. Text can be formatted to provide the worksheet with a particular look.

Enter Numbers

Numbers are the data upon which calculations are performed. Numbers are entered according to the text labels that define the overall worksheet structure. Numbers can be formatted with leading characters, as currency, dates, percentages, or in a number of other standard formats.

Construct Formulas

Formulas are what give an electronic worksheet its power. Formulas, which always begin with an equal sign (=), can include one or more of Excel's functions. Formulas can also include conditional statements (IF-THEN) and Boolean logic (GREATER THAN OR EQUAL TO, LESS THAN, and so on).

Test the Worksheet

Since any of three data types can be entered into an electronic worksheet, and a formula can contain complex functions and expressions, it is important to test a worksheet thoroughly before using it. Excel includes auditing tools for isolating potential problems in a worksheet.

Create Charts

Often, it is easier to understand the relationships that exist among numeric data when they are represented graphically. Excel's powerful charting features allow you to create the most common graph types, and dynamically link them to your data. If the underlying data changes, the charts will automatically reflect the changes.

Print and Distribute the Workbook

The data represented in an Excel workbook can be shared with other Microsoft Office applications. For instance, sales results by region can be linked to or embedded in either a Microsoft Word report, a Microsoft PowerPoint presentation, or a Microsoft Access database. By using the tools together, last-minute changes can be reflected in all documents where the data appears. You can also distribute your Excel data electronically by sending a workbook via e-mail or by publishing workbook data to the World Wide Web. By saving Excel 2000 data in HTML format, your worksheet formats are retained when the data is viewed in Microsoft Internet Explorer or a similar Web browser.

Launching Excel 2000

You can launch Excel the same way you launch other Office applications. You can use the Start menu, Documents list or the Office Shortcut bar.

TASK 1:   To Launch Microsoft Excel

1 Click the Start ![Start] button.

2 Choose Programs from the Start menu and select Microsoft Excel, as shown in Figure O.3.

FIGURE O.3

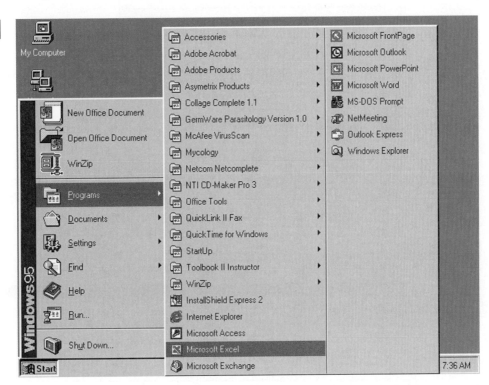

3 Choose Customize from the Tools menu.

4 Click the Options tab.

5 Select the options shown in Figure O.4. This will turn off Excel's customization features and display the Standard and Formatting toolbars in their entirety.

FIGURE O.4

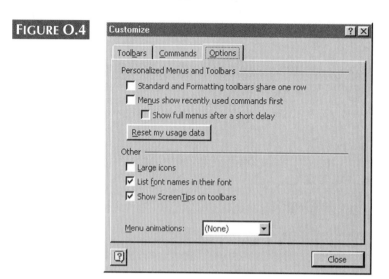

6 Click the Close button. Excel will display the default workbook Book1.

The Excel 2000 User Interface

After you launch Excel as described in the previous task, your screen should look similar to Figure O.5. You will recognize some elements if you have used other Office applications. Some of the items on the interface are unique to Excel. Table O.1 describes each of these elements.

FIGURE O.5

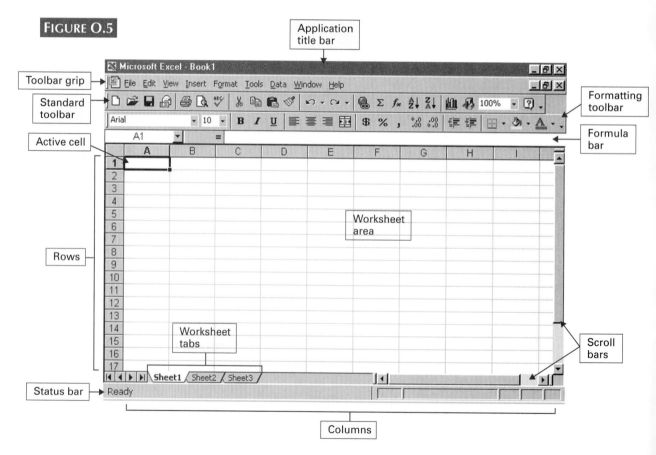

Table O.1

Element	Description
Application title bar	Displays the name of the Office application, name of the active workbook, and the Minimize, Maximize, Restore, and Close buttons.
Worksheet area	The entire worksheet and all its elements, including cells, gridlines, row and column headings, scroll bars, and sheet tabs.
Standard Toolbar	Toolbar containing shortcuts to common commands and tasks.
Formatting Toolbar	Toolbar containing shortcuts to the most common formatting commands.
Formula bar	Displays the constant value or formula used in the active cell. Also used to enter or edit values or formulas.
Sheet tabs	Displays the name of a sheet. Click the sheet tab to make a sheet active.
Rows	Horizontal dimension of Excel's two-dimensional grid.
Columns	Vertical dimension of Excel's two-dimensional grid.
Active cell	The cell currently in use. The active cell can receive data.
Status bar	Displays information about a selected command or an operation in progress. The right side of the status bar shows whether keys such as (CAPS LOCK), (SCROLL LOCK), or (NUM LOCK) are turned on.
Scroll bars	Horizontal and vertical bars for moving within a worksheet.

TASK 2: To Close Your Workbook and Exit Microsoft Excel

1 Click the Close button ⊠ for the Worksheet area.

2 Choose Exit from the File menu or click the Close button ⊠ in the application window to exit Microsoft Excel.

Summary and Exercises

Summary

- Microsoft Excel is an electronic spreadsheet application that allows you to develop powerful tools for performing calculations.
- Spreadsheets are often used to conduct a "what if?" analysis.
- An Excel workbook is composed of one or more worksheets, which provides three-dimensional capabilities.
- Data in an Excel worksheet is located in rows, columns, and cells.
- Excel workbooks contain text, numbers, dates, times, formulas, and functions.
- By following seven steps for designing workbooks, you minimize the potential for error.
- You can launch Excel the same way you launch other Office applications.

Key Terms

active cell
address
application title bar
cell
column
data integrity
Formatting toolbar
formula
formula bar
function
label
number

row
scroll bars
sheet tabs
Standard toolbar
status bar
template
text
"what if?"
workbook
worksheet
worksheet area

Study Questions

Multiple Choice

1. The intersection of a row and a column is a
   a. function.
   b. address.
   c. cell.
   d. row.

2. Which Excel interface object is used to modify the contents of a cell?
   a. status bar
   b. Standard toolbar
   c. Formatting toolbar
   d. formula bar

3. The vertical dimension of an Excel worksheet is called a
   a. cell.
   b. column.
   c. address.
   d. row.

4. An Excel worksheet contains approximately how many cells?
   a. 256
   b. 16,000
   c. one hundred thousand
   d. 16 million

5. Which kind of Excel data actually performs calculations?
   a. labels
   b. numbers
   c. dates/times
   d. formulas

Short Answer

1. What is the cell currently in use called?

2. How do you identify a particular cell?

3. Rows are arranged along which dimension?

4. What kind of data defines the structure of a worksheet?

5. What symbol always precedes a formula?

Fill in the Blank

1. An Excel formula will often contain a _____ to perform a calculation.

2. All data is entered into worksheet _____.

3. An Excel workbook will always contain at least one _____.

4. Excel is often used to conduct a _____ analysis.

5. The five kinds of data contained in Excel worksheets are _____, _____, _____, _____, and _____.

For Discussion

1. How do worksheets differ from a workbook?

2. What is a function and how does it differ from a formula?

Designing Worksheets and Workbooks

To use Excel effectively you must know how to plan, create, save, and print worksheets. In this project you will enter text and numbers into cells, and then create formulas with functions to perform calculations.

Objectives

After completing this project, you will be able to:

➤ Design a workbook

➤ Navigate within worksheets and workbooks

➤ Enter text as labels

➤ Use the fill handle to complete a data series

➤ Adjust column width

➤ Create a folder and save a workbook

➤ Enter numbers into cells

➤ Enter formulas and functions into cells

➤ Preview and print worksheets

➤ Close a workbook and exit Excel

Running Case

Travis Traylor of the Selections, Inc. knows that Microsoft Excel is made to perform calculations and conduct "what-if" analyses, and therefore is often used to list financial or numeric data in order to make business decisions. He wants you to help him analyze sales data using Excel.

The Challenge

Selections, Inc., is a multifaceted department store with four regional offices. Travis Traylor, manager of accounting and finance, has asked you to create a workbook listing the sales figures for four fiscal quarters for each region. He further specified that the workbook should be flexible enough so that he can "drill down" to specific department totals in each region, yet also see the annual sales by department for all sales regions. He wants to meet with you after you design the workbook so that he can review your progress and approve your design.

The Strategy

Since an Excel workbook can contain multiple worksheets, you will want to design this workbook so that it provides both summary and detail information. You will develop a prototype workbook listing the departmental sales for the north region, and then meet with Mr. Traylor before adding additional worksheets to the workbook. Since you are merely seeking his approval for the workbook's design, you will not need to be concerned with formatting this workbook. The worksheet you will create in this project is shown in Figure 1.1.

FIGURE 1.1

Microsoft Excel - Selections.xls

	A	B	C	D	E	F
1	Selections Inc.					
2	Quarterly Sales					
3						
4	Department	1st Qtr.	2nd Qtr.	3rd Qtr.	4th Qtr.	Total
5	Clothing	405112	321670	401934	393714	1522430
6	Cosmetics	373211	34812	29718	38248	475989
7	Watches & Jewelry	45213	21397	18923	44971	130504
8	Electronics and Computers	211396	189201	174916	193712	769225
9	Appliances	48761	39675	36582	38619	163637
10	Furniture	23819	18912	21975	24187	88893
11	Housewares	34907	26585	39638	33935	135065
12	China and Crystal	33185	32081	41972	18381	125619
13	Knives and Cutlery	12954	9273	10593	11976	44796
14	Books & Magazines	36719	37383	38121	29753	141976
15	Bed and Bath	21082	18910	19718	17544	77254
16	Total	1246359	749899	834090	845040	3675388
17						
18						
19						

Sheet1 / Sheet2 / Sheet3 /

Ready

Regional sales worksheet

The Setup

Launch Microsoft Excel, and make sure that you select the Excel settings listed in Table 1.1. This will ensure that your screen matches the illustrations and that the tasks in this project function as described.

Table 1.1

Location	Make these settings:
Office Shortcut Bar	Right-click the Office icon on the shortcut bar and click Exit.
Office Assistant	Hide the Assistant.
Tools, Customize	Click the Options tab and deselect the option to show recently used menu commands first. Deselect the option to display the Standard and Formatting toolbars on one row.
Tools, Options	Click the Edit tab and select Move selection after Enter.
View, Formula Bar	Display the formula bar.
View, Status Bar	Display the status bar.
View, Normal	View the workbook in Normal view.
Maximize	Maximize the application and workbook windows.

Designing a Workbook

You will recall from "Introducing Excel 2000" that before you enter data into worksheet cells, you need an overall plan for the workbook. To design a workbook you will want to think about how the data will be used for reporting and how often it may need to be updated. For example, Mr. Traylor indicated that he wants to be able to see departmental sales for each sales region, summarized by fiscal quarter. In addition, he wants to see a summary for each department across all sales regions.

Your best strategy will be to use five worksheets—four for each sales region and one for the summary of sales across regions. Some data will remain constant across sales regions, such as the names of the departments. Other data, namely the sales figures, will vary by region. The overall structure of the four regional worksheets will be similar, in that the departments will most likely appear in the same order.

After you design each regional worksheet you can determine how best to list the total sales by department in a fifth worksheet. You will want your workbook to be flexible enough to accept changes and revision without jeopardizing the accuracy of the sales totals. In Project 2 you will learn how to link data between worksheets. For now, think in terms of how best to organize the regional worksheets.

You may want to initially plan the structure using a legal pad. Your proposed worksheet might resemble the one shown in Figure 1.2, which lists total sales by department for four fiscal quarters.

FIGURE 1.2

Selections Inc.					
Quarterly Sales					
Department	1st Qtr.	2nd Qtr.	3rd Qtr.	4th Qtr.	Total
Clothing	405112	321670	401934	393714	?
Cosmetics	373211	34812	29718	38248	?
Watches & Jewelry	45213	21397	18923	44971	?
Electronics and Computers	211396	189201	174916	193712	?
Appliances	48761	39675	36582	38619	?
Furniture	23819	18912	21975	24187	?
Housewares	34907	26585	39638	33935	?
China and Crystal	33185	32081	41972	18381	?
Knives and Cutlery	12954	9273	10593	11976	?
Books & Magazines	36719	37383	38121	29753	?
Bed and Bath	21082	18910	19718	17544	?
Total	?	?	?	?	?

To design an electronic worksheet using this structure, begin by entering the text data to define the overall structure. Then enter the sales data as numbers. Finally, construct formulas every place you see a question mark symbol (?) to calculate the sales totals.

 Web Tip

You will recall that Dan Bricklin came up with the idea of the electronic spreadsheet, making what you will do in this project possible. Did you know that Dan received an award for his work? Visit the site http://www.acm.org/awards/fellows_citations/bricklin.html for more information.

Navigating in a Workbook

As you work in Excel you will need to move within a worksheet and among worksheets in the workbook. As you add text, numbers, dates, times, and formulas into cells, you will need to first select a specific cell to make it the *active cell*. The active cell has the focus, as indicated by its thick border. In Figure 1.3, cell A1 is the active cell. Cell A1 is also called the *home cell*, since it is the uppermost left cell in the worksheet. The workbook shown in Figure 1.3 contains three worksheets by default. You will use Sheet1 in this project.

FIGURE 1.3

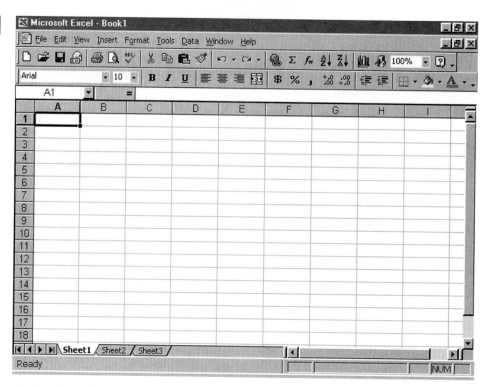

An Excel workbook with the home cell active in Sheet 1

To move between cells on a worksheet, click any cell or use the arrow keys. When you move to a cell, it becomes the active cell. To see a different area of the sheet, use the scroll bars.

TIP You can also use the Go To dialog box to move to a specific cell. Press the (F5) key and enter the cell reference in the Reference: text box, and click OK.

Navigating in a Worksheet Using Keystrokes

Using the scroll bars or clicking the left mouse button are effective methods for navigating in a relatively small worksheet, but at times you will want to move large distances. Excel supports a number of keystrokes you can use to quickly change the active cell. Table 1.2 lists keystrokes you can use to navigate within a worksheet.

Table 1.2

To move:	Use these keystrokes:
One cell to the right	→ or TAB
One cell to the left	← or SHIFT + TAB
One cell down	↓ or ENTER
One cell up	↑ or SHIFT + ENTER
To the home cell	CTRL + HOME
Down one screen	PGDN
Up one screen	PGUP
Right one screen	ALT + PGDN
Left one screen	ALT + PGUP
Last column of the worksheet	CTRL + →
Last row of the worksheet	CTRL + ↓
First column of the worksheet	CTRL + ←
First row of the worksheet	CTRL + ↑

> **TIP** You can move around and zoom on your worksheet or chart sheet by using the Microsoft IntelliMouse pointing device. For more information, open the Help system, search for Intellimouse, and choose the first topic in the list.

Navigating Among Worksheets in a Workbook

To navigate among the sheets in a workbook, simply click the appropriate worksheet tab. Depending upon how Excel is configured on your computer, you may see more than three worksheet tabs. You can use the controls shown in Figure 1.4 to display the tabs for the worksheets in a workbook. As you navigate through the sheets in a workbook, keep in mind that only one sheet is the *active sheet*, or the worksheet with the focus. Once a sheet is active, you can enter text, numbers, dates, and formulas into any of its cells.

> **TIP** You can also right-click the tab scrolling buttons to select a specific sheet.

FIGURE 1.4

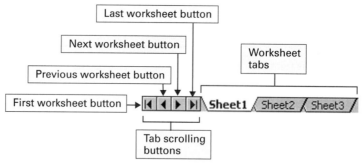

Worksheet navigation buttons and sheet tabs

 Web Tip

Worksheet tabs are an effective tool for workbook navigation. For more information, visit the site http://msdn.microsoft.com/library/books/winguide/platfrm2/d5/s11887.htm.

Entering Text in a Worksheet

When you are creating a workbook, the text you enter into specific cells defines the overall structure. In Microsoft Excel, text is any combination of numbers, spaces, and nonnumeric characters, and text entries often serve as labels that define a worksheet's structure. You will now enter text as labels to create the worksheet prototype shown in Figure 1.2.

 TASK 1: To Enter Text as Labels

1 Select cell A1 of Sheet1 and type **Selections, Inc.** Notice that the mode in the status bar changes to Enter since you are in the process of entering data. Press (ENTER) to complete your entry.

> **TIP** As you enter text in a cell, it will spill over to the next cell if the column is not wide enough to display the entire entry, if the adjacent cell is empty.

2 Type **Quarterly Sales** in cell A2 and press (ENTER).

3 Enter the following text as labels into rows 4 through 16 of column A. Press (ENTER) after you type each label.

Department
Clothing
Cosmetics

Watches & Jewelry
Electronics and Computers
Appliances
Furniture
Housewares
China and Crystal
Knives and Cutlery
Books & Magazines
Bed and Bath

Your worksheet should now look like Figure 1.5.

FIGURE 1.5

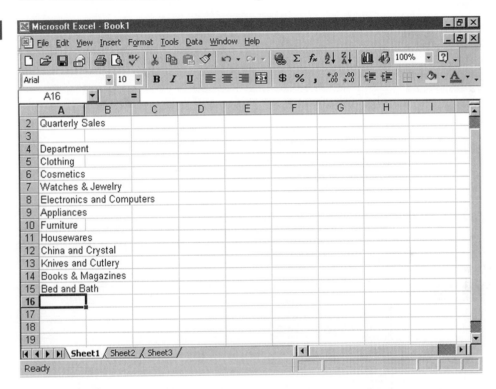

TROUBLESHOOTING Data in column A spills over into the adjacent cells in column B for some rows, since these cells do not yet contain data. Once they contain data, the entries will be truncated.

4   Select cell B4 and type **1st Qtr.** and press (ENTER) and select cell B4 again.

TROUBLESHOOTING If you make a mistake and need to edit the contents of the cell, highlight the cell and type the correct entry, or highlight the cell, click to edit the cell contents on the formula bar, and press (ENTER).

Filling in Data Based on Adjacent Cells

Excel has numerous features that make entering data into a worksheet an easy task. One very useful feature is filling in data based upon the contents of adjacent cells. In this next task you will see how you can use the **fill handle**, which is the small rectangle in the lower right corner of the active cell, to complete a data series.

TASK 2: To Use the Fill Handle to Complete a Data Series

1 Move the mouse pointer over the small rectangle in the lower-right corner of cell B4 until it changes to a small cross, as shown in Figure 1.6.

FIGURE 1.6

	A	B	C
1	Selections Inc.		
2	Quarterly Sales		
3			
4	Departmen	1st Qtr.	
5	Clothing		
6	Cosmetics		

2 Click the left mouse button and drag the selection to the right through cell E4, as shown in Figure 1.7. Notice the **cell tip**, or descriptive label, that appears as you drag the selection.

FIGURE 1.7

	A	B	C	D	E	F
1	Selections, Inc.					
2	Quarterly Sales					
3						
4	Departmen	1st Qtr.				
5	Clothing				4th Qtr.	
6	Cosmetics					
7	Watches & Jewelry					

3 Release the left mouse button. Excel used the entry in cell B4 to determine the appropriate data series for the adjacent cells. Notice that cells C4 through E4 are shaded, as shown in Figure 1.8. This indicates that the range of cells from B4 to E4 is selected, with cell B4 as the active cell. Any time you select multiple cells, the selection will appear as shaded.

FIGURE 1.8

	A	B	C	D	E	F
1	Selections Inc.					
2	Quarterly Sales					
3						
4	Departmen	1st Qtr.	2nd Qtr.	3rd Qtr.	4th Qtr.	
5	Clothing					
6	Cosmetics					

4 Click outside the selected range to deselect it.

> **TIP** When you refer to a range of adjacent cells, list the first cell in the range, a colon character to indicate an adjacent range, and the last cell in the range.

Adjusting Column Width and Entering Additional Text

As you enter data into a worksheet, you will often need to adjust the width of one or more columns. By default, all columns have a width of 8.43. The displayed column width equals the width of the digits 0 through 9 of the standard font. As you can see, the data in cell A4 is truncated, or cut off, since there is data in the adjacent cell. You can easily remedy this situation by changing the column width.

TASK 3:   To Change the Width of Worksheet Columns

1 Move the insertion point to the border between the headings for columns A and B. The insertion point's icon will change to a double-headed arrow to indicate that you can resize the column, as shown in Figure 1.9.

FIGURE 1.9

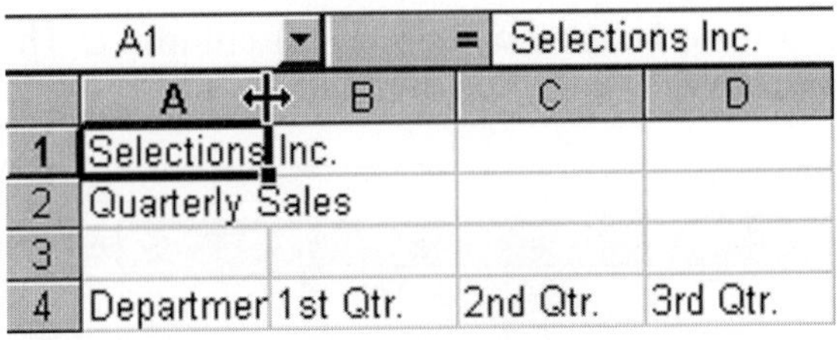

A1	▼		=	Selections Inc.

	A	↔	B	C	D
1	Selections	Inc.			
2	Quarterly	Sales			
3					
4	Departmer	1st Qtr.		2nd Qtr.	3rd Qtr.

2 Double-click the left mouse button. The column will resize to display the contents of the widest entry, as shown in Figure 1.10.

FIGURE 1.10

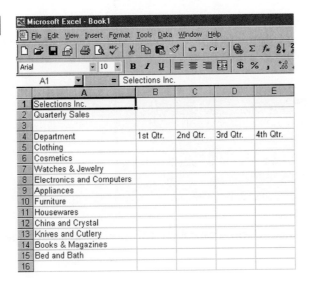

3 Point to the border between columns B and C. Click and drag the width of column B to 12.00, as shown in Figure 1.11.

FIGURE 1.11

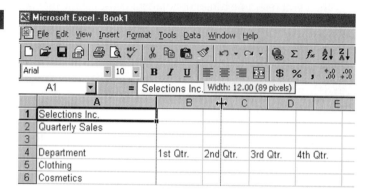

4 Click the heading for column C. The entire column is selected, as shown in Figure 1.12.

FIGURE 1.12

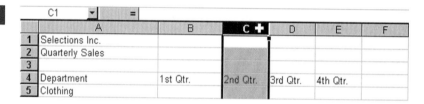

5 Depress the (SHIFT) key and click the heading for column E. This will select the range of columns from C to E (Figure 1.13).

FIGURE 1.13

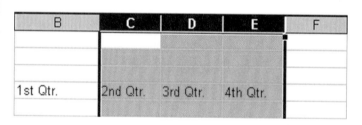

6 Select any of the column borders in the selection, and then click and drag the column widths to 12.00, as shown in Figure 1.14.

FIGURE 1.14

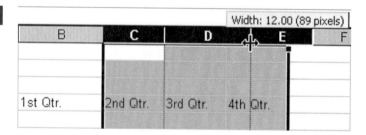

7 Release the mouse button. Columns C through E have now been resized.

TASK 4: To Enter Additional Text Labels and Adjust Column Width

1 Select cell F4, type **Total**, and press (ENTER).

2 Using the click-and-drag method of resizing a column described in the preceding task, change the width of this column to 12.00.

> **TROUBLESHOOTING** Depending upon your screen resolution, you may need to use the horizontal scroll bar to display additional worksheet columns before resizing column F.

3 Select cell A16, type **Total**, and press (ENTER). Your worksheet will now appear as shown in Figure 1.15.

FIGURE 1.15

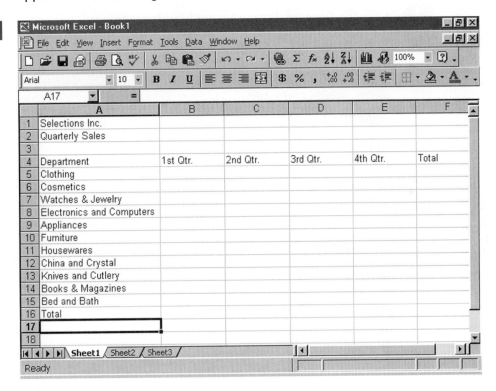

Check Point

You have not yet saved your workbook. Where does your data currently reside?

Saving Your Workbook

At this point you should probably save your workbook. As you know, everything you have done so far resides in memory, and if the computer were to lose power, you would have to recreate this workbook! Therefore, we're going to pause and save our workbook.

It is often customary to create a folder to store files related to a specific project. In the steps that follow you will create a folder on a floppy disk and save your workbook in that folder.

TASK 5: To Create a Folder and Save Your Workbook

1 Click the Save 🖫 button on the Standard toolbar.

2 The Save As dialog box appears, as shown in Figure 1.16.

FIGURE 1.16

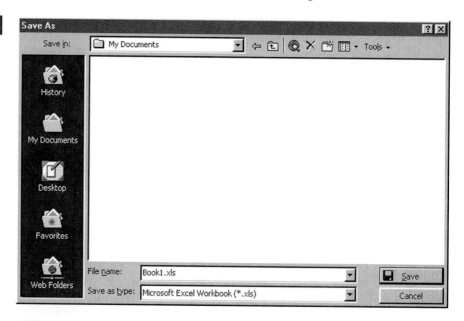

> **TIP** Since you have not saved your workbook yet, Excel displays the Save As dialog box so that you can specify the file name, file location, and file type for your workbook. Depending on your operating system, your screen may differ.

3 Place a blank, formatted floppy disk in the 3½-inch drive on your computer.

> **TROUBLESHOOTING** If you do not have access to a floppy drive, use the local or network drive your instructor specifies.

4 Select the appropriate drive from the Save in: drop-down list, as shown in Figure 1.17.

FIGURE 1.17

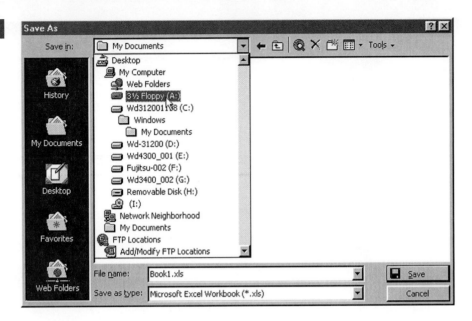

> **TROUBLESHOOTING** The drives listed will be specific to your computer or network.

5   Click the Create New Folder button near the upper-right corner of the Save As dialog box, as shown in Figure 1.18.

FIGURE 1.18

6   Type **Selections** as the name of the folder you will create, as shown in Figure 1.19. Click OK to create the folder.

FIGURE 1.19

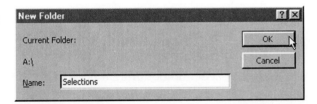

7   The default file name *Book1.xls* appears highlighted in the File name: box. Type **Selections** as the file name for your workbook, as shown in Figure 1.20.

FIGURE 1.20

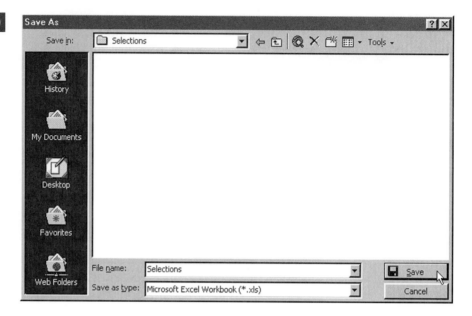

> **TIP** You do not need to add a period (.) and xls as the file name extension .xls. Since the Save as type: list box indicates that the file will be saved as an Excel workbook, the file name extension will be added automatically.

8 Click the Save button. Your workbook is now saved, as indicated by the file name that appears in Excel's title bar.

Check Point

At this point you should recognize that you have defined the structure for one regional worksheet, and saved the workbook in a folder that you have created. You are now ready to enter numbers into the worksheet, and then define formulas to perform calculations.

Break Point

If necessary, you can exit Excel and continue this project later.

Entering Numbers

You will recall that numbers are the data upon which calculations are performed. In Microsoft Excel, a number can contain only the following characters:

```
0 1 2 3 4 5 6 7 8 9 + - ( ) , / $ % . E e
```

Excel ignores leading plus signs (+) and treats a single period as a decimal. All other combinations of numbers and nonnumeric characters are treated as text.

The worksheet design shown in Figure 1.2 displays four columns of sales figures as numbers. You will enter these into columns B through E of your workbook.

TASK 6:   To Enter Numbers

1   Launch Excel and open the *Selections.xls* workbook if necessary.

2   Type **405112** in cell B5 and press (ENTER).

3   Enter the following numbers in columns B through E of your worksheet. When you are finished, your screen should resemble the worksheet shown in Figure 1.21.

Row	Column B	Column C	Column D	Column E
B5	405112	321670	401934	393714
B6	373211	34812	29718	38248
B7	45213	21397	18923	44971
B8	211396	189201	174916	193712
B9	48761	39675	36582	38619
B10	23819	18912	21975	24187
B11	34907	26585	39638	33935
B12	33185	32081	41972	18381
B13	12954	9273	10593	11976
B14	36719	37383	38121	29753
B15	21082	18910	19718	17544

FIGURE 1.21

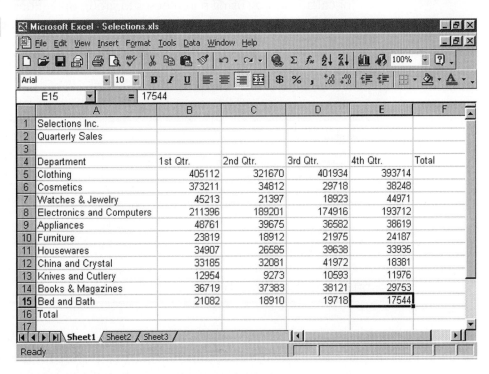

4   Save your workbook.

Creating Formulas

Your prototype worksheet is almost complete! You need to add formulas in row 16 and column F to add together the sales figures.

About Formulas

As you learned in the Introduction to Excel, a **formula** uses existing values to calculate new ones. Formulas often contain **functions**, which essentially are predefined formulas that perform calculations by using specific values, called **arguments**. Both formulas and functions are therefore mathematical or logical statements that perform calculations. Formulas always begin with an equal sign (=).

The order of the elements in a formula determines the final result of the calculation. Formulas in Microsoft Excel follow a specific **syntax**, or order, that includes an equal sign (=) followed by the elements to be calculated (the **operands**), which are separated by calculation operators. Each operand can be a value that does not change (such as a number entered in a cell), a cell or range reference, a label, a name, or a worksheet function. For example, the formula =SUM(B5:B15) will total the range of cells from B5 to B15, inclusive. The equal sign is followed by the function name (SUM), which requires an argument, a cell range in this case (B5:B15).

Excel performs the operations from left to right—according to the order of **operator precedence**—starting with the equal sign (=). You can control the order of calculation by using parentheses to group operations that should be performed first. Many formulas use arithmetic operators. Table 1.3 lists the arithmetic operators recognized by Excel.

Table 1.3

Operator	Purpose	Formula (using cell references)	Result (A1 = 2, A2 = 4)
+ (plus sign)	Addition	= A1 + A2	6
– (minus sign)	Subtraction	= A1 – A2	–2
	Negation	= –A2	–4
* (asterisk)	Multiplication	= A1 * A2	8
/ (forward slash)	Division	= A1 / A2	.5
% (percent sign)	Percent	= A1%	.02
^ (caret)	Exponentiation	= A1 ^ A2	16

Although you can enter formulas in Excel using numeric values, most formulas make extensive use of cell references. A **cell reference** is the address of a specific cell that you want to include in a formula or function. By using cell references, the formula will calculate based upon the values in cells, so that if you change a cell's value, the result of the calculation will change as well. This capability is what gives Excel such power as an analytical tool.

About Functions

Formulas often contain functions, since functions both simplify creating formulas and also improve the accuracy of the results. Excel includes over 200 functions!

Functions include elements called arguments, which provide the necessary values required by the specific function. A function's arguments are enclosed in parentheses, and for functions requiring more than one argument, the arguments are separated from one another with a comma.

Functions in Excel are classified according to a specific type of calculation. The most common classifications include Financial, Date & Time, Math & Trig, Statistical, Lookup & Reference, and Logical. In addition, Excel supports user-defined functions. Some of the more common Excel functions are listed in Table 1.4.

Table 1.4

Function	Purpose	Example (using cell references)	Result (A1 = 2, A2 = 4, A3 = 6)
=SUM(argument)	Calculates the sum of a range of values	=SUM(A1:A3)	12
=MIN(argument)	Returns the minimum value in a range	=MIN(A1:A3)	2
=MAX(argument)	Returns the maximum value in a range	=MAX(A1:A3)	6
=AVERAGE(argument)	Calculates the arithmetic mean of a range of values	=AVERAGE(A1:A3)	4
=PMT(argument)	Calculates the payment of a loan based upon periodic payments and a constant interest rate	=PMT(A1,A2,-A3)	$12.15
=IF(argument)	Returns a value based upon a logical test	=IF(A1>0,"Positive")	Positive
=COUNT(argument)	Counts the number of cells in a range that have a numeric value	=COUNT(A1:A3)	3

 Check Point

Based upon the functions listed in Table 1.4, which function is most appropriate for the worksheet you are designing?

Compare the functions in Table 1.4 with the worksheet design shown in Figure 1.2, and you will see that you should use the SUM function in each formula you will create. Although the following formula would return a correct result:

$$=B5+B6+B7+B8+B9+B10+B11+B12+B13+B14+B15,$$

you should use functions for simplicity and accuracy whenever possible. You can enter a formula in a cell by typing directly in the cell, inserting a function using the **formula palette**, or by using the pointing method. If the formula will include the SUM function, you can use Excel's **AutoSum** feature. Once you create a formula, it can be copied to other worksheet cells.

TASK 7: To Enter Formulas Using a Variety of Methods

1 Click cell B16 to make it the active cell.

2 Type **=SUM(B5:B15)**, press (ENTER), and select B16 again.

> **TIP** As you type a formula directly in a cell, the word *Enter* appears in the Status bar to indicate that you are using data entry mode.

The result shown in Figure 1.22 is displayed.

FIGURE 1.22

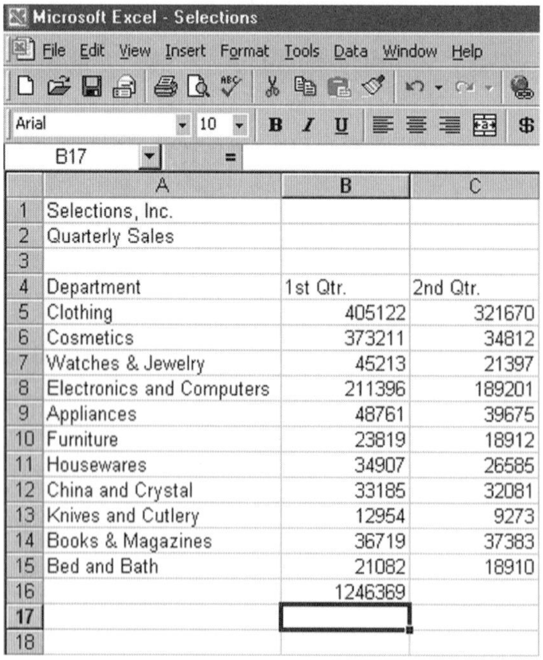

	A	B	C
1	Selections, Inc.		
2	Quarterly Sales		
3			
4	Department	1st Qtr.	2nd Qtr.
5	Clothing	405122	321670
6	Cosmetics	373211	34812
7	Watches & Jewelry	45213	21397
8	Electronics and Computers	211396	189201
9	Appliances	48761	39675
10	Furniture	23819	18912
11	Housewares	34907	26585
12	China and Crystal	33185	32081
13	Knives and Cutlery	12954	9273
14	Books & Magazines	36719	37383
15	Bed and Bath	21082	18910
16		1246369	
17			
18			

Microsoft Excel - Selections
File Edit View Insert Format Tools Data Window Help
Arial 10
B17 =

3 Select cell C16.

4 Click the Insert Function f_x button on the Standard toolbar.

5 The Paste Function dialog box appears. Select All as the function category, and select SUM as the function name, as shown in Figure 1.23.

FIGURE 1.23

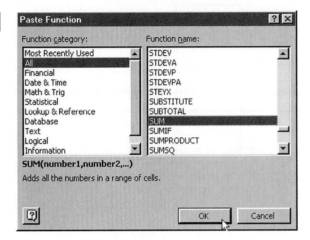

6 Click OK. When the formula palette shown in Figure 1.24 appears, click OK, as the range appearing in the highlighted text box is correct. The results of the calculation are now displayed. Notice that the formula palette displays the results of the calculation.

FIGURE 1.24

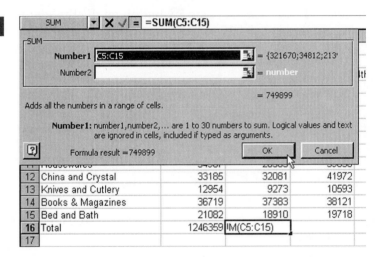

7 Select cell D5 and click and drag the selection through cell D16, as shown in Figure 1.25.

FIGURE 1.25

	B	C	D	E
2				
3				
4	1st Qtr.	2nd Qtr.	3rd Qtr.	4th Qtr.
5	405112	321670	401934	393714
6	373211	34812	29718	38248
7	45213	21397	18923	44971
8	211396	189201	174916	193712
9	48761	39675	36582	38619
10	23819	18912	21975	24187
11	34907	26585	39638	33935
12	33185	32081	41972	18381
13	12954	9273	10593	11976
14	36719	37383	38121	29753
15	21082	18910	19718	17544
16	1246359	749899		
17				

TIP You have just selected an adjacent range in Excel. In Project 2 you will learn more about selecting ranges.

8 Click the AutoSum Σ button on the Standard toolbar. Excel creates a formula with a SUM function and displays the results of the calculation.

9 Select cell D16 and click the Copy button on the Standard toolbar. The formula in cell C16 is placed on the Clipboard.

10 Select cell E16 and click the Paste button on the Standard toolbar. The formula is pasted in cell E16 and the results of the calculation are displayed, as shown in Figure 1.26.

FIGURE 1.26

13	12954	9273	10593	11976
14	36719	37383	38121	29753
15	21082	18910	19718	17544
16	1246359	749899	834090	845040
17				
18				

Sheet1 / Sheet2 / Sheet3 /

11 Using any of the methods shown here, enter a formula in cell F5 that sums the range B5:E5.

12 Using the fill handle, drag this formula from F5 down the worksheet through cell F16. Excel automatically creates a formula that sums the values in each row, as shown in Figure 1.27.

FIGURE 1.27

	F5		=	=SUM(B5:E5)		
	B	C	D	E	F	G
1						
2						
3						
4	1st Qtr.	2nd Qtr.	3rd Qtr.	4th Qtr.	Total	
5	405112	321670	401934	393714	1522430	
6	373211	34812	29718	38248	475989	
7	45213	21397	18923	44971	130504	
8	211396	189201	174916	193712	769225	
9	48761	39675	36582	38619	163637	
10	23819	18912	21975	24187	88893	
11	34907	26585	39638	33935	135065	
12	33185	32081	41972	18381	125619	
13	12954	9273	10593	11976	44796	
14	36719	37383	38121	29753	141976	
15	21082	18910	19718	17544	77254	
16	1246359	749899	834090	845040	3675388	
17						

13 Press CTRL + HOME to return to the home cell.

14 Save your workbook.

Previewing and Printing Worksheets

Before you print a worksheet, you should preview it to make sure it will print as you expect. By using Excel's **Print Preview**, you can see exactly how your worksheet will appear in printed form. In addition to being able to see the entire worksheet on the screen, Print Preview allows you to zoom in on selected areas of the workbook and print directly from the Preview screen. Once you preview the worksheet, you can send a copy to the printer. For more control over how your worksheet is printed, select Print from the File menu to open the Print dialog box.

TASK 8: To Preview and Print Worksheets

1 Click the Print Preview button on the Standard toolbar. The Print Preview displays the worksheet, as shown in Figure 1.28.

FIGURE 1.28

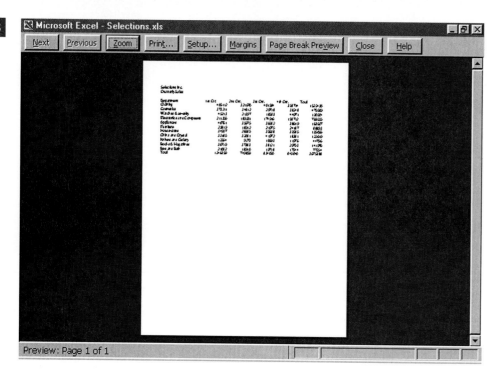

2 Click the insertion point, which now appears as a magnifying glass near the top of the Preview window. Excel zooms the preview.

3 When you are finished previewing the worksheet, click the Close button in the upper-right corner of the Print Preview window. This closes the preview.

TROUBLESHOOTING Make sure you do not click the Close button on the title bar, or you will close Excel.

4 Choose Print from the File menu.

5 In the Print dialog box, verify the printer attached to your computer or network, and click OK. The worksheet prints.

Closing Your Workbook

When you are finished with your workbook, it is a good idea to save it one last time before closing it and exiting Excel. If you have made changes to your workbook and attempt to close Excel, you will be prompted to save your changes.

TASK 9: <u>To Save and Close Your Workbook</u>

1 Click the Save button 💾 on the Standard toolbar to update your workbook.

2 Click the Close button ❌ in the workbook window, or select Close from the File menu.

3 Click the Close button ❌ in the application window to exit Excel.

> **TIP** You can also exit Excel by simply closing Excel, and save any changes you have made to any open workbooks when you are prompted to do so.

You are now ready to meet with Mr. Traylor to have him approve your design. In the next project you will modify this workbook by adding additional regional sheets, a summary sheet, and formulas to link the worksheets.

Summary and Exercises

Summary

- It is generally a good idea to plan your workbook before entering data into Excel.
- You can navigate within a worksheet using the mouse, the scroll bars, or keyboard shortcuts.
- To navigate among worksheets in a workbook, use the sheet tabs or the navigation buttons.
- You can enter text in a worksheet by selecting the appropriate cell and typing an entry.
- You can use the fill handle to fill data in cells based upon the value in an adjacent cell.
- You can easily adjust column widths to display the entire contents of all cells.
- When you first save a workbook, you can specify the file name, location, and file type in the Save As dialog box.
- Enter numbers in a cell by selecting the cell and typing a valid entry.
- You can use a variety of methods to enter formulas with functions into worksheet cells.
- You should always preview a worksheet before printing it.
- Consider saving your workbook prior to closing it and exiting Excel. Excel will prompt you to save your workbook upon closing if it contains any updated information.

Key Terms and Operations

Key Terms

active cell	formula palette
active sheet	function
argument	home cell
AutoSum	operand
cell reference	operator precedence
cell tip	Print Preview
fill handle	syntax
formula	

Operations

adjust column width	enter text
close a workbook	preview a workbook
create a workbook	print a workbook
enter formulas	save a workbook
enter numbers	use functions

Study Questions

Multiple Choice

1. To return to the home cell from anywhere in a worksheet, press
   a. CTRL + →.
   b. PGDN.
   c. CTRL + HOME.
   d. PGUP.

2. Which Excel function calculates the total for a range of values?
   a. MIN
   b. PMT
   c. MAX
   d. SUM

3. If cell A1 is 10, cell A2 is 20, and cell A3 is 30, what value is returned by the formula =SUM(A2:A3)?
   a. 30
   b. 40
   c. 50
   d. 60

4. When you highlight a cell, =A1*2 is displayed in the formula bar. This cell contains what kind of operator?
   a. arithmetic
   b. division
   c. exponentiation
   d. multiplication

5. If the data in a cell appears truncated, what should you do to find the optimum column width?
   a. Edit the data so it is not so long.
   b. Adjust the width of all columns in the worksheet.
   c. Double-click the right border of the column displaying the truncated data.
   d. Construct a formula to calculate the optimum width.

6. When you type a formula containing a function, what must the function contain?
   a. cell references
   b. a range, indicated as such by the colon character
   c. the letters SUM
   d. one or more arguments

7. Which of the following is a valid reference to an adjacent range?
   a. A1:A1
   b. B3;C3
   c. A1:A10
   d. B1-E1

8. Cell A10 contains the following data:
        SUM(B10:LL10)
   Excel will treat this data as:
   a. text.
   b. a formula.
   c. a function.
   d. a date.

9. By default, an Excel workbook contains how many worksheets?
   a. 1
   b. 3
   c. 5
   d. 8

10. When you highlight a cell, =(D211/A7)*(C41/2) is displayed in the formula bar. This cell contains what kind of data?
    a. text
    b. a formula
    c. numbers
    d. a function

Short Answer

1. A cell contains both letters and numbers. What kind of data does it contain?

2. What is the address of the home cell?

3. Write a formula that totals the values in cell A1 to A5.

4. What is the default name for a workbook?

5. Approximately how many functions does Excel contain?

6. What are text entries in cells called when they define a worksheet's structure?

7. PMT is what kind of function?

8. What do functions always contain?

9. What should you do before printing a worksheet?

10. What should you do before closing Excel?

Fill in the Blank

1. A _____ is a predefined formula.

2. Arguments are contained inside _____.

3. All functions require _____.

4. When you save a workbook for the first time, the _____ dialog box appears.

5. The _____ function calculates the arithmetic mean for a range of values.

6. You can use Excel's _____ to fill in a data series based upon the value in an existing cell.

7. The _____ displays the results of a function as you are building it.

8. An Excel formula always begins with _____.

9. Formulas often contain _____ to perform specific calculations.

10. Cell A1 is called the _____.

For Discussion

1. List two reasons why you should use functions in formulas whenever possible.

2. How do functions differ from formulas?

3. How do text, numbers, and formulas differ?

4. How does the fill handle simplify data entry?

5. List three methods for navigating within worksheets.

Hands-On Exercises

1. Creating a Sales Summary

The Java Bar is a coffee and espresso shop located in the Selections, Inc. retail stores. Angie Stover has asked you to create a simple worksheet summarizing the first quarter sales on a weekly basis. In this exercise you will create the worksheet shown in Figure 1.29.

FIGURE 1.29

Microsoft Excel - Java Sales.xls

File Edit View Insert Format Tools Data Window Help

Arial | 10 | B I U | $ %

D11 | = | =AVERAGE(D5:D8)

	A	B	C	D	E	F
1	Java Coffee Bar					
2	First Quarter Sales					
3						
4		January	February	March	Total	Average
5	Week 1	8560	7080	7813	23453	7817.667
6	Week 2	10341	11985	9812	32138	10712.67
7	Week 3	9481	10845	10691	31017	10339
8	Week 4	12901	7609	9814	30324	10108
9						
10	Total	41283	37519	38130		
11	Average	10320.75	9379.75	9532.5		
12						

Sales summary worksheet for the Selections, Inc. Java Bar

1. Launch Excel if it is not currently running, or create a new worksheet by selecting New from the File menu.
2. Enter the text labels shown in Figure 1.29.
3. Enter the numeric data shown in the range B5:D8.
4. Enter a SUM function in cell E5 to total the Week 1 data for the quarter.
5. Use the fill handle to copy this formula through cell E8.
6. Create a formula containing a SUM function in cell B10. Copy this formula through cell D10.
7. Type **=AVERAGE(B5:D5)** in cell F5. Copy this formula through cell F8.
8. Type **=AVERAGE(B5:B8)** in cell B11. Copy this formula through cell D11.
9. Create a folder on your floppy disk named Java Bar.
10. Save your workbook to the Java Bar folder as *Java Sales.xls*. Close the workbook.

 **Web Tip**

Do you like coffee? You can order Starbucks coffee directly from the Web. For more information, visit http://www.starbucks.com.

2. Adding an Additional Worksheet to the Java Bar Workbook

Angie Stover likes the workbook you created, and now wants you to enter data for the second quarter of operations. In this exercise you will copy the existing data, paste it to a new worksheet, and change the appropriate information. Your completed worksheet appears in Figure 1.30.

FIGURE 1.30

Microsoft Excel - Java Sales - 2.xls

D11   =AVERAGE(D5:D8)

	A	B	C	D	E	F
1	Java Coffee Bar					
2	Second Quarter Sales					
3						
4		April	May	June	Total	Average
5	Week 1	8821	7127	8712	24660	8220
6	Week 2	9085	12082	10678	31845	10615
7	Week 3	10381	11634	10988	33003	11001
8	Week 4	12789	7509	9964	30262	10087.33
9						
10	Total	41076	38352	40342		
11	Average	10269	9588	10085.5		
12						

1. Launch Excel if it is not currently running.

2. Open the *Java Sales.xls* workbook you created in the previous exercise. If you do not have a copy, ask your instructor how to obtain this file.

3. Copy the range A1:F11 in Sheet1.

4. Select Sheet2 to make it the active worksheet.

5. Make cell A1 the active cell, and paste the data you just copied to the Office Clipboard.

6. Highlight the range B5:D5, and Choose Clear, Contents from the Edit menu to clear the contents of these cells. Enter the data shown in Figure 1.31.

FIGURE 1.31

Microsoft Excel - Java Sales - 2.xls

A1   = Java Coffee Bar

	A	B	C	D	E	F
1	Java Coffee Bar					
2	Second Quarter Sales					
3						
4		April	May	June	Total	Average
5	Week 1	8821	7127	8712	24660	8220
6	Week 2	9085	12082	10678	31845	10615
7	Week 3	10381	11634	10988	33003	11001
8	Week 4	12789	7509	9964	30262	10087.33
9						
10	Total	41076	38352	40342		
11	Average	10269	9588	10085.5		
12						

7. Save your workbook to the Java folder on your diskette as *Java Sales–2.xls*.

On Your Own Exercises

1. Creating a List of Web Sites

If you enter a fully registered URL into an Excel worksheet, it will be formatted as a hyperlink you can follow by simply clicking it. Search the Web for three financial or investment sites. Create a workbook listing three financial or investment sites. Enter the name of the site in column A, and the URL in column B. Save your workbook to the Investments folder with the name *Financial Sites.xls*.

2. Creating a Class Schedule

Create a workbook listing your current class schedule. Enter the day, time, name of each class, and credit hours. Create a folder on your disk named *Personal*. Save the workbook as *Class Schedule.xls*.

3. Creating a Time Card

Many students work while attending school. Create a workbook listing your time card for one week. Include the days, total hours worked, hourly rate, and gross pay. Save the workbook to your Personal folder as *Time Card.xls*.

4. Creating an Address List in Excel

Excel is often used to store lists of structured information, such as an address list. Create an address list that stores the first name, last name, address, city, zip code, and phone number for three personal contacts. Save the workbook to your Personal folder. Name the workbook *Addresses.xls*.

5. Calculating the Minimum Value in a Range

Ask your instructor or lab assistant where the file named *January Sales.xls* is located.

 **Web Tip**

If you cannot obtain a copy from your instructor, visit the SELECT Web site at http://www.prenhall.com/select to download a copy.

Modify the worksheet so that it calculates the minimum value for each department. Save your updated worksheet to the Personal folder on your disk. Name the updated workbook *January – Update 1.xls*.

6. Conducting a "What-If" Analysis

Open the workbook named *Utility Costs.xls* from your network or disk.

 **Web Tip**

If you cannot obtain a copy from your instructor, visit the SELECT Web site at
http://www.prenhall.com/select to download a copy.

Modify the worksheet so that it calculates all utility costs if the price of
electricity and natural gas is increased by 10% and 15%, respectively. Save
your updated workbook to your Personal folder as *Updated Utility Costs.xls*.

Modifying Worksheets and Workbooks

Now that you have created the Selections, Inc. Sales Summary workbook, you can modify it so that it is easier to use and provides more information. In this project you will enhance the functionality of the workbook by adding worksheets for additional sales regions, deleting worksheets you no longer need, and repositioning the worksheets in the workbook. In addition, you will move, copy, and delete data, and create formulas that share information among worksheets in the Sales Summary workbook.

Objectives

After completing this project, you will be able to:

➤ Open an Excel workbook

➤ Insert worksheets into a workbook

➤ Delete worksheets from a workbook

➤ Change the position of worksheets in a workbook

➤ Edit worksheets by copying and moving data

➤ Edit worksheets by revising data

➤ Enter additional text and number data into a workbook

➤ Create 3-D formulas that link information among worksheets

Running Case

Mr. Traylor is pleased with the progress you have made so far. He enthusiastically accepted your initial design, and now wants you to finish defining the structure of your workbook to include quarterly sales for the remaining sales regions, and a summary of sales for all regions.

The Challenge

The regional worksheets need to be in order by region (North, South, East, West), with the summary worksheet appearing first in the workbook. The summary sales worksheet must contain formulas that dynamically list the regional sales data, so if the figures change for one or more regions, the changes are automatically reflected in the summary. When you are finished updating the workbook, Mr. Traylor will review your changes and approve the next phase of design.

The Strategy

You can easily add worksheets to the workbook and then enter the appropriate data, create formulas, and modify the workbook structure by deleting any extra worksheets and ordering the remaining ones.

You can create 3-D linking formulas to dynamically include all regional sales data in the Sales Summary worksheet. Your workbook will look similar to the one shown in Figure 2.1 after you complete this project.

FIGURE 2.1

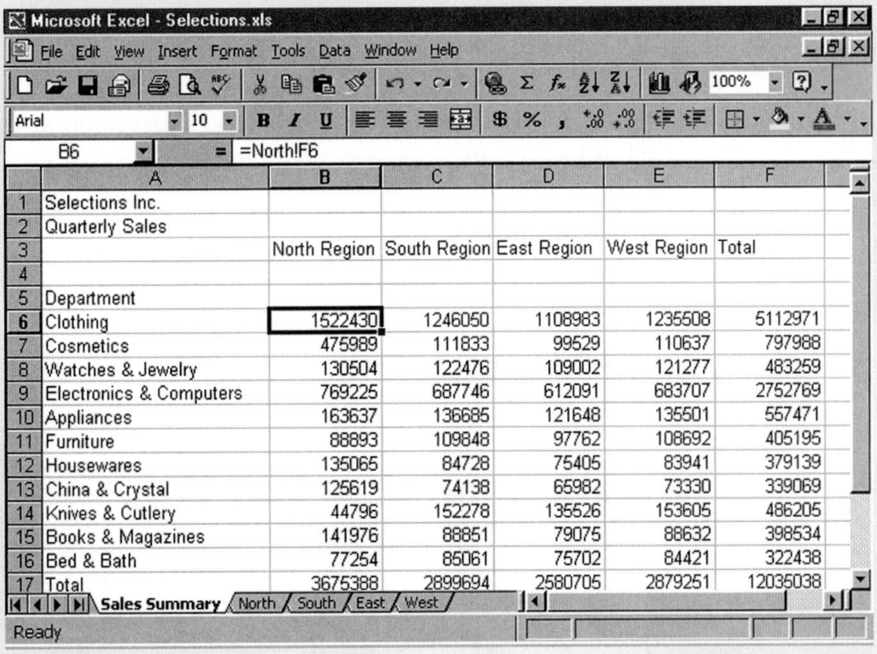

	A	B	C	D	E	F
1	Selections Inc.					
2	Quarterly Sales					
3		North Region	South Region	East Region	West Region	Total
4						
5	Department					
6	Clothing	1522430	1246050	1108983	1235508	5112971
7	Cosmetics	475989	111833	99529	110637	797988
8	Watches & Jewelry	130504	122476	109002	121277	483259
9	Electronics & Computers	769225	687746	612091	683707	2752769
10	Appliances	163637	136685	121648	135501	557471
11	Furniture	88893	109848	97762	108692	405195
12	Housewares	135065	84728	75405	83941	379139
13	China & Crystal	125619	74138	65982	73330	339069
14	Knives & Cutlery	44796	152278	135526	153605	486205
15	Books & Magazines	141976	88851	79075	88632	398534
16	Bed & Bath	77254	85061	75702	84421	322438
17	Total	3675388	2899694	2580705	2879251	12035038

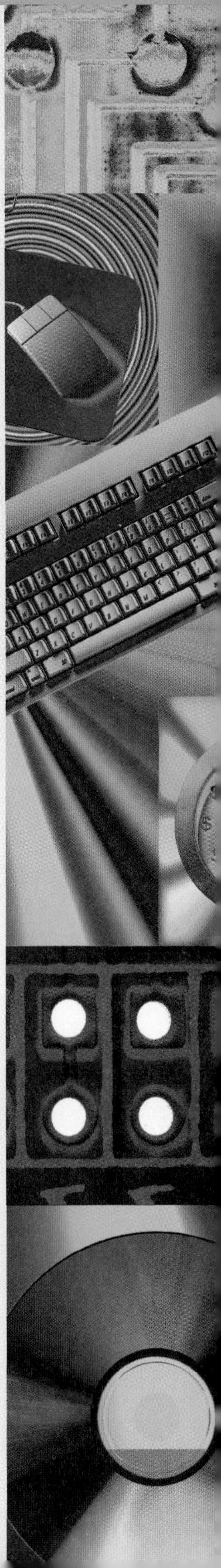

The Setup

Launch Microsoft Excel and make sure that you select the Excel settings listed in Table 2.1. This will ensure that your screen matches the illustrations and that the tasks in this project function as described.

Table 2.1

Location	Make these settings:
Office Shortcut Bar	Right-click the Office icon on the shortcut bar and click Exit.
Office Assistant	Hide the Assistant.
Tools, Customize	Click the Options tab and deselect the option to show recently used menu commands first. Deselect the option to display the Standard and Formatting toolbars on one row.
Tools, Options	Click the Edit tab and select Move selection after Enter.
View, Formula Bar	Display the formula bar.
View, Status Bar	Display the status bar.
View, Normal	View the workbook in Normal view.
Maximize	Maximize the application and workbook windows.

Opening a Workbook

Before you can modify your workbook, you must open it. To open an existing workbook you must specify the file name and location.

TASK 1: To Open an Excel Workbook

1 Select Open from the File menu.

2 In the File Open dialog box, select drive A.

> **TROUBLESHOOTING** If you saved your workbook to another location at the conclusion of Project 1, select the appropriate drive letter.

3 Open the Selections folder by double-clicking it, highlight the *Selections.xls* file, and click Open, as shown in Figure 2.2. Depending on your settings, your screen may differ slightly.

FIGURE 2.2

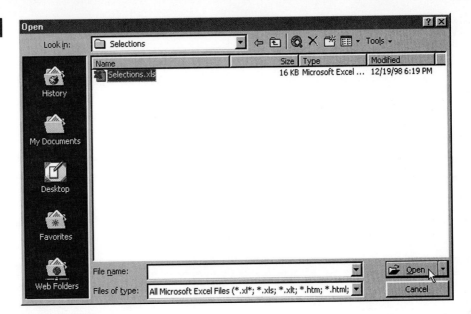

4 Excel opens your workbook.

Working with Worksheets

You will recall from "Introduction to Excel 2000" that an Excel workbook contains one or more worksheets. A workbook with multiple worksheets is useful for a variety of reasons. First, multiple worksheets allow you to keep related but distinct business data in one electronic file. Second, most workbooks contain data for multiple entities, and will often contain charts or graphics as additional worksheets. Finally, Excel supports **_linking formulas_**, whereby you can link data among worksheets to create three-dimensional data models and solutions. A **_3-D workbook_** has multiple worksheets containing one or more linking formulas.

You can easily add, delete, rename, and reposition worksheets in a workbook. You will recall that each worksheet is represented by a sheet tab, which you can select to edit or print the worksheet.

Web Tip

Are you new to Microsoft Excel, but know how to use Lotus 1-2-3? The site http://msdn.microsoft.com/library/officedev/office/orkhtml/018.htm has information about how Excel and Lotus differ.

Editing a Workbook by Inserting Worksheets

Adding worksheets to a workbook is a common task. When you add worksheets to an existing workbook, they will be inserted into the workbook immediately before the current worksheet. Once you enter a worksheet, you can easily rename its tab and change its position.

TASK 2: To Insert Worksheets into the Current Workbook

1 Select Worksheet from the Insert menu. Excel adds a worksheet named Sheet4, as shown in Figure 2.3.

FIGURE 2.3

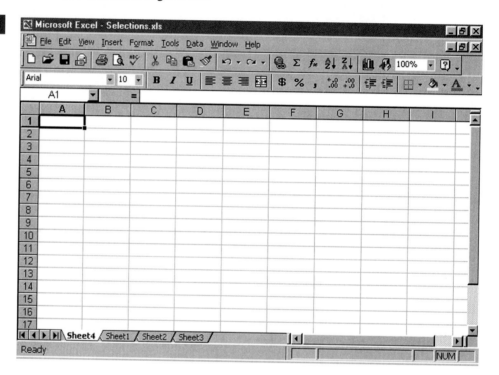

2 Right-click the Sheet4 tab, as shown in Figure 2.4.

FIGURE 2.4

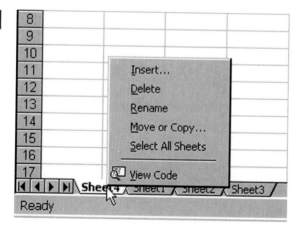

3 Choose Insert from the shortcut menu.

4 Select Worksheet from the Insert dialog box, as shown in Figure 2.5.

FIGURE 2.5

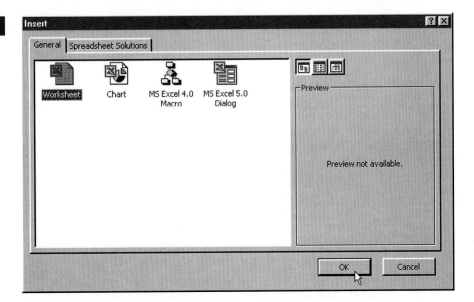

> **TROUBLESHOOTING** If you do not see an icon representing a general worksheet, make sure the General tab is active.

5 Click OK. Sheet5 is now added to the workbook.

6 Using either method just shown, add an additional worksheet to the workbook.

Renaming Worksheets

Excel provides two methods for renaming worksheets using the worksheet tabs. You can either double-click a worksheet tab and type a new name, or right-click the worksheet tab and select Rename from the menu.

TASK 3: To Rename Worksheets

1 Place the insertion point directly over the Sheet1 worksheet tab.

2 Right-click.

3 Select Rename from the shortcut menu.

4 Type **North**. The worksheet tab is renamed, as shown in Figure 2.6.

FIGURE 2.6

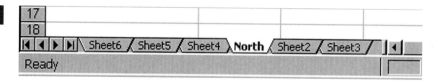

5 Double-click the Sheet2 tab.

6 Type **South** as the worksheet name.

7 Rename the Sheet3, Sheet4, and Sheet5 tabs **East**, **West**, and **Sales Summary**, respectively. Your worksheet appears as shown in Figure 2.7.

FIGURE 2.7

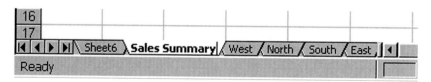

8 Press (ENTER) to accept the last tab name. Save the workbook.

> **TIP** You cannot revert to a previous worksheet tab name using Undo.

Deleting Worksheets

As you might expect, there will be times when you will need to delete worksheets from a workbook. This is a destructive task, and once you delete a worksheet and then save the workbook, there is no way to recover the deleted sheet. Before deleting a worksheet, Excel will verify your intent to do so.

TASK 4: To Delete a Worksheet

1 Select the Sheet6 tab by clicking it.

2 Select Delete Sheet from the Edit menu, as shown in Figure 2.8.

FIGURE 2.8

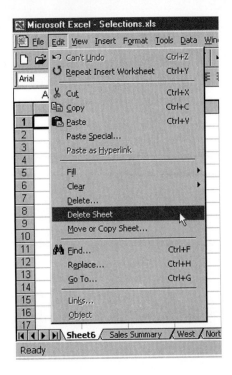

3 The dialog box shown in Figure 2.9 appears. Click OK to permanently delete the worksheet.

FIGURE 2.9

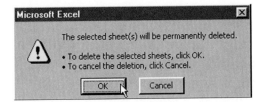

4 The worksheet has now been deleted from the workbook. Save your changes.

> **TIP** You can also delete a worksheet by right-clicking the worksheet tab and selecting Delete from the shortcut menu. If you ever inadvertently delete a worksheet that you need, close the file without saving the workbook, and then reopen the file.

Repositioning Worksheets in a Workbook

In Excel, you can easily change the position of a worksheet in a workbook. You may need to do this when the order of the worksheets represents some logical order, such as fiscal quarters, days, or months. At other times, a specific order is desired to assist users in navigating among worksheets using the controls.

TASK 5: <u>To Change the Order of Worksheet Tabs</u>

1 Click the West worksheet tab to select it.

2 Hold down the left mouse button and drag the worksheet tab to the right of the East worksheet. Notice the icon next to the mouse pointer indicating that a move operation is in progress, and the pointer displaying the new worksheet position, as shown Figure 2.10.

FIGURE 2.10

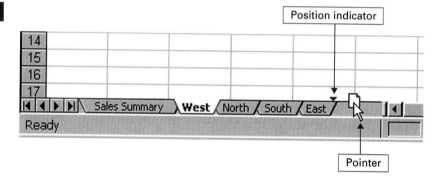

3 Release the left mouse button. The worksheet tabs are now reordered, as shown in Figure 2.11.

FIGURE 2.11

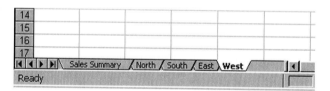

> **TIP** You can also change the position of worksheets by selecting Move or Copy Sheet from the Edit menu, or by right-clicking the worksheet tab and selecting Move or Copy.

4 Save the workbook.

Check Point

Can you remember two methods for renaming worksheets and the procedure for changing their position in a workbook? You can rename worksheet tabs by double-clicking and right-clicking. You can quickly reposition worksheets in a workbook using drag-and-drop.

Editing Worksheet Data

When you are constructing electronic workbooks, you often must enter additional data or change the location of existing data in worksheets. Editing is distinct from formatting: editing includes changing workbook data by copying, moving, or revising text, numbers, and formulas. Formatting, which you will learn in Project 3, changes the way workbook data appears for display and printing, without changing the underlying data.

Editing Worksheets by Copying and Moving Data

When constructing a 3-D workbook it is often possible to enter data in one location and then copy it to additional locations. For example, the column headings in the range B4 to F4 and the department headings in A4 to A16 will be the same for the regional worksheets. The department headings will also appear in the Sales Summary worksheet.

Copying Worksheet Data

You can easily complete the structure of your workbook by copying the existing text labels. Before copying data, you must **select**, or highlight, the data you want to copy. The data you select is a **range** consisting of one or more cells. The ranges you select can include **adjacent cells**, which is a continuous range, or **non-adjacent cells**, which is a selection of more than one continuous range.

A new feature in Office 2000 is the **Office Clipboard**. The Office Clipboard differs from the Windows Clipboard in that the Office Clipboard holds up to 12 items, where the Windows Clipboard holds only one item. When using the Office Clipboard, you can store up to 12 items from any Office application. Each item appears on the Office Clipboard, which you can display as a toolbar.

> **TIP**   For copy operations in Excel, you must work with a single adjacent range. For formatting procedures, you can work with non-adjacent selections.

TASK 6:   To Copy Ranges

1   Click the North worksheet tab to make it the active sheet.

2   Click cell B4 and drag the selection through cell F4, as shown in Figure 2.12.

FIGURE 2.12

	A	B	C	D	E	F
		1R x 5C ▾	=	1st Qtr.		
1	Selections Inc.					
2	Quarterly Sales					
3						
4	Department	1st Qtr.	2nd Qtr.	3rd Qtr.	4th Qtr.	Total
5	Clothing	405112	321670	401934	393714	1522430
6	Cosmetics	373211	34812	29718	38248	475989

3 Click the Copy 🖺 button on the Standard toolbar. You will notice a marquee surrounding the selection, indicating that data is now on the Office Clipboard. In addition, the status bar instructs you to select a destination for the copy procedure, as shown in Figure 2.13.

FIGURE 2.13

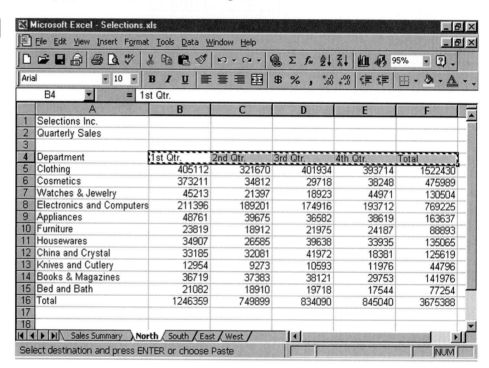

4 Click the South worksheet tab and select cell B4. This indicates the upper-left cell of the selection that will be pasted into this worksheet.

5 Press the (SHIFT) key and click the West worksheet tab. The range of worksheets shown in Figure 2.14 is now selected.

FIGURE 2.14

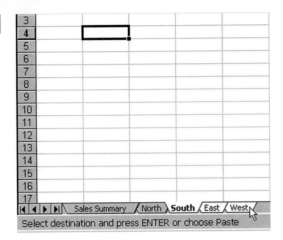

6 Click the Paste 📋 button on the Standard toolbar. The range has been pasted into each selected worksheet.

7 Click the North worksheet tab, highlight the range A4 to A16, and click the Copy 📋 button. The Clipboard toolbar appears.

8 Click the South worksheet tab and place the insertion point in cell A4.

9 Press (SHIFT), click the West worksheet tab, and click the Paste 📋 button.

10 Click the Sales Summary worksheet tab, select cell A4, and click Paste 📋.

11 Click the Sales Summary worksheet tab, press the (CTRL) key, and click the South, East, and West worksheet tabs, respectively. The non-adjacent range of worksheets shown in Figure 2.15 is now selected.

FIGURE 2.15

12 Double-click the border between columns A and B. Column A for each worksheet is resized.

Check Point

What does this double-click procedure do? It resizes column A in each se-lected worksheet to display the widest entry.

13 Select cell A1, press the (SHIFT) key, and click the Sales Summary worksheet tab to deselect the highlighted range in the selected worksheets.

14 Save the workbook.

TASK 7: To Copy an Additional Range

1 Select the range A1 to A2 in the North worksheet.

2 Copy the range to the Clipboard.

> **TIP** The selected data is added to the Office Clipboard.

3 Select the Sales Summary worksheet tab and place the insertion point in cell A1.

4 Press the (CTRL) key and click the South, East, and West worksheet tabs.

5 Paste the selection into the destination cells.

6 Select cell A1, press the (SHIFT) key, and click the Sales Summary worksheet tab.

7 Hide the Office Clipboard and save the workbook.

> **TIP** If you make a mistake while copying and pasting data, you can reverse your actions using Undo, as follows:
> * To undo recent actions one at a time, click Undo 🔄.
> * To undo several actions at once, click the arrow next to Undo 🔄 and se-lect from the list. Microsoft Excel reverses the selected action and all ac-tions above it.
> * To cancel an entry in a cell or the formula bar before you press (ENTER), press (ESC).
> If you change your mind, click Redo 🔄.

Break Point

If necessary you can save your file, exit Excel, and continue this project later.

Moving Worksheet Data

Although you have successfully copied text labels, the structure of the workbook is not quite complete. To make the data on each worksheet easier to understand, you should add a text label for each regional worksheet, and for the Sales Summary sheet as well. To make room for this entry, you will need to move the existing worksheet data. You will add data to this row when you enter the remaining sales figures.

TASK 8:   To Move Ranges

1   Launch Excel if it is not currently running, and open the *Selections.xls* workbook.

2   Click the Sales Summary worksheet tab, press the (SHIFT) key, and click the West worksheet tab to select all worksheets in the workbook.

3   Highlight the range A4 to F16, as shown in Figure 2.16.

> **TIP**   The word *Group* in the title bar indicates that your actions will be applied to multiple worksheets.

FIGURE 2.16

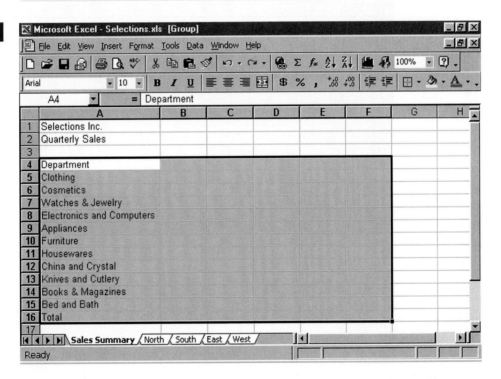

4   Point to any border of the selection and click with the left mouse button.

5   Drag the selection down one row, as shown in Figure 2.17. As you drag, notice the shaded border surrounding the selection you are moving, and the verification of the range you are currently moving.

FIGURE 2.17

3						
4	Department					A5:F17
5	Clothing					
6	Cosmetics					
7	Watches & Jewelry					
8	Electronics and Computers					
9	Appliances					
10	Furniture					
11	Housewares					
12	China and Crystal					
13	Knives and Cutlery					
14	Books & Magazines					
15	Bed and Bath					
16	Total					
17						
18						
19						

6 Drop the selection in its new location by releasing the mouse button. The range of cells has been moved, as shown in Figure 2.18. The range A4:F16 on each of the selected worksheets appears in this new location.

FIGURE 2.18

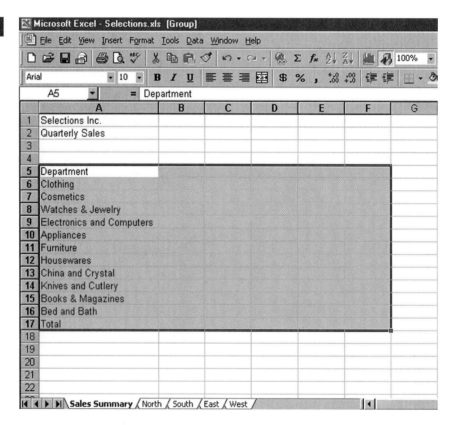

7 Select cell A1, press the (SHIFT) key, and click the Sales Summary worksheet tab to deselect the worksheet selection.

8 Save the workbook.

Editing Worksheets by Revising Existing Data

Another common workbook editing task is revising existing worksheet data. To edit existing data you highlight the cell and either type a new value and press (ENTER), or use the formula bar to change the existing data. In your workbook for Selections, Inc., the product descriptions are inconsistent in the use of the word *and* in the description, a problem that can quickly be remedied.

TASK 9:   To Revise Existing Worksheet Data

1 Select cell A9 of the Sales Summary worksheet.

2 Press the (SHIFT) key and click the West worksheet tab to select all worksheets in the workbook. Release the (SHIFT) key after making the selection.

Check Point

Why in this case are you selecting each worksheet in the workbook? Because the text labels requiring revision appear on every worksheet.

3 Select Replace from the Edit menu. The Replace dialog box appears.

4 Type **and** in the Find What: text box and **&** in the Replace with: text box, as shown in Figure 2.19.

FIGURE 2.19

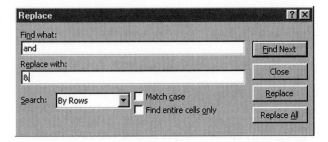

5 Click the Replace All button. The replacement is made for each worksheet in the workbook.

6 Click the North worksheet tab and select cell A1 to verify the changes. The worksheet appears, as shown in Figure 2.20.

FIGURE 2.20

	A	B	C	D	E	F	G	H	I
1	Selections Inc.								
2	Quarterly Sales								
3	North Region								
4									
5	Department	1st Qtr.	2nd Qtr.	3rd Qtr.	4th Qtr.	Total			
6	Clothing	405112	321670	401934	393714	1522430			
7	Cosmetics	373211	34812	29718	38248	475989			
8	Watches & Jewelry	45213	21397	18923	44971	130504			
9	Electronics & Computers	211396	189201	174916	193712	769225			
10	Appliances	48761	39675	36582	38619	163637			
11	Furniture	23819	18912	21975	24187	88893			
12	Housewares	34907	26585	39638	33935	135065			
13	China & Crystal	33185	32081	41972	18381	125619			
14	Knives & Cutlery	12954	9273	10593	11976	44796			
15	Books & Magazines	36719	37383	38121	29753	141976			
16	Bed & Bath	21082	18910	19718	17544	77254			
17	Total	1246359	749899	834090	845040	3675388			
18									
19									

7 Save the workbook.

Entering Additional Text and Number Data

You are now ready to complete the workbook structure by entering the remaining text labels. Then you will enter sales figures for the South, East, and West sales regions. Once these tasks are complete, you will be ready to enter the remaining formulas.

TASK 10: To Enter Additional Text and Numeric Data

1 Type **North Region**, **South Region**, **East Region**, **West Region**, and **Total** in cells B3 through F3, respectively.

> **TIP** Remember that you can use (TAB) or the right directional arrow to move one cell to the right as you enter data into a worksheet.

2 Select columns B through F and change the column widths to 11.00.

3 Select cell A3 of the North worksheet, and type **North Region** as the text label.

4 Type **South Region**, **East Region** and **West Region** in cell A3 of the South, East, and West worksheets, respectively.

5 Change the column widths of columns B through F of the South, East, and West worksheets to 11.00.

Checkpoint

How can you change all column widths simultaneously? First select the worksheets, then the columns, and then change the width of one column in the selection.

6 Using Figure 2.21 as a guide, enter the sales figures for the South region into the South worksheet.

FIGURE 2.21

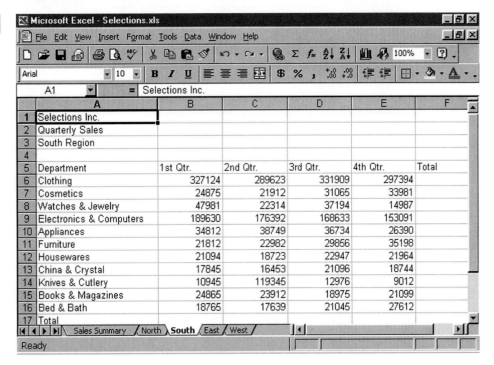

7 Enter the data shown in Figure 2.22 into the East worksheet.

FIGURE 2.22

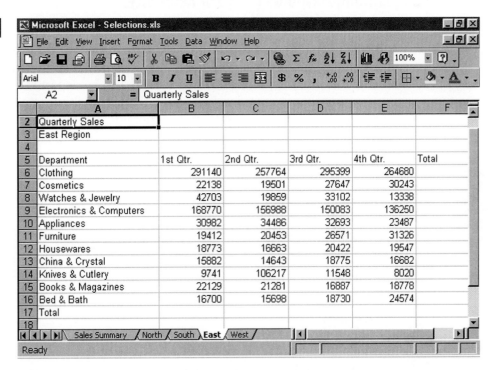

8 Enter the data shown in Figure 2.23 into the West worksheet.

FIGURE 2.23

	A	B	C	D	E	F
1	Selections Inc.					
2	Quarterly Sales					
3	West Region					
4						
5	Department	1st Qtr.	2nd Qtr.	3rd Qtr.	4th Qtr.	Total
6	Clothing	338246	294546	301605	301111	
7	Cosmetics	25720	22284	28228	34405	
8	Watches & Jewelry	49612	22693	33798	15174	
9	Electronics & Computers	196077	179390	153236	155004	
10	Appliances	35995	39407	33380	26719	
11	Furniture	22553	23372	27130	35637	
12	Housewares	21811	19041	20851	22238	
13	China & Crystal	18451	16732	19169	18978	
14	Knives & Cutlery	11317	121373	11791	9124	
15	Books & Magazines	25710	24318	17242	21362	
16	Bed & Bath	19403	17938	19123	27957	
17	Total					

Tabs: Sales Summary / North / South / East / **West**

Cell A1: Selections Inc.

9 Save the workbook.

Constructing Linking Formulas with 3-D References

You are almost finished designing the text, numbers, and formulas for the *Selections, Inc.* workbook. You do, however, have a few more formulas to create. You will first enter the necessary formulas containing the SUM function to total the sales figures by quarter and also by department for each sales region. After these are complete, you will add linking formulas to the workbook. Linking formulas are formulas containing 3-D references, which display data from one part of the workbook in another.

TASK 11: To Create Formulas Containing the SUM Function on Multiple Worksheets Simultaneously

1 Select cell F6 of the South worksheet.

2 Press the (SHIFT) key and click the West worksheet tab to select three worksheets.

3 Type **=SUM(B6:E6)** in the cell.

4 Click the Enter Formula ✓ button on the formula bar to accept the formula, as shown in Figure 2.24.

FIGURE 2.24

	SUM	▼	X	✓	=	=sum(B6:E6)	
	B		C	D	E	F	G
1			Enter				
2							
3							
4							
5	1st Qtr.	2nd Qtr.		3rd Qtr.	4th Qtr.	Total	
6	327124	289623		331909	297394	=sum(B6:E6)	
7	24875	21912		31065	33981		

5 Use the fill handle to copy the formula through row 16, as shown in Figure 2.25.

FIGURE 2.25

	F6	▼	=	=SUM(B6:E6)			
	B	C	D	E	F	G	
1							
2							
3							
4							
5	1st Qtr.	2nd Qtr.	3rd Qtr.	4th Qtr.	Total		
6	327124	289623	331909	297394	1246050		
7	24875	21912	31065	33981			
8	47981	22314	37194	14987			
9	189630	176392	168633	153091			
10	34812	38749	36734	26390			
11	21812	22982	29856	35198			
12	21094	18723	22947	21964			
13	17845	16453	21096	18744			
14	10945	119345	12976	9012			
15	24865	23912	18975	21099			
16	18765	17639	21045	27612			
17							

6 Release the mouse button and select cell A1.

7 Click the North worksheet tab.

8 Save your workbook.

TASK 12: Creating 3-D References

1 Select the range F6:F16 in the North worksheet.

2 Click Copy 📋.

3 Click the Sales Summary worksheet tab.

4 Place the insertion point in cell B6.

5 Choose Paste Special from the Edit menu, as shown in Figure 2.26.

FIGURE 2.26

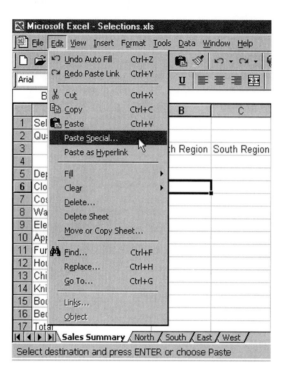

6 The Paste Special dialog box appears. Click the Paste Link button, as shown in Figure 2.27.

FIGURE 2.27

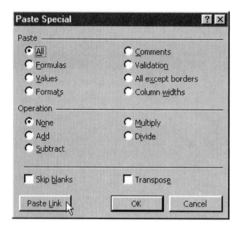

TROUBLESHOOTING Make sure you click the Paste Link button to create a linking formula!

7 Repeat the procedure outlined in the preceding steps to create linking formulas between column F of the South, East, and West worksheets, respectively.

TROUBLESHOOTING Make sure you select Paste Special from the Edit menu and click the Paste Link button to create the linking formulas.

8 When you are finished, the worksheet should display the values shown in Figure 2.28.

TROUBLESHOOTING If your values differ, check the formulas and values you have entered for errors.

FIGURE 2.28

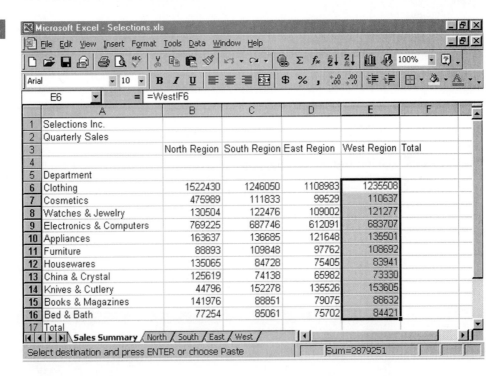

9   Save the workbook.

Notice the syntax for the formula displayed in Figure 2.28. The formula begins with an equal sign, as all formulas do, but the cell reference is preceded by the name of the worksheet, followed by an exclamation point. This formula is a dynamic link; if the value in cell F6 of the West workbook changes, the correct value will be displayed here.

 **Web Tip**

In the previous task you linked data between Excel worksheets. For future reference, you can also share information between Excel and Access. If you do not need to update the data between applications, you can paste data between applications. See http://www.microsoft.com/magazine/oct1998/zd-net/exchange.htm for more information.

Entering Formulas to Sum the Sales Summary Data

To complete your workbook, you need to create formulas containing the SUM function in cells F6:F16 and B17:F17. You can complete this task by creating one formula in each range, and then use the fill handle to replicate it.

TASK 13: Creating Formulas to Sum the Sales Summary Data

1 Place the insertion point in cell F6 of the Sales Summary worksheet.

2 Type **=SUM(B6:E6)**, and click the Enter Formula button to accept the formula.

> **TIP** In Excel, formulas are not case sensitive. You may enter formulas with upper or lower case letters.

3 Using the fill handle, copy this formula through cell F16.

4 Type **=SUM(B6:B16)** in cell B17 and press (ENTER).

5 Use the fill handle to copy this formula through cell F17.

6 Chance the width of columns B through F to 12.00.

7 Select cell A1 and save the workbook. Your screen should now appear as shown in Figure 2.29.

FIGURE 2.29

Microsoft Excel - Selections.xls

File Edit View Insert Format Tools Data Window Help

Arial   10   **B** *I* U

A1   =   Selections Inc.

	A	B	C	D	E	F
1	Selections Inc.					
2	Quarterly Sales					
3		North Region	South Region	East Region	West Region	Total
4						
5	Department					
6	Clothing	1522430	1246050	1108983	1235508	5112971
7	Cosmetics	475989	111833	99529	110637	797988
8	Watches & Jewelry	130504	122476	109002	121277	483259
9	Electronics & Computers	769225	687746	612091	683707	2752769
10	Appliances	163637	136685	121648	135501	557471
11	Furniture	88893	109848	97762	108692	405195
12	Housewares	135065	84728	75405	83941	379139
13	China & Crystal	125619	74138	65982	73330	339069
14	Knives & Cutlery	44796	152278	135526	153605	486205
15	Books & Magazines	141976	88851	79075	88632	398534
16	Bed & Bath	77254	85061	75702	84421	322438
17	Total	3675388	2899694	2580705	2879251	12035038

Sales Summary / North / South / East / West /

Ready

8 Close the workbook and exit Excel.

Summary and Exercises

Summary

- Modifying a workbook's structure includes adding worksheets, deleting worksheets, and repositioning worksheets.
- You can rename worksheet tabs to identify each worksheet's contents.
- Editing includes additions and changes to the data contained in workbooks.
- 3-D linking formulas display results from one cell in another worksheet cell.

Key Terms and Operations

Key Terms

adjacent cells
Enter Formula button
linking formulas
non-adjacent cells
Office Clipboard

range
row header
select
selection
3-D workbook

Operations

change the position of
    worksheets
copy ranges using the Office
    Clipboard
create formulas to total linked
    data
delete worksheets

insert linking formulas
insert worksheets into a
    workbook
move ranges
open a workbook
revise ranges

Study Questions

Multiple Choice

1. A workbook contains five worksheets. Which key would you press to select the first, third, and fifth worksheet in the workbook?
   a. ENTER
   b. SHIFT
   c. DEL
   d. CTRL

2. Which menu adds worksheets to a workbook?
   a. the Edit menu
   b. a shortcut menu
   c. the Insert menu
   d. b and c

3. Which statement is false?
   a. Once you delete a worksheet from a workbook, it cannot be restored.
   b. You can restore a deleted worksheet using the Undo menu.
   c. If you delete a worksheet from a workbook but do not update the file, you can open the old version and retain the deleted worksheet.
   d. Deleting worksheets is considered a destructive command.

4. You can easily reposition a worksheet in a workbook using
   a. the View menu.
   b. clicking and dragging.
   c. the File menu.
   d. a and b.

5. You can edit the contents of a cell using
   a. the View menu.
   b. the status bar.
   c. the formula bar.
   d. the (CTRL) key.

6. 3-D references always contain all but which of the following?
   a. an equal (=) sign
   b. an exclamation point (!)
   c. an ampersand (&)
   d. the sheet name

7. A linking formula creates which kind of link?
   a. dynamic
   b. static
   c. fixed
   d. movable

8. What happens if you delete a worksheet from a workbook and update the file?
   a. The workbook is irretrievably lost.
   b. The workbook can be restored using Undo.
   c. The worksheet is saved to a backup file.
   d. The workbook is renamed.

9. A selection that contains data from cell A1 to A5, and also from cell C10 to D10, is called a(n)
   a. adjacent selection.
   b. range.
   c. non-adjacent selection.
   d. linking formula.

10. 3-D references will always begin with
    a. an exclamation point.
    b. an asterisk.
    c. an ampersand.
    d. an equals sign.

Short Answer

1. When you change the location of data in a worksheet, are you editing or formatting?
2. Which method quickly changes the location of a worksheet in a workbook?
3. 3-D references always include which character after the sheet name?
4. What does it mean if you see an exclamation point and a worksheet name in a formula?
5. Can a deleted worksheet be restored using Undo?
6. How can you quickly change the contents of a cell?
7. If you delete a worksheet but do not save the file, can you retrieve the worksheet?
8. To create a 3-D reference, which option under the Edit menu do you select?
9. What is a link?
10. How do you rename a worksheet tab without using a menu?

Fill in the Blank

1. A _____ formula dynamically links data from one worksheet cell to another.
2. A linking formula contains the _____ character between the worksheet name and cell reference.
3. You can easily rename a worksheet tab by _____ and typing a new name.
4. To insert a worksheet into a workbook, select _____ from the Insert menu.
5. A selection of cells is called a _____.
6. In a(n) _____ range, the cell range is continuous.
7. In a(n) _____ range, the selection includes multiple ranges.
8. To select a non-adjacent range of worksheets, press the _____ key while you add each worksheet to the selection.
9. To select an adjacent range of worksheets, press the _____ key as you click each worksheet tab.
10. You can change the position of a worksheet in a workbook by _____ the worksheet tab to a new location.

For Discussion

1. How does an adjacent selection differ from a non-adjacent selection?
2. How does editing differ from formatting?
3. Why might you want to select multiple worksheets when modifying workbooks?
4. What happens to the data in a 3-D reference if the source data changes?
5. How do linking formulas differ from other formulas you have created?

Hands-On Exercises

Web Tip

If you cannot obtain a copy of these files from your instructor, visit the SELECT Web site at http://www.prenhall.com/select.

1. Adding a Worksheet to the Java Sales Workbook

Angie Stover has asked you to add a summary worksheet to the Java Sales workbook you created in Project 1. Using the procedures you learned in this project, create the structure of the Sales Summary worksheet. The additional worksheet is shown in Figure 2.30.

FIGURE 2.30

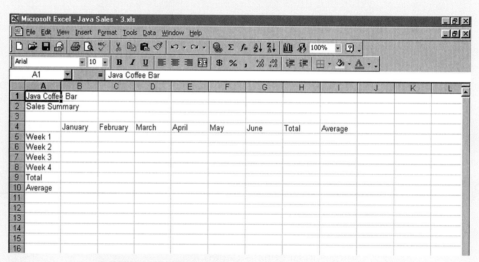

Sales Summary worksheet for Java Sales

1. Launch Excel if it is not currently running.
2. Open the *Java Sales—2.xls* workbook in the Java Bar folder on your disk.
3. Rename the Sheet3 tab as *Sales Summary*.
4. Reposition the Sales Summary worksheet so it appears at the first sheet in the workbook.
5. Add the text labels shown in Figure 2.30.
6. Save the workbook as *Java Sales—3.xls*.

2. Adding Linking Formulas to the Sales Summary Worksheet

In this exercise you will link formulas to the Sales Summary worksheet that you added to the Java Sales workbook in the previous exercise. When you finish adding these formulas, the Sales Summary worksheet appears as shown in Figure 2.31.

FIGURE 2.31

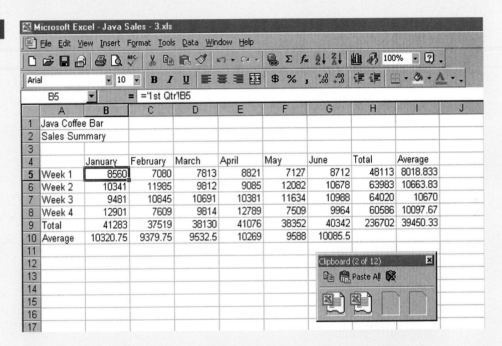

1. Open the *Java Sales—3.xls* workbook, if it is not currently open.
2. Choose Toolbars from the View menu, and select Clipboard.
3. Copy the range the range B5:D8 in the 1st Qtr worksheet. The selection appears on the Office Clipboard, as shown in Figure 2.32.

FIGURE 2.32

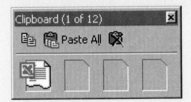

TIP As you add copy additional items, they will be added to the Office Clipboard.

4. Use Paste Special, Paste Link to paste this data beginning in cell B5 of the Sales Summary worksheet.
5. Repeat this procedure to paste the sales figures from April, May, and June to the Sales Summary worksheet. Make sure you create linking formulas!

6. Create the necessary formulas to calculate the total and average weekly and monthly data.

7. Save the workbook as *Java Sales—4.xls*.

8. Close the workbook.

On Your Own Exercises

1. Summarizing a List of Web Sites

Open the *Financial Sites.xls* workbook you created in Project 1. Edit the workbook so it contains four additional sites. Save the workbook to the Investments folder with the name *Financial Sites 2.xls*.

2. Creating a Class Schedule

Open the *Class Schedule.xls* workbook you created in Project 1. Add a summary page at the beginning of the workbook that summarizes your class schedule by day. Include linking formulas to list the class data. Save the workbook as *Class Schedule—By Day.xls*.

3. Create a Time Card

Open the *Time Card.xls* workbook. Add payroll data from an additional week, and then create a worksheet that summarizes the gross pay information for each week. Save the workbook as *Time Cards—Weekly Summary.xls*.

4. Creating an Address List in Excel

Open the *Address.xls* workbook. Add three professional contacts. Then create two additional worksheets for listing the personal versus professional contacts on two separate worksheet plys. Save the workbook as *Updated Addresses.xls*.

5. Calculating the Minimum Value in a Range

Open the file *January—update1.xls* you created in Project 1.

Web Tip

If you cannot obtain a copy from your instructor, visit the SELECT Web site at http://www.prenhall.com/select to download a copy.

Modify the worksheet so that it summarizes the minimum value for each department on a separate worksheet in the workbook. Save the updated workbook as *January—Update 2.xls*.

6. Modifying a "What-If" Analysis

Open the workbook named *Updated Utility Costs.xls* from your network or floppy disk.

Modify the worksheet so that it displays a summary of the 10% and 15% utility price increase estimates. Save the updated workbook to your Personal folder as *Summary of Updated Utility Costs.xls*.

Formatting Worksheets and Workbooks

Now that you have completed the structure of the Selections Sales Summary workbook, it is time to enhance its appearance by applying formats to the cells. Cell formats make it easier to interpret the data in a worksheet, and include tasks such as changing the format of numeric data, adding borders around specific cells, and applying shading to highlight important elements.

Objectives

After completing this project, you will be able to:

➤ Apply number formats

➤ Apply font formats

➤ Change cell alignment

➤ Create and apply styles

➤ Work with rows and columns

➤ Format cells with borders and shading

➤ Use the Web Page Preview

Running Case

When you complete this project, the Selections Sales Summary workbook will be ready to publish to the company's corporate Intranet. Mr. Traylor has reviewed your most recent revisions to the Selections, Inc. Sales Summary workbook. He agrees that the structure is sound, and now wants you to format the workbook so it is more visually appealing. Specifically, Mr. Traylor wants all currency values to be displayed as such, with no decimal places.

The Challenge

For consistency with current reports, Mr. Traylor wants each regional worksheet to look like accounting "green bar" paper, and the Sales Summary sheet to utilize shading, borders, and font styles appropriate for the Web.

The Strategy

Excel includes numerous features and tools for simplifying formatting. Since the four regional worksheets share a common structure, you can apply formats to the North worksheet, and then copy these formats to each additional regional worksheet. For the Sales Summary worksheet, you will want to think about fonts, borders, and shading options that will display well in a Web browser. Using the Web preview, you can see how your formats will display in a browser. Figure 3.1 displays the Sales Summary worksheet, and Figure 3.2 the North regional sales worksheet, as they will appear prior to exporting to the Web.

FIGURE 3.1

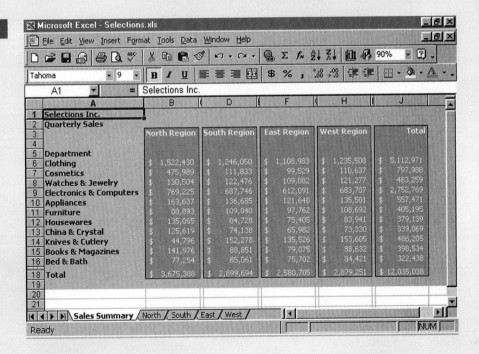

FIGURE 3.2

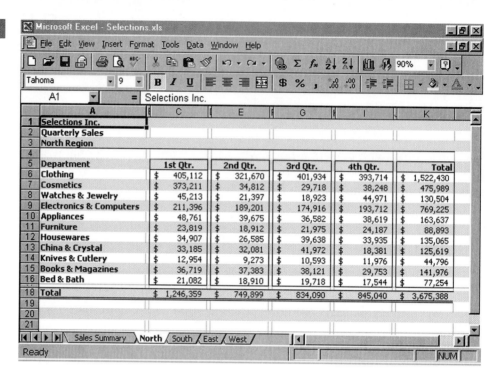

The Setup

Launch Microsoft Excel and select the Excel settings listed in Table 3.1. This will ensure that your screen matches the illustrations and that the tasks in this project function as described.

Table 3.1

Location	Make these settings:
Office Shortcut Bar	Right-click the Office icon on the shortcut bar and click Exit.
Office Assistant	Hide the Assistant.
Tools, Customize	Click the Options tab and deselect the option to show recently used menu commands first. Deselect the option to display the Standard and Formatting toolbars on one row.
Tools, Options	Click the Edit tab and select Move selection after Enter.
View, Formula Bar	Display the formula bar.
View, Status Bar	Display the status bar.
View, Normal	View the workbook in Normal view.
Maximize	Maximize the application and workbook windows.
File, Open	Open the *Selections.xls* workbook.

About Worksheet Formats

The formats you apply to Excel worksheets communicate much to those who view your data. Using appropriate formats portrays excellence and professionalism. Bad formatting is like bad Web page design—it can send the wrong message.

Formatting in Excel is a simple task. To make text stand out, you can format all of the text in a cell or only selected characters. To distinguish between different types of information in a worksheet, you can apply borders to cells, shade cells with a background color, or shade cells with a color pattern. You can use number formats to change the appearance of numbers, including dates and times, without changing the number behind the appearance. Finally, if your data is in a list, there are several ways to quickly format the list by using AutoFormats, styles, and the Format Painter button.

Formatting Numbers

Since the primary data in Excel workbooks tend to be numbers, let's start enhancing the Selections workbook by changing the number formats. **Number formats** change the appearance of numbers, including dates and times, without changing the underlying data. You can apply some number formats using tools such as the Currency Style button, which formats a selection in **currency style**. Currency style formats a number with a dollar sign and two places to the right of the decimal point.

TASK 1:   To Apply Number Formats

1 Click the Sales Summary worksheet tab if it is not currently the active sheet.

2 Select the range B6:F17.

3 Click the Currency Style button 🔲 on the Formatting toolbar. The values are displayed in currency style, as shown in Figure 3.3.

FIGURE 3.3

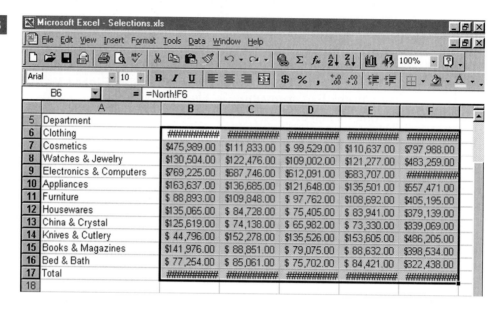

	A	B	C	D	E	F
5	Department					
6	Clothing	############	############	############	############	############
7	Cosmetics	$475,989.00	$111,833.00	$ 99,529.00	$110,637.00	$797,988.00
8	Watches & Jewelry	$130,504.00	$122,476.00	$109,002.00	$121,277.00	$483,259.00
9	Electronics & Computers	$769,225.00	$687,746.00	$612,091.00	$683,707.00	############
10	Appliances	$163,637.00	$136,685.00	$121,648.00	$135,501.00	$557,471.00
11	Furniture	$ 88,893.00	$109,848.00	$ 97,762.00	$108,692.00	$405,195.00
12	Housewares	$135,065.00	$ 84,728.00	$ 75,405.00	$ 83,941.00	$379,139.00
13	China & Crystal	$125,619.00	$ 74,138.00	$ 65,982.00	$ 73,330.00	$339,069.00
14	Knives & Cutlery	$ 44,796.00	$152,278.00	$135,526.00	$153,605.00	$486,205.00
15	Books & Magazines	$141,976.00	$ 88,851.00	$ 79,075.00	$ 88,632.00	$398,534.00
16	Bed & Bath	$ 77,254.00	$ 85,061.00	$ 75,702.00	$ 84,421.00	$322,438.00
17	Total	############	############	############	############	############
18						

TROUBLESHOOTING You will notice that some cells display a series of pound signs (#). This indicates that these columns are too narrow to display the values in the cells as formatted. You can remedy this problem by either changing the cell format or adjusting the column width.

Modifying Formats

When you apply formats, you may need to modify the results. By modifying the formats you just applied to the selected range, the values will display without resizing the columns.

TASK 2: To Modify Number Formats

1 With the range B6:F17 of the Sales Summary worksheet selected, choose Cells from the Format menu.

2 Click the Number tab in the Format Cells dialog box, if it is not active.

3 The format displays values with two places to the right of the decimal point. Click the down arrow at the bottom of the text box displaying the decimal value twice. The value changes to 0, as shown in Figure 3.4.

FIGURE 3.4

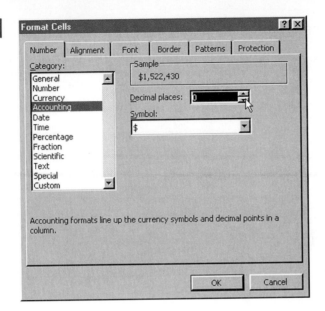

4   Click OK. Your worksheet now looks similar to the one displayed in Figure 3.5.

FIGURE 3.5

	A	B	C	D	E	F
5	Department					
6	Clothing	$ 1,522,430	$ 1,246,050	$ 1,108,983	$ 1,235,508	$ 5,112,971
7	Cosmetics	$ 475,989	$ 111,833	$ 99,529	$ 110,637	$ 797,988
8	Watches & Jewelry	$ 130,504	$ 122,476	$ 109,002	$ 121,277	$ 483,259
9	Electronics & Computers	$ 769,225	$ 687,746	$ 612,091	$ 683,707	$ 2,752,769
10	Appliances	$ 163,637	$ 136,685	$ 121,648	$ 135,501	$ 557,471
11	Furniture	$ 88,893	$ 109,848	$ 97,762	$ 108,692	$ 405,195
12	Housewares	$ 135,065	$ 84,728	$ 75,405	$ 83,941	$ 379,139
13	China & Crystal	$ 125,619	$ 74,138	$ 65,982	$ 73,330	$ 339,069
14	Knives & Cutlery	$ 44,796	$ 152,278	$ 135,526	$ 153,605	$ 486,205
15	Books & Magazines	$ 141,976	$ 88,851	$ 79,075	$ 88,632	$ 398,534
16	Bed & Bath	$ 77,254	$ 85,061	$ 75,702	$ 84,421	$ 322,438
17	Total	$ 3,675,388	$ 2,899,694	$ 2,580,705	$ 2,879,251	$12,035,038
18						

5   Save the workbook.

Copying Formats

Once you define the formats for a range of cells, you can copy these formats to other cells in the worksheet or workbook. The **Format Painter** is one tool you can use to quickly copy formats from one cell to others.

TASK 3:   <u>To Copy Cell Formats Using the Format Painter</u>

1   Select cell B6 in the Sales Summary worksheet.

2   Click the Format Painter button on the Formatting toolbar.

3 Select cells B6:F17 of the North worksheet, as shown in Figure 3.6.

	A	B	C	D	E	F
1	Selections Inc.					
2	Quarterly Sales					
3	North Region					
4						
5	Department	1st Qtr.	2nd Qtr.	3rd Qtr.	4th Qtr.	Total
6	Clothing	405112	321670	401934	393714	1522430
7	Cosmetics	373211	34812	29718	38248	475989
8	Watches & Jewelry	45213	21397	18923	44971	130504
9	Electronics & Computers	211396	189201	174916	193712	769225
10	Appliances	48761	39675	36582	38619	163637
11	Furniture	23819	18912	21975	24187	88893
12	Housewares	34907	26585	39638	33935	135065
13	China & Crystal	33185	32081	41972	18381	125619
14	Knives & Cutlery	12954	9273	10593	11976	44796
15	Books & Magazines	36719	37383	38121	29753	141976
16	Bed & Bath	21082	18910	19718	17544	77254
17	Total	1246359	749899	834090	845040	38 8
18						

Sales Summary \ **North** / South / East / West /

TIP Notice the appearance of the insertion point, which now includes an icon of a paintbrush. The next cell you select will receive the formats of the cell that was active when you chose the Format Painter.

4 Release the left mouse button. The currency format you copied is now applied to this range.

5 Click the Format Painter button again.

TIP You can also double-click the Format Painter to apply a format to multiple selections.

6 Select cells B6:F17 of the South worksheet and release the left mouse button.

7 Using the procedures outlined in the preceding steps, copy these formats to the range B6:F17 of the East and West worksheets, respectively.

8 Save your changes.

TIP You can also copy formats to multiple worksheets by selecting a range of worksheets, as you learned how to do in Project 2.

Applying Font Formats

In Excel, font formats include the font face, style, size, and color. By changing the format of fonts, you can emphasize areas of the worksheet and categorize groups of data. To apply font formats, select the range of cells that you want to format. You can use the **Select All button**, which is the small rectangular button ☐ immediately above the Row 1 label and to the left of the Column A heading, to select every cell in the worksheet. The **Font box** on the Formatting toolbar displays the name of the current font, and the **Font Size box** displays the current font size. Use these boxes to change these font properties. You can change **cell alignment** using the left, center, and right align buttons on the Formatting toolbar.

TASK 4:   <u>To Apply Font Formats and Change Cell Alignment</u>

1 Select the Sales Summary worksheet tab.

2 Select all worksheets in the workbook.

Check Point

How do you select all worksheets in the workbook? You can select all worksheets by selecting the tab for the first worksheet in a range, pressing the (SHIFT) key, and clicking the last tab in the range of worksheets you want to select.

3 Press the Select All button, shown in Figure 3.7. This selects every cell in the worksheet range.

| FIGURE 3.7 |

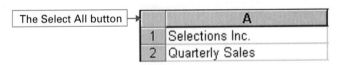

4 Click the drop-down arrow in the Font box to display the current fonts, as shown in Figure 3.8.

> **TROUBLESHOOTING** The fonts displayed depend on your computer's settings. You may see different fonts in this list.

FIGURE 3.8

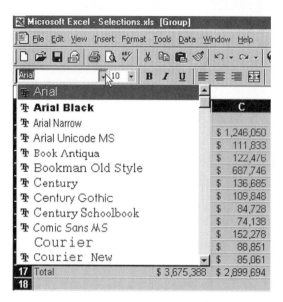

5 Scroll down the list and select the Tahoma font by clicking it with the left mouse button, as shown in Figure 3.9.

FIGURE 3.9

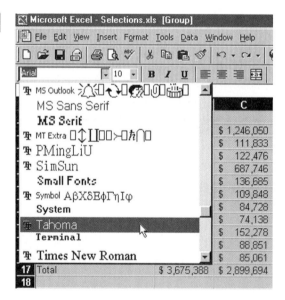

6 Select 9 as the font size in the Font Size box.

7 Click the heading in column A to select it, and change the column width to 21.00.

8 Click the heading for column B, hold down the (SHIFT) key, and click the column F heading to select this range of columns. Change their width to 12.00.

9 Press the (SHIFT) key and click the Sales Summary worksheet tab to deselect the regional worksheets.

10 Highlight the range A1:F3 and click the Bold **B** button on the Formatting toolbar.

11 Highlight the range A5:A17 and click Bold **B**.

12 Select cells B3:E3 and click the Center Align button on the Formatting toolbar, as shown in Figure 3.10. Select cell F3 and click Right Align.

FIGURE 3.10

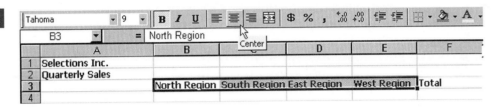

13 Select the North through West worksheets and change the format of cells B5:F5 to Bold **B**.

14 Change the alignment of cells B5:E5 to center aligned, and cell F5 to right aligned.

15 Select cell A1 of the Sales Summary worksheet, and save your changes. The worksheet appears as shown in Figure 3.11.

FIGURE 3.11

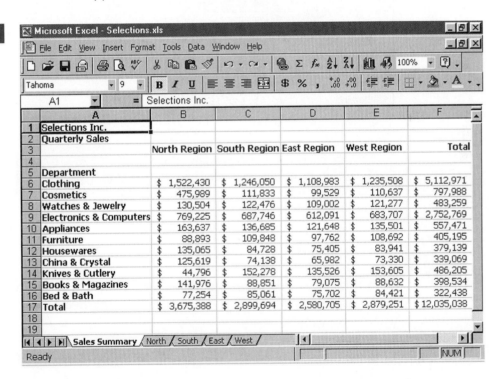

Creating and Applying Styles

You will recall that Mr. Traylor wants each regional worksheet to look like accounting "green bar" paper. This means that you will need to change the **cell shading**, or the color that fills one or more cells, to green. The easiest way to accomplish this task will be to create a style. An Excel **style** is a collection of cell formats—font sizes, patterns, and alignments—that you apply and save as a group. Once a style is defined, it can be applied to additional cells or ranges.

You can shade the appropriate worksheet cells by first applying shading, and then creating and applying a style.

TASK 5: _Shading Worksheet Cells_

1 Select the North through West worksheets.

2 Click the row heading for row 1, hold down the (CTRL) key, and select rows 3 and 5, as shown in Figure 3.12.

FIGURE 3.12

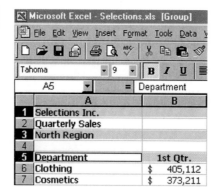

TIP By clicking the row heading, you will select a row. Using the (CTRL) key allows you to make a non-adjacent selection of multiple rows.

Check Point

Why does the word _Group_ appear in the title bar? This indicates that the current operation applies to a group of selected worksheets.

3 Click the drop-down arrow on in the Fill Color button on the Formatting Toolbar.

TROUBLESHOOTING Make sure you click the drop-down arrow to see a list of available colors. If you click the button, the current fill color will be applied to the selection.

4 Choose Light Green in the color list, as shown in Figure 3.13.

FIGURE 3.13

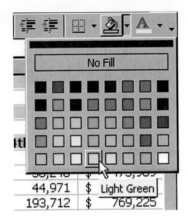

5   Select cell A1. The first three odd rows in the selected worksheets are shaded, as shown in Figure 3.14.

FIGURE 3.14

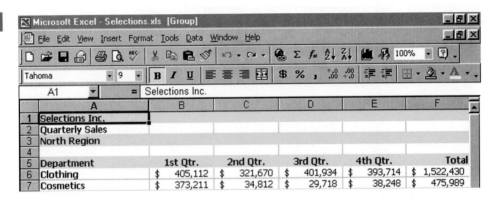

> **TIP**   The entire rows in the selected worksheets are shaded, since you used the row heading to select the entire row for each row in the selection.

TASK 6: <u>To Create and Apply Styles</u>

1   Click the row heading for row 7.

2   Click the Fill Color button to apply the Light Green shading to the row.

> **TIP**   The Fill Color button now displays Light Green as the active color.

3   Choose Style from the Format menu, as shown in Figure 3.15.

FIGURE 3.15

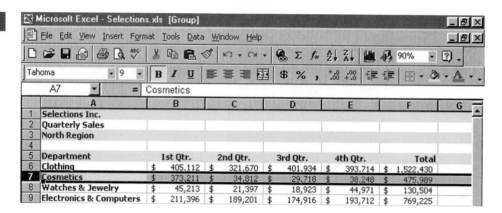

4 The Style dialog box appears. Select the options shown in Figure 3.16, type **GreenBar** as the style name in the name box, and click OK.

FIGURE 3.16

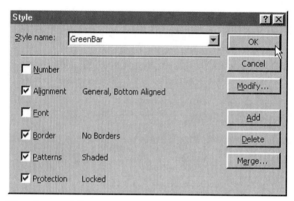

Naming a style

5 Select the row heading for row 9, press the (CTRL) key, and click the row headers for rows 11, 13, 15, 17, and 19.

6 Choose Style from the Format menu, click the drop-down list button on the Style name: text box, and choose GreenBar from the list of available styles by clicking the name with the left mouse button, as shown in Figure 3.17.

FIGURE 3.17

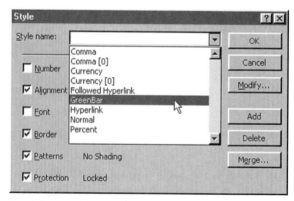

Applying a style

7 Click OK, and select cell A1. The style has been applied to the selected worksheets, as shown in Figure 3.18.

FIGURE 3.18

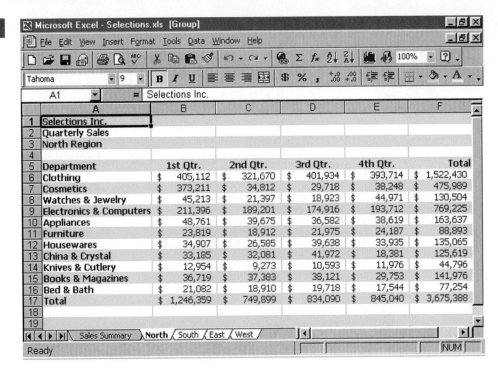

Department	1st Qtr.	2nd Qtr.	3rd Qtr.	4th Qtr.	Total
					Selections Inc.
					Quarterly Sales
					North Region
Clothing	$ 405,112	$ 321,670	$ 401,934	$ 393,714	$ 1,522,430
Cosmetics	$ 373,211	$ 34,812	$ 29,718	$ 38,248	$ 475,989
Watches & Jewelry	$ 45,213	$ 21,397	$ 18,923	$ 44,971	$ 130,504
Electronics & Computers	$ 211,396	$ 189,201	$ 174,916	$ 193,712	$ 769,225
Appliances	$ 48,761	$ 39,675	$ 36,582	$ 38,619	$ 163,637
Furniture	$ 23,819	$ 18,912	$ 21,975	$ 24,187	$ 88,893
Housewares	$ 34,907	$ 26,585	$ 39,638	$ 33,935	$ 135,065
China & Crystal	$ 33,185	$ 32,081	$ 41,972	$ 18,381	$ 125,619
Knives & Cutlery	$ 12,954	$ 9,273	$ 10,593	$ 11,976	$ 44,796
Books & Magazines	$ 36,719	$ 37,383	$ 38,121	$ 29,753	$ 141,976
Bed & Bath	$ 21,082	$ 18,910	$ 19,718	$ 17,544	$ 77,254
Total	$ 1,246,359	$ 749,899	$ 834,090	$ 845,040	$ 3,675,388

8 Save your changes.

Web Tip

Did you know that it is common for accountants to use Excel for accounting? Visit http://www.accountingadvisors.com/exlinks.htm for examples of how accountants use Excel.

Break Point

If necessary you can save your file, exit Excel, and continue this project later.

Working with Rows and Columns

Your workbook is really taking shape! Before applying borders to selected cells, you can add additional rows and columns to enhance the look of the worksheets even more. By adding **dummy cells**, or cells that don't contain data but merely enhance appearance, you can separate worksheet areas that will be formatted with shading to accentuate the different worksheet areas.

TASK 7:   To Insert Columns into Worksheets

1   If necessary, launch Excel and open the *Selections.xls* workbook.

2   Select the North through West worksheets, if they are not currently selected.

3   Select column B and choose Columns from the Insert menu, as shown in Figure 3.19.

FIGURE 3.19

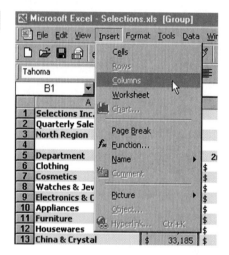

4   Change the width of the column you just added to 0.5.

5   Click inside the Zoom Control text box [100% ▾] on the Standard toolbar, type **90** as the view percentage, and press (ENTER).

6   Change the width of column A to 23.00.

> **TIP** Depending upon your monitor and screen resolution, the contents of Column A appear to spill over into column B at 90% zoom. This is not actually the case, but we are making this change to assist viewing the regional worksheets at this magnification.

7   Add additional dummy columns between each column displaying the quarterly and total sales figures.

8   Change the width of the columns you just added to 0.5.

9   Save your changes. The workbook now looks similar to the one shown in Figure 3.20.

FIGURE 3.20

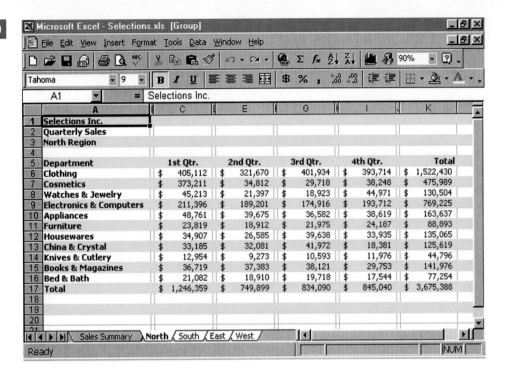

You may wonder what impact these dummy columns have upon the linking formulas in the Sales Summary worksheet. Since these formulas contain relative references to the source data, the formulas are updated automatically. To verify this, you can switch to the Sales Summary worksheet and check the formulas.

> **TIP**   To delete a column, highlight the column you want to delete and choose Delete from the Edit menu.

TASK 8:   To Add a Row to the Selected Worksheets and Resize the Row

1 Select the row heading for row 17.

2 Choose Rows from the Insert menu. Excel adds a row to the worksheet.

3 Place the insertion point on the border between the row headings for rows 17 and 18.

4 Click the left mouse button and resize the row height to 4.50, as shown in Figure 3.21.

FIGURE 3.21

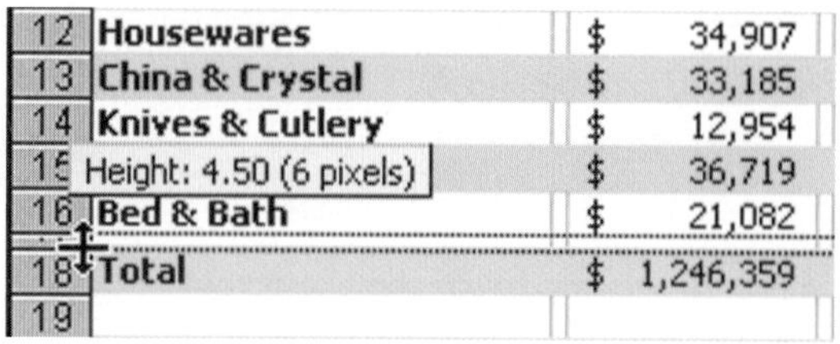

12	Housewares		$	34,907	
13	China & Crystal		$	33,185	
14	Knives & Cutlery		$	12,954	
15	Height: 4.50 (6 pixels)		$	36,719	
16	Bed & Bath		$	21,082	
18	Total		$	1,246,359	
19					

5 Update the workbook by saving your changes.

Adding Borders to Cells

You can further enhance the appearance of Excel worksheets by adding borders to one or more cells. A ***cell border*** is a format that applies lines of various styles to one or more sides (top, bottom, left, right) of the active cell or selection. You can quickly apply cell borders with the ***Borders button*** on the Formatting toolbar.

TASK 9: <u>To Apply Borders to Selected Cells</u>

1 Highlight the range C5:C16.

2 Click the drop-down list arrow on the Borders button [⊞▾] on the Formatting toolbar.

3 Choose the Outside Borders option, as shown in Figure 3.22.

FIGURE 3.22

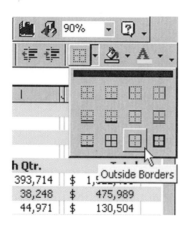

4 Highlight cell C5 and apply the Outside Borders.

5 Highlight the range C5:C16 and click the Format Painter button [✦].

6 Apply the formats to the range E5:E16.

7 Repeat the procedure to apply the format to cells G5:G16 and I5:I16, respectively.

8 Highlight cells K5:K16 and apply the Outside Borders option.

TIP Since Outside Borders was the last format you applied, it is now the default, and you can simply click the Borders button to apply this format.

9 Select cell K5 and apply the Outside Borders format. The workbook now appears as shown in Figure 3.23.

FIGURE 3.23

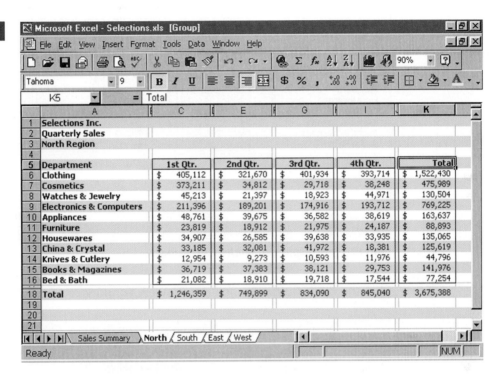

10 Select cells A18:K18. Apply the Top and Double Bottom Border, shown in Figure 3.24, to the selection.

FIGURE 3.24

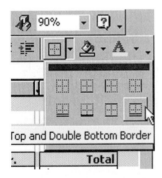

11 Select the range A3:K3 and apply the Bottom Border style.

12 Select cell A1.

13 Save your changes.

14 Click the Print Preview button. The worksheet appears as shown in Figure 3.25.

FIGURE 3.25

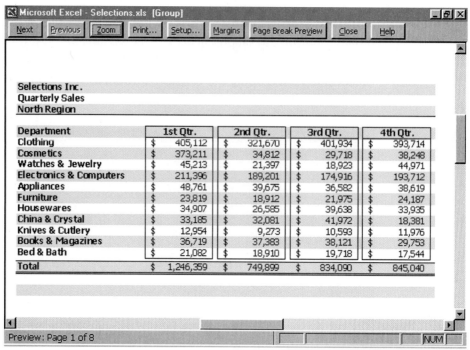

Print Preview displaying worksheet formats

15 Click the Close button in the Print Preview window.

> **TROUBLESHOOTING** You will notice that column K does not appear in the preview, and that the message in the status bar indicates that Excel will require 8 pages to print this data. In Project 4 you will learn how to change the page layout to landscape, so each regional worksheet will print on a single page.

Applying Cell Formats to the Sales Summary Worksheet

The formats you have applied in this project have mostly been for the regional worksheets. Remember that Mr. Traylor wants you to format the Sales Summary worksheet for display on the World Wide Web. In the next task you will apply various formats to the Sales Summary worksheet.

TASK 10: To Apply Cell Formats to the Sales Summary Worksheet

1 Click the Sales Summary worksheet to make it the active sheet.

Check Point

Have any formats been applied to this worksheet? Yes, you have changed both the font and the number format for this sheet.

2 Change the zoom magnification for the sheet to 90%.

3 Change the alignment of cells B3:E32 to Center Align.

4 Apply dummy columns between each regional column, and also before the Total column. Change the width of these columns to 0.5.

5 Change the width of column A to 23.00.

6 Apply a dummy row after row 16, and change the height of this row to 4.50.

7 Select cells A1:K19 and apply Gray-25% as the shading for the selection.

> **TIP** Remember that you can easily change the fill color and grayscales of a selection by using the Fill Color button on the Formatting toolbar.

8 Using the (CTRL) key, highlight the non-adjacent selection shown in Figure 3.26. Apply an outside border.

FIGURE 3.26

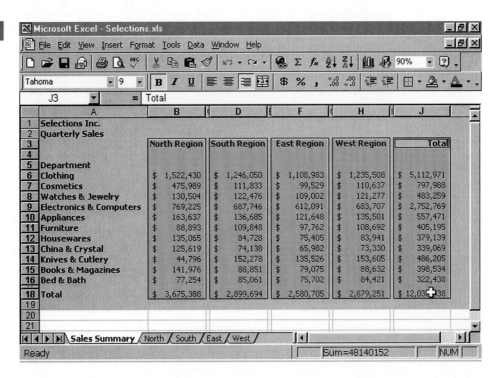

> **TROUBLESHOOTING** Make sure you select the following ranges: B3:B18, D3:D18, F3:F18, H3:H18, and J3:J18.

9 Apply Blue-Gray as the fill color for the selection.

10 Click the drop-down list arrow on the Font button and select Light Yellow as the font color, as shown in Figure 3.27.

FIGURE 3.27

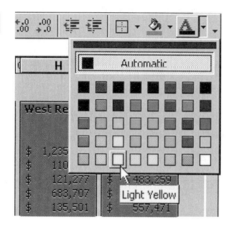

11 Select cell A1.

12 Save your changes. The worksheet appears, as shown in Figure 3.28.

FIGURE 3.28

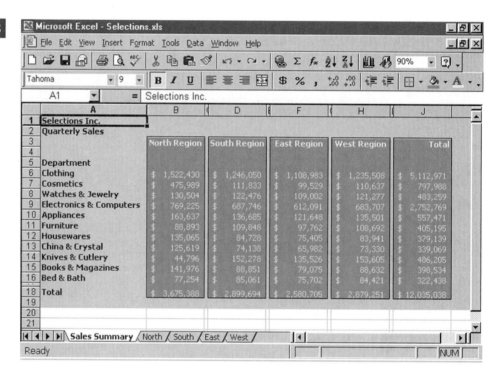

Using the Web Page Preview

An exciting new feature in Office 2000 is **Universal Document Viewing**. You can now save Office documents in HTML file format and retain the formatting features of your native Office file. By saving as HTML, you ensure that anyone with a Web browser can view your documents. Editing those documents is not a problem either because Office 2000 allows you to open them again in the original Office program without losing any of the rich functionality of the Office file formats.

TASK 11: To Use Excel's Web Page Preview

1 Select Web Page Preview from the File menu. Microsoft Internet Explorer or a similar Web browser generates a preview document for your workbook, as shown in Figure 3.29.

FIGURE 3.29

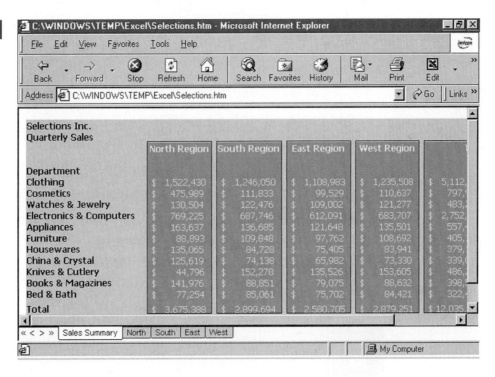

2 Click the North tab in the lower-left corner of the browser window. The browser now displays an HTML preview for the North worksheet, as shown in Figure 3.30.

FIGURE 3.30

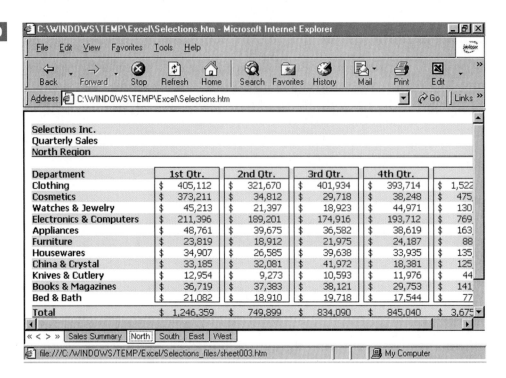

C:\WINDOWS\TEMP\Excel\Selections.htm - Microsoft Internet Explorer

File   Edit   View   Favorites   Tools   Help

Back   Forward   Stop   Refresh   Home   Search   Favorites   History   Mail   Print   Edit

Address C:\WINDOWS\TEMP\Excel\Selections.htm

Selections Inc.
Quarterly Sales
North Region

Department	1st Qtr.	2nd Qtr.	3rd Qtr.	4th Qtr.	
Clothing	$ 405,112	$ 321,670	$ 401,934	$ 393,714	$ 1,522
Cosmetics	$ 373,211	$ 34,812	$ 29,718	$ 38,248	$ 475
Watches & Jewelry	$ 45,213	$ 21,397	$ 18,923	$ 44,971	$ 130
Electronics & Computers	$ 211,396	$ 189,201	$ 174,916	$ 193,712	$ 769
Appliances	$ 48,761	$ 39,675	$ 36,582	$ 38,619	$ 163
Furniture	$ 23,819	$ 18,912	$ 21,975	$ 24,187	$ 88
Housewares	$ 34,907	$ 26,585	$ 39,638	$ 33,935	$ 135
China & Crystal	$ 33,185	$ 32,081	$ 41,972	$ 18,381	$ 125
Knives & Cutlery	$ 12,954	$ 9,273	$ 10,593	$ 11,976	$ 44
Books & Magazines	$ 36,719	$ 37,383	$ 38,121	$ 29,753	$ 141
Bed & Bath	$ 21,082	$ 18,910	$ 19,718	$ 17,544	$ 77
Total	$ 1,246,359	$ 749,899	$ 834,090	$ 845,040	$ 3,675

« < > »   Sales Summary   North   South   East   West

file:///C:/WINDOWS/TEMP/Excel/Selections_files/sheet003.htm   My Computer

3 Close the browser.

TASK 12: To Save the Workbook as HTML

1 Choose Save As Web Page from the File menu.

2 Accept the default file name and file location in the Save As dialog box by clicking Save, as shown in Figure 3.31.

FIGURE 3.31

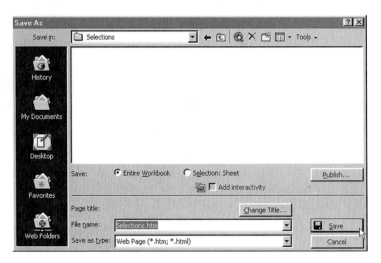

Save As

Save in: Selections   Tools ▾

History

My Documents

Desktop

Favorites

Web Folders

Save: ⦿ Entire Workbook   ○ Selection: Sheet   Publish...
                          □ Add interactivity

Page title: Change Title...

File name: Selections.htm   💾 Save

Save as type: Web Page (*.htm; *.html)   Cancel

3 Close the workbook and exit Excel.

TIP You can verify the HTML document by opening it using your Web browser.

Summary and Exercises

Summary

- You can easily apply formats to numbers to make them easier to interpret.
- Font formats include size, style, and weight.
- You can easily change the alignment of data in one or more cells.
- A style is a set of formats that are stored with a name.
- Once you create a style, you can apply it to other selections.
- You can insert, delete, and resize the rows and columns in a worksheet.
- You can format cells by applying borders and shading.
- You can use the Web Page Preview to see how a worksheet will display if exported to the Web.

Key Terms and Operations

Key Terms

Borders button
cell alignment
cell border
cell shading
currency style
Font box

Font Size box
Format Painter
number formats
Select All button
style
Universal Document Viewing

Operations

add borders to cells
apply font formats
apply number formats
apply styles
ahange cell alignment
copy number formats
create styles

insert columns
modify number formats
resize columns
save worksheets as HTML
shade worksheet cells
use Web Page Preview

Study Questions

Multiple Choice

1. Which of the following is not considered a number format?
   a. percent
   b. altitude
   c. scientific notation
   d. currency

2. Which cell alignment option is not supported by Excel?
    a. left
    b. center
    c. right
    d. justified

3. You use which menu to add columns to a worksheet?
    a. View
    b. File
    c. Insert
    d. Edit

4. If a range of cells is surrounded by a rectangle, the range contains which of the following?
    a. number formats
    b. shading
    c. text formats
    d. borders

5. Which formatting option changes the color of a cell?
    a. number formats
    b. text formats
    c. borders
    d. shading

6. If you change a cell to display two places to the right of the decimal and a percent symbol, what are you changing?
    a. cell alignment
    b. a number format
    c. a font format
    d. a cell's shading

7. Which screen element contains the tools you can use to change the display of data in cells?
    a. the Drawing toolbar
    b. the Standard toolbar
    c. the Format menu
    d. the formula bar

8. Which button copies formats from a selection to another cell or range?
    a. Copy
    b. Paste
    c. Paste Special
    d. Format Painter

9. Which of the following best describes a style?
    a. the number of decimal places a value displays
    b. the alignment of text in a cell
    c. a set of formatting characteristics
    d. a consistent background for worksheets

10. Which of the following is not a font format?
    a. size
    b. font face
    c. percent
    d. italics

Short Answer

1. Which view displays worksheet data as it will appear when saved as HTML?
2. How can you easily store the formats from a cell or range?
3. Which format enhances cells or ranges using lines?
4. When you change the display of financial data to include a dollar sign, you are applying what kind of format?
5. Which formatting feature governs where data appears relative to the cell border?
6. Which format includes two places to the right of the decimal and a percent symbol?
7. Which menu should you use to add columns to a worksheet?
8. How do borders and shading differ?
9. How can you change font color?
10. How do you create a style?

Fill in the Blank

1. A _____ surrounds a one or more cells to enhance appearance.
2. Currency format is one of many _____ formats.
3. You can save a series of formats as a _____.
4. Once you create a _____, the formats it contains can be applied to other worksheet ranges.
5. The _____ is a tool that allows you to copy formats from one location to another.
6. To insert rows into a worksheet, use the _____ menu.
7. Bold, italics, and alignment are examples of _____ formats.
8. The _____ displays worksheet data exactly as it will appear in a Web browser when saved as HTML.
9. Right is an example of _____.
10. When you add color to the background of a range, you are applying cell _____.

For Discussion

1. What is a style? Why are styles useful?
2. List three font formats you can apply to a selection.

3. How does inserting columns into a worksheet differ from inserting worksheets into a workbook?

4. What is Web Page Preview? How does a Web Page Preview differ from a Print Preview?

5. List three common number formats.

Hands-On Exercises

1. Indenting and Rotating Text

Excel supports indenting and rotating text as a method for formatting worksheet data to make it more visually appealing. In this exercise you will indent and rotate text in the Java Sales workbook.

1. Open the *Java Sales—4.xls* workbook.
2. Click the First Qtr worksheet tab to make it the active sheet.
3. Select cells B4:D4.
4. Select Cells from the Format menu.
5. Click the Alignment tab.
6. Change the Horizontal alignment to Center, and click the polygon next to 90 Degrees, as shown in Figure 3.32.

FIGURE 3.32

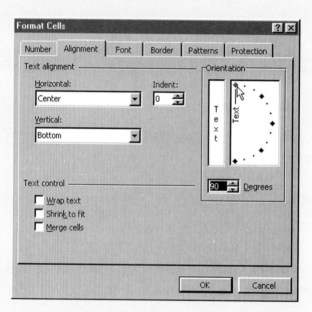

7. Click OK. Change the font format to bold for the selection.
8. Select cells A5:A8 and click the Increase Indent button on the Formatting toolbar, as shown in Figure 3.33.

FIGURE 3.33

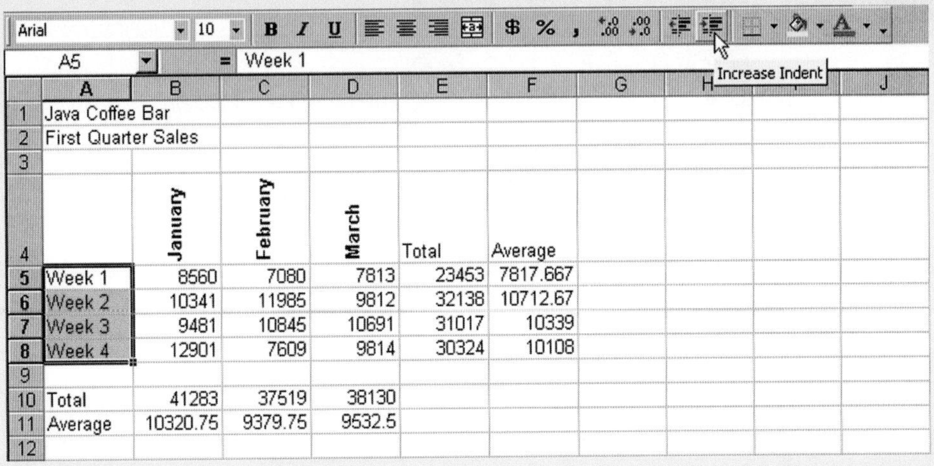

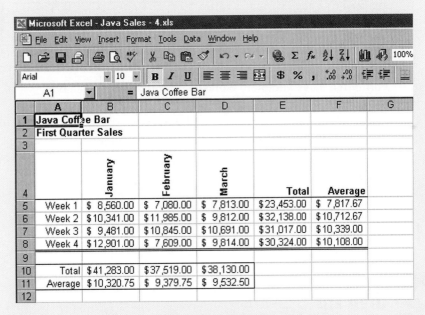

9. Format all cells with numbers to currency style, and adjust column widths as necessary.

10. Add the borders and additional font formats shown in Figure 3.34.

FIGURE 3.34

11. Copy these formats to the Second Qtr sheet.

12. Save the workbook as *Java Sales—5.xls*.

2. Merging Worksheet Cells

There are times when you will want to center cell information across columns, and have the information remain centered regardless of the column width. To do this, you can use the **_Merge Cells_** feature.

1. Open the *Java Sales—5.xls* workbook if it is not currently open.

2. Click the Sales Summary tab to make it the active sheet.

3. Select the range A1:I1.

4. Click the Merge and Center button on the Formatting toolbar, as shown in Figure 3.35.

FIGURE 3.35

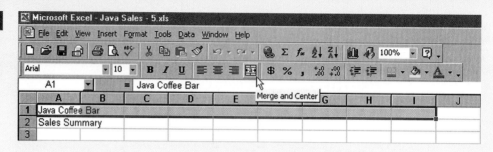

5. Use the Format Painter to apply this format to the range A2:I2.

6. Apply formats to the Sales Summary worksheet so that your worksheet appears like the one shown in Figure 3.36.

FIGURE 3.36

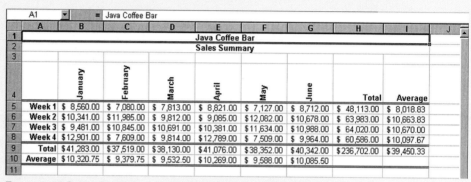

Formatted Sales Summary worksheet for the Java Coffee Bar

7. Select cells I4:I10, choose Delete from the Edit menu, and select the option to shift the cells left. This will delete the cells.

8. Save your workbook as *Java Sales—6.xls*.

9. Close the workbook.

On Your Own Exercises

 **Web Tip**

If you cannot obtain a copy of these files from your instructor, visit the SELECT Web site to download the necessary files: http://www.prenhall/select

1. Formatting the Web Sites Workbook

Open the *Financial Sites 2.xls* workbook you modified in Project 1. Edit the workbook so it contains borders and shading to accentuate the sites. Save your workbook to the Investments folder with the name *Financial Sites 3.xls*.

2. Formatting Your Class Schedule

Open the *Class Schedule—By Day.xls* workbook you modified in Project 2. Apply any formats you deem appropriate to each worksheet in the workbook. Save the workbook as *Class Schedule—By Day 2.xls*.

3. Formatting Time Cards

Open the *Time Cards—Weekly Summary.xls* workbook file. Make sure all numeric data has appropriate number formats. Add borders and shading to make the workbook easier to read. Save the updated workbook as *Time Cards—Weekly Summary 2.xls*.

4. Formatting an Excel Address List

Open the *Updated Address.xls* workbook. Format each worksheet in the workbook with text formats appropriate to the data. Save the workbook as *Updated Addresses—2.xls*.

5. Formatting the January Sales Workbook

Ask your instructor or lab assistant where the file named *January—Update 2.xls* is located if you did not complete Exercise 1 of Project 2.

Modify the worksheet so that all numeric values are in currency format, and that all summary data has a border above the totals. Save the updated workbook as *January—Update 3.xls*.

6. Formatting the Utility Costs Workbook

Open the workbook named *Summary of Updated Utility Costs.xls* from your network or disk. Modify the worksheet by applying formats appropriate to the worksheet. Save your updated workbook to your Personal folder as *Formatted Summary of Updated Utility Costs.xls*.

Creating More Complex Workbooks

Now that you have mastered the basics of designing workbooks with multiple worksheets, you are ready to construct more complex workbook solutions for the Selections, Inc. department stores. In this project you will learn how to create and name ranges that can be used in formulas. In addition, you will learn how to prepare workbooks for printing by modifying the page setup, adding headers and footers, and defining print ranges.

Objectives

After completing this project, you will be able to:

➤ Create range names

➤ Use ranges to select data

➤ Use ranges in formulas using the MIN, MAX, and AVERAGE functions

➤ Use logical functions

➤ Modify the page setup

➤ Set print areas

➤ Set and use print options

Running Case

Mr. Traylor is very pleased with the work you have completed so far on the Selections, Inc. Sales Summary workbook. Now he wants you to roll up your sleeves and really get productive! As he reviewed the workbook structure, he told you he wants to be able to easily compare the sales summary data from quarter to quarter. When you finish making these changes, you will be ready to print copies of the workbook for Mr. Traylor.

The Challenge

Mr. Traylor would like you to add a text description indicating whether each quarter's sales figures are an increase or decrease from the previous quarter. Finally, he wants you to prepare the workbook for printing by including headers and footers and making any other necessary changes.

The Strategy

Before enhancing this workbook, you can simplify many of the tasks Mr. Traylor requests by creating and naming ranges. Range names can be used in formulas and will also assist you when sorting the worksheet data. Adding summary data to each worksheet is an easy task, since Excel supports the MIN, MAX, and AVERAGE functions. By adding a lookup function you can reduce multiple instances of the department names, and the IF function will return a text label indicating whether the quarterly sales figures have increased or decreased from the previous quarter. You can add headers and footers to the workbook by modifying the current page setup, and change the orientation to landscape for better viewing. Finally, you can ensure that the worksheets will always print correctly by defining print areas. Figures 4.1 and 4.2 display how the Sales Summary and North worksheets will appear when printed.

FIGURE 4.1

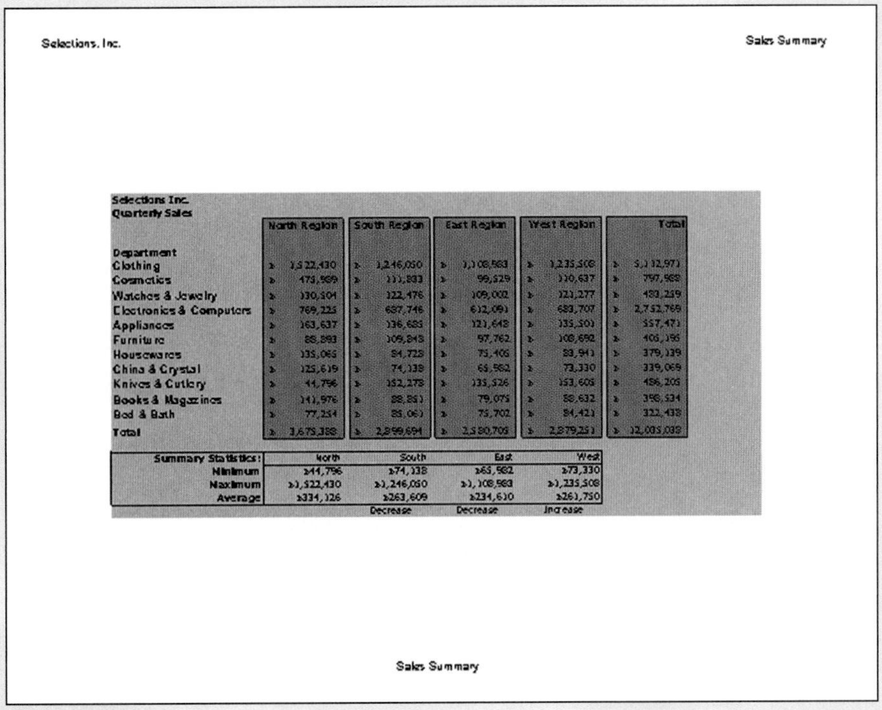

FIGURE 4.2

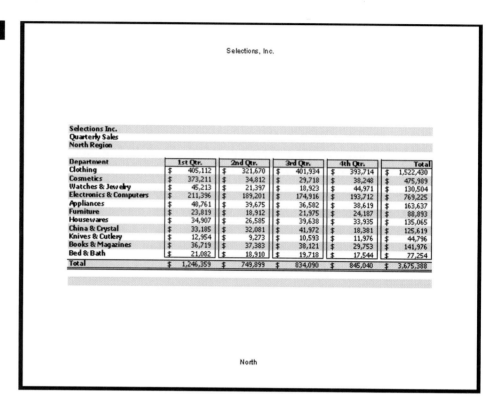

The Setup

Launch Microsoft Excel and select the Excel settings listed in Table 4.1. This will ensure that your screen matches the illustrations and that the tasks in this project function as described.

Table 4.1

Location	Make these settings:
Office Assistant	Hide the Office Assistant.
Tools, Customize	Click the Options tab and deselect the option to show recently used menu commands first.
Tools, Customize	Click the Options tab and deselect the option to display the Standard and Formatting toolbars on one row.
View, Formula Bar	Display the formula bar.
View, Status Bar	Display the status bar.
View, Normal	View the workbook in Normal view.
Maximize	Maximize the application and workbook windows.
File, Open	Open the *Selections.xls* workbook.

FIGURE 4.5

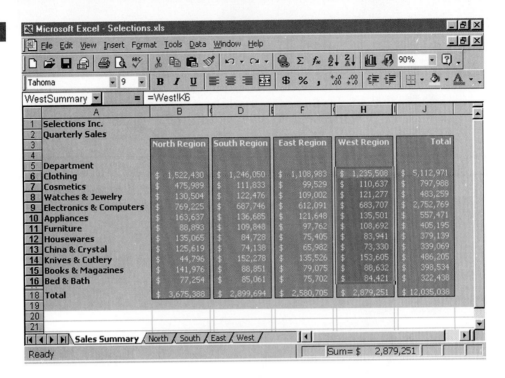

3 Select EastSales from the Name list. The selection changes so that cells F6:F16 are highlighted.

Web Tip

Ranges are a powerful feature in Microsoft Excel. The macro language for Office, Visual Basic, includes additional capabilities for ranges. To see an example of what you can do with ranges in Excel using Visual Basic, visit http://www.microsoft.com/exceldev/tips/rngtot.htm.

Using Range Names in Formulas

Another beneficial use for range names is that they can be used instead of cell references in formulas. Since Mr. Traylor wants to include a listing of the minimum, maximum, and average sales figures across all regions, you can use the range names you have created in the additional formulas that the Sales Summary worksheet requires.

> **TIP** If you insert columns or rows inside a named range, the range corresponding to the name increases accordingly. The same is true if you delete columns or rows inside the named range. You can always edit the range of cells corresponding to a name by selecting Name from the Insert menu, and then selecting Define.

TASK 3: <u>To Use Range Names in Formulas</u>

1 In the Sales Summary worksheet, type **Summary Statistics:** in cell A20, **Minimum** in cell A21, **Maximum** in cell A22, and **Average** in cell A23.

2 Select cells A20:A23 and change the alignment to right aligned and the font style to bold.

3 Place the insertion point in cell B21.

4 Click the Function _fx_ button.

5 In the Paste Function dialog box, choose Statistical in the Function category and MIN as the Function name, as shown in Figure 4.6.

FIGURE 4.6

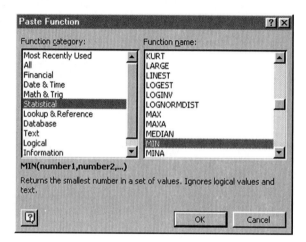

6 Click OK. The formula palette will display the range B6:B20 as the first parameter for the function.

7 Choose Name, Paste from the Insert menu, as shown in Figure 4.7.

FIGURE 4.7

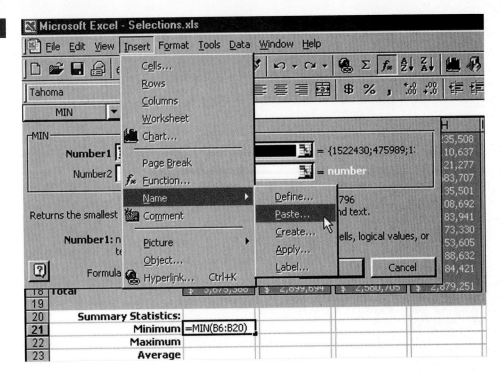

8 Select NorthSummary in the Paste Name dialog box and click OK, as shown in Figure 4.8.

FIGURE 4.8

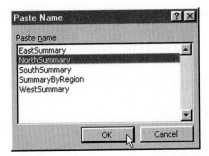

9 The range name now appears in the formula palette. Click OK.

10 The minimum value in the range is displayed in cell B21, as shown in Figure 4.9. Note the syntax for the formula.

FIGURE 4.9

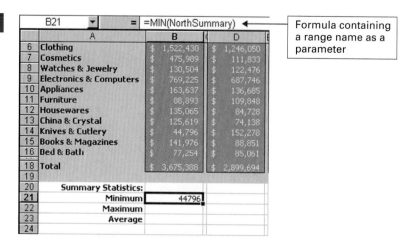

	A	B		D	
6	Clothing	$ 1,522,430	$	1,246,050	
7	Cosmetics	$ 475,989	$	111,833	
8	Watches & Jewelry	$ 130,504	$	122,476	
9	Electronics & Computers	$ 769,225	$	687,746	
10	Appliances	$ 163,637	$	136,685	
11	Furniture	$ 88,893	$	109,848	
12	Housewares	$ 135,065	$	84,728	
13	China & Crystal	$ 125,619	$	74,138	
14	Knives & Cutlery	$ 44,796	$	152,278	
15	Books & Magazines	$ 141,976	$	88,851	
16	Bed & Bath	$ 77,254	$	85,061	
18	Total	$ 3,675,388	$	2,899,694	
19					
20	Summary Statistics:				
21	Minimum	44796			
22	Maximum				
23	Average				
24					

B21 = =MIN(NorthSummary) ← Formula containing a range name as a parameter

Check Point

How else could you have created this formula? You could also create this formula by typing it directly into the cell or the formula bar.

11 Type **=max(NorthSummary)** in cell B22 and press (ENTER).

12 Type **=average(NorthSummary)** in cell B23 and press (ENTER).

13 Select the range B21:B23 and change the number format to currency, 0 decimal places.

14 Select cell B23. Your workbook appears as shown in Figure 4.10.

FIGURE 4.10

B23 = =AVERAGE(NorthSummary)

	A	B		D		F		H		J	
5	Department										
6	Clothing	$ 1,522,430	$	1,246,050	$	1,108,983	$	1,235,508	$	5,112,971	
7	Cosmetics	$ 475,989	$	111,833	$	99,529	$	110,637	$	797,988	
8	Watches & Jewelry	$ 130,504	$	122,476	$	109,002	$	121,277	$	483,259	
9	Electronics & Computers	$ 769,225	$	687,746	$	612,091	$	683,707	$	2,752,769	
10	Appliances	$ 163,637	$	136,685	$	121,648	$	135,501	$	557,471	
11	Furniture	$ 88,893	$	109,848	$	97,762	$	108,692	$	405,195	
12	Housewares	$ 135,065	$	84,728	$	75,405	$	83,941	$	379,139	
13	China & Crystal	$ 125,619	$	74,138	$	65,982	$	73,330	$	339,069	
14	Knives & Cutlery	$ 44,796	$	152,278	$	135,526	$	153,605	$	486,205	
15	Books & Magazines	$ 141,976	$	88,851	$	79,075	$	88,632	$	398,534	
16	Bed & Bath	$ 77,254	$	85,061	$	75,702	$	84,421	$	322,438	
18	Total	$ 3,675,388	$	2,899,694	$	2,580,705	$	2,879,251	$	12,035,038	
19											
20	Summary Statistics:										
21	Minimum	$44,796									
22	Maximum	$1,522,430									
23	Average	$334,126									
24											
25											

Sales Summary / North / South / East / West /

15 Save your changes.

TASK 4:   To Create Additional Formulas Using Range Names

1 Using either procedure outlined in the previous task, enter the appropriate formulas in cells D21:D23, F21:F23, and H21:H23, respectively.

> **TIP**   Remember that you can copy formulas from one column to another. If you use this method in this case, you will need to change the name of each range in the formulas. When you are finished, make sure you check each additional formula for accuracy!

2 Highlight cells A20:K24. Set the shading to Gray-25%.

3 Enter an outside border around cells A20:H23, B20:H23, and B20:H20.

4 Type **North** in cell B20, **South** in cell D20, **East** in cell F20, and **West** in cell H20.

> **TIP**   After you apply a border to one range, you can highlight the next range that will receive the border and select Repeat Borders from the Edit menu.

5 Change the alignment of cells B20:H20 to right aligned. Your worksheet should now resemble the one shown in Figure 4.11.

FIGURE 4.11

	H20	▼	=	West				
	A	B		D		F		H		J
5	Department								
6	Clothing	$ 1,522,430	$ 1,246,050	$ 1,108,983	$ 1,235,508	$ 5,112,971
7	Cosmetics	$ 475,989	$ 111,833	$ 99,529	$ 110,637	$ 797,988
8	Watches & Jewelry	$ 130,504	$ 122,476	$ 109,002	$ 121,277	$ 483,259
9	Electronics & Computers	$ 769,225	$ 687,746	$ 612,091	$ 683,707	$ 2,752,769
10	Appliances	$ 163,637	$ 136,685	$ 121,648	$ 135,501	$ 557,471
11	Furniture	$ 88,893	$ 109,848	$ 97,762	$ 108,692	$ 405,195
12	Housewares	$ 135,065	$ 84,728	$ 75,405	$ 83,941	$ 379,139
13	China & Crystal	$ 125,619	$ 74,138	$ 65,982	$ 73,330	$ 339,069
14	Knives & Cutlery	$ 44,796	$ 152,278	$ 135,526	$ 153,605	$ 486,205
15	Books & Magazines	$ 141,976	$ 88,851	$ 79,075	$ 88,632	$ 398,534
16	Bed & Bath	$ 77,254	$ 85,061	$ 75,702	$ 84,421	$ 322,438
18	Total	$ 3,675,388	$ 2,899,694	$ 2,580,705	$ 2,879,251	$ 12,035,038
19						
20	Summary Statistics:	North	South	East	West
21	Minimum	$44,796	$74,138	$65,982	$73,330
22	Maximum	$1,522,430	$1,246,050	$1,108,983	$1,235,508
23	Average	$334,126	$263,609	$234,610	$261,750
24						
25						

◄◄ ◄ ► ►► \ Sales Summary / North / South / East / West /

6 Save your changes.

Using Logical Functions

Mr. Traylor specified that he wants a way of seeing the sales trends for each quarter at a glance, and to know how they compared with the figures from the previous quarter. You can use a logical function to accomplish this task. A *logical function* is a function that analyzes a value and, based upon a condition, returns a result. Excel's *IF function* compares the value in one cell with either a predefined condition or the value in another cell.

In the next task you will add a conditional function to compare each quarter's sales figures with the sales for the preceding quarter. If the value exceeds the average, the text *Increase* is returned. If the value decreases, the word *Decrease* is returned.

TASK 5: To Add an IF Function to Test Conditions

1 Place the insertion point in cell D24 of the Sales Summary worksheet.

2 Type **=IF(D23>B23,"Increase","Decrease")** as the formula for this cell, and press (ENTER).

3 Copy this formula to cells F24 and H24 respectively. Change the alignment of cells D24, F24, and H24 to centered. When you are finished, the Sales Summary returns the text shown in Figure 4.12.

FIGURE 4.12

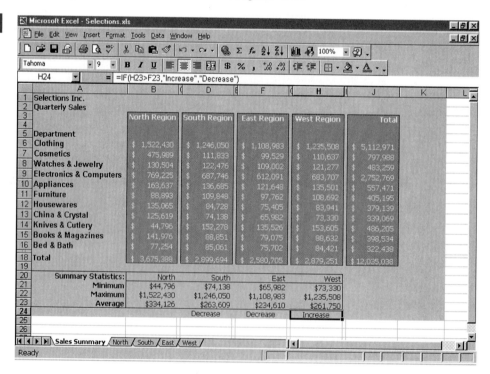

4 Save your changes.

Web Tip

Excel includes the IIF function, which returns multiple responses. See http://msdn.microsoft.com/library/devprods/vs6/vb/html/vafctiif.htm for more information.

Break Point

If necessary, you can save your file, exit Excel, and continue this project later.

Modifying the Page Setup of Worksheets

With more complex workbooks you often need to modify the page setup prior to printing. Changing the page setup includes the worksheet's *orientation*, or its layout on the page when printed. *Landscape orientation* aligns the paper so that it is wider than tall, *portrait orientation* so that it is taller than wide.

Excel's *Page Break Preview* allows you to determine whether you should change the orientation. Once the worksheet has the appropriate layout, you can add *headers* and *footers*, which is text that appears at the top and bottom of the printed page. Finally, you can define a *print area*, which prints a specific area of the worksheet.

TASK 6: To Change Worksheet Orientation

1 Choose Page Break Preview from the View menu.

2 Depending upon how your computer is configured, you may see the dialog box shown in Figure 4.13. If so, click OK.

FIGURE 4.13

Welcome to Page Break Preview

You can adjust where the page breaks are by clicking and dragging them with your mouse.

☐ Do not show this dialog again.

OK

3 Excel displays the current page breaks, with each page designated in gray text, as shown in Figure 4.14. The dashed blue line indicates the current page break.

FIGURE 4.14

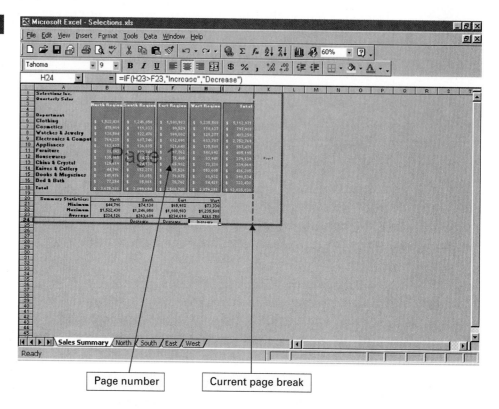

Page number

Current page break

TROUBLESHOOTING The page numbers are difficult to see, as the background color for much of this worksheet is also gray.

4 Choose Page Setup from the File menu.

5 The Page Setup dialog box appears. Make sure the Page tab is active, change the orientation to Landscape, change the scaling to 95% of normal size, and click the Print Preview button, as shown in Figure 4.15.

FIGURE 4.15

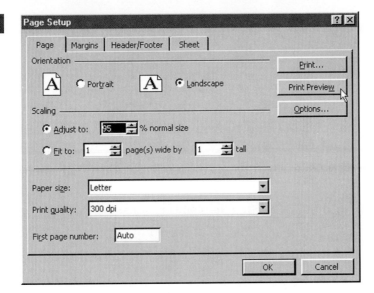

6 The preview appears, as shown in Figure 4.16.

FIGURE 4.16

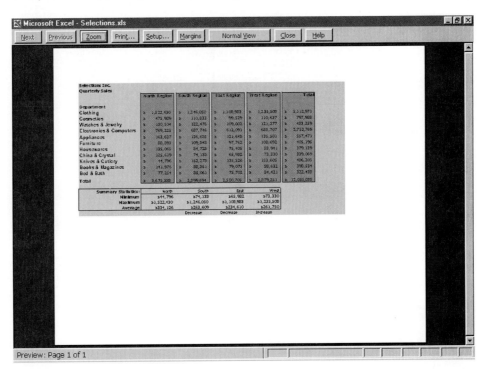

TROUBLESHOOTING Click the Zoom button in the Print Preview if necessary to display the entire worksheet.

You will notice that the worksheet data is not centered on the page. You can easily change this by centering the worksheet on the page.

7 Click the Setup button at the top of the Preview window to return to the Page Setup dialog box.

8 Click the Margins tab. Change the left and right margins to 1 inch.

TIP You can either use the spin controls to increase the margins, or place the insertion point inside the text box that displays the current margin setting and type a new value.

9 Click the checkboxes shown in Figure 4.17 to center the worksheet on the page.

FIGURE 4.17

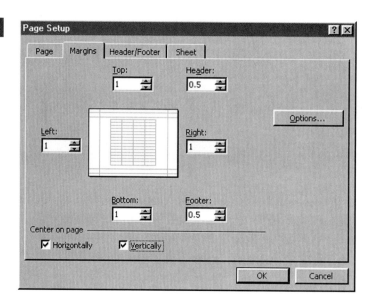

10 Click OK.

11 Click the Close [Close] button in the Preview window to close the Print preview.

12 Select Normal from the View menu to switch to Normal view.

13 Using the same procedure, change the page orientation, margins, and centering options of the North through West worksheets to the same settings.

14 Save your changes.

Check Point

Remember that you can apply changes to multiple worksheets by first selecting the range of worksheets.

> **TIP**   Consider checking spelling before printing worksheets. To check spelling, click the Spelling button on the Standard toolbar. To print multiple worksheets, select the worksheet tabs for the sheets you desire to print. Then, click the Print button on the Standard toolbar.

Adding Headers and Footers to Worksheets

Headers and footers enhance the appearance of worksheets when they are printed. You can select predefined headers and footers, or create custom ones on your own.

TASK 7:   To Add Headers and Footers to Worksheets

1   Click the Sales Summary worksheet tab to make it the active sheet.

2   Choose Page Setup from the File menu.

3   Click the Header/Footer tab.

4   The Header/Footer dialog box appears. You can select a header or footer from the list, or define a custom header and footer.

5   Click the Custom Header button.

6   In the Header dialog box, place the insertion point in the Left text box and type **Selections, Inc.**

7   Place the insertion point in the Right text box and type **Sales Summary**. Click OK. The Header/Footer dialog box appears, as shown in Figure 4.18.

FIGURE 4.18

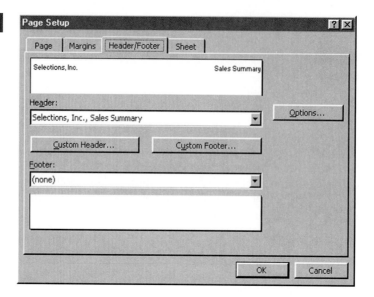

TIP You can add additional elements such as the current date, the time, or the page number to the header or footer using the buttons provided.

8 Click OK to return to the Page Setup dialog box. Notice that the custom header is displayed in the preview pane.

9 Click the Custom Footer button in the Page Setup dialog box.

10 Place the insertion point in the Center section and click the Worksheet Name button.

11 Click OK to return to the Page Setup dialog box.

12 The Header/Footer tab of the Page Setup dialog box appears, as shown in Figure 4.19.

FIGURE 4.19

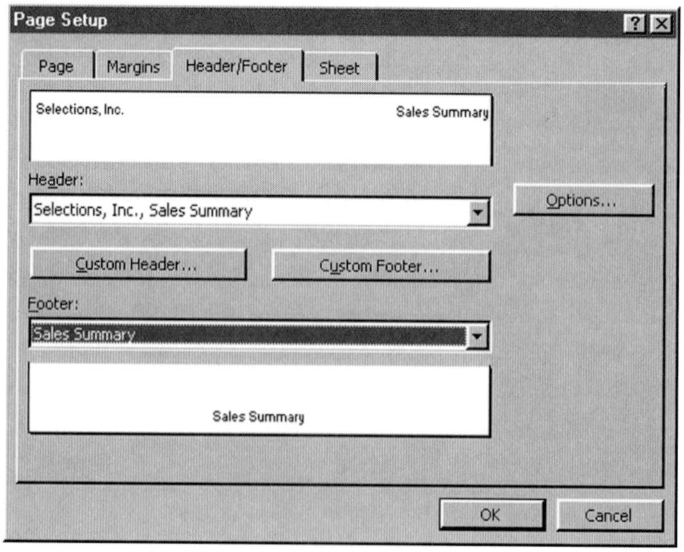

13 Click OK, and then click the Print Preview button. The header and footer appear, as shown in Figure 4.20.

FIGURE 4.20

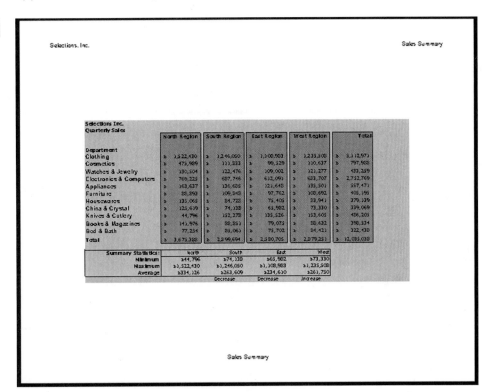

14 Close the Preview.

15 Using the same procedures, add a custom header to each of the regional worksheets with Selections, Inc. in the center pane of the header. Add the worksheet name to the center pane of the footer. Save your changes when you are finished. The North worksheet previews as shown in Figure 4.21.

FIGURE 4.21

Selections, Inc.

Selections Inc.
Quarterly Sales
North Region

Department	1st Qtr.	2nd Qtr.	3rd Qtr.	4th Qtr.	Total
Clothing	$ 405,112	$ 321,670	$ 401,934	$ 393,714	$ 1,522,430
Cosmetics	$ 373,211	$ 34,812	$ 29,718	$ 38,248	$ 475,989
Watches & Jewelry	$ 45,213	$ 21,397	$ 18,923	$ 44,971	$ 130,504
Electronics & Computers	$ 211,396	$ 189,201	$ 174,916	$ 193,712	$ 769,225
Appliances	$ 48,761	$ 39,675	$ 36,582	$ 38,619	$ 163,637
Furniture	$ 23,819	$ 18,912	$ 21,975	$ 24,187	$ 88,893
Housewares	$ 34,907	$ 26,585	$ 39,638	$ 33,935	$ 135,065
China & Crystal	$ 33,185	$ 32,081	$ 41,972	$ 18,381	$ 125,619
Knives & Cutlery	$ 12,954	$ 9,273	$ 10,593	$ 11,976	$ 44,796
Books & Magazines	$ 36,719	$ 37,383	$ 38,121	$ 29,753	$ 141,976
Bed & Bath	$ 21,082	$ 18,910	$ 19,718	$ 17,544	$ 77,254
Total	$ 1,246,359	$ 749,899	$ 834,090	$ 845,040	$ 3,675,388

North

TIP The worksheets you have created each print on a unique page, as you see from the Print Preview. If you ever need to add a page break to a worksheet, place the insertion point in the row below the location of the break, and select Page Break from the Insert menu.

Setting and Clearing Print Areas

There are times when you want to print only a portion of a worksheet. By setting a print area, you can easily print an adjacent range or non-adjacent selection.

TASK 8: To Set and Clear Print Areas

1 Select Normal from the View menu to switch to Normal view, if necessary.

2 Select the range A1:C19 of the Sales Summary worksheet.

3 Choose Print Area, Set Print Area from the File menu, as shown in Figure 4.22.

FIGURE 4.22

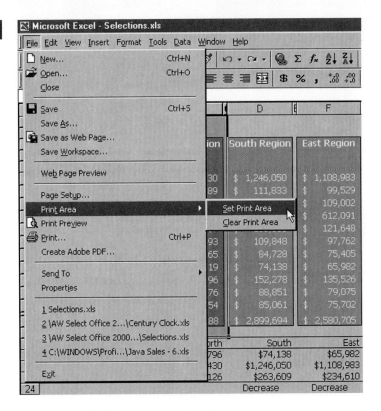

4 Click the Print Preview 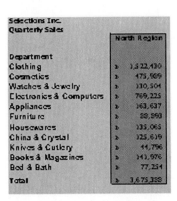 button on the Standard toolbar.

5 Click the Zoom button in the Print Preview window. A portion of the worksheet appears, as shown in Figure 4.23.

FIGURE 4.23

	North Region
Selections Inc.	
Quarterly Sales	
Department	
Clothing	$ 1,522,430
Cosmetics	$ 475,589
Watches & Jewelry	$ 130,904
Electronics & Computers	$ 769,225
Appliances	$ 163,637
Furniture	$ 88,893
Housewares	$ 135,066
China & Crystal	$ 125,619
Knives & Cutlery	$ 44,796
Books & Magazines	$ 141,976
Bed & Bath	$ 77,254
Total	$ 3,675,333

TROUBLESHOOTING Depending upon your monitor and current display settings, you may need to use the scroll bars to reposition the preview.

6 Close the Print Preview window.

7 Choose Print Area, Clear Print Area from the File menu, as shown in Figure 4.24.

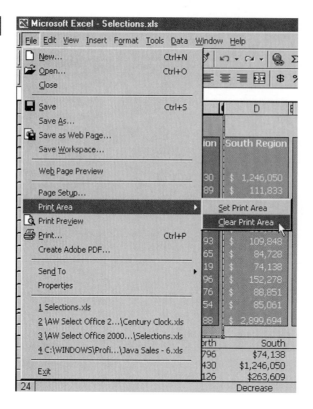

FIGURE 4.24

8 Click cell A1 and save your changes.

Setting Other Print Options

There are additional options you can set in Excel before printing one or more worksheets in a workbook. This is useful when you want to further change Excel's default settings.

TASK 9: <u>To Set Print Options</u>

1 Choose Page Setup from the File menu.

2 Click the Sheet tab. The Page Setup dialog box appears, as shown in Figure 4.25.

FIGURE 4.25

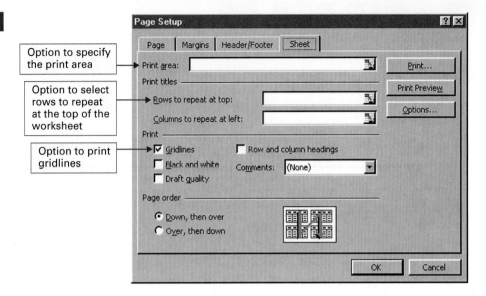

Option to specify the print area →

Option to select rows to repeat at the top of the worksheet →

Option to print gridlines →

3 Check the option for gridlines.

4 Click OK.

5 Select each worksheet in the workbook.

6 Select Print from the File menu.

7 Click OK to print a copy of each worksheet in the workbook.

TROUBLESHOOTING Make sure you select an active printer before printing!

8 Close the Selections workbook.

Summary and Exercises

Summary

- After naming an Excel range, you can use the range name in formulas and can also select the range using the Name box.
- Logical functions compare data based upon the conditions you specify.
- You can modify a worksheet's Page Setup settings to enhance its appearance when printed.
- Headers and footers contain information that will print at the top and bottom of every page of a worksheet.
- Print areas define a range to be printed.

Key Terms and Operations

Key Terms

AutoFormat	name
footer	orientation
header	Page Break Preview
IF function	portrait orientation
landscape orientation	print area
logical function	

Operations

add custom headers and footers	set print areas
change worksheet orientation	use ranges in formulas
name ranges	use ranges to select data
	use the IF function

Study Questions

Multiple Choice

1. Which Excel feature allows you to simplify references to ranges in formulas?
   a. the IF function
   b. a range name
   c. a print area
   d. the Page Setup dialog box

2. Once you set a print area, how do you remove it?
   a. use an IF function
   b. use the Edit menu
   c. use the File menu
   d. use the Web Page Preview

3. Which menu do you use to change the orientation of a worksheet?
   a. File
   b. Edit
   c. View
   d. Insert

4. The MIN function is an example of a
   a. logical function.
   b. financial function.
   c. statistical function.
   d. lookup function.

5. The AVERAGE function does what?
   a. sums a range of cells
   b. calculates the maximum value in a range of cells
   c. calculates the future value for a range of cells
   d. calculates the mean value for a range of cells

6. How many conditions does the IF function support?
   a. 0
   b. 1
   c. 2
   d. 3

7. The formula =IF(A1>=0,"Acceptable") tests for which value in cell A1?
   a. a value equal to zero
   b. any value less than zero
   c. values greater than or equal to zero
   d. only the value zero

8. The IF function belongs to which category of function?
   a. logical
   b. lookup
   c. statistical
   d. financial

9. The IF function can be used to
   a. conduct a logical test.
   b. calculate a mean value.
   c. set a print area.
   d. minimize redundant data.

10. A formula contains the following function:
    =IF(A1>0,2,1)
    If cell A1 contains a negative number, what value is returned?
    a. 0
    b. 1
    c. 2
    d. −1

Short Answer

1. Which function compares the values in two cells and returns data specific to the comparison?

2. How do you change the orientation of a worksheet?

3. What kind of function is IF?

4. What does the IF function do?

5. How do you set a print area?

6. What does the AVERAGE function do?

7. Once you define a print area, how do you print other portions of the workbook?

8. Which screen element do you use to name ranges?

9. How do you refer to a range by name in a formula?

10. AVERAGE belongs to what category of function?

Fill in the Blank

1. The _____ function compares values and returns the appropriate text or value.

2. You can modify a worksheet's page setup using the _____ menu.

3. The _____ function conducts a logical test.

4. MIN and MAX are _____ functions.

5. The IF function is a _____ function.

6. You can use _____ to simplify range references in formulas.

7. If you want to add text at the top of every page of a worksheet, add a _____ to the sheet.

8. You use the _____ to name a range.

9. To set a print area, select _____ from the _____ menu.

10. Once you set a _____ , only a portion of a worksheet will be printed.

For Discussion

1. Can you use range names in 3-D formulas? Explain.

2. Why should you consider setting print areas for worksheets?

3. When should you include MIN, MAX, and AVERAGE functions in a workbook?

4. State a case where an IF function is useful.

5. How do the MIN and MAX functions differ?

Hands-On Exercises

1. Adding the MIN and MAX Functions to a Workbook

As you learned in this project, the MIN, MAX, and AVERAGE functions are useful for summarizing data. The workbook already includes the AVERAGE function; in this exercise you will modify the Java Sales worksheet to include the MIN and MAX functions. When you are finished, you will send the worksheet as an e-mail attachment to Mr. Traylor.

1. Open the *Java Sales   6.xls* workbook.

2. Select the 1st Qtr and 2nd Qtr worksheets.

3. Highlight cells F4:F8 and select Cells from the Insert menu, as shown in Figure 4.26.

FIGURE 4.26

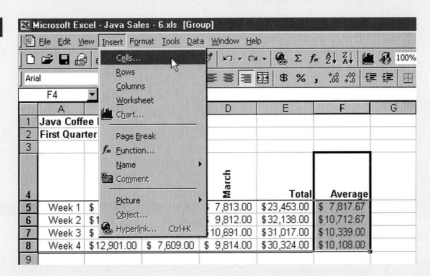

4. Choose the option in the Insert dialog box to shift the cells right and click OK, as shown in Figure 4.27.

FIGURE 4.27

5. Repeat this procedure to add two additional rows to the worksheet.

6. Type **Min** in cell F5 and **Max** in cell F6.

7. Add formulas to the appropriate cells to calculate the minimum and maximum values.

8. Press (CTRL) + G to open the Go To dialog box.

9. Type **A11** in the Reference: text box and click OK, as shown in Figure 4.28.

FIGURE 4.28

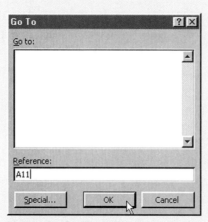

Using the Go To dialog box to move to a specific cell

10. Select A11:D12 and insert cells into the worksheet. Choose the option to shift cells down.

11. Type **Min** in cell A11 and **Max** in cell A12.

12. Add the appropriate formulas to the worksheet.

13. Adjust column widths and reapply formats as appropriate. Save the workbook as *Java Sales—7.xls*. When you are finished, the workbook will look similar to Figure 4.29.

FIGURE 4.29

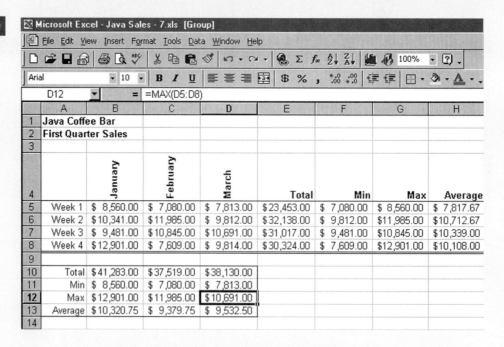

2. Preparing the Java Sales Summary Worksheet for Printing

Mr. Traylor wants to print the Java Sales worksheets after you make the following changes. First, you need to add a worksheet listing sales figures for the third quarter. Then you need to apply a different format to the worksheets using one of Excel's preset formats, called an **AutoFormat**. Finally, he wants to print the quarterly worksheets without the minimum and maximum data. Complete this exercise as follows:

1. Open the *Java Sales—7.xls* workbook.

2. Click the 2nd Qtr worksheet tab and then select Move or Copy Sheet from the Edit menu.

3. Choose the options to create a copy at the end of the workbook, as shown in Figure 4.30. Click OK.

FIGURE 4.30

4. Rename the tab for this new worksheet as **3rd Qtr**, and change the text labels to reflect the correct months and sales quarter.

5. Highlight the range B5:E8 in this worksheet, select Clear from the Edit menu, and then select Contents, as shown in Figure 4.31. This clears the contents of these cells.

FIGURE 4.31

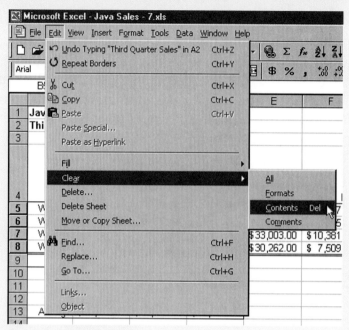

Clearing a range of cells

> **TIP** Notice that you can also clear cell contents by highlighting a range and pressing the (DEL) key.

6. Enter the sales data shown in Figure 4.32 into cells B5:D8.

FIGURE 4.32

	A	B	C	D
1	Java Coffee Bar			
2	Third Quarter Sales			
3				
4		July	August	September
5	Week 1	$ 9,125.34	$ 8,099.45	$ 7,095.23
6	Week 2	$10,789.33	$12,986.34	$13,908.45
7	Week 3	$11,673.12	$11,034.81	$12,855.12
8	Week 4	$ 9,087.12	$12,344.09	$11,094.98

7. Select the quarterly worksheets and highlight the range A4:H8. Click the Edit menu and choose Clear. This will clear the existing formats from the selection.

8. Select AutoFormat from the Format menu. Choose the Classic 3 AutoFormat by clicking it. When your screen matches Figure 4.33, click OK.

FIGURE 4.33

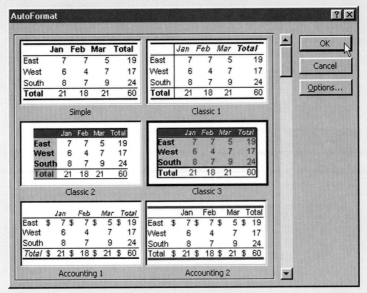

Applying an AutoFormat to a range of cells

9. Select the range A10:D13 and apply the same AutoFormat to this range.

10. Select columns F and G by clicking the heading for column F, pressing the (SHIFT) key, and clicking the heading for column G.

11. Select Column from the Format menu, and then select Hide, as shown in Figure 4.33. This will hide these columns for printing.

FIGURE 4.34

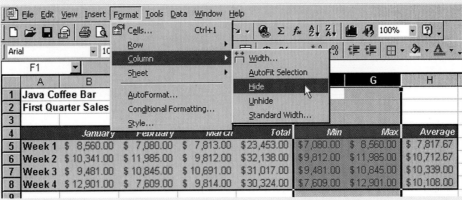

Hiding columns

12. Select rows 11 and 12 by clicking the row selector for row 11, pressing the (SHIFT) key, and clicking the row selector for row 12. Select Row from the Format menu and then select Hide. The workbook appears as shown in Figure 4.35. Notice the column and row headings.

FIGURE 4.35

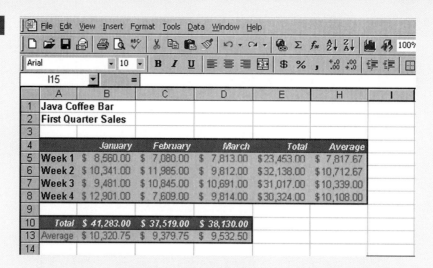

13. Print the selected worksheets.

14. Highlight columns E through H, select Column from the Format menu, and then select Unhide, as shown in Figure 4.36. This will display the hidden columns.

FIGURE 4.36

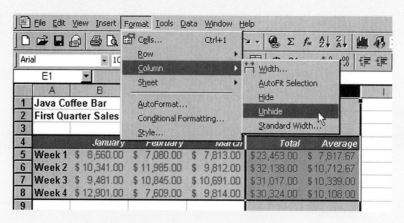

15. Repeat the same procedure to display rows 11 and 12, which are currently hidden.

16. Save the workbook as *Java Sales—8.xls*.

3. Creating a Workbook from a Template and Sending the Workbook as an Electronic Mail Attachment

Mr. Traylor wants you to create an invoice workbook and send him an electronic copy for review. You can use one of Excel's templates, or preformatted workbooks, to create the invoice, and then use the File menu to send a copy to Mr. Traylor via e-mail.

1. Launch Excel if it is not currently running.

2. Select New from the File menu.

3. Click the Spreadsheet Solutions tab and highlight the Invoice template in the list. When your screen matches Figure 4.37, click OK.

FIGURE 4.37

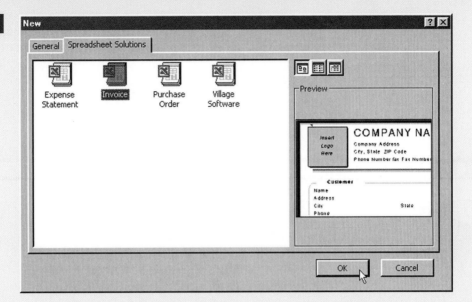

TROUBLESHOOTING Your icons may appear different from the ones shown here, depending on how your computer or network is configured and on the current view setting for the Spreadsheet Solutions dialog box.

4. When you see the dialog box indicating that this worksheet contains macros, click Enable Macros.

5. Save a copy of the workbook to your disk as *Selections Invoice.xls.*

6. Select Send To from the File menu, and select the option to send the workbook as an e-mail attachment, as shown in Figure 4.38.

FIGURE 4.38

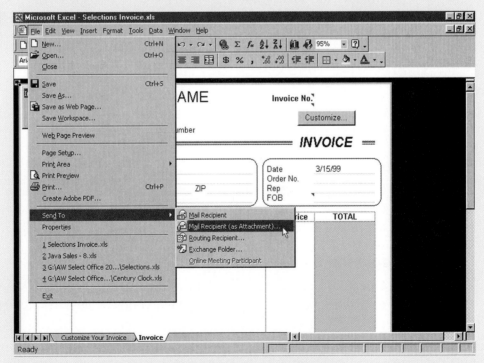

Sending a workbook to a mail recipient as an attachment

TIP To send a workbook as a mail attachment, you need to have a valid e-mail account and the appropriate mail server on your computer or network.

7. If Exchange Server launches, choose Cancel.
8. Close the workbook.

On Your Own Exercises

 Web Tip

If you cannot obtain a copy of these files from your instructor, visit the SELECT Web site at http://www.prenhall.com/select to download the necessary files.

1. Modifying Page Setup for the Web Sites Workbook

Open the *Financial Sites 3.xls* workbook you modified in Project 3. Edit the workbook so it contains headers and footers and prints in landscape orientation. Save the workbook to the Investments folder with the name *Financial Sites 4.xls*.

2. Adding an IF Function to the Class Schedule Workbook

Open the *Class Schedule—By Day 2.xls* workbook you modified in Project 3. Add an IF function to the class schedule by day summary that tests to see whether the total number of hours taken on a given day exceed 9. If so, return the text "Difficult Schedule." If not, return "Average Schedule." Save the updated workbook as *Class Schedule—By Day 3.xls*.

3. Preparing Time Cards for Printing

Open the *Time Cards—Weekly Summary 2.xls* workbook file. Create three named ranges and use the names in the workbook's formulas. Save the updated workbook as *Time Cards—Weekly Summary 3.xls*.

4. Modifying an Excel Address List

Open the *Updated Addresses—2.xls* workbook. Add a header and footer to the worksheet. Set the orientation to landscape, and create a print area for all addresses. Save the workbook as *Updated Addresses—3.xls*.

5. Modifying the January Sales Workbook

Open the *January—Update 3.xls* workbook. Add MIN and MAX functions to each worksheet. Save the updated workbook as *January—Update 4.xls*.

6. Formatting the Utility Costs Workbook

Open the workbook named *Formatted Summary of Updated Utility Costs.xls* from your network or disk. Modify the worksheet by adding formulas to calculate the minimum, maximum, and average utility costs for each period. Save the updated workbook to your Personal folder as *Formatted Summary of Updated Utility Costs 2.xls*.

> **TIP** When printing worksheet data, you can print either the entire work-sheet, or only selected cells.

Select the range of cells listing the minimum, maximum, and average utility costs for each period. Click the File menu, and choose Print. In the Print dialog box, click the Selection option on the Print What section. Click OK to print only the selected cells.

Analyzing and Distributing Worksheet Data

After completing this project, you will be able to:

➤ Describe four common Excel chart types

➤ Create charts

➤ Change chart properties

➤ Delete charts

➤ Preview charts

➤ Print charts

➤ Add graphics to workbooks

➤ Publish worksheets to the Web

➤ View worksheet data on the Web

Running Case

As you will recall from the step for designing electronic workbooks presented in the introduction, summarizing and distributing data are common tasks. Graphs and charts convey information visually, making it easy to understand relationships between numbers. You can add charts to the existing Selections, Inc. workbook to emphasize sales trends. By adding graphics and drawing objects to the workbook before saving it to the Web, you can communicate this important information to other Selections personnel.

The Challenge

Mr. Traylor has reviewed all the work you have done for him, and now wants you to finalize the Selections workbook so it can be distributed internally on the corporate Intranet. Before posting this data, however, he wants to easily communicate to middle and upper management the sales trends by department for each region, and also the percentage of total sales across all regions for each department.

The Strategy

Fortunately Excel has powerful charting capabilities to visually represent worksheet data. You can summarize the sales trends by department and region using a column chart. To summarize the total sales by department across regions, you can create and edit pie charts.

Joy Quinn of the advertising department at Selections gave you an electronic image file of the company logo. By adding this and additional drawing objects to the workbook prior to printing and exporting to the Web, you can easily enhance the overall appearance of the information. Figure 5.1 displays the Sales Summary worksheet prior to printing. Figures 5.2 and 5.3 show the column and pie charts you will export to the intranet.

FIGURE 5.1

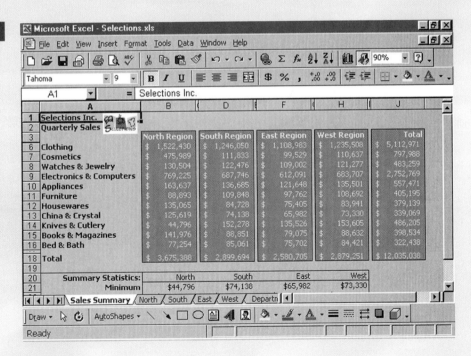

FIGURE 5.2

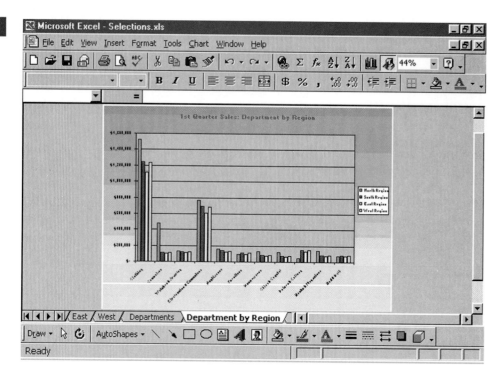

FIGURE 5.3

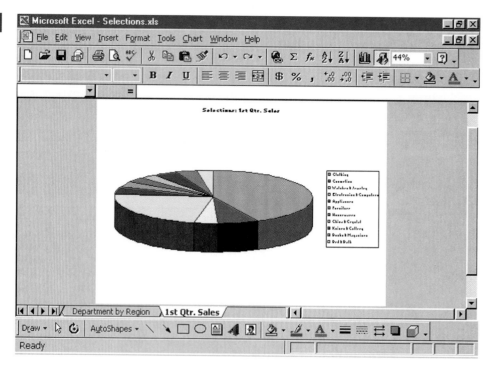

The Setup

Launch Microsoft Excel and select the Excel settings listed in Table 5.1. This will ensure that your screen matches the illustrations and that the tasks in this project function as described.

Table 5.1

Location	Make these settings:
Office Assistant	Hide the Office Assistant.
Tools, Customize	Click the Options tab and deselect the option to show recently used menu commands first.
Tools, Customize	Click the Options tab and deselect the option to display the Standard and Formatting toolbars on one row.
View, Formula Bar	Display the formula bar.
View, Status Bar	Display the status bar.
View, Normal	View the workbook in Normal view.
View, Toolbars	Display the Drawing toolbar.
Maximize	Maximize the application and workbook windows.
File, Open	Open the *Selections.xls* workbook.

Using Charts to Analyze and Summarize Worksheet Data

Charts make it easy for users to see comparisons, patterns, and trends in data. For instance, rather than having to analyze several columns of worksheet numbers, you can see at a glance whether sales are falling or rising over quarterly periods, or how department sales vary.

You can create a chart on its own sheet or as an embedded object on a worksheet. You can also publish a chart on a Web page. To create a chart, you must first enter the data for the chart on the worksheet. Then select that data and use the **Chart Wizard**, Excel's wizard that walks you through the steps of creating a chart. The Chart Wizard will step through the process of choosing the chart type and the various chart options.

You select the **chart type** depending upon the data you want to compare. For instance, when you want to show the parts of a whole, a **pie chart** is most appropriate. Trends over time are easily seen with a **line chart**. Both **column charts** and **bar charts** represent the same categories from different sources, such as the total gross national product from several countries. **X-Y scatter charts** compare pairs of values and often display correlations, such as the correlation between time in the computer lab and overall grade in a computer course.

Once you determine which kind of chart is most appropriate for your data, you can select a **chart sub-type**, which defines the look and feel of the specific chart, such as whether it is three-dimensional or contains summary data within the chart. Finally, you can easily change the **chart options**, such as whether a legend is displayed, the chart title, and any labels that accompany the chart's axes.

Creating Charts

The easiest and most flexible way to create charts is by using the Chart Wizard. In the next task you will add a column chart comparing departmental sales by sales region to the Selections, Inc. workbook.

TASK 1: To Insert a Column Chart into the Workbook

1 Highlight the row headings for rows 4 and 5, as shown in Figure 5.4.

FIGURE 5.4

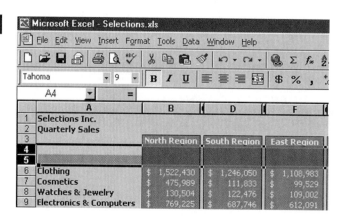

2 Select Rows from the Format menu, and then choose Hide, as shown in Figure 5.5. This hides the blank rows that separate the column headings from the worksheet data so you can select the headings and data as an adjacent selection.

FIGURE 5.5

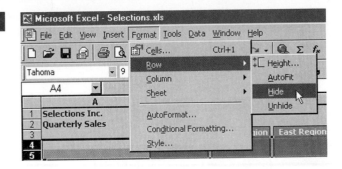

3 Select the range A3:A16.

> **TROUBLESHOOTING** Make sure you do not accidentally select the dummy row 17, as it does not contain any data. If you select it, a blank data series will appear in your chart.

4 While holding down the (CTRL) key, select the following ranges: B3:B16, D3:D16, F3:F16, H3:H16. The non-adjacent selection appears as shown in Figure 5.6.

FIGURE 5.6

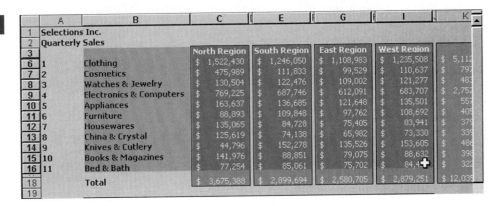

5 Click the Chart Wizard button 📊 on the Standard toolbar to start the Chart Wizard. The first step of the Chart Wizard is displayed.

> **TIP** Notice that only four steps are required to complete this chart!

6 Accept the defaults displayed in Figure 5.7 and click the Next button.

TROUBLESHOOTING If these are not the default settings on your computer, select the options shown in Figure 5.7.

FIGURE 5.7

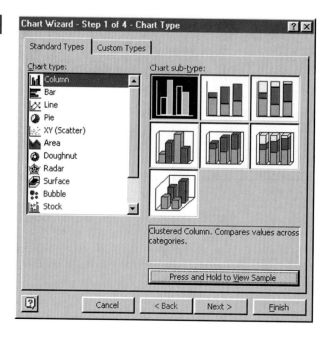

7 Accept the defaults in Step 2 of the Chart Wizard, shown in Figure 5.8. You will notice that the data range you selected has a marquee surrounding it.

FIGURE 5.8

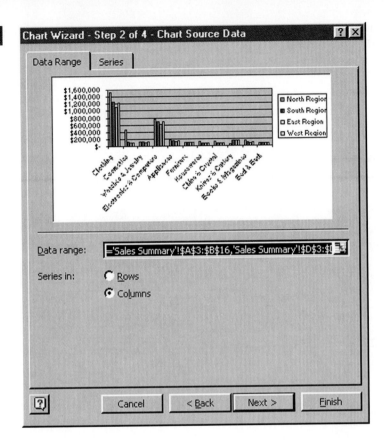

8 Click Next. In Step 3 of the Chart Wizard, place the insertion point inside the Chart title: box and type **1st Quarter Sales: Department by Region** as the chart title.

9 Press the ⎵TAB⎵ key once to move the insertion point into the next text box. The title appears in the preview pane, as shown in Figure 5.9.

FIGURE 5.9

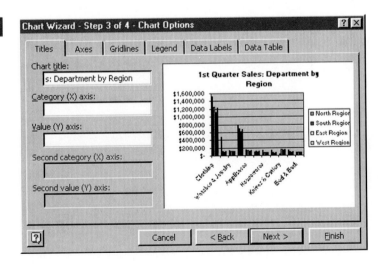

Since this chart contains so many categories, you will not add any additional labels.

10 Click Next.

11 The final step of the Chart Wizard asks about the location for this chart. Since it contains much data, the best option is to add it as a new worksheet. Select the As new sheet: button.

12 Type **Department by Region** as the sheet name. When your screen matches Figure 5.10, click the Finish button.

FIGURE 5.10

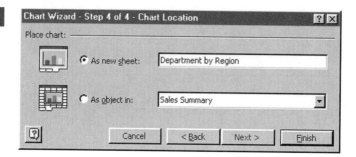

Check Point

When you add a chart to a new worksheet, it becomes a graphic of the sheet, but is linked to the data series you used to create the chart. Thus, if the underlying data changes, the chart reconfigures to display the changes.

If you select the option to add the chart to an existing sheet it becomes a drawing object in that sheet. The chart is still dynamically linked to the data series.

13 The chart is added to the workbook, as shown in Figure 5.11.

FIGURE 5.11

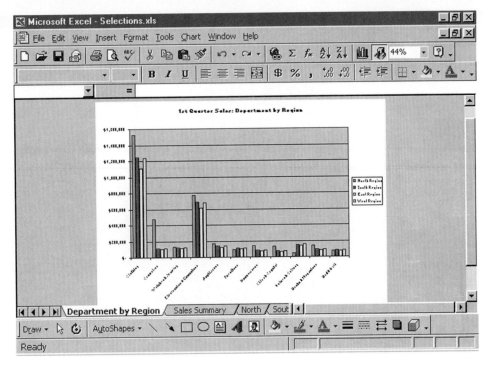

Workbook with chart added

14 Change the position of the chart so it is the last worksheet in the workbook.

15 Save your changes.

TASK 2:   To Enter a Pie Chart into the Workbook

1 Use the navigation buttons in the workbook window to display the Sales Summary worksheet tab.

2 Click the Sales Summary tab to make it the active sheet.

3 Select the range B6:B16, hold down the (CTRL) key, and select the range K6:K16, as shown in Figure 5.12.

FIGURE 5.12

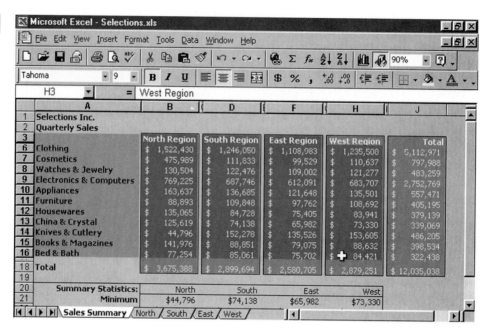

4 Click the Chart Wizard button 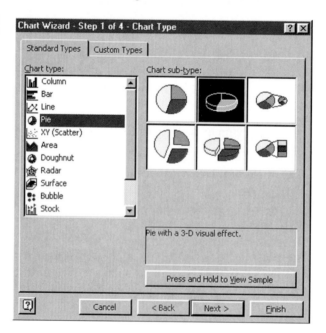 on the Standard toolbar to start the Chart Wizard.

5 Select Pie as the chart type, and Pie with a 3-D visual effect as the chart sub-type, as shown in Figure 5.13. Click Next.

FIGURE 5.13

 Check Point

There is a marquee on the worksheet behind the Chart Wizard. What does this indicate? The marquee indicates the data range upon which the chart will be based. The data range can be either an adjacent or a non-adjacent selection.

6 Verify the default settings in Step 2 of the Chart Wizard, as shown in Figure 5.14, and click Next.

FIGURE 5.14

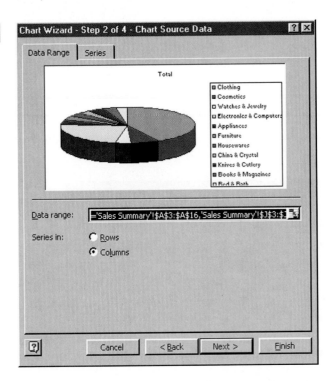

7 In Step 3 of the Chart Wizard, type **Selections: 1st Qtr. Sales** as the title for the chart. When your screen matches Figure 5.15, click Next.

FIGURE 5.15

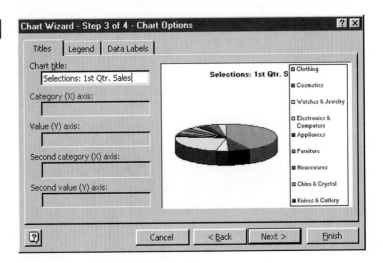

Check Point

In Step 3 of the Chart Wizard shown in Figure 5.15, the text boxes for the axes are grayed out. Why is this the case? A pie chart is used to display parts of a whole, and depends upon only one data series. The chart title is sufficient to convey this information, so additional labels are not available.

8 In the final step of the Chart Wizard, select the option to add the chart as a new sheet and type **1st Qtr. Sales** as the name for the worksheet, as shown in Figure 5.16. Click Finish.

FIGURE 5.16

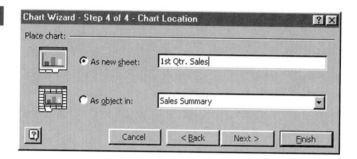

The chart shown in Figure 5.17 is added to the workbook.

FIGURE 5.17

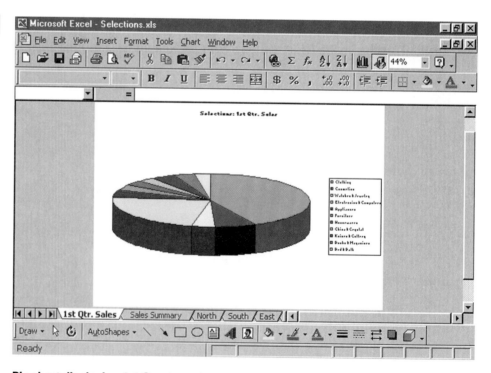

Pie chart displaying 1st Quarter sales

9 Position the chart as the last worksheet in the workbook.

10 Save your changes.

Modifying Charts

Once you have created Excel charts, they can be easily modified. A chart is an **object**—something other than text, numbers, or formulas—that is added to a worksheet. A chart is a **linked object**, meaning that it is bound to the data in the series used to define it. If the underlying data changes, the chart is updated automatically.

When Excel creates a chart using the Chart Wizard, it adds elements to the chart that vary depending upon the chart type. Each element has **properties**, or settings that define how it appears. In the two tasks that follow, you will see how easily you can modify a chart's properties.

TASK 3:   To Modify a Column Chart by Changing Its Properties

1 Click the Department by Region worksheet tab to make the column chart you created the active sheet. Change the zoom to 44%.

2 Click somewhere in the white area of the chart, as shown in Figure 5.18. Notice that the Name box and the comment next to the pointer both identify this chart element as the Chart Area.

> **TIP** If the Chart toolbar appears, close it.

FIGURE 5.18

Name box and comment identifying the chart element

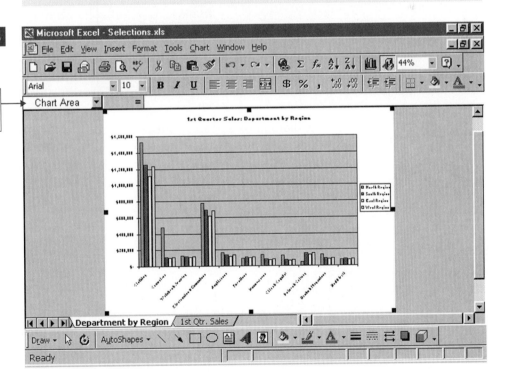

3 Choose Selected Chart Area from the Format menu, as shown in Figure 5.19.

FIGURE 5.19

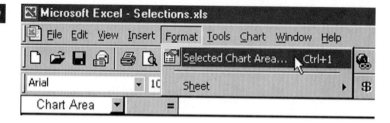

4 Click the Fill Effects button in the Format Chart Area dialog box, as shown in Figure 5.20.

FIGURE 5.20

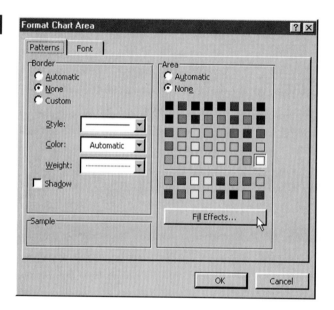

5 The Fill Effects dialog box appears. Check the Preset color option, and select Daybreak from the Preset colors: drop-down list, as shown in Figure 5.21.

FIGURE 5.21

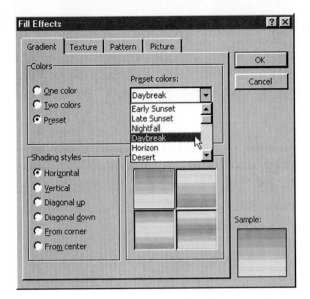

6 Click OK to return to the Format Chart Area dialog box.

7 Click OK. The chart is modified, as shown in Figure 5.22.

FIGURE 5.22

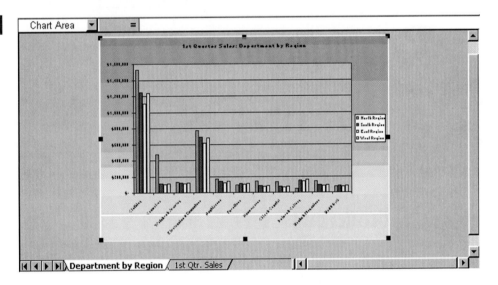

8 Right-click the chart title and select Format Chart Title from the shortcut menu, as shown in Figure 5.23.

FIGURE 5.23

9 Click the Font tab in the Format Chart title dialog box.

10 Change the font size to 14 and the color to Red, as shown in Figure 5.24.

FIGURE 5.24

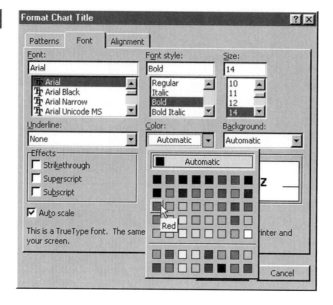

11 Click OK. Your changes are displayed in the chart.

12 Save your changes.

> **TIP** If you preview the chart, you may not see the colors you have selected, depending upon the current printer. To see color in a preview and have it print, you must have a color printer installed on your computer or network.

Break Point

If necessary you can save your file, exit Excel, and continue this project later.

Deleting Charts

As with any data or object in an Excel workbook, charts can be deleted. Because it is so easy to create charts using the Chart Wizard, you can design several charts, and then delete the ones you no longer need.

TASK 4:   To Add a Chart to the Workbook and Then Delete It

1   Click the North worksheet tab to make it the active sheet.

Check Point

If the worksheet tab is not currently visible, how can you display it? To display worksheet tabs that currently are not visible, use the navigation controls in the lower-left corner of the worksheet window.

2   Highlight the range A6:A16.

3   Hold down the (CTRL) key and select the range K6:K16.

4   Press the (F11) key.

> **TIP** The (F11) key is used to activate Excel's Create a chart in one step feature, which adds a worksheet to the current workbook based upon the default chart type.

5   The chart named Chart3 shown in Figure 5.25 is added to the workbook.

FIGURE 5.25

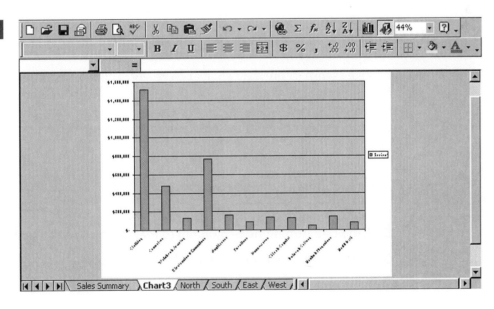

TROUBLESHOOTING If you have created additional charts, the worksheet tab for this chart may display a different name.

6 Select Delete Sheet from the Edit menu, as shown in Figure 5.26.

FIGURE 5.26

7 Verify that you want to delete the worksheet by clicking OK.

8 The chart is deleted from the workbook. Save your changes.

Previewing Charts

It makes sense to preview charts before you actually print them. Since charts often contain multiple colors or shades of gray, they require more toner or ink when printed than worksheet data. Previewing charts also allows you to conduct a final check of the data before finalizing your reports.

TASK 5: <u>To Preview Charts</u>

1 Click the Department by Region tab to make this chart the active sheet.

2 Click the Preview button on the Standard toolbar.

3 The print preview window displays the chart, as shown in Figure 5.27.

FIGURE 5.27

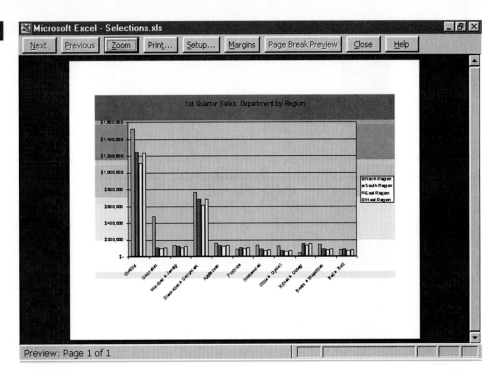

> **TROUBLESHOOTING** Depending upon your current printer and settings, the preview may look different on your computer.

4 Close the preview window.

5 Click the 1st Qtr. Sales worksheet tab.

6 Click the Print Preview button.

7 The print preview window displays the chart, as shown in Figure 5.28.

FIGURE 5.28

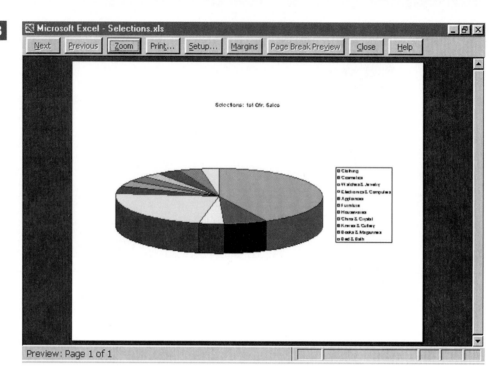

8 Close the preview window.

Web Tip

As you may know, the Web has become an important medium for distributing information from almost every knowledge domain imaginable. Here is a Web site that emphasizes graphs and charts related to investing: http://www.investorlinks.com/quotes.html.

Printing Charts

Once you have previewed your charts, you are ready to print them. You print charts as you print any Excel worksheet data: by using the File menu, or by using the Print button on the Standard toolbar.

TASK 6: To Print Charts

1 Click the Department by Region worksheet tab.

2 Choose Print from the File menu.

3 The Print dialog box for charts that you inserted as separate worksheets is identical to the Print dialog box for worksheets. As you can see from Figure 5.29, you can print more than one worksheet tab (if more than one is selected), and you can also set the number of copies to print.

FIGURE 5.29

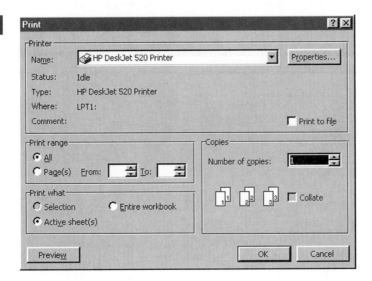

The Print dialog box

4 Click OK to print one copy of the current chart.

> **TROUBLESHOOTING** Your chart will print only if you have access to an active printer.

Adding Graphics to Workbooks

In addition to chart objects, you can add a variety of graphics to Excel workbooks to enhance their appearance. Many organizations have company logos that are used for official correspondence. In this task you will add the Selections logo to the workbook.

TASK 7:   To Add a Graphic to the Sales Summary Worksheet

1 Click the Sales Summary worksheet tab to make it the active sheet.

2 Select cell A1.

3 Select Picture from the Insert menu, and then select From File, as shown in Figure 5.30.

FIGURE 5.30

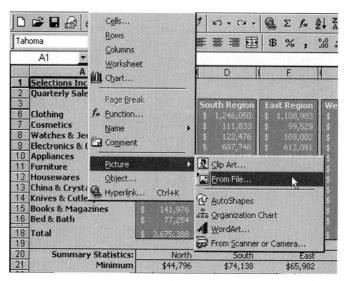

4 Locate the *Sm Selections Logo.gif* file on your floppy disk.

 **Web Tip**

If you do not have a copy of this file, you can download it from the SELECT Web site at http://www.prenhall.com/select.

5 Highlight the file name in the Insert Picture dialog box and click the Insert button, as shown in Figure 5.31.

FIGURE 5.31

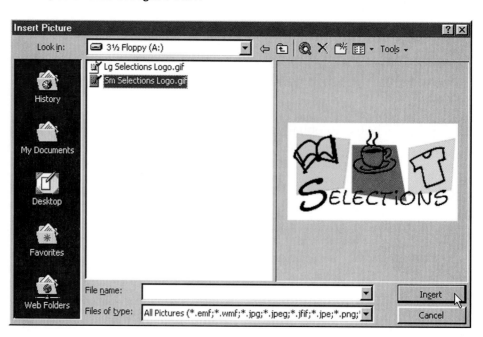

6 The image is inserted in the upper-left corner of the active sheet, as shown in Figure 5.32.

> **TIP** Depending on how your computer is configured, the Picture toolbar may appear on the screen.

FIGURE 5.32

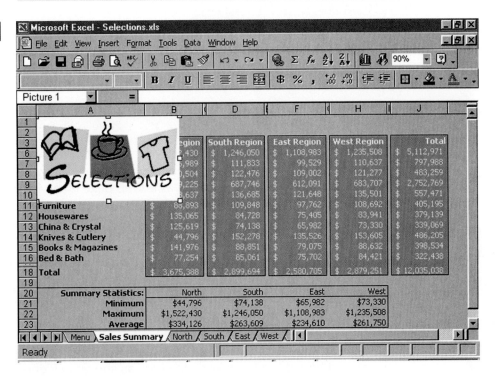

7 Since the image has just been added to the worksheet, it is currently selected. Move the mouse pointer to the lower-right selection handle and size the image smaller, as shown in Figure 5.33.

FIGURE 5.33

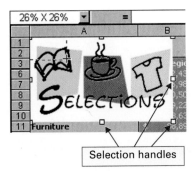

Selection handles

8 Position the mouse pointer immediately over the image, click the left mouse button, and drag the image to the location shown in Figure 5.34.

FIGURE 5.34

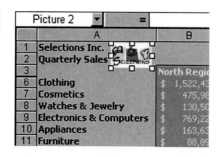

9 Save your changes.

Publishing Workbooks to the Web

Your work is almost finished! Mr. Traylor wants you to publish a copy of the worksheet to the intranet so it can be reviewed internally. As you know from Project 2, by saving the workbook as a Web page it can be posted to a Web server.

TASK 8: To Publish Workbooks to the Web

1 Select Save As Web Page from the File menu.

2 Use the workspace in the Save As dialog box to create a new folder named *Selections Web*. Type **Selections Sales Summary.htm** in the File name text box of the Save As dialog box, as shown in Figure 5.35.

FIGURE 5.35

3   Click the Publish button.

4   The Publish as Web Page dialog box appears. You can use this dialog box to specify which components of your workbook you want to publish and whether you want users to interact with your worksheets through a Web browser. Since you are posting sales data, do not add interactivity. Accept the defaults as shown in Figure 5.36 and click the Publish button.

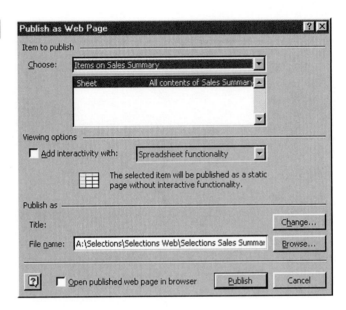

FIGURE 5.36

Your worksheet has successfully been published as an HTML file, which you can view with any browser.

> **TROUBLESHOOTING**   When developing Web resources you may want to consider omitting spaces from HTML filenames. Some browsers may return unpredictable results when opening files with spaces in the name.

5   Save and close the workbook.

TASK 9:   To View Excel Data on the Web

1   Minimize Excel on the desktop and open your floppy disk using My Computer.

2   Locate the *Selections Sales Summary.htm* document.

3   Double-click the file to open it. If Microsoft Internet Explorer or a comparable Web browser is installed on your computer, your HTML file appears similar to Figure 5.37.

FIGURE 5.37

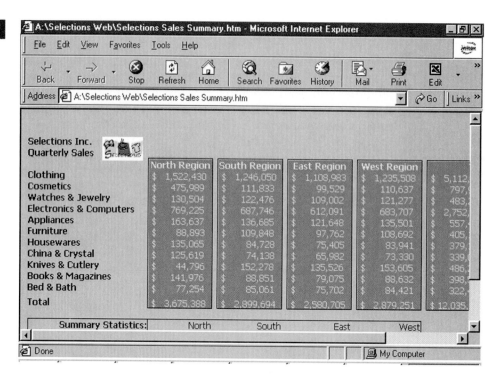

4 Close the Web browser when you are finished viewing the HTML file.

5 Close Excel.

Web Tip

Did you know that the United States Department of the Treasury has graphical information available on the Web? Go to http://www.fms.treas.gov/bulletin/index.html and download the Adobe Acrobat versions of the reports you want to view.

Summary and Exercises

Summary

- Graphs and charts are often used to efficiently communicate numeric data.
- Excel supports many chart types that are appropriate for representing any data your workbook will contain.
- Once you create a chart, you can easily change its properties.
- Printing and previewing charts are common tasks.
- You can enhance the visual appeal of workbooks by adding graphics.
- You can publish Excel workbooks containing charts and other graphic elements to the Web.

Key Terms and Operations

Key Terms

bar chart
chart options
chart sub-type
chart type
Chart Wizard
column chart

line chart
linked object
object
pie chart
properties
X-Y scatter chart

Operations

add graphics to workbooks
create a column chart
create a pie chart
delete charts
modify charts
preview charts
print charts
publish worksheets on the Web
view published worksheets on the Web

Study Questions

Multiple Choice

1. Which menu contains an option to publish worksheet data to the Web?
   a. File
   b. Edit
   c. View
   d. Insert

2. To add an existing graphic to a workbook, you first need to know the image's:
   a. file format.
   b. location.
   c. size.
   d. color.

3. Which chart type is best for representing the parts of a whole?
   a. column
   b. bar
   c. pie
   d. line

4. The bar chart is most similar to which other chart type?
   a. pie
   b. line
   c. column
   d. X-Y scatter

5. The _____ chart compares pairs of values.
   a. line
   b. pie
   c. bar
   d. X-Y scatter

6. Which chart type is best for showing trends over time?
   a. column
   b. bar
   c. pie
   d. line

7. Which menu do you use to preview a chart?
   a. File
   b. Edit
   c. View
   d. Insert

8. Which statement is false?
   a. A pie chart is best at representing the parts of a whole.
   b. Charts are visual representations of numeric data.
   c. A chart can never be deleted from a workbook.
   d. A column chart compares data from multiple data sources.

9. To delete a chart as a worksheet from a workbook, which menu do you use?
   a. File
   b. Edit
   c. Insert
   d. Help

10. What is the maximum percentage a pie chart will display?
   a. 10
   b. 25
   c. 75
   d. 100

Short Answer

1. Which chart type is most like a column chart?

2. How many data series are represented in a pie chart?

3. Which chart type is used to represent correlations?

4. Which chart type is used to show trends over time?

5. What is a chart?

6. How can you delete a chart from a workbook?

7. How do you look at a chart before printing it?

8. How do you add graphics to a worksheet?

9. Which tool helps you create charts?

10. Which application do you use to view worksheet data that has been published to the Web?

Fill in the Blank

1. A _____ chart represents parts of a whole.

2. To insert a chart on a separate worksheet, use the _____ option in the Step 4 of the Chart Wizard.

3. The data used to create a pie chart is called the _____.

4. A(n) _____ chart is never used to plot more than one data series.

5. A(n) _____ chart shows the relationship between pairs.

6. A(n) _____ chart belongs to a particular worksheet.

7. You can add graphic files to workbooks using the _____ menu.

8. You can publish a worksheet to the Web using the _____ menu.

9. A(n) _____ chart is almost identical to a(n) _____ chart, the only difference being the orientation of the data series.

10. To allow multiple users to interact with a workbook, you can _____ it to the Web.

For Discussion

1. Why are charts useful? What kind of information do they convey?

2. When should you consider using a pie chart? A line chart? A column chart? Describe a situation where each type of chart is useful.

3. How does inserting a chart as a separate worksheet differ from embedding a chart into an existing worksheet?

4. Why might you want to add graphics to a workbook?

5. When might you want to publish a worksheet to the Web that supports interactivity?

Hands-On Exercises

1. Adding a Menu Worksheet to a Workbook

There may be times when a workbook has become so complex that you want to add an initial worksheet to the workbook that explains how to navigate within the book. In this exercise you will create a worksheet that will act as a menu to the various worksheets in the Selections workbook.

1. Launch Excel if it is not currently running, and open the Selections workbook.

2. Add a worksheet as the first sheet in the book. Rename the sheet *Menu*.

3. Insert the *Lg Selections Logo.gif* file into the worksheet.

4. Enter the text labels shown in Figure 5.38 into the worksheet.

FIGURE 5.38

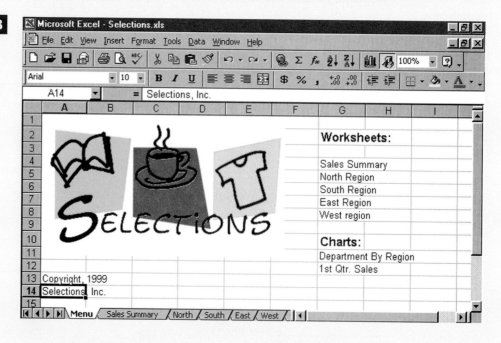

5. Save a copy of the workbook as *Selections—First Quarter.xls*.

6. Select Toolbars from the View menu, and display the Drawing toolbar.

7. Select Block Arrows from the AutoShapes menu on the Drawing toolbar. Select the Pentagon arrow, as shown in Figure 5.39.

FIGURE 5.39

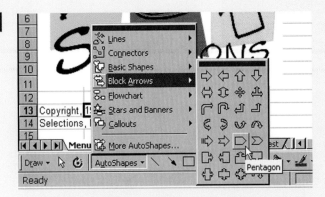

8. Draw a block arrow in the approximate position shown in Figure 5.40.

FIGURE 5.40

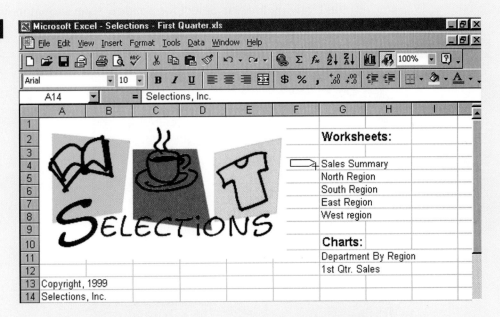

9. With the arrow selected, choose the Fill button on the drawing toolbar, and choose Indigo as the arrow's fill color, as shown in Figure 5.41.

FIGURE 5.41

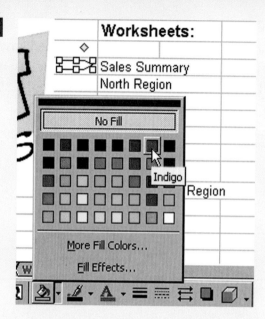

10. With the draw object still highlighted, click the Shadow button on the Drawing toolbar. Select the shadow style shown in Figure 5.42.

FIGURE 5.42

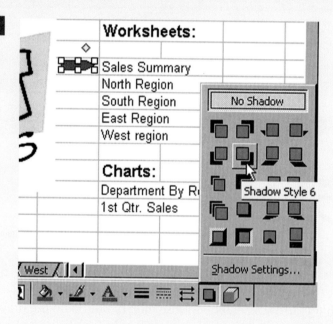

11. Select Shadow Settings from the Shadow button. Using the tools on the Shadow Settings toolbar, nudge the shadow so it looks similar to Figure 5.43.

FIGURE 5.43

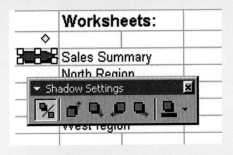

12. Using the Copy and Paste buttons, select the current arrow and create additional arrows for each of the text entries.

13. Close the Shadow Setting toolbar when you are finished using it.

14. Select the buttons to the left of the two chart names, and change the fill color to Dark Red. When you are finished, the worksheet should look similar to the one shown in Figure 5.44.

FIGURE 5.44

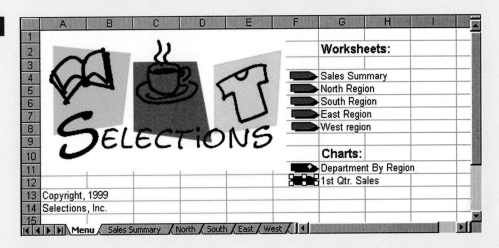

15. Save your changes. Close the workbook if you do not intend to finish the next exercise at this time.

2. Adding Hyperlinks to a Worksheet

In this exercise you will add hyperlinks to the worksheet you created in the previous exercise.

1. Open the *Selections—First Quarter.xls* workbook if it is not currently open.

 Web Tip

You may obtain a copy of this file from the SELECT Web site at http://www.prenhall.com/select if you do not have it.

2. Click the Menu tab if it is not currently the active sheet.

3. Select Options from the Tools menu.

4. Click the View tab and deselect the Gridlines option. When your screen matches Figure 5.45, click OK.

FIGURE 5.45

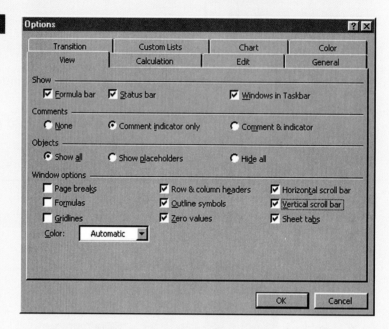

5. Select cell G4 and right-click. Choose Hyperlink from the shortcut menu, as shown in Figure 5.46.

FIGURE 5.46

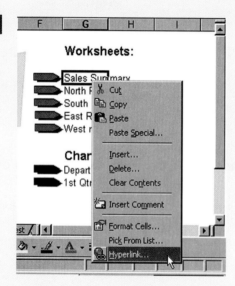

The Insert Hyperlink dialog box appears. Click the Place in This Document button in the bar to the left, as shown in Figure 5.47.

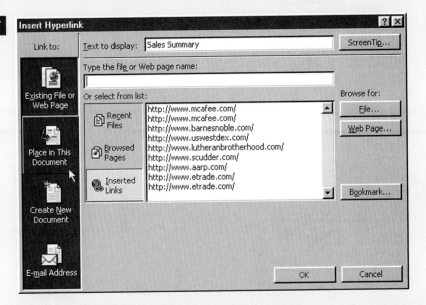

6. Click the plus sign (+) next to Cell Reference to open the list, and select Sales Summary, as shown in Figure 5.48.

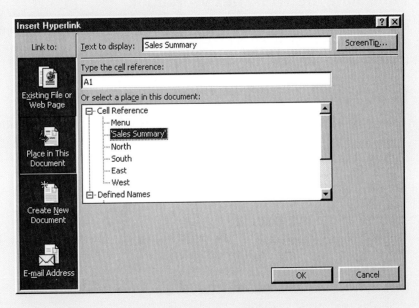

7. Click OK. The text label is changed to a hyperlink, as shown in Figure 5.49. Now that the label is a hyperlink, you can click it to go the cell A1 of the Sales Summary sheet.

FIGURE 5.49

Worksheets:

Sales Summary
North Region
South Region
East Region
West region

8. Add hyperlinks to the remaining text labels so that each links to the appropriate worksheet tab.

TIP You cannot add hyperlinks to the chart sheets.

9. Select a cell in each of the existing worksheets and type Menu as the text label. Add a hyperlink from each sheet back to the menu.

10. Save your changes and close the workbook.

On Your Own Exercises

1. Publishing the Web Sites Workbook

Open the *Financial Sites 4.xls* workbook you modified in Project 3. Publish all worksheet data to the Web. Open the HTML version using your Web browser. Close both files when you are finished.

2. Printing Your Class Schedule to the Web

Open the *Class Schedule—By Day 3.xls* workbook you modified in Project 3. Print the sheet containing course information to the Web. Close the workbook when you are finished.

3. Adding a Graphic to the Time Cards Workbook

Open the *Time Cards—Weekly Summary 3.xls* workbook file. Insert a ClipArt image of your choosing to the workbook. Save the updated workbook as *Time Cards—Weekly Summary 4.xls*.

4. Publishing Addresses to the Web

Open the *Updated Addresses—3.xls* workbook. Publish your address list to the Web. Close the workbook when you are finished.

5. Charting January Sales

Open the *January—Update 4.xls* workbook. Create a column chart comparing all sales by category. Publish the chart to the Web. Save the updated workbook as *January—Update 5.xls*.

6. Creating a Chart to Show Utility Costs

Open the workbook named *Formatted Summary of Updated Utility Costs 2.xls* from your network or floppy disk. Add a line chart showing the changes in utility costs over time. Save the updated workbook to your Personal folder as *Formatted Summary of Updated Utility Costs 3.xls*.

Using Financial Functions

By using Excel's financial functions, you can quickly and easily run the numbers for a loan of any magnitude.

Objectives

After completing this project, you will be able to:

➤ Define the structure of the amortization schedule

➤ Enter the numeric data for the loan

➤ Calculate the monthly payment using the PMT function

➤ Calculate the beginning balance using the PV function

➤ Calculate the principal and interest paid in each loan payment using the PPMT and IPMT functions

➤ Construct formulas to calculate the cumulative principal, cumulative interest, total payments, and ending balance

➤ Use the fill handle to complete the amortization schedule

➤ Freeze worksheet panes to assist in viewing the amortization schedule

➤ Conduct a "what-if" analysis by changing the loan scenario

Running Case

Even businesses need to borrow money at times! The regional accounting office for Selections has allocated money for many of its stores to expand next year. To pay for this expansion, Mr. Traylor wants you to analyze a multitude of loan options to determine the best scenario for the Selections, Inc. department stores.

The Challenge

Mr. Traylor has asked you to construct an amortization schedule so he can compare different loan scenarios. After you complete the workbook, he will determine the optimum loan scenario on a store-by-store basis before contacting specific lending institutions for funding.

The Solution

Excel has a number of financial functions that will make creating this workbook a simple task! By entering four numeric constants and using the PMT, PPMT, IPMT, and PV financial functions, you can create the workbook Mr. Traylor needs. Your completed amortization schedule will look like the one shown in Figure 6.1.

FIGURE 6.1

Microsoft Excel - Loan Amortization.xls

A1 = Selections, Inc.

	Payment Number	Beginning Balance	Principal Paid	Cumulative Principal	Interest Paid	Cumulative Interest	Total Paid to Date	Ending Balance
1	Selections, Inc.							
2	Amortization Schedule							
3	01/15/99							
5		Payment	$3,110.62					
6		Interest	7.500%					
7		Term	3 Years					
8		Principal	$100,000.00					
11	1	$100,000.00	$ 2,485.62	$ 2,485.62	$625.00	$625.00	$ 3,110.62	$ 97,514.38
12	2	$ 97,514.38	$ 2,501.16	$ 4,986.78	$609.46	$1,234.46	$ 6,221.24	$ 95,013.22
13	3	$ 95,013.22	$ 2,516.79	$ 7,503.57	$593.83	$1,828.30	$ 9,331.87	$ 92,496.43
14	4	$ 92,496.43	$ 2,532.52	$ 10,036.09	$578.10	$2,406.40	$ 12,442.49	$ 89,963.91
15	5	$ 89,963.91	$ 2,548.35	$ 12,584.43	$562.27	$2,968.67	$ 15,553.11	$ 87,415.57
16	6	$ 87,415.57	$ 2,564.27	$ 15,148.71	$546.35	$3,515.02	$ 18,663.73	$ 84,851.29
17	7	$ 84,851.29	$ 2,580.30	$ 17,729.01	$530.32	$4,045.34	$ 21,774.35	$ 82,270.99
18	8	$ 82,270.99	$ 2,596.43	$ 20,325.44	$514.19	$4,559.54	$ 24,884.97	$ 79,674.56
19	9	$ 79,674.56	$ 2,612.66	$ 22,938.09	$497.97	$5,057.50	$ 27,995.60	$ 77,061.91

Loan Amortization

Ready

The Setup

Launch Microsoft Excel and select the Excel settings listed in Table 6.1. This will ensure that your screen matches the illustrations and that the tasks in this project function as described.

Table 6.1

Location	Make these settings:
Office Assistant	Hide the Office Assistant.
Tools, Customize	Click the Options tab and deselect the option to show recently used menu commands first.
Tools, Customize	Click the Options tab and deselect the option to display the Standard and Formatting toolbars on one row.
View, Formula Bar	Display the formula bar.
View, Status Bar	Display the status bar.
View, Normal	View the workbook in Normal view.
Maximize	Maximize the application and workbook windows.
Worksheet Tab for Sheet1	Double-click and rename this tab Loan Amortization, and delete the remaining worksheets.

Using Excel to Amortize a Loan

As you learned in the introduction, a great advantage of Excel and other electronic spreadsheets is their ability to perform "what-if" analyses. The computer can easily store and retrieve data and perform calculations, so Microsoft Excel can be used to develop sophisticated models to assist in decision making.

Amortizing a Loan

One decision that individuals and managers often undertake involves assessing the terms under which they will borrow money. Loan payments are amortized; **amortization** is the process of distributing monthly payments over the life of a loan. The factors determining a loan's repayment include the amount of the loan, the percent interest charged by the bank or lending organization, and the length of time over which the loan will be repaid. Each of these factors has a technical name:

• The amount borrowed is the **principal**

- The percent interest is the **rate**
- The time period over which payments are made is the **term**

Depending on the values associated with each factor, varying portions of each loan payment apply to the principal and the interest payment. In general, borrowers aim to pay off the principal in as short an amount of time as financially possible.

Understanding Loan Payments

An **amortization schedule** lists the outstanding balance, monthly payment, amount of each payment that applies to the principal, and the amount of each payment that applies to the outstanding principal for the life of a loan. In this project, you will learn to use financial functions to create an amortization schedule.

The Power of Excel

In this project you will create a loan amortization worksheet by entering four numeric constants and hundreds of formulas. By carefully planning the structure of the worksheet, you can efficiently utilize **absolute cell references**, which are references in formulas preceded with a dollar sign ($) symbol before both the row and column reference. Absolute references always refer to the same cell when the formula is copied elsewhere in the worksheet; an important consideration, when the amount of the principal, the interest rate, and the term of the loan all impact the monthly payment. Other formulas you create will use **relative cell references**, which will change the row and column.

This worksheet will also contain **checks and balances**, to ensure that the calculations are accurate. The checks and balances you will use are specific calculations performed by more than one method, and compared with one another, to assure accuracy throughout the worksheet. Recall that checking the accuracy of a worksheet's data is an important step in designing electronic workbooks.

Defining the Structure of the Amortization Schedule

The amortization schedule's structure is defined by entering text labels specifying where the payment, interest, term, and loan repayment data appears in the worksheet. Remember that Excel uses two categories of constants: **text constants** define the structure of the worksheet, and **numeric constants** comprise the data upon which the **loan scenario** is based.

When you enter the constants, you format them to enhance the appearance of the worksheet.

TASK 1: To Define the Structure of the Amortization Schedule

1 Type **Selections, Inc.** in cell A1.

2 Type **Amortization Schedule** in cell A2.

3 Type **=NOW()** as a formula in cell A3 and click the Enter button on the formula bar.

> **TIP** The =NOW() function is a Date & Time function that displays the date and time according to the computer's system clock. This date is dynamic; as the system clock changes, the date is updated.

4 Select Cells from the Format menu. Click the Number tab in the Format Cells dialog box, choose Date as the category, and choose the date type shown in Figure 6.2.

FIGURE 6.2

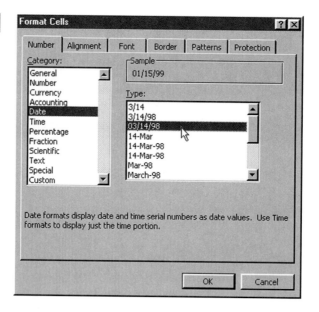

5 Click the Alignment tab and set the horizontal alignment of the cell to Left.

6 Click OK.

7 Type **Payment** in cell B5, **Interest** in cell B6, **Term** in cell B7, and **Principal** in cell B8. Set the alignment of these cells to right aligned.

8 Type **Payment Number** in cell A10, **Beginning Balance** in cell B10, **Principal Paid** in cell C10, **Cumulative Principal** in cell D10, **Interest Paid** in cell E10, **Cumulative Interest** in cell F10, **Total Paid to Date** in cell G10, and **Ending Balance** in cell H10.

TASK 2: <u>To Apply Additional Formats to the Text Constants</u>

1 Select the range A10:H10 and set the font style to bold. Using the Fill Color button on the Formatting Toolbar, set the fill color of the selection to Gray-25%. The worksheet appears as shown in Figure 6.3.

FIGURE 6.3

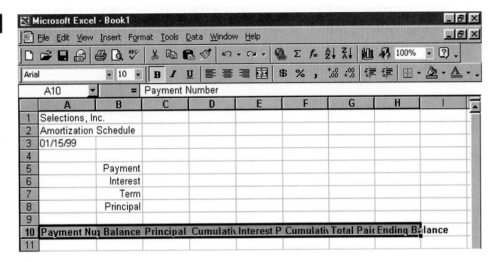

2 Select the range B5:C8. Set the fill color of the selection to Gray-25%.

3 Select the range B5:C5. Using the Font Color button on the Formatting toolbar, set the font color of this selection to Dark Red, as shown in Figure 6.4.

FIGURE 6.4

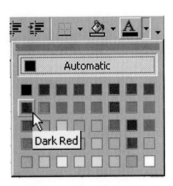

4 Select the Borders button on the Formatting toolbar. Insert a thin border around the selection.

5 Set the font style of the selection to bold.

6 Select the range A10:H10, and select Cells from the Format menu. Select the Alignment tab.

7 Set the Horizontal text alignment to center, and check the option to wrap text, as shown in Figure 6.5. Click OK.

FIGURE 6.5

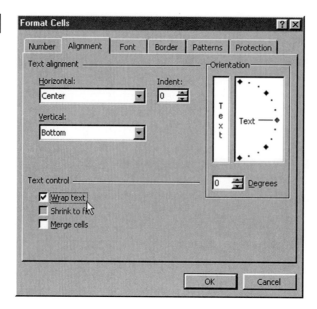

8 Select the Borders tool 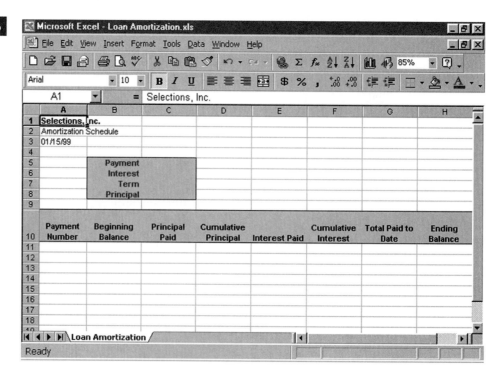 on the Formatting toolbar. Select the option to add a Top and Bottom Border to the selection.

9 Use the column headings to select columns B through H.

10 Set the width of the selected columns to 12.00. Save the workbook to your floppy disk in a folder titled *Loan*. Save the workbook as *Loan Amortization.xls*.

11 Change the Zoom control on the Standard toolbar to 85%.

12 Select cell A1 and change the font to bold. The workbook should look like the one shown in Figure 6.6.

FIGURE 6.6

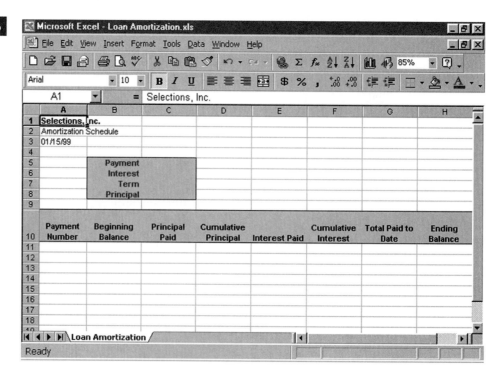

Entering Numeric Constants

Excel will calculate a loan payment using three factors: the loan principal, the interest rate, and the term. You will enter these values in the range C6:C8 of your worksheet. All loan repayment data is calculated using these values.

TASK 3:   **To Enter and Format Numeric Constants**

1 Place the cell pointer in cell C6, type **.075**, and press ⒠ENTER⒡.

2 Click cell C6 again to make it the active cell, select Cells from the Format Menu, and click the Number tab.

3 Select Percentage as the category, and specify three decimal places, as shown in Figure 6.7. Click OK.

FIGURE 6.7

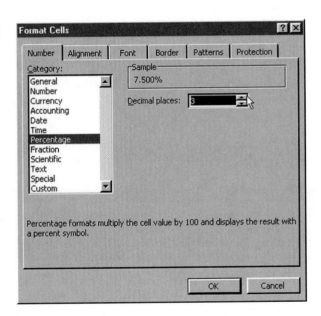

4 Make cell C7 the active cell, type the value **3**, and press ⒠ENTER⒡.

5 Place the cell pointer in cell C7, select Cells from the Format menu, and click the Number tab if necessary.

6 Choose Custom as the category, and place the insertion point in the Type: text box.

7 Enter **## "Years"** as the custom format, as shown in Figure 6.8. The Sample box shows how the current value will appear.

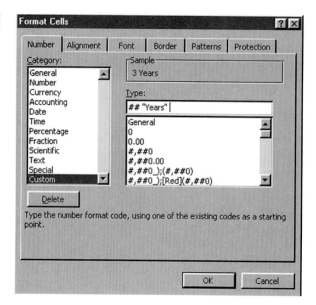

FIGURE 6.8

8 Click OK. This places the text string *Years* after the numeric value in the cell.

9 Place the cell pointer in cell C8, type **100000**, and press (ENTER).

10 Make cell C8 the active cell and select Cells from the Format menu. Click the Number tab and select Currency as the category. Make sure two decimal places are specified.

11 Click OK. After entering and formatting the three numeric constants, the worksheet should look like the one shown in Figure 6.9.

FIGURE 6.9

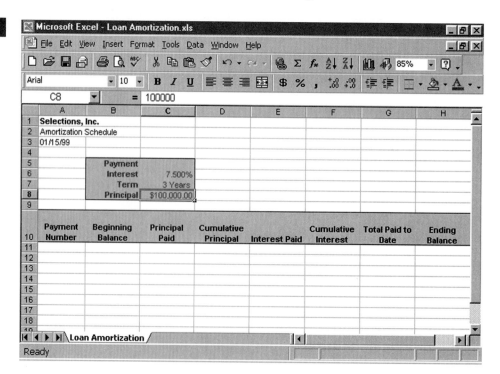

Calculating the Loan Payment Using Excel's PMT Function

After you specify the rate, term, and principal in the Excel worksheet, you can calculate the loan payment. The PMT (payment) function is a financial function used to calculate the periodic payment of a loan, assuming a constant interest rate and constant payments over the life of the loan. You will recall that functions perform calculations by using specific values, called **arguments**, in a particular order, called the **syntax**. The PMT function uses five arguments, three of which are required. Each argument is separated from the others with a comma. The general syntax for the PMT function is:

=PMT(interest rate, number of payments, present value)

> **TIP** Search for PMT in the Help system for more information about the arguments accompanying this function.

TASK 4: To Calculate the Loan Payment Using the PMT Function

1 Place the cell pointer in cell C5 to make it the active cell.

2 Type **=PMT(C6/12,C7*12,-C8)** as the formula for this cell and press (ENTER). The value shown in Figure 6.10 is displayed.

Check Point

If you need help constructing this formula, what should you do? To get assistance using one of Excel's functions, use the formula palette to construct the formula.

FIGURE 6.10

C5	▼	= =PMT(C6/12,C7*12,-C8)

	A	B	C	D	E
1	**Selections, Inc.**				
2	Amortization Schedule				
3	01/15/99				
4					
5		Payment	$3,110.62		
6		Interest	7.500%		
7		Term	3 Years		
8		Principal	$100,000.00		
9					

3 Save your changes.

Web Tip

Speaking of loans, do you need to finance your education? Visit http://www.finaid.org for information about student loans and other sources of funding.

Calculating the Beginning Balance Using Excel's PV Function

Although the beginning balance of the loan that appears in cell B11 is the same as the principal displayed in cell C8, the PV function can be used to enter a "check" into the worksheet. By using the PV function in cell B12 rather than merely including a reference to cell C5, you verify the accuracy of the worksheet.

As with the PMT function, the PV (present value of an annuity) function requires three arguments: rate, term, and payment. The general syntax for the PV function is:

=PV(interest rate, number of payments, periodic payment)

TASK 5: To Calculate the Beginning Balance Using the PV Function

1 Place the cell pointer in cell B11.

2 Type **=PV(C6/12,C7*12,-C5)** and press (ENTER).

TIP As with the PMT function, the annual interest rate must be divided by the number of annual periods (12) per year. You must multiply the term (in years) by the number of payments made each year (12). The payment must be preceded by a minus sign.

The value displayed in cell B11 should appear as shown in Figure 6.11.

FIGURE 6.11

	A	B	C	D
	B11	=	=PV(C6/12,C7*12,-C5)	
1	Selections, Inc.			
2	Amortization Schedule			
3	01/15/99			
4				
5		Payment	$3,110.62	
6		Interest	7.500%	
7		Term	3 Years	
8		Principal	$100,000.00	
9				
10	Payment Number	Beginning Balance	Principal Paid	Cumulative Principal
11		$ 100,000.00		
12				

3 Save the workbook.

Calculating the Principal Paid in Each Payment Using Excel's PPMT Function

The amount of each loan payment that applies to the loan principal (rather than the accrued interest) varies throughout the term of the loan. As with most annuity functions, the actual variance depends upon the loan's rate, term, and principal. The PPMT (periodic principal payment) returns the payment on the principal for a given period. The PPMT function requires four arguments: the rate, the specific period, the number of payments, and the present value of the annuity for the period. Practically speaking, this means that you pay more interest to the bank than you do toward your debt in the early loan payments. This is how the lending institution makes its money, and minimizes its risk if you default on the loan.

In this function, the **present value** refers to the total amount that a series of future payments is worth now—this is the loan principal. The general syntax is:

=PPMT(interest rate, payment period, number of payments, present value)

This function, which is copied to other cells in the amortization schedule, includes both absolute cell references and one mixed cell reference. A **mixed reference** means that the column reference remains constant, but the row reference varies. The function also will need to reference the specific payment (by payment number) within the period. This data is supplied to the function from column A of the amortization schedule.

> **TIP** The term *mixed reference* is a carryover from Lotus 1-2-3 and is not used in Microsoft Excel. Therefore, this term will not be found in the Help System. It is a useful term, however, because it conveys the idea that part of the reference is relative and part is absolute. In Excel, mixed references are also referred to as absolute references.

Web Tip

Is all this financial-speak making your head spin? There is a wealth of information about finances and investing available on line. Visit the Motley Fool at http://www.fool.com for a variety of perspectives concerning finances and investing.

TASK 6: To Calculate the Periodic Principal Payment Using the PPMT Function

1 Click cell A11 to make it the active cell.

2 Type **1** as a numeric constant representing the first periodic payment.

3 Place the insertion point in cell C11, making it the active cell. Type **=-PPMT($C$6/12,$A11,$C$7*12,$C$8)** and press (ENTER). The worksheet should display the value shown in Figure 6.12.

FIGURE 6.12

	C11		=	=-PPMT($C$6/12,$A11,$C$7*12,$C$8)		
	A	B	C	D	E	F
1	Selections, Inc.					
2	Amortization Schedule					
3	01/15/99					
4						
5		Payment	$3,110.62			
6		Interest	7.500%			
7		Term	3 Years			
8		Principal	$100,000.00			
9						
10	Payment Number	Beginning Balance	Principal Paid	Cumulative Principal	Interest Paid	Cumulative Interest
11	1	$100,000.00	$ 2,485.62			
12						

Check Point

Let's analyze this formula. The entire payment is preceded by a minus sign, because annuity payments must be specified as a negative value. The references to the rate (cell C6), term (cell C7), and present value (cell C8) are absolute, because the formula must always reference the same cells, regardless of where the formula is copied in the worksheet. Cell C11 contains a mixed reference: The row reference must change to reflect the periodic payment as the formula is copied down the amortization schedule, but column A must be referenced when the formula is copied to cell E11 to construct the IPMT function. It is not mandatory that cells C6, C7, and C8 contain absolute references. Technically, these could contain mixed references to specify which part of the reference should remain constant (C$6, for example); only the row designation must remain constant as the formulas are copied. The worksheet also uses the IPMT function, which shares the same arguments as the PPMT function, so absolute references are used to assist in creating these formulas. In general, it is a good practice to use absolute references unless the column reference must change if the formula is copied to another column in the worksheet.

Calculating the Interest Paid in Each Payment Using the IPMT Function

The method for calculating the portion of a loan payment that applies to the interest payment is almost identical to the method for calculating a periodic principal payment. The only difference is that the IPMT (periodic interest payment) function is used. The general syntax for the IPMT function is:

=IPMT(interest rate, payment period, number of payments, present value)

TASK 7: <u>To Calculate the Periodic Interest Payment</u>

1 Select cell C11.

2 Copy the contents of the cell.

3 Place the insertion point in cell E11.

4 Select Paste using either the Edit menu or the Standard toolbar.

5 Edit the formula in the formula bar by changing the function from PPMT to IPMT. The worksheet should now look like the one shown in Figure 6.13.

FIGURE 6.13

E11		=	=-IPMT($C$6/12,$A11,$C$7*12,$C$8)		
	A	B	C	D	E	F

	A	B	C	D	E	F
1	Selections, Inc.					
2	Amortization Schedule					
3	01/15/99					
4						
5		Payment	$3,110.62			
6		Interest	7.500%			
7		Term	3 Years			
8		Principal	$100,000.00			
9						
10	Payment Number	Beginning Balance	Principal Paid	Cumulative Principal	Interest Paid	Cumulative Interest
11	1	$100,000.00	$ 2,485.62		$625.00	
12						

6 Save the workbook.

Constructing Formulas to Calculate the Cumulative Principal, Cumulative Interest, Total Payments, and Ending Balance

When building an amortization schedule in Excel, it is helpful to display not only the current principal and interest payments, but the cumulative payments as well. For the first payment, the periodic principal and interest payment equal the cumulative payments. In subsequent rows, however, the cumulative payment figures increase. The total payments to date can be calculated by adding the cumulative principal and the cumulative interest payments.

Break Point

If necessary, you can save the workbook, exit Excel, and continue this project later.

TASK 8: To Construct Formulas to Determine the Cumulative Interest, Cumulative Principal, Total Payments, and Ending Balance

1 Select cell D11 as the active cell.

2 Type **=C11**.

3 Place the insertion point in cell F11 and type **=E11**.

4 Place the insertion point in cell G11 and type **=D11+F11**.

Check Point

The value displayed in cell G11 should be identical to the value in cell C5. This provides another "check" to verify the accuracy of your worksheet.

5 Place the insertion point in cell H11.

6 Type **=B11-C11**. The ending balance is the principal that must be paid to fulfill the repayment obligation. This is equal to the beginning balance minus the principal payment. The worksheet should appear similar to the one shown in Figure 6.14.

FIGURE 6.14

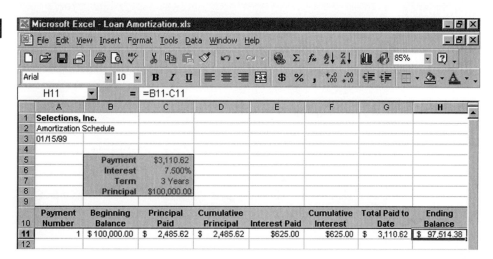

7 Save the worksheet.

Using the Fill Handle to Complete the Amortization Schedule

After you enter formulas in row 12 of the amortization schedule, you can use the fill handle to copy the formula to other portions of the worksheet. The default amortization schedule covers a loan with a term of three years, a principal of $12,000, and an annual interest rate of 7.50%.

> **TIP**   Here is where you will finally see the power of Excel to replicate formulas!

TASK 9: To Use the Fill Handle to Complete the Amortization Schedule

1 Place the insertion point in cell A12 to make it the active cell.

2 Type **=A11+1**.

3 Type **=H11** in cell B12. The beginning balance for this payment equals the ending balance after the last payment was made.

4 Highlight the range C11:H11. Using the fill handle, copy the range down to row 12, as shown in Figure 6.15.

FIGURE 6.15

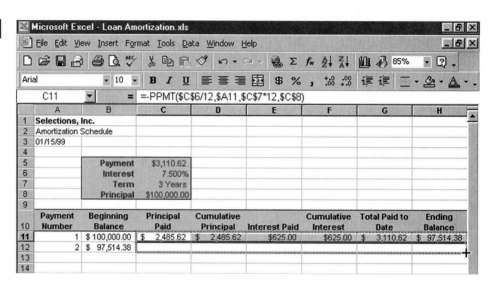

5 Highlight cell D12, change the formula to **=D11+C12**, and click the Enter button on the formula bar to update the formula. The result shown in Figure 6.16 is returned.

FIGURE 6.16

	D12		=	=D11+C12	
	B	C	D	E	
1	Inc.				
2	Schedule				
3					
4					
5	Payment	$3,110.62			
6	Interest	7.500%			
7	Term	3 Years			
8	Principal	$100,000.00			
9					

	Beginning Balance	Principal Paid	Cumulative Principal	Interest Paid
10				
11	$ 100,000.00	$ 2,485.62	$ 2,485.62	$625.00
12	$ 97,514.38	$ 2,501.16	$ 4,986.78	$609.46
13				
14				

6 Highlight cell G12 and change the formula to **=D12+F12** (Figure 6.17).

FIGURE 6.17

G12	▼	=	=D12+F12					
	A	B	C	D	E	F	G	H
1	Selections, Inc.							
2	Amortization Schedule							
3	01/15/99							
4								
5		Payment	$3,110.62					
6		Interest	7.500%					
7		Term	3 Years					
8		Principal	$100,000.00					
9								
10	Payment Number	Beginning Balance	Principal Paid	Cumulative Principal	Interest Paid	Cumulative Interest	Total Paid to Date	Ending Balance
11	1	$ 100,000.00	$ 2,485.62	$ 2,485.62	$625.00	$625.00	$ 3,110.62	$ 97,514.38
12	2	$ 97,514.38	$ 2,501.16	$ 4,986.78	$609.46	$1,234.46	$ 6,221.24	$ 95,013.22
13								

7 Highlight the range A12:H12. Using the fill handle, use AutoReplication to copy this row of formulas through row 46, and release the mouse button. The values should calculate as shown in Figure 6.18.

FIGURE 6.18

A12	▼	=	=A11+1					
	A	B	C	D	E	F	G	H
29	19	$ 52,800.81	$ 2,780.62	$ 49,979.80	$330.01	$9,122.01	$ 59,101.81	$ 50,020.20
30	20	$ 50,020.20	$ 2,798.00	$ 52,777.80	$312.63	$9,434.64	$ 62,212.44	$ 47,222.20
31	21	$ 47,222.20	$ 2,815.48	$ 55,593.28	$295.14	$9,729.78	$ 65,323.06	$ 44,406.72
32	22	$ 44,406.72	$ 2,833.08	$ 58,426.36	$277.54	$10,007.32	$ 68,433.68	$ 41,573.64
33	23	$ 41,573.64	$ 2,850.79	$ 61,277.15	$259.84	$10,267.15	$ 71,544.30	$ 38,722.85
34	24	$ 38,722.85	$ 2,868.60	$ 64,145.75	$242.02	$10,509.17	$ 74,654.92	$ 35,854.25
35	25	$ 35,854.25	$ 2,886.53	$ 67,032.29	$224.09	$10,733.26	$ 77,765.55	$ 32,967.71
36	26	$ 32,967.71	$ 2,904.57	$ 69,936.86	$206.05	$10,939.31	$ 80,876.17	$ 30,063.14
37	27	$ 30,063.14	$ 2,922.73	$ 72,859.59	$187.89	$11,127.20	$ 83,986.79	$ 27,140.41
38	28	$ 27,140.41	$ 2,940.99	$ 75,800.58	$169.63	$11,296.83	$ 87,097.41	$ 24,199.42
39	29	$ 24,199.42	$ 2,959.38	$ 78,759.96	$151.25	$11,448.08	$ 90,208.03	$ 21,240.04
40	30	$ 21,240.04	$ 2,977.87	$ 81,737.83	$132.75	$11,580.83	$ 93,318.65	$ 18,262.17
41	31	$ 18,262.17	$ 2,996.48	$ 84,734.31	$114.14	$11,694.96	$ 96,429.28	$ 15,265.69
42	32	$ 15,265.69	$ 3,015.21	$ 87,749.52	$95.41	$11,790.38	$ 99,539.90	$ 12,250.48
43	33	$ 12,250.48	$ 3,034.06	$ 90,783.58	$76.57	$11,866.94	$ 102,650.52	$ 9,216.42
44	34	$ 9,216.42	$ 3,053.02	$ 93,836.60	$57.60	$11,924.54	$ 105,761.14	$ 6,163.40
45	35	$ 6,163.40	$ 3,072.10	$ 96,908.70	$38.52	$11,963.06	$ 108,871.76	$ 3,091.30
46	36	$ 3,091.30	$ 3,091.30	$ 100,000.00	$19.32	$11,982.39	$ 111,982.39	$ 0.00
47								

TIP Notice that the Ending Balance equals zero at payment 36. This verifies that the amortization schedule is calculating the loan repayment figures correctly.

8 Scroll to the top of the worksheet, highlight Column A, and set the alignment of the selection to Center, as shown in Figure 6.19.

FIGURE 6.19

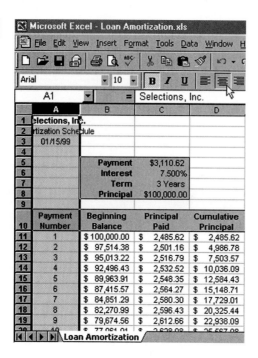

9 Highlight the range A1:A3. Set the alignment to Left (Figure 6.20).

FIGURE 6.20

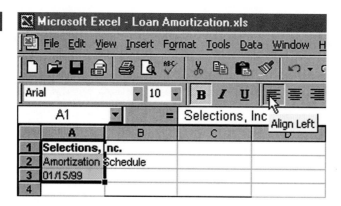

10 Highlight cell A1 and save your changes. The workbook should now look like the one shown in Figure 6.21.

FIGURE 6.21

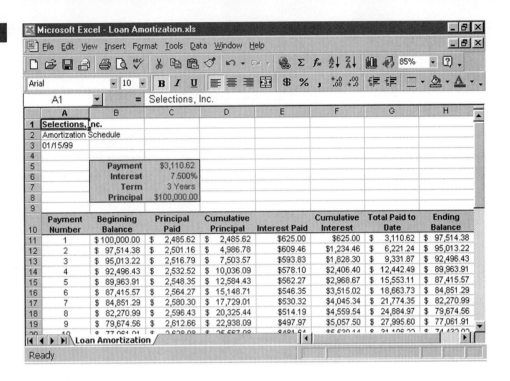

Freezing Worksheet Panes to Assist in Viewing Large Worksheets

Your amortization schedule is now fully functional. Take a moment to note the power of Microsoft Excel: By using financial functions and copying these formulas down the worksheet, the entire loan repayment table is based upon four numeric constants—even though your worksheet presently contains almost three hundred formulas.

Viewing large worksheets can be problematic because the heading rows scroll out of view as you move down the worksheet. To alleviate this problem, certain rows can be *frozen* so they always appear on the screen. In the next task, you will freeze the worksheet headings so the entire amortization schedule can be viewed with the headings visible on the screen.

TASK 10: To Freeze Worksheet Panes to Assist Viewing

1 Place the insertion point in cell A11.

2 Select Freeze Panes from the Window menu, as shown in Figure 6.22.

FIGURE 6.22

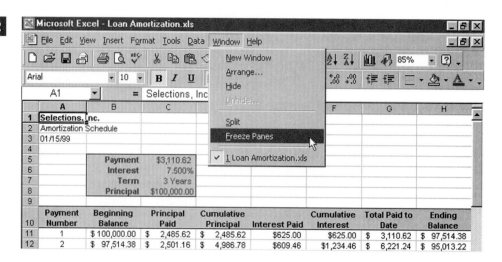

3 Select Go To from the Edit menu, as shown in Figure 6.23.

FIGURE 6.23

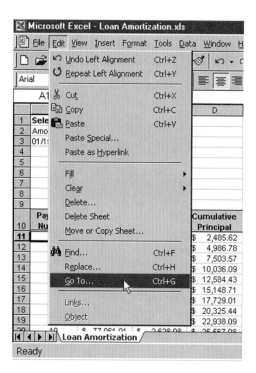

4 The Go To dialog box appears. Type **A46** in the Reference: text box and click OK, as shown in Figure 6.24.

FIGURE 6.24

5   Cell A46 becomes the active cell, and rows 1 through 10 and additional rows up to row 46 become visible, as shown in Figure 6.25.

FIGURE 6.25

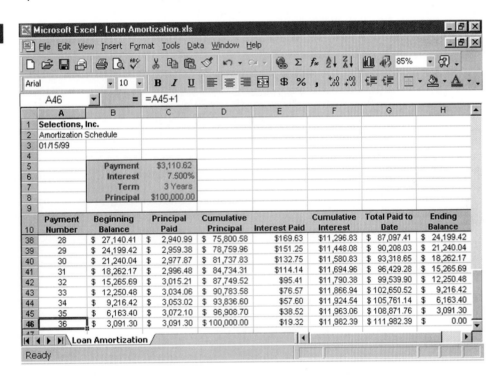

As you scroll through the worksheet, rows 1 through 10 always remain visible.

TIP   To unfreeze the panes, select Unfreeze Panes from the Window menu.

Changing the Loan Scenario

Using this workbook, Mr. Traylor can easily compare alternative loan scenarios. To see how easy it is to view another loan scenario, simply change the principal and term values, and then add additional rows to the worksheet.

TASK 11: **To Change the Loan Scenario**

1 Enter **4** in cell C7 and press (ENTER).

2 Type **250000** in cell C8 and press (ENTER). Notice that the monthly payment changes to $6,044.73, as shown in Figure 6.26.

FIGURE 6.26

	A	B	C
1	Selections, Inc.		
2	Amortization Schedule		
3	01/15/99		
4			
5		Payment	$6,044.73
6		Interest	7.500%
7		Term	4 Years
8		Principal	$250,000.00
9			

3 Scroll to the bottom of the worksheet and highlight the range A46:H46.

4 Using the fill handle, drag the selection through row 58 and release the left mouse button. Your amortization schedule should now resemble the one shown in Figure 6.27.

FIGURE 6.27

	A	B	C	D	E	F	G	H
1	Selections, Inc.							
2	Amortization Schedule							
3	01/15/99							
4								
5		Payment	$6,044.73					
6		Interest	7.500%					
7		Term	4 Years					
8		Principal	$250,000.00					
9								
10	Payment Number	Beginning Balance	Principal Paid	Cumulative Principal	Interest Paid	Cumulative Interest	Total Paid to Date	Ending Balance
50	40	$ 52,740.69	$ 5,715.10	$ 202,974.40	$329.63	$38,814.61	$ 241,789.02	$ 47,025.60
51	41	$ 47,025.60	$ 5,750.82	$ 208,725.22	$293.91	$39,108.52	$ 247,833.74	$ 41,274.78
52	42	$ 41,274.78	$ 5,786.76	$ 214,511.98	$257.97	$39,366.49	$ 253,878.47	$ 35,488.02
53	43	$ 35,488.02	$ 5,822.93	$ 220,334.90	$221.80	$39,588.29	$ 259,923.20	$ 29,665.10
54	44	$ 29,665.10	$ 5,859.32	$ 226,194.22	$185.41	$39,773.70	$ 265,967.92	$ 23,805.78
55	45	$ 23,805.78	$ 5,895.94	$ 232,090.16	$148.79	$39,922.49	$ 272,012.65	$ 17,909.84
56	46	$ 17,909.84	$ 5,932.79	$ 238,022.95	$111.94	$40,034.42	$ 278,057.37	$ 11,977.05
57	47	$ 11,977.05	$ 5,969.87	$ 243,992.82	$74.86	$40,109.28	$ 284,102.10	$ 6,007.18
58	48	$ 6,007.18	$ 6,007.18	$ 250,000.00	$37.54	$40,146.82	$ 290,146.82	$ 0.00

Loan Amortization

Ready   Sum=7671321.58

5 Using the vertical scroll bar, move to the top of the worksheet and make cell A1 the active cell.

6 Save and close the workbook.

Summary and Exercises

Summary

- Excel contains many financial functions for comparing scenarios involving investments or payments.
- Three numeric values—principal, interest, and term—are required to determine a loan payment.
- The PMT function is used to calculate a loan payment.
- The PV function is used to calculate the present value of an annuity.
- The PPMT function is used to calculate the portion of a loan payment that applies to the outstanding principal.
- The IPMT function is used to calculate the portion of a loan payment that applies to interest.
- A complex workbook such as an amortization schedule will contain hundreds of formulas.
- You can freeze worksheet panes to assist viewing large worksheets.

Key Terms and Operations

Key Terms

absolute reference	present value
amortization	principal
amortization schedule	rate
annuity functions	relative reference
argument	syntax
macro	term
mixed reference	text constants
loan scenario	Visual Basic
numeric constants	

Operations

construct a formula using the IPMT (interest payment) function
construct a formula using the PMT (payment) function
construct a formula using the PPMT (periodic payment) function
construct a formula using the PV (present value of an annuity) function
create an amortization schedule
create formulas to calculate the cumulative interest and cumulative
   principal
determine the ending balance
freeze worksheet panes
use AutoFill to copy formulas

Study Questions

Multiple Choice

1. A worksheet is being constructed to determine the monthly payment required to return $250,000 in the year 2025. Which financial function should be used to perform this calculation?
   a. PMT
   b. IPMT
   c. PV
   d. FV

2. A worksheet includes a formula for calculating the payment on a loan. To see the amount of the monthly payment that applies to the interest payment, you will use which function?
   a. PMT
   b. IPMT
   c. NOW()
   d. PPMT

3. Which statement concerning the use of the PV annuity function is false?
   a. An annuity payment should be entered as a negative value.
   b. The present value of the investment is required.
   c. The total number of payment periods in the annuity is required.
   d. The interest rate can fluctuate over the life of the annuity.

4. Which of the following most likely refers to the principal of a loan in a financial function?
   a. H6/12
   b. I7*12
   c. –J7
   d. g3/12

5. Which of the following formulas includes an absolute reference to an annuity payment?
   a. =PMT(a1/12,c7*12, d7)
   b. =PPMT(a1/12,c7*12, e7)
   c. =PMT(h6/12,I$7*12,–j7)
   d. =IPMT(a1/12,c7*12, –e7)
   e. =PMT(a1/12,$b7*12,–$r$5)

6. A relative reference will never contain
   a. a dollar sign before the row reference.
   b. a dollar sign before the column reference.
   c. a dollar sign before both the row and the column reference.
   d. all of the above.

7. The principal payment (PPMT) function is most similar to which function?
   a. PMT
   b. PV
   c. IPMT
   d. PPMT

8. Which function calculates the portion of a loan payment applied toward the principal?
   a. PMT
   b. PV
   c. IPMT
   d. PPMT

9. You can freeze worksheet panes using which menu?
   a. Format
   b. Edit
   c. Data
   d. View
   e. Window

10. The =NOW() function is in which category of functions?
    a. Financial
    b. Statistical
    c. Date/Time
    d. Logical

Short Answer

1. Examine the function =PMT(H6/12,I7*12,–J7). Which element refers to the present value of the loan?

2. Explain how the term of a loan affects the total amount paid.

3. What does the PPMT function calculate?

4. What is a mixed reference?

5. Why should the formulas in an amortization schedule contain absolute references?

6. What is the maximum number of arguments that can be included with the PMT function?

7. What value does the PPMT function return?

8. If you are having difficulty viewing the headings in a large worksheet, what should you do?

9. What character precedes a mixed reference?

10. How should annuity payments be entered in a formula?

Fill in the Blank

1. The _____ function is very similar to the PPMT function.

2. A(n) _____ payment is usually preceded by a minus (–) sign.

3. A(n) _____ reference contains a dollar sign symbol before both the row and column reference.

4. The PPMT function requires _____ arguments.

5. A table listing loan payments shows how the repayment is _____ over time.

6. The PV function calculates the _____ of an annuity.

7. The IPMT function is used to determine the portion of a loan payment that applies to the _____.

8. You can _____ worksheet panes if viewing a large worksheet becomes cumbersome.

9. The time period over which a loan is repaid is the _____.

10. The FV function is similar to the _____ function.

For Discussion

1. What is the FV function? How does the data it returns differ from data returned by the PV function?

2. What is a macro? How is a macro recorded and applied?

3. How can worksheets, such as the amortization schedule you created in this project, be protected from changes?

4. What arguments are required by the PMT function? Is the order in which these appear in a formula significant?

Hands-On Exercises

1. Protecting Cells in a Workbook

In many settings, portions of a worksheet should be protected to prohibit users from inadvertently making destructive changes to the workbook. By unlocking the cells to which users need access and protecting the worksheet, you can easily achieve this objective! Open the *Java Bar Loan Amortization* workbook and do the following:

1. Select the nonadjacent ranges C6:C8 and A13:H46.

2. Select Cells from the Format menu.

3. Click the Protection tab.

4. Deselect the Locked checkbox in the Format Cells dialog box.

5. Click OK.

6. Select Protection from the Tools menu.

7. Select Protect Sheet.

8. Do not enter a protection password in the Protect Sheet dialog box.

9. Click OK.

10. Save the updated workbook as *Protected Loan Analysis.xls*.

2. Creating Excel Macros

When using Excel you often may need to complete a series of tasks more than once. By recording a macro, you can easily apply these procedures again by simply playing the macro. A **macro** is a series of commands and functions stored in a Visual Basic module that can be run whenever you need to perform the task again. (**Visual Basic** is the programming language used throughout the Office environment for recording macros. If you know Visual Basic, you can easily edit a macro you have created.)

It would be nice if your amortization worksheet could easily be returned to a predictable state after the loan's term is modified, since the worksheet will either display errors or not display the entire repayment schedule. You can create a macro to set the default values and create the appropriate number of loan repayment formulas.

Complete the following:

1. Launch Excel if it is not already running.
2. Open the *Loan Amortization.xls* workbook.
3. Save a copy of the workbook as *Loan Defaults.xls*.
4. Select Macro from the Tools menu, and choose Record New Macro.
5. Type **SetDefaults** as the name of the macro, and make sure the macro is stored in the current workbook, as shown in Figure 6.28. Click OK.

FIGURE 6.28

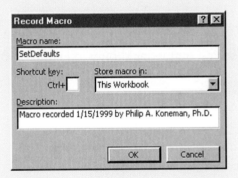

TIP   Every procedure you now apply will become a part of the macro. You will also notice that the Stop Recording toolbar is now visible on the screen.

6. Click cell A13 to make it the active cell.
7. While simultaneously holding down the (SHIFT) and (CTRL) keys, press the (END) key. The range A13:H58 is now selected, as shown in Figure 6.29.

FIGURE 6.29

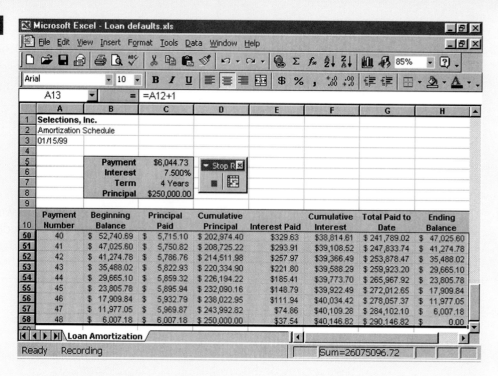

	A	B	C	D	E	F	G	H
1	Selections, Inc.							
2	Amortization Schedule							
3	01/15/99							
4								
5		Payment	$6,044.73					
6		Interest	7.500%					
7		Term	4 Years					
8		Principal	$250,000.00					
9								
10	Payment Number	Beginning Balance	Principal Paid	Cumulative Principal	Interest Paid	Cumulative Interest	Total Paid to Date	Ending Balance
50	40	$ 52,740.69	$ 5,715.10	$ 202,974.40	$329.63	$38,814.61	$ 241,789.02	$ 47,025.60
51	41	$ 47,025.60	$ 5,750.82	$ 208,725.22	$293.91	$39,108.52	$ 247,833.74	$ 41,274.78
52	42	$ 41,274.78	$ 5,786.76	$ 214,511.98	$257.97	$39,366.49	$ 253,878.47	$ 35,488.02
53	43	$ 35,488.02	$ 5,822.93	$ 220,334.90	$221.80	$39,588.29	$ 259,923.20	$ 29,665.10
54	44	$ 29,665.10	$ 5,859.32	$ 226,194.22	$185.41	$39,773.70	$ 265,967.92	$ 23,805.78
55	45	$ 23,805.78	$ 5,895.94	$ 232,090.16	$148.79	$39,922.49	$ 272,012.65	$ 17,909.84
56	46	$ 17,909.84	$ 5,932.79	$ 238,022.95	$111.94	$40,034.42	$ 278,057.37	$ 11,977.05
57	47	$ 11,977.05	$ 5,969.87	$ 243,992.82	$74.86	$40,109.28	$ 284,102.10	$ 6,007.18
58	48	$ 6,007.18	$ 6,007.18	$ 250,000.00	$37.54	$40,146.82	$ 290,146.82	$ 0.00

8. Press the (DEL) key to delete the selected portion of the amortization schedule.

9. Type **.075** in cell C6 as the rate, **3** in cell C7 as the term, and **100000** in cell C8 as the principal.

10. Select the range A12:H12 and use the fill handle to copy the formulas through row 46.

11. Scroll to the top of the worksheet and make cell A1 the active cell.

12. Click the Stop Recording button, as shown in Figure 6.30.

FIGURE 6.30

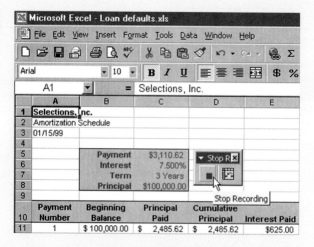

	A	B	C	D	E
1	Selections, Inc.				
2	Amortization Schedule				
3	01/15/99				
4					
5		Payment	$3,110.62		
6		Interest	7.500%		
7		Term	3 Years		
8		Principal	$100,000.00		
9					
10	Payment Number	Beginning Balance	Principal Paid	Cumulative Principal	Interest Paid
11	1	$ 100,000.00	$ 2,485.62	$ 2,485.62	$625.00

13. You have now successfully recorded a macro. Any time you change the worksheet scenario and then want to restore it to a predictable state, select Macros from the Tools menu and run the macro.

14. Save the workbook.

3. Calculating the Future Value of an Investment

The future value of an annuity (FV) function is one of Excel's financial functions that will calculate the future value of an investment. In this example the FV function requires four arguments: the interest rate, the number of contribution periods, the contribution made each period, and the initial value of the investment. In this exercise you will compare three investment scenarios using the FV function. The completed worksheet is shown in Figure 6.31.

FIGURE 6.31

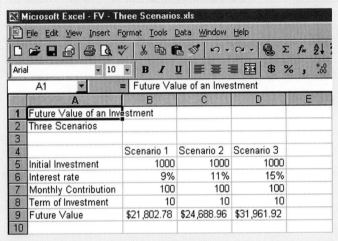

Comparing three investment scenarios

1. Launch Excel if it is not currently running, or create a new worksheet by selecting New from the File menu.

2. Enter the text labels shown in Figure 6.31.

3. Select the range B5:D5 and type **1000**.

4. Type **9%** in cell B6, **11%** in cell C6, and **15%** in cell D6.

> **TIP**   You can enter percentages in a cell by either typing the decimal equivalent or typing the percent value followed by the percent (%) symbol.

5. Select the range B7:D7 and type **100** as the monthly contribution.

6. Select the range B8:D8 and type **10** as term of the investment.

7. Select cell B9, type **=FV(B6/12,B8*12,-B7,-B5)**, and press (ENTER). Cash you pay out (deposits to savings or other payments) is represented by a negative number.

8. Use the fill handle to copy this formula through cell D9.

9. Create a folder on your disk named *Investments*.

10. Save your workbook to the Investments folder with *FV—Three Scenarios.xls* as the file name.

4. Using the Date Function

Excel stores dates as sequential serial numbers so that it can perform calculations on them. Excel stores January 1, 1900, as serial number 1. The Date function in Excel is used to return the serial number corresponding to a given date. In this exercise, you will create a simple clock that counts the number of days remaining until the new century. The workbook you will create is shown in Figure 6.32.

FIGURE 6.32

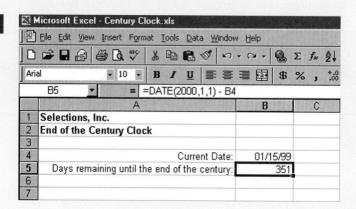

1. Launch Excel if it is not currently running, or create a new worksheet by selecting New from the File menu.

2. Enter the text labels shown in Figure 6.32. Format the text as shown.

3. Type **1/15/99** in cell B4, and change the format to a date format if necessary.

4. Type **=DATE(2000,1,1) – B4** as the formula in cell B5. This formula uses the Date function to return the serial number for January 1, 2000, and subtracts from this number the date listed in cell B4.

5. Format cell B5 as a number with zero decimal places, if necessary.

6. Save the workbook as *Century Clock.xls*.

7. Close the workbook.

On Your Own Exercises

1. Creating Macros to Enable and Disable Protection for a Worksheet

Open the *Protected Loan Analysis.xls* workbook. Create two macros: one that sets the protection for the worksheet, and one that removes the worksheet protection. Save the workbook as *Protected Loan Y-N.xls*.

2. Repaying a Loan Early

Visit Microsoft's New Spreadsheet Solutions site, which contains spreadsheet solutions created by Village Software, to download a file called *Loan Manager*.

Web Tip

You can download the *Loan Manager* file from the Web at
http://www.microsoft.com/excel/freestuff/templates/villagesoftware/.
If you cannot access this site, ask your instructor for a copy of the file.

Download the Loan Manager self-extracting file (*Loan.exe*), and install the
Loan.xlt template to your disk. Open the *Loan.xlt* file, and enter the loan data
from this project. Make three additional payments of $100.00 each. Save
the workbook as *Prepaid.xls.*

3. Modifying a Workbook

Open the *Prepaid.xls* workbook and make the following changes:

1. Create a macro to set the workbook to a predictable state.
2. Protect the cells containing critical formulas so they cannot be
   modified.

Save the updated workbook as *Prepaid Updates.xls.*

4. Comparing Multiple Amortizations

Create an Excel workbook containing two amortization schedule worksheets
with two separate loan scenarios. Save the workbook as *Loan
Comparisons.xls.*

5. Adding a Lump Sum Feature to the Loan Comparisons Workbook

When repaying a loan, it is common to make lump sum payments against
the principal at periodic intervals. Modify the two worksheets in the *Loan
Comparisons.xls* workbook to accept lump sum payments. Save the updated
workbook as *Updated Loan Comparisons.xls.*

6. Summarizing Loan Comparison Data

Open the *Updated Loan Comparisons.xls* workbook and create a summary
worksheet that summarizes the loan scenarios on one sheet. Use linking
formulas and name the updated workbook as *Summarized Loan
Comparisons.xls.*

Integrated Project

Integrating Word and Excel

One of the advantages of using software programs that are part of a suite is that the programs are designed to work together as a team. You've already discovered a few of the shared components in Microsoft Office—the spelling dictionary, Find, and so on. Now it's time to see how you can use data from an Excel worksheet in a Word document and how to create links so that data in both files updates automatically.

Objectives

After completing this project, you will be able to:

➤ Identify differences between linking and embedding

➤ Copy Excel data to a Word document

➤ Link an Excel chart to a Word document

➤ View links

➤ Save documents and workbooks as Web pages

➤ View documents and workbooks as Web pages

➤ E-mail documents and worksheets

Running Case

You've been instrumental in formulating a number of Word documents and have put your skills to the test with Excel. Because of your expertise with both applications, you've been placed on special assignment in the finance department, where they are gearing up for their mid-summer sale.

The Challenge

Selections, Inc., is on the verge of its annual midsummer sale. To ensure its success and to encourage an all-out effort to increase sales in each region, Mr. Travis Taylor, accounting and finance department manager, and Ms. Joy Quinn, production and advertising department manager, have teamed up. They plan to provide current sales figures to regional sales offices and promote the sale by initiating a sales competition. You have been selected to create the documents and brochures pictured in Figure 1.1. The letter will be e-mailed to each regional office and the sales competition information will be posted on the Selections, Inc., Web site for easy reference.

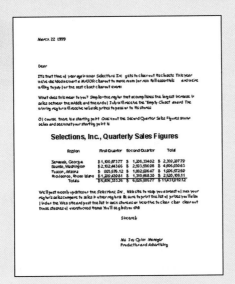

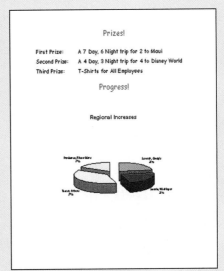

The Strategy

You'll use skills you've just learned to create a new Excel worksheet that contains all regional sales totals for the first two quarters of the current year. Using the figures, you will create the chart shown in Figure 1.1 to visually display profits. After you complete the Excel worksheet and chart, you will use Word to create the letter to all regional sales directors and the Web flyer.

Integrating data from the worksheet with text in the letter and flyer is as easy as dragging the data from the worksheet and dropping it on the report. You can also copy the Excel chart to the report and create a link so that the chart in the Web page automatically updates when you change data in the Excel worksheet.

The Setup

To ensure that your screen will match the figures pictured in this project, make sure the settings shown in Table 1.1 are active.

Table 1.1

Location:	Make these settings:
Office Assistant	Hide the Office Assistant.
View	Click the Print Layout View button at the bottom of the Word window. Ensure that the Formula Bar and Status Bar are both displayed in the Excel window.
Toolbars	Ensure that both the Standard and Formatting toolbars are active in both application windows. If you don't see them, choose View, Toolbars, and then select them. Close all other active toolbars.
	Choose Tools, Customize, and then click the Options tab and ensure that the Personalized Menus and Toolbars options are all deselected. Then click the Reset my usage data button and choose Yes to restore automatic changes to menus. Choose Close.
Zoom	Set the zoom to Page Width in Word and 100% in Excel.
Ruler	Hide the Ruler in Word.

 Web Tip

If you do not have a copy of *Selections 2nd Quarter Sales Letter.doc* and *Selections Quarterly Sales Figures.xls* on your student disk, you can download them from the SELECT Web site at http://www.prenhall.com/select.

Identifying Differences between Linking and Embedding

When data you want to include in a new file already exists in another file—even if that file was created in another application—you can open the file in its original application and place it in the new file. The procedure you use to place the data depends on whether you want the information to reflect the most up-to-date information or to remain constant. Table 1.2 identifies terms associated with sharing information among Office 2000 applications.

You've already embedded items in files you've created. When you added graphics, WordArt, and other items to your Word and Excel files, they were embedded and saved with the file. You'll use both embedding and linking to create the files in this project. Here are some basic considerations for choosing whether linking or embedding is better:

- Are you going to use the document with different data or updated information at a later date? If so, consider linking the data to the document file you plan to reuse.

- How is your memory? Your computer memory, of course. If it is limited, you might also want to link files. Embedding graphics and data files increases the size of the file, which can sorely tax limited resources.

- Are you planning to use the file on a disk or away from the computer containing the files? If so, consider embedding so that you are sure to have everything you need when you reach your destination and need to print or present the information. Unless you're very careful, linked files often get left behind.

Table 1.2

Term	Description
Source file	The file containing the information you want to use in a new file.
Source application	The application used to create the source file.
Target file	The file to receive information that is currently stored in another file.
Target application	The application used to create the target file.
Embedded objects	Data, graphics, or other objects placed in target files and saved with the file. Embedded objects remain constant when they are added to other files, even when the original (source) file changes.
Linked objects	Data, graphics, charts, or other objects placed in target files with a reference and attachment to the source file. When you create a link between the source file and the target file, the target file checks the source file each time you open the target file to determine whether data in the source file has changed. You then have the option to update the target file to reflect changes made to the source file when necessary.

Copying Excel Data to a Word Document

Because the data you want to add to the Word document already exists in the Excel file, you're ready to integrate the data into the document. Because the letter to each regional manager will contain sales data as of the end of the second quarter and will not change, you can embed the data in the letters rather than link it.

TASK 1:   To Embed Excel Data in a Word Document

1. Launch Excel and open the *Selections Quarterly Sales Figures.xls* worksheet, as shown in Figure 1.2.

FIGURE 1.2

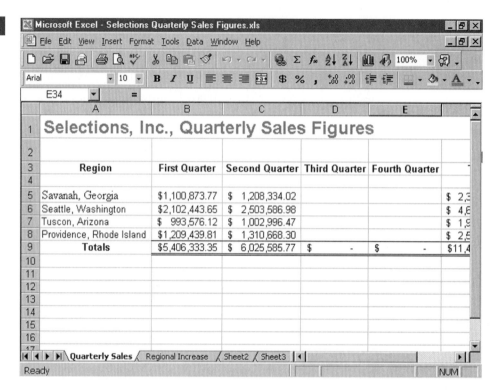

2 Launch Word and open the *Selections 2nd Quarter Sales Letter.doc* document.

3 Minimize all other program windows that are open and maximize both Word and Excel. Minimizing all extra program windows ensures that you'll be able to divide the screen evenly between Word and Excel.

4 Point to a blank area of the Windows taskbar and right-click.

FIGURE 1.3

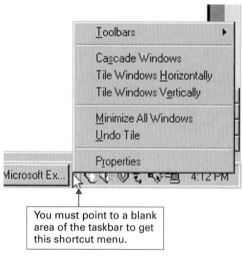

You must point to a blank area of the taskbar to get this shortcut menu.

5 Choose Tile Windows Vertically.

FIGURE 1.4

The application active
at the time you tiled
appears on the left.

The menu bars
wrap to cover
multiple lines.

Additional
toolbar buttons
are off-screen.

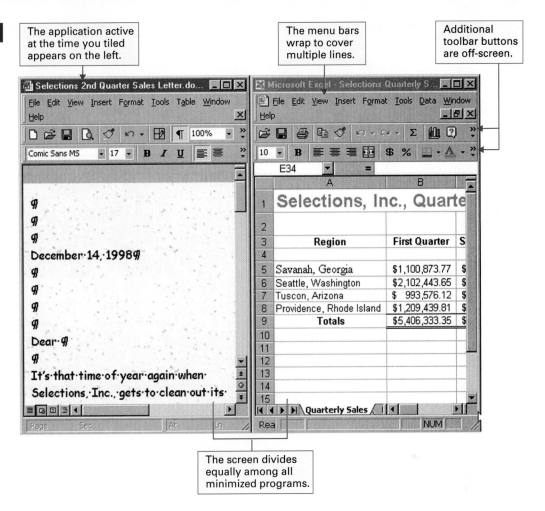

The screen divides
equally among all
minimized programs.

TROUBLESHOOTING Tiled applications on different size monitors
may vary somewhat from the screen pictured in Figure 1.4.

6 Click the Word title bar and scroll the document to display the wide space
between the third and fourth paragraphs and click to position the insertion
point on one of the blank paragraphs.

TIP Displaying nonprinting characters makes determining proper position
easier.

7 Click the Excel title bar and then select cells A1 through D9.

FIGURE 1.5

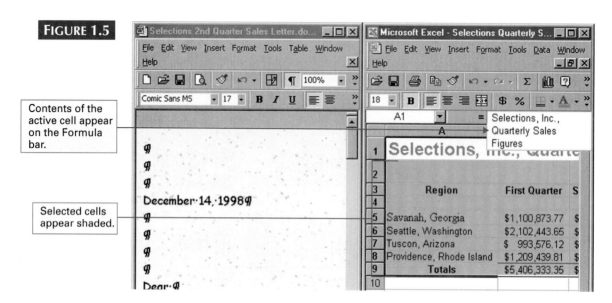

Contents of the active cell appear on the Formula bar.

Selected cells appear shaded.

8 Position the pointer close to the border of the selected area of the Excel worksheet, press and hold the (CTRL) key, and drag and drop the selected cells to Word.

FIGURE 1.6

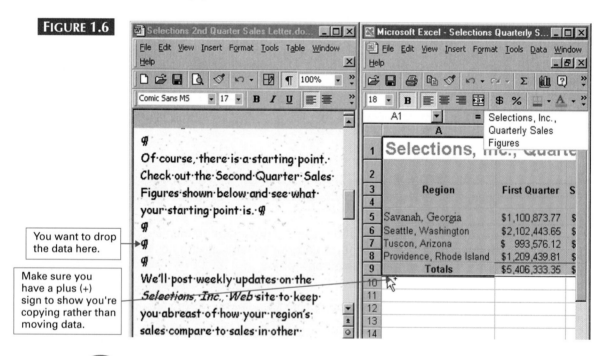

You want to drop the data here.

Make sure you have a plus (+) sign to show you're copying rather than moving data.

9 Adjust the size and position of the copied cells so that they appear as shown in Figure 1.1, then press (CTRL) + (END). The insertion point is positioned at the end of the document.

10 Switch to Excel and type the following data in column E for Third Quarter Sales:

$500,934.18

$1,000,475.97

$750,222.36

$338,642.13

11 Save changes to the worksheet.

Check Point

Change the title of the worksheet to a WordArt object. Save changes to the file and print a copy of the worksheet.

Linking an Excel Chart to a Word Document

The data you copied from the worksheet to the letter is now an embedded object in the letter, and the data in the Word document remains the same regardless of what happens to the worksheet. When you want data in a document to change as data in the original worksheet changes, you have to create a **link** between the worksheet and the document. That way, each time you open the document, Word will ask whether you want to update the object with data from the source file. After you inserted third quarter sales data in the worksheet, a percentage increase chart was automatically updated to show the sales increase for each region. Because you will be updating the figures in the worksheet each day to reflect up-to-the-minute sales figures that you want reflected in the flyer that you post to the Web site, you need to link the chart to the document.

TASK 2: To Link an Excel Chart to a Word Document

1 Tile the program windows again, if necessary display the *Percent Increase* chart sheet in Excel, and close the Chart toolbar.

2 Position the pointer on the chart until *Chart Area* appears as a ScreenTip and click. Handles appear on the corners and sides of the chart.

3 Click ⬛. A marquee that looks like marching dashes appears around the chart area.

4 Click the Word title bar and choose Edit, Paste Special.

FIGURE 1.7	

Options enable you to paste an object or paste a link.

Possible object types are listed.

A description of the selected object is given.

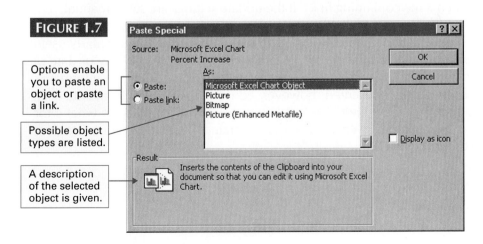

5 Click the Paste link option, ensure that Microsoft Excel Chart Object is selected in the As list box, and choose OK. Wow! Did your screen seem to go nuts? You need to make some adjustments to the size of the chart to bring it back onto the page.

6 Maximize Word, switch to Print Layout view, and size the chart so that it appears as shown in Figure 1.8.

FIGURE 1.8

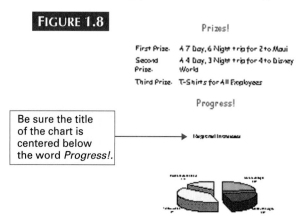

Prizes!

First Prize.   A 7 Day, 6 Night trip for 2 to Maui
Second   A 4 Day, 3 Night trip for 4 to Disney
Prize.   World
Third Prize.   T-Shirts for All Employees

Progress!

Be sure the title of the chart is centered below the word *Progress!*.

7 Save changes to the document.

Web Tip

The concept of links in documents is similar to the concept of hyperlinks on the Web. You can access the original file linked to another file by simply double-clicking it in the document. On the Web, you single-click a hyperlink to connect to the site.

Editing and Breaking Links

When a file or object is linked to another file, each time a change occurs in the source file, it can be updated in the target file. Depending on which settings are active on your computer, updates may be made automatically when you open a file containing links. If the update settings are set as manual, a dialog box will open each time you open a file containing links so that you have the option to update the links. This update feature is particularly useful when you create a file that is constantly changing up to the day or date on which you plan to send a document or present data. After the information has been sent or presented, however, you often will want to maintain the data contained in the letter so that you can refer to it later to see what information was shared. To ensure that data contained in a file never updates, you can break the link.

TASK 3:   To Edit and Break Links

1 Switch to Excel, maximize the window, display the Quarterly Sales worksheet, and change the third quarter sales data in column E as follows:

$625,448.54
$1,234,587.99
$890,234.77
$500,334.12

2 Switch to Word to view the chart. If the chart in the Word document changed to reflect changes to the Excel worksheet, your Links settings are automatic. If the chart in the Word document did *not* change, your settings are manual.

3 Choose Edit, Links.

FIGURE 1.9

Update Now enables you to manually update a link whenever you want to.

The source file and location

Open Source launches the source application and opens the source file, if necessary.

Change Source lets you link a different drive, folder, file, and/ or chart to the document.

Update settings— Automatic is active on my computer

Locked links cannot be updated.

Break Link removes the link between the source and target files and leaves the object embedded in the target file.

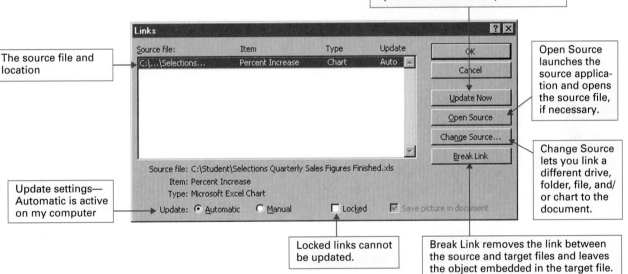

4 Choose Manual, then choose OK, save changes, and close the document.

5 Switch to Excel, add $1,000 to each of the values in column E, and save changes to the worksheet.

6 Open the *Selections 2nd Quarter Sales Letter.doc* again. Did the chart update?

7 Choose Edit, Links, and then click Update Now.

8 Save changes to the file.

Check Point

Preview the document, and then click the Shrink to Fit button on the Preview toolbar to make the letter fit on one page. Save changes to the file, print it, and then close it.

Break Point

If necessary, you can save your file, exit Word and Excel, and continue this project later.

Saving Documents and Workbooks as Web Pages

Office 2000 applications contain a feature that automatically codes and formats your files so that they can be posted to the Web. All you have to do is answer a few questions, and a wizard creates the Web document—like magic!

TASK 4: To Save Files as Web Pages

1 Launch Word, if necessary, and open *Selections 2nd Quarter Sales Letter.doc*.

2 Delete the text that makes up the letter but leave the second page intact.

3 Choose File, Save as Web Page.

4 Click the Change Title button.

FIGURE 1.10

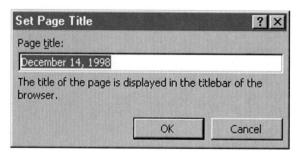

5 Type ***Your name*'s Regional Sales Progress** and click OK. The new title appears as the Page title.

6 Click Save.

TROUBLESHOOTING Tiled applications on different size monitors may vary somewhat from the screen pictured in Figure 1.5. Depending on the browser identified as your default, you may see the following message:

Choose Continue to view the Web page and decide what action you need to take. Often this message is simply a reflection of the file name you gave your Web page. If your browser does not support spaces in Web page names, for example, you may want to adjust the file name accordingly.

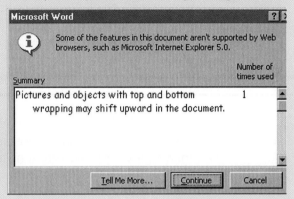

Viewing Documents and Workbooks as Web Pages

After you save files as Web pages, you can view them in your default browser without actually connecting to the Web.

TASK 5:   To View Documents as Web Pages

1 Choose File, Web Page Preview and maximize the window, if necessary.

2 Close the browser.

FIGURE 1.11

Your default browser launches and displays the Web page

The page title you entered appears in the title bar

The folder in which the file is stored appears in the Address box

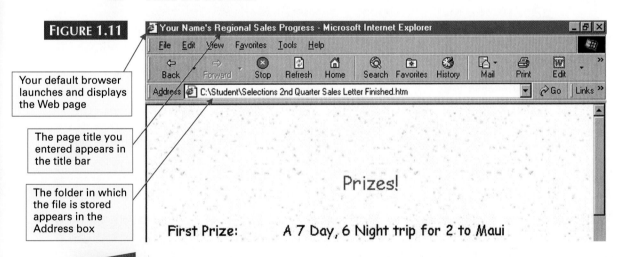

 **Check Point**

Make the necessary adjustments to the Web document, save your changes and close the file. Save the entire Excel Workbook file *Selections Quarterly Sales Figures.xls* as a Web page with the page title *Your Name's Quarterly Sales Figures*, preview it, and then close the browser.

Web Tip

If your school or place of work has an intranet or you have access to an Internet site to which you can save files, you can save your files to an FTP site directly from an Office 2000 application. To access this feature, you must first add the FTP site to your list of Internet sites:

1. Choose File, Open, and select Add/Modify FTP Locations from the Look in drop-down list.

2. Type the name of the FTP site to which you can save files.

3. Select the type of access you have to the site (Anonymous or User), and then type your password, if necessary.

4. Choose Add.

After the site is added to the list, simply select FTP Locations from the Save in drop-down list when you save your file and select the appropriate site.

E-Mailing Documents and Workbooks

Another special feature built into Office 2000 applications is the capability to e-mail a document or file directly from the application to an e-mail address or as an attachment to an e-mail message.

TASK 6: To E-Mail Files

1 Launch your default e-mail program, if necessary. Some setups require that the default e-mail program be running and connected to the network.

2 Switch to Excel and open *Selections Quarterly Sales Figures.xls*, if necessary.

> **TROUBLESHOOTING** The last file you used in Excel was saved as a Web page. You may need to switch to the .xls file in Excel or close the .htm file and open the .xls file.

3 Choose File, Send To, Mail Recipient.

FIGURE 1.12

The Office Assistant pops up and offers assistance

Options for sending specific worksheets or the complete workbook

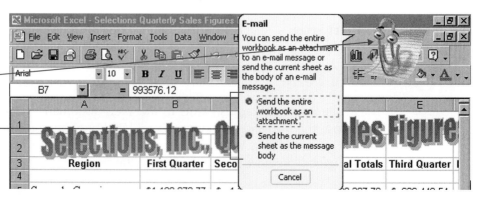

4 Choose Send the current sheet as a message body. A new mail message opens in Excel.

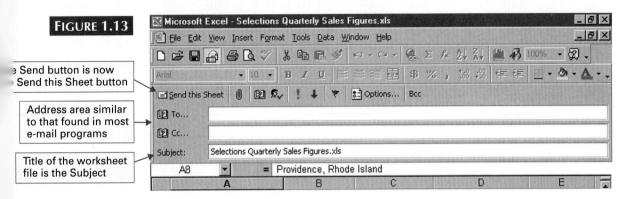

FIGURE 1.13

e Send button is now Send this Sheet button

Address area similar to that found in most e-mail programs

Title of the worksheet file is the Subject

5 Address the e-mail message to yourself and click Send this Sheet. The e-mail is sent to the recipient and you should receive the worksheet as an e-mail message.

6 Close Excel, saving changes to the workbook as necessary.

7 Switch to Word and open the *Selections 2nd Quarter Sales Letter.doc* file.

> **TROUBLESHOOTING** The last file you used in Word was saved as a Web page. You may need to switch to the .doc file in Word or close the .htm file and open the .doc file.

8 Choose File, Send To, Mail Recipient (as Attachment). A different format e-mail message window opens.

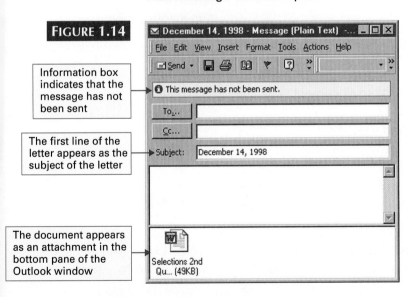

FIGURE 1.14

Information box indicates that the message has not been sent

The first line of the letter appears as the subject of the letter

The document appears as an attachment in the bottom pane of the Outlook window

9 Address the message to yourself and type **Please review the attached file, add comments to the document, and return the file to me at your earliest convenience.** in the message window.

10 Send the message, close the file and exit Word.

Summary

- One advantage of using programs that are part of an office suite is that the shared features make integrating information quick and easy.

- You can share data between applications using a variety of different techniques: dragging and dropping, copying and pasting, and linking.

- Linking data between applications ensures that data updated in one application is reflected in the other application.

- Embedding creates a copy of the data and places it in the target document without creating a link. Embedded data isn't updated automatically when data changes in the other application.

- Office 2000 applications contain a feature that automatically codes and formats your files so that they can be posted to the Web. All you have to do is answer a few questions, and a wizard creates the Web document.

- After you save files as Web pages, you can view them in your default browser without actually connecting to the Web.

- You can e-mail a document or file directly from the application to an e-mail address or as an attachment to an e-mail message.

Key Terms and Operations

Key Terms

embed
integrate
link
source file

source application
target file
target application

Operations

copy Excel data to a Word document
edit and break links
e-mail documents and worksheets
identify differences between linking and embedding
link an Excel chart to a Word document
save documents and workbooks as Web pages
view documents and workbooks as Web pages

For additional review and exercises using Word and Excel (or Word, Excel, and Access or Word, Excel, Access, and PowerPoint) visit the SELECT Web site at http://www.prenhall.com/select.

Projects for
Microsoft
Access 2000

Introducing Access 2000

Microsoft Access is the database management tool that ships with Microsoft Office 2000 Professional. As part of the Microsoft Professional and Premium Suites, Access has features that will appeal to a variety of users. For those new to database management, Access includes numerous wizards for completing a variety of database tasks. For experienced database developers, Access includes powerful features for manipulating data in Access tables, data in legacy systems, and data residing on Web servers. Since Access and Visual Basic both share some of the same features and capabilities, seasoned programmers can develop sophisticated stand-alone applications that utilize Access data, or custom front-end applications that meet a variety of business needs in a client-server environment. In short, Access 2000 is a versatile database development tool suited for both beginning and seasoned developers.

Since Access is based upon the relational database model, you can create powerful applications that can be implemented in a variety of ways. This overview will introduce you to basic database concepts and the Microsoft Access user interface.

Objectives

After completing this project, you will be able to:

➤ Define database terminology

➤ Identify Microsoft Access database objects

➤ Identify the steps required to design a database

➤ Launch Microsoft Access and create a new database

➤ Identify Microsoft Access screen elements

➤ Close a database and exit Access

Defining Database Terminology

A ***database*** is a collection of information related to a particular subject or purpose. For example, most people keep a list of the names, addresses, and phone numbers of the people they contact frequently. The categories of information that you keep on each individual are most likely consistent. In database terms, each individual item of information in the list such as first name or last name is called a ***field***. The field information for one person in the list is a **record**. Therefore, a database contains fields and records. Figure O.1 refers to five fields and one record in a sample phone list.

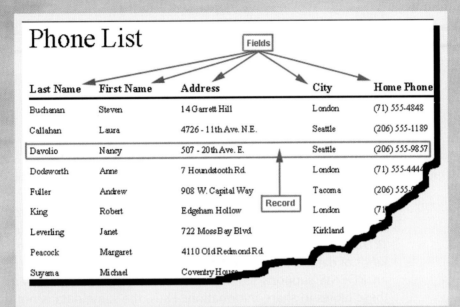

Fields and a record

TIP Some sources will refer to a field as a column and a record as a row. Although these are not technical database terms, they are useful when you are viewing an Access datasheet, which lists data in this row-and-column format.

When using Microsoft Access to store information, field and record information is contained in a database object called a table. A **table** is a two-dimensional grid containing field data. Figure O.2 displays phone list data in a Microsoft Access table.

| FIGURE O.2 |

Employees : Table

		Last Name	First Name	Address	City	Home Phone
▶	⊞	Buchanan	Steven	14 Garrett Hill	London	(71) 555-4848
	⊞	Callahan	Laura	4726 - 11th Ave. N.E.	Seattle	(206) 555-1189
	⊞	Davolio	Nancy	507 - 20th Ave. E.	Seattle	(206) 555-9857
	⊞	Dodsworth	Anne	7 Houndstooth Rd.	London	(71) 555-4444
	⊞	Fuller	Andrew	908 W. Capital Way	Tacoma	(206) 555-9482
	⊞	King	Robert	Edgeham Hollow	London	(71) 555-5598
	⊞	Leverling	Janet	722 Moss Bay Blvd.	Kirkland	(206) 555-3412
	⊞	Peacock	Margaret	4110 Old Redmond Rd.	Redmond	(206) 555-8122
	⊞	Suyama	Michael	Coventry House	London	(71) 555-7773
✳						

Record: |◄ ◄ 1 ► ►| ►✳ of 9

Table data

A computer application that you use to create and maintain databases is a **database management system (DBMS)**. Access allows you to store information in separate tables and use the data from one or more tables through relationships. A database management system that allows you to establish relationships among tables is a **relational database management system (RDBMS)**. Relational database management systems are the most powerful kinds of database applications available for microcomputers. This is because an RDBMS supports storing field data in separate tables and then linking these tables to share information. Thus, the same data is not duplicated unnecessarily, which improves the overall accuracy of the information.

Identifying Access Database Objects

In addition to tables, Microsoft Access databases contain other components, each of which is called an object. A **database object** is a component of the database that gives it functionality. Each database object belongs to a category of objects known as a **class**. For example, a table for storing phone list information is a specific instance of a table object. Microsoft Access has seven classes of database objects. A table, a query, a form, a report, a page, a macro, and a module are all classes of database objects. The purpose of each object is listed in Table O.1.

Table O.1: Seven classes of database objects

Object class	Purpose
Table	An organized collection of rows and columns used to store field data.
Query	An object that is used to view, change, or organize data.
Form	A graphical object that displays data from a table or a query in an easy-to-use format.
Report	An object used to present data in a printed format.
Pages	Data Access Pages are HTML files designed in Access and formatted to display in a Web browser.
Macro	A set of one or more actions that are used to automate common tasks such as opening a form or printing a report.
Module	A collection of Visual Basic for Applications programming components that are stored together as a unit.

> **TIP** Macros and modules are complex database objects. In this learning module you will learn to design and use tables, queries, forms, and reports.

In Microsoft Access, the database objects you create are stored in a single database file with a .mdb file name extension.

Before you design a database, you need to understand how Access database objects relate to one another. Since tables are used to store field and record information, you must create at least one table before you create any other object. For this reason, tables are the primary objects in an Access database. Since queries allow you to organize and view data in different ways, a query is always based upon one or more tables. Queries can also display data from other queries.

Working with records in a row-and-column format is often tedious. For this reason, forms are used to make a table or query more accessible. In a well-designed database, users work with record and field data via forms, and not at the table level. While tables are required to store field data, forms based upon tables and queries are the objects users interact with directly, since forms are designed to make data access and maintenance easy, and are also usually designed to prevent users from inadvertently making destructive changes to table data. While forms and access pages are appropriate for viewing data on the screen, reports are used to format table-to-query data for printed output.

TIP Macros and modules are resources you can use to add more functionality to a database application. Working with these objects requires a solid working knowledge of Microsoft Access and Visual Basic. Therefore, you will not learn about them in this learning module.

Designing a Database

Making a database easy to use requires careful planning. The time you spend planning a database prior to designing it will greatly benefit you! In general, you will complete five steps when designing a database. Database planning includes determining the overall specifications and requirements. Database design includes implementing these specifications using a software application such as Microsoft Access.

1. Defining the purpose

Define the overall purpose of the database, including a list of user specifications for input and output. Input and output specifications include tasks such as entering data from a common source such as employment applications or printing a report of payroll data for the current pay period. This data is often gathered by interviewing end users.

2. Planning the database objects

The objects contained in your database must be carefully planned. You will need to determine the appropriate number of tables, the ways in which the records will be reorganized using queries, and the kinds of forms and reports your database will contain.

3. Creating and relating tables

As you know, tables are the primary objects. As you will see in Project 1, when designing a table you must first specify the kind of data each field will contain. You may decide to add some of the fields to additional tables. If your database contains more than one table, you will need to establish relationships among the tables.

4. Creating queries to reorganize data

You rarely need to see all of the field data in a database for all records at the same time. For this reason, queries are used to determine how data is reorganized to fulfill a specific request. You may need a listing of all customers from California, or a calculation of a member's outstanding balance. Queries are often used for this purpose.

5. Creating forms, pages, and reports

Since forms and reports are used by end users to work with records on the screen and in printed form, they are essential to a database. To share database information with other users, you can create access pages to list records in HTML format for display in a Web browser. Forms, access pages, and reports get their data from tables and queries.

A full-fledged database design is a complex and time-consuming process that requires careful planning and documentation. For the databases you will design in this module, use a word processor such as Microsoft Word to document your intended design.

In the projects that follow, you will complete these stages of database design for a simple database in which the data is stored in one table. After launching Microsoft Access, you will see that the user interface has been designed to facilitate creating and maintaining relational databases.

Launching Microsoft Access and Creating a New Database

As with each of the Office applications, you can launch Microsoft Access in a variety of ways from the Windows desktop. In the steps that follow, you will use the Start button to launch Access and create a new database.

TASK 1:   To Launch Microsoft Access and Create a New Database

1   Click the Start 🏁 Start button.

2   Choose Programs from the Start menu and choose Microsoft Access, as shown in Figure O.3.

FIGURE O.3

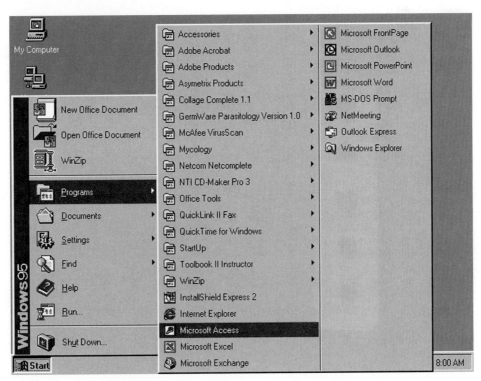

Launching Microsoft Access

The Microsoft Access dialog box shown in Figure O.4 appears. You have three options: opening an existing database using the list of recently used databases, creating a new database using the Database Wizard, or creating a blank database.

FIGURE O.4

③ Select the Blank Access database option button and click OK. The File New Database dialog box shown in Figure O.5 appears. Notice that the dialog box specifies a default location and database name. The folders appearing to the left may vary, depending on your settings.

FIGURE O.5

Default location

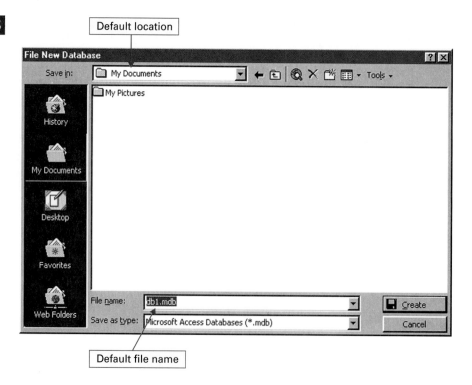

Default file name

4 Select your floppy disk or network folder as the storage location, and type **Selections** as the database name, as shown in Figure O.6.

FIGURE O.6

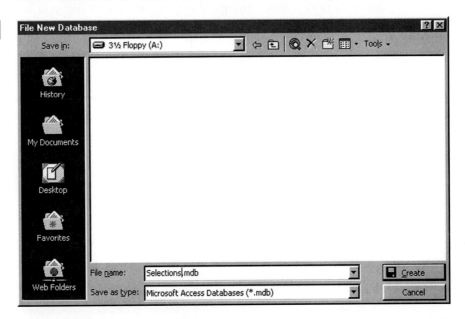

TIP When you name your database file, Access will automatically add the .mdb extension to the file name.

5 Click the Create button. Access creates a new database and displays the database window shown in Figure O.7.

FIGURE O.7

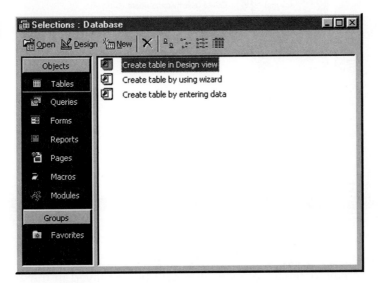

TIP Unlike other applications in the Office suite, only one database file can be open at a time.

Identifying Microsoft Access Screen Elements

You will notice three things about the database file you have just created. First, the database window appears in a restored state within the application window. Second, the name of the database appears in the title bar of the database window. Third, the database window contains buttons that display the database objects you will create, and the uppermost Tables button is active.

> **TIP** Notice that the object buttons in the database window appear in the same order as the seven classes of database objects listed in the steps for designing a database. Since tables are the primary repositories for the data in a database, the Tables button is listed first.

You will notice that the Microsoft Access screen shown in Figure O.8 has unique elements that are not seen in other Office applications.

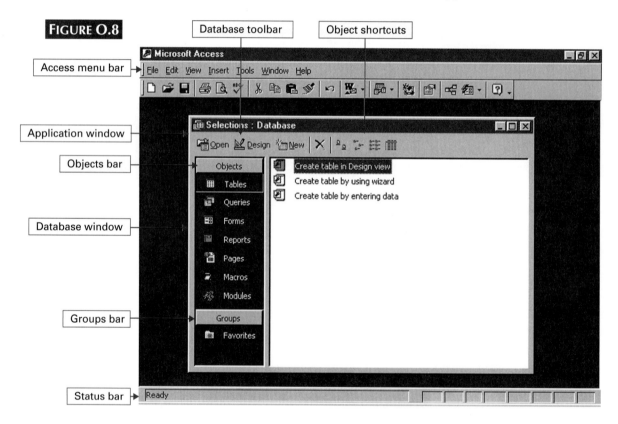

FIGURE O.8

The most striking feature of the Access interface is the database window. As you create database objects, they will be displayed in the appropriate page for a specific object selection on the **Objects bar**. You will also notice that the application window contains only one toolbar. You will use this is the same way as other toolbars in the Windows environment. Table O.2 identifies the purpose of each screen element.

Table O.2

Screen element	Purpose
Access menu bar	Provides access to the commands used to perform tasks.
Application title bar	Identifies the current application and contains control menu items for maximizing, minimizing, and restoring the application window and exiting the application.
Database toolbar	Provides shortcuts to the most common database tasks.
Database window	Displays object tabs for the seven kinds of database objects you can create.
Objects bar	Display the database objects you create in the Objects bar, which has an easy-to-use vertical orientation.
Groups bar	Click the Groups bar to view your groups, which can contain shortcuts to database objects of different types.
Object wizards and shortcuts	In the database window, quickly create a new database object by using a wizard, or open a new database object in Design view. Once you create an object, open it using its object shortcut.
Status bar	Displays program status and instructions and information for performing specific tasks.

Closing Your Database File and Exiting Microsoft Access

Since you are finished with your database for the time being, you may close it and exit Microsoft Access. As you have not yet created any database objects, there is nothing to update in the file. Any time you close a database that you have modified, it is updated automatically.

TASK 2:   To Close Your Database File and Exit Microsoft Access

1 Click the Close button of the database window to close the open database file.

2 Choose Exit from the File menu or click the Close button in the application window to exit Microsoft Access.

Summary and Exercises

Summary

- Microsoft Access is a relational database management system (RDBMS).
- A database is a collection of information related to a common purpose.
- When launching Access, you must specify whether you want to open an existing database or create a new one.
- Access includes two methods for creating a new database.
- An Access database file can contain multiple objects, including tables, queries, forms, reports, access pages, macros, and modules.
- Tables are the primary kind of database object in Access.
- Only one database can be open at a time.
- The database window provides a graphical method for designing and using database objects.

Key Terms

Access menu bar
application title bar
class
database
database management system
   (DBMS)
database object
database toolbar
database window
field
form
macro

module
Objects bar
object shortcut
page
query
record
relational database
   management system
   (RDBMS)
report
table

Study Questions

Multiple Choice

1. Which Access object is considered primary?
   a. table
   b. query
   c. form
   d. report

2. Which screen element is used to easily design or open the objects within a database?
   a. Close button
   b. status bar
   c. database toolbar
   d. database window

3. A database contains the first name, last name, and phone number for a group of students. The first name entries are what kind of data?
   a. fields
   b. records
   c. queries
   d. tables

4. During which phase of the database design are the output specifications identified?
   a. defining the purpose
   b. planning the objects
   c. creating and relating tables
   d. creating queries

5. How many database files can be open simultaneously?
   a. one
   b. two
   c. three
   d. four

Short Answer

1. What is the database window?

2. How many object classes are there in Access?

3. All database objects are displayed in which screen element?

4. Which database object is used to create and format printed output?

5. Microsoft Access is based upon which model?

Fill in the Blank

1. Database users typically interact with field data using a(n) _____.

2. A(n) _____ is used to display fields in a Web browser.

3. A table is an instance of an object _____.

4. You can use a(n) _____ to quickly open a database object.

5. A(n) _____ is the primary object in Access.

For Discussion

1. How do fields and records differ?

2. What steps are required to design a database?

Creating Access Tables

A defining feature of relational databases is the ability to represent data in separate tables and then relate the tables when the data is needed.

Objectives

After completing this project, you will be able to:

➤ Design a multiple-table database

➤ Open a database

➤ Create a table using Table Design view

➤ Create a table using the Table Wizard

➤ Create a table by importing data from Excel

➤ Add records to a table in Datasheet view

➤ Create an AutoForm

Running Case

Selections, Inc. is a multifaceted department store with four regional offices and 34 locations in the United States and Canada. You have been hired as a database designer to create a database for storing employee information. As a database designer you want to think carefully about how to structure the data in your database so as to avoid unnecessary duplication.

The Challenge

Mr. Travis Traylor is the head of the finance and accounting department for Selections, Inc. He wants you to design a database for tracking payroll information. Specifically, he wants to be able to print payroll information for any employee in the company, by department and by employee. The database must list payroll information for any pay period and list the payroll history for each employee. Ultimately, Mr. Traylor wants this information to be available both in printed form and on the company's corporate intranet.

The Strategy

You begin planning a database by determining the inputs and outputs, which include the reports you want to generate from the data and the forms you will create to enter and maintain data. To create a database that meets Mr. Traylor's requirements, you will need to store data in multiple tables. By entering the departments in one table, the payroll data for each payroll period in a second table, and the employees in a third table, you will be able to generate the reports Mr. Traylor has requested, and also avoid errors in the data. Figure 1.1 graphically depicts how data in multiple tables can be combined to generate the payroll reports Mr. Traylor requested.

FIGURE 1.1

Department Names	Employee Data	Time Card Data

Three tables contain the data required to generate a payroll report

Department	Employee Name	Total Hours	Pay Rate	Gross Pay

A payroll report is generated using data from each table

Database table structure

In this project you will create the three tables shown in Figure 1.1. Since you will create the Employee table by importing data, it will already contain records. The Department table has a small number of records, so you will enter them in Table Datasheet view. The Time Card table will contain records for each employee for each pay period. The table structure and records your database will contain at the conclusion of this project are shown in Figure 1.2.

FIGURE 1.2

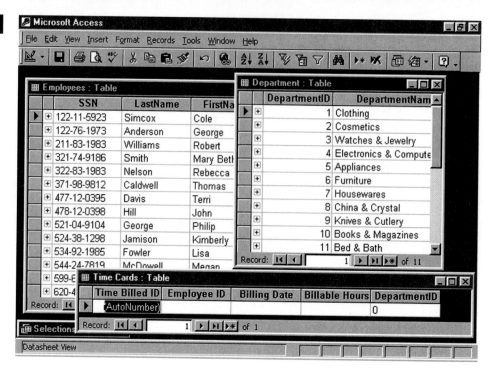

The Setup

So that your screen matches the illustrations in this project, you should set up Access as shown in Table 1.1 after you launch Access and open your database. These are the default settings in Access, but they may have been changed on your computer.

Table 1.1

Location	Make these settings:
Tools, Customize	Click the Toolbars tab and display the database toolbar and the menu bar, if they are not currently visible, as shown in Figure 1.3.
Tools, Options	Display the status bar, the startup dialog box, new object shortcuts, and windows in the taskbar, as shown in Figure 1.4.
Tools, Options	Click the General tab and deselect the setting for displaying dates in four-digit format.
Tools, Customize	Click the Options tab, and make sure the checkbox to display recently used menu commands first is deselected, as shown in Figure 1.5.

FIGURE 1.3

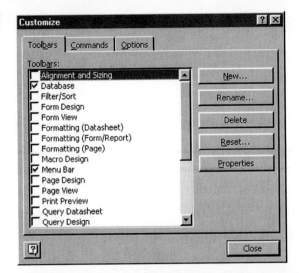

FIGURE 1.4

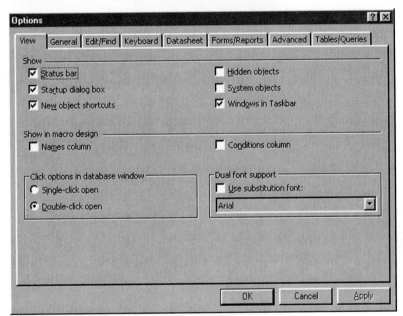

FIGURE 1.5

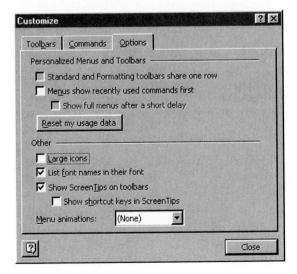

Opening an Access Database

When you launch Access, the Microsoft Access dialog box shown in Figure 1.6 appears. From this dialog box you can either create a new database or open an existing one. Remember that a list of recently opened databases appears at the bottom of the Microsoft Access dialog box.

FIGURE 1.6

TASK 1: <u>To Open a Database</u>

1 Launch Access.

> **TROUBLESHOOTING** If Access is running and the Microsoft Access dialog box is not visible, choose Open Database from the File menu.

2 With the Open an existing file option selected, click OK.

3 When the Open dialog box appears, select your floppy disk drive in the Look in: drop-down list.

4 Click *Selections.mdb* in the file list, if it is not selected, as shown in Figure 1.7.

FIGURE 1.7

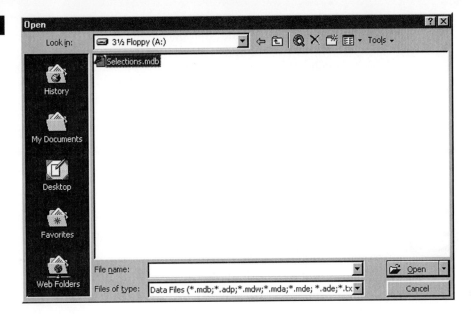

5 Click Open. Access opens the database file, displays the name of the database in the title bar of the database window, and makes the Tables tab active, as shown in Figure 1.8.

FIGURE 1.8

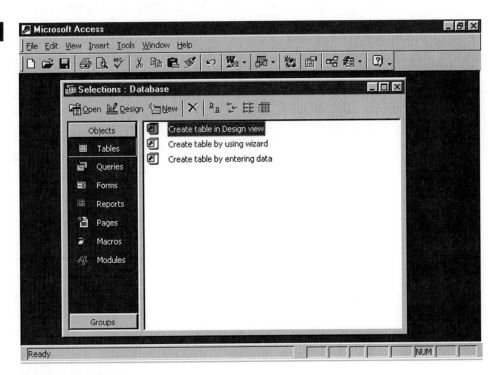

TIP As you learned in the "Introducing Access 2000," designing a database requires careful planning. In the tasks that follow, you will create tables without planning their design. Designing tables involves a detailed and technical process known as normalization, whereby you determine the optimum number of related tables to best minimize redundant data, and how best to utilize primary and foreign key fields to appropriately relate the tables. In this project, the database planning has been done for you, as these concepts are beyond the scope of this book.

 Web Tip

Are you interested in the relational database model? Visit this site for information about E. F. Codd and the relational database model:
http://www.iemagazine.com/9810/frm_feat4.shtml

Creating Tables

After you have determined which tables to include in your database, you need to define each table's structure. **Table structure** refers to the names of each field in the table, the type of data the field will contain, and the number of characters required for each field. Each table in a database should also have a **primary key**, which is a field that is unique for each record in the database, and never contains an empty or *null* value. A **table** is a two-dimensional grid consisting of named fields. Tables are the primary repositories for data in an Access database.

The first step in defining the table structure is determining the appropriate fields. Table 1.2 displays the structure for each of the tables you will create in this project. The field designated as the primary key is underlined.

Both the Department and Employees tables contain data that will change infrequently. For example, the name of a department will not change unless the store makes organizational changes. The employee data will change when employees are hired or fired, or change address, phone number, or pay rate. The Time Card table will change each period as new records are added to the table.

It is desirable from a database maintenance perspective that the Time Card table, which is updated most frequently, has access to the department and employee data that changes infrequently, but also allows this data to be easily updated when changes are necessary. To share records in this manner, the tables that are related need to have one field in common. The fields used to link the tables listed in Table 1.2 appear in italics. This link is called a **join**.

Table 1.2

Department table	Employees table	Time Cards table
Department ID	*Employee ID*	*Time Card ID*
Department Name	Last Name	*Employee ID*
	First Name	*Department ID*
	Address	Pay Period
	City	Hours Worked
	State	
	Zip Code	
	Home Phone	
	Date of Birth	
	Pay Rate	

You can create tables in Access using Table Design view, using the Table Wizard, or by importing data from an existing file such as a Microsoft Excel workbook. Regardless of the method you choose, you may need to modify the table in the future to accommodate updated database requirements. You will create the Department table using Table Design view, the Time Cards table using the Table Wizard, and the Employees table by importing an Excel workbook.

Naming Fields and Determining Data Types

Access does not place many restrictions for naming the fields in a table. A field name can be up to 64 characters in length and may include any combination of letters, numbers, spaces, and special characters except a period (.), an exclamation point (!), an accent grave (`), and brackets ([ ]).

> **TIP** If your database will include Visual Basic code or more complex expressions, consider omitting spaces from the field name.

To store your table data in the most efficient manner, Access supports different data types. A *data type* is a characteristic of how data is stored in a database. Depending upon what kind of data your fields will contain, various data types are appropriate. For example, a text data type is required to store name and address information. If you need to perform calculations involving monetary units, you will need to use the currency data type. Table 1.3 summarizes the ten data types you may use for table data.

Table 1.3: Access Data types

Data Type	Description
Text	Any combination of alphabetic and numeric characters such as names, addresses, and phone numbers. The text data type holds a maximum of 255 characters. This is the default data type.
Memo	Used for long text entries exceeding 255 characters. Holds up to 64 kilobytes of data in a random format.
Number	Numeric values such as inventory quantity or the number of items ordered. Numeric data can be used in calculations.
Date/Time	Date and time values for the years 100 through 9999.
Currency	Currency values and numeric data used in mathematical calculations involving data with one to four decimal places.
AutoNumber	A unique and sequential number is created as records are added to a table. AutoNumber data cannot be changed, edited, or deleted.
Yes/No	Single-character data in a Yes/No (Boolean) format. This data type displays a checkbox.
OLE object	Embedded or linked objects such as a Microsoft Excel spreadsheet, a Microsoft Word document, graphics, or sounds.
Hyperlink	Text or combinations of text and numbers stored as text and used as a hyperlink address. This data type is used to link to Web pages or other documents.
Lookup Wizard	A field that allows you to choose a value from another table or from a list of values.

When you create a table using a wizard, Access may determine the data types for you. When using Table Design view, you must specify the data types. When you create a table by importing data into Access, it will determine the appropriate data type.

Creating a Table Using Table Design View

A common method for creating tables in Access is by using **Table Design view**. To create a table by this method, enter the names and properties for each field in the table. Once this process is complete, save the table structure.

 TASK 2: To Create the Department Table Using Table Design View

1 Click the Tables button in the Objects bar, if it is not currently active.

2 Select the Create table in Design view shortcut in the database window and click the Open button, as shown in Figure 1.9.

FIGURE 1.9

TIP You can also double-click this shortcut to open it.

3 Access opens a new table in Table Design view, which consists of the two panes displayed in Figure 1.10.

FIGURE 1.10

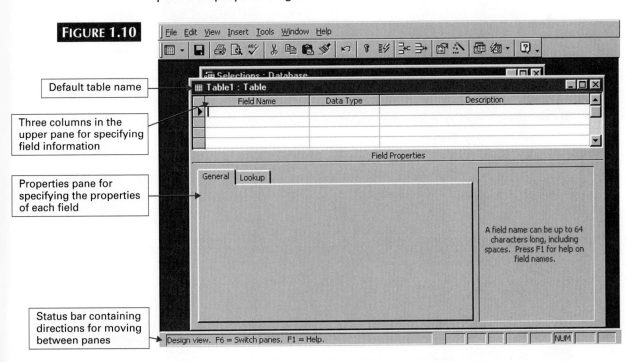

Default table name

Three columns in the upper pane for specifying field information

Properties pane for specifying the properties of each field

Status bar containing directions for moving between panes

The **_Table Design window_** is a visual workspace where you can enter information about each field in your table. Table Design View always displays this window.

4 The insertion point will be in the left column of the first row of the upper pane. Type **DepartmentID** in the left column of the first row and press (TAB) to move the insertion point into the Data Type column of the upper pane.

5 Click the drop-down list (Data Type) button in the Data Type column, and select AutoNumber as the data type for this field, as shown in Figure 1.11.

> **TIP** In Access, the AutoNumber data type is often used as a primary key, since it always contains a unique, non-null value.

FIGURE 1.11

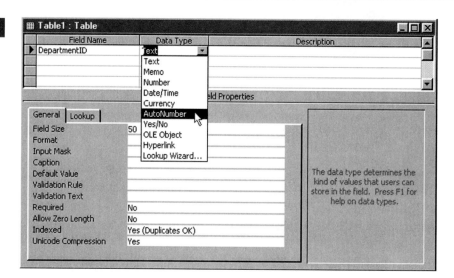

6 Press (TAB) to move the insertion point into the Description column. Type **Primary Key**.

> **TIP** Although Access does not require anything in the Description column, you should consider documenting information about the table's structure for future reference.

7 Click the Primary Key button on the database toolbar to make this field the primary key.

> **TIP** An icon representing this field as the primary key appears to the left of the field name in the upper pane of the Table Design window.

8 Press (TAB) once to move the insertion point into the Field Name column for the second row. Type **DepartmentName** as the field name.

9 Press ⬚TAB⬚ to move the insertion point into the Data Type column. Press ⬚F6⬚ once to activate the Properties pane for the current field. You will notice that the data type is set to text by default, and that the insertion point appears immediately after the default field size entry.

10 The default field size is selected. Type **35** as the field size for the field.

11 Press ⬚F6⬚ to move back to the upper pane.

12 Click the Save ⬚ button on the database toolbar to save the table structure.

13 Type **Department** as the table name in the Save As dialog box and click OK, as shown in Figure 1.12.

FIGURE 1.12

14 Click the Close ⬚X⬚ button in the Table Design window to close the table. The table name now appears in the database window, as shown in Figure 1.13.

FIGURE 1.13

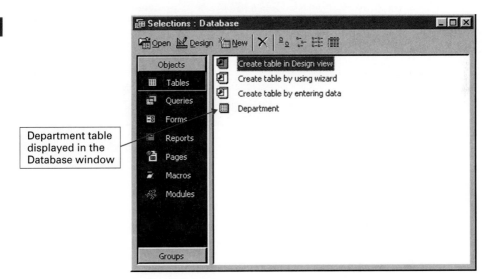

Department table displayed in the Database window

Check Point

How many records does this table contain? None, since you have merely defined the table structure.

Creating a Table Using the Table Wizard

You have successfully created a table using Table Design view. You will create two more tables before entering records into the Department table. Access includes additional options for creating tables other than Table Design view. In this task you will create a table using the **Table Wizard**, which walks you through the table design process.

TASK 3: To Create the Time Cards Table Using the Table Wizard

1 Select the Create table by using wizard shortcut, and click the Open ⬚Open button. The Table Wizard shown in Figure 1.14 appears.

FIGURE 1.14

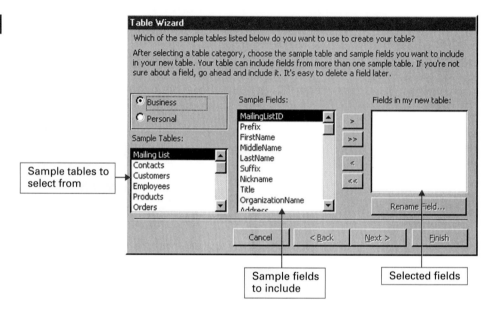

Sample tables to select from

Sample fields to include

Selected fields

2 You must first select a table from the Sample Tables: list to see a list of fields appropriate to your table design. Use the vertical scroll bar in the Sample Tables: list to display additional tables. Select the Time Billed table.

3 The Table Wizard now displays fields appropriate to your table. Click the Add ⬚ button to move the TimeBilledID field from the Sample Fields: list to the Fields in my new table: list. The field is added, as shown in Figure 1.15.

FIGURE 1.15

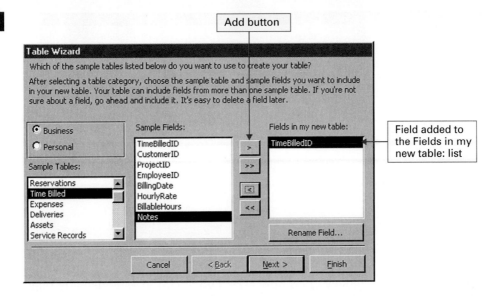

④ Copy the EmployeeID, BillingDate, and BillableHours fields to the Fields in my new table: list, as shown in Figure 1.16. Click Next.

FIGURE 1.16

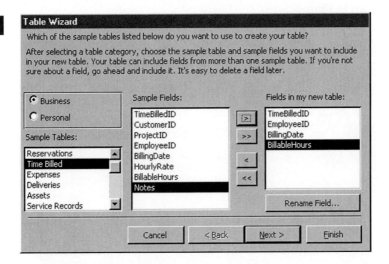

TROUBLESHOOTING You will notice that Table 1.2 shows an additional field for this table, DepartmentID. You will add this as a lookup field in Project 2.

⑤ Access will suggest Time Billed as a name for this table. It will also request that it set a primary key. Type **Time Cards** as the name. Leave the option to set a primary key, as shown in Figure 1.17, and click Next.

FIGURE 1.17

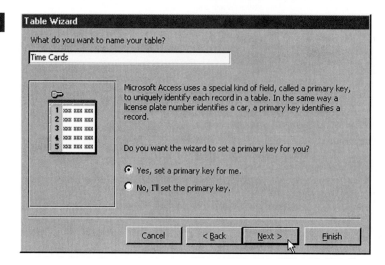

FIGURE 1.18

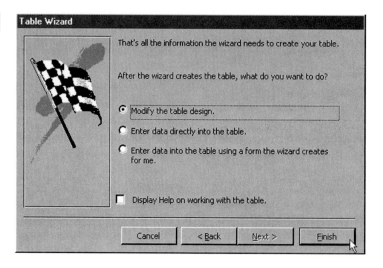

6 The Table Wizard now asks if you want to establish any relationships. Since you will complete this task in Project 2, click Next.

7 The Table Wizard now allows you to select a view for the table once it is created. Select the option to modify the table design and click Finish, as shown in Figure 1.18.

8 The table appears in Design view. Change the data type for the EmployeeID field to text.

9 Press (F6) and change the field size of the EmployeeID field to 11 characters.

10 Press (F6) to return to the upper pane of the Table Design window.

11 Highlight the BillingDate field name and type **PayPeriod**.

12 Highlight the BillableHours field name and type **HoursWorked**. Your table design should now appear as shown in Figure 1.19.

FIGURE 1.19

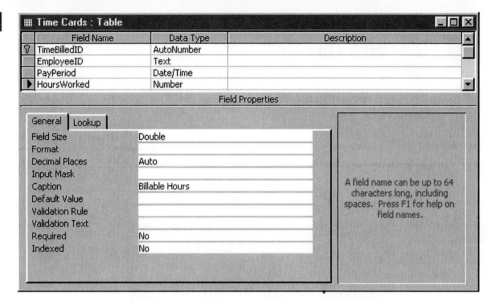

13 Click the Save 🖫 button to update the table.

14 Click the Close ✕ button to return to the database window.

Break Point

If necessary, you can exit Access and continue this project later.

Creating a Table by Importing Data from Excel

In many circumstances you will have data within the organization that you want to incorporate into a database. Access allows you to import data from a variety of formats. Since a listing of addresses is often stored in an Excel workbook, importing records from Excel to Access is a common task.

TASK 4: To Create the Employees Table by Importing a Microsoft Excel Worksheet

1 Launch Access if it is not currently running.

2 Create a folder named *Data Files* on your floppy disk or network location.

3 Ask your instructor where the file *Employees.xls* is located on your network. Copy this file to the folder you just created.

 **Web Tip**

If a copy of this file is not available on your computer or network, you can download a copy from the SELECT Web site at http://www.prenhall.com/select.

4 Choose Get External Data, Import from the File menu, as shown in Figure 1.20.

FIGURE 1.20

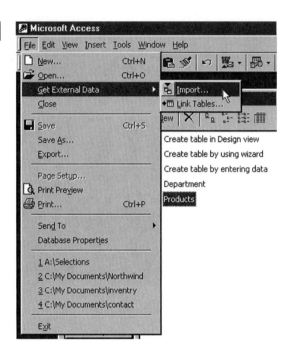

5 Select Microsoft Excel in the Files of type: list box, and locate the *Employees.xls* file on your disk or network drive. Click Import, as shown in Figure 1.21.

FIGURE 1.21

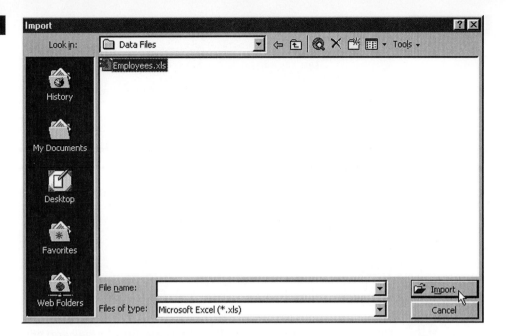

6   When the Import Spreadsheet Wizard appears, make sure the checkbox specifying that the first row contains column headings is checked, as shown in Figure 1.22. Click Next.

FIGURE 1.22

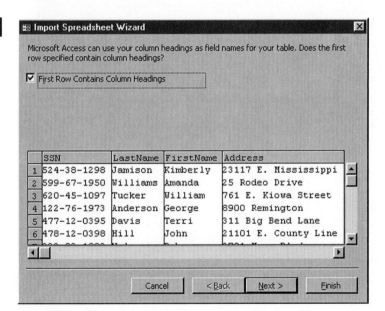

7   Select the default option to store the data in a new table, and click Next.

8   When you are prompted to specify field information, click Next.

9   Choose the option to select your own primary key, and make sure SSN is the selected field, as shown in Figure 1.23.

FIGURE 1.23

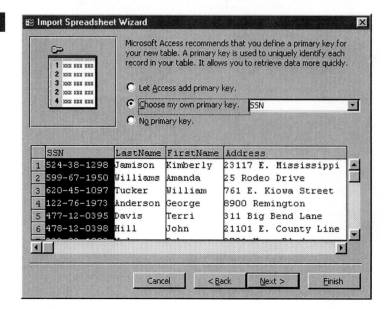

10 Click Next. Accept the default table name *Employees* and click Finish, as shown in Figure 1.24.

FIGURE 1.24

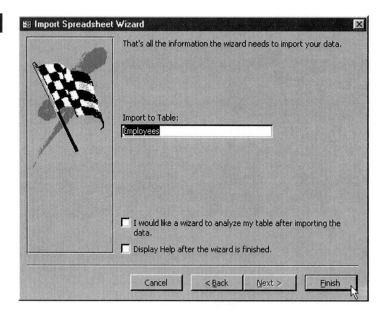

11 The dialog box shown in Figure 1.25 appears.

FIGURE 1.25

TROUBLESHOOTING If you do not see the dialog box shown in Figure 1.25, repeat the import procedure.

12 Click OK to return to the database window.

Check Point

You have added several objects to your database. Which tables contain records? Currently only the Employees table contains records.

Web Tip

The Association for Computing Machinery awarded a citation to E.F. Codd for developing the relational database model, which is a more powerful method for storing field and record data than in tools such as Microsoft Excel. Visit the following site for more information:
http://www.acm.org/awards/fellows_citations/codd.html

Adding Records to the Department Table

When you create a table using the Table Design window or the Table Wizard, the table comprises a structure with no records. If a table does not contain more than three or four fields, you can easily add records using *Datasheet view*, which is a two-dimensional grid for entering and editing table data. For larger tables, it is easiest to create an AutoForm to add records to the table. In the task that follows, you will add records to the Department table in Datasheet view.

TASK 5: <u>Adding Records to the Department Table Using Datasheet View</u>

1 Click the Tables button on the database toolbar to display the table objects in your database, if it is not currently active.

2 Select the Department table, and click the Open ⬚ Open button. The table opens in Datasheet view, as shown in Figure 1.26.

FIGURE 1.26   Table name

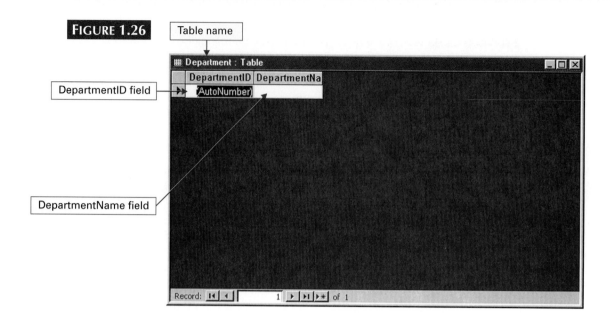

DepartmentID field

DepartmentName field

 Check Point

What is Datasheet view? Datasheet view is a view of the records in a table or query in a two-dimensional grid, in which each column represents a field and each row represents a record.

3 Press (TAB) to place the insertion point inside the DepartmentName field for the first record. Type **Clothing** as the field entry.

> **TROUBLESHOOTING** If you make an error while entering data into the field, you can use the mouse or directional arrows to move to the error, highlight the error, and retype the entry.

You will notice that the number 1 appears as the primary key value for this record, as shown in Figure 1.27.

FIGURE 1.27

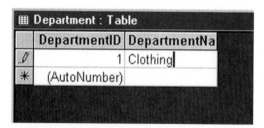

4 Press (TAB) twice to move the insertion point to the DepartmentName field for the next record. Type **Cosmetics** and press (TAB) twice.

> **TIP** In Access, a record is saved to disk anytime you enter or edit data and then move to another record.

5 Enter the remaining department names, as listed here.
- **Watches & Jewelry**
- **Electronics & Computers**
- **Appliances**
- **Furniture**
- **Housewares**
- **China & Crystal**
- **Knives & Cutlery**
- **Books & Magazines**
- **Bed & Bath**

6 Place the insertion point at the right border of the field selector until the mouse pointer changes shape, as shown in Figure 1.28.

FIGURE 1.28

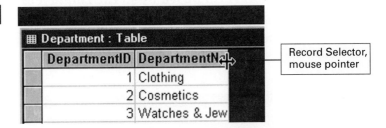

7 Drag the Field Selector to resize the field so all data is visible. When you are finished, your Datasheet should resemble the one shown in Figure 1.29.

> **TIP** You can also double-click the border between fields for AutoFit to determine the optimum field width.

FIGURE 1.29

8 Close the table. When asked if you want to save changes to the table layout, click Yes.

Creating an AutoForm to Display Records in the Employees Table

You will recall that it is important to consider the required inputs when designing a database. You will also recall from "Introducing Access 2000" that forms are often used to enter and edit table data. With many tables, it is tedious to enter and maintain records using a datasheet. By using the Auto-Form Wizard you can quickly create an **AutoForm**, which is a form based upon a query or a table that Access will create automatically. You will now create a form to enter and edit records in the Employees table, which you will do in Project 3.

TASK 6: <u>To Create an AutoForm Based Upon the Employees Table</u>

1 Click the Forms button on the Objects bar, and then click New, as shown in Figure 1.30.

FIGURE 1.30

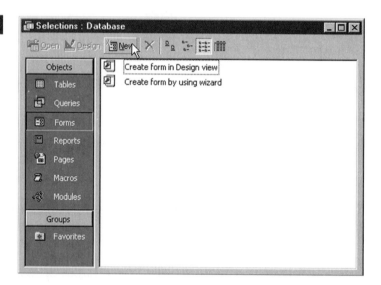

2 The New Form dialog box appears. In the upper portion, select AutoForm: Columnar, and in the drop-down list for specifying the table or query upon which the form will be based, select Employees, as shown in Figure 1.31.

FIGURE 1.31

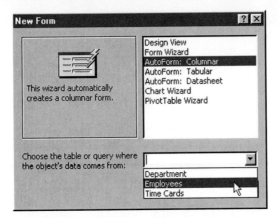

Specifying the database object for creating a columnar AutoForm

3 Click OK. The form shown in Figure 1.32 appears. Notice that it displays the first record in the database. Depending upon your settings, the date and currency formats may vary.

FIGURE 1.32

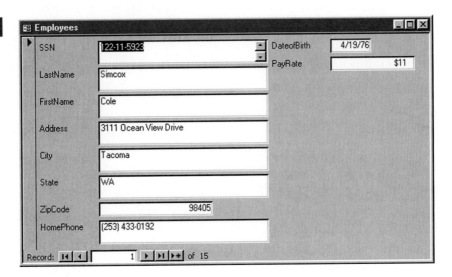

4 Click the Close ☒ button.

5 You will be prompted to save the form. Click Yes, and accept the default name by clicking OK. You can now enter records into the table using the form, or modify the existing records. Since you are finished for now, close the *Selections.mdb* database and exit Access.

Summary and Exercises

Summary

- Tables are the primary repositories for data in an Access database.
- Table structure includes field names and data types.
- Access supports ten data types.
- Tables are created using the Table Design Wizard, using Table Design view, or by importing data into Access.
- Record data can be entered, displayed, and edited in Datasheet view.
- You can create an AutoForm based upon a table for entering records into the table.

Key Terms and Operations

Key Terms

AutoForm
currency
data type
date/time
Datasheet view
hyperlink
join
memo
numeric

OLE object
primary key
table
Table Wizard
Table Design view
Table Design window
table structure
text
yes/no

Operations

add records to a table using Datasheet view
create a table by importing an Excel workbook into Access
create a table using Design view
create a table using the Table Wizard
create an AutoForm
open a database

Study Questions

Multiple Choice

1. Which data type is used to store long text entries?
   a. text
   b. memo
   c. numeric
   d. OLE object

2. The upper pane in the Table Design window is used to enter
    a. field names.
    b. field data types.
    c. field properties.
    d. a and b.

3. Which of the following statements is false?
    a. When you open an Access database, the database window is normally is displayed.
    b. To create database objects, you must first open the database file containing them.
    c. All Access database objects are contained in one file.
    d. When you open a database file, a new table is automatically created.

4. What field type uses a checkbox to store field data?
    a. text
    b. number
    c. date/time
    d. yes/no

5. Which of the following data types allows you to specify a field size?
    a. text
    b. number
    c. date/Time
    d. currency

6. You are designing a table containing name and address information. How many characters should you reserve for the LastName field, which is a text data type?
    a. 255
    b. 50
    c. 15
    d. 5

7. You have been commissioned to create a database for a hardware store. To easily enter data into the specific tables, which object should you create?
    a. query
    b. report
    c. AutoReport
    d. form

8. You are creating an Employee table by importing an Excel workbook. Which of the following fields should you designate as the primary key?
    a. last name
    b. address
    c. zip code
    d. Social Security number

9. Which view do you use to enter data into a table?
   a. Table Design view
   b. Datasheet view
   c. Database Location view
   d. Database Design view

10. When you get external data to create an Access table, which Access wizard appears?
    a. Table Design Wizard
    b. Table Datasheet Wizard
    c. Import Spreadsheet Wizard
    d. Import Table Wizard

Short Answer

1. How does a database differ from a table?
2. How does a record differ from a field??
3. What is the default data type listed in the Table Design window?
4. Where do you change the properties of a field in a table?
5. Why is the AutoNumber data type often used for a table's primary key?
6. How do you create a table in Access?
7. What is displayed on the screen when you open an Access database file?
8. Where in the database window are tables displayed?
9. When displaying records in a form, which view is active?
10. How do you add a new record to a table using Datasheet view?

Fill in the Blank

1. A(n) _____ field will never contain duplicate entries.
2. The _____ column in the Table Design window does not require an entry.
3. A _____ is often used to enter records into a table.
4. If you import data from an Excel workbook, the _____ Wizard will appear.
5. You can use _____ view to define a table.
6. In Datasheet view, each row represents a(n) _____.
7. The _____ data type is often used to define a table's primary key.
8. You can use _____ view to enter records into an Access table.
9. In Datasheet view, each column represents a _____.
10. The primary key field cannot contain _____ or _____.

For Discussion

1. How do text and memo data types differ? When is each appropriate?

2. Why are tables the primary data repository in Access?

3. What additional fields might you want to include in the Employees table and why?

4. How can you minimize redundant data in a relational database?

5. What do you define before creating a table?

Hands-On Exercises

1. Creating an Inventory Database

Create an Access database for recording the current value of inventory for Selections, Inc. Use the Table Wizard to create a table that lists product data. The table you will create is shown in Figure 1.33.

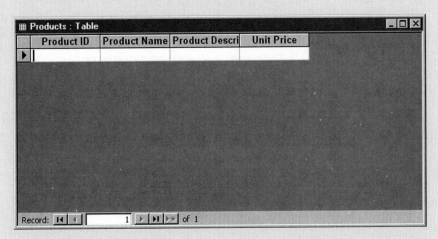

FIGURE 1.33

To create the Inventory database, complete the following:

1. Launch Access if it is not currently running. Create a blank database named *Inventory.mdb*. Save the database to a folder named *Inventory* on your disk or network drive.

2. Make sure the Tables button is selected in the Objects bar. Select the Create table by using wizard shortcut.

3. In the Table Wizard dialog box, select Products from the Sample tables: list, and select the Business option. You now need to specify which fields to add to the table. Select the ProductID, ProductName, ProductDescription, and UnitPrice fields.

4. Set ProductID as the primary key.

5. Click Next. In this step of the Table Wizard, specify Products as the name for the table, and select the option to set your own primary key. Click Next.

6. By default, the Table Wizard should specify ProductID as the primary key field. Select the option to enter letters and numbers in the field.

7. In the last step of the Table Wizard, select the option to enter data directly into the table. Click Finish and close the table.

8. Close the Inventory database.

2. Entering Records into a Table

Open the Inventory database you created in the previous exercise.

To add records to the Products table:

1. With the Tables button active, open the Products table, and widen the second and third columns.

2. Enter five records into the table, as shown in Figure 1.34.

FIGURE 1.34

	Product ID	Product Name	Product Description	Unit Price
	1	Sampson Carryall	Leather Attache Case	$199.95
	2	WeatherGuard	Cordura & Leather Backpack	$129.95
	3	WeatherGuard Pro	Cordura, Leather, & GoreTex Backpack	$179.95
	4	Case Logic Gear	GoreTex CD-ROM carrying case (20)	$39.95
	5	Extreme Image	GoreTex Laptop computer case	$119.95

Products : Table

Record: 6 of 6

3. Close the table and the database.

On Your Own Exercises

1. Creating a Database Using the Hyperlink Data Type

The Hyperlink data type was first introduced in Access 97. In this assignment you will create a new database that incorporates this data type. Create a new database with the name *Web Sites.mdb*. Create a table named Sites with the following structure:

Field Name	Data Type	Size
Company	Text	50
Primary Product	Text	50
Company URL	Hyperlink	N/A

When you save the table, allow Access to create a primary key. Close the database when you are finished.

2. Adding Records to a Table

In this assignment you will modify the database you created in the previous exercise by adding records to the table. Open the *Web Sites.mdb* database and add the following three records to the table:

Company	Primary Product	Company URL
Microsoft	Software	http://www.microsoft.com
Adobe Graphics	Software	http://www.adobe.com
Fidelity Financial	Services	http://www.fidelity.com

After you have added these records, use the navigation controls on the table to move to the first record. If you can access the World Wide Web from your lab or computer, click the company URL field for Microsoft. When you are finished, close your Web browser and the database.

3. Adding a Table to an Existing Database

In this exercise you will add a table to the Inventory database. The table has the following structure:

Field Name	Data Type
InventoryID	AutoNumber
DateAcquired	Date/Time
Quantity	Number

Save the table as Inventory. Close the table and the database.

4. Exporting Data from Access to Excel

Open the *Web Sites.mdb* database. Search the Help system for information on how to export Access data to an Excel workbook. Export the Sites table to an Excel workbook named *Sites.xls*. Close Access when you are finished.

5. Creating a Database Using an Access Database Wizard

Access includes wizards to assist you in creating entire databases. Launch Access and create a Contact Management database by using a database template. Save your database to a blank floppy disk with *Contact Management.mdb* as the file name. Close the database when you are finished.

6. Adding Contact Type Records to the Contact Management Database

Open the *Contact Management.mdb* database you created in the previous exercise. Add three records to the Contact Types table. When you are finished, close the database and exit Access.

Establishing Relationships and Modifying Tables

Now that you have created tables for the Selections database, you need to establish relationships between them. Relationships allow you to share information among tables and specify rules about how records are related. When you are finished, you will be well on your way to providing Mr. Traylor with the employee information he has requested.

Running Case

Mr. Traylor has reviewed the work you have done so far on the database, and has approved the initial design. He is concerned, however, that you build the database in such a way that the time card data will be both easy to enter and entered accurately. As a cost-saving initiative, Selections, Inc. cross-trains all employees to work in two or more departments, and employees rotate from department to department each pay period.

The Challenge

Mr. Traylor wants you to establish a relationship between the Time Cards and Department tables so that the department names can be included on each employee's time card statement. He also has specified that the database should ensure accurate time card data. He requests that you modify the tables and forms so that the data entry personnel can easily add new employee data as new employees are hired. Finally, he wants to be assured that the data entry personnel cannot inadvertently create a time card record using an invalid employee number, or enter billable hours exceeding 80 hours for each pay period.

The Strategy

Although it may seem that Mr. Traylor is asking you to make significant modifications to the database, you can easily accommodate his request. Your first task will be to add a lookup field to the Time Cards table, so that the data entry personnel can select each employee's department from a list as they enter time card records, thereby ensuring that the department names are always accurate. When you add this field, Access will create a relationship between the Time Cards and Department tables. You can modify this relationship so that it is impossible to modify the department name by enforcing referential integrity. You will then establish a relationship between the Time Cards and the Employees tables, so time card records for specific employees can be created. You can then create multiple time cards for each employee, as shown in Figure 2.1.

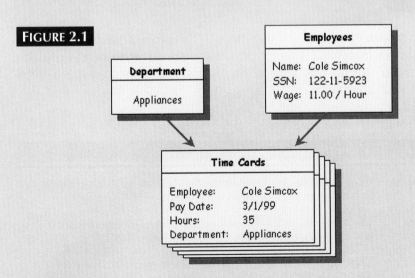

FIGURE 2.1

Once you have established the relationships between tables you can print the relationships layout as a way of documenting your database design.

You will now be ready to modify field properties to assist data entry. By changing field properties by assigning input masks and data validation rules, you can improve the accuracy of data entry in both the Employees and Time Cards tables. When you finish modifying the tables, you will enter six time card records. The Time Cards table with these records is shown in Figure 2.2. In Project 4 you will create a query to display all the data for each employee for each pay period.

FIGURE 2.2

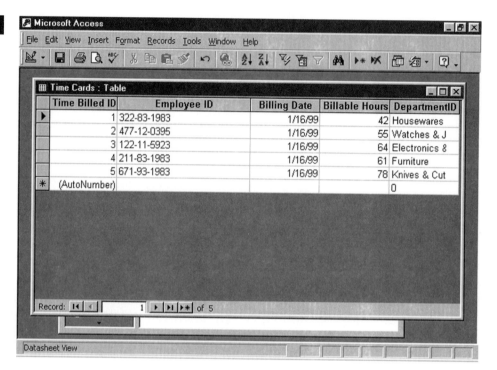

The Setup

So that your screen matches the illustrations in this project, you should set up Access as shown in Table 2.1 after you launch Access and open your database. These are the default settings in Access, but they may have been changed on your computer.

Table 2.1

Location	Make these settings:
Tools, Customize	Click the Toolbars tab and display the database toolbar and the menu bar, if they are not currently visible, as shown in Figure 2.3.
Tools, Options	Display the status bar, the startup dialog box, new object shortcuts, and windows in the taskbar, as shown in Figure 2.4.
Tools, Options	Click the General tab and deselect the setting for displaying dates in four-digit format.
Tools, Customize	Click the Options tab, and make sure the checkbox to display recently used menu commands first is deselected, as shown in Figure 2.5.

FIGURE 2.3

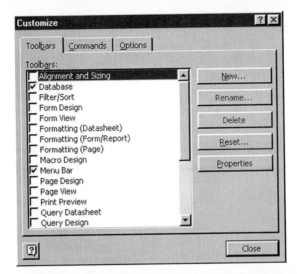

FIGURE 2.4

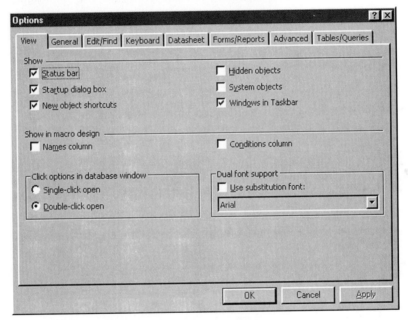

FIGURE 2.5

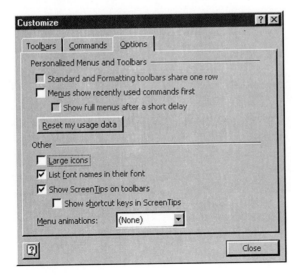

Adding a Lookup Field to the Time Cards Table

As you know, a database with data stored in multiple tables is efficient because you have access to table data when it is needed. By adding a lookup field to the Time Cards table, you can look up a specific department by name and associate this data with each time card record. A **lookup field** displays values looked up from a related table and displays them in a list. The data can be looked up because the foreign key in the table displaying the looked up list corresponds to the primary key in the table that contains the values. A **foreign key** is simply the field in a related table that links the two tables. A lookup list is based upon existing data in a table or query, or upon a value list that you create.

> **TIP** A lookup field requires either a relationship between tables, or a list of values you will create. In this example, you will use values that exist in an existing table.

TASK 1: To Add a Lookup Field That Lists Department Names to the Time Cards Table

1 Click the Tables button in the Objects bar, if it is not currently selected.

2 Highlight the Time Cards table and click the Design Design button.

3 When the Table Design window appears, use the scroll bar in the upper pane to display the next available field row, as shown in Figure 2.6.

FIGURE 2.6

Field Name	Data Type	Description
EmployeeID	Text	
PayPeriod	Date/Time	
HoursWorked	Number	

Field Properties

General | Lookup

Field Size	Long Integer
New Values	Increment
Format	
Caption	Time Billed ID
Indexed	Yes (No Duplicates)

A field name can be up to 64 characters long, including spaces. Press F1 for help on field names.

4 Type **DepartmentID** as the field name for the next field in the table.

5 Press (TAB) once and select Lookup Wizard as the data type, as shown in Figure 2.7.

FIGURE 2.7

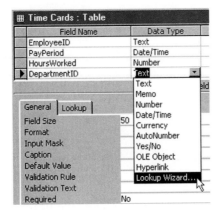

6 The Lookup Wizard appears. Accept the default option to look up values in a table or query (Figure 2.8), and click Next.

FIGURE 2.8

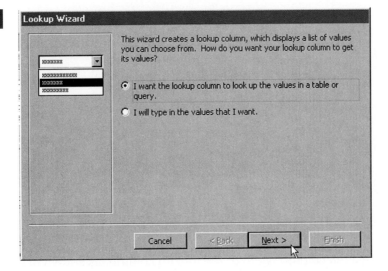

7 Specify the Department table as the one containing the values, and click Next (Figure 2.9).

FIGURE 2.9

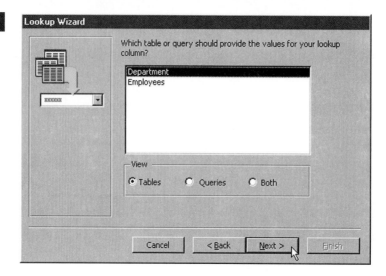

8 Move DepartmentName from the Available Fields: list to the Selected Fields: list, as shown in Figure 2.10, and click Next.

FIGURE 2.10

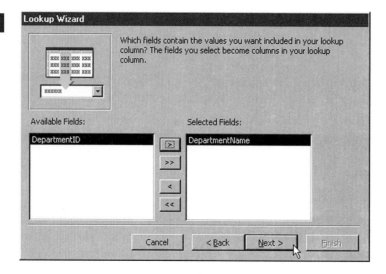

9 Adjust the column width of the lookup column, as shown in Figure 2.11. Make sure you accept the default to hide the key column. Click Next.

FIGURE 2.11

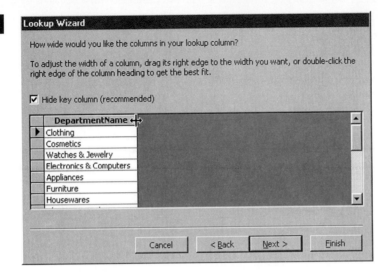

TIP The field you are creating is a foreign key that displays the department names by associating them with the key value. By hiding the foreign key, the department names will be displayed in the table even though the field contains the key value.

10 Accept the default caption, DepartmentID, and click Finish.

11 Access asks whether you want to save the table before creating relationships. Click Yes.

12 Click the View 🔲▾ button to switch to Datasheet view.

13 Click inside the DepartmentID field for the first record. When the drop-down list button appears, click it. The department names are displayed, as shown in Figure 2.12.

FIGURE 2.12

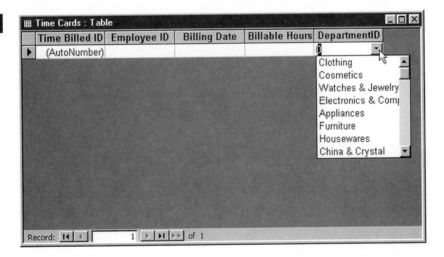

> **TIP** Notice that the field currently contains a zero. This represents a **null value**, meaning that the field does not yet contain an entry. Once you select a department name, the appropriate primary key value (currently 1 through 9) will be entered into the field, and the corresponding department name displayed.

Before you add records to the table, you will modify the table relationships and add a lookup list to the EmployeeID field.

14 Click the Close **X** button to close the table and return to the database window.

Web Tip

For a more complex example of designing a database and establishing relationships, see: http://msdn.microsoft.com/library/partbook/inscript/html/ch8creatingaccessdatabase.htm

Creating and Modifying Relationships

After you have created different tables in your Microsoft Access database, you need a way of telling Microsoft Access how to bring that information back together again. The first step in this process is to define relationships between your tables. A relationship exists between two tables, and is technically called a join. Depending upon how the data is related, Access will use the appropriate kind of join. After you've established the appropriate relationships in your database to join the tables, you can create queries, forms, and reports to display information from several tables at once.

When you added a lookup field to the Time Cards table, Access automatically created a relationship between it and the Department table. You will now create a relationship between the Time Cards and Employees tables, modify the relationship between the Time Cards and Department table, and print information about the relationships in your database.

TASK 2: <u>To Open the Relationships Window and Add Tables</u>

1 Click the Relationship 🔲 button on the database toolbar to open the Relationships window. The Show Table dialog appears, as shown in Figure 2.13.

TROUBLESHOOTING If the Show Table dialog box does not appear, click the Show Table 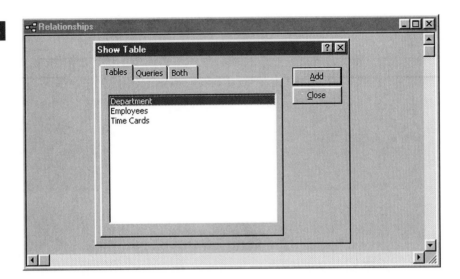 button, or choose Show Table from the Relationships menu.

FIGURE 2.13

2 Select all three table names with the left mouse button, and click Add, as shown in Figure 2.14. The tables are added to the Relationships window.

FIGURE 2.14

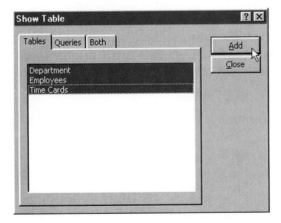

TROUBLESHOOTING Make sure you click Add only once, as it is possible to add multiple instances of a table to the Relationships window. If you inadvertently add multiple instances, you will need to delete the extra tables from the window.

3 Click the Close button to close the Show Table dialog box. A line representing the relationship between the Department and Time Cards tables becomes visible.

4 Click the title bar in the Employees table and drag the table to the right of the Time Cards table, if necessary.

5 Click the Title bar of the Time Cards table and drag it to a position similar to that shown in Figure 2.15.

FIGURE 2.15

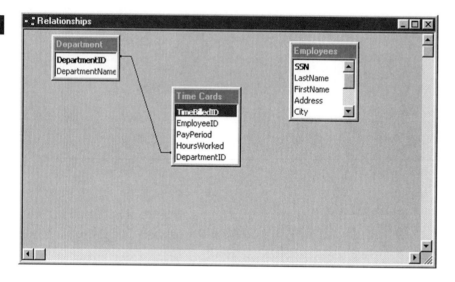

Using the Relationships Window

The **Relationships window** is a visual workspace for creating and modifying relationships. Access recognizes three kinds of relationships, as summarized in Table 2.2.

Table 2.2

Type of relationship	Definition
One-to-one	Each record in table A can have only one matching record in table B, and each record in table B can have only one matching record in table A. This type of relationship is not common, because most information related in this way would be in one table.
One-to-many	A one-to-many relationship is the most common type of relationship. In a one-to-many relationship, a record in table A can have many matching records in table B, but a record in table B has only one matching record in table A.
Many-to-many	In a many-to-many relationship, a record in table A can have many matching records in table B, and a record in table B can have many matching records in table A. A many-to-many relationship is really two one-to-many relationships with a third table.

Your database will contain two one-to-many relationships.

Check Point

Why will your database contain one-to-many relationships? Because each employee can have one or more than one time card record, and the time card records will display more than one of the possible department names.

Once you add tables to the Relationships window and modify the layout, you can save these settings. You will now create a new relationship, and modify the existing one.

TASK 3: To Create a One-to-Many Relationship between the Time Cards and Employees Tables and Enforce Referential Integrity

1 Click the SSN field name in the Employees table, and drag the field name next to the EmployeeID field name in the Time Cards table, as shown in Figure 2.16. Notice the icon representing the common field.

FIGURE 2.16

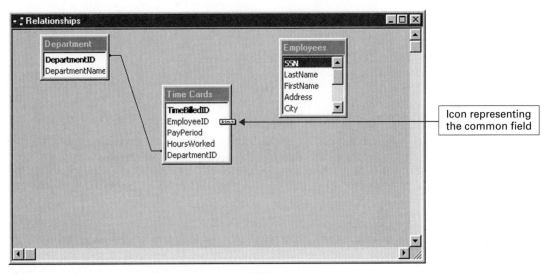

Defining a relationship in the Relationships Window

2 Release the left mouse button. The Edit Relationships dialog box appears.

3 Click the checkbox to enforce referential integrity and click the Create button, as shown in Figure 2.17.

> **TIP** *Referential integrity* is a system of rules that Access uses to ensure that relationships between records in related tables are valid, and that you don't accidentally delete or change related data. In this case, Access will not allow you to enter a value in the Time Cards EmployeeID field that does not exist in the Employees table, or to delete an employee record if it is currently used in one or more fields in the Time Cards table.

FIGURE 2.17

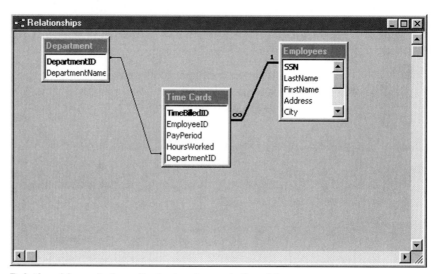

You have successfully created the relationship shown in Figure 2.18.

FIGURE 2.18

Relationships window displaying two relationships

> **TIP** The 1 and the infinity symbol (∞) indicate that this is a one-to-many relationship with referential integrity enforced. The relationship between the Department and Time Cards tables is also a one-to-many relationship, but since it does not display these symbols, referential integrity is not currently enforced.

TASK 4: To Modify the Relationship between the Time Cards and the Department Tables to Enforce Referential Integrity

1 Place the mouse pointer immediately over the line representing the relationship between the Time Cards and Department table.

2 Right-click. The menu shown in Figure 2.19 appears.

FIGURE 2.19

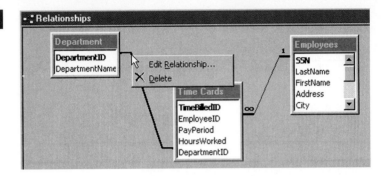

> **TROUBLESHOOTING** If this menu does not appear, try again, making sure the mouse pointer is directly over the relationship line when you right-click.

3 Choose Edit Relationship from the menu. The Edit Relationships dialog box appears.

4 Check the box to enforce referential integrity, and click the OK button. The line now appears with the symbols indicating that referential integrity is enforced.

5 Click the Close ☒ button in the Relationships window.

6 When the dialog box shown in Figure 2.20 appears, click Yes to save the layout and return to the database window.

FIGURE 2.20

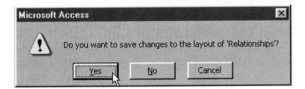

 Web Tip

For more information on relationships, visit http://msdn.microsoft.com/library/devprods/vs6/davinci/html/dvcontablerelationships.htm.

Printing Relationships

In Access 2000 Microsoft has added a feature allowing you to print the relationships layout. This is useful for documenting the structure of your database.

TASK 5: <u>To Print the Relationships</u>

1 Click the Relationships ⊞ button on the database toolbar to open the Relationships window.

2 Choose Print Relationships from the File menu, as shown in Figure 2.21.

FIGURE 2.21

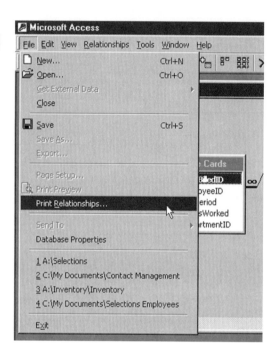

3 Access now generates a report of the relationships layout, as shown in Figure 2.22.

FIGURE 2.22

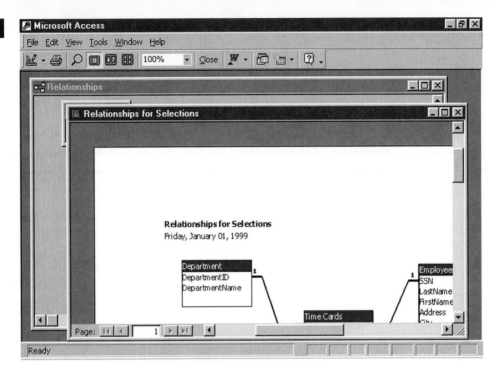

Check Point

What do the 1 and the infinity symbol mean when they appear in a relationship? This means that the one-to-many relationship enforces referential integrity.

4 Click the Print button on the Print Preview toolbar.

> **TROUBLESHOOTING** Make sure your printer is online before you print!

5 Close the Relationships report without saving it.

6 Close the Relationships window.

Break Point

If necessary, you can save the file, exit Access, and continue this project later.

Improving Data Accuracy Using Input Masks and Validation Rules

Access support two methods for improving the accuracy of field data as it is entered into tables or forms: input masks and validation rules. An ***input mask*** is a field property that displays literal characters in the field with blanks to fill in. A ***validation rule*** is a field property that specifies requirements for data entered into a record, field, or control. When data is entered that violates the ***Validation Rule property***, you can use the ***Validation Text property*** to specify the message, or ***validation text***, to be displayed to the user. Validation rules are particularly important for number and currency data types that are used in calculations, where you want to specify values such as positive numbers, or to avoid null values.

For example, Selections employees can work a maximum of 80 hours during a two-week pay period. By changing the ValidationRule and ValidationText properties of the HoursWorked field, you can ensure that the values entered are within this range.

TASK 6: To Set the Validation Rule and Validation Text Properties for the HoursWorked Field

1 Highlight the Time Cards table in the database window and click the Design ⬚ Design button to open the table in Design view.

> **TIP** You can also open a table, query, form, or report in Design view by highlighting the object's name and right-clicking to open the appropriate shortcut menu.

2 Place the insertion point in any column of the HoursWorked field row and press (F6) to move to the lower pane of the Table Design window.

3 Click inside the Validation Rule row and type **>=0 And <=80** as the expression.

4 Move the insertion point into the Validation Text row and type **Hours worked must be greater than or equal to zero and less than or equal to 80 hours** as the validation rule.

Check Point

Although validation text is not required when you enter a validation rule, why should validation text always accompany a validation rule? Validation text will give the user appropriate feedback if he or she enters an invalid value. Your screen should now resemble Figure 2.23.

FIGURE 2.23

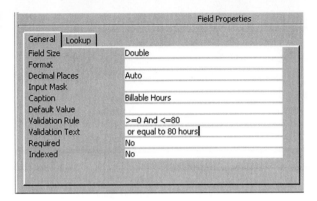

Field Properties

General | Lookup |

Field Size	Double
Format	
Decimal Places	Auto
Input Mask	
Caption	Billable Hours
Default Value	
Validation Rule	>=0 And <=80
Validation Text	or equal to 80 hours
Required	No
Indexed	No

5 Click the Save 🖫 button to update the table.

6 Close the table. You will test the validation rule when you enter data into the table.

TASK 7: To Add Input Masks to the Employees Table

1 Open the Employees table in Design view.

2 Press (F6) to move to the lower pane of the Table Design window.

3 Place the insertion point in the Input Mask row for the SSN field.

4 Click the Ellipsis ... button that appears immediately to the right of the Input Mask row.

5 Select Social Security Number as the input mask and click Next, as shown in Figure 2.24.

FIGURE 2.24

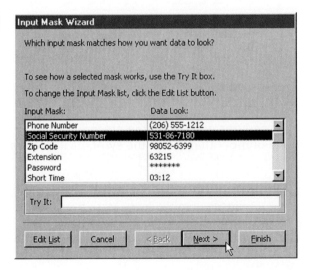

Input Mask Wizard

Which input mask matches how you want data to look?

To see how a selected mask works, use the Try It box.

To change the Input Mask list, click the Edit List button.

Input Mask:	Data Look:
Phone Number	(206) 555-1212
Social Security Number	531-86-7180
Zip Code	98052-6399
Extension	63215
Password	*******
Short Time	03:12

Try It: [   ]

Edit List | Cancel | < Back | Next > | Finish

6 On the next page of the Input Mask wizard, click Next to accept the defaults.

7 Select the option to store the symbols in the mask and click Finish, as shown in Figure 2.25.

FIGURE 2.25

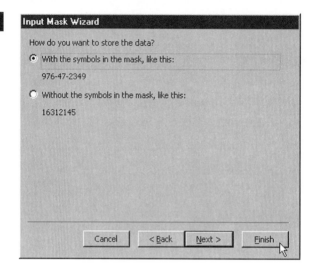

8 Click the Save 🖫 button to update the table.

9 Switch to Datasheet view.

10 Click the New Record ▶* button on the database toolbar.

11 Type **1** to display the input mask, as shown in Figure 2.26.

FIGURE 2.26

⊞	534-92-1985	Fowler	Lisa
⊞	544-24-7819	McDowell	Megan
⊞	599-67-1950	Williams	Amanda
⊞	620-45-1097	Tucker	William
⊞	671-93-1983	Terpstra	Mike
⊞	1 ▌ - __ - ____		

Record: ◀◀ ◀ | 16 | ▶ ▶◀ ▶* of 16

12 Press (ESC) to cancel entering data into this field.

13 Click the Design 🖾 ▾ button. Press (F6) to return to the upper portion of the Table Design window and place the insertion point into the HomePhone field row.

14 Using the same procedures outlined in the preceding steps, add an input mask for the phone number that stores the symbols in the mask.

> **TIP** You can also enter an input mask manually by typing the expression shown in Figure 2.27 directly into the Input Mask row. Use the Office Assistant for more information concerning input masks.

FIGURE 2.27

Field Properties	
General	Lookup
Field Size	255
Format	
Input Mask	!\(999") "000\-0000;0;
Caption	
Default Value	
Validation Rule	
Validation Text	
Required	No
Allow Zero Length	No
Indexed	No
Unicode Compression	Yes

A pattern for all data to be entered in this field

Web Tip

For more specific information about input mask options as well as examples, visit http://msdn.microsoft.com/library/officedev/access/d1/s1198b.htm.

15 Click the Save 💾 button to save these changes to the table design. Close the table.

Adding a Lookup Field to a Table in Design View

Earlier in the project you added a lookup field to the Time Cards table using the Lookup Wizard. You will now learn how to add to add a lookup field by changing the table properties directly.

TASK 8: To Add a Lookup Field to the Time Cards Table by Modifying the Table Properties Directly

1 Open the Time Cards table in Design view.

2 Place the insertion point in the EmployeeID field row.

3 Click the Lookup tab in the lower pane of the Table Design window.

4 Place the insertion point inside the Display Control field.

5 Click the drop-down list button and select Combo Box as the control type, as shown in Figure 2.28.

FIGURE 2.28

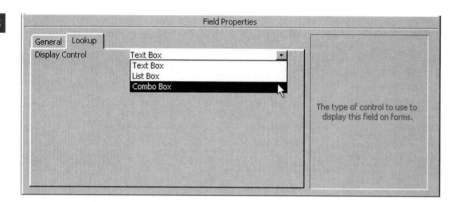

6 Select the Employees table in the Row Source row, type **3** in the Column Count row, and type **1";1.5";1.5"** in the Column Widths row. Make sure your settings match those shown in Figure 2.29.

FIGURE 2.29

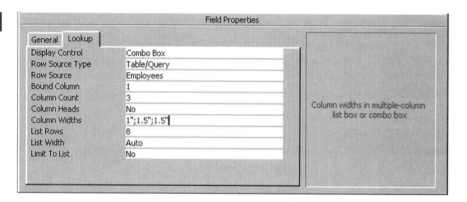

TIP Entering 3 in the Column Count row displays the first three fields in the table in the lookup list, so that you can verify an employee's name when selecting a Social Security number. Entering the column widths sets the widths of the columns included in the lookup list.

7 Click the Save 🖫 button to save these changes to the table design.

8 Switch to Datasheet view.

9 Place the insertion point over the right border of the Employee ID field, click the left mouse button, and drag the field to a size similar to what is shown in Figure 2.30.

FIGURE 2.30

10 Save your changes.

Adding Records to the Time Cards Table Using Lookup Lists

Now that you are finished modifying the tables in the Selections database, you can enter records into the Time Cards table. Although you may normally create a form for entering data, you can also enter records directly into the table's datasheet.

TASK 9:   To Add Records to the Time Cards Table

1   Click the Employee ID field for the first record.

2   Select the fifth employee in the list, as shown in Figure 2.31.

FIGURE 2.31

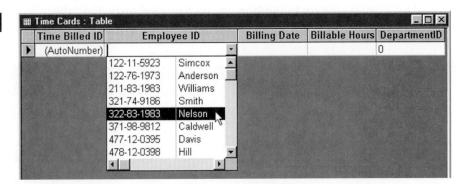

3   Press (TAB), type **1/16/99** for the billing date, type **42** as billable hours, and select Housewares as the department, as shown in Figure 2.32.

FIGURE 2.32

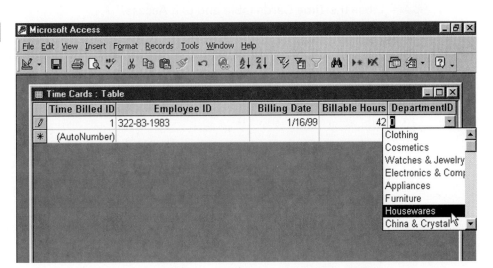

4 Using the following data, create four additional time card records:

Employee ID	Billing Date	Billable Hours	DepartmentID
477-12-0395	**1/16/99**	**55**	**Watches & Jewelry**
122-11-5923	**1/16/99**	**64**	**Electronics & Computers**
211-83-1983	**1/16/99**	**61**	**Furniture**
671-93-1983	**1/16/99**	**78**	**Knives & Cutlery**

> **TROUBLESHOOTING** If you inadvertently enter a billable hours value less than zero or exceeding 80, the validation text will inform you of this error.

When you are finished entering these records, the table should appear as shown in Figure 2.33.

FIGURE 2.33

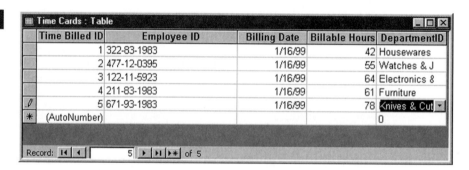

5 Close the Time Cards table and exit Access.

You have modified the Selections database according to Mr. Traylor's specifications. After you learn more about maintaining tables you will create queries, additional forms, and reports for listing gross pay information.

Summary and Exercises

Summary

- You can easily have a field in one table look up values in another by using the Lookup Wizard.
- You create relationships in Access by adding tables to the Relationships window and then assigning relationships.
- A one-to-many relationship is the most common kind of relationship among tables.
- In Access 2000 you can print a report of all relationships.
- When referential integrity is enforced, data entry errors are minimized.
- Validation rules and associated validation text improve data accuracy.
- You can improve data entry by setting the input mask property of text and number fields.
- Since lookup fields are field properties, you can create a lookup field by modifying field properties in Design view.
- Lookup fields make it easier to enter data in one table that exists in another.

Key Terms and Operations

Key Terms

input mask
lookup field
null value
referential integrity
Relationships window

validation rule
Validation Rule property
validation text
Validation Text property

Operations

add records to a table using lookup fields
add tables to the Relationships window
create a lookup field in Table Design view
create and modify relationships
print relationships
set input mask properties
set Validation Rule and Validation Text properties
use the Lookup Wizard

Study Questions

Multiple Choice

1. You should always change the Validation Text property of a field when you enter a(n)
   a. input mask.
   b. lookup field.
   c. relationship.
   d. validation rule.

2. You can easily create relationships between tables by using
   a. Datasheet view.
   b. Table Design view.
   c. the lower pane of the Table Design window.
   d. the Relationships window.

3. Which statement is false concerning a one-to-many relationship?
   a. One or more records in table B are related to one record in table A.
   b. Referential integrity must be enforced before creating a one-to-many-relationship.
   c. One and only one record in table A is related to table B.
   d. It is the most common kind of relationship.

4. Validation rules are especially important when defining fields using which data type?
   a. Memo
   b. Date/Time
   c. Text
   d. Currency

5. The "many" side of a one-to-many relationship is represented with
   a. a line.
   b. the number 1.
   c. the word *many*.
   d. the infinity symbol.

6. A lookup field list cannot contain
   a. data from a table.
   b. data in a value list you create.
   c. data from a query.
   d. data from an AutoForm.

7. Which kind of relationship is most common in Access databases?
   a. one-to-many
   b. one-to-one
   c. many-to-many
   d. one-to-many-to-one

8. You can change the Validation Text property of a field using
   a. Datasheet view.
   b. the upper pane of the Table Design window.
   c. the lower pane of the Table Design window.
   d. the Relationships window.

9. A relationship will exist between a maximum of how many tables?
   a. two
   b. three
   c. four
   d. eight

10. A database table for mutual fund contributions contains the following fields: LastName, FirstName, AccountID, ContributionAmount. Which field(s) should you add a validation rule to?
    a. LastName
    b. AccountID
    c. FirstName
    d. ContributionAmount

Short Answer

1. List three sources for a lookup list.

2. Between how many tables does a relationship always exist?

3. What happens when you specify Lookup Wizard as a data type?

4. Where do you modify relationships?

5. How do you print table relationships?

6. What does a lookup field require?

7. What is referential integrity?

8. What happens if you violate a validation rule?

9. Which view do you use to change the Validation Text property of a field?

10. How do you add field data to a table by using a lookup list?

Fill in the Blank

1. Validation rules are important for _____ data types that may be used in calculations.

2. A(n) _____ allows data in one table to look up values in another.

3. You can create lookup fields directly in tables using _____ view.

4. A(n) _____ supplies a template for entering data into a field.

5. A _____ is the most common type of relationship.

6. A _____ appears whenever a validation rule is violated.

7. You create and modify relationships in the _____.

8. To assist users in entering a telephone number into a field, add a(n) _____.

9. You modify field properties in the _____ of the Table Design window.

10. Whenever you change the _____ property of a field, you should also consider changing the _____ property.

For Discussion

1. Explain how lookup fields utilize primary and foreign keys.

2. Why should you consider enforcing referential integrity in relationships?

3. How does a primary key differ from a foreign key?

4. In this project you created a lookup field that hides the primary key value. Why does Access suggest that you do this?

5. Why should you change the Validation Text property of a field if you change the Validation Rule property?

Hands-On Exercises

1. Adding a Table to the Inventory Database

Open the Inventory database you created in Project 1. You will create a new table in Table Design view that lists the current items in stock as they arrive. Once you create the table you can establish a relationship and add a lookup field.

 **Web Tip**

If you do not have a copy of this file, you can download it from the SELECT Web site at http://www.prenhall.com/select.

1. With the Tables button active, click the New button in the database window.

2. Select Design View in the New Table dialog box and click OK.

3. Create the fields shown in Figure 2.34. Set the InventoryID field as the primary key.

FIGURE 2.34

Field Name	Data Type	Description
InventoryID	AutoNumber	
ProductID	Text	
UnitsInStock	Number	
DateAcquired	Date/Time	

Current Inventory : Table

Field Properties

4. Save the table and type **Current Inventory** as the name.

5. Open the Relationships window.

6. Add the Products and Current Inventory tables to the window.

7. Create a one-to-many relationship between these tables and enforce referential integrity, as shown in Figure 2.35.

FIGURE 2.35

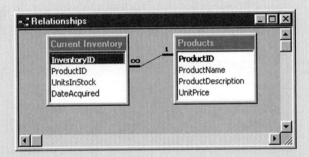

8. Close the Relationships window and save your changes.

2. Adding a Lookup Field to the Inventory Database

As you learned in this project, lookup fields make it easier to enter data into tables. In this exercise you will add a lookup field to the Current Inventory table that looks up products from the Products table.

1. Open the Current Inventory table in Table Design view.

2. Place the insertion point in the ProductID row in the upper pane of the Table Design window.

3. Select the Lookup tab in the Field Properties pane.

4. Modify the properties as shown in Figure 2.36.

FIGURE 2.36

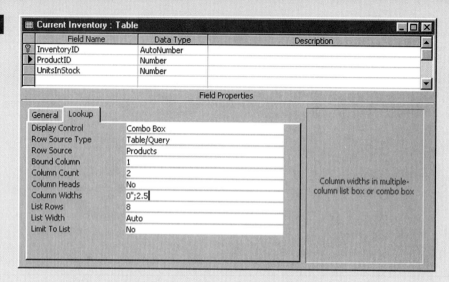

5. Save your changes and switch to Datasheet view.

6. Adjust the column width for the ProductID field.

7. Use the lookup field to add the records shown in Figure 2.37.

FIGURE 2.37

InventoryID	ProductID	UnitsInStock	DateAcquired
1	WeatherGuard Pro	15	1/5/99
2	WeatherGuard	10	1/5/99
3	Case Logic Gear	35	1/8/99
4	Extreme Image	10	1/8/99
5	Samson Carryall	3	1/9/99
6	Samson Carryall	7	1/11/99
(AutoNumber)		0	

Record: ◄◄ ◄ 6 ► ►◄ ►* of 6

8. Close the table, save changes to the layout, and exit Access.

On Your Own Exercises

1. Creating a Table of Web Site Ratings

Open the *Web Sites.mdb* database you created in Project 1. Create a table with two fields that lists five ratings for Web sites. The first field will be an AutoNumber type, and the second a text data type. Save the table as *Ratings*.

2. Adding a Lookup Field to a Table

Modify the Sites table in the *Web Sites.mdb* database by adding a lookup field that looks up the Web site ratings from the Ratings table. Rate each site in the database and save your changes when you are finished.

3. Establishing a Relationship in the Inventory Database

Open the *Inventory.mdb* database. Add a lookup field to the Inventory table that looks up the product name from the Products table. Edit the relationship to enforce referential integrity.

4. Using the Office Assistant

Open the *Inventory.mdb* database. Choose Show the Office Assistant from the Help menu. Search the Help system for information on changing the Validation Rule property. Determine whether you should add any validation rules to the database. Save any changes.

5. Checking Referential Integrity

Open the *Contact Management.mdb* database you created in Project 1. Check all relationships and determine whether referential integrity is currently enforced, and if it is not, whether it should be. Save any changes you make to the database.

6. Adding Contact Records to the Contact Management Database

Open the *Contact Management.mdb* database you created in Project 1. From the Switchboard, select the option to enter contacts. Add five contacts to the database. When you are finished, close the database and exit Access.

Manipulating Table Data

Now that you have established relationships among tables in the Selections database and added records, you need to anticipate how best to add new records, edit existing record data, or view existing records in different ways. In this project you will learn how to organize and work with table data.

Objectives

After completing this project, you will be able to:

➤ Navigate among records using Datasheet view

➤ Test validation records by adding new records

➤ Search a table for a specific record

➤ Update records in a table using the Replace feature

➤ Sort records in a table

➤ View table properties

➤ Filter records

➤ Create a data access page

➤ View a data access page using a Web browser

Running Case

Mr. Traylor has appointed you as the developer at Selections, Inc. You are therefore responsible for implementing and maintaining the database of the employees. As with any database, Mr. Traylor will expect you both to test the existing design and to adapt the database as the need for information in new formats arises. You will be able to provide Mr. Traylor with relevant, timely, and accurate information.

The Challenge

Mr. Traylor has four tasks for you.

- First, he wants you to make sure the data validation rules you have established are valid.

- Second, he wants to see how quickly and efficiently you are able to make changes to the existing table data. The finance committee made the decision today to raise the hourly wage of all employees at certain pay levels, which need to be changed. One employee is now married, and thus her last name needs to be changed.

- Third, he wants to see employee records listed in three ways: sorted by last name, sorted by last name for a specific state, and sorted by age for a specific state and city.

- Finally, he wants to post all employee data to the company intranet, so the regional departmental managers can modify them. Figure 3.1 shows the data access page you will create as it appears in Microsoft Internet Explorer.

FIGURE 3.1

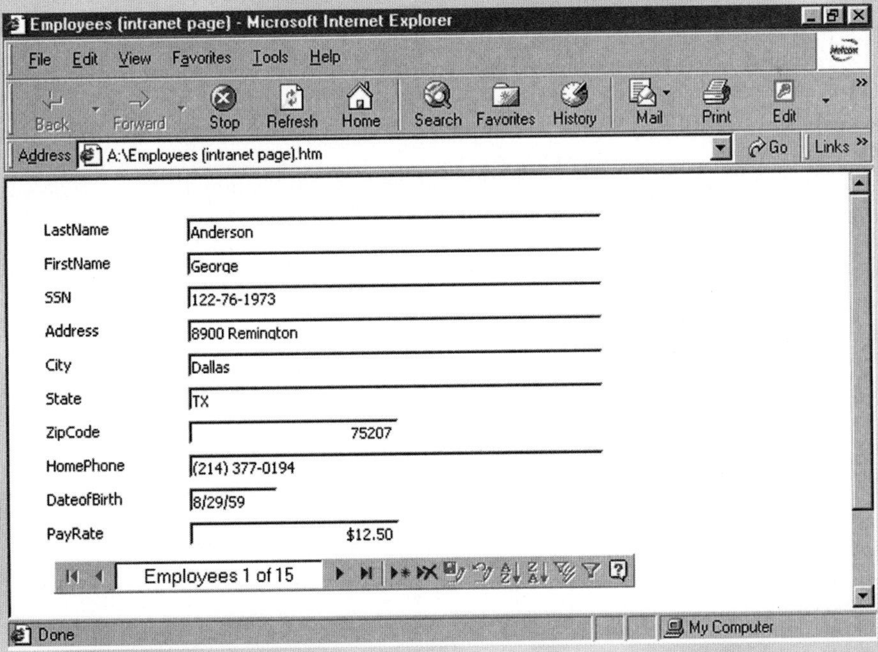

Employees (intranet page) - Microsoft Internet Explorer

File   Edit   View   Favorites   Tools   Help

Back   Forward   Stop   Refresh   Home   Search   Favorites   History   Mail   Print   Edit

Address A:\Employees (intranet page).htm

LastName	Anderson
FirstName	George
SSN	122-76-1973
Address	8900 Remington
City	Dallas
State	TX
ZipCode	75207
HomePhone	(214) 377-0194
DateofBirth	8/29/59
PayRate	$12.50

Employees 1 of 15

Done   My Computer

The Strategy

Since you will be working with records in Table Datasheet view, you will need to know how to navigate among records using this view. To test the validation rules you have established, you can add additional employee records to the database. To change the pay rates and the one employee's last name, you can use the Find and Replace feature. To display the records in a different order, you can use the Sort feature; to see records from specific cities and for specific pay rates, you can filter the database. Finally, to post employee data to the corporate intranet, you can create a data access page.

> **TIP** In practice, databases are beta-tested within an organization prior to a full-scale implementation.

The Setup

So that your screen matches the illustrations in this project, you should set up Access as shown in Table 3.1 after you launch Access and open your database. These are the default settings in Access, but they may have been changed on your computer.

Table 3.1

Location	Make these settings:
Tools, Customize	Click the Toolbars tab and display the database toolbar and the menu bar, if they are not currently visible, as shown in Figure 3.2.
Tools, Options	Display the status bar, the startup dialog box, new object shortcuts, and windows in the taskbar, as shown in Figure 3.3.
Tools, Options	Click the General tab and deselect the setting for displaying dates in four-digit format.
Tools, Customize	Click the Options tab, and make sure the checkbox to display recently used menu commands first is deselected, as shown in Figure 3.4.
Office Assistant	Hide the Office Assistant.

FIGURE 3.2

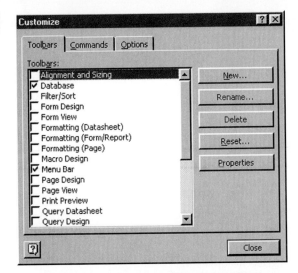

FIGURE 3.3

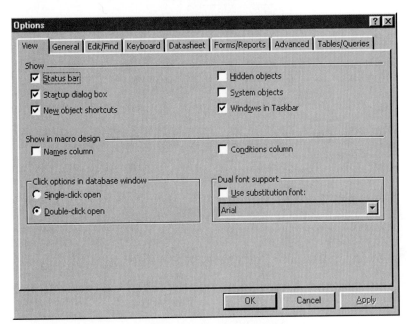

FIGURE 3.4

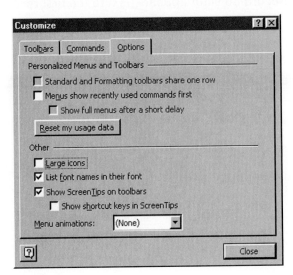

Navigating among Table Records Using Datasheet View

Although end users typically use Access forms to interact with record data, database designers will frequently use Table Datasheet view to interact with records. One common task is navigating among the records the datasheet displays. Access supports multiple methods for navigating among records. To **navigate** among records is to move from one record to another in a table. Datasheet view includes navigation buttons, or **controls**, that you can use to move among records. You can use these controls to move to the first, previous, next, and last records in the table. You can also use the New Record button to add records to the table. Figure 3.5 shows the navigation buttons appearing in the lower-left corner of the Employees table when it is opened in Datasheet view.

FIGURE 3.5

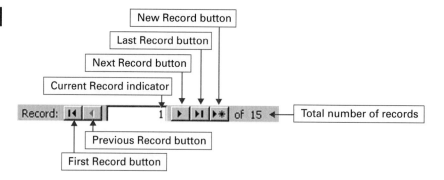

TASK 1: To Navigate among Records in Datasheet View

1. Open the Selections database.

2. From the database window with the Tables button active, double-click the Employees table to open it in Datasheet view.

3. The datasheet's Record Selector appears next to the first record, as shown in Figure 3.6.

FIGURE 3.6

Record Selector

TIP The Record Selector will at times display these symbols:

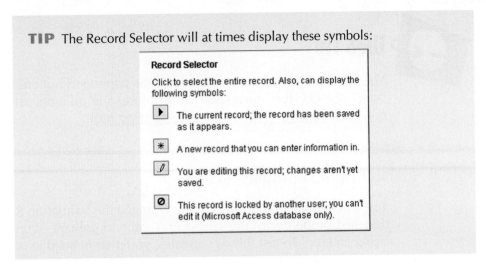

Record Selector

Click to select the entire record. Also, can display the following symbols:

▶ The current record; the record has been saved as it appears.

✳ A new record that you can enter information in.

✎ You are editing this record; changes aren't yet saved.

⊘ This record is locked by another user; you can't edit it (Microsoft Access database only).

4 Click the Last Record button. The last record in the database is selected, as shown in Figure 3.7.

FIGURE 3.7

	SSN	LastName	FirstName	Address	City	
⊞	122-11-5923	Simcox	Cole	3111 Ocean Vie	Tacoma	WA
⊞	122-76-1973	Anderson	George	8900 Remington	Dallas	TX
⊞	211-83-1983	Williams	Robert	6001 Riverwalk	Austin	TX
⊞	321-74-9186	Smith	Mary Beth	145 Angelo Rio	Tucson	AZ
⊞	322-83-1983	Nelson	Rebecca	3701 Mesa Blvd	Phoenix	AZ
⊞	371-98-9812	Caldwell	Thomas	425 Falls Churc	Houston	TX
⊞	477-12-0395	Davis	Terri	311 Big Bend L:	Houston	TX
⊞	478-12-0398	Hill	John	21101 E. Count	San Antonio	TX
⊞	521-04-9104	George	Philip	675 Hurricane F	Tacoma	WA
⊞	524-38-1298	Jamison	Kimberly	23117 E. Missis	Denver	CO
⊞	534-92-1985	Fowler	Lisa	400 Columbia G	Redmond	WA
⊞	544-24-7819	McDowell	Megan	31101 Lombard	Seattle	WA
⊞	599-67-1950	Williams	Amanda	25 Rodeo Drive	Aurora	CO
⊞	620-45-1097	Tucker	William	761 E. Kiowa S:	Tucson	AZ
▶ ⊞	671-93-1983	Terpstra	Mike	2111 E. Baselin	Boulder	CO

Employees : Table

Record: 14 ◄ 15 ► ►I ►✳ of 15

You can also move to a specific record by entering a valid record number in the current record indicator.

5 Double-click inside the current record indicator to highlight the value, and type **8** as the record number, as shown in Figure 3.8.

FIGURE 3.8  Record: 14 ◄ | 8 | ► ►I ►✳ of 15

6 Press (ENTER). Record 8 is now the current record.

TIP Once a record is current, you may edit its contents by tabbing to the appropriate field in Datasheet view.

7 Close the Employees table.

Web Tip

You can add Visual Basic objects such as command buttons to Access database objects for navigation. For more information, see http://www.microsoft.com/accessdev/articles/cmdbtnwz.htm.

Testing Validation Rules by Adding Records

You will recall that in Project 2 you changed the Validation Rule and Validation Text properties of the Time Cards table to prevent erroneous data from being entered. To test these properties, you merely need to add a record and intentionally violate the rule, to make sure it is working properly. This provides a quick check of the accuracy of the information your database may contain.

TASK 2: To Test the Validation Rule and Validation Text Properties of the Time Cards Table

1 Open the Time Cards table in Datasheet view.

2 Click the New Record ▶* button.

3 In the Employee ID field, select Nelson, as shown in Figure 3.9.

FIGURE 3.9

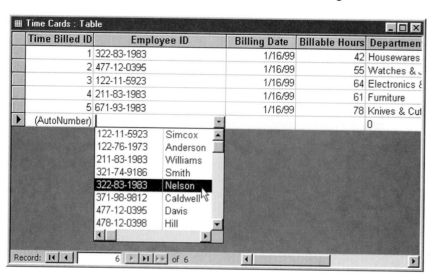

4 Press TAB and type **02/02/99** as the billing date for the new record.

5 Press TAB again, and type **81** as the billable hours.

6 Press TAB. The message shown in Figure 3.10 that indicates the validation rule has been violated appears on the screen.

FIGURE 3.10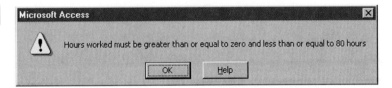

> **TIP** When you add data validation to your database, make sure the validation text you add will be understood by the average database user!

7 Click OK. Highlight the invalid number, and type **39** as the correct value.

Check Point

What would happen if you entered 0 as the billable hours? The value would be accepted, since zero does not violate the validation rule.

8 Press TAB, and select China & Crystal as the department.

9 Close the table.

Searching for Records

As with many databases, record data will change over time. This is particularly true for database tables containing name and address information. Although it is not difficult to find a specific record in a table that has a small number of records, when a table contains hundreds or thousands of records, this method becomes impractical.

Fortunately, Access contains search capabilities. Using the **Find** dialog box to search for a specific record and *edit*, or change, its data is a common database maintenance task. Editing field data is one way of updating records. Updating also includes adding and deleting records. You will need to update the Employees table by changing Kimberly Jamison's last name, as she was recently married.

TASK 3: <u>To Search a Table for a Specific Record</u>

① Open the Employees table in Datasheet view.

② Choose Find from the Edit menu, as shown in Figure 3.11.

FIGURE 3.11

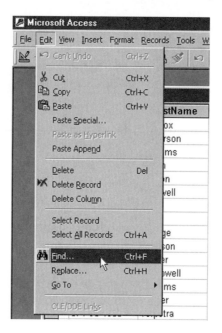

Check Point

What other option do you have to evoke the Search feature? You can use the Find button on the database toolbar.

③ The Find and Replace dialog box appears. Type **Jamison** as the search term, select Employees: Table in the Look in: drop-down list, and select Match: Any Part of Field, as shown in Figure 3.12.

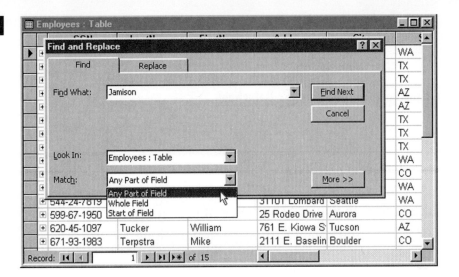

FIGURE 3.12

4   Click Find Next. The Record Selector moves to record 10.

Updating Records in a Table

Once you find a record using the Find option, you can edit it in the same way you edit any record displayed in a table. By entering a new value, you can replace the selected text with a new entry.

TASK 4:   To Update Records

1   Click the Cancel button. The text is highlighted.

2   Type **Miller** as the new last name, and press (ENTER). The record will be updated once you move the focus to another field or record.

3   Click the First Record button.

Updating Multiple Records in a Table Using Replace

You may have noticed that the Find and Replace dialog box contains two tabs: one to locate records, and another to replace the results of a search.

Mr. Traylor wants you to replace certain hourly wage figures with those the finance office has authorized. All employees earning $8.90 per hour will be paid $9.25, and those earning $9.45 will now earn $9.80. All changes are retroactive to the first of the year.

The **_Find and Replace_** feature works with tables, queries, and forms. In the tasks that follow, you will use the Find feature to locate field data and the Replace feature to update the field with a new value. You will locate and change field data in the Employees table's datasheet, and also in the Employees form.

Using Find and Replace with a Table's Datasheet

You can perform find and replace operations on one or more fields in a table's datasheet.

TASK 5: **To Replace Employee Hourly Wages with New Values Using Datasheet View**

1 Click the Find 🔍 button on the database toolbar.

2 Click the Replace tab.

3 Type **8.90** in the Find What: text box, and **9.25** in the Replace With: text box.

> **TROUBLESHOOTING** Do not enter the dollar sign character ($) in front of the number. The dollar sign is displayed because the number appears in currency format. The actual data stored in the database is a decimal value. When you create a form that will require a currency input and you don't want the user to enter a $ by accident, just add a $ as text directly before the input field. That will help you avoid this problem.

4 Click the Replace All button to replace all instances of the pay rate. The warning shown in Figure 3.13 appears on the screen. Notice the message in that status bar, indicating the number of records that will be changed if you complete this operation.

FIGURE 3.13

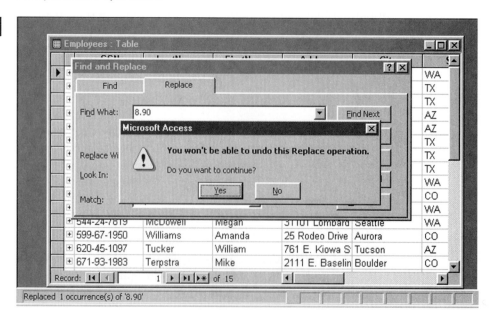

Check Point

Why will only one record be changed? Only one record will be changed because there is only one employee in the database at this pay rate.

5 Click the Yes button to complete the replace operation.

6 Click Cancel to remove the Find and Replace dialog box from the screen.

7 Close the table.

Using Find and Replace with Forms

When you created an AutoForm based upon the Employees table in Project 1, Access set the properties for each field automatically. A *property* is a setting for a specific object or control that affects how its data is displayed, or some other characteristic of the object or control. The Employees form displays currency values according to the AutoForm properties. Although Access will locate the underlying value regardless of how it is displayed on the form, you will change this property before you search for and replace a specific pay rate.

 TASK 6: **To Replace Employee Hourly Wages with New Values Using the Employees Form**

1 Click the Forms button on the Objects bar in the database window to display the current forms, as shown in Figure 3.14.

FIGURE 3.14

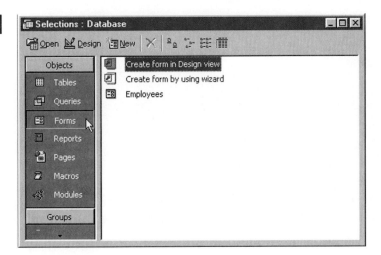

2 Double-click the Employees form to open it in Form view. You will notice that the pay rate for the first employee does not display any places to the right of the decimal.

3 Place the insertion point inside the PayRate text box and click the Properties button on the database toolbar.

4 Click the Format tab in the Properties sheet for the PayRate text box.

5 Click the Decimal Places row and select 2 from the drop-down list, as shown in Figure 3.15.

FIGURE 3.15

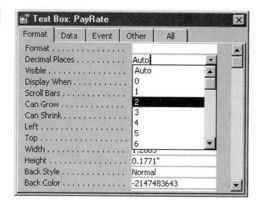

6 Click the Close button for the Properties sheet. The text box now displays the underlying field data with two decimal places.

7 Click the Pay Rate field, and click the Find button on the database toolbar.

8 Click the Replace tab.

9 Type **9.45** in the Find What: text box, and **9.80** in the Replace With: text box.

10 When your settings match those shown in Figure 3.16, click the Replace All button.

FIGURE 3.16

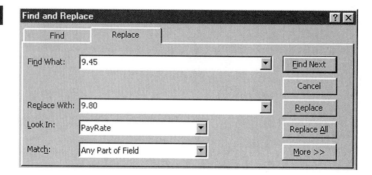

11 Click the Yes button to complete the replace operation, and then click Cancel to remove the Find and Replace dialog box from the screen.

12 Close the form. Click Yes when you see the message displayed in Figure 3.17.

FIGURE 3.17

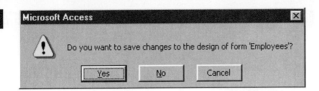

Microsoft Access

⚠ Do you want to save changes to the design of form 'Employees'?

[Yes]   [No]   [Cancel]

Sorting Records

Another common database maintenance task is sorting records. When you apply a **sort**, you reorder the records in a table or form according to the entries in a specific field. The field you select for a sort specifies the **sort criteria**. Although Access objects such as forms and reports can be designed so as to display data in a sorted format, at times you may want to quickly verify the data on the screen. Records can be sorted in either ascending or descending order. When you sort in **ascending order**, names and terms are sorted from A to Z, and dates and times are sorted from earlier to later. When you sort by **descending order**, the opposite is true.

> **TIP** When sorting, the sort order is determined by the language settings. When you are sorting records for display, you should sort on multiple fields in an order. For instance, first sort by Department, then Last name, then First name, so that the data is easier to read when the records are displayed.

When you sort records, Access saves the sort order when you save the form or datasheet, and reapplies it automatically when you reopen the object or base a new form or report on that object.

TASK 7:   To Sort Records in a Table

 Open the Employees table in Datasheet view.

 Place the insertion point somewhere in the LastName field, or select the entire column by clicking the LastName field selector, as shown in Figure 3.18.

FIGURE 3.18

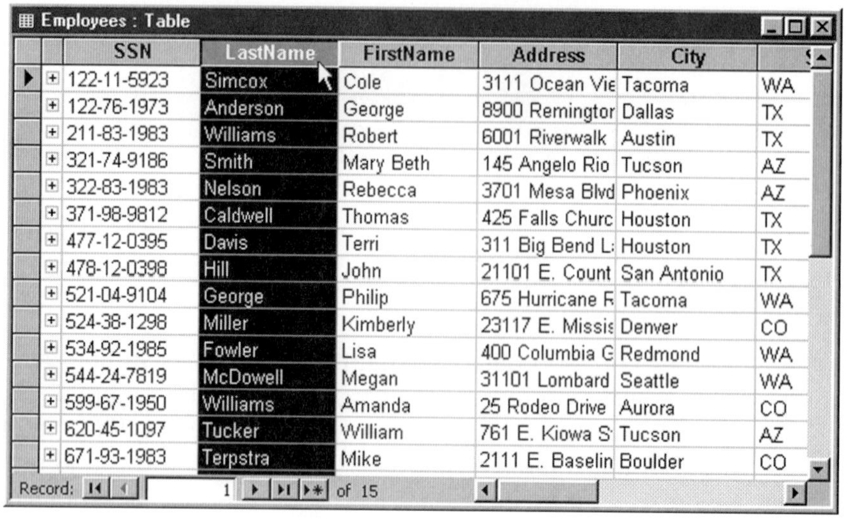

3 Click the Sort Ascending $\frac{A}{Z}\downarrow$ button on the Table Datasheet toolbar.

4 The records are now sorted in ascending order by last name, as shown in Figure 3.19.

FIGURE 3.19

5 Close the table.

6 The Microsoft Access dialog box shown in Figure 3.20 appears. Since you want the table design to be modified, click Yes.

FIGURE 3.20

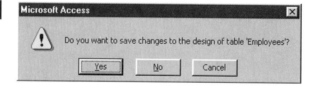

Any time you open the table, the data will now appear in alphabetical order by last name. This is because you modified the table structure by specifying a sort property for the table. Recall that a property is some characteristic of a database control or object. In the event that you would ever need to change this property, you need to know where to change it.

TASK 8:   To View the Table Properties

1   Open the Employees table in Design view.

2   In the Table Design window, place the insertion point inside the title bar, and click the right mouse button. The shortcut menu shown in Figure 3.21 appears.

FIGURE 3.21

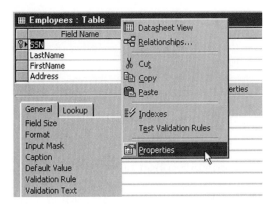

Check Point

How else can you open the Properties Sheet for the table? You can open the table's Properties sheet by clicking the Properties button on the database toolbar.

3   Select the Properties option, as shown in Figure 3.18. The Table Properties sheet shown in Figure 3.22 appears. Notice the setting for the Order By row: Employees:LastName. This specifies the field on which the table is currently sorted. To remove or change the sort specifications, delete this entry, or select another field name.

FIGURE 3.22

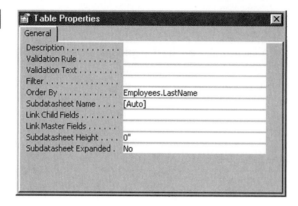

4 Close the Table Properties sheet without making any changes.

5 Close the form.

> **TIP** To sort on more than one field you must use either the Advanced Filter option, or construct a query.

Filtering Records

Sometimes you need to retrieve a subset of records from an underlying table, such as when Mr. Traylor requested a sorted list of employees for a specific state and city. You can apply a *filter* to temporarily view or edit a subset of records while you're viewing a form or datasheet. Access supports two methods for quickly filtering records. With *Filter by Selection* you select all or part of a value, and then click the Filter by Selection button on the toolbar to find all records with the selected value. If you would rather specify a value you're searching for by typing it or picking it from a list in the field, you can use the *Filter by Form* option. This option also allows you to specify multiple criteria for a filter.

When you are finished viewing the filtered data, you remove the filter to restore the datasheet or form to its previous order.

TASK 9: To Use Filter by Selection to Display All Employees from Texas

1 Open the Employees table in Datasheet view.

2 Maximize the datasheet to display as many fields as possible.

3 Select the state name TX in the first record, as shown in Figure 3.23.

FIGURE 3.23

	SSN	LastName	FirstName	Address	City	State	Z
▶ ⊞	122-76-1973	Anderson	George	8900 Remingtor	Dallas	TX	
⊞	371-98-9812	Caldwell	Thomas	425 Falls Churc	Houston	TX	
⊞	477-12-0395	Davis	Terri	311 Big Bend L	Houston	TX	
⊞	534-92-1985	Fowler	Lisa	400 Columbia G	Redmond	WA	
⊞	521-04-9104	George	Philip	675 Hurricane F	Tacoma	WA	

4   Click the Filter by Selection ▼ button on the Table Datasheet toolbar. The filter is applied, as shown in Figure 3.24. Notice that FLTR appears in the status bar and the word *Filtered* appears in parentheses following the New Record button.

FIGURE 3.24

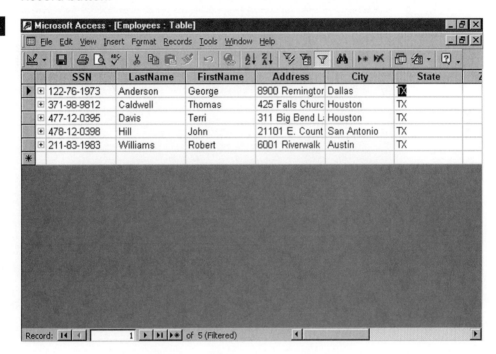

5   Click the Remove Filter ▽ button to remove the filter.

6   Close the table without saving the changes.

TASK 10: To Use Filter by Form to Display All Employees from Texas in Sorted Order

1   Open the Employees table again in Datasheet view.

2   Click the Filter by Form 🖩 button on the Table Datasheet toolbar.

3   Use the ⌷TAB⌷ key or the mouse to select the State field.

4   Click the button appearing in the field and select TX from the list, as shown in Figure 3.25.

FIGURE 3.25

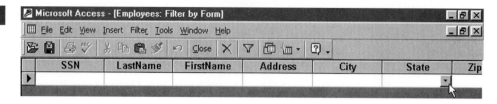

The text string "TX" now appears in quotes in the empty field list, as shown in Figure 3.26.

FIGURE 3.26

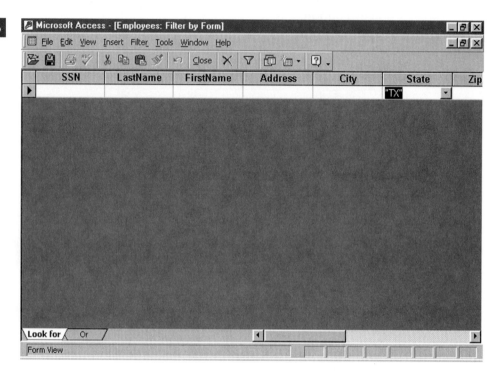

TIP Notice that Look for and Or tabs appear just above the status bar. These can be used to select records meeting multiple conditions.

5 Click the Apply Filter ⦿ button on the Table Datasheet toolbar. Once again, the datasheet displays records for all employees from Texas.

6 Click the Filter by Form ⦿ button again to return to select an additional filter criterion.

7 Place the insertion point inside the City field and select Houston from the list, as shown in Figure 3.27.

FIGURE 3.27

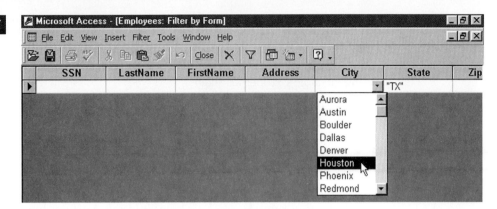

> **8** Click the Apply Filter button to apply the filter with the two criteria you specified.

> **9** Use the horizontal scroll bar to display the DateofBirth field.

> **10** With the mouse pointer anywhere inside this field, click the Sort Ascending button. The two filtered records are now displayed in ascending order by date of birth, as shown in Figure 3.28.

FIGURE 3.28

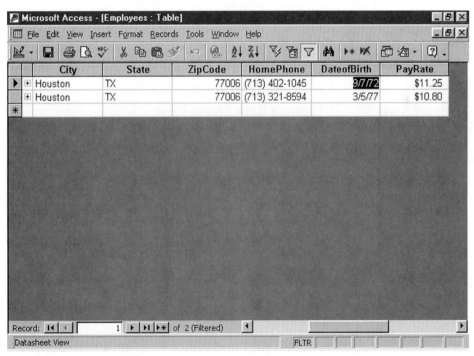

Datasheet displaying filtered and sorted records

> **11** Close the datasheet. Do not save your changes to the table.

> **TIP** If you click the Yes button, the filter and sort information will be stored with the table design. Whenever you apply sort or filter criteria and then update a table, these properties can always be edited or deleted at a later time using the table's Properties sheet.

Web Tip

For more information on sorting and filtering records, visit http://msdn .microsoft.com/library/books/techlang/dnjet/c5_body_6.htm.

Creating a Data Access Page

You are almost finished making the changes Mr. Traylor specified for the database. The remaining task is to create a form for posting the employee data on the company's intranet. You can use the new database object now available in Access 2000: a data access page. A **data access page** is an Access object you create to enter, edit, and interact with live data via the Internet or an intranet outside an Access database or project. Once you have created a data access page you can export it as an HTML file.

TASK 11: To Create a Data Access Page

1 Click the Pages button on the Objects bar.

2 Click the New button in the database window.

3 Select Page Wizard in the upper portion of the New Data Access Page dialog box, and the Employees table in the drop-down list. When your settings match Figure 3.29, click OK.

FIGURE 3.29

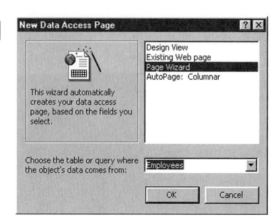

4 In the first page of the wizard, select the Employees table in the Tables/Queries drop-down list, if necessary.

5 Click the ▸▸ button to move all available fields to the Selected Fields: list. When your settings match Figure 3.30, click Next.

FIGURE 3.30

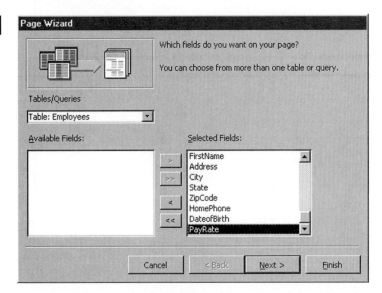

6 When you are asked to specify grouping levels, click Next, as shown in Figure 3.31.

FIGURE 3.31

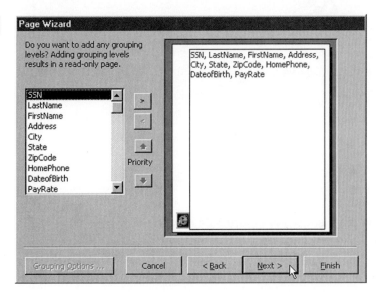

7 Select LastName and FirstName as the sort fields, as shown in Figure 3.32. Click Next.

FIGURE 3.32

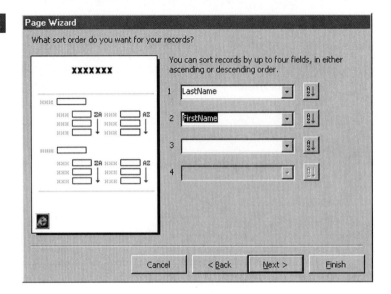

8 Edit the title for the page, select the option to display the page, and click Finish, as shown in Figure 3.33.

FIGURE 3.33

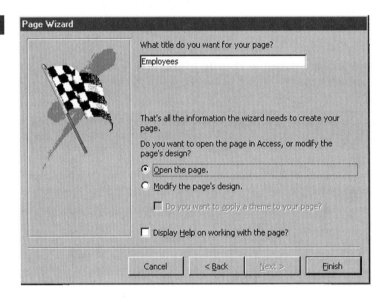

The page shown in Figure 3.34 is created.

FIGURE 3.34

Microsoft Access - [Employees]

File   Edit   View   Insert   Format   Tools   Window   Help

LastName	Anderson
FirstName	George
SSN	122-76-1973
Address	8900 Remington
City	Dallas
State	TX
ZipCode	75207
HomePhone	(214) 377-0194
DateofBirth	8/29/59
PayRate	$12.51

Employees 1 of 15

Ready

TROUBLESHOOTING Maximize the data access page, if necessary.

9 Click the Close button. Access displays the message shown in Figure 3.35.

FIGURE 3.35

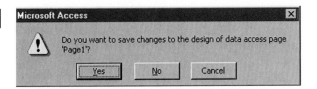

Microsoft Access

⚠ Do you want to save changes to the design of data access page 'Page1'?

[Yes]   [No]   [Cancel]

10 Click Yes.

11 Type **Employees (Intranet page)** as the file name and click OK. The data access page closes, and is saved.

> **TIP** When you create a data access page, it is stored in the default folder for the application, and a shortcut is added to the database window (you can change the default folder for Access by selecting Options from the Tools menu).

Viewing a Data Access Page on the Web

The data access page you just created is stored externally from the Selections database file. Before viewing it on the Web, you can export the page to your floppy disk and then open it in your Web browser.

TASK 12: Exporting the Data Access Page

1 With the Pages button active in the Objects bar, highlight the *Employees (Intranet page)* data access page.

2 Choose Export from the File menu.

3 Set the location and file type as shown in Figure 3.36.

FIGURE 3.36

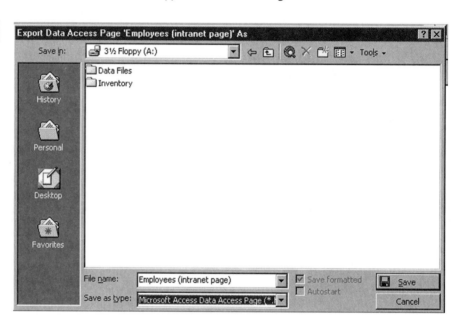

4 Click the Save button.

5 Close the database.

6 Exit Access.

TASK 13: Opening the Data Access Page Using Internet Explorer

1 Using My Computer, open your disk.

2 Double-click the *Employees (intranet page).htm* file, as shown in Figure 3.37.

FIGURE 3.37

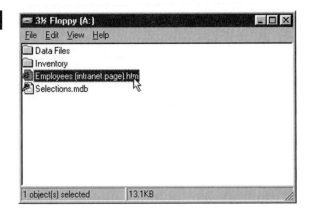

3 The page appears in Internet Explorer, as shown in Figure 3.38.

FIGURE 3.38

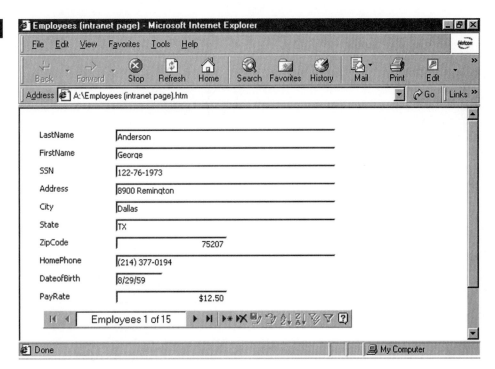

TROUBLESHOOTING You must have Microsoft Internet Explorer 5 or higher installed on your computer to open the data access page.

4 Close your Web browser when you are finished viewing the page.

TIP This page contains a link to the employee data in the Employees table. If you make changes to the data in the access page displayed in your Web browser, the changes are made in the Access table underlying the page.

Summary and Exercises

Summary

- Table Datasheet view includes navigation buttons, or controls, to move among records and add new records to the table.
- You can enter a valid record number in the current record area of the datasheet's navigation controls and press (ENTER) to move to a specific record.
- To test the Validation Rule and Validation Text properties of a table, add new records that violate the rule.
- You can use the Find and Replace feature to locate fields meeting specific criteria or to change the field entry.
- You can sort records by any field in the table.
- To change a table's sort order, change the Order By property of the table.
- Filter by Form allows you to view records in a table datasheet that meet one condition.
- Filter by Selection allow you to view records in a table's datasheet that meet one or more conditions.
- A data access page displays table data in an HTML form.

Key Terms and Operations

Key Terms

ascending order	Find
controls	Find and Replace
data access page	navigate
descending order	property
filter	sort
Filter by Form	sort criteria
Filter by Selection	

Operations

create a data access page
filter records by form
filter records by selection
navigate among records in a table's datasheet by replacing the current record number and pressing (ENTER)
navigate among records in a table's datasheet using the Navigation buttons
search for field data in a table's datasheet
sort table records
test Validation Rule and Validation Text properties by adding new records to a table

use Find and Replace to locate and change field data using a datasheet
use Find and Replace to locate and change field data using a form
view a data access page using Microsoft Internet Explorer
view table properties

Study Questions

Multiple Choice

1. To quickly locate a record in a table or form, use the
   a. Find dialog box.
   b. Replace All button.
   c. Table Datasheet view.
   d. Apply Filter button.

2. Updating records in a table includes all of the following except
   a. changing an employee's address.
   b. creating a new table.
   c. inserting records.
   d. deleting records.

3. The easiest way of making a global change in a database is by using the
   a. Replace All feature.
   b. Sort Ascending button.
   c. Remove Filter button.
   d. New Page button.

4. Which of the following is not true concerning the sort feature in Access?
   a. Records can be sorted in ascending or descending order according to the values in a specific field.
   b. Information about the sort can be saved with the table design properties.
   c. Dates are sorted from most recent to least recent when using the Sort Descending feature.
   d. The case of text entries does not matter when sorting records.

5. The filter option that allows you to select records matching multiple criteria is
   a. Apply Filter.
   b. Filter by Form.
   c. Remove Filter.
   d. Filter by Selection.

6. The filter feature that enables you to select records containing the same text or value as one highlighted in a specific field is
   a. Apply Filter.
   b. Filter by Form.
   c. Remove Filter.
   d. Filter by Selection.

7. To create a resource for displaying table data on a corporate intranet, you should
   a. create a new table.
   b. split the database into two files.
   c. create a new database and copy all the records into it.
   d. create a data access page.

8. To identify the field you want to use for sorting records,
   a. click the Sort Ascending button.
   b. select the entire table.
   c. position the insertion point somewhere in the desired field.
   d. click the Sort Descending button.

9. Which feature allows you to select a criterion for viewing records by using a drop-down list?
   a. Sort Ascending
   b. Filter by Selection
   c. Sort Descending
   d. Filter by Form

10. Which feature allows you to use a selected portion of a field to specify which records in the table to display?
    a. Sort Ascending
    b. Filter by Selection
    c. Sort Descending
    d. Filter by Form

Short Answer

1. What is the difference between finding and replacing data?

2. How does sorting records differ from applying a filter?

3. How does the case of a text entry affect the sort order?

4. How many criteria can you specify when using the Filter by Selection option?

5. Does the Replace All feature conduct a global find-and-replace?

6. What is an easy method for locating records to update?

7. Which option should you use to view records in a table that meet one criterion?

8. How can you interact with table data on the Web?

9. Can you include multiple criteria when using the Filter by Form option?

10. How will date values appear if a database is sorted in descending order?

Fill in the Blank

1. A(n) _____ link is established between an Access table and a data access page if no grouping options are specified when the page is created.

2. When you sort table data in descending order, _____ are displayed before numbers.

3. To open a data access page, you need to use the _____ _____ Web browser.

4. When using Filter by Form, you may specify _____ conditions.

5. To test validation rules, add a record containing _____ to the table.

6. A table's _____ include the setting for record sort order.

7. If a validation rule is violated, a dialog box will appear only if the _____ property has been changed.

8. Most objects and _____ in Access have properties you can set.

9. You can use the _____ button to view all records in a filtered datasheet.

10. You can export a data access page as _____ for display on the Web.

For Discussion

1. When should you consider using Filter By Form rather than Filter By Selection?

2. How does the data type of a field affect how the records are ordered when you sort a table?

3. How can you interact with Access table data using a web page?

4. Explain how editing, filtering, and sorting records differ.

5. When might you want to create a data access page that does not support user interaction with table data?

Hands-On Exercises

1. Compacting a Database

Whenever you modify your database objects, the database file grows in size. If you open your database from a floppy disk, it is a good idea to compact it periodically. By keeping the file size as small as possible, you can locate and manipulate records more quickly.

To compact the Selections database:

1. Open the Selections database file on your floppy disk.

2. Choose Database Utilities from the Tools menu.

3. Choose Compact and Repair Database from the menu, as shown in Figure 3.39.

FIGURE 3.39

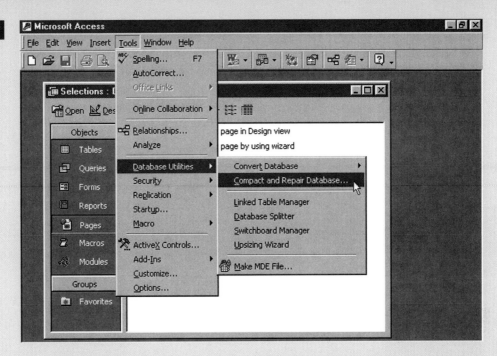

While the database is compacting, the mouse pointer displays an hourglass icon and you will see various messages appear in the Status bar.

4. When control returns to the database window, the database has been compacted. Close the database file.

2. Deleting Records from a Table

Deleting records from a table is a common database maintenance task. In this exercise you will learn how to delete records from a table in Datasheet view. Complete the following tasks:

1. Open the *Inventory.mdb* file on your disk.

Web Tip

If you do not have this file, you may download it from the SELECT Web site at http://www.prenhall.com/select.

2. Click the Tables button on the Objects bar, and open the current Inventory table in Datasheet view.

3. Use the Record Selector to highlight the fifth record, as shown in Figure 3.40.

FIGURE 3.40

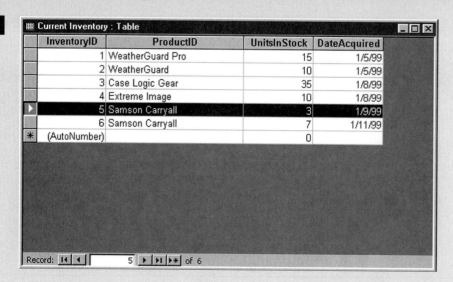

InventoryID	ProductID	UnitsInStock	DateAcquired
1	WeatherGuard Pro	15	1/5/99
2	WeatherGuard	10	1/5/99
3	Case Logic Gear	35	1/8/99
4	Extreme Image	10	1/8/99
5	Samson Carryall	3	1/9/99
6	Samson Carryall	7	1/11/99
(AutoNumber)		0	

Record: 5 of 6

4. Click the Delete Record 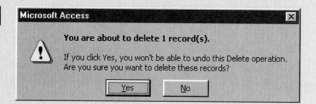 button on the Table Datasheet toolbar.

5. The Microsoft Access dialog box shown in Figure 3.41 appears. Click Yes to delete the record.

FIGURE 3.41

Microsoft Access

⚠ **You are about to delete 1 record(s).**

If you click Yes, you won't be able to undo this Delete operation. Are you sure you want to delete these records?

[Yes] [No]

6. Choose Database Utilities from the Tools menu, and then choose Compact Database from the menu. This action closes the table.

On Your Own Exercises

1. Sorting the Web Sites Database

Modify the Sites table in the Web Sites database by sorting the records by site name, in ascending order. Save your changes when you are finished.

2. Creating a Data Access Page of Web Site Ratings

Open the *Web Sites.mdb* database you modified in the previous project.

 **Web Tip**

If you did not complete Exercise 1 of this project, download the file from the SELECT Web site at http://www.prenhall.com/select.

Create a data access page that displays each Web site and its associated rating. Save the updated database as *Web Sites 2.mdb*. Export the data access page as an HTML page to the same folder containing the database file. Close the database when you are finished.

3. Sorting the Inventory Database

Open the *Inventory.mdb* database. Sort the records in the Current Inventory table in descending order for the Product ID field. Save your changes.

4. Using the Office Assistant

Open the Inventory database. Choose Show the Office Assistant from the Help menu. Search the Help system for information on creating a data access page with grouping levels. Save any changes you make to the database.

5. Sorting Contacts

Open the Contact Management database you created in Project 1 and modified in Project 2. Sort the data in the Contacts Type table in ascending order by contact. Save the changes you make to the database.

6. Sorting and Compacting the Contact Management Database

Open the *Contact Management.mdb* database you modified in Project 2. Sort the contacts by date, and then compact and repair the database. When you are finished, exit Access.

Creating Queries

Most databases contain much more information than is useful at any given time. Stated another way, end users need some way of viewing information from the database that meet specific criteria, or combine records for multiple tables. By designing and running queries, you are able to see the data you need to create reports and make business decisions. In this project you will design a query that returns payroll data for each Selections employee in the database.

Objectives

After completing this project, you will be able to:

➤ Create a select query based upon one table

➤ Add fields to a select query

➤ View the results of a query

➤ Create a select query based upon multiple tables

➤ Add calculated fields to a query

➤ Specify the sort order for a query

➤ Specify query conditions

➤ Create an AutoForm based upon a query

Running Case

Mr. Traylor is very pleased with the work you have done on the Selections database. Now he wants to see a list of all the time card data for each employee. You are almost ready to provide Mr. Traylor with the specific payroll data he requested!

The Challenge

You will need to calculate each employee's gross pay based upon his or her pay rate, and the hours worked each pay period. Finally, Mr. Traylor wants a separate listing of the payroll data by department. This information will be sorted by last name.

The Strategy

Fortunately, Access has powerful database query capabilities that will allow you to deliver the exact information that Mr. Traylor has requested. You can create a query that will calculate each employee's payroll data according to the specifications he gave you. In addition, you can specify criteria that will return records that meet specific conditions, from multiple tables. Figure 4.1 shows a form displaying a payroll record for one employee.

FIGURE 4.1

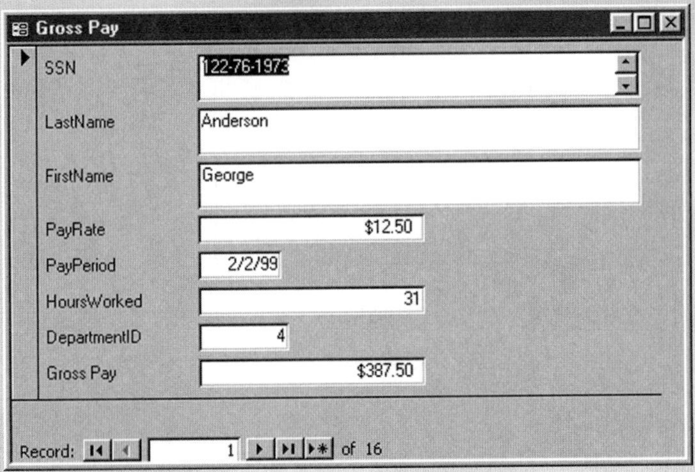

Gross Pay	
SSN	122-76-1973
LastName	Anderson
FirstName	George
PayRate	$12.50
PayPeriod	2/2/99
HoursWorked	31
DepartmentID	4
Gross Pay	$387.50

Record: 1 of 16

The Setup

So that your screen matches the illustrations in this project, you should set up Access as shown in Table 4.1 after you launch Access and open your database. These are the default settings in Access, but they may have been changed on your computer.

Table 4.1

Location	Make these settings:
Tools, Customize	Click the Toolbars tab and display the database toolbar and the menu bar, if they are not currently visible, as shown in Figure 4.2.
Tools, Options	Display the status bar, the startup dialog box, new object shortcuts, and windows in the taskbar, as shown in Figure 4.3.
Tools, Options	Click the General tab and deselect the setting for displaying dates in four-digit format.
Tools, Customize	Click the Options tab, and make sure the checkbox to display recently used menu commands first is deselected, as shown in Figure 4.4.
Office Assistant	Hide the Office Assistant.

FIGURE 4.2

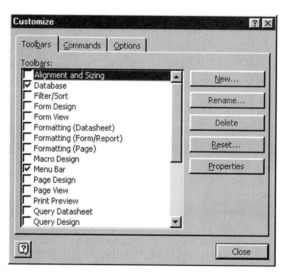

FIGURE 4.3

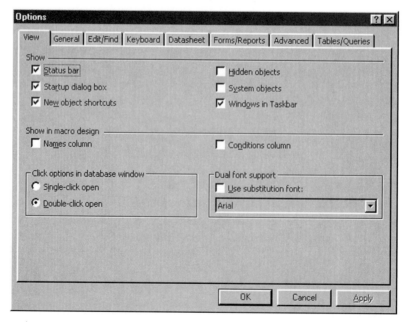

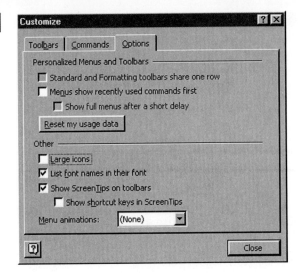

FIGURE 4.4

Creating Select Queries

What is a query? An Access **query** is a database object that you create to view, change, and analyze data in different ways. You can also use queries as the source of records for forms and reports. Sometimes you will want to see information from the database that requires a *calculated field*—a field that displays data resulting from an expression rather than stored data.

Think of a query as a subset of data from one or more tables. Data returned by a query isn't stored in the query, but in the tables underlying the query. Therefore, the query will always display the most recent data in the database.

> **TIP** Access creates a statement using SQL (Structured Query Language) behind the scenes for running your query. After you create a query, you can view the SQL statement by using SQL view.

The most common kind of query is a **select query**—a query that retrieves data from one or more tables and displays the results in a datasheet where you can update the records.

TASK 1:   To Create a Select Query Based upon One Table Using Query Design View

1. Open the Selections database.

2. Click the Queries button on the Objects bar.

3. Click the New ⊞ New button.

4. In the New Query dialog box, select Design View and click OK, as shown in Figure 4.5.

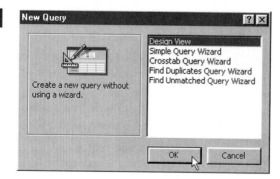

FIGURE 4.5

5 When the Show Table dialog box appears, click the Employees table to select it. Click Add, as shown in Figure 4.6.

FIGURE 4.6

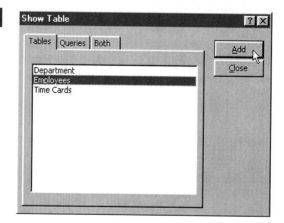

6 Click the Close button. The Query Design window appears. Figure 4.7 identifies important screen elements you will use.

FIGURE 4.7

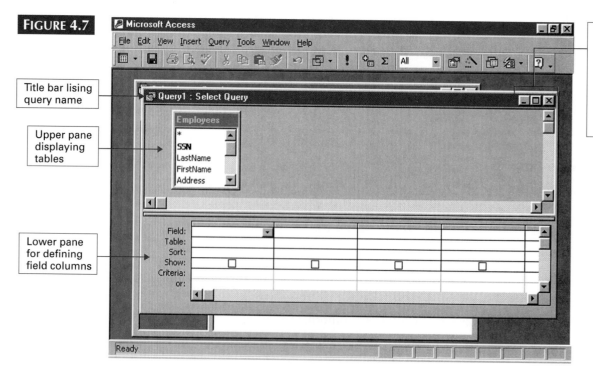

The Query Design window consists of two panes. The upper pane includes the tables containing the fields that you will use in the query. The lower pane consists of columns where you will define the fields of data the query will display. This is the *query design grid*. Notice that the default name of the query is displayed in the query's title bar.

> **TIP** You can add additional tables to the upper pane at any time.

7 Click the Save 💾 button on the Query Design toolbar.

8 Type **Employee Pay Rates** in the Save As dialog box, as shown in Figure 4.8.

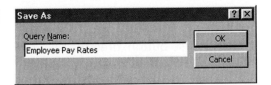

FIGURE 4.8

9 Click OK.

Adding Fields to a Select Query

Just like a table, an Access query has multiple views. You use *Query Design view* to create the query specifications. You can then run a query. When you *run* a query, Access will load your specifications and display the results in a query datasheet. A *query datasheet* is almost identical to a table datasheet—you can use it to modify field data or add records to the underlying table or tables.

> **TIP** Although a query datasheet will display the results of calculated fields, you cannot modify the contents of a calculated field via a query datasheet.

Before a query datasheet will display any records, you need to specify which fields the query will return. These are added to the query design grid. You can add fields in a variety of ways.

TASK 2:   To Add Fields to the Query Design Grid

1 Click the EmployeeID field in the field list of the Employees table in the upper pane of the Query Design window, as shown in Figure 4.9.

FIGURE 4.9

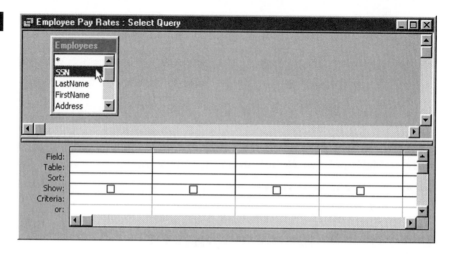

2 While holding down the left mouse button, drag the field name from the upper pane to the first available row and column in the lower pane. Access displays the icon shown in Figure 4.10, representing the field you are currently adding to the lower pane of the design grid.

FIGURE 4.10

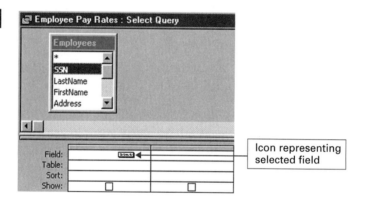

Icon representing selected field

3 Release the left mouse button. The SSN field is now displayed in the leftmost column of the Query Design grid, as shown in Figure 4.11.

FIGURE 4.11

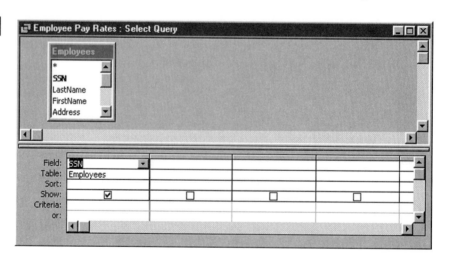

4 Move the mouse pointer inside the first row of the next available column in the lower pane and click the left mouse button. A drop-down list button appears.

5 Click the drop-down list button and select the LastName field, as shown in Figure 4.12.

FIGURE 4.12

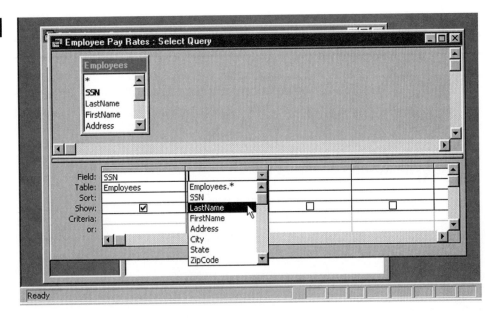

The title field is added to the lower pane.

6 Using either method, add the FirstName and PayRate fields to the query design grid. When you are finished, four fields are displayed, as shown in Figure 4.13.

FIGURE 4.13

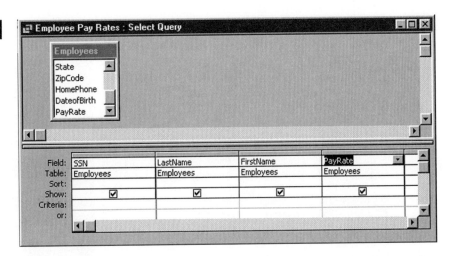

TIP Notice that the Show: button for each field is checked. If you need to use a field for the query but do not want it to show in the query datasheet, deselect the field's Show: button.

Click the Save ⊟ button on the Query Design toolbar to update the changes to your query.

> **TIP** Choose SQL View from the View menu to see the SQL statement that underlies this query.

 Web Tip

For more information concerning SQL statements, visit http://msdn .microsoft.com/library/officedev/office/d1/sba39.htm.

Viewing the Results of a Query

So far you have not seen how the query datasheet will look when you run the query. One of the advantages of using a graphical query design tool such as the Query Design window is that you can run your query at any time while you are designing it to see what data it will display.

TASK 3: To View the Results of a Query

 Click the Run 🛚 button on the Query Design toolbar. The query returns records in a datasheet displaying only the fields you selected, as shown in Figure 4.14.

FIGURE 4.14

SSN	LastName	FirstName	PayRate
122-11-5923	Simcox	Cole	$11.45
122-76-1973	Anderson	George	$12.50
211-83-1983	Williams	Robert	$11.50
321-74-9186	Smith	Mary Beth	$13.20
322-83-1983	Nelson	Rebecca	$12.50
371-98-9812	Caldwell	Thomas	$10.80
477-12-0395	Davis	Terri	$11.25
478-12-0398	Hill	John	$11.75
521-04-9104	George	Philip	$11.45
524-38-1298	Miller	Kimberly	$12.75
534-92-1985	Fowler	Lisa	$12.15
544-24-7819	McDowell	Megan	$12.25
599-67-1950	Williams	Amanda	$9.80
620-45-1097	Tucker	William	$9.25
671-93-1983	Terpstra	Mike	$12.65

Employee Pay Rates : Select Query
Record: 1 of 15

> **TIP** You can also use the View menu to switch between Query Design and Query Datasheet view.

Notice that the title bar identifies the datasheet as belonging to a select query. You will also notice that the Query Datasheet contains many of the same elements that a table datasheet does.

2 Click the Design ![Design button] button on the Query Datasheet toolbar.

3 Close the query. The query object appears in the database window, as shown in Figure 4.15.

FIGURE 4.15

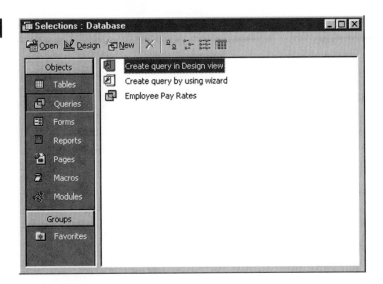

Creating a Query Displaying Data from Multiple Tables

The query you just created uses data from a single table. You will recall that one of the purposes of normalizing a database (splitting the information into multiple tables) is to increase overall efficiency, reduce data redundancy, and increase data integrity.

Since queries return records in a datasheet, you can think of them as behaving in a manner similar to tables. By adding fields to a table from multiple tables, you will be able to generate the payroll information Mr. Traylor requested, and have it appear in a datasheet.

TASK 4: <u>To Create a Query Based upon Multiple Tables</u>

1 With the Queries button active on the Objects bar, click the New ![New button] button in the database window.

2 Select Design View in the New Query dialog box and click OK.

3 Highlight the three table names appearing in the Show Table dialog box, and click Add. Depending upon the location of the Show Table dialog box on your screen, you may see a portion of each table in the upper portion of the table design grid, as shown in Figure 4.16.

FIGURE 4.16

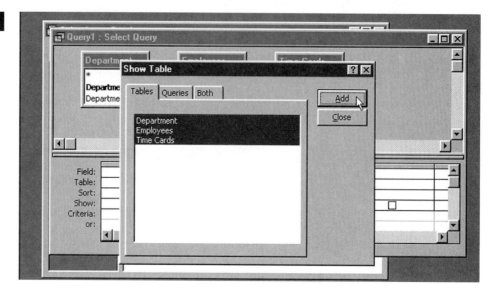

4 Click the Close button in the Show Table dialog box.

5 Maximize the Query Design window.

6 Using the procedures you learned earlier in this project, add the fields shown in Table 4.2 to the query design grid.

Table 4.2

Field	Located in Table
SSN	Employees
LastName	Employees
FirstName	Employees
PayRate	Employees
PayPeriod	Time Cards
HoursWorked	Time Cards
DepartmentID	Time Cards

7 Click the Save button and type **Gross Pay** as the name for the query. When you are finished, your screen will appear as shown in Figure 4.17.

FIGURE 4.17

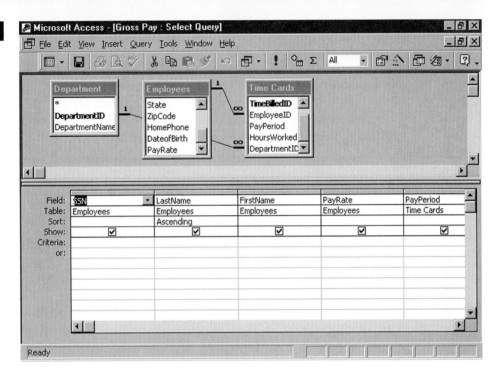

8 Click the Run ⚡ button to view the results of the query. The query datasheet shown in Figure 4.18 appears. The column widths appearing here have been adjusted so all fields appear in the datasheet.

FIGURE 4.18

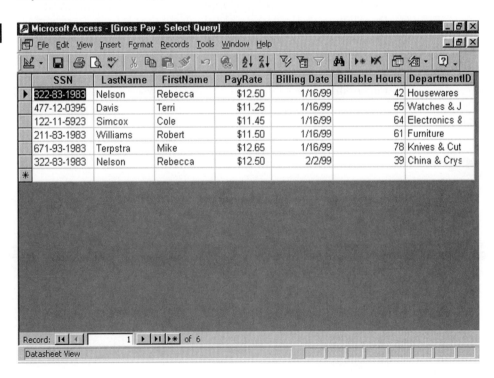

Check Point

Why does the query return only 6 records, when there are records for 15 employees in the Employees table? Only 6 records are returned because a Select query based upon multiple tables will return only records that contain data for all fields specified in the query's design.

9 Click the Design button to return to Design view.

10 Save any changes you have made to the query's design (such as changing the width of columns in the datasheet).

Break Point

If necessary, you can close Access and continue this project later.

Adding a Calculated Field to the Query

To determine each employee's gross pay, you must create a calculated field for this data. A **calculated field** is a field you create in the query design grid. Recall that a calculated field is a field that returns data according to some expression. An **expression** is a combination of object identifiers, arithmetic or logical operators, and values that produce a result. Access includes an **Expression Builder**—a graphical workspace—that you can use to create an expression.

TASK 5: <u>To Add an Expression to Calculate Gross Pay</u>

1 Use the scroll bar in the query design grid to display additional columns in the pane, as shown in Figure 4.19.

FIGURE 4.19

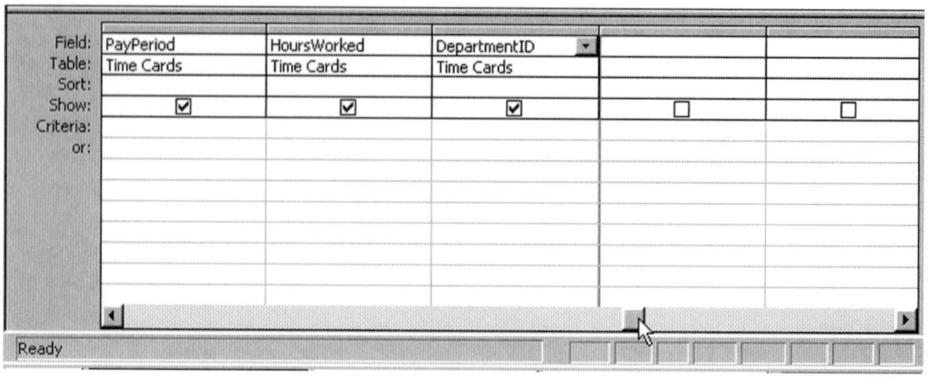

Field:	PayPeriod	HoursWorked	DepartmentID ▾		
Table:	Time Cards	Time Cards	Time Cards		
Sort:					
Show:	☑	☑	☑	☐	☐
Criteria:					
or:					

Ready

2 Place the insertion point over the next available column, click the right mouse button, and choose Build from the shortcut menu, as shown in Figure 4.20.

FIGURE 4.20

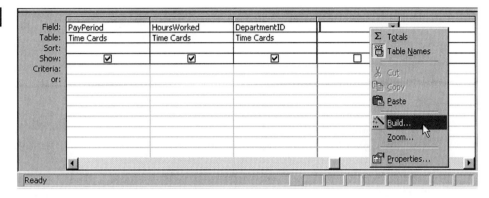

3 Double-click the Tables folder in the leftmost pane of the Expression Builder. The table list expands, as shown in Figure 4.21. The data you need to calculate gross pay is located in separate tables.

FIGURE 4.21

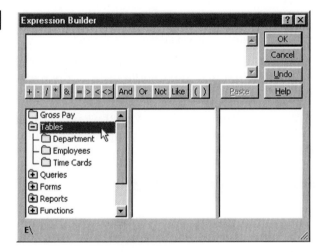

4 Click the Employees table name. The list of fields the folder contains, as shown in Figure 4.22, is now displayed in the middle pane of the Expression Builder.

FIGURE 4.22

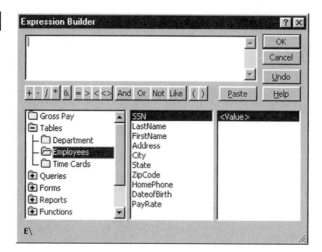

5 Place the insertion point inside the workspace in the upper portion of the Expression Builder. You will enter an expression to calculate gross pay by multiplying the hours worked by the pay rate.

6 Click the Equal Sign ▤ button appearing on the toolbar inside the Expression Builder.

> **TIP** For many expressions, the equal sign is optional.

7 Select the PayRate field name in the middle pane of the Expression Builder, and click Paste.

8 Click the Multiplication ▤ button or type ***** on the keyboard. The expression shown in Figure 4.23 specifies that the PayRate will be multiplied by an additional value you will specify.

FIGURE 4.23

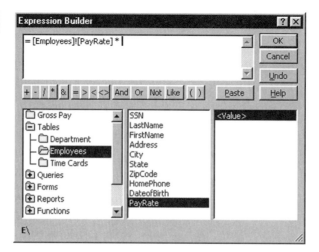

9 Click the Time Cards folder, select the HoursWorked field, and click Paste. Your expression now matches the one shown in Figure 4.24.

FIGURE 4.24

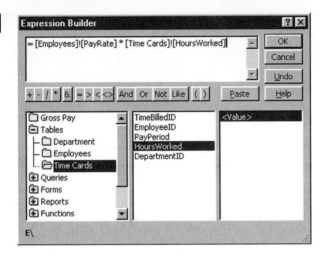

10 Click OK. The expression appears in the query design grid.

> **TROUBLESHOOTING** The expression will appear truncated, since it is too wide to appear in the current column width.

11 Check the Show: checkbox for the calculated field, as shown in Figure 4.25. You need to do this so that the results will be displayed in the query datasheet when the query is run.

FIGURE 4.25

12 Save your changes to the query.

TASK 6: To View the Results of the Expression and Modify Its Format

1 Click the Run ! button on the Query Design toolbar.

2 Using the scrollbar in the datasheet, position the columns so that you can see the calculated field data, as shown in Figure 4.26.

FIGURE 4.26

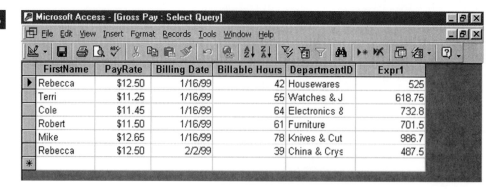

The calculated field has the default name of *Expr1*, and the data does not appear in currency format.

3 Click the View 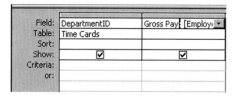 button on the Query Datasheet toolbar.

4 Highlight the text *Expr1* in the first row of the column containing the calculated field expression and type **Gross Pay** as the new field label, as shown in Figure 4.27.

FIGURE 4.27

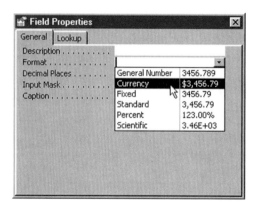

TROUBLESHOOTING Make sure you do not highlight the colon character!

5 Click the Properties button on the Query Datasheet toolbar.

6 Click the Format row in the Field Properties dialog box.

7 Click the drop-down list button. Select Currency from the list, as shown in Figure 4.28.

FIGURE 4.28

8 Close the Field Properties dialog box and run the query to view your changes. Adjust the view using the scroll bar if necessary. The field is formatted as shown in Figure 4.29.

FIGURE 4.29

	FirstName	PayRate	Billing Date	Billable Hours	DepartmentID	Gross Pay
▶	Rebecca	$12.50	1/16/99	42	Housewares	$525.00
	Terri	$11.25	1/16/99	55	Watches & J	$618.75
	Cole	$11.45	1/16/99	64	Electronics 8	$732.80
	Robert	$11.50	1/16/99	61	Furniture	$701.50
	Mike	$12.65	1/16/99	78	Knives & Cut	$986.70
	Rebecca	$12.50	2/2/99	39	China & Crys	$487.50
✳						

9 Save your changes.

10 Close the query.

> **TIP** Remember that you can view the SQL statement underlying any query by choosing SQL View from the View menu in Query Design view.

Defining the Sort Order for a Query

You will frequently need to see records in a query that meet certain conditions and appear in a specific order. Remember that Mr. Traylor requested a listing of the payroll data alphabetized by last name.

TASK 7: To Add Sort Order to the Query Design

1 Open the Gross Pay query in Design view.

2 Place the insertion point in the Sort: row of the LastName field in the query design grid and click the drop-down list, as shown in Figure 4.30.

FIGURE 4.30

Field:	SSN		LastName		FirstName
Table:	Employees		Employees		Employees
Sort:				▾	
Show:	☑		Ascending		☑
Criteria:			Descending		
or:			(not sorted)		

3 Select Ascending as the sort order.

4 Update the query design and run the query. The records returned are now listed in alphabetical order by last name, as shown in Figure 4.31.

FIGURE 4.31

Microsoft Access - [Gross Pay : Select Query]

File Edit View Insert Format Records Tools Window Help

SSN	LastName	FirstName	PayRate	Billing Date	Billable Hours	DepartmentID
477-12-0395	Davis	Terri	$11.25	1/16/99	55	Watches & J
322-83-1983	Nelson	Rebecca	$12.50	2/2/99	39	China & Crys
322-83-1983	Nelson	Rebecca	$12.50	1/16/99	42	Housewares
122-11-5923	Simcox	Cole	$11.45	1/16/99	64	Electronics &
671-93-1983	Terpstra	Mike	$12.65	1/16/99	78	Knives & Cut
211-83-1983	Williams	Robert	$11.50	1/16/99	61	Furniture

5 Close the query.

Specifying Query Conditions

Queries are powerful not only because they return records with data from fields in multiple tables, but also because you can specify criteria further defining which records will be returned. Remember that Mr. Traylor wants to see a listing of employee data by department. You can easily accomplish this task by adding one or more conditions to the query design grid. A **condition** is a specification that must be met for data to be returned, such as a department name or a specific pay rate. In the tasks that follow you will add additional records to the Time Cards table and then specify query conditions.

TASK 8: To Add Records to the Time Cards Table

1 Open the Time Cards table in Datasheet view.

2 Using Figure 4.32 as a guide, add the records with a Time Billed ID of 7 through 16 to the table.

FIGURE 4.32

Microsoft Access - [Time Cards : Table]

File Edit View Insert Format Records Tools Window Help

Time Billed ID	Employee ID	Billing Date	Billable Hours	DepartmentID
1	322-83-1983	1/16/99	42	Housewares
2	477-12-0395	1/16/99	55	Watches & Jewelry
3	122-11-5923	1/16/99	64	Electronics & Compute
4	211-83-1983	1/16/99	61	Furniture
5	671-93-1983	1/16/99	78	Knives & Cutlery
6	322-83-1983	2/2/99	39	China & Crystal
7	122-11-5923	2/2/99	55	Appliances
8	122-76-1973	2/2/99	31	Electronics & Compute
9	321-74-9186	2/2/99	34	Clothing
10	371-98-9812	2/2/99	72	Appliances
11	477-12-0395	2/2/99	65	Electronics & Compute
12	478-12-0398	2/2/99	47	Clothing
13	521-04-9104	2/2/99	52	Electronics & Compute
14	524-38-1298	2/2/99	41	Clothing
15	534-92-1985	2/2/99	72	Clothing
16	671-93-1983	2/2/99	67	Electronics & Compute

> **TROUBLESHOOTING** If you cannot remember how to add records to the table using the datasheet, review Task 9 of Project 2.

3 Close the table when you are finished adding records.

TASK 9: To Specify a Single Query Condition

1 Open the Gross Pay query in Datasheet view. The query now returns the 16 records shown in Figure 4.33.

FIGURE 4.33

Microsoft Access - [Gross Pay : Select Query]

File Edit View Insert Format Records Tools Window Help

SSN	LastName	FirstName	PayRate	Billing Date	Billable Hours	Departmen
122-76-1973	Anderson	George	$12.50	2/2/99	31	Electronics & Co
371-98-9812	Caldwell	Thomas	$10.80	2/2/99	72	Appliances
477-12-0395	Davis	Terri	$11.25	1/16/99	55	Watches & Jewe
477-12-0395	Davis	Terri	$11.25	2/2/99	65	Electronics & Co
534-92-1985	Fowler	Lisa	$12.15	2/2/99	72	Clothing
521-04-9104	George	Philip	$11.45	2/2/99	52	Electronics & Co
478-12-0398	Hill	John	$11.75	2/2/99	47	Clothing
524-38-1298	Miller	Kimberly	$12.75	2/2/99	41	Clothing
322-83-1983	Nelson	Rebecca	$12.50	1/16/99	42	Housewares
322-83-1983	Nelson	Rebecca	$12.50	2/2/99	39	China & Crystal
122-11-5923	Simcox	Cole	$11.45	1/16/99	64	Electronics & Co
122-11-5923	Simcox	Cole	$11.45	2/2/99	55	Appliances
321-74-9186	Smith	Mary Beth	$13.20	2/2/99	34	Clothing
671-93-1983	Terpstra	Mike	$12.65	2/2/99	67	Electronics & Co
671-93-1983	Terpstra	Mike	$12.65	1/16/99	78	Knives & Cutlery
211-83-1983	Williams	Robert	$11.50	1/16/99	61	Furniture

Record: 1 of 16

Check Point

Why are the records not listed in order by date, as the records were entered into the Time Card table? The records returned by this query are sorted by last name.

2 Switch to Design view.

3 Use the horizontal scroll bar in the lower pane of the Query Design window to display the DepartmentID field.

4 Place the insertion point in the Criteria: row and type **1**, as shown in Figure 4.34.

FIGURE 4.34

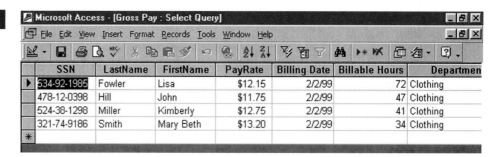

Field:	PayPeriod	HoursWorked	DepartmentID	Gross Pay: [Employ	
Table:	Time Cards	Time Cards	Time Cards		
Sort:					
Show:	☑	☑	☑	☑	☐
Criteria:			1		
or:					

5 Run the query. The records shown in Figure 4.35 are returned in the query datasheet.

FIGURE 4.35

Microsoft Access - [Gross Pay : Select Query]

File Edit View Insert Format Records Tools Window Help

	SSN	LastName	FirstName	PayRate	Billing Date	Billable Hours	Departmen
▶	534-92-1985	Fowler	Lisa	$12.15	2/2/99	72	Clothing
	478-12-0398	Hill	John	$11.75	2/2/99	47	Clothing
	524-38-1298	Miller	Kimberly	$12.75	2/2/99	41	Clothing
	321-74-9186	Smith	Mary Beth	$13.20	2/2/99	34	Clothing
*							

Check Point

Why did you enter the value 1 in the DepartmentID field? You entered 1 because this is the AutoNumber value associated with the department name.

6 Switch to Design view.

TASK 10: To Specify an AND Condition

1 Use the horizontal scroll bar to display the PayRate field.

2 Type **>12** in the Criteria row for this field in the lower pane of the Query Design Window.

3 Display the DepartmentID field, highlight the current value of 1, and type **4**. The conditions appear as shown in Figure 4.36.

FIGURE 4.36

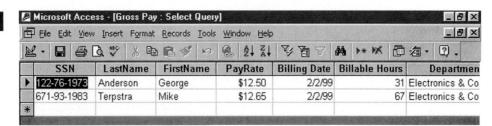

Field:	FirstName	PayRate	PayPeriod	HoursWorked	DepartmentID
Table:	Employees	Employees	Time Cards	Time Cards	Time Cards
Sort:					
Show:	☑	☑	☑	☑	☑
Criteria:		>12			4
or:					

TIP This is called an AND condition, because the only records that will be returned when the query is run are those where the DepartmentID is equal to 4 AND the PayRate is greater than $12.00 per hour.

4 Run the query. The two records displayed in Figure 4.37 are returned in the datasheet.

FIGURE 4.37

Microsoft Access - [Gross Pay : Select Query]

File   Edit   View   Insert   Format   Records   Tools   Window   Help

	SSN	LastName	FirstName	PayRate	Billing Date	Billable Hours	Departmen
▶	122-76-1973	Anderson	George	$12.50	2/2/99	31	Electronics & Co
	671-93-1983	Terpstra	Mike	$12.65	2/2/99	67	Electronics & Co
*							

5 Switch to Design view.

TASK 11: <u>To Specify an OR Condition</u>

1 Delete the entry in the Criteria row of the PayRate field.

2 In the DepartmentID field, Type **1** in the row immediately below the current entry in the Condition: row, as shown in Figure 4.38.

FIGURE 4.38

Field:	PayRate	PayPeriod	HoursWorked	DepartmentID	Gross Pay: [Employ
Table:	Employees	Time Cards	Time Cards	Time Cards	
Sort:					
Show:	☑	☑	☑	☑	☑
Criteria:				4	
or:				1	

Ready

3 Run the query. The records shown in Figure 4.39 are returned.

FIGURE 4.39

SSN	LastName	FirstName	PayRate	Billing Date	Billable Hours	Departmen
▶ 122-76-1973	Anderson	George	$12.50	2/2/99	31	Electronics & Co
477-12-0395	Davis	Terri	$11.25	2/2/99	65	Electronics & Co
534-92-1985	Fowler	Lisa	$12.15	2/2/99	72	Clothing
521-04-9104	George	Philip	$11.45	2/2/99	52	Electronics & Co
478-12-0398	Hill	John	$11.75	2/2/99	47	Clothing
524-38-1298	Miller	Kimberly	$12.75	2/2/99	41	Clothing
122-11-5923	Simcox	Cole	$11.45	1/16/99	64	Electronics & Co
321-74-9186	Smith	Mary Beth	$13.20	2/2/99	34	Clothing
671-93-1983	Terpstra	Mike	$12.65	2/2/99	67	Electronics & Co

Microsoft Access - [Gross Pay : Select Query]

File Edit View Insert Format Records Tools Window Help

4 Close the query. Do not save your changes.

Web Tip

As you may suspect, AND and OR conditions are specified using SQL. Visit http://msdn.microsoft.com/library/sdkdoc/sql/tsqlfund/src/tfund04_0d4j.htm for more information about specifying conditions in SQL statements.

Creating an AutoForm Based upon a Query

You can think of an Access query as being similar to a table, in that you can base other database objects upon it. Remember how easy it was to create a form based upon a table? It's just as easy to create an AutoForm from a query!

TASK 12: To Create an AutoForm Based upon the Gross Pay Query

1 Click the Forms button on the Objects bar in the database window and click the New button.

2 In the New Form dialog box, select AutoForm: Columnar as the form type, and Gross Pay as the form's source, as shown in Figure 4.40.

FIGURE 4.40

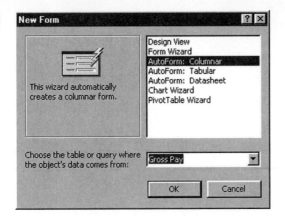

3   Click OK. After a moment, the form appears.

4   Switch to Design view, and change the Decimal Places property of the PayRate and Gross Pay fields to **2**.

5   Switch to Form view. The form appears as shown in Figure 4.41.

FIGURE 4.41

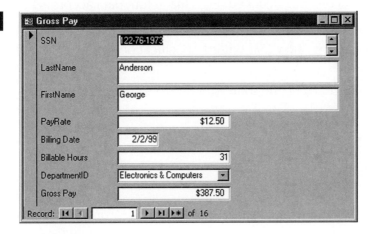

6   Close the form. Click Yes to save the changes, and accept the default name *Gross Pay*.

> **TIP** By default, an AutoForm always uses the name of object upon which it was created as its name.

7   Close the database.

Summary and Exercises

Summary

- Queries are database objects that you use to view, change, and analyze data in different ways.
- Queries are often used as the source of records for forms and reports.
- A select query retrieves data from one or more tables and displays the results in a datasheet.
- You use the Query Design window to create queries in Access.
- The Query Design window consists of two panes—the upper pane contains a list of tables and fields; the lower pane contains the query design grid.
- Fields appearing in the query design grid return information in a query datasheet when the query is run.
- Queries can be based upon one or more tables.
- Queries can contain calculated fields that return data according to an expression.
- You can easily create expressions using the Expression Builder.
- You can add sort order and criteria specifications to return specific records in a specified order.
- A query object can be the source for an Access AutoForm.

Key Terms and Operations

Key Terms

calculated field	query datasheet
condition	query design grid
expression	Query Design view
Expression Builder	select query
query	run

Operations

add calculated fields to a query using the Expression Builder
add fields to a query using the query design grid
add tables to a query
create a new query
create an AutoForm based upon a query
define the sort order and criteria for a query
run a query
specify sort order and criteria

Study Questions

Multiple Choice

1. The query design grid appears in the
   a. database window.
   b. query datasheet.
   c. upper pane of the Query Design window.
   d. lower pane of the Query Design window.

2. To sort the data returned by a query, you specify sort order in the
   a. database window.
   b. query design grid.
   c. query datasheet.
   d. upper pane of the Query Design window.

3. When you run a query based upon one table, the results are displayed in
   a. the database window.
   b. a query datasheet.
   c. a table datasheet.
   d. the query design grid.

4. In Access, an AutoForm can be based upon
   a. tables only.
   b. queries only.
   c. tables and queries.
   d. neither tables nor queries.

5. Where do you add fields when designing a query?
   a. the database window
   b. the upper pane of the Query Design window
   c. the query design grid
   d. the query datasheet

6. What do you use to create a calculated field in a query?
   a. a formula
   b. an expression
   c. a filter
   d. a condition

7. Which of the following statements is true?
   a. Select queries cannot be used to change field data in tables.
   b. Queries return records in a datasheet.
   c. Select queries do not reflect the most recent changes to an underlying table.
   d. Queries can be used as the source object for an Access form.

8. The expression =[Quantity]*[Cost] will most likely return the
   a. purchases made by an employee.
   b. total membership fee charged to a club member.
   c. total number of members belonging to a club.
   d. value of an inventory item.

9. Where is the data in a calculated field stored?
    a. in the Database window
    b. in a query datasheet
    c. in a table
    d. Calculated fields are not stored anywhere in a database.

10. Which of the following statements is false?
    a. Query results are returned in a datasheet.
    b. A query must be based upon one or more tables or another query.
    c. A query is similar to a filter in that it can be used to return specific records from a database.
    d. A query cannot be saved.

Short Answer

1. What is the query design grid?

2. What does the upper pane of the Query Design window display?

3. What do the columns in the query design grid represent?

4. How do you run a query?

5. What options are available for sorting records returned by a query?

6. When you run a query, where is the data displayed?

7. How many criteria rows are required in the query design grid for an AND condition?

8. How do you specify conditions in a query?

9. What database objects can be used to create an AutoForm?

10. What kind of query returns data from one or more tables?

Fill in the Blank

1. The table or tables used in a query are added to the Query Design window using the _____ dialog box.

2. A query returning records that meet one condition or another is called a(n) _____ query.

3. Queries are modified in _____ view.

4. A(n) _____ uses an expression to return data in a query.

5. Fields appearing in a query are displayed in the _____ pane of the Query Design window.

6. You can change the sort order of records in a query datasheet by changing the _____ of the query design grid.

7. When you run a query, the results are displayed in a(n) _____.

8. The _____ property of a field determines whether currency data is displayed as such.

9. Queries can be based upon one or more _____.

10. A query returning records meeting two conditions simultaneously is called a(n) _____ query.

For Discussion

1. How does a query datasheet differ from a table datasheet?
2. What is a calculated field and where does it store data?
3. How do you specify the sort order for a query?
4. How does an AND condition differ from an OR condition?
5. How do you create a query based upon more than one table?

Hands-On Exercises

1. Modifying a Query's AutoForm

The AutoForm you created in the project displays a list box for changing the employee's Social Security number. In this exercise you will modify the design of the Gross Pay form so that no data can be changed. Complete the following steps:

1. Open the *Selections.mdb* database file on your disk.
2. Click the Forms button on the Objects bar.
3. Open the Gross Pay form in Design view.
4. Select the SSN field and right-click. Choose Properties.
5. With the Format tab active, select None in the Scroll Bars row, as shown in Figure 4.42.

FIGURE 4.42

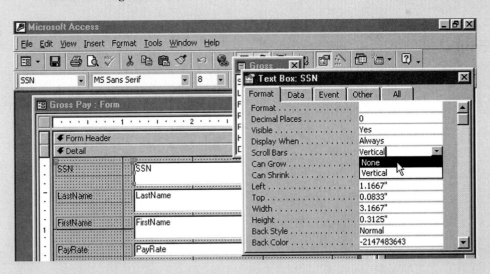

6. Highlight every field containing data by holding the (SHIFT) key while clicking every text box field.
7. Click the Data tab in the Properties dialog box.
8. Change the Enabled and Locked properties for the selection, as shown in Figure 4.43.

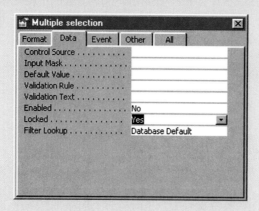

9. Switch to Design view. The data is displayed, but you are unable to change any of the entries using the form.

10. Save the form and close the database.

2. Creating a Multitable Query in the Inventory Database

In this exercise you will create a query in the Inventory database that contains a calculated field displaying the current value of the inventory.

1. Open the *Inventory.mdb* database file on your floppy disk.

Web Tip

If you do not have this file, you may download it from the SELECT Web site at http://www.prenhall.com/select.

2. Create a new query in Design view.

3. Add the Products and Current Inventory tables to the Query Design window.

4. Include the ProductName and UnitPrice fields from the Products table and the InventoryID and UnitsinStock fields from the Current Inventory table in the Query Design grid.

5. Create a calculated expression to determine the inventory value. Change the name of the calculated field.

6. Run your query. The results should match those shown in Figure 4.44.

FIGURE 4.44

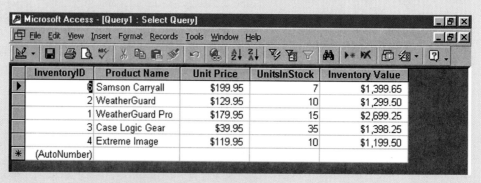

7. Save the query as Inventory Value.

8. Close the query.

9. Close the database.

On Your Own Exercises

1. Querying the Web Sites Database

Create a query in the Web sites database that returns records meeting an AND condition of your choosing. Save the query with an appropriate name. Save your changes when you are finished.

2. Creating a Data Access Page of Web Site Ratings

Open the *Web Sites.mdb* database you modified in the previous exercise.

 Web Tip

If you did not complete Exercise 1 of this project, download the file from the SELECT Web site at http://www.prenhall.com/select.

Create a data access page based upon the query created in Exercise 1. Save the updated database as *Web Sites 3.mdb*. Export the data access page as an HTML page to the same folder containing the database file. Close the database when you are finished.

3. Sorting the Inventory Database

Open the *Inventory.mdb* database. Sort the records in the Inventory Value query in descending order by inventory value. Now reverse the sort order for this field. Save your changes.

4. Using the Office Assistant

Open the *Inventory.mdb* database. Choose Show the Office Assistant from the Help menu. Search the Help system for information about AND versus OR queries. Build an OR query, and save it with a unique name. Save the changes you make to the database.

5. Specifying Query Conditions

Open the *Contact Management.mdb* database you created in Project 1 and modified in Projects 2 and 3. Create a query that returns records according to contact type. Save the query with an appropriate name. Save the updated database.

6. Specifying AND Query Conditions

Open the *Contact Management.mdb* database you modified in the previous exercise. Create a multitable query with an AND condition. Give the query an appropriate name, save and close the database, and exit Access.

Creating and Modifying Forms

Remember that tables hold data and queries return data; forms make it easy for database users to work with records in a database. While most of the information in a form comes from an underlying record source—a table or query—other information in the form is stored in the form's design. In this project you will learn how to create and modify a form for entering employee records into the Selections database.

Objectives

After completing this project, you will be able to:

➤ Delete a form from a database

➤ Rearrange fields on a form

➤ Select and remove fields from a form

➤ Create a new form in Design view

➤ Add controls to a form in Design view

➤ Save a form

➤ Add unbound controls to a form

➤ Add a picture to a form

➤ Add records to a table using a form

Running Case

Mr. Traylor is impressed with how easily you can work with the record data in the Selections database. He now wants you to make the database easy to use for the data entry personnel at Selections, Inc. Now that you have designed the required employee tables and queries, you are ready to create forms for end users.

The Challenge

Mr. Traylor has reviewed the forms in your database. He wants you to create a new form listing information about employees at Selections that will be as easy as possible for the data entry team to use. He wants a simpler layout that has fewer descriptive labels. Finally, he wants the Selections logo to appear on the Employees form.

The Strategy

You can easily modify existing forms and create new ones using Form Design view. Rather than modifying the Employees form, it will be easier to delete the existing one and create a new one in Design view that meets Mr. Traylor's specifications. You can use Design view to add fields to a form, modify the appearance of the form, and add the Selections logo. Figure 5.1 shows the form you will create in this project.

FIGURE 5.1

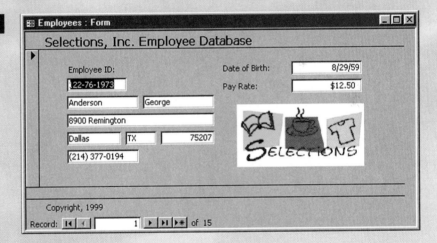

The Setup

So that your screen matches the illustrations in this project, you should set up Access as shown in Table 5.1 after you launch Access and open your database. These are the default settings in Access, but they may have been changed on your computer.

Table 5.1

Location	Make these settings:
Tools, Customize	Click the Toolbars tab and display the database toolbar and the menu bar, if they are not currently visible, as shown in Figure 5.2.
Tools, Options	Display the status bar, the startup dialog box, new object shortcuts, and windows in the taskbar, as shown in Figure 5.3.
Tools, Options	Click the General tab and deselect the setting for displaying dates in four-digit format.
Tools, Customize	Click the Options tab, and make sure the checkbox to display recently used menu commands first is deselected, as shown in Figure 5.4.
Office Assistant	Hide the Office Assistant.

FIGURE 5.2

FIGURE 5.3

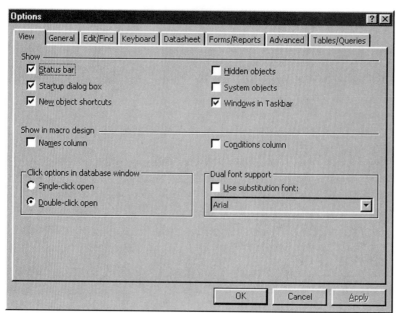

FIGURE 5.4

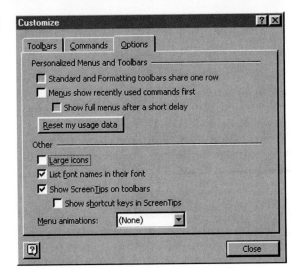

Creating Forms

In Project 1 you used the AutoForm Wizard to create the Employees form that is currently in the database. Remember that a form is always based upon a **record source**—a table or query that contains the records the form displays. You create the link between a form and its record source by using graphical objects called controls. A **control** is an object such as a text box that displays information in a form.

Although you have the option of modifying the current Employees form in Design view, it will be easier to delete the existing one and create a new form using Form Design view.

TASK 1:   To Delete an Existing Database Form

1. Click the Forms button on the Objects bar.
2. Select the Employees form in the database window.
3. Choose Delete from the Edit menu, as shown in Figure 5.5.

FIGURE 5.5

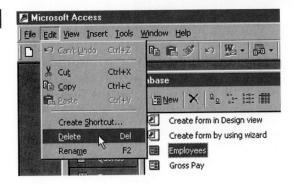

TIP You can also delete a database object using the Cut button, or by choosing Delete from the object's shortcut menu.

4 The dialog box shown in Figure 5.6 appears.

FIGURE 5.6

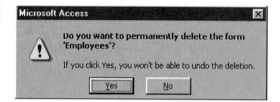

Microsoft Access

Do you want to permanently delete the form 'Employees'?

If you click Yes, you won't be able to undo the deletion.

Yes   No

5 Click Yes.

TROUBLESHOOTING Make sure you have selected the Employees form, as you cannot reverse this action with Undo!

Since the form has been deleted from the database, it is no longer visible in the database window.

Creating a New Form Using Design View

You are now ready to create a form. As you will see, Access provides numerous tools for creating a form in Design view. You create a form by adding controls to the form's **Detail section**, which is the area of the Form Design window that appears when you create a new form in Design view.

TASK 2: <u>To Create a New Form Using Design View</u>

1 Click the New [New] button in the database window.

2 Select Design View to create a form without using a wizard, and base the form upon the Employees table, as shown in Figure 5.7.

FIGURE 5.7

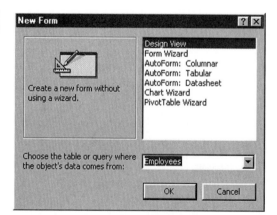

New Form

Create a new form without using a wizard.

Design View
Form Wizard
AutoForm: Columnar
AutoForm: Tabular
AutoForm: Datasheet
Chart Wizard
PivotTable Wizard

Choose the table or query where the object's data comes from: Employees

OK   Cancel

3 A blank form will appear in Form Design view. Figure 5.8 indicates important elements of the Form Design window.

FIGURE 5.8

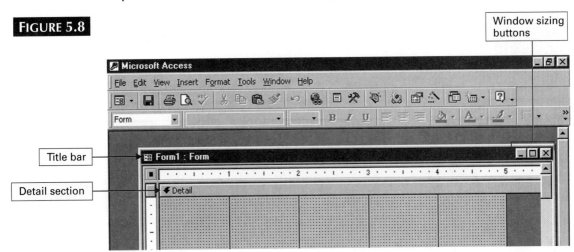

TROUBLESHOOTING If any tool palettes are displayed in the window, close them.

A default name for the form appears in the form's title bar. The Form Design window contains buttons for minimizing, maximizing, and closing the form. You will add controls for the form's Detail section.

4 Click the Maximize button in the form's title bar.

TASK 3:   To Add Controls to the Form

1 Click the Field List 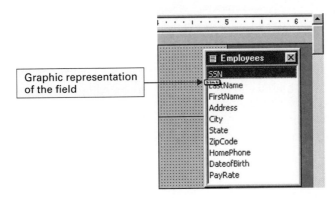 button on the Form Design toolbar, if necessary.

2 Reposition the Field List box near the top of the screen, and resize it so that all field names are visible.

3 Click the SSN field name to select it. While holding down the left mouse button, begin to drag it toward the form's Detail section. Notice that as you drag, the mouse pointer changes to a graphic representation of the field, as shown in Figure 5.9.

FIGURE 5.9

4 Drag the SSN field into the upper left portion of the Detail section.

5 Release the mouse button. Two controls appears on the form, as shown in Figure 5.10.

FIGURE 5.10

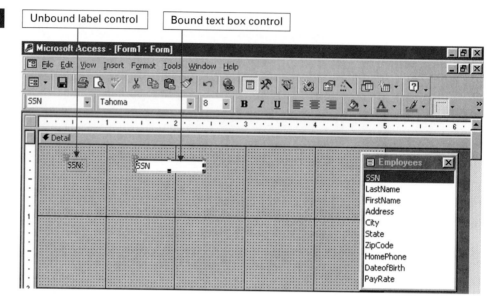

In Figure 5.10 that both controls have SSN inside them. The control on the right is a **bound control**, meaning that it is bound, or linked to a specific database object (a field, in this case). The leftmost control is a **label control**, which will display descriptive text. The bound control is a **text box control**, which is used to display field data that can be edited in the form.

6 Using the same procedure, drag the remaining controls shown in Figure 5.11 to the Detail section of the form, approximately in the position shown.

FIGURE 5.11

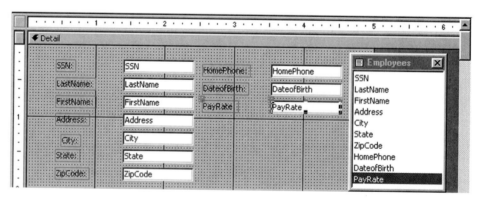

TROUBLESHOOTING As you move the controls on the form you will notice that the label and the text box for each field move as a unit. If you click the square selection handle in the upper-left portion of each control, it will move independently of the associated control.

TASK 4: <u>To Save the Form and Switch to Form View</u>

1 Save the form. Type **Employees** in the Save As dialog box, and click OK.

2 Click the View button on the Form Design toolbar. The form displays the first record in the Employees table in Form view, as shown in Figure 5.12.

FIGURE 5.12

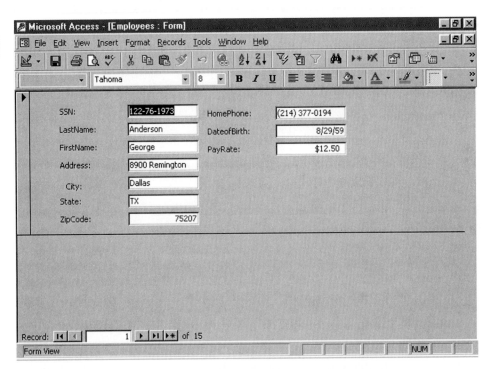

TIP The form is maximized, since you maximized the Form Design window.

3 Click the View button on the Form Design toolbar to return to Design view.

Modifying a Form's Controls

Form Design view has the advantage of giving you complete control over the location and format of each control on a form. Once you add controls to a form in Design view, the next step in designing a form is modifying the controls.

Some of the labels appearing on the Employees form are not really necessary. Also, the size and location of each text box should be changed. In the tasks that follow, you will delete some of the labels on the form and change the text properties of others. You will also reposition the text box controls to make the form easier to read. Finally, you will add a ControlTip to the text boxes that no longer have labels. A **ControlTip** is a descriptive message that appears when you move the mouse pointer over a control.

TASK 5: __To Delete Label Controls from the Employees Form__

1 Move the mouse pointer over the SSN label, as shown in Figure 5.13.

FIGURE 5.13

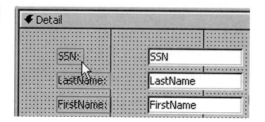

2 Click the left mouse button. The control is now selected, as shown in Figure 5.14.

FIGURE 5.14

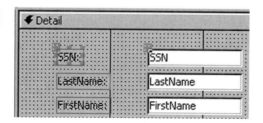

3 Click once inside the label. The insertion point appears in a location similar to that shown in Figure 5.15.

FIGURE 5.15

4 Edit the label so it reads *Employee ID*.

5 Click the FirstName label. While holding down the (SHIFT) key, click the LastName, Address, City, State, ZipCode, and HomePhone labels. The labels should now be selected, as shown in Figure 5.16.

FIGURE 5.16

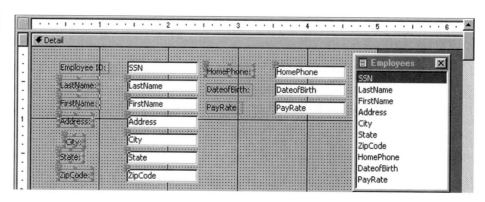

6 Click the Cut button on the database toolbar.

Check Point

Will you be able to reverse this action? Yes, this action can be reversed using Undo.

7 Click the Close button on the field list to close it. Your form appears as shown in Figure 5.17.

FIGURE 5.17

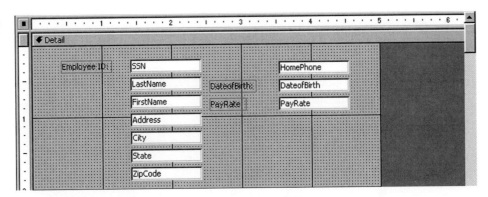

8 Save your changes.

TASK 6: To Reposition Text Box Controls on the Form

1 Click to select the SSN field. Position the insertion point immediately over the rectangle in the upper-left corner of the SSN field and click. Notice that the horizontal and vertical rulers highlight the current selection, as shown in Figure 5.18.

FIGURE 5.18

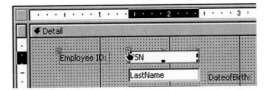

2 While holding down the left mouse button, drag the text box below its label, as shown in Figure 5.19.

FIGURE 5.19

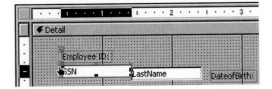

TROUBLESHOOTING Make sure the insertion point appears as shown in Figure 5.16 and not as an open hand, or you may move the text box and its associated label.

3 Move the insertion point over the right border of the SSN text box, and resize it as shown in figure 5.20.

FIGURE 5.20

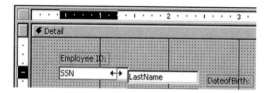

4 Using Figure 5.21 as a guide, reposition and resize the remaining controls as shown.

FIGURE 5.21

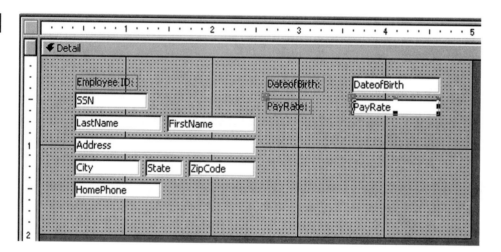

 Check Point

Are the text box controls bound or unbound? Text box controls are bound, because they display record data that will change on the form.

5 Edit the DateofBirth and PayRate labels so they appear as **Date of Birth** and **Pay Rate** respectively, as shown in Figure 5.22.

FIGURE 5.22

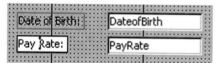

6 Click the Restore button in the form's title bar.

7 Resize the form so it approximates the size shown in Figure 5.23.

FIGURE 5.23

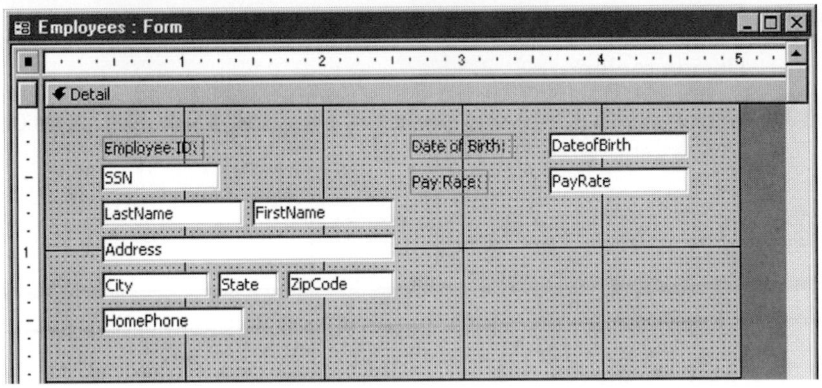

8 Click the View button to view your changes. The form appears as shown in Figure 5.24.

FIGURE 5.24

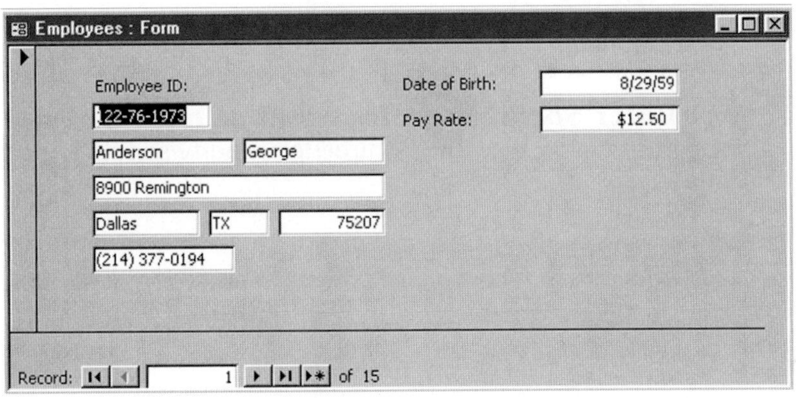

9 Save the form and switch to Design view.

Break Point

If necessary, you can exit Access and continue this project later.

Using ControlTips to Improve Data Accuracy

When the form displays a record, you can see from the field data which control is bound to which field. If you were to add a new record, you might not know exactly what to enter into some of the text boxes. A ControlTip instructs users on what exactly what information to enter into a text box control when a form is used to add records to a database.

TASK 7: To Add ControlTips to the Employees Form

1 Launch Access and open the *Selections.mdb* database if necessary.

2 Select the SSN text box and click the Properties ⊞ button on the Form Design toolbar.

3 Click the Other tab, and place the insertion point inside the ControlTip Text row, as shown in Figure 5.25.

FIGURE 5.25

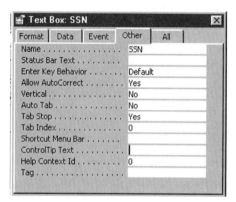

4 Type **Enter Social Security Number here** in the row. Resize the Properties dialog box. The ControlTip property should appear as shown in Figure 5.26.

FIGURE 5.26

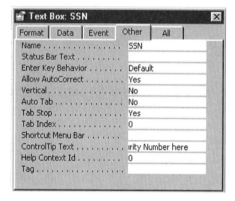

5 Close the Properties dialog box and switch to Form view ⊞▾ .

6 Move the insertion point over the SSN text box to see the ControlTip. It appears as shown in Figure 5.27.

FIGURE 5.27

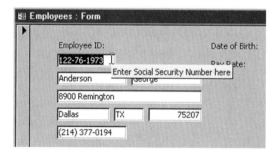

7 Switch to Design view .

8 Using the same procedure, add ControlTips to the FirstName, LastName, Address, City, State, ZipCode, and HomePhone text box controls. Type the appropriate field name in the text for each ControlTip.

9 Save your changes to the form.

Web Tip

The Microsoft Office Developers Forum contains a listing of sample forms you can create in Access. For more information, visit: http://www .microsoft.com/accessdev/articles/solforms.htm.

Adding Unbound Controls to a Form

Remember that a text box control is a bound control since it is bound, or linked to a specific record source. Labels are **unbound controls**, since they do not return data from a table or a query. Unbound controls are often used to add descriptive information to a form.

Working with Unbound Label Controls

When you added fields to the form using the field list, Access created a label to accompany each bound text box control. The text for each label corresponds to the name of the field the text box displays. You will now modify the text in the existing labels, and add a label control as a title for the form.

TASK 8: To Add a Label Control to the Form Header and Footer and Modify Format Properties

1 Choose Form Header/Footer from the View menu, as shown in Figure 5.28.

FIGURE 5.28

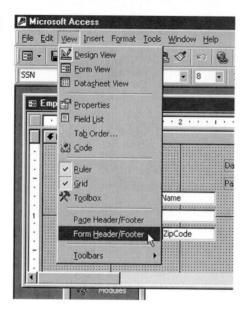

2 Display the Toolbox by clicking the Toolbox ⚒ button on the Forms toolbar.

3 Select the Label tool from the Toolbox, as shown in Figure 5.29.

FIGURE 5.29

4 Draw a label in the form header, as shown in Figure 5.30.

FIGURE 5.30

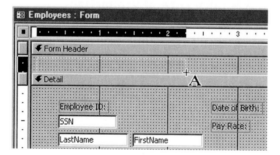

5 Type **Selections, Inc. Employee Database** as the label text.

6 Open the Properties window for the control.

7 Click the Format tab, if necessary. Scroll so that Font Size is visible. Set the Font Size property to 12, and the Font Weight property to Semi-bold, as shown in Figure 5.31.

FIGURE 5.31

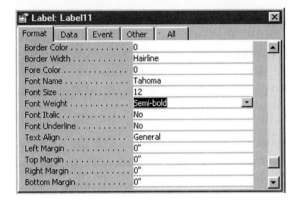

8 Close the Properties window.

9 Resize the control so it displays the entire caption.

10 Use the vertical scroll bar to display the form footer.

11 Add a label control to the form footer, and type **Copyright, 1999** as the caption for the label, as shown in Figure 5.32.

FIGURE 5.32

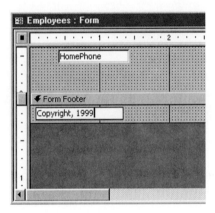

12 Switch to Form view. The form appears as shown in Figure 5.33.

FIGURE 5.33

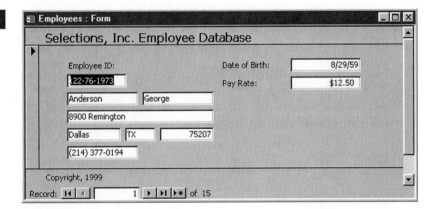

13 Save your changes to the form.

14 Switch to Design view.

Adding an Image to the Form Using an Unbound Control

You can enhance the appearance of a form by adding an image to it. If the image will not need to be updated, you can embed it into the form using an unbound image control. An *image control* displays an embedded or linked image file.

TASK 9: To Embed an Image into the Form Using an Unbound Control

1 Click the Image Control 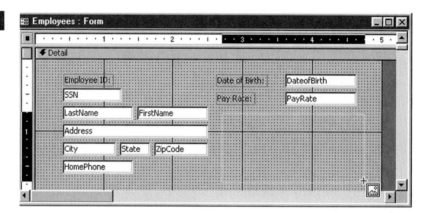 button in the Toolbox.

2 Drag an image control near the lower right corner of the form, as shown in Figure 5.34.

FIGURE 5.34

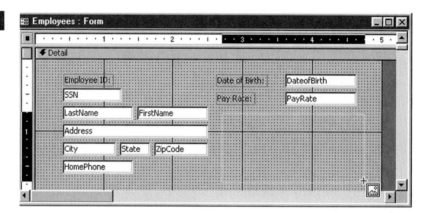

3 In the Insert Picture dialog box, select the *Sm Selections Logo.gif* file from the Images folder on your floppy disk, as shown in Figure 5.35.

FIGURE 5.35

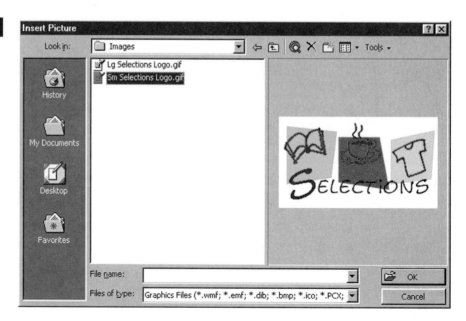

Web Tip

If you do not have a copy of this image file on your floppy disk, download it from the SELECT Web site at http://www.prenhall.com/select.

4 Click OK.

5 Open the Properties window for the control and click the Format tab. Change the Size Mode property to Stretch.

6 Close the Properties window.

7 Size the control as necessary.

8 Switch to Form view, and resize the form per your liking. When you are finished, your form should look similar to the one shown in Figure 5.36.

FIGURE 5.36

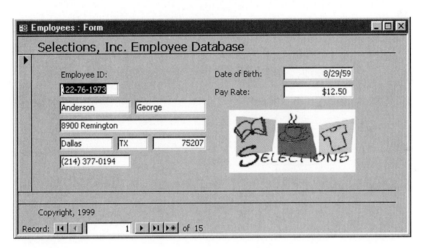

9 Save these changes and close the form.

Check Point

Why is an image control unbound? The image control is an unbound control because an image is not based upon a record source.

Web Tip

What to create forms like the pros? Visit
http://msdn.microsoft.com/library/conf/html/sa00d.htm
for more information.

Maintaining Table Data Using a Form

A common database task is using a form to enter, modify, and delete records. Recall that in a well-designed database, users do not interact with records at the table level. In the tasks that follow, you will add a record to the Employees table using the modified Employees form, and then delete this record from the database.

TASK 10: To Add a Record to the Employees Table Using the Employees Form

1 From the database window, open the Employees form.

2 Click the New Record ▶* button on the form.

3 Enter the data shown in Figure 5.37 into the form. Remember to use TAB to move from field to field.

FIGURE 5.37

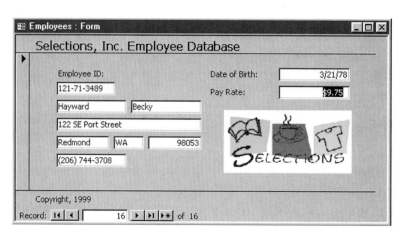

4 Using the First Record button, move to the first record in the database.

> **TIP** Remember that the table is updated once you move to a new record on the form.

5 Close the form.

TASK 11: To Delete a Record from the Employees Table Using the Employees Form

1 Open the Employees form.

2 Using one of the methods you learned previously, navigate to the sixth record in the database.

> **TIP** Although you entered this record at the sixteenth record in the table, it appears as the sixth record, since the data is sorted alphabetically by last name.

3 Choose Delete Record from the Edit menu.

4 The dialog box shown in Figure 5.38 will appear. Click Yes to delete the record.

FIGURE 5.38

> **TIP** Remember that Access updates a table as you make changes. If you delete a record, you will not be able to restore it!

> **TROUBLESHOOTING** If you attempt to delete a record for an employee for whom you have entered time card data, you will be unable to do so, as referential integrity rules will not allow this action to occur. You must first delete the associated time card records, and then delete the employee record.

5 Close the form, and exit Access.

Summary and Exercises

Summary

- You have a great deal of flexibility in how you create a form using Design view.
- Forms often contain both bound and unbound controls.
- Bound controls are linked to an underlying record source such as a table or a query.
- Unbound controls are normally used to add descriptive information to a form.
- When a form will be used to enter data into a record source, ControlTips are useful for providing instructions for end users.
- You can add text to a form's header and footer using an unbound label control.
- You can embed an image in a form using an unbound image control.
- You can use a form to enter, modify, and delete records in a table.

Key Terms and Operations

Key Terms

bound control	image control
control	label control
ControlTip	record source
Design view	text box control
Detail section	unbound control
Form view	

Operations

add a record to a table using a form
add fields to a form
add unbound controls to a form's header and footer
create a new form using Design view
delete a form
delete a record from a table using a form
embed an image in a form using an unbound control
modify bound controls
view a form

Study Questions

Multiple Choice

1. Which form element displays a message when a text box control is highlighted?
    a. label control
    b. image control
    c. bound control
    d. ControlTip

2. To add controls to a form, you use
   a. Form view.
   b. the Toolbox.
   c. Design view.
   d. b and c.

3. In Access, a form normally
   a. is bound to a field.
   b. is based upon a record source.
   c. uses another form as its record source.
   d. contains only unbound controls.

4. You can easily add fields to a form using
   a. the Toolbox.
   b. Form view.
   c. the Field List.
   d. the View button.

5. Label controls are used to display
   a. descriptive text.
   b. data that is bound.
   c. field data.
   d. images or graphics.

6. A form displays records in
   a. Form Design view.
   b. Form Datasheet view.
   c. the database window.
   d. a bound control.

7. To embed an image on a form, you normally use a
   a. label control.
   b. text box control.
   c. image control.
   d. bound control.

8. Which of the following statements is false?
   a. Label controls can be deleted from a form.
   b. A label can be resized on a form.
   c. A label can be moved on a form using the mouse.
   d. A label is a bound control.

9. You created a form using Form Design view, and specified a table as the form's data source. How many record sources does the form have?
   a. one
   b. two
   c. four
   d. eight

10. A form can be based upon all except which of the following?
    a. a table
    b. a query
    c. a table and a query
    d. a form

Short Answer

1. What do you use to add fields to a form in Design view?
2. What kind of control do you use to add descriptive text to a form?
3. What database objects can be used to create a form?
4. A text box is which kind of control?
5. What screen element assists in adding fields to a form?
6. Where do you find the tools you need to add controls to a form?
7. Do you use a bound or an unbound control to display field data?
8. A label is which kind of control?
9. The data in a form is displayed on the screen using which view?
10. What kind of control is used to display a bitmap graphic on a form?

Fill in the Blank

1. Bound controls get their data from a(n) _____.
2. An image embedded in a form from a graphic file uses the _____ control.
3. To display a form's header and footer, choose _____ from the View menu.
4. The _____ contains buttons for selecting the kinds of controls you will add to a form.
5. To create a form without using a wizard, select _____ view.
6. A(n) _____ is descriptive text accompanying text box controls.
7. Once you _____ a form from a database, it cannot be restored using Undo.
8. You can display the _____ to quickly and easily add fields to a form in Design view.
9. All of a form's controls possess _____.
10. A(n) _____ control accompanies a text box when you add field from the field list to a form in Design view.

For Discussion

1. How does Form Design view differ from Query Design view and Table Design view?
2. How do you remove controls from a form?
3. How do bound controls differ from unbound controls?
4. What is a ControlTip? Why is it sometimes helpful to include ControlTips on a form?
5. Describe a situation where you might want to display images on a form that are bound to a record source.

Hands-On Exercises

1. Creating a Form that Displays a Subform

You will recall that the record source for a form can be data from multiple tables. In this exercise you will create a form for displaying employee records, and the associated time cards for each employee. To do this, you must create a main form that contains a subform. The main form will display the employee data, the subform the time cards for each employee.

1. Copy the Selections database and name the copy *Time Cards.mdb*.
2. Open the *Time Cards.mdb* database on your disk.

Web Tip

If you do not have a copy of this file, you can download it from the SELECT Web site at http://www.prenhall.com/select.

3. Click the Forms button on the Objects bar. Create a new form using the Form Wizard.
4. Select the Employees table, and add the fields shown in Figure 5.39 to the form. Click Next.

FIGURE 5.39

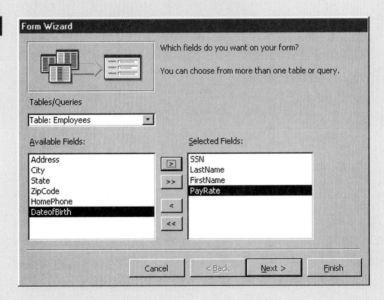

5. Select the Time Cards table, and add the PayPeriod and HoursWorked fields to the form, as shown in Figure 5.40. Click Next.

FIGURE 5.40

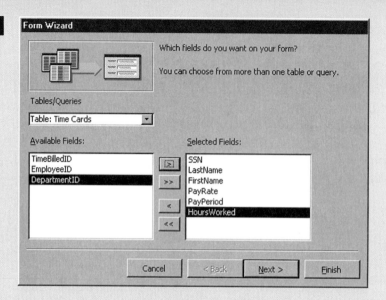

6. Select the defaults shown in Figure 5.41 and click Next.

FIGURE 5.41

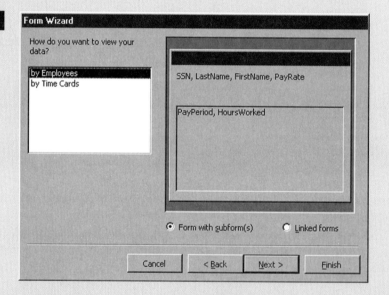

7. Select Datasheet as the style for the subform and click Next.

8. Select Standard as the style, and click Next.

9. Type **Employee Pay Record** as the name of the form. When your screen matches Figure 5.42, click Finish.

FIGURE 5.42

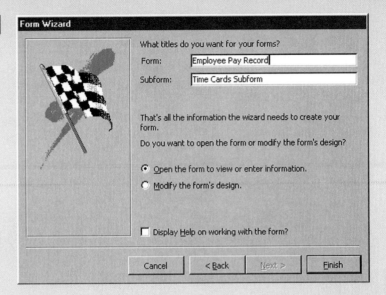

9. Adjust the size of the form, and the width of the columns in the subform. When you are finished, your form and its linked subform will look similar to Figure 5.43.

FIGURE 5.43

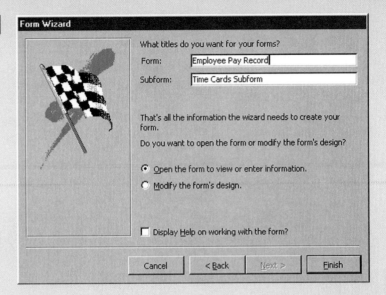

10. Save the form and close the database if you are finished working the exercises for this project.

2. Adding a Calculated Control to the Time Cards Subform

The form you created in the previous exercise will be much more useful if the subform displays the gross pay for each time card. In this exercise you will add a text box to the subform, and then add an expression to calculate the gross pay.

1. Copy the *Time Cards.mdb* database, and name the copy *Gross Pay.mdb*.

2. Open the *Gross Pay.mdb* database on your disk.

3. Open the *Employee Pay Record* form in Design view.

4. In the Detail section of the subform, add a text box control to the right of the Hours Worked field.

5. Delete the label associated with the unbound control.

6. Open the Properties window for the control. Click the Data tab, and type

   =[Forms]![Employee Pay Record]![PayRate]*[HoursWorked]

   in the Control Source row.

7. Change the format of the control to Currency.

8. Click the Format tab and change the format to Currency.

9. Click the Other tab and type **Gross Pay** in the Name property row for the control.

10. Close the Properties window and save the form.

11. Switch to Form view and select SSN. The form appears similar to the one shown in Figure 5.44.

FIGURE 5.44

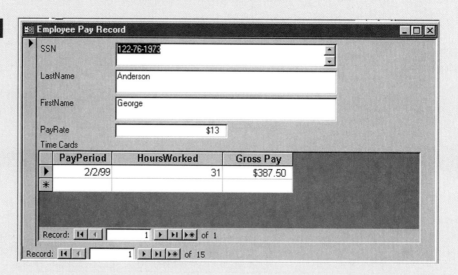

12. Close the database.

13. Exit Access.

On Your Own Exercises

1. Building a Form Based upon a Query with an AND Condition

Open the Web Sites database file. Using Form Design view, create a form based upon the query displaying records meeting the AND condition you specified in Project 4. Update the database when you are finished.

2. Creating a Form Based upon a Multitable Query

Open the *Inventory.mdb* database on your disk. Create an AutoForm based upon the Inventory Value query you created in Project 4. Modify the form as appropriate. Save your changes.

3. Creating a Switchboard Form

Open the *Inventory.mdb* database. Using the Help System, determine how to create a Switchboard. Create a working switchboard form for the database that automatically appears when the database is opened. Save your changes.

4. Using the Office Assistant

Open the Inventory database. Choose Show the Office Assistant from the Help menu. Search the Help system for information about creating calculated controls on forms. Create a control in the form footer that lists the total value of the inventory. Save the changes you make to the database.

5. Modifying a Form in the Contact Management Database

Open the Contact Management database you created in Project 1 and modified in Projects 2, 3, and 4. Add a ClipArt image to the Contacts form using an unbound control. Save your changes.

6. Creating a Form Based upon a Multitable Query

Open the *Contact Management.mdb* database you modified in the previous exercise. Create an AutoForm based upon the multitable query you created in Project 4. Save the database when you are finished.

Creating and Modifying Reports

A report is an effective way to present your data in a printed format. Because you have control over the size and appearance of everything included in a report, you can display the information exactly how you want to see it printed.

Objectives

After completing this project, you will be able to:

➤ Create a report using the Report Wizard

➤ View a report in the Print Preview window

➤ Modify a report

➤ Print a report

➤ Create a report using Report Design view

➤ Sort and group data in a report

➤ Add a calculated control to a report

Running Case

Mr. Traylor is very pleased with the work you have done on the Employees database, and now wants to begin distributing printed information from it. You are now ready to prepare payroll information for him. In this project you will create a report listing the specific information Mr. Traylor has requested.

The Challenge

Mr. Traylor has requested two reports. The first is an employee address list that will be distributed to the human resources department. The second is a report listing the time cards for each employee in the database, with the total year-to-date payroll amount listed at the end of the report.

The Strategy

You can easily create the first report using the Report Wizard. Once you have designed the report you can modify its appearance using Report Design view. You can create the second report using Report Design view in a manner similar to how you learned to create forms. After adding the appropriate controls to the report's design, you can determine the year-to-date payroll amount using a calculated expression in a text box control. Figure 6.1 shows the report design listing each employee's gross pay that you will create in this project.

FIGURE 6.1

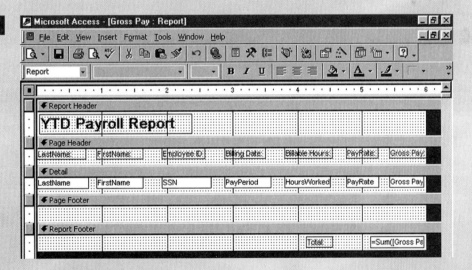

The Setup

So that your screen matches the illustrations in this project, you should set up Access as shown in Table 6.1 after you launch Access and open your database. These are the default settings in Access, but they may have been changed on your computer.

Table 6.1

Location	Make these settings:
Tools, Customize	Click the Toolbars tab and display the database toolbar and the menu bar, if they are not currently visible.
Tools, Options	Display the status bar, the startup dialog box, new object shortcuts, and windows in the taskbar.
Tools, Options	Click the General tab and deselect the setting for displaying dates in four-digit format.
Tools, Customize	Click the Options tab, and make sure the checkbox to display recently used menu commands first is deselected.
Office Assistant	Hide the Office Assistant.
File, Open	Open the *Selections.mdb* database.

Creating Reports

Creating reports is similar to creating forms. The **Report Design window** contains a graphical workspace displaying the report's bound and unbound controls. The Report Design window contains five sections where you can add controls. You add the controls to a specific section depending upon whether the information will appear at the beginning or end of the report, which requires a control in either the **Report Header** or **Report Footer** section. If your information needs to appear on every page of the report, add a control to the **Page Header** or **Page Footer** section. For information that is bound to a specific field in the record source, use a bound control such as a text box and add it to the **Detail section** in the Report Design window. These sections are identified in Figure 6.2.

FIGURE 6.2

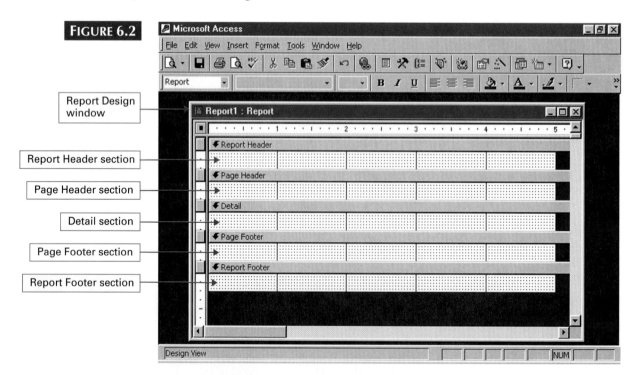

Report Design window
Report Header section
Page Header section
Detail section
Page Footer section
Report Footer section

Creating a Report Using the Report Wizard

The easiest way to create a report is to use the Report Wizard, view the report, and then switch to the Report Design window to make any necessary modifications.

TASK 1:   To Create a Report Using the Report Wizard

1 Click the Reports button on the Objects bar.

2 Click the New button ![New].

3 Select the Report Wizard, and base the report upon the Employees table, as shown in Figure 6.3. Click OK.

FIGURE 6.3

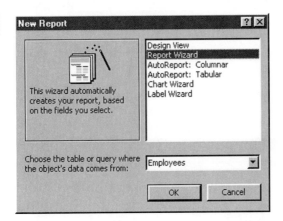

4 Select the Employees table in the Tables/Queries list if necessary. Move the SSN, LastName, FirstName, Address, City, State, ZipCode, and HomePhone fields from the Available Fields list to the Selected Fields list, as shown in Figure 6.4.

FIGURE 6.4

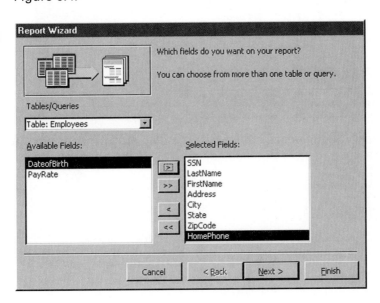

5 Click the Next button. The next Report Wizard dialog box asks if you want any grouping levels. Accept the default settings shown in Figure 6.5.

FIGURE 6.5

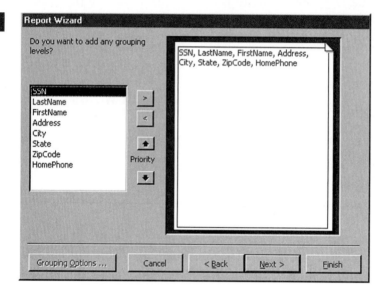

6 Click Next. Select LastName in the first drop-down list and FirstName in the second list to sort on two fields, as shown in Figure 6.6.

FIGURE 6.6

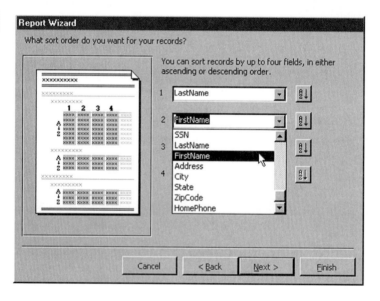

7 Click Next. Select a Tabular layout in Landscape orientation. Also select the checkbox to have all fields adjust to fit on the page, as shown in Figure 6.7.

FIGURE 6.7

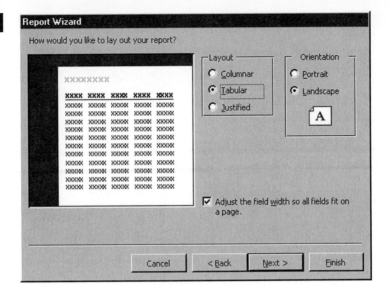

8   Click Next. Select Formal as the style from the options shown in Figure 6.8.

FIGURE 6.8

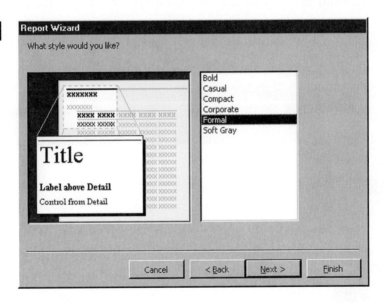

9   Click Next. Accept *Employees* as the default name for the report by clicking Finish, as shown in Figure 6.9.

FIGURE 6.9

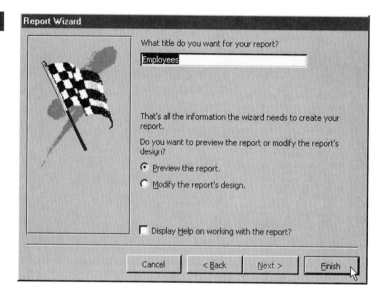

10 Access displays the report in Print Preview. Figure 6.10 highlights a number of important screen elements contained in the Print Preview view.

FIGURE 6.10

Print Preview toolbar

Print Preview window

First Page, Previous Page, Next Page, and Last Page buttons

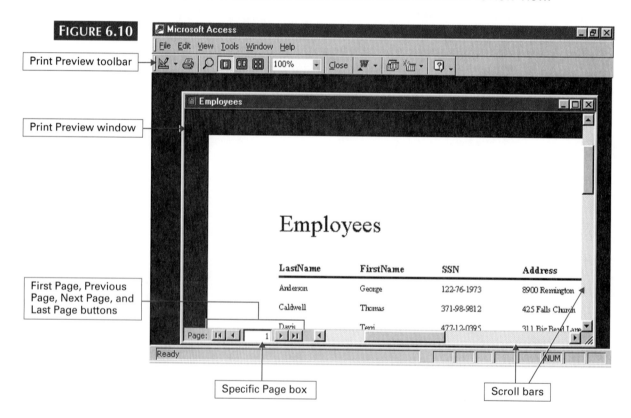

Specific Page box

Scroll bars

Viewing a Report in the Print Preview Window

When you create a new report using the Report Wizard or preview an existing report, Access displays the report information in the Print Preview/Layout window. The information is displayed here exactly as it will appear when printed.

The Preview normally displays at 100% of its size. You can use the scroll bars in the Print Preview window or the Zoom box on the Print Preview toolbar to change how the preview displays.

TASK 2: <u>To Change the Preview Display</u>

1 Drag the horizontal scroll bar to reposition the preview. At 100% it is difficult to see the entire layout of the report.

2 Click the Zoom 100% box on the Print Preview toolbar and change the view to 75%.

3 Maximize the Preview window.

4 Reposition the Preview using the scroll bars. The entire report layout is now visible, as shown in Figure 6.11.

FIGURE 6.11

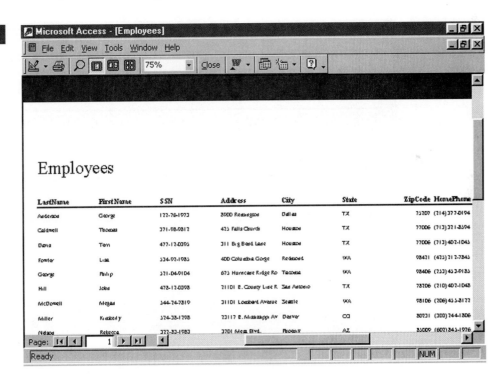

5 Close the report.

6 Restore the database window.

Break Point

If necessary, you can exit Access and continue this project later.

Modifying the Report Design for Printing

Rarely does a wizard create a report that does not need to be modified. You can easily modify a report's layout by adjusting the size and position of the report's bound and unbound controls in the Report Design window. Once you have modified the Employees report, it will be ready for printing.

TASK 3: <u>To Modify the Design of the Employees Report for Printing</u>

1 Launch Access and open the *Selections.mdb* database if necessary. Click the Reports button on the Objects bar if it is not currently active, click Employees, and click the Design button. Maximize the Report Design window so it appears as shown in Figure 6.12. Hide the Toolbox and Field list if necessary.

FIGURE 6.12

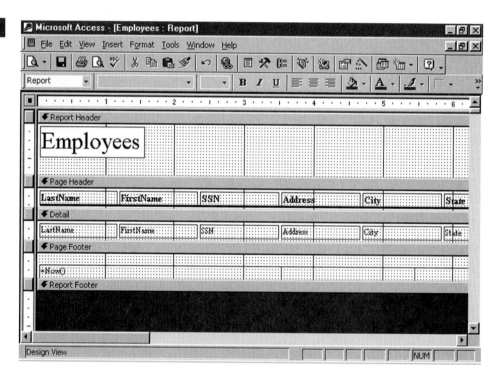

Notice that the current report uses four report sections.

Check Point

Is the label control bound or unbound? Since the label control displays descriptive text that does not originate from a record source, it is an unbound control.

2 Highlight the caption of the label in the Report Header section to select the caption. Type **Selections, Inc. Employee List** as the new caption for the control, as shown in Figure 6.13.

FIGURE 6.13

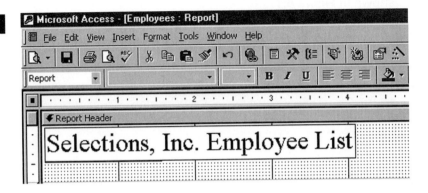

3 Press (ENTER).

4 Select the FirstName label in the Page Header section.

5 Click the Cut ✂ button.

6 Select the caption for the LastName label, and type **Name**.

7 Select the SSN label caption and type **Employee ID**, as shown in Figure 6.14. Press (ENTER).

FIGURE 6.14

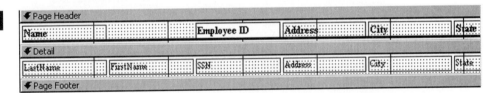

8 Use the horizontal scroll bar to display the address information. Reposition and resize the Address, City, State, ZipCode, and HomePhone text boxes to approximate the positions shown in Figure 6.15.

FIGURE 6.15

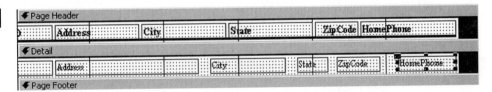

9 Resize and reposition the label controls shown in Figure 6.16, to correspond with the text box controls.

FIGURE 6.16

10 Click the View 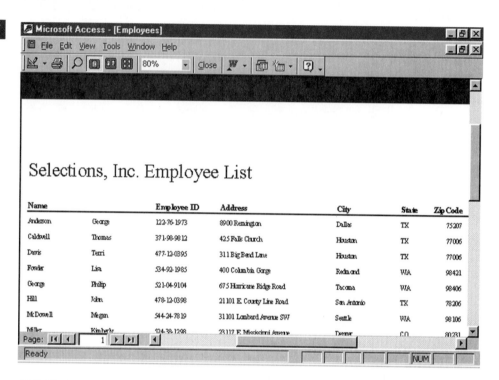 button on the Report Design toolbar.

11 Select the current zoom setting Change the zoom to 80% by typing **80** as the zoom value. Press (ENTER) to accept the value. The report now appears as shown in Figure 6.17.

FIGURE 6.17

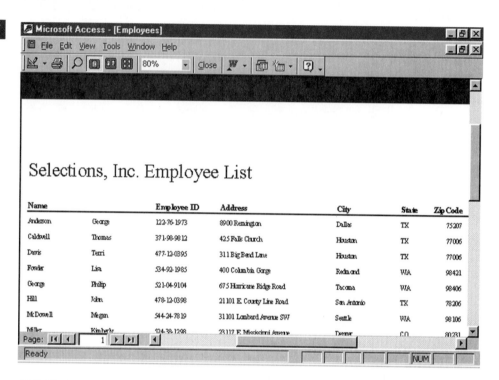

TIP Reports have three views: Design, Preview, and Layout. You use Design view to create or change a report. Print Preview displays the report's data as it will appear on every page. Layout Preview displays the report's layout, which includes just a sample of the data in the report.

---

12 Click the Print button on the Print Preview toolbar to print the report.

13 Close the report when it is finished printing.

14 The Microsoft Access dialog box shown in Figure 6.18 appears, asking whether you want to save changes to the report.

FIGURE 6.18

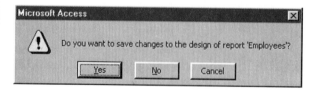

15 Click Yes to save and close the report.

Creating a Report Using Report Design View

Although the Report Wizard quickly generates reports, you have the most control over what a report contains when you create a new report using Design view. By placing bound and unbound controls in the various sections of the report, you specify exactly how you want the report to look.

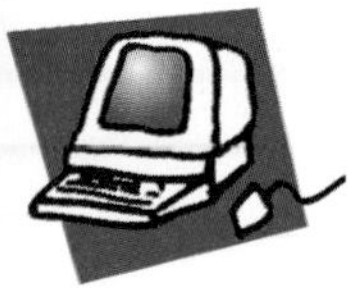

TASK 4: To Create a New Report Using Design View

1. Click the New button in the database window.
2. Select Design View and base the report on the Gross Pay query, as shown in Figure 6.19.

FIGURE 6.19

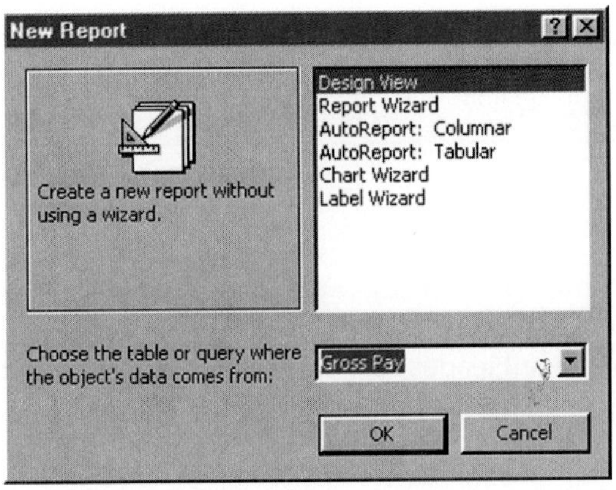

3. Click OK. Click the Field List button on the Report Design toolbar to display the field list, if it is not currently visible.
4. Drag the SSN, LastName, FirstName, PayRate, PayPeriod, HoursWorked, and Gross Pay fields into the Detail section.

> **TIP** Don't be concerned with where these fields are currently placed, since you will modify the report design.

5. Select the LastName label and click the Cut button.
6. Place the insertion point inside the Page Header section and click the Paste button. The label is pasted into the Header section, as shown in Figure 6.20.

FIGURE 6.20

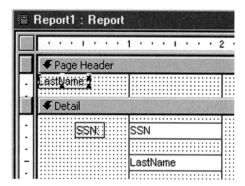

7 Maximize the Report window, if necessary. Cut the remaining labels from the Detail section, paste them into the Page Header section, and reposition each one. Resize the report as necessary. When you are finished, your report design should resemble Figure 6.21.

FIGURE 6.21

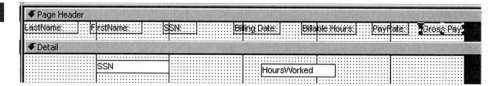

TROUBLESHOOTING You will have to reposition each control when you past it into the Page Header section, since by default Access pastes the control in the upper-left corner of the section.

8 Position the text box controls as shown in Figure 6.22.

FIGURE 6.22

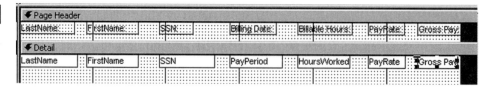

9 Highlight the text in the SSN label caption and type Employee ID as the new caption. Deselect the control.

10 Place the insertion point near the lower edge of the Detail section. Click and drag the lower border of the Detail section, as shown in Figure 6.23.

FIGURE 6.23

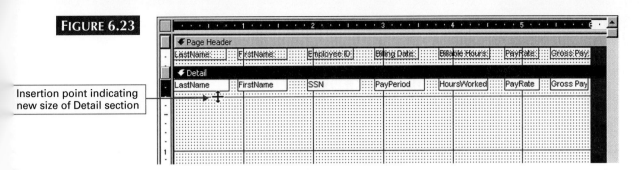

Insertion point indicating new size of Detail section

11 Save the report. Type **Gross Pay** as the name of the report, as shown in Figure 6.24.

FIGURE 6.24

12 Click OK.

13 Click the View button to preview the report, and change the zoom to 75%. The report appears as shown in Figure 6.25.

FIGURE 6.25

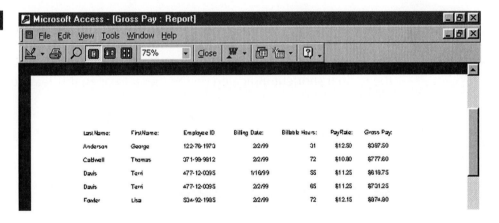

Adding Sorting and Grouping Levels to the Report for Previewing and Printing

Remember that Mr. Traylor wants to see a listing of all time cards for each employee. You can modify the report using the Sorting and Grouping feature in Access to create a report that meets Mr. Traylor's specifications.

TASK 5: To Add Sorting and Grouping Levels to the Report for Previewing and Printing

1 Switch to Design view.

2 Choose Sorting and Grouping from the View menu, as shown in Figure 6.26.

FIGURE 6.26

Check Point

How else can you open the Sorting and Grouping dialog box? You can use the toolbar shortcut indicated on the menu to open this feature.

3 Click the drop-down list button in the first Field/Expression row, and select SSN, as shown in Figure 6.27.

FIGURE 6.27

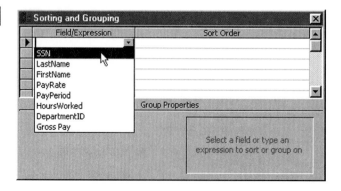

4 Accept the Group Properties defaults shown in Figure 6.28.

FIGURE 6.28

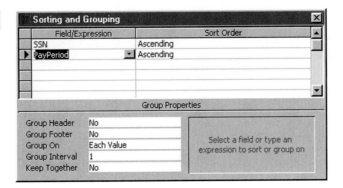

5 Select PayPeriod in the next row of the Field/Expression column of the Sorting and Grouping dialog box. Do not display a Group Header for this detail. When your settings match those shown in Figure 6.29, close the Sorting and Grouping dialog box.

FIGURE 6.29

Check Point

Why did you add this field to the Sorting and Grouping settings? By adding the PayPeriod field, the report will sort the records for each employee in ascending order by date.

6 Save the report.

7 Preview the report. Your report should look similar to the one shown in Figure 6.30.

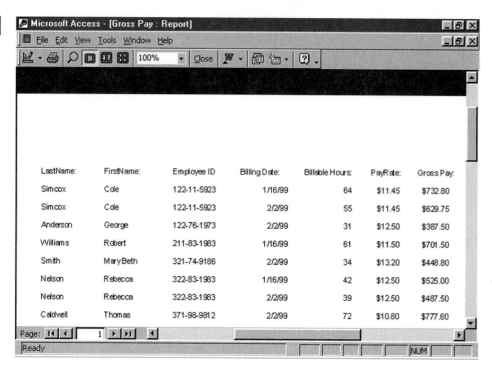

FIGURE 6.30

8 Close the Preview.

9 Click the Print 🖨 button to print the report.

Web Tip

Do you want some tips on the kinds of reports small businesses may need? Visit http://www.microsoft.com/smallbiz/software/office/access.htm for more information.

Adding a Calculated Control to the Report

Do you remember the additional specifications Mr. Traylor gave for this report? He wants the report to display the total payroll amount to date. You can add this figure at the end of the report in a calculated control, which is a control containing an expression.

TASK 6: To Create a Calculated Control to Sum the Total Payroll Amount

1 Choose Report Header/Footer from the View menu.

2 Display the Toolbox.

3 Select the Text Box control tool.

4 Add a text box control to the right side of the Report Footer section, immediately below the Gross Pay text box in the Detail section, as shown in Figure 6.31.

FIGURE 6.31

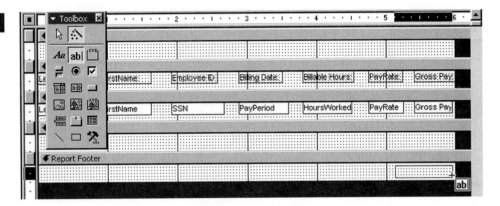

TIP Notice that the text box is currently not bound to a specific object.

5 Highlight the caption for the label that is associated with the text box control, and type **Total:** as the new caption.

6 Select the text box control and click the Properties 🔲 button on the Report Design toolbar.

7 Click the Data tab in the Text Box Properties dialog box to display the data properties. Click the ellipsis button that appears to the right of the Control Source row.

8 Type **=sum([Gross Pay])** in the Expression Builder, and click OK, as shown in Figure 6.32.

FIGURE 6.32

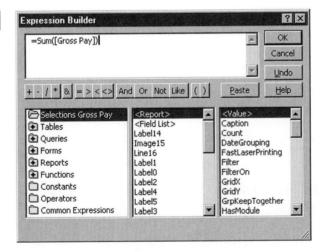

9 Click the Format tab in the Properties dialog box and set the Format property of the control to Currency.

10 Save and preview your report.

11 Adjust the preview to display the total payroll calculation. The value $10,419.90 should appear, as shown in Figure 6.33.

FIGURE 6.33

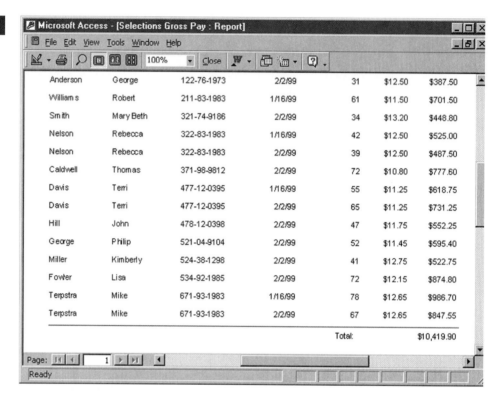

Anderson	George	122-76-1973	2/2/99	31	$12.50	$387.50
Williams	Robert	211-83-1983	1/16/99	61	$11.50	$701.50
Smith	Mary Beth	321-74-9186	2/2/99	34	$13.20	$448.80
Nelson	Rebecca	322-83-1983	1/16/99	42	$12.50	$525.00
Nelson	Rebecca	322-83-1983	2/2/99	39	$12.50	$487.50
Caldwell	Thomas	371-98-9812	2/2/99	72	$10.80	$777.60
Davis	Terri	477-12-0395	1/16/99	55	$11.25	$618.75
Davis	Terri	477-12-0395	2/2/99	65	$11.25	$731.25
Hill	John	478-12-0398	2/2/99	47	$11.75	$552.25
George	Philip	521-04-9104	2/2/99	52	$11.45	$595.40
Miller	Kimberly	524-38-1298	2/2/99	41	$12.75	$522.75
Fowler	Lisa	534-92-1985	2/2/99	72	$12.15	$874.80
Terpstra	Mike	671-93-1983	1/16/99	78	$12.65	$986.70
Terpstra	Mike	671-93-1983	2/2/99	67	$12.65	$847.55
					Total:	$10,419.90

Adding a Report Header Displaying a Title for the Report

The report still needs slight modification. It will look better if you add a label in the Report Header section and add a descriptive label explaining exactly what information the calculated control displays.

TASK 7: <u>To Modify the Report</u>

1 Click the View button to return to the Report Design window.

2 Add a label control to the Report Header section.

3 Type **YTD Payroll Report** as the caption in the label.

4 Change the Font Size property to 16.

5 Change the Font Weight property to Semi-bold.

6 Adjust the Report Header section and the label control as necessary. The report design should now look similar to Figure 6.34.

FIGURE 6.34

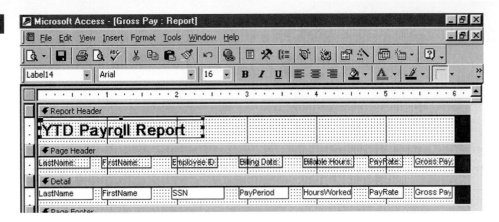

---

7 Save your changes to the report design.

8 Preview the report and change the zoom to 60%. Your report should resemble Figure 6.35.

FIGURE 6.35

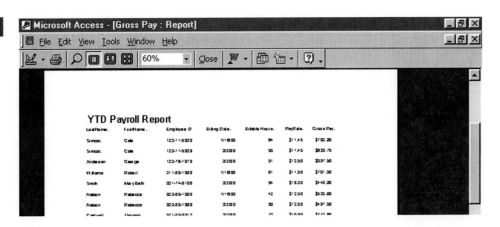

---

9 Close the report.

10 Close the database.

 Web Tip

You can create sophisticated Access reports for delivery on the Web. See http://msdn.microsoft.com/library/periodic/period98/html/vbpj0498.htm for more information.

Summary and Exercises

Summary

- Database reports are used to print information from a database.
- You can create a report by using one of the Report Wizards or by using Report Design view.
- A report contains bound and unbound controls that specify where information will appear on the report.
- Once you create a report you can view it in the Print Preview window.
- You can modify a report by changing the properties of each control in the report.
- Calculated controls perform calculations based upon an expression.
- A report can be sorted on up to four fields when you create a report using the Report Wizard.
- You can change the sort order of information in a report by using the Sorting and Grouping option.

Key Terms and Operations

Key Terms

Detail section
Page Footer
Page Header

Report Design window
Report Footer
Report Header

Operations

change the Preview display
create a calculated control
create a new report using
  Report Design View

create a report using the Report
  Wizard
modify a report in Design view
specify sort order

Study Questions

Multiple Choice

1. Which view displays all the data in a report exactly as it will be printed?
   a. Design view
   b. Preview view
   c. Layout view
   d. Form view

2. When you create a report using the Report Wizard, how many fields can you specify for the sort order?
   a. one
   b. two
   c. three
   d. four

3. To arrange controls on a report you must use
   a. Design view.
   b. Layout view.
   c. Form view.
   d. Preview view.

4. In which section of a report do bound controls normally appear?
   a. Page Header
   b. Detail
   c. Page Footer
   d. Report Header

5. You can add fields to a report easily using the
   a. Toolbox.
   b. Properties dialog box.
   c. database window.
   d. Field list.

6. Unbound controls usually appear in all sections of a report except which section?
   a. Page Header
   b. Report Header
   c. Page Footer
   d. Detail

7. Data entered in the Page Header section of a report appears at the
   a. beginning of the report only.
   b. end of the report.
   c. top of every page
   d. bottom of every page.

8. Field data from a query appears in which section of a report?
   a. Page Header
   b. Detail
   c. Page Footer
   d. Report Header

9. A query displays an employee's Last Name, First Name, Address, Social Security Number, and Annual Salary. To easily locate a given employee in a report based upon the query, the report should be sorted on which field?
   a. Last Name
   b. Social Security Number
   c. First Name
   d. Annual Salary

10. You want to add a descriptive title that appears only on the first page of the report. To which section should you add the control to?
    a. Page Header
    b. Detail
    c. Page Footer
    d. Report Header

Short Answer

1. What is the main purpose of a report?

2. What is a calculated control?

3. Where do bound controls normally appear in a report?

4. When should you use a query as the basis for a report?

5. How do you specify sort order in a report?

6. What is the fastest method for creating a report?

7. What dialog box do you use to create a calculated control in a report?

8. How do you move labels from the Detail section of a report to the Page Header section?

9. How do you save a report?

10. What kind of unbound controls does a report usually contain?

Fill in the Blank

1. A calculated control contains a(n) _____ that performs the calculation.

2. The _____ section displays information that appears only at the beginning of the report.

3. If you want to sort data that is displayed in a report, you must change the _____ and _____ properties for one or more fields.

4. A label appearing in the Page Header section of a report is a(n) _____ control.

5. Information displayed in a report's Detail section requires a(n) _____.

6. A report can be based upon either a(n) _____ or a(n) _____.

7. To create a report using Design view, you add _____ to the various sections of a report.

8. A text box control appearing in the Report Detail section is a(n) _____ control.

9. The _____ view displays all the records in a report exactly as they will be printed.

10. The _____ contains summary information for each page of a report.

For Discussion

1. What two database objects can you use to create a report? When might you use one rather than the other?

2. What are some ways you might use calculated controls in a report?

3. When you do use bound versus unbound controls on a report?

4. Describe the three views associated with reports.

5. When should you consider changing the sorting and grouping options for a report?

Hands-On Exercises

1. Adding an Image to a Report

In Project 5 you learned how to add an image to a form using an unbound image control. You can also add images to any section of a report. In this exercise you will create a copy of the Gross Pay report in the Selections database, rename the copy, and add the Selections logo to the report.

1. Open the *Selections.mdb* database on your floppy disk.
2. Click the Reports button on the Objects bar.
3. Select the Gross Pay report, and choose Copy from the Edit menu.
4. Click the Paste button.
5. Type **Selections Gross Pay** as the new name for the report in the Paste As dialog box, as shown in Figure 6.36.

FIGURE 6.36

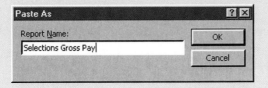

6. Click OK, and open the Selections Gross Pay report in Design view.
7. Add an image control to the Report Header section.
8. Locate the *Sm Selections Logo.gif* file on your floppy disk.

Web Tip

If you do not have a copy of this file, download it from the SELECT Web site at http://www.prenhall.com/select.

9. Click OK, as shown in Figure 6.37.

FIGURE 6.37

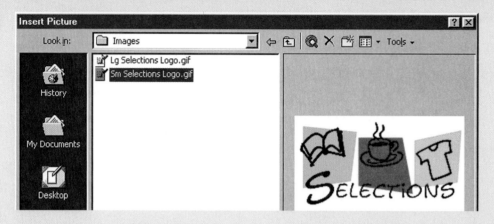

10. Change the Clip property of the image control to Stretch.

11. Reposition and resize the image control, and reposition the label control as shown in Figure 6.38.

FIGURE 6.38

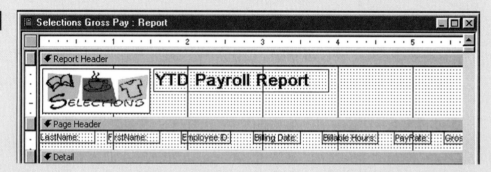

12. Save your changes.

13. Preview the report.

14. Close the report.

2. Modifying a Report's Design

The report you created in the previous exercise can still use modification. In this exercise you will add additional unbound controls to the report, modify text box properties, and change the location of some of the report's controls.

1. Open the *Selections.mdb* database file, if necessary.

2. Open the Selections Gross Pay report in Design view.

3. Using the Line tool in the Toolbox, create a line at the bottom edge of the Report Header section. Change the Border Width property of the line to 3 point.

4. Adjust the size of the Report Header section if necessary.

5. Select the label control displaying the report caption. Change the Back Color property to Gray, the Fore Color property to Blue, the Italics property to True, the Border style property to Solid, and the Font Size property to 24.

6. Select all labels appearing in the Page Header section.

7. Change the Fore Color property of the selection to Blue, and the Italics property to Yes.

8. Draw a line control at the bottom of the Page Header section, and also at the top of the Report Footer section. Change the Border Color property of both lines to blue.

9. Save your changes.

10. Preview the report, and change the zoom to 70%. Your preview should resemble Figure 6.39.

FIGURE 6.39

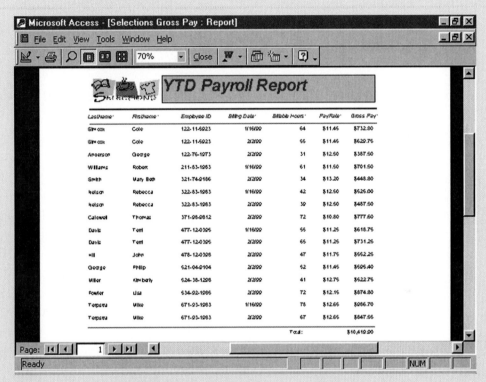

11. Close the preview and the report.

12. Close the database.

On Your Own Exercises

1. Building a Report Based upon a Query with an AND Condition

Open the Web Sites database file. Using Report Design view, create a report based upon the query displaying records meeting the AND condition you specified in Project 4. Update the database when you are finished.

2. Creating a Report Based upon a Multitable Query

Open the *Inventory.mdb* database on your floppy disk. Create a report using the Report Wizard based upon the Inventory Value query you created in Project 4. Modify the report as appropriate. Save your changes.

3. Adding Functionality to a Switchboard Form

Open the *Inventory.mdb* database. Using the Help system, determine how to add a button to the existing switchboard that will open the report you created in the previous exercise. Test the button after you create it. Save your changes.

4. Using the Office Assistant

Open the Inventory database. Choose Show the Office Assistant from the Help menu. Search the Help system for information about creating calculated controls on reports. Create a control in the report footer of the Inventory Value report that lists the total value of the inventory. Save the changes you make to the database.

5. Modifying Reports in the Contact Management Database

Open the Contact Management database you created in Project 1 and modified in Projects 2, 3, 4, and 5. Add a ClipArt image to the Contacts report using an unbound control. Save your changes.

6. Creating a Form Based upon a Multitable Query

Open the *Contact Management.mdb* database you modified in the previous exercise. Create a report based upon the multitable query you created in Project 4. Save your changes to the database.

7. Backing Up and Restoring a Database

Even database professionals can lose data! To protect your database against loss, you should periodically back it up. You can back up a database using Windows Explorer, My Computer, Microsoft Backup, the MS-DOS Copy command, or other backup software to copy the database file (an .mdb file) to a backup medium of your choice. Use one of these methods to back up any of the databases you have created. After creating your backup, make sure you can open the database copy.

If you use Microsoft Backup or a third-party backup application to create your backup, you will need to use the restore option to restore the database.

TIP Restoring a database is a Windows feature, and not specific to Access.

8. Saving Database Objects as Web Pages

In Access, you can easily create static Web pages for table, query, form, and report objects. To do so, open the specific database object and choose Export from the File menu. Then, specify HTML Documents as the file type, and follow the instructions on the screen. Note that when you use this method to create Web pages, some formatting may be lost.

Open the *Selections.mdb* database. Export a table, query, form, and report as a Web page to a folder on your floppy disk named *Web Pages*. When you are finished, view each document using a Web browser.

Integrated Project

Integrating Word, Excel, and Access

In Integrated Project 1, you learned how to share Word and Excel data using linking and embedding techniques. Many of the techniques you used to copy and paste data between Word and Excel can also be used when you want to share data between Access and Word or Excel. In addition, you'll appreciate the features built into Access that make sharing data automatic.

Objectives

After completing this project, you will be able to:

➤ Copy Excel data to an Access database

➤ Import and link an Access table to a new database

➤ Merge data from an Access database table with a Word document

➤ Merge Access data from an Access query to a Word document

Running Case

You've been identified as the person in Selections, Inc., who has the broadest background with Office 2000 applications. As a result of the fine work you did while working with the accounting and finance department on the summer sale, you've been reassigned to that department temporarily to work on another special project.

The Challenge

Ms. Joy Quinn, production/advertising manager, and Mr. Travis Taylor, accounting and finance Manager, would like to send letters of congratulation to the store managers of all regional offices for their efforts in the annual Closet Cleanout sales competition. The letter, pictured in Figure 2.1, should contain detailed sales data for each region.

FIGURE 2.1

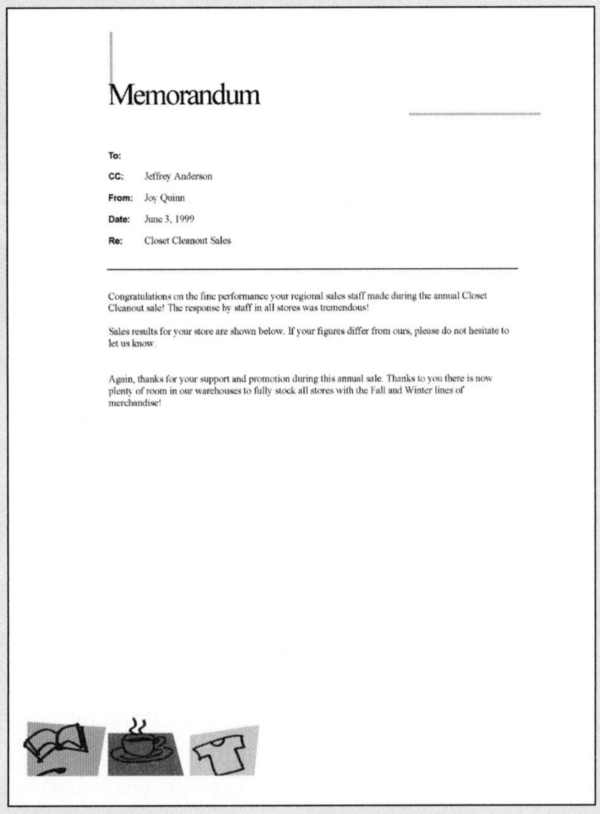

Memorandum

To:
CC: Jeffrey Anderson
From: Joy Quinn
Date: June 3, 1999
Re: Closet Cleanout Sales

Congratulations on the fine performance your regional sales staff made during the annual Closet Cleanout sale! The response by staff in all stores was tremendous!

Sales results for your store are shown below. If your figures differ from ours, please do not hesitate to let us know.

Again, thanks for your support and promotion during this annual sale. Thanks to you there is now plenty of room in our warehouses to fully stock all stores with the Fall and Winter lines of merchandise!

The Strategy

The corporate headquarters maintains a database that contains information about all manager-level personnel in each regional office and their positions within the company. The sales data is contained in an Excel workbook that you used in Integrated Project 1. You can copy the data from the workbook to create a new Access database and then copy an existing table from an Access database into the new database. When all the data is contained in the same database, you can use the same techniques you used in Integrated Project 1 to copy sales data to the appropriate letter. In addition, you can use information from the Access table to create a data source file for merging with the letter.

The Setup

To ensure that your screen will match the figures pictured in this project, make sure the settings shown in Table 2.1 are active.

Table 2.1

Location:	Make these settings:
Office Assistant	Hide the Office Assistant.
View	Click the Print Layout View button at the bottom of the Word window. Ensure that the formula bar and status bar are both displayed in the Excel window.
Toolbars	Ensure that both the Standard and Formatting toolbars are active in both application windows. If you don't see them, choose View, Toolbars, and then select them. Close all other active toolbars. Choose Tools, Customize, and then click the Options tab and ensure that the Personalized Menus and Toolbars options are all deselected. Then click the Reset my usage data button and choose Yes to restore automatic changes to menus. Choose Close.
Zoom	Set the zoom to Page Width in Word and 100% in Excel.
Ruler	Display the Ruler in Word.

Web Tip

If you do not have a copy of *Closet Cleanout Congrats.doc, Selections Quarterly Sales Figures.xls,* and *Selections Managers.mdb* on your student diskette, you can download them from the SELECT Web site at http://www.prenhall.com/select or check with your instructor to find out how to obtain a copy.

Copying Excel Data to an Access Database

You can drag data from Excel into Access using the same basic techniques you used to drag Excel data into Word. When you drag the Excel worksheet into Access, Access creates a new table using the worksheet data. Access imports the data, converting it to a format you can use to perform standard database activities.

TASK 1:   To Import Excel Data into a New Access Database

1 Launch Access and create a new blank Access database named *Closet Cleanout.mdb.* Maximize the program windows, and minimize any other open applications.

2 Launch Excel, maximize the program window, and open the *Selections Quarterly Sales Figures.xls* workbook. Only Access and Excel should be maximized at this point.

3 Click the Sheet2 tab. This sheet contains a listing of sales data for three quarters for each region.

FIGURE 2.2

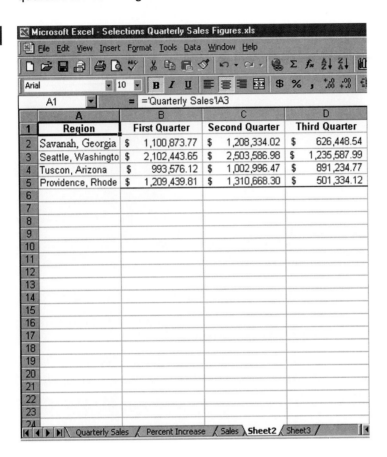

4 Right-click a blank area of the taskbar and choose Tile Windows Vertically. The Excel and Access application windows are tiled, as shown in Figure 2.3.

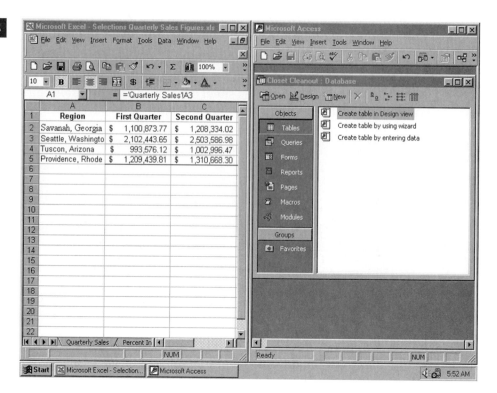

FIGURE 2.3

5 Spell check the worksheet and correct all misspelled words.

6 Select the Excel data in cells A1–D5. The selected rows are highlighted. Be sure only cells A1–D5 are selected.

7 Position the pointer on the border of the selected Excel data, press and hold (CTRL), and drag the data to the Access database window, as shown in Figure 2.4.

FIGURE 2.4

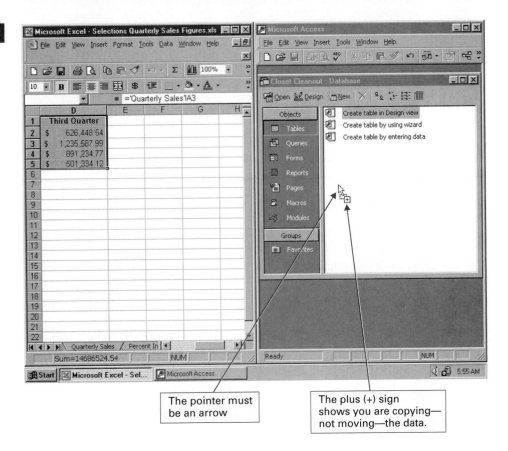

The pointer must be an arrow

The plus (+) sign shows you are copying—not moving—the data.

8 Release the mouse button and then the (CTRL) key. An Access dialog box wants to know if the first row contains headings.

FIGURE 2.5

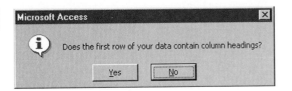

TIP Headings from the Excel worksheet become field names in the Access table.

9 Choose Yes. Access presents a message box informing you that the import was successful.

10 Click OK. Sheet2 appears in the Tables list of the new database.

11 Right-click the table name in the database window, right-click, and select Rename. Rename the table as **Quarterly Sales**.

12 Maximize Excel and then close Excel without saving. If you don't maximize Excel before exiting, it will launch in half-screen size the next time.

Check Point

If you explore the structure of the Selections Quarterly Sales workbook, you will notice that Sheet2 contains linking formulas to the first worksheet in the workbook. Thus, any changes to the sales data will automatically be reflected in the Sheet2 worksheet.

Importing and Linking an Access Table to a New Database

When tables in one database contain information you need to use in another database, you can **import** the table from one database to another. In addition, to ensure that the information is kept up to date regardless of which database is used to edit information, you can link the tables.

TASK 2: To Import and Link an Access Table to a New Database

1 In Access, choose File, Get External Data.

FIGURE 2.6

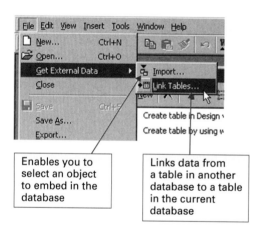

Enables you to select an object to embed in the database

Links data from a table in another database to a table in the current database

2 Choose Link Tables.

FIGURE 2.7

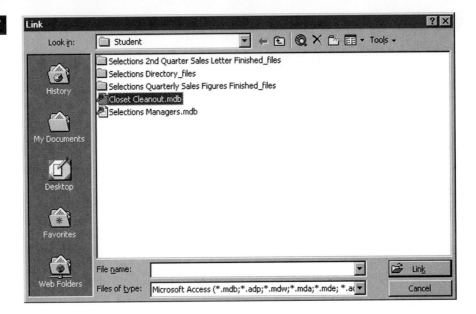

3 Select *Selections Managers.mdb* and click Link. The Link Tables dialog box displays a list of tables in the selected database.

FIGURE 2.8

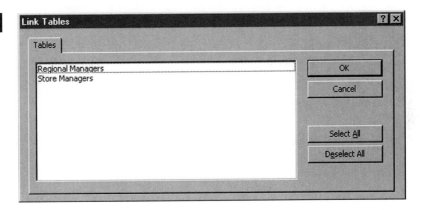

4 Select *Regional Managers* and click OK.

FIGURE 2.9

The new linked table appears in the Tables list with an arrow beside it

5 Open the *Regional Managers* table and view the contents.

6 Close the table.

Break Point

If necessary you can save your file, exit Access, and continue this project later.

Merging Data from an Access Database Table with a Word Document

Now that you have in one database all the information you need, you can complete the letters by merging names and addresses with the Word document and copying regional information to each merged letter. When you merge data from Access tables to Word documents, field names in the table are inserted into the document to tell Word where to look for the data in the Access database. The Word document to which you add merge fields is the **merge document** and the database table that contains the data and fields is the **merge data source**.

TASK 3:   To Merge Access Data with Word

1   Launch Access and open the *Closet Cleanout.mdb* database, if necessary.

2   Close all tables in the database and select the Regional Managers table in the database window, but do not open it.

3   Click the OfficeLinks 🖳 drop-down list arrow on the Database toolbar.

FIGURE 2.10

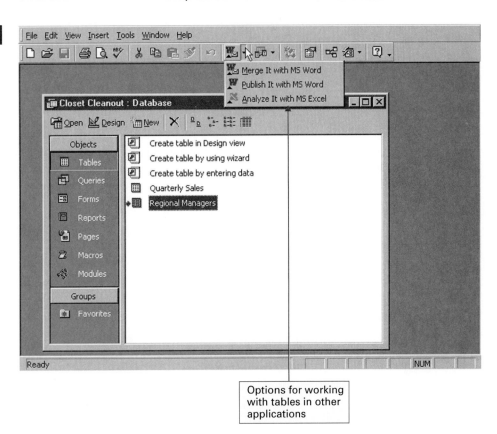

Options for working with tables in other applications

4   Select Merge It with MS Word. The Microsoft Word Mail Merge Wizard dialog box appears, as shown in Figure 2.11.

FIGURE 2.11

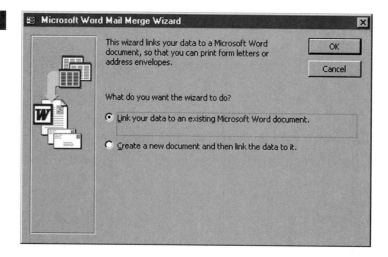

5 Choose Link your data to an existing Microsoft Word document and then choose OK. The Select Microsoft Word Document dialog box opens.

6 Open the folder containing the *Closet Cleanout Congrats.doc* and double-click the file name.

FIGURE 2.12

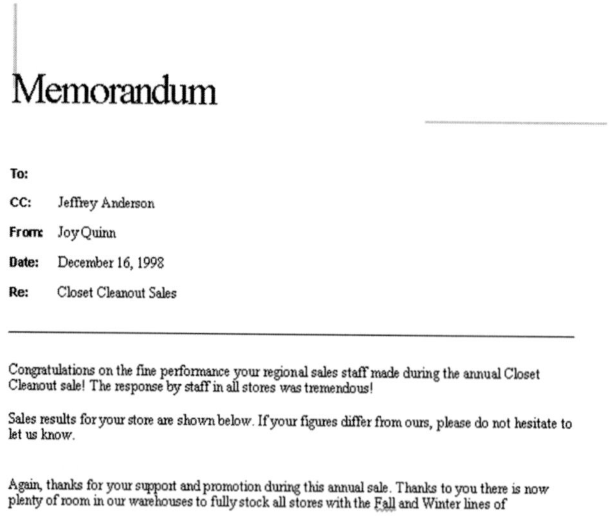

Memorandum

To:
CC: Jeffrey Anderson
From: Joy Quinn
Date: December 16, 1998
Re: Closet Cleanout Sales

Congratulations on the fine performance your regional sales staff made during the annual Closet Cleanout sale! The response by staff in all stores was tremendous!

Sales results for your store are shown below. If your figures differ from ours, please do not hesitate to let us know.

Again, thanks for your support and promotion during this annual sale. Thanks to you there is now plenty of room in our warehouses to fully stock all stores with the Fall and Winter lines of

7 Insert the two merge fields into the document, as shown in Figure 2.13.

FIGURE 2.13

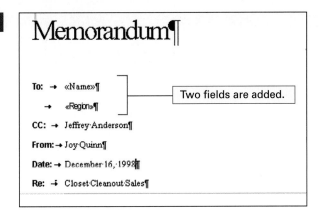

Check Point

Save the document as a new file named *Closet Cleanout Congrats Form.doc*, merge the data with the form to a new document, and review the form letters. Save the merged file using the file name *Closet Cleanout Letters Done.doc*. Close *Closet Cleanout Congrats Done.doc*.

Merging Access Data from a Query to a Word Document

You can copy data from Access to other files using the same techniques you used to copy data from Excel into a Word document. Because of the different objects and ways to view data in Access, you can also create a query and use it to merge data in a different format to Word. This makes placing region-specific data into your merged letters quick and easy.

TASK 4:   To Merge Access Records from a Query to a Word Document

1 Make Access the active window, if necessary, and create a new query based on both tables.

2 Create a relationship between the Region fields of each table in the query design window and add fields to the query, as shown in Figure 2.14.

FIGURE 2.14

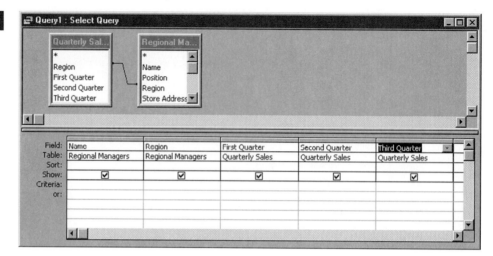

3 Save the query using the query name *Sales Merge Query*, and close the query.

4 Select (but do not open) the Sales Merge Query.

5 Click the OfficeLinks ⬛ drop-down list arrow and select Merge It with MS Word. The Microsoft Word Mail Merge Wizard dialog box opens.

6 Select Link your data to an existing Microsoft Word document and choose OK.

7 Open the folder containing *Closet Cleanout Congrats.doc*, select the document, and choose Open. Word launches, if necessary, and opens the document. The Merge toolbar appears at the top of the window and the Insert Merge Field list contains only the four fields contained in the query.

> **TROUBLESHOOTING** Be sure to open the original *Closet Cleanout Congrats.doc* rather than the *Closet Cleanout Congrats Form.doc*. If you try to open the *Closet Cleanout congrats Form.doc*, you will receive an ActiveX error message because that document is already associated with the Regional Managers table. If you saved the previous merge activity and overwrote the original *Close Cleanout Congrats.doc*, download another copy of it from the SELECT Web site at http://www.prenhall.com/select.

8 Maximize Word, create a 4 x 2 table, type the text in row 1, and linsert the merge fields in row 2, as shown in Figure 2.15.

FIGURE 2.15

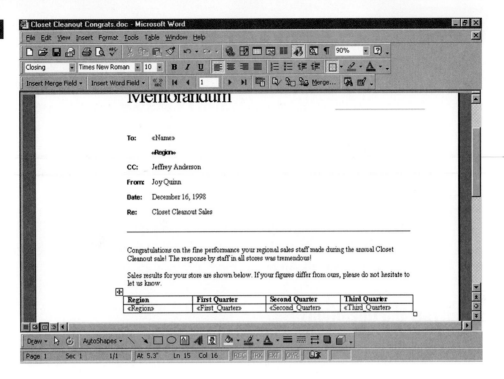

9 Save the file using the file name *Closet Cleanout Query Merge Form.doc*.

10 Merge the documents and review the results.

Check Point

Print a copy of each letter. When you're finished, close the Form Letter file without saving it, maximize both applications, and exit Access and Word.

Summary

- You can use the same techniques to drag and drop Excel worksheet data to an Access database that you used to drag worksheet data to a Word document.
- When you drag and drop data from a worksheet to a database, Access creates a new table in the active database.
- When you use data from an Access database as the merge file for a Word merge document, you have the choice of selecting an existing Word file or creating a new Word document.
- Using an Access database table as a data source automatically creates a link between the database table and the merge document.
- To use data from multiple tables in a database as a data source, you can create a query and select the query as the file to merge to Word.

Key Terms and Operations

Key Terms

import
merge data source
merge document
merge to Word

Operations

copy data from an Excel worksheet to create a new Access database table
import and link Access tables
merge Access database table and query data with a new Word document

For additional review and exercises using Word and Excel (or Word, Excel, and Access or Word, Excel, Access, and PowerPoint) visit the SELECT Lab Series Web Site at http://www.prenhall.com/select.

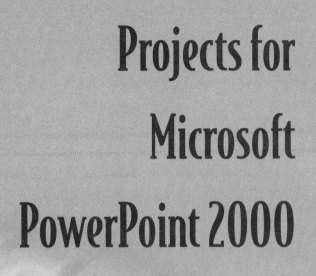

Projects for
Microsoft
PowerPoint 2000

Introducing PowerPoint 2000

Microsoft PowerPoint 2000 is a presentation graphics program that enables you to prepare slide shows and present them with style and impact. In addition, you can use PowerPoint to:

- Print handouts for the audience—and include slide miniatures and lines for notetaking on the handouts.
- Create notes for yourself to aid in your presentation delivery.
- Create an interactive presentation that runs automatically as well as a presentation containing slides timed to coincide with your talk.
- Jazz up your presentation using animation, graphics, and other multimedia components.

The term *presentation* can mean different things to different people and can vary in as many different ways as there are people to make a presentation. **Presentation** as it is used in PowerPoint means a collection of related slides that summarize key points and act as a visual aid for a written or oral report. Whether you display slides on a computer screen, project slides onto a flat surface, or print the slides for distribution, PowerPoint can help you develop your presentation.

Defining PowerPoint Terminology

To use PowerPoint effectively, you need to become familiar with the PowerPoint terminology identified in Table O.1:

Table O.1

Term	Description
Slides	Basic units of a presentation. Presentations typically consist of numerous slides. Each slide in a presentation is equivalent to a page of a document, a worksheet in a workbook, or a database record.
Placeholders	Predefined areas outlined on slides that are designed to hold slide text, bulleted lists, graphs, tables, charts, and so forth.
AutoLayouts	Preformatted layouts that contain specific object placeholders.
Masters	Layouts that contain text, bullets, alignment, header/footer text, and background format for all slides in a presentation.
Templates	Professionally developed slide designs that you can apply to presentations to give a consistent look to all slides in a presentation.

Designing a Presentation

Because PowerPoint 2000 comes with a variety of designs you can use to dress up a presentation, you can focus on the content. Careful planning will enable you to develop a presentation targeted to your audience, design a look that best conveys the purpose of the presentation, and determine the method you plan to use to deliver the presentation. Consider the following as you plan each presentation:

- *Why* are you giving the presentation? Determining the message you want to communicate and the action you want the audience to take helps ensure that the focus of the material will be on target.

- *What* materials do you want to use with the presentation? Deciding whether slides, handouts, notes, and/or overhead transparencies would be most effective makes creating all materials as you create the presentation more efficient.

- *Who* will be in the audience and how many people will attend? Categorizing the attendees as managers, corporate executives, salespeople, peers, and so forth enables you to develop a presentation geared to the proper level.

- *When* will the presentation occur? Identifying the time of day, placement of the presentation in relation to other presentations, and so on helps to determine presentation strategy and length.

- *Where* is the presentation to be given? Considering the size of the room, acoustics of the room, location of the speaker platform, and other factors helps you determine the size of slide and screen elements to include in a presentation. Keep in mind the old adage that "Less is more." Small printed characters are difficult to see from the back of the room, and information is often lost on crowded slides. Limit lists to short statements rather than complete sentences, make the font larger, and keep graphics and other components simple.

- *How* does the method you use to deliver the presentation affect presentation design? Adding color to slides can be more effective in on-screen presentations, while color used for handouts and transparencies might be too dark.

After you have considered each of these questions and outlined your presentation, you're ready to launch PowerPoint and put it to work for you.

Web Tip

Search the Internet using the term *presentations* as the search topic. You'll find lots of good ideas for developing dynamic presentations!

Launching PowerPoint 2000

After powering up your computer, logging onto required networks, and responding to messages built into your computer system, Windows starts automatically. Basically, you can launch PowerPoint 2000 using the same techniques you use to launch other programs. However, because of the sophisticated nature of PowerPoint, you have to make some decisions about how you want to develop your presentation before the full PowerPoint 2000 window appears.

TASK 1: To Launch PowerPoint 2000

1 Choose Start, Programs, PowerPoint.

FIGURE O.1

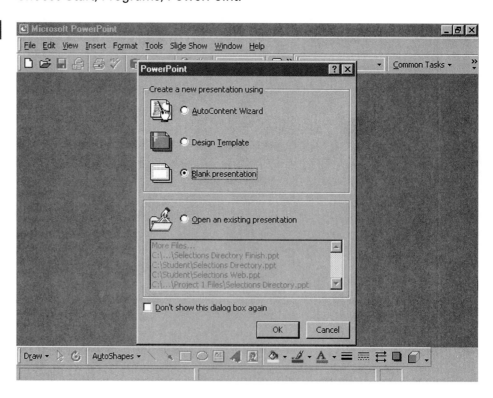

> **TROUBLESHOOTING** Selecting the Don't show this dialog box again checkbox at the bottom of the dialog box bypasses this dialog box. If a person who used the computer previously checked this option, the dialog box will not appear. To turn on the option, choose Tools, Options, and check the Startup dialog option on the View page.

Creating a New Presentation

The PowerPoint dialog box offers different methods you can use to create your presentation, as described in Table O.2.

Table O.2

Option	Description
AutoContent Wizard	Creates a presentation based on choices you select from options the wizard presents. The wizard formats slides and enters instructional presentation content based on the type of presentation you select. You then replace the instructional and informative text with the text you want to include on each slide.
Design Template	Formats a presentation based on a professionally designed "theme." Each template contains background color, text format, and graphics for the slides. You then build the presentation from scratch by adding text and other objects to slides in the presentation.
Blank presentation	Creates a plain presentation that formats slides with placeholders only. You can then add color, format text, and create objects manually.

TASK 2:   To Create a New Presentation

1   From the PowerPoint dialog box, choose Blank Presentation and choose OK.

FIGURE O.2

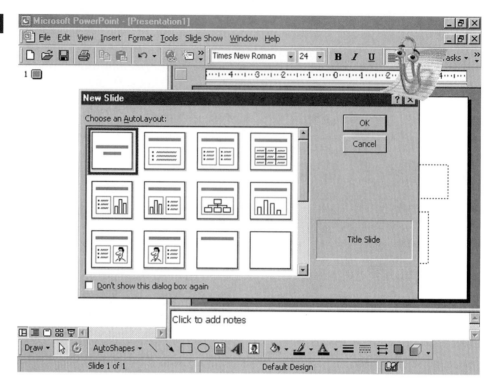

The AutoLayout slide formats contain placeholders for different types of objects that you might want to include on a slide. By default, the Title Slide AutoLayout format is selected for the first slide of each new presentation. The name of the AutoLayout format, *Title Slide*, appears at the right of the New Slide dialog box.

2 Choose OK.

While many PowerPoint 2000 features are similar to features found in other Office 2000 programs, PowerPoint contains a number of unique features. Table O.3 describes the features in Figure O.3.

FIGURE O.3

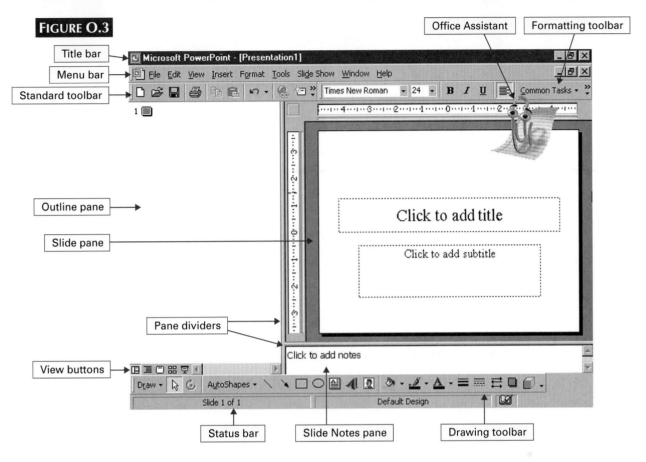

Table O.3

Screen Feature	Description
Title bar	Identifies the application name and the name of the active presentation. The presentation name is generic until it is saved, and then the filename you assign appears in the title bar. The application icon appears at the left end of the title bar, and the Maximize/Restore, Minimize, and Close buttons appear at the right end of the title bar.
Menu bar	Groups by type the most frequently used commands for completing PowerPoint 2000 tasks.
Standard toolbar	Contains buttons that serve as shortcuts for performing common menu commands, displaying special toolbars, and changing screen features. Toolbar buttons change as you access different features.
Formatting toolbar	Appears at the right end of the Standard toolbar and displays buttons and list boxes to access the most frequently used formatting commands. Buttons on this toolbar change as different formatting commands are used.
Office Assistant	Displays tips as you work and answers your questions about the program.
Status bar	Displays information about the program status, instructions for performing selected tasks, active key information, functions of toolbar buttons, trouble messages, active templates, active slide number, and so forth.

Table O.3 (continued)

Screen Feature	Description
Drawing toolbar	Displays tools for creating and formatting drawn objects.
Outline pane	Presents slide text added to text placeholders in an outline structure. You can use Outline view to create new slides, add and edit text in slide placeholders, and rearrange slides without graphic objects getting in the way.
Slide pane	Displays all slide text, formatting, graphics, charts, and other objects as they appear on a slide. Slide view lets you create and edit slides and enhance slides by adding slide objects, such as drawings, tables, charts, and other visuals.
Slide Notes pane	Provides space to type notes about the active slide and supportive information to use during presentation delivery.
Normal View button	Displays the default tri-pane window.
Outline View button	Enlarges the Outline pane and reduces the size of the Slide pane and slide notes.
Slide View button	Enlarges the Slide pane and reduces the Outline pane and Slide notes pane.
Slide Sorter View button	Displays thumbnail images of multiple slides on-screen at the same time. Slide Sorter view makes rearranging slides more efficient and displays tools for enhancing the presentation. Editing slides is restricted in this view.
Slide Show button	Displays slides using the full screen and hides the title bar, menus, toolbars and other presentation development tools.
Pane dividers	Separate the three sections of the PowerPoint Normal view window. Panes can be sized by positioning the mouse pointer on the divider and dragging the divider to create panes the desired sizes.

Summary and Exercises

Summary

- Microsoft PowerPoint is a presentation graphics program designed to prepare slide shows.
- Presentations may include handouts, slides, speaker notes, and outlines.
- Presentations can be created using an AutoContent Wizard, a Design Template, or a blank presentation.
- Each presentation may contain numerous slides, each designed to focus on a particular aspect of the broad presentation theme.
- PowerPoint displays presentations in five different views: Normal view, Outline view, Slide view, Slide Sorter view, and Notes Pages view (available on the View menu). Each view is designed to help you accomplish specific tasks.
- Toolbars containing tools needed to accomplish specific tasks appear automatically.

Key Terms and Operations

Key Terms

AutoContent Wizard	placeholder
AutoLayout	presentation
Drawing toolbar	slide
Formatting toolbar	Standard toolbar
master	status bar
menu bar	template
Office Assistant	title bar

Operations

launch Microsoft PowerPoint
create a blank PowerPoint presentation
exit Microsoft PowerPoint

Study Questions

Multiple Choice

1. A collection of related slides that summarize key points and act as a visual aid for a report is called a
    a. summary report.
    b. presentation.
    c. placeholder.
    d. template.

2. To launch PowerPoint,
    a. double-click the Outlook icon.
    b. open My Computer.
    c. start Office 2000 and press (ALT) + W.
    d. choose Start, Programs, PowerPoint.

3. The PowerPoint view that displays small slide images of all slides in a presentation is the
    a. Slide view.
    b. Outline view.
    c. Slide Sorter view.
    d. Notes Pages view.

4. The PowerPoint view that makes rearranging slides easier is
    a. Slide view.
    b. Outline view.
    c. Slide Sorter view.
    d. Notes Pages view.

5. The term that refers to the layout of objects on slides is
    a. AutoLayout.
    b. Master.
    c. Template.
    d. Slide.

6. Most slides contain
    a. slide tables.
    b. pictures.
    c. slide titles.
    d. slide names.

7. Slide Sorter view displays
    a. all slide objects.
    b. the slide title and body text only.
    c. small slide images.
    d. slide images and notes about the slide.

8. Slide view displays
    a. all slide objects.
    b. the slide title and body text only.
    c. small slide images.
    d. slide images and notes about the slide.

Short Answer

1. What is the difference between the Standard toolbar and the title bar?

2. What supporting materials can you generate from a presentation?

3. How many views are available in PowerPoint?

4. What are AutoLayouts?

5. What six things should you consider as you plan your presentation?

Fill in the Blank

1. Checking the _____ will bypass the selection of methods you can use to create a new presentation when you launch PowerPoint.

2. PowerPoint can be used to generate slides, handouts, _____, and notes pages.

3. The PowerPoint view that displays only title and body placeholder text is _____ view.

4. Professional designs that contain graphics and background color schemes you can use to dress up a presentation are called _____.

5. The _____ is the basic unit of a presentation.

For Discussion

1. Why is planning your presentation important?

2. What is the difference between AutoLayout formats, templates, and masters?

3. What are the four options in the PowerPoint dialog box that appears when you launch PowerPoint and what does each option enable you to do?

Creating Presentations

PowerPoint provides a variety of approaches for creating presentations. Regardless of which technique you choose for creating a presentation, the procedures for adding text to slide placeholders, creating new slides, and proofing and printing slides are the same. In this project, you create several new presentations, add text to the presentations, and save and print presentations.

Objectives

After completing this project, you will be able to:

➤ Create blank presentations

➤ Add text to slide placeholders

➤ Add slides to presentations

➤ Add text to outlines and slide notes

➤ Navigate presentations

➤ Proof presentations

➤ Create presentations using Wizards

➤ Set up pages and print presentation materials

Running Case

Selections, Inc., administrative personnel have identified two projects for which they need a temporary staff assistant. Because of your unique artistic ability, you have been temporarily assigned to the administrative offices of Selections, Inc., as a graphic artist. After accepting the position, you realize that both of the primary projects you have been hired to complete require the use of PowerPoint 2000. It's time to start learning something about PowerPoint . . .

The Challenge

Administrative personnel at Selections, Inc., have assigned you two projects: to create a presentation about Selections, Inc., departments and to design and create a PowerPoint presentation about Selections, Inc., that is suitable for display on the World Wide Web.

The Strategy

The first project, creating a directory of Selections, Inc., departments, seems the easier of the two projects to complete. All you have to do is obtain a listing of items found in each department and put your creative talents to work to design the directory so that it is user friendly. When you're finished with the first three slides, you can have them reviewed and then use PowerPoint's AutoContent Wizard to design the home page. The first three slides of the directory presentation and the first slide of the home page are shown in Figure 1.1.

FIGURE 1.1

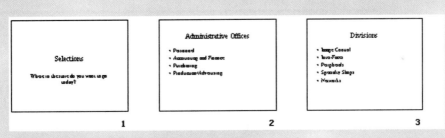

 Web Tip

You can obtain the Selections, Inc., corporate structure from the SELECT Web site at http://www.prenhall.com/select.

The Setup

To ensure that your screen looks like those pictured in this project, you need to check some of the settings.

Table 1.1

Item	Action
Office Assistant	Hide the Assistant
Toolbars	Reset default toolbars by choosing Tools, Customize, and then display the Toolbars page of the dialog box. Check the Standard, Formatting, and Drawing toolbars, and the menu bar. Select each of these items individually and choose Reset. Choose OK to confirm each change. Click the Options tab and ensure that Personalized Menus and Toolbars options are all deselected. Then click the Reset my usage data button and choose Yes to restore automatic changes to menus. When all toolbars and the menu bar have been reset, choose Close.
View	Click the Normal View button at the bottom of the presentation window to display the tri-pane window.

Creating Blank Presentations

Each time you launch PowerPoint, the PowerPoint dialog box presents methods you can use to create new presentations. These procedures were discussed in "Introducing PowerPoint 2000."

 Web Tip

Need some free tips and hints for creating business presentations? Connect to http://www.cusp.com.

 TASK 1: **To Create a Blank Presentation with a Title Slide**

1 Launch PowerPoint 2000, if necessary. The PowerPoint dialog box presents methods for creating new presentations.

> **TIP** If PowerPoint is already running, click the New ⬜ button on the Standard toolbar and skip step 2. PowerPoint automatically creates a blank presentation.

2 Choose Blank presentation from the PowerPoint dialog box and then choose OK. The New Slide dialog box presents AutoLayout formats with the Title Slide AutoLayout format active.

3 Choose OK. The new presentation appears in the PowerPoint window in Normal view.

Adding Text to Slide Placeholders

The title slide appears in the Slide pane of the Normal view window and contains two placeholders that contain instructions for adding text. Text you type in the placeholders automatically appears in the Outline pane of the PowerPoint window.

TASK 2:   To Add Text to Slide Placeholders

1 Click the title placeholder. The insertion point replaces instruction text in the placeholder, as shown in Figure 1.2.

FIGURE 1.2

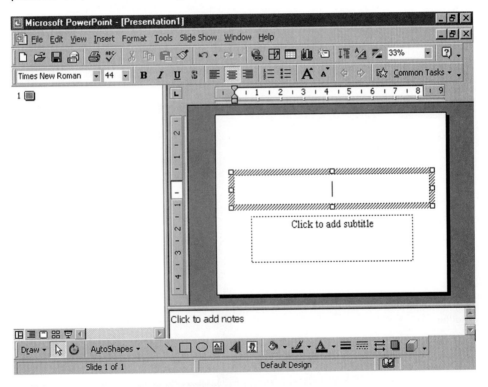

TIP Text automatically appears in the first placeholder on the slide if you start typing without clicking a placeholder.

2 Type **Selections**.

FIGURE 1.3

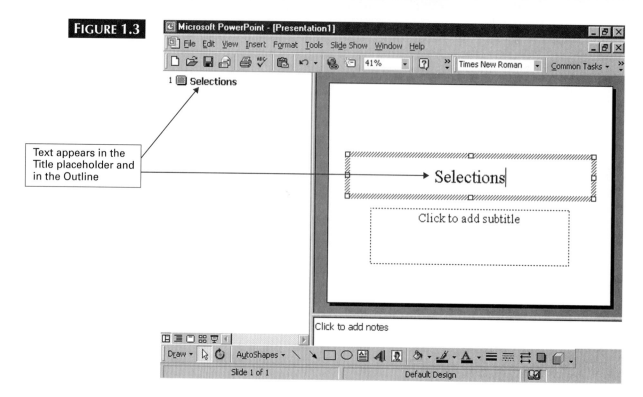

Text appears in the Title placeholder and in the Outline

3 Press (CTRL) + (ENTER). The subtitle placeholder is active and the insertion point replaces instruction text in the placeholder.

4 Type **Where in the store do you want to go today?**

FIGURE 1.4

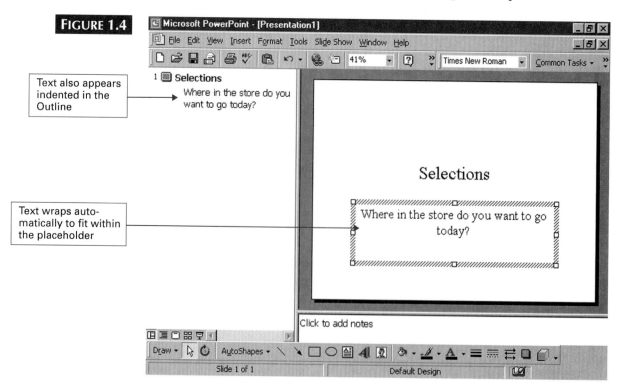

Text also appears indented in the Outline

Text wraps automatically to fit within the placeholder

TROUBLESHOOTING A tip light bulb may appear when you type the question mark at the end of the subtitle placeholder. PowerPoint checks the format of text you add to slides as you work. When it finds inconsistencies in the default end punctuation settings, it notifies you by placing a light bulb on-screen. You'll learn to change the style settings later in this project.

Adding Slides to Presentations

Most presentations consist of a series of slides, each devoted to a particular topic you want to cover in the presentation. Behind each title slide, you often need to add slides to provide explanatory information about the topic or supporting documentation. Slides you add to a presentation follow the active slide. PowerPoint provides four different ways to add a slide:

- Click the New Slide 🖾 button on the Standard toolbar.
- Choose Insert, New Slide from the menus.
- Press (CTRL) + M.
- Press (CTRL) + (ENTER) from the last placeholder on the active slide to create a new Bulleted List slide.

TASK 3:   To Add Slides to Presentations

1   Click the New Slide 🖾 button on the Standard toolbar. The Active AutoLayout format is identified, as shown in Figure 1.5.

FIGURE 1.5

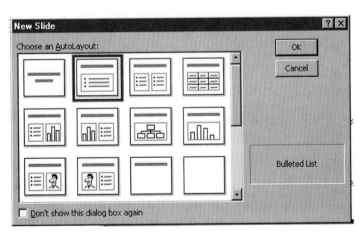

2   Choose OK.

FIGURE 1.6

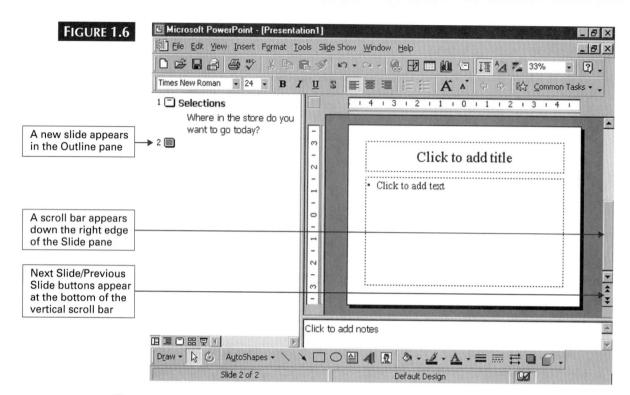

A new slide appears in the Outline pane

A scroll bar appears down the right edge of the Slide pane

Next Slide/Previous Slide buttons appear at the bottom of the vertical scroll bar

3 Type **Administrative Offices** in the title placeholder. The title appears in the slide placeholder and in the outline.

4 Press (CTRL) + (ENTER). The text placeholder is active.

5 Type **Personnel.** and press (ENTER). The first bulleted item is complete and a new bullet appears.

6 Type the following text to create three additional bulleted items:
- **Accounting and Finance**
- **Purchasing**
- **Production/Advertising**

TROUBLESHOOTING PowerPoint may be set to automatically check bulleted list items for consistent use of end punctuation. When inconsistencies are found, a light bulb appears on-screen. You'll learn how to correct this later in this project.

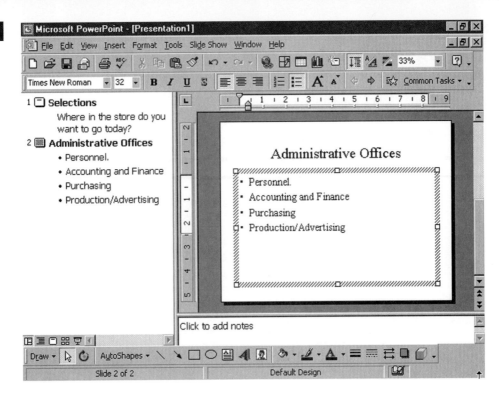

FIGURE 1.7

 Check Point

Do you remember how to save files? Well, it's time to save your presentation before continuing. Choose File, Save to open the Save dialog box. Don't forget to open the folder identified by your instructor. Name the presentation *Selections Directory.ppt* and add the file designator (for example, your initials) identified by your instructor.

Adding Text to Outlines and Slide Notes

So far, you have typed text into text placeholders directly on the slide in the Slide pane. You can also type text in the Outline pane of the window when you want to create a series of bulleted list slides. In addition, you can type information about the active presentation slide in the Slide Notes pane of the window and use the notes as you deliver your oral presentation.

> **TIP** Slide notes are used during an oral presentation to remind you of important information you want to be sure to tell the audience. Audience handouts are printed copies of your presentation in a format your audience can use. Audience handouts do NOT contain your slide notes.

When you work in the Outline pane, you can easily promote and demote text using both the keyboard and mouse. Promoting items moves them from bullet points to slide titles or higher-level bullet points. Demoting items moves them from slide titles to bullet points or to lower-level bullet points.

TASK 4: To Add Text to Outlines and Slide Notes

1 Click the Outline pane below the existing text. The insertion point appears at the end of the word *Advertising* in Slide 2.

2 Press (CTRL) + (ENTER). Slide 3 appears in the Outline pane and a new bulleted list slide appears in the Slide pane. Slide 3 is now active in the outline.

> **TIP** Pressing (CTRL) + (ENTER) in the last placeholder on a slide or after the last bulleted list item in the outline automatically creates a new bulleted list slide.

3 Type **Divisions** as the title of Slide 3 and then press (ENTER). The title appears beside the Slide 3 icon in the outline and in the title placeholder of the slide as you type. Slide 4 appears in both the Outline and Slide panes after you press (ENTER).

4 Press (TAB) to demote the new slide to a bullet point for Slide 3. Slide 3 appears in the Slide pane and a new bullet for Slide 3 replaces the Slide 4 icon in the outline.

5 Type the following bulleted items for Slide 3:
- **Image Control**
- **Inter-Faces**
- **Peripherals**
- **Specialty Shops**
- **Net-Works**

6 Click the Slide Notes pane of the presentation window. Notes you add at this time apply to the active slide.

7 Type **Link to appropriate division location and page.**

8 Click the Peripherals bullet point in the Outline pane and then click the Promote ◄ button on the Formatting toolbar. Peripherals becomes the title of Slide 4 with Specialty Shops and Networks as bullets of the new slide.

9 Click the Demote {demote.tif} button on the Formatting toolbar. Peripherals becomes a bullet point again.

10 Click the Peripherals bullet point in the Slide pane and press (TAB). Peripherals is demoted to a second-level bullet point.

11 Press (SHIFT) + (TAB) to promote Peripherals to a first-level bullet point again.

FIGURE 1.8

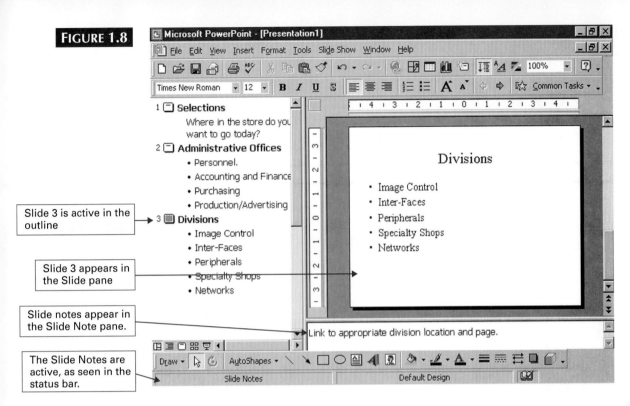

Slide 3 is active in the outline

Slide 3 appears in the Slide pane

Slide notes appear in the Slide Note pane.

The Slide Notes are active, as seen in the status bar.

12 Click 🖫 to save changes to your presentation.

Check Point

Do you remember the quick and easy way to automatically create a new bulleted list slide in the Outline pane? If not, review the tip presented earlier in this project and then create a new bulleted list slide. You'll use the slide to add additional information to the presentation later in the project.

Break Point

If you do not have time to complete this project, save the presentation and then close it. Then exit PowerPoint and log off the network, if necessary.

Navigating Presentations

You've already discovered that the status bar displays the active pane as well as the slide number when the Slide pane is active. As you build your presentation and your presentation grows, navigating slides in the presentation becomes important. Using a variety of keyboard and mouse navigation techniques, you can display different slides in the presentation for editing or review.

TASK 5: <u>To Navigate Presentation Slides</u>

1 Position the insertion point in the title of Slide 2 in the Outline pane to display Slide 2 in the Slide pane.

2 Click the slide in the Slide pane. "Slide 2 of 4" appears in the status bar.

3 Press (PGDN) to display Slide 3.

4 Press (CTRL) + (HOME) to display Slide 1.

5 Click the Next Slide ⬇ button at the bottom of the vertical scroll bar in the Slide pane to display Slide 2.

6 Drag the scroll box in the vertical scroll bar to the bottom of the scroll bar to display Slide 4. As you drag the scroll box, the slide number, total number of slides in the presentation, and slide titles appear as screen tips to help you identify the active slide.

Check Point

Spell-checking presentations requires the same techniques used to spell-check documents. Click the Spelling and Grammar ABC button on the Standard toolbar to spell-check your presentation before continuing and correct any misspelled words. (See *Common Elements* CE-34-35 to review the Spell Check feature in more detail.)

Proofing Presentations

Proofing tools in PowerPoint not only include the spelling checker and the Find and Replace features. They also include a feature that enables you to quickly and efficiently proof your presentation for consistency of **style**. Using the style checker, you can check placeholder text for consistency in end punctuation and capitalization, and check spelling at the same time. **Visual Clarity** options help you ensure that presentation information is easily seen and read for the way you plan to present it.

TASK 6: <u>To Check Presentation Style</u>

1 Click the title of Slide 1 in the Outline pane. You can start the style checker on any slide; starting with Slide 1 simply ensures that your screen will match the figures shown here.

2 Choose Tools, Options, and then click the Spelling and Style tab.

FIGURE 1.9

Checks indicate active features

Make sure **Check style** is active.

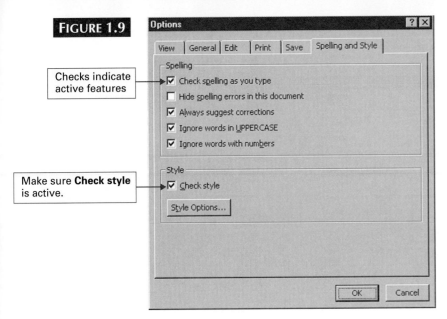

3 Click Style Options.

FIGURE 1.10

Case default options are active

End punctuation features

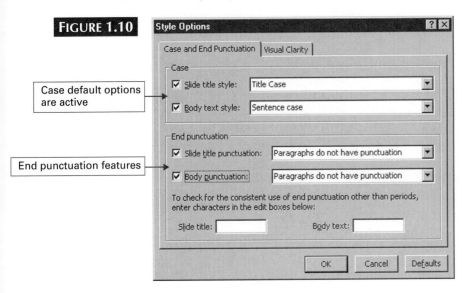

4 Ensure that the Slide title punctuation and Body punctuation checkboxes have been checked.

5 Select Paragraphs do not have punctuation from the Slide title punctuation and Body punctuation drop-down lists.

6 Click the Visual Clarity tab and review the options to ensure that your settings match those shown in Figure 1.11.

FIGURE 1.11

All options are active →

Default settings are identified to maximize visual clarity.

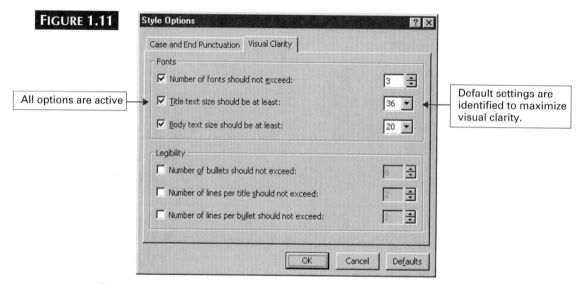

7 Choose OK twice. After activating end punctuation checking, tip light bulbs may appear on additional slides that do not conform to active settings.

8 Display Slide 2 and click the light bulb.

FIGURE 1.12

The Office Assistant appears with a list of options for correcting the first inconsistency.

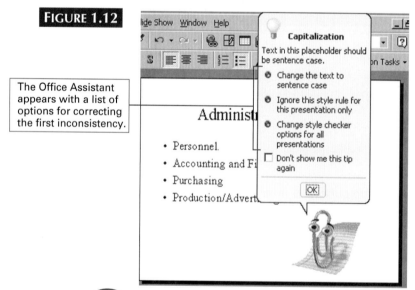

9 Choose Ignore this style rule for this presentation only. Another tip light bulb appears.

10 Click the light bulb and choose Remove end punctuation.

11 Display Slide 1 and leave the presentation open.

Creating Presentations Using Wizards

The PowerPoint AutoContent Wizard helps you build generic outlines for specific types of presentations based on information that you provide. The wizard enables you to choose the type of presentation you want to create and presents a series of dialog boxes that contain options for you to choose. After the outline is complete, you can substitute more specific text for the generic text the wizard provides. The AutoContent wizard will help you develop a scheme for your Selections, Inc., home page on the World Wide Web.

TASK 7: <u>To Create a Presentation Using a Wizard</u>

1 Choose File, New.

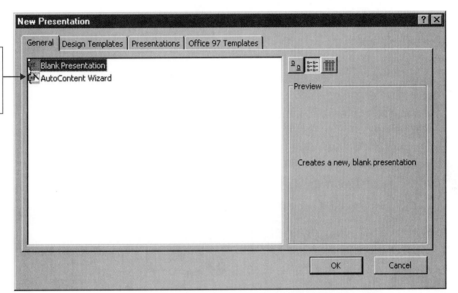

FIGURE 1.13

AutoContent Wizard is available on the General page of the New Presentation dialog box.

TIP If you're just launching PowerPoint and want to create a new presentation using a wizard, you can select the AutoContent Wizard right from the PowerPoint dialog box and choose OK. The AutoContent Wizard dialog box shown in Figure 1.14 appears. Start with step 3—you'll see the same screens from there on.

2 Double-click AutoContent Wizard.

FIGURE 1.14

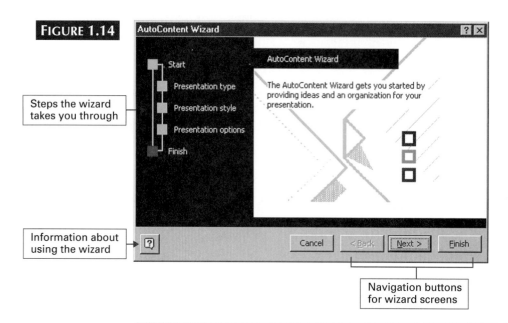

Steps the wizard takes you through

Information about using the wizard

Navigation buttons for wizard screens

TROUBLESHOOTING The Office Assistant may pop up and ask if you want help. Just select No, don't provide help now.

3 Click Next.

FIGURE 1.15

Presentations are grouped by type.

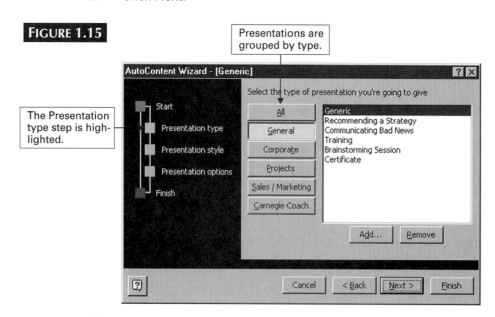

The Presentation type step is highlighted.

4 Click the Corporate button. A list of corporate presentation types appears.

5 Click Group Home Page and then click Next.

FIGURE 1.16

Output options identify the medium you plan to use to deliver the presentation.

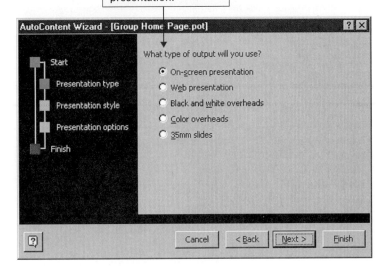

6 Click Next to accept the on-screen presentation output.

FIGURE 1.17

You can type in your title and footer information.

The Presentation options step is high-lighted.

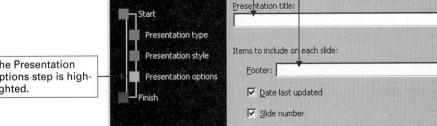

7 Type **Selections, Inc.** in the Presentation title text box, and then type **All rights reserved.** in the Footer text box; click Next. The last screen the wizard presents instructs you to click Finish to view the document. If you need to make changes to previous Wizard screens, click the Back button until the screen appears, make the changes, and then click Finish from any screen.

FIGURE 1.18

The presentation is formatted with an appropriate template

PowerPoint automatically adds the user name to the title slide

The outline identifies topics you can develop to complete the presentation before sending it to the Web

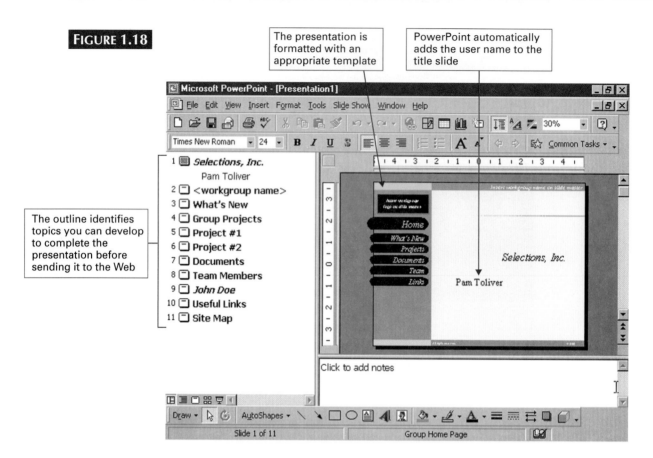

8 Click Finish.

9 Save the presentation using the filename *Selections Web.ppt*.

Setting Up Pages and Distributing Presentation Materials

Because PowerPoint is primarily a graphically oriented program, you can set up and distribute presentation materials in a variety of formats. As a result, it is important to set up the page format and paper size before printing your presentation materials or preparing them for service bureaus.

Setting Up Pages

Most presentation materials can be printed on a variety of different paper sizes using either *portrait* or *landscape orientation*. The Page Setup command on the File menu enables you to set the paper size and orientation for the particular material you are printing—slides, handouts, or slide notes. PowerPoint has a single-page dialog box with separate controls for orienting different materials.

TASK 8:   To Change Paper Size and Orientation

1 Choose File, Page Setup.

FIGURE 1.19

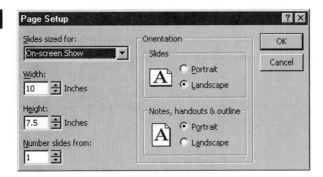

2 Select Letter Paper (8.5x11 in) from the Slides sized for drop-down list. The Width and Height settings change to the new paper size.

3 Choose OK and save changes to the presentation.

Distributing Presentation Materials

Presentations can be prepared for distribution in a variety of ways. You can:

- Send the presentation to Genigraphics or another service bureau so that the service bureau can prepare overhead transparencies or 35 mm slides. Choose File, Send to, Genigraphics and follow the Wizard instructions to create special output. Be sure to contact the service bureau before initiating this command to see if the bureau you're using has any special requirements.

- E-mail the presentation to a business, colleague, or friend for review. Choose File, Send to, Mail Recipient [or Mail Recipient (as Attachment)] and then address the e-mail message and type an appropriate subject and message.

- Print the presentation and presentation materials. Choose File, Print to display the Print dialog box.

The Print dialog box contains features and options unique to PowerPoint. For example, you can print each slide individually on a sheet of paper or transparency film, multiple slides on the same page in a format called **handouts**, or print the Outline view of your presentation. Figure 1.20 identifies additional print options that you can set to control the quality of the print for different types of printers.

FIGURE 1.20

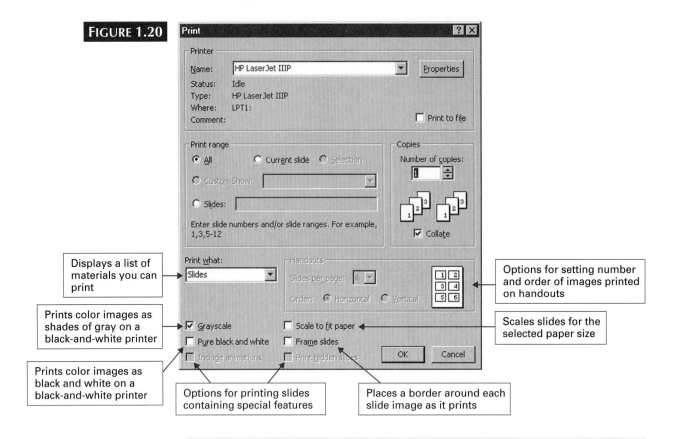

Displays a list of materials you can print

Prints color images as shades of gray on a black-and-white printer

Prints color images as black and white on a black-and-white printer

Options for setting number and order of images printed on handouts

Scales slides for the selected paper size

Options for printing slides containing special features

Places a border around each slide image as it prints

TIP To print your presentation slides on transparency film using a black and white printer, check the Grayscale or Pure black and white option. Your transparencies will be crisp and clear when you display them using an overhead projector. Also be sure you have transparency film sheets that are safe to use on your printer before you print.

TASK 9: To Print Presentation Materials

1 Choose the Window menu and select the *Selections Directory.ppt* presentation.

2 Choose File, Print. The Print dialog box shown in Figure 1.20 appears.

3 Click the Print what drop-down list arrow.

FIGURE 1.21

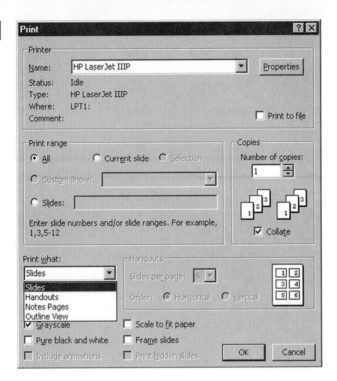

4 Select Handouts. The previously dimmed Handouts options are now available and the Frame slides option is checked.

5 Click the Slides per page drop-down list arrow and select 3.

6 Click the Slides option in the Print range area and type **1-3** in the Slides textbox.

7 Choose OK. All three slide images print on one page, with lines on the side for note-taking.

> **TROUBLESHOOTING** If the Office Assistant offers a tip, just choose OK to ignore it and continue.

8 Choose File, Print. The Print dialog box opens and displays the settings last used.

> **TROUBLESHOOTING** Each time you launch PowerPoint, the print settings return to the default settings.

9 Choose Outline View from the Print what drop-down list and leave other settings as entered.

10 Choose OK. The portion of the outline that was last displayed prints.

> **TIP** To change the part of the outline that prints, switch to Outline view and expand and collapse slide text until the text you want to print is displayed.

Summary and Exercises

Summary

- PowerPoint enables you to create blank presentations formatted with no special design as well as presentations formatted using special designs called templates.

- AutoLayout formats make creating slides with preformatted text easier.

- You can add, delete, format, and select presentation text using many of the same techniques used in other Office 2000 applications.

- Presentations normally contain numerous slides; you can add slides and move from slide to slide using a variety of different mouse and keyboard techniques.

- You can save, open, close, and print presentations using many of the same procedures used in other Office 2000 applications; you can print a variety of different presentation materials by selecting the desired format from the Print dialog box.

Key Terms

handouts
landscape
orientation
portrait
Style
Visual Clarity

Study Questions

Multiple Choice

1. To create a new, blank presentation,
   a. launch PowerPoint—a new presentation automatically appears.
   b. choose New Presentation from the PowerPoint dialog box.
   c. select Blank presentation from the PowerPoint dialog box and press (ENTER).
   d. select Template from the PowerPoint dialog box and press (ENTER).

2. Slides added to a presentation are formatted using
   a. an AutoLayout format.
   b. text and title boxes.
   c. blank slides that resemble blank pieces of paper.
   d. outlines.

3. New slide layouts contain
   a. fields.
   b. placeholders.
   c. tables.
   d. templates.

4. Placeholders identify
   a. slide names.
   b. slide fields.
   c. slide titles.
   d. slide objects.

5. To add a new slide to a presentation, use any of the following techniques except
   a. double-clicking the active slide.
   b. clicking the New Slide button on the toolbar.
   c. pressing (CTRL) + M.
   d. choosing Insert, New Slide from the menu.

6. Outline view displays
   a. all slide objects.
   b. the slide title and body text only.
   c. small slide images.
   d. slide images and notes about the slide.

7. Normal view displays
   a. all slide objects.
   b. the slide title and body text only.
   c. small slide images.
   d. slide images, notes about the slide, and an outline.

Short Answer

1. How do you create a new presentation if PowerPoint is already running?

2. What's a template?

3. What are AutoLayout formats and what do they contain?

4. What are the panes of the Normal view and when should you use each pane?

5. How do you switch from one pane to the next?

6. How do you print handouts?

7. How can you use the vertical scroll bar to display a specific slide?

8. How do you move from one placeholder on a slide to another without using the mouse?

Fill in the Blank

1. PowerPoint provides a variety of approaches for creating _____.

2. After you select the toolbars you want to use in your presentation, you should select the _____ button before clicking OK.

3. The _____ button is selected to view the tri-pane window.

4. The dialog box that presents AutoLayout formats is the _____ dialog box.

5. The title slide contains two _____ that contain instructions for adding text.

6. The _____ replaces instruction text in a placeholder when you begin typing.

7. To list a number of key points on a single slide, select the _____ slide AutoLayout.

8. You can type text in the _____ pane of a window when you want to create a series of bulleted list slides.

9. As you build your presentation and it grows, _____ slides becomes important.

10. To spell-check, find, search for, and replace words and check your presentation for consistency of style, _____ tools are used.

For Discussion

1. How do you identify the material you want to print, and what options should you check if you're using a black-and-white printer?

2. What are the advantages of formatting a presentation by using the AutoContent Wizard?

3. What kind of presentations could you create with PowerPoint for your other classes?

4. Name a situation in which you might want to use each: AutoContent Wizard, Design Template, and Blank presentation.

5. How do you check the presentation style to ensure consistency of the presentation?

Hands-On Exercises

1. Creating, Proofing, Saving, and Adding Slides and Text to a Presentation

The mall in which the Selections, Inc., store in Omaha, Nebraska, is located has a number of annual events that it likes to advertise to draw customers into the stores. This year Selections, Inc., has been "selected" to develop a series of advertisements to appear in the local newspaper. You've been assigned the task of developing this series of advertisements and have decided to use PowerPoint to create a slide for each of the four events and see what the mall administrative officers think about your approach. You'll add the dates and dress up the slides later! Figure 1.22 shows the information to be included on each of the four slides in the presentation:

FIGURE 1.22

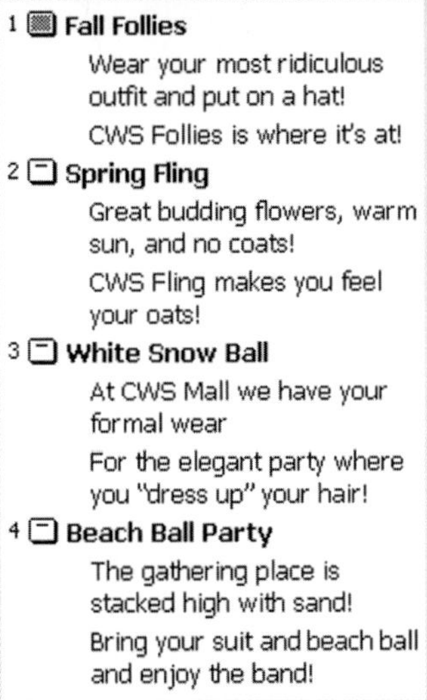

1 🔲 **Fall Follies**

Wear your most ridiculous
outfit and put on a hat!

CWS Follies is where it's at!

2 🔲 **Spring Fling**

Great budding flowers, warm
sun, and no coats!

CWS Fling makes you feel
your oats!

3 🔲 **White Snow Ball**

At CWS Mall we have your
formal wear

For the elegant party where
you "dress up" your hair!

4 🔲 **Beach Ball Party**

The gathering place is
stacked high with sand!

Bring your suit and beach ball
and enjoy the band!

Using PowerPoint, create a new blank presentation. Follow these instructions to complete the presentation:

1. Launch PowerPoint and create a new blank presentation that contains a title slide.

2. Click in the Outline pane and add the text shown in Figure 1.22.

3. Spell-check the document.

4. Click the slide icon beside Slide 2 in the Outline pane and choose Format, Slide Layout. When the Slide Layout dialog box opens, select the Title Slide AutoLayout format. Repeat this procedure to format Slides 3 and 4 as title slides.

5. Save the presentation using the file name *CWS Mall Special Activities.ppt*.

6. Close the presentation and exit PowerPoint when you have completed your work.

2. Switching Views, Navigating Presentation Slides, and Printing Handouts

Before showing your CWS Mall Special Activities presentation to the mall administration, you believe adding color would improve the presentation appearance. After adding color to your presentation background, your slides should appear as shown in Figure 1.23. You can have your supervisor print a color copy of the presentation slides while you print the presentation as black-and-white handouts with four slides per page before deciding which printouts to use.

FIGURE 1.23

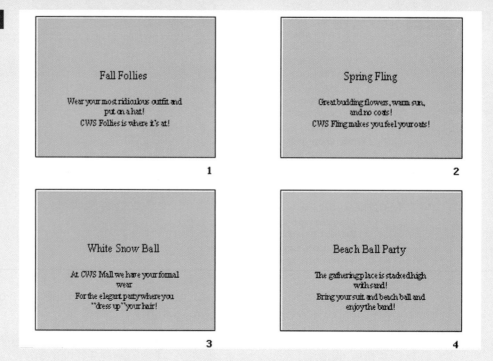

Follow these instructions to complete the first draft of your presentation:

1. Open the presentation CWS Mall Special Activities, if necessary, and review it.

2. Display Slide 1 in Slide view, choose Format, Background, and select the Follow Fills Scheme Color from the Color drop-down list.

3. Choose Apply to All.

4. Review each slide on-screen using different navigation techniques.

5. Save changes and print a copy of the presentation as black-and-white handouts with four slides per page.

6. Choose File, Send To, Mail Recipient (as Attachment) and address the e-mail message to your instructor to print a copy of presentation slides on the color printer.

> **TIP** To send a presentation as a mail attachment, you must have a valid e-mail account and the appropriate mail server on your computer or network. Without these features, the menu command may not be available.

7. Close the presentation and exit PowerPoint when you have completed your work.

On Your Own Exercises

1. Creating, Proofing, Saving, and Adding Slides and Text to a Presentation

The Willows Resort area has a number of restaurants, each featuring menu selections from a specific region of the world. Jeremy Stills, senior editor of *World Dining Guide*, has been asked to include the Willows restaurants in the Year 2000 guide. He has developed the preliminary outline shown in Figure 1.24 and asks that you create a presentation using the outline.

FIGURE 1.24

1. **The Willows Restaurants**
   Something for Everyone - Add the Spice of Variety to Your Life!
2. **A Taste of Thailand**
   - An exotic selection of dishes straight from Bangkok
   - Noodles, stir frys and rice dishes - your choice of meat
3. **South of the Border**
   - Viva Mexico! Authentic Northern Mexico specialties
   - Burritos, tacos, fajitas and the best fried ice cream outside of Tijuana
   - Homemade tortillas, chips and salsa available for purchase
4. **California Dreamin'**
   - Lonely for the beach and the sun? Our casual atmosphere will take you away...
   - Fresh seafood, salad and pasta - all with a light, healthy flair
5. **Manilla Pho Hoacali**
   - If you've never sampled the tastes of Vietnam, this restaurant is a must!
   - Rice vermicelli, soft noodles, Vietnamese curry and specialty drinks
   - Add your own fresh herbs to create your own unique flavor
6. **Thibodeaux's Crawfish Pot**
   - Oh yeah, cher, you gotta go to the best cajun restaurant this side of Mardi Gras!
   - Authentic gumbo, fried alligator, crawfish etouffee and blackened steak
   - Check out Brunet's attic - Louisiana specialty items so you can take the bayou home with you
7. **Chang's Wok**
   - For a real Chinese experience - cooked right at your table!
   - Choose your own meats, vegetables and spices, all cooked fresh by your very own chef
8. **Catch of the Day**
   - Our fish are flown in twice daily to give you the freshest selection possible
   - New England lobster, crabs, scallops, and over 30 different fishes every day (based on seasonal availability)
   - Lobster bisque, clam chowder and seafood gumbo made from scratch

Using PowerPoint, create a new blank presentation. Add the text pictured in the outline shown in Figure 1.24 and save the presentation using the filename *The Willows Restaurants.ppt*.

2. Creating, Formatting, and Saving a Multi-Slide Presentation

The human resources manager at your office likes the design of your résumé. Create a résumé presentation that includes at least three slides that contain information found in your résumé.

Save the presentation using the filename *Resume Design.ppt*. Print an outline for the HR manager to review for content. Close the presentation and exit PowerPoint.

3. Using a Wizard to Create an On-Screen Presentation

Use the AutoContent Wizard to create a marketing presentation to pursuade other students to take a college course you particularly enjoyed. Design the presentation to show on-screen and provide handouts for each person at the meeting. Save the presentation using the filename *My Favorite Class.ppt* and print black-and-white handouts with three slides per page. Print a color copy of the slides, if you have access to a color printer. Close the presentation and exit PowerPoint when you have completed your work.

4. Creating a Presentation from Information Obtained from the Internet

Search the Internet for information about our National Forests. Then use the information to create a presentation that contains at least ten slides. Be sure to include the following information in your presentation:

- The number and location of National Forest Regions in the nation.
- The names of at least two National Forests in each region.
- The number of guests and visitors to at least one region of the National Forests last year.
- The number of acres of U.S. soil covered by National Forests.

Organize the material appropriately and save the presentation using the filename *Our National Forests.ppt*. Print a copy of the presentation as black-and-white handouts.

 Web Tip

Most government agencies have Web sites. The US Forest Service is no exception! Go directly to their Web site at http://www.fs.fed.us. You'll find National Forests listed in the Enjoyment list.

5. Creating a New Presentation

Create a new presentation that identifies at least three generations of your family tree. Include as many names, birthdates, and birthplaces as you can find for yourself, your siblings, your parents (or guardians), and grandparents. Save the presentation using the filename *Family Tree of [your name].ppt*.

 **Web Tip**

Having trouble locating your relatives? Check out the Family Tree Web site at http://www.familytreemaker.com. Are you listed? Can you now take your family tree a few generations further?

6. Printing Presentation Materials

Print copies of all slides in the *Selections Web.ppt* presentation as grayscale handouts with three slides per page. Save and close the presentation. Use the handouts of the *Selections Web.ppt* presentation to substitute appropriate text about Selections, Inc., for the generic text. Text you add should cover information related to the generic topics provided by the wizard, but should be specific enough to adequately advertise Selections, Inc.

Enhancing Presentations

PowerPoint contains a variety of tools that you can use to edit and enhance presentation slides. You've probably already learned how to select and format text in all Office 2000 applications as well as how to add and manipulate art objects. In this project, you learn special PowerPoint techniques for selecting and formatting text, how to format slide place-holders, and how to make your text dance! You'll even learn how to add tables to slides and how to dress up your presentation slides using ideas from professional designers. When you get your presentation into tip-top shape, you'll pack your presentation to take on the road.

Objectives

After completing this project, you will be able to:

➤ Apply presentation templates

➤ Select, edit, and format presentation slide text

➤ Create a table slide

➤ Format slide text placeholders

➤ Add art to slides

➤ Edit and manipulate art objects

➤ Animate slide text

➤ Pack a presentation to go

Running Case

Because you have done such an excellent job designing presentations and seem to have a knack for working with PowerPoint, Seth Goebel, administration manager, has asked that your assignment to the Administrative De-partment be extended to enable you to complete the projects that you have begun. You're delighted because you've just discovered some new features in PowerPoint that make dress-ing up a presentation a snap. . . .

PROJECT 2

The Challenge

Ms. Joy Quinn, the Production and Advertising Department manager, has reviewed the presentation slides you created in Project 1 and has made some changes to the slide text and placeholder format. In addition, she has some data she would like you to add to the presentation, and she would like you to dress up your *Selections Directory.ppt* presentation. When you're finished, she'd like to have the presentation put on a disk so that she can share the design with regional offices. When you complete the changes Ms. Quinn has recommended, your presentation slides will appear as shown in Figure 2.1.

FIGURE 2.1

The Strategy

Because you already know the basics of how to select and edit text, many of the changes Ms. Quinn has requested will take very little time. You'll use special features built into PowerPoint to complete the other formatting requirements and add the new table slide. You'll tackle adding color and animation to slides as well.

The Setup

To ensure that your screen looks like those pictured in this project, you need to check some of the settings.

Table 2.1

Item	Action
Office Assistant	Hide the Assistant.
Toolbars	Reset default toolbars by choosing Tools, Customize, and then display the Toolbars page of the dialog box. Check the Standard, Formatting, and Drawing toolbars and the menu bar. Select each of these items individually and choose Reset. Choose OK to confirm each change. Click the Options tab and ensure that the Personalized Menus and Toolbars options are all deselected. Then click the Reset my usage data button and choose Yes to restore automatic changes to menus. When all toolbars and the menu bar have been reset, choose Close.
View	Click the Normal View button at the bottom of the presentation window to display the tri-pane window. Choose View Ruler to display the ruler, if necessary.

 Web Tip

If you do not have a copy of the Selections Logo (*selections.gif*) on your student data disk, you can download it from the SELECT Web site at http://www.prenhall.com/select.

Applying Presentation Templates

If you have worked with word processing programs such as Word, you are already familiar with the concept of **templates**—preformatted layouts that hold text font format and alignment, color combinations, layout, and design elements. In PowerPoint, presentation templates provide style and color, and add the pizazz your presentation needs to attract the attention of your audience. Applying a template to your presentations helps maintain consistency among the slides in the presentation.

Templates are stored in the Office 2000 Templates folder that opens automatically when you choose a template command from the menu or status bar. When you apply a template to a presentation, all slides in the presentation are automatically formatted with the template design. You can apply a template to an existing presentation or change the template of an existing presentation by:

- Double-clicking the Default Design area of the status bar at the bottom of the presentation window.

> **TIP** When a presentation is already formatted with a template, the name of the template appears on the status bar.

- Choosing Format, Apply Design Template.
- Clicking Apply Design Template from the Common Tasks drop-down list.

You can also apply a template to a new presentation by

- Selecting the Design Template option on the PowerPoint dialog box when you launch PowerPoint and then selecting the design you want to use.
- Choosing File, New and selecting the design from the Design Templates page of the New Presentation dialog box.

Of course, if you will be printing presentation materials on a black-and-white printer, it's also a good idea to see what your printouts will look like. You can preview templates in black-and-white or grayscale before printing.

TASK 1:   To Apply a Template to a Presentation

1 Launch PowerPoint and open the *Selections Directory.ppt* presentation in Normal view.

2 Double-click Default Design on the status bar at the bottom of the presentation window in the Presentation Design folder. The Apply Design Template dialog box displays a list of available templates, as shown in Figure 2.2.

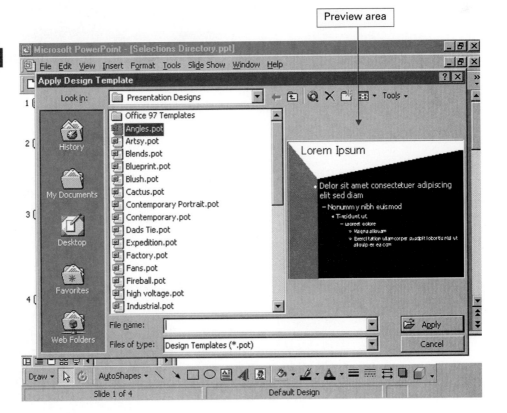

FIGURE 2.2

TROUBLESHOOTING The list of design templates varies depending on whether a previous version of Microsoft PowerPoint was installed on your computer and the options selected during installation of PowerPoint 2000.

TIP Templates have a .pot file name extension to distinguish them from presentation (.ppt) files.

3 Select *Factory.pot*. The Factory template design appears in the preview area.

4 Choose Apply. The presentation is reformatted as shown in Figure 2.3. The text in the Outline pane remains unchanged, but the text in the Slide pane is reformatted. Now the status bar shows *Factory* as the template in use.

FIGURE 2.3

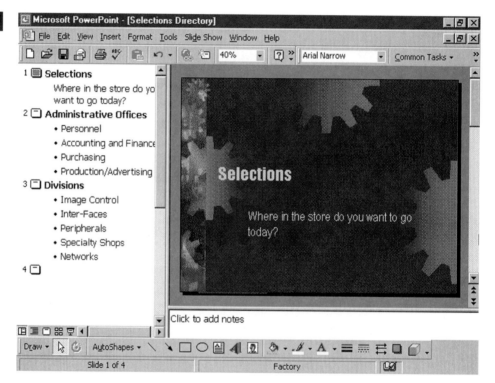

5 Click the Grayscale Preview ⬛ button on the Standard toolbar. The slide appears with the template elements visible but with no color.

6 Click ⬛ again to turn off the grayscale preview.

7 Save changes to the presentation.

Creating a Table Slide

Tools available in PowerPoint enable you to quickly add information to slides and arrange the information in column format. There are a number of ways to add tables to PowerPoint slides, but the most efficient procedure is to use the Table AutoLayout format.

TASK 2:   To Create a Table Slide

1   Display the last slide in the *Selections Directory.ppt* presentation.

2   Choose Format, Slide Layout and choose the Table AutoLayout format. The word *Table* appears in the description area of the New Slide dialog box.

3   Choose Apply.

FIGURE 2.4

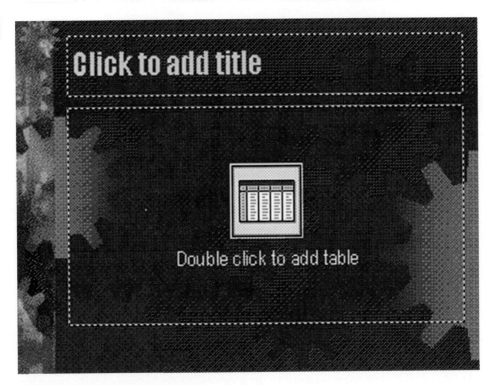

4   Double-click the table placeholder.

FIGURE 2.5

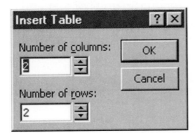

5   Choose OK to accept the default settings. A 2-column, 2-row table appears in the table placeholder on the slide, and the Tables and Borders toolbar opens.

6 Type **Nibbles & Bytes**, **Java**, **ClipArt Gallery**, and **Bookmarks** in the corresponding table cells shown in Figure 2.6. The format will look different.

FIGURE 2.6

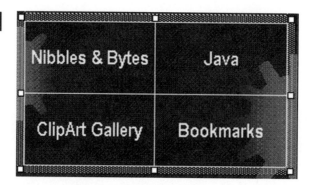

| Nibbles & Bytes | Java |
| ClipArt Gallery | Bookmarks |

7 Now format the table text so that it appears as shown in Figure 2.6.

- Click the placeholder border and click the Center ▤ button on the Formatting toolbar.

- Click the Bold **B** button on the Formatting toolbar.

- Click the Increase Font Size **A** button on the Formatting toolbar until the font size is 38.

- Click the Center Vertically ▤ button on the Tables and Borders toolbar.

8 Select the title placeholder and type **Specialty Shops**.

9 Save changes to the presentation.

Selecting, Editing, and Formatting Presentation Slide Text

Applying a template to a presentation automatically reformats text font, size, and alignment so that it conforms to the style of the template. After the presentation is formatted, you can use text selection techniques identified in the Common Elements projects to select basic units of text and edit them manually. PowerPoint also provides some special techniques for selecting specific units of text. You'll use a variety of techniques to make the text edits Ms. Quinn has requested.

TASK 3: To Select, Edit, and Format Text

1 Display Slide 1 of *Selections Directory.ppt* in Normal view.

2 Click after the *s* at the end of the word *Selections* in the title placeholder and type **, Inc.**

FIGURE 2.7

3 Click the Slide 2 bullet at the left of the words *Accounting and Finance* in the presentation outline. Text associated with the bullet is selected, and Slide 2 appears in the Slide pane.

FIGURE 2.8

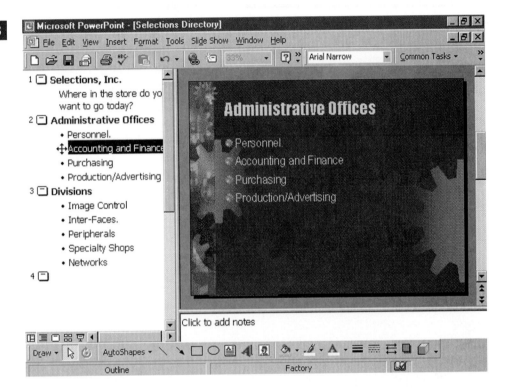

TIP The pointer appears as a four-headed arrow when you point to a bullet or slide icon in the outline, and changes to a two-headed arrow when you drag the item, as shown in Figure 2.9.

4 Drag the bullet for the selected item and drop the item when a horizontal bar, identifying the active position of the text, appears between the slide title and word *Personnel*.

FIGURE 2.9

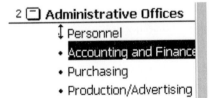

5 Click the slide icon for Slide 3 in the outline. The slide title and all bullet points are selected.

6 Drag the slide icon and position the slide below the Slide 4 icon in the outline. All slide text moves to a new position, and slides renumber automatically, as shown in Figure 2.10.

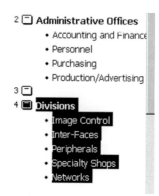

FIGURE 2.10

Check Point

Use the same techniques to arrange bulleted list items on Slides 2 and 4 in alphabetical order and move Slide 4 back to its original position. Save changes to the presentation and leave it open. Spell-check the presentation.

Formatting Slide Text Placeholders

Placeholder objects contained on slides can be selected, sized, and moved using the same techniques you use to size graphic objects. In PowerPoint, however, sizing and positioning text placeholders enables you to adjust the position of slide text the way setting margins controls the placement of text on word processing documents. In addition, you can change and adjust the *line spacing*—the space between lines of type within a placeholder—for each text placeholder individually, and replace fonts throughout the presentation with one action!

TROUBLESHOOTING Refer to the Common Elements projects for more information about moving and sizing graphic objects and aligning text.

TASK 4: To Format Text Placeholders

1 Display Slide 1 in the *Selections Directory.ppt* presentation and choose View, Ruler to display the ruler, if necessary. Displaying the ruler helps to position and size placeholders more precisely.

2 Press (SHIFT) and click the subtitle placeholder. The pointer changes to a four-headed arrow, indicating that you're selecting an object rather than positioning the insertion point in the placeholder. The subtitle placeholder is selected and has handles for sizing.

FIGURE 2.11

3 Drag the center right handle toward the center of the slide and position it at the 2½-inch mark on the ruler. Text in the placeholder wraps to fit the new placeholder size.

4 Center and bold the subtitle placeholder text using the toolbar buttons. The formats automatically apply to all text in the selected placeholder.

FIGURE 2.12

5 Choose Format, Line Spacing.

FIGURE 2.13

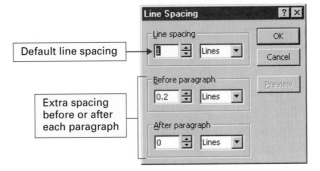

6 Type **2** in the Line spacing value box, type **0** in the Before paragraph value box, and then choose OK. Text in the placeholder is double-spaced.

7 Choose Format, Change Case.

FIGURE 2.14

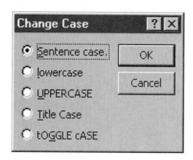

8 Choose UPPERCASE and then choose OK. Text in the placeholder is reformatted in all uppercase letters.

9 Click the placeholder border and then click the Decrease Font Size button on the Formatting toolbar until the text appears on two lines, if necessary.

10 Choose Format, Replace Fonts. The Replace Font dialog box displays the default text font for the active presentation.

11 Select Arial from the With drop-down list.

> **TIP** If you don't have Arial in your fonts list, select the font indicated by your instructor.

12 Save changes to the presentation.

 ## Break Point

If necessary, you can save your file, exit PowerPoint, and continue this project later.

Adding Art to Slides

PowerPoint makes dressing up your presentation with pictures quick and easy. Not only can you apply your own artistic talents to design powerful creations, but you can pull designs from the **Clip Gallery**, use images from other sources, or download art from the Internet. You can also use the Word-Art feature to change text into "words of art."

Many of the procedures for inserting graphics—both clip art and saved images—were introduced in the Common Elements projects. You'll use those techniques to add art to slides.

Web Tip

The Microsoft PowerPoint Web site contains a wealth of additional clip art images you can use to enhance your presentations. In addition, you can find graphics on Web sites, photo galleries, and so forth. A word of caution is in order, however, before you "borrow" a graphic designed by someone else. Check the copyright regulations governing the graphics and ask permission. Plagiarism is plagiarism, whether you use someone else's words or works of art—including photographs!

TASK 5: To Add Clip Art to Slides

1 Open the *Selections Directory.ppt* presentation and switch to Normal view, if necessary.

2 Display Slide 4 and choose Insert, Picture, Clip Art. The Insert Picture dialog box opens.

3 Click the Buildings category and scroll until you see the Expanding Horizons clip art image pictured in Figure 2.15.

> **TIP** If you don't see the graphic pictured in Figure 2.15 in the Buildings category, click the Keep Looking button at the bottom of the Insert ClipArt dialog box to display additional clips. If you don't see the clip after all clips are presented, check with your instructor for a copy of the required graphic.

4 Choose Insert Clip and close the Insert ClipArt window.

5 Choose Format, Picture and then click the Size tab.

6 Type **175** in the Scale Height value box to scale the graphic for the slide; then click OK. Notice as you type that the value in the Scale Width value changes, too.

7 Position the graphic as shown in Figure 2.15 and adjust the size manually by dragging a handle, if necessary.

FIGURE 2.15

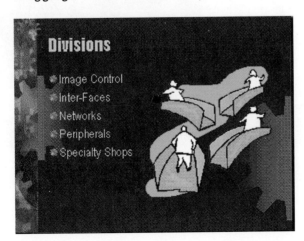

8 Save changes to the presentation.

Check Point

Format, size, and position the bulleted list placeholder on Slide 2 to better fit the list. Save changes to the presentation.

Editing and Manipulating Art Objects

The Common Elements projects introduced you to some of the ways you can edit and manipulate art objects. To create effective presentations, you will want to use more advanced techniques to edit art objects.

TASK 6: To Edit and Manipulate Art Objects

1 Display Slide 3 of the *Selections Directory.ppt* presentation in Normal view.

2 Click the clip art image to select it and then click the Draw menu button on the Drawing toolbar.

FIGURE 2.16

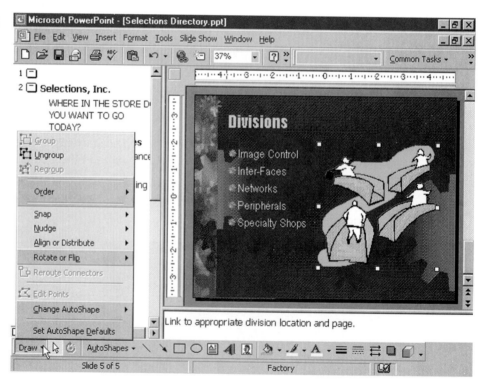

3 Choose Ungroup. A message box tells you that the graphic is an imported picture and asks if you want to convert it to a Microsoft Office drawing.

4 Choose Yes to convert the object.

FIGURE 2.17

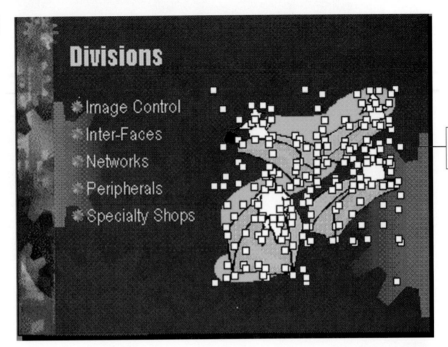

Handles for each piece of the image are shown.

5 Click a blank area of the slide to deselect image pieces, and then click to select the green background. Only the green area is selected, but the handles appear to encompass the entire image.

6 Click the Fill Color drop-down list arrow and choose the Follow Shadows Scheme Color. The green area blends in with the slide template.

7 Use the procedures identified in steps 5 and 6 to change the colors of other pieces of the image, if necessary.

8 Position the pointer in the lower left corner of the slide, and then click and drag across the clip art image.

FIGURE 2.18

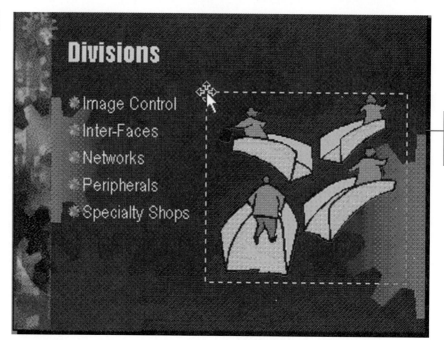

A marquee surrounds the pieces of the image.

9 Release the mouse button when all pieces of the image are within the marquee. All pieces of the original clip are selected.

10 Choose Draw, Group. The image is one object again. Now let's flip it over!

11 Choose Draw, Rotate or Flip, Flip Horizontal.

FIGURE 2.19

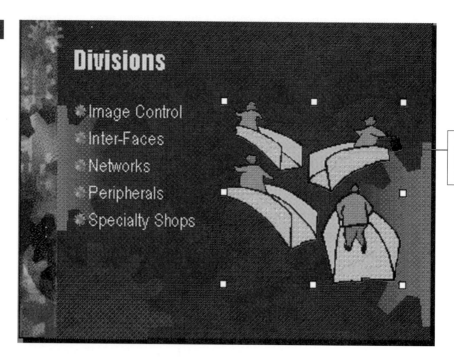

The selected image is now facing the other direction.

12 Save changes to the presentation.

Animating Slide Text

PowerPoint is equipped with a **text preset animation** feature that makes "animating" slide placeholder text a snap! In PowerPoint 2000, you can set each text placeholder to animate individually. Animating the title enables you to control how the title moves onto the slide, and animating bulleted list text presents each bulleted item individually. Text preset animations help focus the attention of your audience on each individual bulleted item as you discuss it and remove the distractions of presenting all bulleted points at once.

PowerPoint enables you to set text animation using basic tools and also enables you to create custom animations.

Using Basic Text Animation Tools

The **Animation toolbar** contains a basic set of animation tools that enable you to add sound to animated text automatically. You can use these tools to create simple text animations.

TASK 7: To Animate Slide Text

1 Display Slide 5 in Normal view, if necessary.

2 Click the Animation Effects ☆ button. The Animation Effects toolbar opens.

FIGURE 2.20

FIGURE 2.21

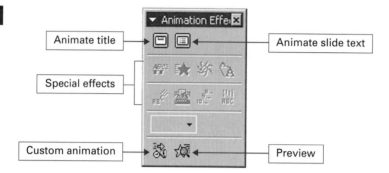

Animate title → Animate slide text

Special effects →

Custom animation → Preview

4 Click the Animate Title 🖼 button and then click the slide title placeholder. Special effects are available after you identify the text placeholder to animate.

FIGURE 2.22

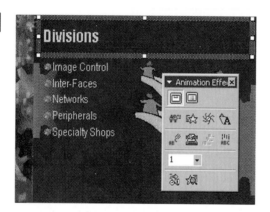

5 Click the Laser Text Effect 🔤 button and then click the Animation Preview 🎞 button. An Animation Preview window opens to demonstrate the animation effect.

FIGURE 2.23

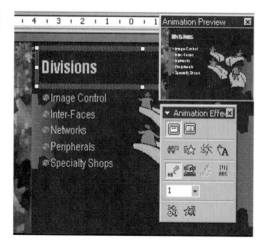

6 Close the Animation Preview window and the Animation Effects toolbar, and then save changes to the presentation.

Creating Custom Animations

The **Custom Animation dialog box** contains controls that enable you to control how previously presented bullet points display on-screen and allow you to set the order in which you want to display text in different placeholders. In addition, you can control when other objects appear on-screen using the Custom Animation dialog box.

TASK 8:   To Create Custom Animations

1 Display Slide 3 in Normal view, if necessary.

2 Choose Slide Show, Custom Animation, and click the Order & Timing tab.

FIGURE 2.24

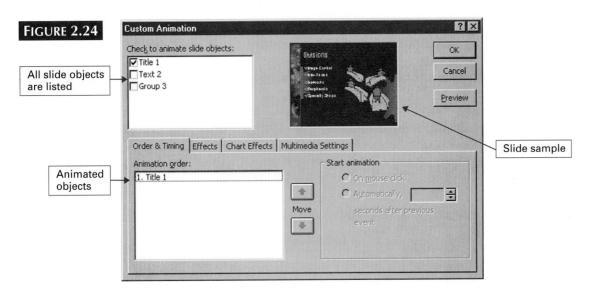

All slide objects are listed

Animated objects

Slide sample

> **TIP** You can also access this dialog box by clicking the Custom Animation button on the Animation Effects toolbar.

3 Click the checkbox for Text 2 in the Check to animate slide objects box until a check mark appears.

FIGURE 2.25

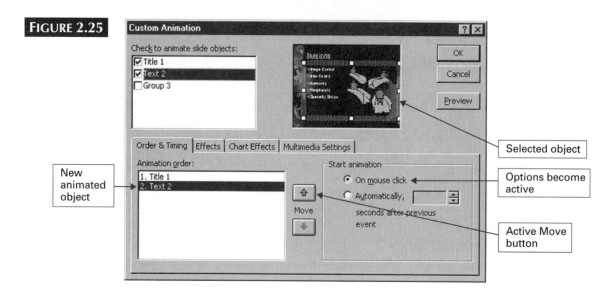

New animated object

Selected object

Options become active

Active Move button

4 Click the Effects tab. The active animation effect appears.

FIGURE 2.26

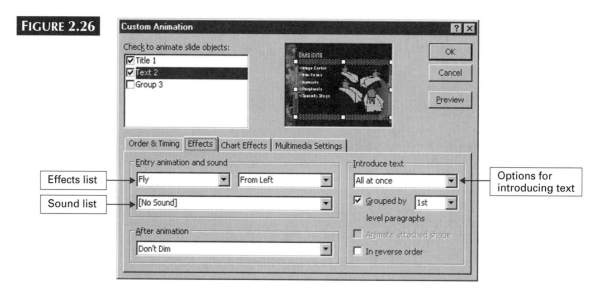

Effects list

Sound list

Options for introducing text

5 Click the animation effect drop-down list arrow (it now says "Fly") and select Dissolve. When you select a different effect, it's demonstrated on the slide image in the dialog box.

6 Select Screeching Brakes from the sound drop-down list and Hide After Animation from the After animation drop-down list. With each selection, the effect is demonstrated on the slide image.

7 Choose Preview to see the results of your settings.

8 Choose OK to save changes to the presentation.

Check Point

If you didn't like the results of your animation effects, change them and then save changes to the presentation. Use similar techniques to create animation effects and edit art objects on all slides in the presentation. When you're finished, save changes to the presentation.

Packing a Presentation to Go

Now that you have the presentation design pretty well set, you can pack it on a disk so that Ms. Quinn can take it with her when she visits the regional offices. Graphics, templates, and animation effects increase the size of presentations and make them difficult to copy to a disk. Luckily, PowerPoint has a ***Pack and Go Wizard*** that can have her on the road in just a few minutes with disk in hand. When you pack a presentation using the Pack and Go Wizard, PowerPoint compresses the presentation, making it more compact and easier to fit on one disk. Of course, the larger the presentation, the more space required. If your presentation requires more than one disk, the Pack and Go Wizard will tell you when to put a new disk in the disk drive.

TASK 9:   To Pack a Presentation to Go

1 Choose File, Pack and Go. The Wizard displays the steps and navigation buttons.

FIGURE 2.27

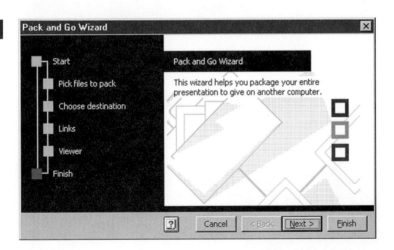

2 Click Next.

FIGURE 2.28

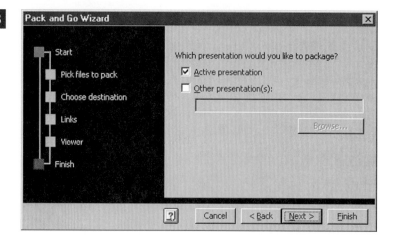

3 Ensure that Active presentation is selected and click Next. Now you can select the drive on which to pack the presentation.

FIGURE 2.29

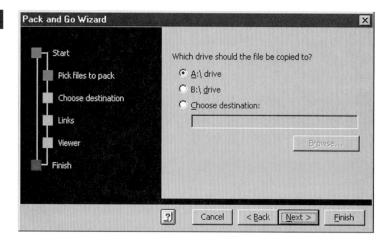

4 Ensure that A:\ drive is active, place a disk in the floppy drive, and click Next.

FIGURE 2.30

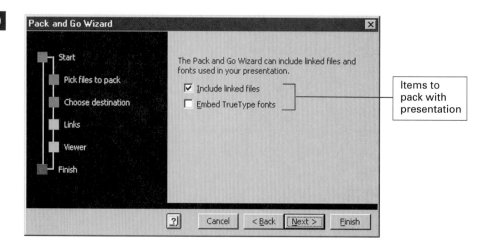

5 Deselect the Include linked files, because your presentation does not contain links, and select Embed TrueType fonts to ensure that your presentation is displayed properly. Then click Next.

FIGURE 2.31

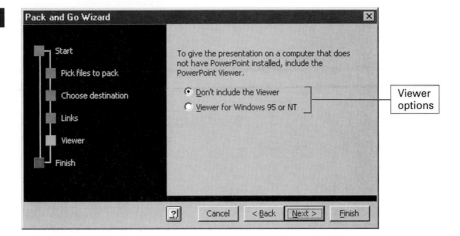

TIP   Choose Don't include the Viewer if the computer you'll be using has PowerPoint installed; include the viewer if the computer does not have PowerPoint installed.

TIP   If the Viewer is not installed on your computer, you will need the Office 2000 CD to access the PowerPoint Viewer.

6 Click Don't include the Viewer and click Next. The Finish step displays information about what PowerPoint will do when you choose Finish.

7 Click Finish.
PowerPoint whirs and burps a bit as it packages the presentation on the disk. When the presentation is packaged, a message window tells you that Pack and Go has successfully packed your presentation. If your presentation is too large to fit on one disk, you will be told when to insert another disk.

8 Click OK to acknowledge the message.
Packing the presentation to go automatically creates two files on your disk: *pngsetup.exe* and *pres0.ppz*. The *pngsetup.exe* file can be used to install and show the presentation on any computer that has enough memory and disk space. The *pres0.ppz* file contains slides and other important information about the presentation.

Summary and Exercises

Summary

- PowerPoint contains a variety of tools that you can use to edit and enhance presentation slides.
- Presentation templates provide style and color and add pizazz to your presentation.
- PowerPoint provides some special techniques for selecting specific units of text.
- Placeholder objects can be selected, sized, and moved using the same techniques you use to size graphics.
- The Change Case feature allows you to format placeholders in sentence case, lowercase, uppercase, title case and toggle case.
- You can apply your own artistic talents to design creations, pull designs from the Clip Gallery, use images from other sources, or download art from the Internet.
- To create effective presentations, you can use advanced techniques to edit art objects such as changing the scheme color, rotating and grouping objects, and animating objects.
- PowerPoint is equipped with a text preset animation feature that makes animating the slide placeholder text a snap.
- The Animation toolbar also allows you to add sound to animated text.
- The Custom Animation dialog box allows you to control how previously presented bullet points display on-screen, and the order in which you wish to display them.
- When you pack a presentation using the Pack and Go Wizard, PowerPoint compresses the presentation, making it more compact and easier to fit on one disk.

Key Terms and Operations

Key Terms

Animation toolbar
Clip Gallery
Custom Animation dialog box
line spacing

Pack and Go Wizard
templates
text preset animation

Operations

add art to slides
animate slide text
apply presentation templates
edit and manipulate art
  objects

format slide text placeholders
select, edit, and format
  presentation slide text

Study Questions

Multiple Choice

1. To help maintain consistency among slides in a presentation, apply a
   a. placeholder.
   b. template.
   c. color style.
   d. layout.

2. All of the following can be used to add a template to an existing presentation *except*
   a. double-clicking Default Design.
   b. triple-clicking Default Design.
   c. choosing Format, Apply Design Template.
   d. clicking Apply Design Template from the drop-down Common Tasks list.

3. Templates are easily identified by the extension
   a. .doc.
   b. .ppt.
   c. .xls.
   d. .pot.

4. Which case would you use if you would like all letters in your placeholder to appear capitalized?
   a. sentence case
   b. lowercase
   c. title case
   d. uppercase

5. To add art to your presentation, you can pull designs from the
   a. Internet.
   b. Clip Gallery.
   c. Presentation Gallery.
   d. both a and b.

6. What makes animating a slide placeholder a snap?
   a. text preset animation
   b. animate placeholder selection
   c. slide layout
   d. basic slide animation

7. To set the order in which you want to display text in different placeholders, you would use
   a. preset animation.
   b. select order.
   c. custom animation.
   d. outline order.

8. Graphics, templates, and animation effects increase the size of presentations, so to save on disk you would use which feature?
   a. Save as Compact
   b. Pack and Go
   c. Save without Animation
   d. Pick and Save

9. Which case would you select for all letters in a placeholder to appear in small letters with no capitalization?
   a. lowercase
   b. uppercase
   c. toggle case
   d. title case

10. What allows you to adjust the position of a slide placeholder the way setting a margin does in Word?
    a. margin control
    b. ruler
    c. slide placement
    d. sizing and positioning placeholder

Short Answer

1. How does the mouse pointer appear when you point to a bullet or slide icon in the outline?

2. How can you display the ruler in PowerPoint?

3. What are the five options in the Change Case menu?

4. What helps focus the attention of your audience on each individual bulleted item?

5. How can you easily view the effects you have created in animating your presentation?

6. What feature would you use to control the order in which objects will appear on-screen?

7. Which feature compresses your presentation for easy storage on disk?

8. What are the two options available to determine when an object will appear on-screen?

9. Why would you include the Viewer when you pack your presentation to go?

10. What are the preformatted layouts that hold text format, color combinations, layout, and design?

Fill in the Blank

1. To make an item fly in from the left of the screen, you would change the _____ in the Custom Animation dialog box.

2. The active template is identified on the _____.

3. Displaying the _____ helps to position and size placeholders.

4. You can download additional clip art from the PowerPoint _____ _____.

5. A variety of images are available in the _____ Gallery.

6. To change the distance between lines of type within a placeholder, adjust the _____.

7. Presentation _____ provide style and color to your slides.

8. To ensure your presentation displays properly when you Pack and Go, you would select _____ in the Pack and Go Wizard.

9. The _____ contains a basic set of animation tools.

10. If the computer you are using for a presentation does not have PowerPoint installed, you will need to include the _____ when you Pack and Go.

For Discussion

1. What are the different techniques to add art to your presentation?

2. Discuss how you can rearrange and renumber items in the Outline view.

3. How can you change the color scheme of a picture?

4. Discuss why you would use the Pack and Go feature instead of saving your presentation as you normally would on a disk.

5. List several reasons you would use animation effects on your presentation.

Hands-On Exercises

1. Adding a New Slide and Inserting a Graphic

Selections, Inc., has just received a copy of their new corporate logo from the design studio. It's a colorful, cheerful design that might add character to your presentation and serve to introduce the store. As a result, you want to add the slide to the beginning of your Selections Directory presentation and format the logo to appear as shown in Figure 2.32.

FIGURE 2.32

Follow these instructions to complete the slide.

1. Create a new blank slide in the presentation.
2. Click the slide icon for the new slide in the Outline pane and drag the new slide to the beginning of the presentation.
3. Choose Insert, Picture, From File; open the folder containing the Selections logo (*selections.gif*); and double-click the file name.
4. Size the logo to cover the complete slide.
5. Save changes to the presentation.

2. Adding Drawings to the Slides, Downloading Clips from the Internet, Formatting Text Placeholders and Using Text Animation Tools

Mr. Goebel would like to change the graphics on the *CWS Mall Special Activities* presentation and add appropriate graphics and drawings for the upcoming events.

Follow these steps to complete the task:

1. Launch PowerPoint, if necessary, and open the *CWS Mall Special Activities* presentation.
2. Display Slide 1 in Normal view. Animate the title of the slide to fly in from the right. Animate the subtitle to appear randomly with each mouse click.
3. Display Slide 2 and create and format a drawn object using a shaded AutoShape arrow. Edit the colors to show gradient fill effects.
4. Select Insert, Picture, Clip Art and then choose Clips Online. Browse the Microsoft Clip Gallery Live site for clips that might be useful to your presentation.

TIP The first time you log onto the Clip Gallery Live, you will be asked to accept a License Agreement. Read the agreement carefully—know what you're "signing." Clips you select from the Microsoft Web site are automatically downloaded to your Clip Gallery. As a result, the clips you see on your computer will not necessarily be the same clips the person sitting next to you sees.

 **Web Tip**

The Microsoft Clip Gallery Live changes almost daily as new clips are added. You can use the Search dialog box on the site to search for additional clips using keywords about the site. Try searching for "Snow" and see if you come up with any useful clips.

5. Replace the Times New Roman font throughout the presentation with a condensed font.

6. Save the presentation on a disk using Pack and Go. Do not include linked files. Do not include the Viewer. Embed TrueType Fonts.

7. Close the presentation and exit PowerPoint when you've completed your work.

On Your Own Exercises

1. Applying a Template and Adding, Moving, and Sizing Clip Art Images

Jeremy Stills, editor of the Year 2000 Dining Guide, would like you to apply a template and add clip art images to enhance slides in the Willows Restaurants presentation. Use the techniques explored in this project to locate and insert appropriate clip art on at least four slides.

2. Adding, Formatting, and Manipulating Clip Art and Drawings

Create a four-slide presentation featuring a New Year's fundraiser designed to raffle off items donated by local retail stores. Title the presentation *2000*, and use tools presented in this project to add clip art images and drawings to your presentation slides. Edit the clip art images by ungrouping them and changing the colors. Size and position the graphics to enhance the presentation. Save the presentation and print copies of the slides. Close the presentation and exit PowerPoint when you've completed your work.

3. Searching the Internet for Pictures to Enhance Presentations and Use Animation Effects

Your supervisor has asked you to design a presentation for an upcoming employee appreciation barbecue. The presentation will include an invitation, a menu, and a slide thanking employees for their continued support of the company. Search the Internet for additional graphics to use on the handout. Animate text effects and sound effects. Animate the bulleted items to appear automatically within five seconds of each other. Save the presentation as *Barbecue* and print a copy of your presentation to be color-copied by the human resources department for each employee. Close the presentation and exit PowerPoint when you've completed your work.

4. Applying a Template, Arranging Bulleted Lists, and Changing Line Spacing

Open the presentation *Barbecue.ppt*. Apply the Expedited template to the presentation. Arrange the bulleted list items in the Menu slide in alphabetical order and change the line spacing so that the menu items fit on one page. Animate the bulleted items with sound effects. Change the case of the Title slide to appear in all capital letters. Change the scheme color of the Title slide so that the objects show up better. Pack your presentation to go. Include the Viewer, embed TrueType fonts, and deselect Include linked files. Exit PowerPoint.

5. Finding Templates on the Internet

Search the Microsoft PowerPoint Web site and locate additional templates that you can use to format presentations. Download a template and apply it to the *Resume Design.ppt* presentation created in the preceding assignment. Save the presentation and print a copy of the title slide.

 **Web Tip**

Can't find any templates? Try going to Microsoft's home page at http://www.microsoft.com and then click Products.

6. Copying Graphics from the Internet, Editing Presentation Format, and Applying a Template to a Presentation

Return to the Web site from which you gathered information for the *Our National Forests* presentation. Locate an emblem that represents the U.S. Forest Service and copy it to the Windows clipboard. Leave the Web site open.

Open the *Our National Forests* presentation and paste the U.S. Forest Service emblem on the presentation title slide. Size and position the graphic appropriately.

Format the presentation by:

* Applying an appropriate template.
* Displaying each slide in the presentation and inserting clip art and graphics downloaded from the Internet to presentation slides.
* Format the body placeholder on each slide to fit the text.
* Edit clip art objects as necessary to fit the presentation slide.
* Animate slide text for at least three of the presentation slides.

Pack the presentation to go and store it on disk as directed by your instructor.

7. Editing a Presentation

Open the *Selections Web.ppt* presentation and apply a different template to the file. Save changes to the presentation. Then replace the generic text in the presentation with the text you wrote on the presentation printout in Project 1, On Your Own Exercise 6. Save changes to the presentation and print a copy of the presentation as black-and-white slides with six slides per page.

> **TIP**   Use the Edit, Replace command to search for text you want to replace and enter the replacement text in the dialog box. (See *Common Elements* CE-35-36 to review Find and Replace Text in more detail.)

Viewing and Organizing Slide Shows

Most of the presentations you create are designed to provide powerful visuals to enhance oral presentations. Slides in a presentation can be formatted and shown on-screen by individuals or projected on an audiovisual screen or flat surface as you present a report to an audience.

Showing your presentations with style has a positive impact on your audience. The PowerPoint slide show feature enables you to show your presentation on a computer screen. Seeing your presentation "live" the first time can be quite satisfying and exciting. In this project, you learn how to dress up your presentation for on-screen viewing and how to use Slide Sorter view to rearrange slides in the presentation.

Objectives

After completing this project, you will be able to:

➤ Present a slide show

➤ Use the slide show shortcut menu

➤ Rearrange slides using Slide Sorter view

➤ Add slides from one presentation to an existing presentation

➤ Set action buttons

➤ Add slide transitions

➤ Hide slides and display hidden slides

➤ Set presentations to run automatically

Running Case

There are only a few days before your temporary assignment to the administrative offices of Selections, Inc., is complete. You've pretty much got your presentations finished—now it's time to see what the presentations look like on-screen. You'll find PowerPoint full of features that make changing the on-screen presentation more dynamic!

The Challenge

Ms. Quinn has reviewed the Selections Directory presentation and has tentatively approved the design, graphics, and format of slides in the presentation. She now asks that the presentation be tweaked closer to its final form so that she can present it to the managers at their next meeting.

The Strategy

To get the Selections Directory presentation into shape, you need to view the presentation as a slide show and then use Slide Sorter view to make final edits to the presentation organization. Figure 3.1 shows the final presentation in Slide Sorter view.

FIGURE 3.1

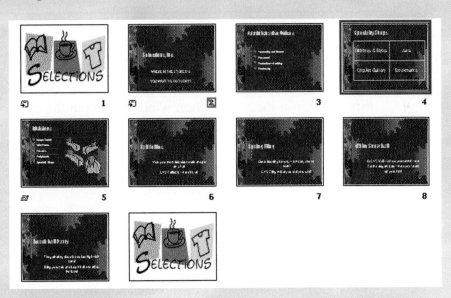

The Setup

You're switching to a different view for many of the activities in this section, and you'll be using the slide show feature in PowerPoint. As a result, some additional settings have been added to the setup table to ensure that your screen will match the figures pictured in this project.

Table 3.1

Item	Action
Office Assistant	Hide the Assistant.
View	Click the Slide Sorter View button at the bottom of the presentation window.
Toolbars	Switch to Slide Sorter view and ensure that both the Standard and Slide Sorter toolbars are active. If you don't see them, choose View, Toolbars, and then select them.
	Reset both toolbars by choosing Tools, Customize, and then display the Toolbars page of the dialog box. Check the Standard and Slide Sorter toolbars and the menu bar. Choose each of these items individually and choose Reset. Choose OK to confirm each change.
	Click the Options tab and ensure that the Personalized Menus and Toolbars options are all deselected. Then click the Reset my usage data button and choose Yes to restore automatic changes to menus.
	When all toolbars and the menu bar have been reset, choose Close.
Zoom	Set the zoom to 66%.

Presenting a Slide Show

Viewing your presentation as a slide show makes it come to life. Slide shows display slides in the presentation window without the PowerPoint toolbars, title bar, and status bar. During a slide show, each slide literally fills the screen and you can focus on slide contents to determine impact. PowerPoint offers a number of ways to launch a slide show:

- Choose View, Slide Show.
- Choose Slide Show, View Show.
- Click the Slide Show ⬚ button at the bottom of the presentation window.
- Press (F5).

> **TIP** Some people use the slide show as a way to preview the information on their slides prior to printing them. Of course, on-screen, slides will appear in living color. When you print them on a black-and-white printer, the effect may be something less than you had hoped for. To view your slides as they will appear when printed on a noncolor printer, click the Grayscale Preview button on the Standard toolbar or choose View, Black and White.

 Web Tip

You can search the Web to locate sample presentations and slide shows using any Web browser and search engine.

TASK 1: <u>To View a Presentation as a Slide Show</u>

1 Open the *Selections Directory.ppt* presentation and display the first slide in Normal view.

> **TIP** The slide show starts with the active slide. In this case, the first slide appears on-screen. However, if Slide 3 was active when you started the slide show, the slide show would start with Slide 3.

2 Click the Slide Show ⊟ button at the bottom of the presentation window.

FIGURE 3.2

Advancing Slides

You can use both the keyboard and mouse to move among slides in a presentation during a slide show. Table 3.2 compares the actions for using both techniques. Practice each technique to identify the ones you like best.

Table 3.2

Movement	Mouse Action	Keyboard Action(s)
Advance to next slide	Click the left mouse button.	Press **N**, (ENTER), (SPACE), (PGDN), (↓), or (→).
Return to previous slide	Right-click and select Previous.	Press **P**,(ENTER), (BACKSPACE), (PGUP), (←), or (↑).
Specific slide number		Type \<number\>; then press (ENTER). For example, type **5** to go to slide **5** and then press (ENTER).
Stop show	Right-click and select End show.	Press (ESC).

TIP Because you may not always have access to a computer to display an on-screen show, you may find it necessary to print your presentation on transparencies to show from an overhead projector. To print to transparencies, be sure you have transparency film sheets that are safe to use on your printer, and then place the transparency film into the printer before printing your slides.

Using the Slide Show Shortcut Menu

The **_slide show shortcut menu_** displays commands for navigating the slide show as well as for controlling on-screen features such as the mouse pointer and slide meter. To display the slide show shortcut menu, click the right mouse button during the slide show or press (SHIFT)+(F10).

TASK 2: To Use the Slide Show Shortcut Menu

1 Click 🖥 to start the slide show, if necessary. The slide that was active in Slide view appears in full-screen view.

2 Right-click anywhere on the screen.

FIGURE 3.3

TIP You can also access the slide show shortcut menu by moving the mouse pointer on-screen until a shortcut menu button appears in the lower-left corner of the slide; then click the shortcut menu button.

TROUBLESHOOTING If you switch to a different program while a slide show is active, and then return to PowerPoint, a Slide Show toolbar appears in the active PowerPoint view. Click Resume Slide Show to continue the slide show where you left off.

3 Choose Screen, Black Screen. The entire screen becomes black so that the audience focuses on you, the speaker, rather than on the same slide for an extended period of time.

4 Click the left mouse button to redisplay the slide. The slide that was displayed before you turned the screen black appears again.

5 Right-click again, and then choose Pointer Options, Pen. The mouse pointer changes to a pen that you can use to draw on slides during a slide show.

6 Point to the coffee cup, press the left mouse button, and hold it down as you move the mouse and draw a circle around the coffee cup.

FIGURE 3.4

I hope your circle looks better than mine.

> **TIP** You could also display a black screen while you draw or annotate. Annotations are not saved as changes to the slide. When you advance to the next or previous slide or end the presentation, the annotation disappears. To erase the annotation so that you can draw on the same slide again, press **E**.

7 Press (ESC) to end annotation. The mouse pointer changes back to an arrow.

8 Right-click again, and then choose End Show. The slide displayed when you chose End Show appears in Normal view.

Rearranging Presentation Slides Using Slide Sorter View

After viewing the presentation as a slide show, you may find that you need to make changes in slide arrangement so that the flow is smoother or to match changes in the oral presentation. Slide Sorter view displays miniature images (these are sometimes called *thumbnail* images, remember?) of presentation slides that you can drag to new positions. Slide Sorter view prevents slide editing; as a result, you must return to Normal or Slide view to edit slide text and graphics.

Moving Slides

In Slide Sorter view, moving slides is as simple as dragging and dropping a slide to a new position in the presentation.

TASK 3:   To Rearrange Slides Using Slide Sorter View

1 Click the Slide Sorter View ⊞ button at the bottom of the presentation window.

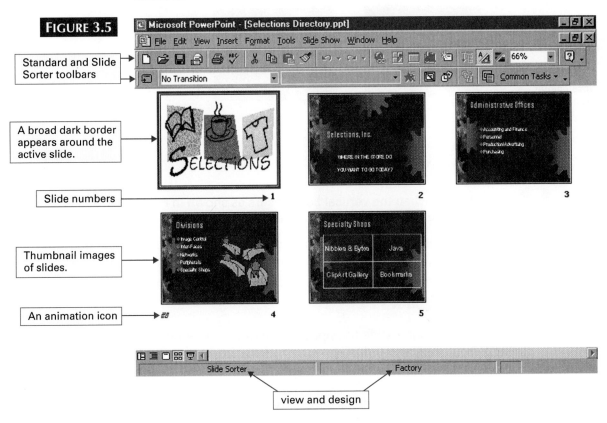

FIGURE 3.5

Standard and Slide Sorter toolbars

A broad dark border appears around the active slide.

Slide numbers

Thumbnail images of slides.

An animation icon

view and design

2 Click Slide 5 to select it, and then drag it to the left of Slide 4.

FIGURE 3.6

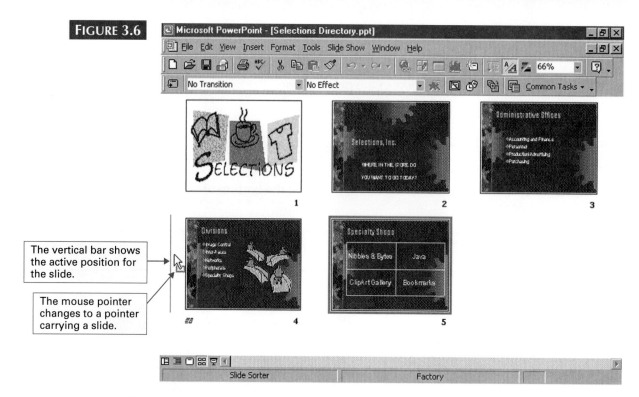

The vertical bar shows the active position for the slide.

The mouse pointer changes to a pointer carrying a slide.

3 Drop Slide 5 when the vertical bar appears as shown in Figure 3.6. Slides appear in the new order and renumber automatically.

4 Save changes to the presentation, and leave it open.

Copying and Duplicating Slides

When you want a slide to appear in more than one position in a presentation, you can copy or duplicate the slide to prevent having to reconstruct it. You can also copy or duplicate slides and delete text to introduce information about a specific bullet point.

TASK 4: To Copy and Duplicate Slides

1 Display the *Selections Directory.ppt* presentation in Slide Sorter view, if necessary.

2 Select Slide 1 and click 🖺. The slide is copied to the Windows Clipboard.

3 Click after the last slide in the presentation and then click 🖺. A copy of Slide 1 now appears as Slide 6.

4 Select Slide 3, and choose Insert, Duplicate Slide. A duplicate of Slide 3 appears as Slide 4.

Deleting Slides

When slides become outdated and are no longer needed, you can delete them. PowerPoint offers a variety of ways to remove slides from a presentation. The active view determines which procedure you should use, and the active or selected slide is the slide that is deleted.

- Choose Edit, Delete Slide from any view.
- Press (DELETE) in Slide Sorter and Outline views.

> **TROUBLESHOOTING** In some cases, a warning message appears on-screen asking if you are sure you want to delete the slide. Choose OK to delete the slide or Cancel to leave the slide.

- Click ✂.

Check Point

Delete Slide 4 (the duplicate you just created).

Start the slide show for the Selections Directory presentation and display the complete presentation. What happens when Slide 5 appears on-screen? What happens after you show Slide 6?

Break Point

If necessary, you can save your file, exit PowerPoint, and continue this project later.

Adding Slides from One Presentation to an Existing Presentation

You will often find that slides you created for one presentation could be used in a different presentation. You can insert slides from one presentation into another presentation using a couple of different techniques:

- Display the presentation containing the slides in Slide Sorter view, select the slides, and copy them to the Clipboard. Then open the presentation into which you want to place the slides and paste them in.
- Display the presentation into which you want to place the slides and insert slides from a different file. You can insert all slides in a file or select the slides you want to include.

TASK 5: <u>To Insert Slides from a File</u>

1 Display the *Selections Directory.ppt* presentation in Slide Sorter view, if necessary.

2 Position the insertion point between Slide 5 and Slide 6. A bar appears between the two slides. Slides you insert will appear between these two slides.

3 Choose Insert, Slides from Files.

FIGURE 3.7

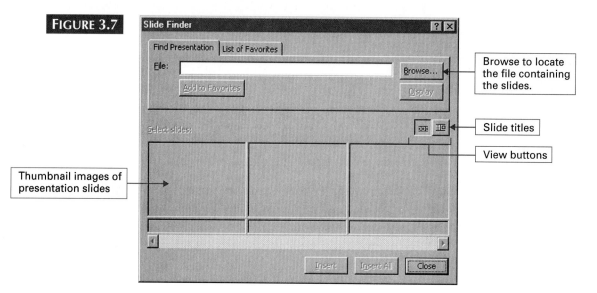

Browse to locate the file containing the slides.

Slide titles

View buttons

Thumbnail images of presentation slides

4 Choose Browse, open the folder containing the CWS Mall Special Activities presentation, and double-click the file name.

5 Choose Display, if necessary, to display slide thumbnail images in the Select Slides palette.

FIGURE 3.8

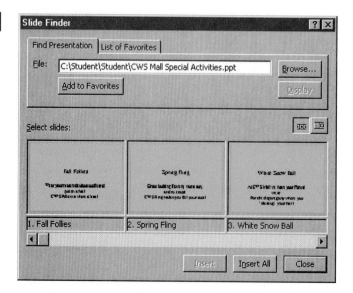

6 Choose Insert All and close. All four slides appear just before the last slide in the active presentation.

> **TIP** But what happened to the format and color of the original slides? They took on the color and format of the active presentation template.

7 Save changes to the presentation.

Check Point

Display Slide 6 in Normal view. Format the text in the text placeholder so that it appears more neatly arranged than it does now. Then select the text in the placeholder and double-click the Format Painter button on the Standard toolbar. Display Slide 7 and drag the mouse pointer over the text in the text placeholder to paint the format on the text placeholder. Repeat the procedure for Slides 8 and 9.

Web Tip

You can get help developing your résumé right there on the World Wide Web. Visit sites such as http://www.4resumes.com and see what's there.

Setting and Creating Action Buttons

Action buttons enable you to control the slide that PowerPoint displays when you click the button during a slide show. For the Selections Directory presentation, you can make the bullets beside the bulleted list items action buttons so customers can jump to the department or division they want to find. PowerPoint creates a *hyperlink* to the slide so that clicking on the action button automatically displays the desired slide. You can set the hyperlink as you create an action button or assign the action to buttons after you create them. You draw and add text to action buttons using the same techniques you use to draw and add text to text boxes, rectangles, and other drawn objects.

> **TIP** You can also add action buttons to enable users to choose the section of a presentation they want to view or to display documents from other applications. Explore these advanced features as you become more comfortable with PowerPoint.

Action buttons are similar to text boxes in that they may both contain text. However, there are a few basic differences between these two drawn objects: Text boxes are designed to place text in an area outside a text placeholder on a slide, and after you draw a text box, the insertion point is positioned inside the text box so that you can type the text. Action buttons are designed to perform an action, so when you draw an action button, the Hyperlink to dialog box opens to enable you to set the action. Text can be added to the action button after the hyperlink is set. By default, text typed in both types of objects automatically wraps to conform to the size and shape of the action button or text box much the same way text in placeholders wraps when it reaches the edge of the placeholder. Text boxes and action buttons enlarge to accommodate additional text when necessary.

> **TROUBLESHOOTING** If text you type in an action button or text box extends beyond the side of the box, the word-wrap feature has been disabled. To enable word-wrap, select the action button or text box and then choose Format, Text Box, click the Text Box tab and check the Word wrap text in AutoShape option.

TASK 6: To Create Action Buttons

1 Launch PowerPoint, open the *Selections Directory.ppt* presentation, and display Slide 5 in Normal view, if necessary.

2 Choose Slide Show, Action Buttons.

FIGURE 3.9

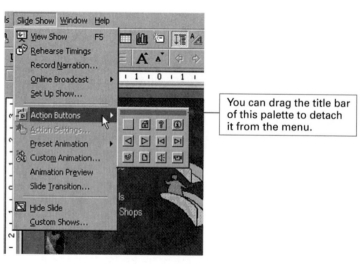

You can drag the title bar of this palette to detach it from the menu.

3 Click the Action Button: Custom ▢ button. The mouse pointer changes to a crosshair ✛.

4 Draw a rectangle around the text of the last bullet point, Specialty Shops.

FIGURE 3.10

Options that control what happens when you click the button.

The action button hides text

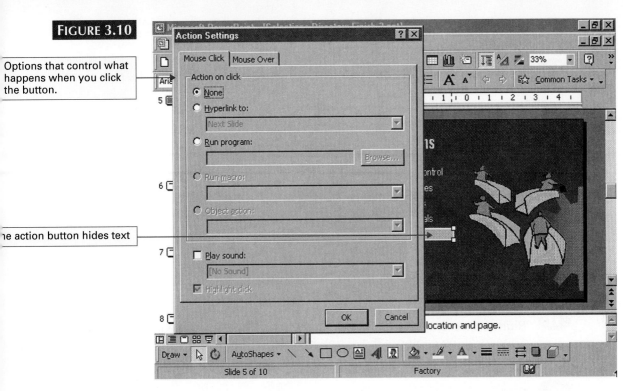

⑤ Choose the Hyperlink to radio button and then choose Slide from the drop-down list immediately below it. Slide titles appear beside the slide numbers in the drop-down list.

⑥ Choose (4) Specialty Shops and then click OK. The slide title appears in the Hyperlink to text box.

⑦ Choose OK. The slide appears with the action button selected.

⑧ Format the button as follows:

• Click the Fill Color [⬛▾] drop-down list arrow on the Drawing toolbar and click the Follow Background Scheme Color button.

TROUBLESHOOTING Having difficulty figuring out where the Follow background Scheme Color is? Point to different colors on the Fill Color palette and wait for the screen tip to appear, as shown in Figure 3.11.

FIGURE 3.11

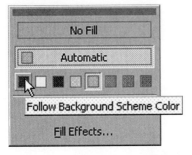

• Click the Line Color [✎▾] drop-down list arrow and choose No Line.

9 Press (CTRL) and drag the action button so that it covers Peripherals. A copy of the action button appears over the next-to-last bullet item.

10 Repeat the procedure from Step 9 to create action buttons for the rest of the bulleted list items.

FIGURE 3.12

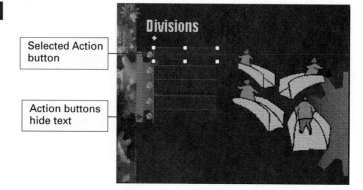

Selected Action button

Action buttons hide text

11 Right-click the first action button and choose Add Text. The insertion point appears at the center of the action button.

12 Type **Image Control** and left-align the text, as shown in Figure 3.13.

13 Right-click the action button containing the text and choose Format, AutoShape. The Format AutoShape dialog box opens.

14 Click the Text Box tab and clear the check mark from the Word wrap text in AutoShape option, if necessary, to keep the text from wrapping in the action button.

> **TIP** When you use the Text Box tool on the Drawing toolbar to add a graphic text box to a slide, you may want to leave this option checked so that the text conforms to the shape and size of your text box.

15 Repeat the procedures in Steps 12-14 to add, align, and format text on all Slide 5 action buttons.

16 Press (SHIFT) and click to select all five action buttons, and then choose Draw, Align or Distribute, Align Left.

FIGURE 3.13

Setting Action Button Actions

When you copy an action button, the action attached to the button goes with it. The hyperlink or action associated with each action button can be edited and changed after the action button is created.

TASK 7:   <u>To Edit Action Button Actions</u>

1 Click the Image Control action button to select it.

> **TROUBLESHOOTING** If you see an insertion point in the action button, click the border around the action button before continuing.

2 Right-click and choose Action Settings from the shortcut menu. The Action Settings dialog box opens.

3 Click the Hyperlink to drop-down list arrow, choose Next Slide, and click OK.

4 Save changes to the presentation, start the slide show, and point to Specialty Shops.

FIGURE 3.14

Because Slide 5 was active, it appears on-screen first.

Because the action button is hyperlinked to other slides, the mouse pointer displays as a pointing hand when you point to the action button.

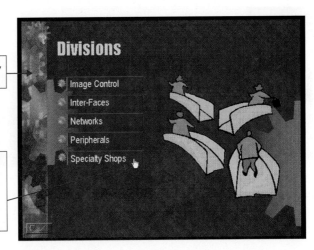

5 Click the Specialty Shops hyperlink to see if the appropriate slide displays.

6 End the slide show and make the necessary edits to the hyperlink.

7 Save changes to the presentation.

Adding Slide Transitions

Slide *transitions* create special effects as your slides move on and off the screen during a slide show. You can use the Slide Sorter toolbar to add transitions to your slides. If slides contain animated text, the animation starts after the slide appears on-screen during the show.

TASK 8: <u>To Add Slide Transitions</u>

1 Display the *Selections Directory.ppt* presentation in Slide Sorter view.

2 Select Slide 1 and then click the Slide Transition Effects drop-down list arrow on the Slide Sorter toolbar.

FIGURE 3.15

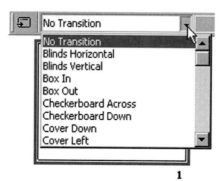

3 Scroll down the effects list and click Dissolve—then watch Slide 1 closely to view the effect!

FIGURE 3.16

Selected effect

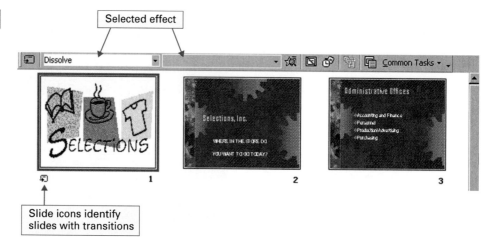

Slide icons identify slides with transitions

4 Click the slide icon below Slide 1. The transition effect repeats to show the effect.

5 Click to select Slide 2, and then press ⟨CTRL⟩ and click Slides 4, 5, 6, and 7. The five selected slides appear with broad dark borders.

6 Click the Slide Transition Effect drop-down list arrow and choose Random Transition.

TROUBLESHOOTING While most of the transition effects are arranged alphabetically on the drop-down list, Random Transition appears way down at the bottom of the list. Scroll down until you find it.

An icon appears below each selected slide.

7 Click the transition slide icon below each slide and view the transition effect. The effect changes each time you click the icon below a slide when you use Random Transition.

8 Save changes to the presentation.

Hiding Slides and Displaying Hidden Slides

Hiding slides enables you to include slides containing detailed information or data in your presentation but display the slides during a slide show only when the audience asks questions or when you need more details about a topic. Hidden slides remain in the background during a slide show and appear only when you access them.

TASK 9:   To Hide Slides and Display Them during a Slide Show

1 Display *Selections Directory.ppt* in Slide Sorter view and select Slide 2.

2 Click the Hide Slide ⬚ button on the Slide Sorter toolbar.

FIGURE 3.17

Slide numbers of hidden slides are marked.

3 Select Slide 1 and then click ⬚. Slide 1 appears in the slide show window.

4 Click the left mouse button until the next slide displays. Slide 3 now appears after Slide 1 during the slide show unless you call up Slide 2.

5 Press (ESC) to stop the slide show, select Slide 1, if necessary, and then click ⬚ to start the show again. Slide 1 appears in the slide show window.

6 Press **H** to display the hidden Slide 2. Slide 2 title appears immediately.

> **TIP** You can also display slides during a slide show by right-clicking on-screen, choosing Go, By Title, and selecting the slide you want to display.

7 Press (ESC) to stop the slide show, select Slide 1, if necessary, and then click 🖳 again. Slide 1 appears in the slide show window.

8 Right-click and choose Go, Slide Navigator.

FIGURE 3.18

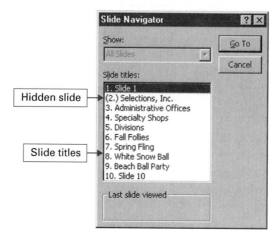

9 Select (2.) Selections, Inc. and then click Go To. Slide 2 appears immediately.

10 Press (ESC) to stop the slide show and then save changes to the presentation.

Setting Presentations to Run Automatically

Setting presentations to run automatically is a great way to communicate information without having to start and stop a slide show manually. Power-Point contains features that enable you to set the presentation to run without interruption. By setting the presentation to run automatically, most controls are unavailable to users, so you don't have to worry about users who are viewing the presentation changing or corrupting the presentation. Self-running presentations restart when they are finished and when they have been idle for more than five minutes. For slides to advance on their own, you will need to tell PowerPoint how long to leave each slide on-screen. You can add timings to each slide manually.

TASK 10: To Set a Show to Run Automatically

1 Choose Slide Show, Set Up Show.

FIGURE 3.19

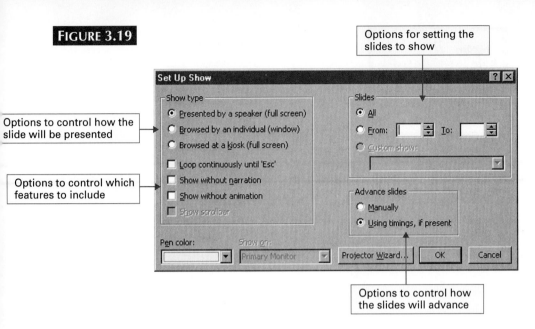

Options for setting the slides to show

Options to control how the slide will be presented

Options to control which features to include

Options to control how the slides will advance

2 Choose Browsed at a kiosk (full screen). The Loop continuously until 'Esc' option is automatically set.

3 Choose OK.

4 Select Slide 1.

5 Click the Slide Transition 🔲 button on the Slide Sorter toolbar.

FIGURE 3.20

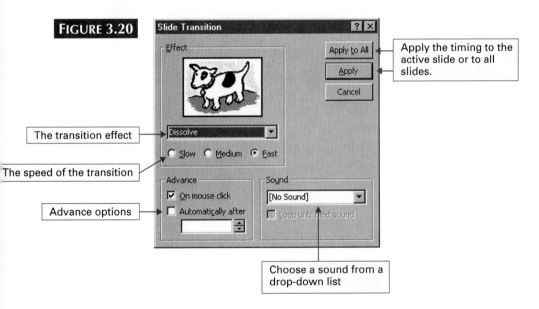

Apply the timing to the active slide or to all slides.

The transition effect

The speed of the transition

Advance options

Choose a sound from a drop-down list

6 Choose the Automatically after option, type **10** in the value box, and then choose Apply.

FIGURE 3.21

:10   1

Timings appear
below images.

7   Click   to start the show.

8   Press (ESC) to stop the show and save changes to the presentation.

☑ Check Point

Add slide timings to other slides in the presentation and save changes to the presentation. Pack your presentation to go and submit it to your instructor.

Summary and Exercises

Summary

- Slides in a presentation can be formatted and shown on-screen or projected on an audiovisual screen or flat surface.
- Use Slide Sorter view to make final changes to the presentation organization— moving slides is as simple as dragging and dropping.
- Viewing your presentation as a slide show makes it come to life.
- You can use both the keyboard and mouse to move among slides in a presentation during a slide show.
- The slide show shortcut menu displays commands for navigating the slide show and controlling on-screen features.
- Slides can be copied or duplicated to appear more than once in a presentation.
- Action buttons enable you hyperlink to other slides during a presentation. You can copy the action buttons to other slides.
- Slide transitions create special effects as your slides move on and off the screen during a slide show.
- Additional slides can be hidden in case the audience asks questions or when you need to present more details about a topic.
- Setting a presentation to run automatically is a great way to communicate information without having to start and stop a slide show manually.

Key Terms and Operations

Key Terms

Action button
Advancing slide
Black Screen
Delete Slide
hiding slides
hyperlink

On-Screen Presentation
slide show shortcut menu
Slide Sorter view
thumbnail
transitions

Operations

add slide transitions
hide slides and display hidden slides
present a slide show
rearrange presentation Slides using Slide Sorter view
set action buttons
set presentations to run automatically
use mouse and keyboard techniques to navigate a slide show
use the slide show shortcut menu

Study Questions

Multiple Choice

1. Which view displays mini images of the slides?
   a. Outline view
   b. Slide Sorter view
   c. Slide view
   d. Notes view

2. Which is not a procedure used to launch a slide show?
   a. press (F6).
   b. choose View, Slide Show.
   c. choose Slide Show, View Show.
   d. click the Slide Show button.

3. To rearrange slides in your presentation, you would use which feature?
   a. Slide preview
   b. Arrange view
   c. Slide Sorter
   d. View toolbar

4. When you want a slide to appear in more than one position in a presentation, you should _____ the slide.
   a. duplicate
   b. move
   c. copy
   d. both a and c

5. Which buttons enable you to control the slide that PowerPoint displays when you click the button during a slide show?
   a. superlink buttons
   b. action buttons
   c. slide control buttons
   d. slide show buttons

6. To return to the previous slide in a slide show using the mouse,
   a. left-click and select Previous.
   b. use the left arrow key.
   c. click the left mouse button.
   d. right-click and select Previous.

7. Which menu is used to display commands for navigating a slide show?
   a. the Standard toolbar menu
   b. the Slide Show shortcut menu
   c. the Navigation menu
   d. the Slide Show commands menu

8. Which view should you use to add transition effects to slides?
   a. Slide Sorter view
   b. Outline view
   c. Slide view
   d. Transition view

9. To easily make bulleted lists appear with different transition effects, you would select which option from the Slide Transition effects list?
   a. Many Transitions
   b. Blinds Horizontal
   c. Random Transition
   d. Checkerboard Across

Short Answer

1. How can you reset the toolbars?

2. In Slide Sorter view, how will you know which slide is active?

3. What options can be used to stop a slide show?

4. What is the easiest way to insert a slide that you want to appear more than once in a presentation?

5. What option is useful to ensure that the audience focuses on you if discussion ensues while presenting a slide show?

6. How do you add transition effects to a slide?

7. What are the four different techniques you can use to start a Slide Show?

8. How can you advance to the next slide in a slide show using the keyboard?

9. Why would you want to hide slides in your presentation?

Fill in the Blank

1. Slides in a _____ can be formatted and shown on-screen.

2. You will find that the _____ view makes organizing your presentation easier.

3. _____ slides enables you to include slides to be shown if you need more information or details about a topic.

4. Slide Sorter view prevents slide _____.

5. To create a duplicate slide, use the _____ command.

6. Viewing your presentation as a(n) _____ makes it come to life.

7. Either the keyboard or the _____ can be used to move among slides during a slide show.

8. PowerPoint creates a(n) _____ to a slide to enable you to jump to a specific area of the presentation.

9. Slide Sorter view displays miniature, or _____, images of the slides.

10. Slide _____ create special effects as your slides move on and off screen during a slide show.

For Discussion

1. List the four ways to launch a slide show.

2. What option allows you to set a presentation to run without interruption, and how do you set the option to view a full screen?

3. Why would you use the expand feature in your presentation?

4. How can you format specific slides in your presentation to jump to specific divisions?

5. How can you control which slide appears first during a slide show?

Hands-On Exercises

1. Adding Slides to the Presentation and Creating Action Buttons

Additional slides are needed in the presentation to enable Ms. Quinn to locate information about specific areas. When you're finished you will have created the slides pictured in Figure 3.22 (not necessarily in the order shown here). After the new slides are completed, you can create hyperlinks from existing slides to the new slides so that Ms. Quinn will easily be able to jump from topic to topic.

FIGURE 3.22

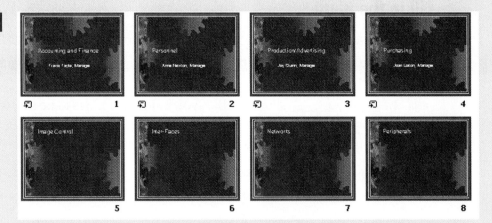

To complete the presentation, follow these steps:

1. Open the *Selections Directory.ppt* presentation and display Slide 3 in Normal view.

2. Create a new title slide, type **Accounting and Finance** in the title placeholder, and type **Travis Taylor, Manager** in the subtitle placeholder.

3. Repeat the procedures from Step 2 to create title slides containing the following text for Slides 5–7:

Slide 5:   **Personnel**
       Anne Newton, Manager

Slide 6:   **Production/Advertising**
       Joy Quinn, Manager

Slide 7:   **Purchasing**
       Joan Liston, Manager

4. Display Slide 3 and create action buttons for each of the bullet points, directing the hyperlink to the appropriate new slide. Create action buttons on Slides 4–7 that jump back to Slide 3.

5. Display Slide 9 (the new Slide 9 title is Divisions) and create a new Title Only slide after Slide 9. Type **Image Control** in the title placeholder.

6. Repeat the procedure from Step 5 to create the following slides to follow Slide 10:

   Slide 11: **Inter-Faces**

   Slide 12: **Networks**

   Slide 13: **Peripherals**

7. Move Slide 8 (Specialty Shops) so that it appears after Slide 13 (Peripherals) and then create or edit action buttons for the bullet points contained on Slide 8 (Divisions) to hyperlink to the appropriate slide. Be sure the action buttons do not extend onto the graphic. Create action buttons on Slides 9–13 that return to Slide 8. Show the slide show and test the hyperlinks.

8. Add speaker notes to the Slide Notes pane for each slide containing a hyperlink. Include information about what action the hyperlink performs. Print a copy of Notes Pages for each slide containing speaker notes.

9. Add slide transitions to the new slides and save changes to the presentation.

2. Rearranging and Hiding Slides and Showing a Presentation

The Willows Restaurants presentation is almost ready for Mr. Taylor to show, but it needs a bit more editing. The final presentation outline appears in Figure 3.23.

FIGURE 3.23

1 ▣ The Willows Restaurants

    Something for Everyone - Add the Spice of Variety to Your Life!

2 ▣ California Dreamin'

- Lonely for the beach and the sun? Our casual atmosphere will take you away...
- Fresh seafood, salad and pasta - all with a light, healthy flair

3 ▣ A Taste of Thailand

- An exotic selection of dishes straight from Bangkok
- Noodles, stir frys and rice dishes - your choice of meat

4 ▣ South of the Border

- Viva Mexico! Authentic Northern Mexico specialties
- Burritos, tacos, fajitas and the best fried ice cream outside of Tijuana
- Homemade tortillas, chips and salsa available for purchase

5 ▢ Manilla Pho Hoacali

- If you've never sampled the tastes of Vietnam, this restaurant is a must!
- Rice vermicelli, soft noodles, Vietnamese curry and specialty drinks
- Add your own fresh herbs to create your own unique flavor

6 ▣ Catch of the Day

- Our fish are flown in twice daily to give you the freshest selection possible
- New England lobster, crabs, scallops, and over 30 different fishes every c (based on seasonal availability)
- Lobster bisque, clam chowder and seafood gumbo made from scratch

7 ▢ Sandwich Shops

- Need to grab a quick bite? Visit one of our many delis and sandwich stop
- Willow Green on the golf course.
- The Cola Shop on the Mezzanine.
- Grey Fox Deli at the Grande Hotel.
- The Boardwalk on the beach.

8 ▢ Thibodeaux's Crawfish Pot

- Oh yeah, cher, you gotta go to the best cajun restaurant this side of Mard Gras!
- Authentic gumbo, fried alligator, crawfish etouffee and blackened steak
- Check out Brunet's attic - Louisiana specialty items so you can take the b home with you

9 ▢ Oh yeah, cher, you gotta go to the best cajun restaurant this s of Mardi Gras!

- Owned by Doug Mayeaux
- All foods cooked to order - if you don't like it spicy, you don't get it spicy!

10 ▢ Authentic gumbo, fried alligator, crawfish etouffee and blackened steak

- What's a crawfish? Looks like a small lobster, has a taste between crawfi and shrimp - you gotta try it to believe it!
- Does blackening the steak burn it? No! It's simply a seasoning and cook technique - if it tastes burnt, send it back!

11 ▢ Check out Brunet's attic - Louisiana specialty items so you c: take the bayou home with you

- Gumbo and Jambalaya mixes so you can make it at home
- Original Tobasco® products straight from Iberville Parish
- Cajun spices and seasonings

12 ▢ Chang's Wok

- For a real Chinese experience - cooked right at your table!
- Choose your own meats, vegetables and spices, all cooked fresh by your own chef

Follow these instructions to complete the presentation:

1. Launch PowerPoint, if necessary, and open the Willows Restaurants presentation.

2. Display the presentation in Slide Sorter view and move Slide 4 so that it becomes Slide 2. Then move Slide 8 so that it becomes Slide 6.

3. Select Slide 6 and then click the New Slide button on the Standard toolbar and choose the Bulleted List AutoLayout. Double-click the plain new slide to display it in Slide view so that you can add slide text.

4. Type **Sandwich Shops** in the title placeholder and then add the following bulleted list to the bulleted list placeholder:

   - **Need to grab a quick bite? Visit one of our many delis and sandwich stops.**
   - **Willow Green on the golf course.**
   - **The Cola Shop on the Mezzanine.**
   - **Grey Fox Deli at the Grande Hotel.**
   - **The Boardwalk on the beach.**

5. Display the presentation in Slide Sorter view again, hide Slide 7, and create new slides that contain the bullet points from Slide 8 as their titles.

6. Switch to Outline view and add the text for new Slides 9–10, as shown in Figure 3.23.

7. View the slide show and then display the presentation in Slide Sorter view to add transitions and text preset animations that you find most effective to each slide.

8. Save the changes to the presentation and print a copy of the outline. Demonstrate the slide show for your instructor.

On Your Own Exercises

1. Locating Information on the Internet; Editing, Enhancing, and Viewing a Presentation as a Slide Show; and Packing a Presentation to Go

Mr. Stills would like to fine-tune the Willows Restaurants presentation to include additional restaurants of interest in the North Carolina area. Search the Internet for resorts, restaurants, and so on in the North Carolina area and create two additional slides in the presentation to summarize the information. In addition, you need to make the following changes to the presentation:

1. Display the presentation Slide Sorter view and rearrange the bulleted list slides into alphabetical order by titles as follows:
   - Slide 3 becomes Slide 2
   - Slide 6 becomes Slide 4
   - Slide 12 becomes Slide 5

- Slide 7 becomes Slide 6
- Slide 8 becomes Slide 7

2. Add two new bulleted list slides to the end of the presentation and type the information you found on the Internet on the appropriate slide.

3. Add the following bulleted list items to Slide 2:
   - An exotic selection of dishes straight from Bangkok
   - Thailand's capital city
   - Three chefs trained in Bangkok
   - Noodles, stir fries and rice dishes—your choice of meat
   - You pick how hot you want it!
   - Mild, Medium, Hot, Very Hot

4. Add transitions and text preset animations to the bulleted list slides and show the presentation.

When you're finished, pack the presentation onto a floppy disk. Save and close the presentation and exit PowerPoint when you have completed your work.

2. Editing and Enhancing a Presentation and Viewing a Slide Show

Open your presentation titled *1999.ppt* and use the tools presented in this project to create additional slides for bulleted lists, rearrange slides, and add text to the slides. Add slide transitions and text preset animations to slides in the presentation. View the presentation as a slide show and save the presentation. Present the slide show to your instructor and print pure black-and-white handouts with six framed slides per page. Close the presentation and exit PowerPoint when you've completed your work.

3. Rearranging and Hiding Slides and Showing a Presentation

Mr. Stills has asked you to reorder the slides in *The Willows Restaurants.ppt*. He would also like to include several hidden slides and rearrange the slides in Slide Sorter view so that the slides are in alphabetical order by title. Then create a new slide that identifies the different types of restaurants (Mexican, Chinese, Cajun, and Seafood, for example) and create action buttons from the slide to at least one example of a restaurant serving that type of food. View the slide show and check the hyperlinks. Then add transitions and text preset animations to each slide.

Save changes to the presentation before closing the presentation. Exit PowerPoint when you've completed your work.

4. Using the Slide Show Shortcut Menu and Setting Action Buttons

Open the presentation *Barbecue.ppt* and start the slide show. Use the slide show shortcut menu and set the presentation to go to black screen so that the audience focuses on you. Insert slides listing the basic ingredients in the menu items and use the action button to create a hyperlink to these slides should the employees ask questions. Add slide transition effect and sound effects. Save the presentation to diskette using Pack and Go.

5. Creating a New Presentation Using Slides from an Existing Presentation and Information from the Internet

Open the Our National Forests presentation and copy the slide containing information about the number of guests who have visited the National Forests to the Windows Clipboard.

Create a new blank presentation containing a title slide and type the title **National Parks and National Forests** in the title placeholder. Type **Where do most visitors go?** as the subtitle. Then switch to Slide Sorter view and paste the slide from the Clipboard to become Slide 2 in the new presentation.

Connect to the Internet and search for information about our national parks, focusing on the number of visitors to the parks each year. Compile this information into another slide in the presentation and add a final slide to the presentation that draws a conclusion from the information you've gathered. Save your presentation using the filename *Parks and Forests—The Visitor Perspective*.

Web Tip

Be careful how you enter Web addresses in the URL text box. You may end up at an inappropriate site just when your instructor is looking over your shoulder!

6. Expanding Your Family Tree Using Action Buttons

Open the presentation you created that contains information about your family tree. Create a bulleted list slide and position it as Slide 2. Add the title **Family Navigator** as the title for the new slide and enter the titles of additional slides in the presentation as your bulleted list points. Create an action button for each bulleted list point and hyperlink each button directly to the slide containing the information.

For each individual on your family tree for whom you have identified and included at least one parent in your presentation, create an action button that hyperlinks the individual to the slide containing information about his or her parent(s).

Save changes to your presentation and then pack the presentation to take home and show to your family.

Working with Masters

So far, you've worked with most of the basic features PowerPoint 2000 has to offer. You've created presentations, enhanced the presentations with art and graphics, and learned to show presentations with style using transitions and special effects. Now you're ready to get to work with Slide Masters and create your own special presentation design. You can apply most of the techniques you've already learned, such as how to add graphics, animate text, and format placeholders, as you develop your masterful design.

Objectives

After completing this project, you will be able to:

➤ Display presentation Slide Masters

➤ Add footers to presentations

➤ Change text style and alignment on Slide Masters

➤ Change bullet formats on Slide Masters

➤ Format the slide background

➤ Customize a color scheme

➤ Insert and format graphics on Slide Masters

➤ Create Title Masters

➤ Save presentation designs as templates

Running Case

Your temporary assignment to the administrative offices is almost complete. Before you go, Mr. Goebel has one last task he wants you to undertake. He wants you to design the Selections, Inc., master design template so that he can distribute it to all the stores and they can use it as a guide for developing their local store template.

The Challenge

Ms. Joy Quinn has sketched out the design she envisions might be appropriate for all Selections, Inc. stores. Her sketches for the title slide and bulleted list slides are shown in Figure 4.1. Your task is to create the design in PowerPoint and save the design as a template.

FIGURE 4.1

1   2

The Strategy

You can create the presentation design for Selections, Inc., by accessing the presentation Slide Master and using PowerPoint features to create the background, format placeholder text, change the bullet shape, insert the graphic on the slide, and add slide numbers so that they appear on all slides in the presentation. When the presentation design is complete, you can save it as a template and apply it to all presentations you create for Selections, Inc.

The Setup

To ensure that your screen will match the figures pictured in this project, make sure the settings shown in Table 4.1 are active.

Table 4.1

Item	Action
Office Assistant	Hide the Assistant.
View	Click the Normal View button at the bottom of the presentation window. Choose View, Ruler to turn off Ruler, if necessary.
Toolbars	Ensure that both the Standard and Formatting toolbars are active. If you don't see them, choose View, Toolbars, and then select them.
	Reset both toolbars by choosing Tools, Customize, and then display the Toolbars page of the dialog box. Check the Standard and Formatting toolbars and the menu bar. Choose each of these items individually and choose Reset. Choose OK to confirm each change.
	Click the Options tab and ensure that the Personalized Menus and Toolbars options are all deselected. Then click the Reset my usage data button and choose Yes to restore automatic changes to menus.
	When all toolbars and the menu bar have been reset, choose Close.
Zoom	Set the zoom to 41%.

Displaying Slide Masters

Each presentation you create contains slides formatted with a template that contains design elements such as background color, text placeholder format, and graphics. These design elements are stored in layouts called ***Slide Masters***. Each template contains a separate master for formatting each type of presentation material (slides, notes, and handouts).

You can create the presentation design requested by Ms. Quinn by editing the masters so that they contain the elements she wants to include in the presentation design. To customize a specific presentation, you must first open the presentation you want to customize or create a new presentation formatted with the template that most resembles the presentation design you want to create. You can then display the presentation Slide Master and make the changes necessary to create your custom design.

PowerPoint contains two different masters for formatting slides:

- The Slide Master design is applied to slides formatted using all AutoLayout formats except the Title AutoLayout format.
- The Title Master design is applied to slides formatted using the Title AutoLayout.

TASK 1:   To Display the Presentation Slide Master

1 Launch PowerPoint and create a new blank presentation that contains a slide formatted using the Title AutoLayout format. The new slide appears with the presentation outline and notes in Normal view.

2 Choose View, Master.

FIGURE 4.2

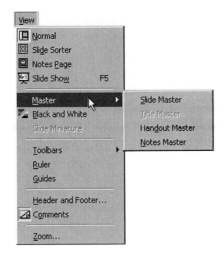

3 Choose Slide Master.

FIGURE 4.3

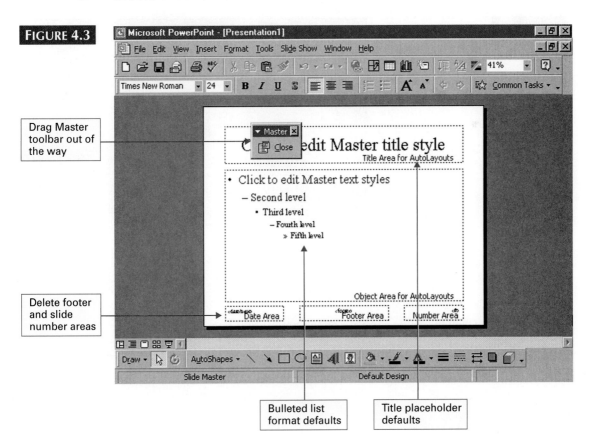

Adding Footers to Presentations

Adding information such as the company name, date, or slide number to slides in a presentation is easy; all you have to do is tell PowerPoint which elements you want to include in the layout and add the features to the *footer*—the area at the bottom of a slide below the text placeholder. Features you add to the footer automatically appear in the default footer position of each slide you can, of course, reposition them. Although you can activate footer features from any view, you can use the Slide Master to change the position of footer area placeholders.

TASK 2: ## To Add and Position the Slide Number in the Footer Area of Presentation Slides

1 Choose View, Header and Footer.

FIGURE 4.4

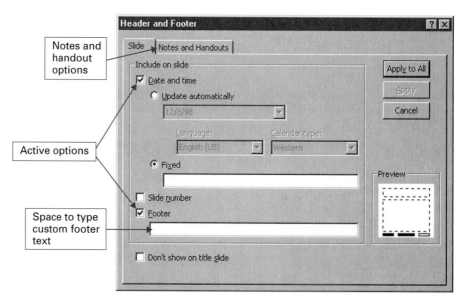

2 Click the Slide number check box until it becomes active.

3 Remove the checkmarks from the Date and time and Footer checkboxes.

FIGURE 4.5

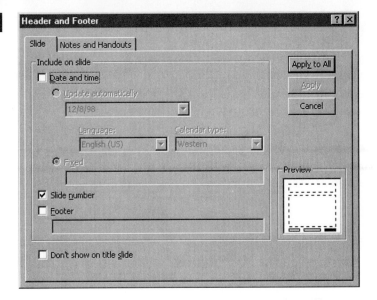

4 Click Apply to All. The Header and Footer dialog box closes and the Slide Master appears.

5 Click the Number Area text box to select it, and then drag it to the right so that the right edge of the box is against the slide edge, as shown in Figure 4.6.

FIGURE 4.6

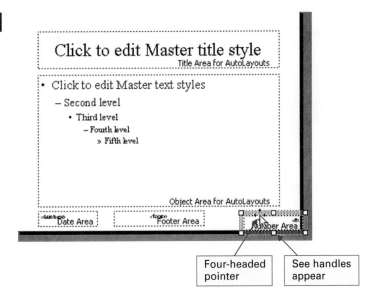

Four-headed pointer

See handles appear

6 Save the presentation using the file name *Selections Design*.

Changing Text Style and Alignment on Slide Masters

To ensure that slide text style and size remain consistent on all slides in the presentation, you can change the text format and **_alignment_** in text placeholders on the Slide Master. Then you can adjust text size and alignment on individual slides within a presentation as necessary.

> **TIP** When you change the appearance and alignment of text on the Slide Master of an existing presentation, any text on slides within the presentation that you have formatted individually will not be affected.

TASK 3: To Change Text Style and Alignment on the Slide Master

1 Display the Slide Master, if necessary, and click a blank area of the slide.

2 Press (SHIFT) and click the Title Area for AutoLayouts placeholder on the Slide Master, as shown in Figure 4.7.

FIGURE 4.7

3 Click the Left Alignment ≣ button on the Formatting toolbar. Text aligns to the left of the placeholder.

4 Triple-click the title placeholder text to select it. All title text is selected.

5 Click the Font drop-down list arrow on the Formatting toolbar and select Comic Sans MS font. The font changes to the new font. Alignment is now easier to see.

FIGURE 4.8

TIP If the Comic Sans MS font is not available, select a script style font.

6 Save changes to the presentation.

Check Point

Add your name to the footer area of the Slide Master, left-align the name, and position the Footer Area box at the left edge of the Slide Master. Experiment with fonts and alignments for the bulleted list placeholder and select a font and alignment that complements the title font and alignment. Save changes to your presentation.

Changing Bullet Format on Slide Masters

Each bulleted list text level is formatted using a separate bullet style. The format for the bullet is built into the template design and can easily be altered. When you change the *bullet format* for bullet levels on the Slide Master, the new bullet shape changes for the selected level on all slides in the presentation. PowerPoint contains a variety of *text categories* from which you can choose your bullet shapes.

You can also change the bullet format for a specific bullet level on the Slide Master or for a bulleted list on an individual slide from bullets to numbers when appropriate. Just select the level or bullet points you want to change and click the Numbering ⬚ button on the Formatting toolbar.

You can also create an AutoNumber format quickly without using the menus. Press (BACKSPACE) to remove the existing bullet or number. Then type the number or letter along with appropriate end punctuation as you want them to appear in the list [for example, 1., I. (i), a)]. Press (TAB) and type the text for the list item. When you press (ENTER) for the next item, PowerPoint automatically enters the number or letter in the sequence you started [for example, 2., II., (ii), b)]. You can even autoformat bullets by typing an asterisk (*) or chevron (>)—such symbols become bullets (•) or fancy chevrons (➤) automatically after you press (ENTER) following the list item text.

> **TIP** When you change the bullet format on the Slide Master of an existing presentation, bullets you have formatted individually on slides are not changed.

TASK 4: To Change the Bullet Format for a Text Level

1 Point to the second bullet level line in the Object Area for AutoLayouts and right-click.

FIGURE 4.9

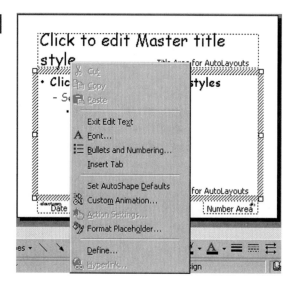

2 Select Bullets and Numbering from the shortcut menu.

FIGURE 4.10

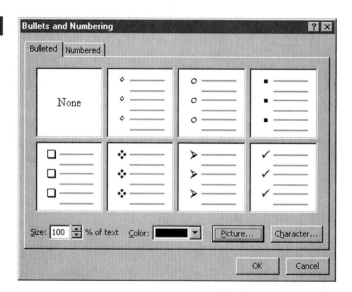

3 Click the Picture button to open the Picture Bullet dialog box.

FIGURE 4.11

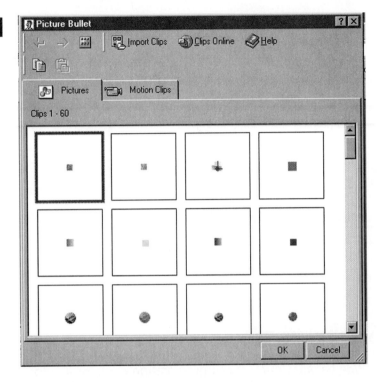

4 Scroll the bullet pictures and click the bullet you want to use. The bullet is displayed in a Preview window.

FIGURE 4.12

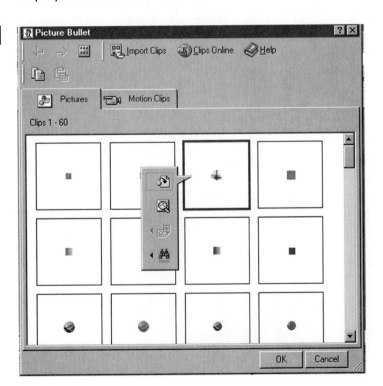

5 Click the Insert Clip button. The selected clip appears beside the second bullet level.

FIGURE 4.13

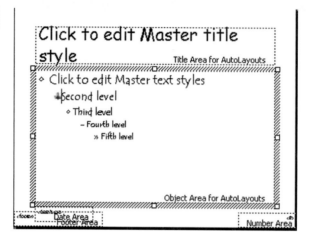

6 Save changes to the presentation.

Formatting the Slide Background

The *slide background* for your presentation contains a color design that provides the backdrop for all text and objects you place on presentation slides. As a result, adding or changing the background color scheme often affects the colors of title text, bulleted list text, colors displayed in charts, and other objects you add to slides. When you like the colors you have set, you can leave the color scheme intact and simply lighten and format the background color.

TASK 5: <u>To Format the Slide Background</u>

1 Choose Format, Background.

FIGURE 4.14

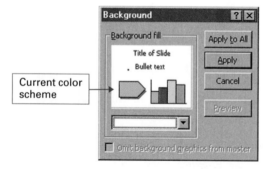

2 Click the Background fill drop-down list arrow.

FIGURE 4.15

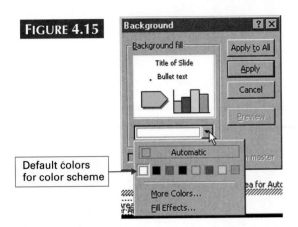

Default colors for color scheme

3 Choose Fill Effects.

FIGURE 4.16

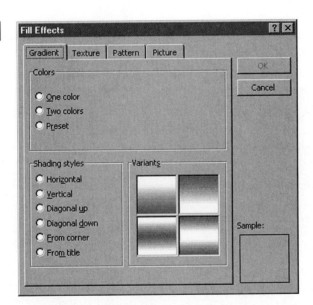

4 Choose Two colors and select the settings shown in Figure 4.17.

FIGURE 4.17

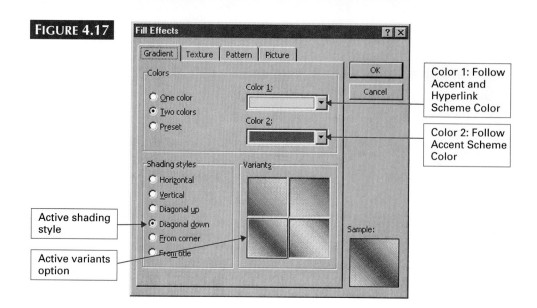

Color 1: Follow Accent and Hyperlink Scheme Color

Color 2: Follow Accent Scheme Color

Active shading style

Active variants option

5 Click OK to close the Fill Effects dialog box and then click Apply to All to format all slide types with the background.

FIGURE 4.18

6 Save changes to the presentation.

Break Point

If necessary you can save your file, exit PowerPoint, and continue this project later.

Customizing a Color Scheme

Each template was designed with a specific color identified for title text, bulleted list text and lines, background, fills, and accent colors. The combination of these colors is called a *color scheme*. Color schemes used in PowerPoint templates were designed by graphic artists for visual effect and to complement other colors. When the colors displayed for different objects on your slides need to be adjusted to better fit your needs, you can edit the individual object colors by customizing the color scheme.

TASK 6: To Customize a Color Scheme

1 Select Format, Slide Color Scheme.

FIGURE 4.19

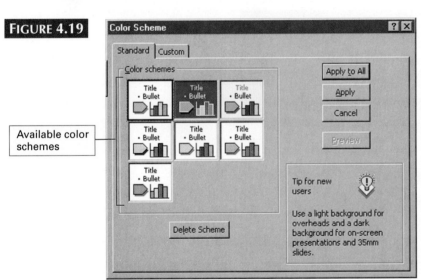

Available color schemes

2 Click the color scheme on the Standard page that most closely fits the colors you want to use for the presentation. You have free rein to be creative here. Take advantage of it—you can always go back and change it if it doesn't look right.

3 Click the Custom tab.

FIGURE 4.20

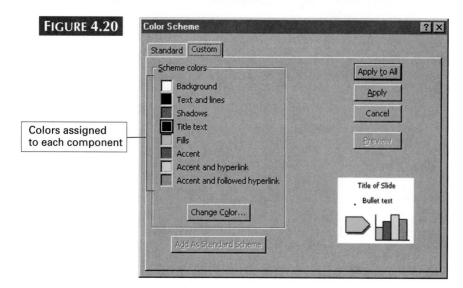

Colors assigned to each component

4 Select the component you want to change from the Scheme colors list and then choose Change Color.

TIP You wouldn't want to choose the Background component after spending so much time creating a gradient fill. Pick one of the other components.

FIGURE 4.21

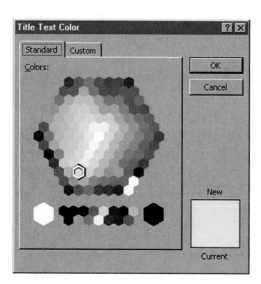

TIP If you choose to create a custom color, you can select a position on the Custom color palette or enter values for hue, saturation, and luminescence as well as for depth of green, red, and blue to create the color you want. Experiment with these values to see how they affect the color.

5 Select the desired color for the component and choose OK. The selected color appears in the color box on the Scheme colors list.

6 Choose Apply to All to apply the color change to all slides in the presentation.

 ## Check Point

Use the same procedure to change the color of each additional item you want to change. Change the bullet format for additional bullet levels, and adjust the background color if necessary. Save changes to your presentation.

Inserting and Formatting Graphics on Slide Masters

You're almost finished with the special design Ms. Quinn requested. All you have left is to add the Selections logo graphic to the presentation design. You can use the same procedures to insert the graphic on the Slide Master that you use to insert graphics on slides.

 ## Web Tip

You can download the *Selections.gif* graphic from the SELECT Web site at http://www.prenhall.com/select, if you have not yet done so.

 TASK 7: ## To Insert and Format a Graphic on a Slide Master

1 Display the Slide Master, if necessary.

2 Choose Insert, Picture, From File. The Insert Picture dialog box displays the contents of the active folder.

3 Open the folder that contains the *Selections.gif* graphic.

4 Select *Selections.gif* and choose Insert. The graphic appears in the center of the slide and is selected.

FIGURE 4.22

5 Move and size the graphic so that they appear as shown in Figure 4.23.

FIGURE 4.23

6 Select the graphic and display the Picture toolbar.

FIGURE 4.24

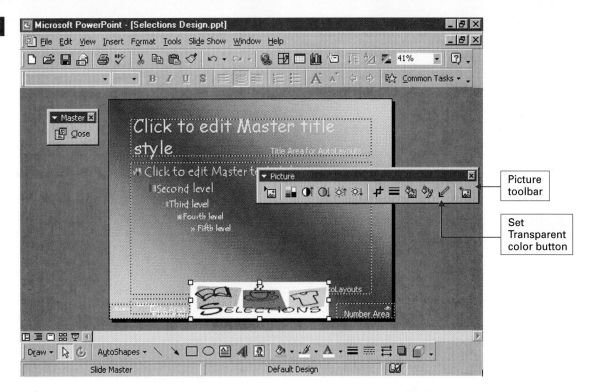

Picture toolbar

Set Transparent color button

7 Click the Set Transparent Color ![button] button on the Picture toolbar. The pointer appears with a *transparent color* brush ![brush].

8 Click a white corner of the graphic.

FIGURE 4.25

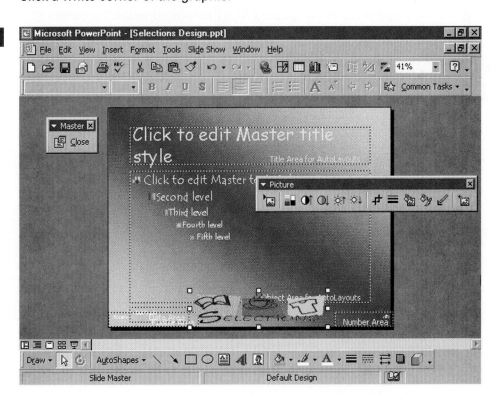

9 Save changes to the presentation.

Web Tip

Want to remember some oldies but goodies? Visit *Life* Magazine's "Places We Remember" in the collective life of the Beatles. You'll find it at http://www.pathfinder.com/Life/thebeatles.

Creating and Formatting Title Masters

Slide Masters contain design features that are applied to all slides in the presentation as long as no special **Title Master** exists. Because text on the title slide is often arranged differently from text on other slides in a presentation, you may want to adjust the layout and design for title slides using the Title Master. PowerPoint applies Title Master format to all slides in a presentation formatted using the Title AutoLayout format.

Check Point

Only one template master can be used in each presentation. In Project 3 you saw slides from a different presentation automatically reformat to the active presentation template when they were inserted, remember?

TASK 8: To Create a Presentation Title Master

1 Choose View, Master, Slide Master, if necessary.

2 Choose Insert, New Title Master. Title Masters format with the background color, text style, and text alignment of the Slide Master. Graphics contained on the Slide Master appear.

> **TROUBLESHOOTING** Most templates contain preformatted Title Masters. If the presentation is formatted with a template, New Title Master may not be listed on the Insert menu, so you can skip Step 2.

FIGURE 4.26

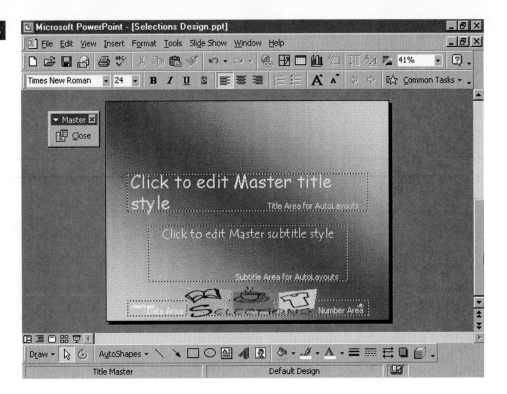

3 Select the graphic and size it to fill the complete Title Master.

4 Display the Picture toolbar, if necessary, and then click the Image Control button on the Picture toolbar.

FIGURE 4.27

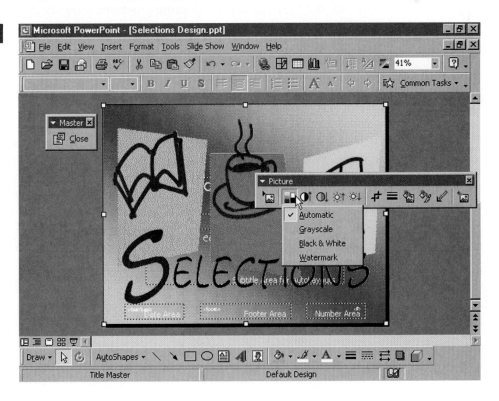

5 Select Watermark.

FIGURE 4.28

FIGURE 4.28

6 Choose Draw, Order, Send to Back. The graphic moves behind text so that you can select placeholders.

7 Adjust the placement of the Footer Area and Number Area on the Title Master so that they appear in the same positions they occupied on the Slide Master.

8 Close the Picture toolbar and then save changes to the presentation.

Saving Presentation Designs as Templates

When you spend hours designing a presentation format for company or personal use, you may want to save the design and apply it to other presentations you develop. To save a design so that you can apply it to other presentations, you can save it as a template. Templates store slide designs—not the text and other objects included in presentations. As a result, when you use an existing presentation design to create a template, you need to remove existing text from the presentation slides before saving the design as a template.

TASK 9: To Save a Presentation Design as a Template

1 Switch to Normal view and choose File, Save As. The Save As dialog box opens.

TROUBLESHOOTING Be sure to choose Save As to open the Save As dialog box. Choosing Save will overwrite your original presentation.

2 Click the Save as type drop-down list arrow and select Design Template (*.pot).

FIGURE 4.29

Templates folder opens

3 Type **(Your Initials) Selections Design** in the File name text box, and press (ENTER). Substitute your initials in place of (Your Initials) in the file name. The template name appears in the presentation title bar.

TROUBLESHOOTING To ensure that your presentation design is listed on the pages of the New Presentation dialog box when you choose File, New, you should save your presentation template to the Program Files\Microsoft Office\Templates\Presentation Designs folder on the hard drive.

4 Close the presentation template.

5 Choose File, New, and then click your template design name. Your template appears alphabetically among the templates listed. An image of the presentation title slide displays in the Preview box.

TROUBLESHOOTING If you save the template file to a different disk or folder, you will need to apply the template to presentations after they are created. Open the presentation, and then choose Format, Apply Design Template. Then you can open the folder containing your template and apply it as needed.

TIP The variant gradient you applied as the slide background may appear distorted in the Preview box.

FIGURE 4.30

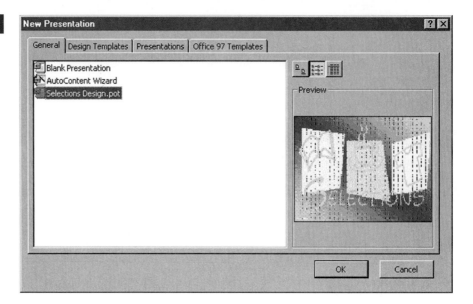

6 Press (ENTER). A new presentation containing a title slide formatted with the custom Title Master design is automatically created.

 Check Point

Type **My New Title Master** in the title placeholder of the slide and type your name in the subtitle placeholder. Then create a new bulleted list slide titled *Slide Master* that contains the following bullet points: Slide Master, Title Master, Handout Master, Notes Master. Save the presentation using the file name *Working with Masters* and print a copy of the presentation as hand-outs with two slides per page. Close the presentation.

TIP You can open the template and edit the template design by choosing File, Open; selecting Presentation Templates from the Files of type list; opening the Presentation Designs subfolder in the Templates folder if necessary; and double-clicking the template name. Changes you make to the presentation template and text you add while the template is open automatically become part of the presentation design. If you have already created a presentation and have altered or edited the colors or format of text in the presentation, you can use this presentation as a basis for creating a new presentation template. Be sure, when you use an existing presentation to create a template, that you delete all slide text before saving the presentation as a template; and be sure to select File, Save As before saving the presentation as a template. You should leave the original presentation intact!

Summary and Exercises

Summary

- Slide Masters enable you to make changes to text placeholder formats and apply the changes to all slides in the presentation.

- The techniques used to make changes to the Slide Master can be used to change the format and design of Notes Pages and Handouts Masters.

- Slide Master changes can be applied to slides following the Title AutoLayout format by choosing the Apply to All button rather than the Apply button when a Title Master is included among the master layouts.

- Format changes you make to Slide Masters do not affect format changes made specifically to individual features of selected slides.

- PowerPoint provides a variety of different text categories that contain bullet shapes and formats you can apply to bullet levels.

- To display information contained in footer area placeholders, set the features you want to display in the Header and Footer dialog box.

- You can change the effect of a presentation template by changing the slide background color. Different features enable you to create special effects with the background fill.

- When you create a presentation design that you want to save and use again, you can save the design as a template in the Templates, Presentation Designs folder. The name you assign to the template appears alphabetically on the Presentations Design page of the New Presentation dialog box.

- Slides formatted with the Title AutoLayout format will follow the color design of the Slide Master unless you create a special Slide Master for the presentation template. Graphics placed on a Slide Master do not appear automatically on Title slides; they must be copied or placed on the Title Master separately.

Key Terms and Operations

Key Terms

alignment	Slide Master
bullet format	text categories
color scheme	Title Master
footer	transparent color
slide background	

Operations

add footers to presentations
change bullet formats on Slide Masters
change text style and alignment on Slide Masters
create Title Masters
customize a color scheme

display presentation Slide Masters
format the slide background
insert and format graphics on Slide Masters
save presentation designs as templates

Study Questions

Multiple Choice

1. You can display the presentation Slide Master by
   a. clicking the Master shortcut icon on the desktop.
   b. choosing View, Master, Slide Master.
   c. choosing Slide Master from the Slide Show menu.
   d. displaying a slide and pressing (ENTER).

2. To apply changes you make on a Slide Master to slides formatted using the Title Master,
   a. click the Apply to All button on the various dialog boxes.
   b. use the Format Painter to copy changes.
   c. choose Format, Apply Format from the menus.
   d. click the Apply button on the various dialog boxes.

3. Format changes you make to the Slide Master
   a. affect every slide in the presentation.
   b. affect every slide in the presentation except title slides.
   c. affect every slide in the presentation except title slides and slides that have been individually formatted.
   d. affect only the slide that was active when you displayed the Slide Master.

4. Placeholders for slide numbers appear in the
   a. header area of a slide.
   b. footer area of Slide Masters.
   c. header and footer area of Slide Masters.
   d. margin of slides.

5. Information you want to add to the footer area of slides must be "turned on" from the
   a. Slide Master.
   b. Title Master.
   c. Header and Footer dialog box.
   d. individual presentation slides.

6. The area of a slide behind the slide objects is called the
   a. mat.
   b. background.
   c. color scheme.
   d. template.

7. To change the color of the slide background,
    a. select the color from the Fill Color palette.
    b. double-click the slide background and set the color.
    c. select the color from the color palette in the Background dialog box.
    d. select a different template.

8. PowerPoint templates are stored
    a. in the Inbox.
    b. in the My Documents folder.
    c. in the root directory of drive C.
    d. in the Presentation Designs subfolder of the Templates folder.

9. To save a presentation design as a template,
    a. choose File, Save As; select Presentation Template from the Save as type drop-down list; and type a name for the design.
    b. click 🖫.
    c. choose File, Close, and answer Yes when asked whether you want to save your work.
    d. delete the presentation and then save the template.

10. To copy a graphic from the Slide Master to the Title Master,
    a. drag the graphic to the Title Master.
    b. copy the graphic to the clipboard and paste it in the Title Master.
    c. you must redraw or insert the graphic on the Title Master.
    d. it's not necessary to do anything.

Short Answer

1. From what menu do you display Slide Masters?

2. What Slide Masters are available for formatting slides in a presentation?

3. How do you access picture bullets?

4. What bullet levels can be changed?

5. What is the term associated with varying the shading of a slide background or filled object?

6. To change the direction of the shading on a slide background, what do you select?

7. What folder contains template designs?

8. What effect does changing the template design in one presentation have on existing presentations formatted using the same template?

9. How do you change the position of the slide number on a slide?

10. How do you display the Header and Footer dialog box?

For Discussion

1. What characteristics and features of slides in a presentation do you need to review after customizing template designs?

2. What is the difference between a slide layout and a Slide Master layout?

3. What are the steps required to open a template so that you can edit it?

4. How does the footer area of a Slide Master differ from the footer area of a Word document?

Hands-On Exercises

1. Formatting Text and Bullets on Slide Masters

Additional changes need to be made to the presentation template for the presentation *(Your Initials) Selections, Inc. Design.*

Use the following techniques to change the template design:

1. Open the template:
   - Choose File, Open.
   - Select Presentation Templates (*.pot) from the Files of type list.
   - Open the Program Files folder, the Microsoft Office folder, the Templates folder, and finally the Presentation Designs folder, if necessary.

   TIP If you stored your presentation template in a different folder or on a different disk, open the appropriate folder.

   - Select the template you want to open and press (ENTER).
2. Display the Slide Master and select bullet characters for bullet level 1 and bullet level 3.
3. Delete bullet list levels 4 and 5.
4. Select the text in the Title Area for AutoLayouts placeholder and change the color of the text to dark blue.
5. Select the text in the Object Area for AutoLayouts placeholder and change the text color to a dark blue that is slightly lighter than the title blue.
6. Save changes to the template.
7. Apply the new template design to the Working with Masters presentation and print a copy of the presentation as handouts with two slides per page.
8. Save and close the presentation.

2. Changing the Slide Background and Adjusting Objects on Slides

Mr. Stills would like you to make changes to the Title Master for the template you used to format the Willows Restaurants presentation. A suggested finished design is shown in Figure 4.31.

To complete the change to the presentation template, follow these steps:

1. Open the Willows Restaurants presentation and display Outline view.
2. Choose File, Save As, and save the presentation as a template using the file name *(Your Initials) Willows Restaurants Design.*
3. Press (CTRL) + A to select all slide text and press (DELETE).
4. Display the Title Master.

FIGURE 4.31

 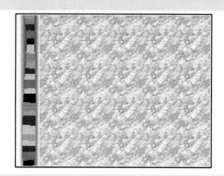

5. Select the title placeholder and delete it.

6. Choose Format, Background, and change the fill effects to a textured fill.

7. Choose Insert, Picture, WordArt. Then select the WordArt object that appears in Figure 4.31, type **The Willows Restaurants**, and choose OK.

8. Display the Slide Master and change the background color to the same textured background applied to the Title Master.

9. Save changes to the template and close it.

10. Print a copy of the presentation template Title Master and Slide Master.

On Your Own Exercises

1. **Changing the Background, Adding a Footer, Formatting Bullets, and Changing Text Alignment for a Template**

Open the *Selections Web.ppt* presentation and customize the template so that it contains each of the following:

- A new background design
- Your name in the footer area
- A different text alignment and font color for title text
- A new bullet design for the first bullet list level
- Additional customization to add a personal touch to the presentation

After you complete your design, save changes to the presentation and review each slide in the presentation. Make necessary adjustments to text, graphics, WordArt, and colors so that they complement the colors you used in your new design. When the presentation is complete, save it again. Print a copy of the title presentation as handouts with six slides per page.

Remove all text from the presentation and save the presentation design as a template using *(Your Initials) Selections, Inc. Shops Design* as the template name.

2. Customizing a Presentation Template

Customize the *Barbeque.ppt* presentation template so that it includes each of the following features:

- A custom text color for all title text.
- Text font and alignment for text placeholders.
- A graphic on the Slide Master, appropriately positioned so that it does not interfere with the text and graphics.
- A footer that includes your name.

Save the design as a template using the file name *(Your Initials) Fun Times.pot*, apply it to the Barbeque presentation, and print a copy of the *Barbeque.ppt* presentation slides.

3. Customizing a Presentation Template

Because your résumé is a document that should uniquely represent you, customize the template that you applied to your résumé presentation so that it conveys both your credentials and your personality. Save the design as a template using the file name *(Your Initials) Resume.pot*, apply the template to your résumé presentation, and print a copy of the presentation as handouts with six slides per page.

4. Searching the Internet for Template Designs

Log on to the Microsoft PowerPoint Web site and search for additional PowerPoint templates stored on the Web. When you locate one you like, download the template, customize it, save it as a template using your name as the template name, and then apply the template to your résumé presentation. Be sure to include your name on each slide in the presentation.

5. Changing the Template Background, Adding Graphics as a Watermark, and Adjusting the Position of the Placeholders on Slide and Title Masters

Open the *Our National Forests* presentation and customize the template so that it contains the following visual elements:

- Some color of green background with a gradient fill
- A tree watermark positioned down the left side of both the Title and Slide Masters (delete the original Forest Service logo graphic from existing slides)
- A special bullet shape (not necessarily from the Picture palette) for the first-level bullet
- The current date and slide number in the footer area

When you've completed the customization, adjust the placement of the title and text placeholders on the Slide and Title Masters so that the text does not run into the tree on the left side of the slides. Make necessary changes to the text color and save changes to your presentation. Pack the presentation to go and demonstrate it for your instructor.

Integrated Project

Integrating Word, Excel, Access, and PowerPoint

As you've already discovered, you can save valuable time by sharing data that already exists in other Office applications with documents and files created within the Office suite. In this integrated project, you learn how to integrate data among all Office products, how to share outlines between Word and PowerPoint, and how to save presentations to the World Wide Web.

Objectives

After completing this project, you will be able to:

➤ Embed a Word table on a PowerPoint slide

➤ Link data from Excel to a PowerPoint slide

➤ Create a Word document from a PowerPoint presentation outline

➤ Save a PowerPoint slide as a graphic

➤ Create a hyperlink between a PowerPoint presentation and an Access database

➤ Save a presentation as a Web page

➤ View the Web presentation

Running Case

Your internship at Selections, Inc., is almost complete. During your last week on the job, you've been asked to tie up all the loose ends of projects you have completed during the semester by pulling information you've created in other applications into PowerPoint presentations and prepare the presentation for use on the Selections Web page.

INTEGRATED PROJECT 3

The Challenge

Joy Quinn, production/advertising manager of Selections, Inc., wants to complete the Selections Directory presentation by adding the slides shown in Figure 3.1 to the presentation and then use the completed outline of the presentation as the basis for the report in Word 2000 shown in Figure 3.2. Ms. Quinn also wants to include a slide from the presentation as a graphic in the report and to be able to launch her Access database for regional office addresses while she is showing the presentation, if necessary.

FIGURE 3.1

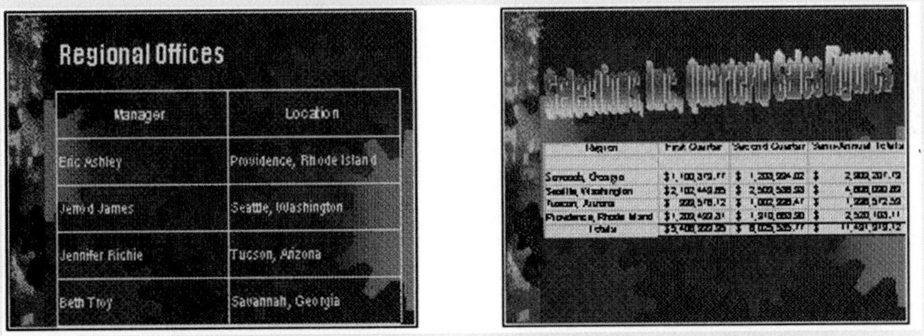

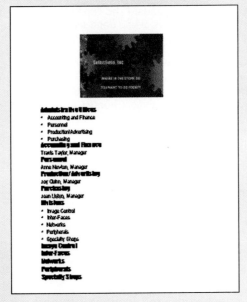

FIGURE 3.2

The Strategy

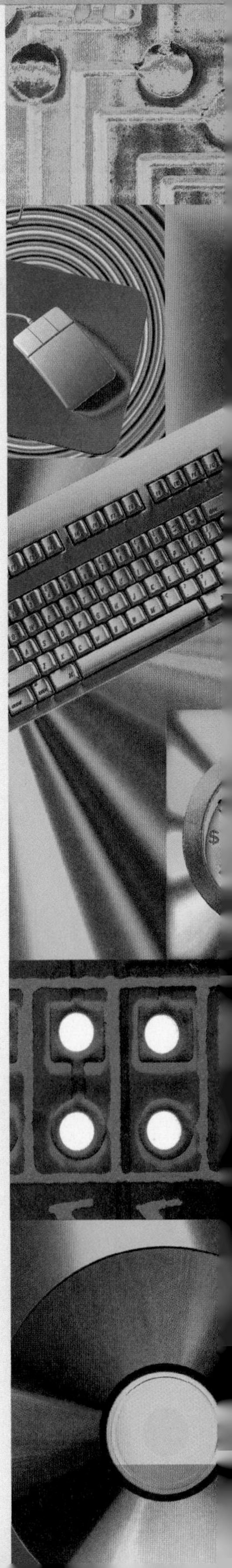

When information such as the table on the first slide in Figure 3.1 already exists in another file, you can copy the data and paste it on the slides. To add information such as the tabled data shown on the second slide in Figure 3.1, you can use tools similar to those found in Word to add the table to the slide. After the slides are complete, you can send the outline of the presentation to Word so that it can eventually be used to develop an extensive report. By saving Slide 2 as a graphic, you can insert a picture of the slide in the Word document. Last, but certainly not least, you can link the table of regional offices in the PowerPoint slide to the Access database that contains regional office addresses so that the addresses can easily be supplied when questions arise during the presentation.

The Setup

To ensure that your screen will match the figures pictured in this project, make sure the settings shown in Table 3.1 are active.

Table 3.1

Location:	Make these settings:
Office Assistant	Hide the Office Assistant.
View	Click the Print Layout View button at the bottom of the Word window.
	Ensure that the formula bar and status bar are both displayed in the Excel window.
	Display Normal view in PowerPoint.
Toolbars	Ensure that both the Standard and Formatting toolbars are active in all application windows. If you don't see them, choose View, Toolbars, and then select them. Close all other active toolbars.
	Choose Tools, Customize, and then click the Options tab and ensure that the Personalized Menus and Toolbars options are all deselected. Then click the Reset my usage data button and choose Yes to restore automatic changes to menus. Choose Close.
Zoom	Set the zoom to Page Width in Word, 100% in Excel, and 33% in PowerPoint Normal view.
Ruler	Display the Ruler in Word and PowerPoint.

 Web Tip

If you do not have a copy of *Selections Managers.mdb* on your student disk, you can download it from the SELECT Web site at http://www .prenhall.com/select or check with your instructor to find out how to obtain a copy.

Embedding a Word Table in a PowerPoint Slide

In Word 2000 Project 5, you discovered how formatting information as a table improves the presentation of the information. You will be delighted to learn, I'm sure, that the same tools you used to create a table in Word are available to you in PowerPoint! In fact, PowerPoint makes creating a new slide and accessing table tools easy by providing a Table AutoLayout format.

TASK 1: To Create a Table Slide

1 Launch PowerPoint, open *Selections Directory.ppt*, and display Slide 1 in Normal view.

2 Click 🖫.

FIGURE 3.3

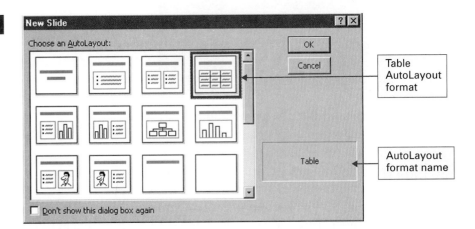

3 Click the Table AutoLayout format and choose OK. A new slide appears in Normal view.

4 Type **Regional Offices** in the title placeholder and then double-click the table placeholder. The Insert Table dialog box, which is the same as the one in Word, appears, as shown in Figure 3.4.

FIGURE 3.4

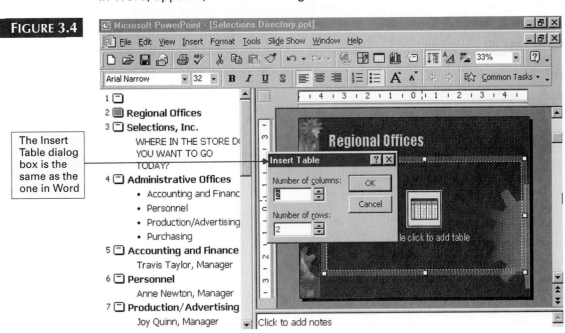

5 Type **4** in the Number of rows value box and choose OK. The table is formatted with four rows and two columns. The pointer appears as a pencil. The Tables and Borders toolbar opens.

6 Use standard Word table procedures to enter and format the table information so that it appears as shown in Figure 3.7. Press ⎯TAB⎯ after the last existing row to create the new row.

FIGURE 3.5

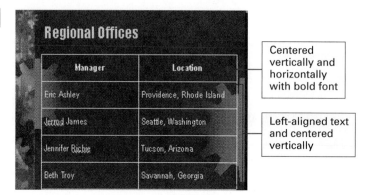

7 Save changes to the presentation.

Linking Data from Excel to a PowerPoint Slide

The data for the second new slide you will create already exists in an Excel worksheet. Thus, you can copy the data from the Excel workbook and place it on the PowerPoint slide. Linking the data ensures that PowerPoint will always display the most recent information, in the event that the Excel source file is changed.

TASK 2: To Link Data from Excel to a PowerPoint Slide

1 Display Slide 2 in *Selections Directory.ppt*, if necessary and create another new slide formatted using the Blank AutoLayout. A new slide containing no placeholders appears on-screen.

2 Launch Excel, open the *Selections Quarterly Sales Figures.xls* workbook, and display the Quarterly Sales worksheet.

> **TIP** Make necessary column adjustments to display all worksheet data.

FIGURE 3.6

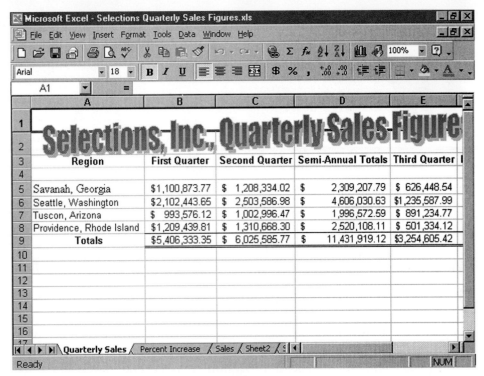

3 Select cells A3 through D9 and click ⬚. A marquee appears around the copied cells, indicating that they have been placed on the Office Clipboard.

4 Switch to PowerPoint and choose Edit, Paste Special. The Paste Special dialog box appears.

5 Choose Paste link, ensure that Microsoft Excel Worksheet Object is selected, and choose OK.

FIGURE 3.7

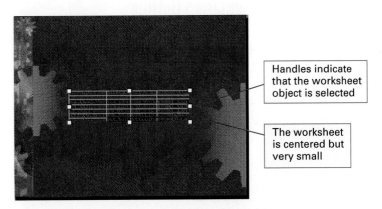

Handles indicate that the worksheet object is selected

The worksheet is centered but very small

TIP Remember that you must choose Paste Link to link, not embed, the Excel worksheet data to the PowerPoint slide.

6 Right-click the worksheet object and select Format Object.

7 Select the following options in the Format Object dialog box:
- Colors and Lines Page: Select the title text color from the Fill Color drop-down list.
- Size Page: Change the Scale settings Height and Width to 175%.

8 Adjust the position of the table on the slide and save changes to the presentation.

Check Point

Change the line and text color for cells in the table on Slide 2 so that they are the same color as the title text. Copy the WordArt object from the Excel worksheet to Slide 3, change the color of the text, and size and position it appropriately. Hide Slide 3. Print a copy of Slides 2 and 3. Close the workbook and exit Excel, but leave PowerPoint open.

Creating a Word Document from a PowerPoint Presentation Outline

Outlines from PowerPoint presentations are effective guides for developing Word reports that parallel the presentation. Because Outline view in Power-Point prints extraneous information and slide icons, you will get a more document-like outline by printing the outline in Word. With the touch of a button, you can send the outline to Word and eliminate the need to retype the entire outline. When you send the outline to Word, a Write-Up dialog box opens and displays a list of formats you can choose for the Word document.

TASK 3: To Create a Word Document from a PowerPoint Presentation Outline

1 Display *Selections Directory.ppt* in Outline view.

2 Choose File, Send To, Microsoft Word.

FIGURE 3.8

Formats for the document layout in Word

Linking options

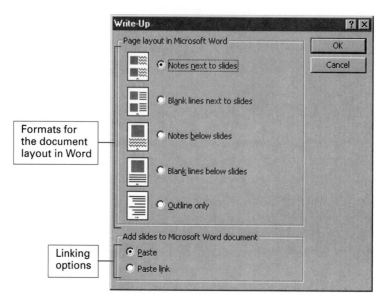

3 Click Outline only and then click OK. The outline appears in a new Word document.

4 Delete all outline text down to *Administrative Offices* (Slide 5) and adjust the text size and format so that it appears on one page.

5 Save the Word document using the file name *Selections Directory Outline.rtf.*

Break Point

The document needs some cleanup and adjustment to make it appear as shown in Figure 3.2. Delete the extra lines where there were slides containing no text placeholders and then save changes to the document. If necessary you can save your file, exit Word and PowerPoint, and continue this project later.

Saving a PowerPoint Slide as a Graphic

Another way to share data among Office 2000 applications is to capture information from one application as a graphic and place it into another application's file. PowerPoint slides make effective graphics that not only enhance a document, but also relay a message. PowerPoint includes file options that enable you to save your slides in the most popular image formats.

Web Tip

To present graphic files with documents you save on the Web, you must save the graphics in either .gif or .jpg (often called "jay peg") format.

TASK 4: To Save a PowerPoint Slide as a Graphic and Add It to a Word Document

1 Launch Word, if necessary, and open *Selections Directory Outline.rtf.*

2 Launch PowerPoint, if necessary, open *Selections Directory.ppt*, and display Slide 4 in Normal view.

3 Choose File, Save As. The Save As dialog box opens.

4 Open the drive and folder you want to use to store the graphic, and then click the Save as type drop-down list arrow.

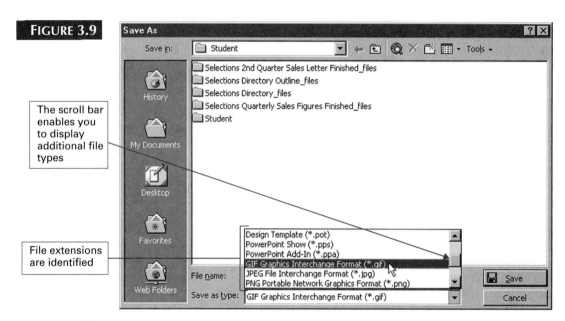

FIGURE 3.9

The scroll bar enables you to display additional file types

File extensions are identified

5 Select GIF Graphics Interchange Format (*.gif) and click Save.

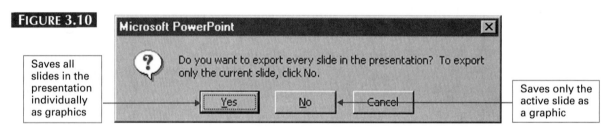

FIGURE 3.10

Saves all slides in the presentation individually as graphics

Saves only the active slide as a graphic

6 Click No to export only Slide 4, close the presentation, and exit PowerPoint.

 **Check Point**

Switch to Word and position the insertion point at the top of *Selections Directory Outline.rtf*. Then insert the slide graphic at the top of the document, center the graphic and size and position it as shown in Figure 3.2. Preview the document and click the Shrink to Fit button on the Print Preview toolbar to reduce the document to one page, if necessary. Adjust the left margin until your document appears as shown in Figure 3.2. Save changes to the document, print a copy of the document, and then exit Word.

Creating a Hyperlink between a PowerPoint Presentation and an Access Database

One of the new slides you added to the presentation contained data from an Access database table. The data you added, however, did not include all the information contained in the database. It might be helpful to have quick and easy access to additional information contained in the database. You can create a hyperlink between the database and the presentation.

TASK 5:   To Create a Hyperlink between PowerPoint and Access

1 Launch PowerPoint, open *Selections Directory.ppt*, and display Slide 2 in Normal view. The slide containing the Regional Offices list appears.

2 Display the Drawing toolbar, if necessary, choose AutoShapes, Action Buttons, and create a blank Custom button, positioning it in the lower-right corner of the slide.

FIGURE 3.11

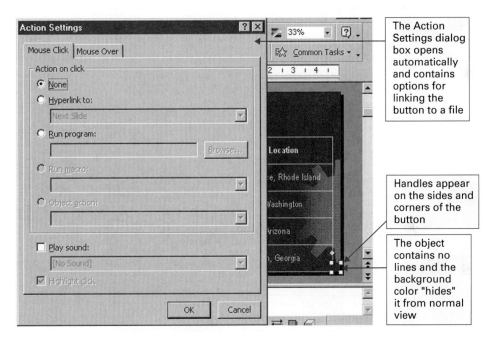

The Action Settings dialog box opens automatically and contains options for linking the button to a file

Handles appear on the sides and corners of the button

The object contains no lines and the background color "hides" it from normal view

TROUBLESHOOTING If your button appears with different line and fill colors, change the colors using the Line Color and Fill Color buttons on the Drawing toolbar.

3 Click the Hyperlink to option and select Other File from the Hyperlink to drop-down list. The Hyperlink to Other File dialog box opens.

4 Locate and select *Selections Managers.mdb*, then choose OK. The file location appears in the Hyperlink to field.

5 Choose OK, save changes to the presentation, and start the slide show. Slide 2 appears on-screen.

6 Click the custom action button in the lower-right corner of the slide. Access launches and opens the linked database. You can open any database object and review the data, as required.

7 Close Access and end the Slide Show.

Saving a Presentation as a Web Page

Because PowerPoint presentation slides are generally so colorful and contain short summarizations of important ideas, they make wonderful Web pages. If you have access to a Web server and a current browser, you can save your presentation for Web-based delivery in no time at all. Office 2000 applications convert files to a format that can be used on the Web automatically. When you save your presentation as a Web page, PowerPoint creates a separate .gif or .jpg file for each slide in the presentation.

Web Tip

You can share presentations with friends by publishing them on a Web site and sending your friends a hyperlink to the site. Simply choose File, Save as Web Page and select an FTP site to which you have save rights from the Save In drop-down list. When you've completed the information in the dialog box, choose Publish. Depending on the site you choose, you may be presented additional options.

TASK 6: To Save a Presentation as a Web Page

1 Choose File, Save as Web Page.

FIGURE 3.12

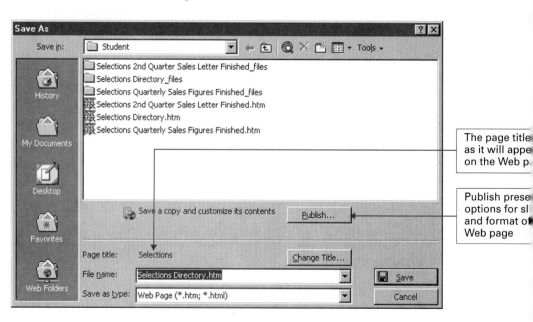

The page title as it will appe on the Web p

Publish prese options for sl and format of Web page

2 Choose Publish.

FIGURE 3.13

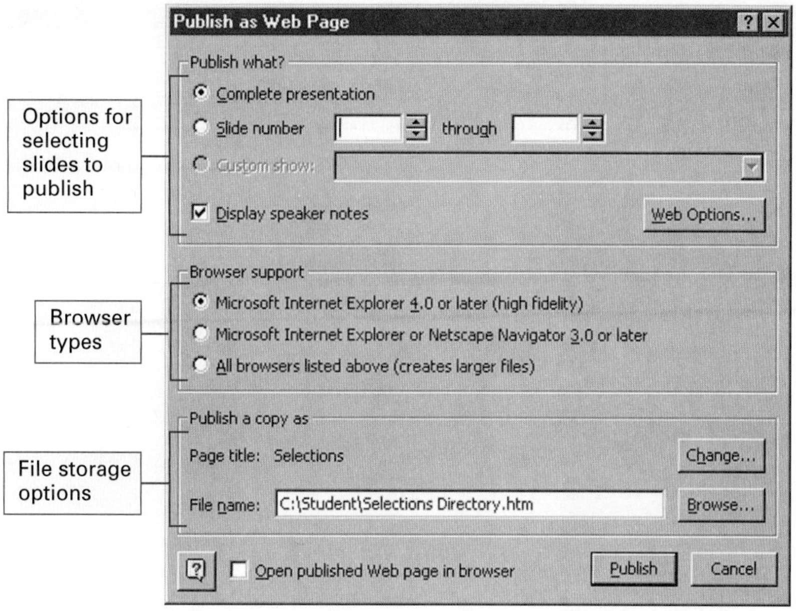

Options for selecting slides to publish

Browser types

File storage options

Publish as Web Page   ? X

Publish what?
- ○ Complete presentation
- ○ Slide number [   ] ⇕ through [   ] ⇕
- ○ Custom show: [▼]
- ☑ Display speaker notes   Web Options...

Browser support
- ○ Microsoft Internet Explorer 4.0 or later (high fidelity)
- ○ Microsoft Internet Explorer or Netscape Navigator 3.0 or later
- ○ All browsers listed above (creates larger files)

Publish a copy as
Page title: Selections   Change...

File name: [C:\Student\Selections Directory.htm]   Browse...

[?] ☐ Open published Web page in browser   Publish   Cancel

3 Select the Browser support option for your computer and choose Publish. It takes anywhere from a few seconds to several minutes to save the presentation as a Web page.

Viewing the Web Presentation

After you save a presentation as a Web page, you can preview the page to see what it will look like on the Web without actually connecting to the Web.

TASK 7: To View a Presentation as It Appears on the Web

1 Choose File, Web Page Preview and maximize the Browser, if necessary. The first slide appears in the default browser.

FIGURE 3.14

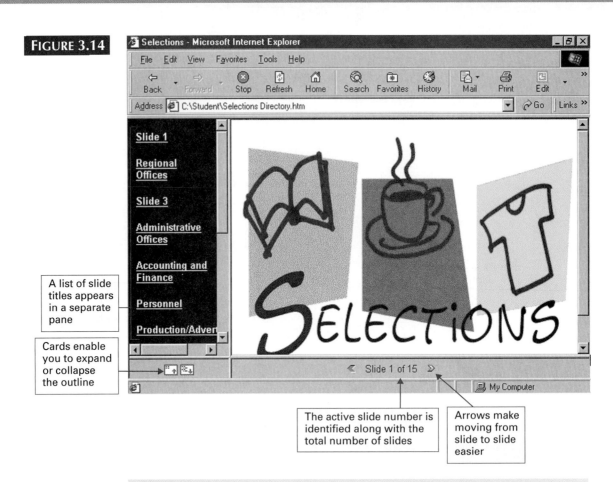

A list of slide titles appears in a separate pane

Cards enable you to expand or collapse the outline

The active slide number is identified along with the total number of slides

Arrows make moving from slide to slide easier

TROUBLESHOOTING If you receive an error message when you try to preview the Web page, try launching your default Web browser before previewing the Web page. If the presentation does not appear, type the location (path) of the folder containing the Web file in the Address text box and type the file name shown in Figure 3.14 at the end of the path statement. Then press (ENTER).

2 Click the Next Slide ▷ arrow. Slide 2 appears in the browser window.

Check Point

Continue clicking the Next Slide arrow to display each additional slide in the presentation. Then explore other features of the browser window. When you are finished, close the presentation file, exit the browser, and close the presentation in PowerPoint.

Summary

- You can drag and drop data from Office 2000 applications to other applications.

- The File, Send To command displays a number of different commands you can use to share information among Office 2000 applications.

- Many of the tools you use to create and format information are available in all Office 2000 applications. As a result, learning to use the tools in one application means you will know how to apply features in other applications.

- Saving files as graphics enables you to enhance other files by inserting the graphics.

- The File, Save as Web Page feature automatically formats Office 2000 files so that they can be used on the Web.

- Hyperlinks enable you to launch applications and open files while you are working in another application.

- When you want to add data using tools from other applications to create objects on slides in a PowerPoint presentation, you can select an AutoLayout format for the slide and then double-click the object placeholder to access the tools.

Key Terms and Operations

Key Terms

Hyperlink

Operations

create a hyperlink between PowerPoint and an Access database
create an embedded object in PowerPoint using tools learned in other
    applications
create a Word document using the outline from a PowerPoint presentation
insert a presentation slide graphic in a Word document
link files from one application to another
save a presentation as a Web page
save a presentation slide as a graphic
view the presentation on the Web

For additional review and exercises using Word and Excel (or Word, Excel, and Access or Word, Excel, Access, and PowerPoint), visit the SELECT Web site at http://www.prenhall.com/select.

Bonus Feature: Sharing Files and Posting Presentations

One of the advantages of using software programs that are part of a suite is that the programs are designed to work together as a team. This bonus feature shows you how to use a Word outline to create a PowerPoint presentation and how to save the presentation in a format that can be used on the World Wide Web! Download a document named *Etch-a-Sketch.doc* from the SELECT Web site at http://www.prenhall.com/select to get started.

 TASK 1: To Create a PowerPoint Presentation from a Word Outline

1 Launch PowerPoint 2000, if necessary, and create a new blank presentation. The New Slide dialog box opens and presents a variety of AutoLayout formats.

2 Click Cancel. An empty presentation opens.

3 Choose Insert, Slides from Outline. The Insert Outline dialog box opens.

4 Select *Etch-a-Sketch.doc* and choose Insert. The document outline appears in PowerPoint and each slide in the presentation is automatically created.

5 Save the presentation using the file name *A Technological Comeback.ppt*.

 Check Point

Create a template design that resembles an Etch-a-Sketch screen and apply it to the presentation.

 TASK 2: To Save a PowerPoint Presentation as a Web Page

1 Choose File, Save as Web Page. The Save As dialog box opens.

2 Open the folder to contain the Web presentation and choose Publish. The Publish as Web Page dialog box opens.

3 Select the Browser support option for your computer and choose Publish.

 Check Point

Choose File, Web Page Preview to see what the presentation will look like on the Web. Click the Next Slide arrow ➢ button to view each presentation slide.

Internet Explorer

Overview of Internet Explorer 5

Internet Explorer 5 is your vehicle for exploring the information superhighway, taking you to places you want to go on the Internet and helping you obtain information. This overview presents methods for using Internet Explorer 5 to access Web pages and download files.

Objectives

After completing this project, you will be able to:

➤ Identify the structure and purpose of the Internet

➤ Launch Internet Explorer 5

➤ Identify the Internet Explorer 5 screen elements

➤ Navigate the Internet

➤ Use Channels

➤ Download a file

➤ Access newsgroups

➤ Exit Internet Explorer 5

Identifying the Structure and Purpose of the Internet

The Internet is a global interconnected **network** of networks consisting of millions of computers, all using a common set of computer code called **Internet Protocol (IP)** to communicate. The Internet began with a network set up by the Department of Defense in the 1980s called ARPANET, or Advanced Research Projects Agency Network.

> **TIP** A network generally consists of many computers, called **clients**, that are attached to a main computer, called the **server**. The server provides the client computers with storage space, programs, a post office, and so on. Client computers may be connected to the server with cables, referred to as a local area network or LAN, or via telephone lines or satellite, which is called a wide area network or WAN.

Soon the National Science Foundation joined the Internet, followed by many universities. The Internet quickly established a culture of free exchange of information and ideas. This trend continues, but the commercial aspect of the Internet is developing at a break-neck speed.

It is amazing that an entity as large as the Internet can operate without "someone in charge." No one person, organization, or country "owns and operates" the Internet; however, **InterNIC**, the first and primary domain name registration authority, issues unique server identifiers (IP addresses) and domain names to organizations and individuals that want to have a presence on the Internet. Additionally, InterNIC keeps a database of all IP addresses and domain names on the Internet and makes this information available.

Connecting to the Internet

To connect to the Internet, you must be connected to a **host computer**. Many businesses, universities, colleges, and schools have host computers so that their employees, students, and staff have access to the Internet. If you don't have access to a host computer, but your computer has a modem, you can connect to the Internet through an **Internet service provider (ISP)**. ISPs usually charge a fee based on usage. If you spend half your waking-hours on the Internet, you'd better look for an ISP that offers unlimited usage for a set fee.

> **TIP** There are many national and local ISPs, including AT&T and EarthlinkSprint. Online service providers (OSPs) such as AOL, MSN, and CompuServe have the services of ISPs but also have an interface with a more organized set of proprietary information such as news, sports, chat rooms, and so on.

Identifying Services on the Internet

A variety of services are available on the Internet, but the most popular services are the World Wide Web, e-mail, newsgroups (bulletin board–type discussion groups), and Internet chat. Two older services that have been virtually replaced by the World Wide Web are FTP and Gopher. **FTP**, which stands for File Transfer Protocol, is used for uploading and downloading files. **Gopher** is a menu-based system for locating resources originated by the University of Minnesota. FTP and Gopher are text-based services that were quite popular before the graphical World Wide Web and Web browser programs became so well established.

New services that are becoming more and more popular as the technology develops include Internet meetings and telephone conferences.

Launching Internet Explorer 5

Internet Explorer 5 is a program designed for the Windows 95/98/NT platforms. It is classified as a Web browser program because its interface is designed specifically for accessing the graphical features (pictures, icons, buttons, and so on) of the World Wide Web. Internet Explorer 5 also can be used for accessing FTP and gopher sites.

TASK 1: To Launch Internet Explorer 5

1 Double-click the Internet Explorer 5 icon  on the desktop.

> **TIP** If the Quick Launch toolbar appears in the taskbar, click the Launch Internet Explorer Browser 🅔 button to start Internet Explorer 5.

2 Respond to any prompts to log onto your service provider's network, if applicable. The default *start page* appears.

> **TIP** You can choose any Web page you want for the start page. Just go to the page you want to use as the start page and choose Tools, Internet Options. Click the General tab, if necessary, and select Use Current, OK. It is probably not advisable to change the start page in the computer lab.

Identifying the Internet Explorer 5 Screen Elements

Figure I.1 shows the basic elements of the Internet Explorer 5 screen. Table I.1 describes the elements of the screen.

Table I.1

Element	Description
Title bar	Displays the name of the application
Menu bar	Contains the options File, Edit, View, Favorites, Tools, and Help
Standard toolbar	Contains the buttons Back, Forward, Stop, Refresh, Home, Search, Favorites, History, Mail, Print, Edit, and Discuss
Address bar	Contains a text box in which you enter the address of the Internet site you want to visit.
Go button	Goes to the default start page.
Links toolbar	Contains the buttons Best of the Web, Channel Guide, Customize Links, Internet Start, Free HotMail, Windows, and Windows Update. If this toolbar is not fully displayed, you can drag the toolbar to display it.
Status bar	Displays information about what is happening at the moment.

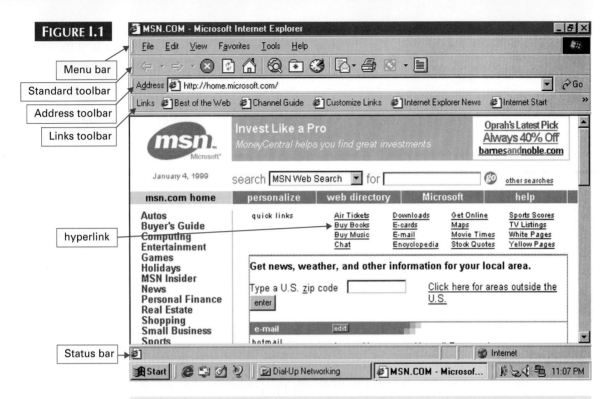

FIGURE I.1

TIP As you navigate to other sites on the Internet, the text box in the Address bar displays the address of the current site.

TROUBLESHOOTING In this and subsequent figures, the buttons do not display button names. In some browsers you cannot see all the buttons on the toolbar if button names are displayed.

Navigating the Internet

As soon as you launch Internet Explorer 5, you begin navigating the Internet automatically because Internet Explorer 5 takes you to its start page on the World Wide Web. To continue navigating on the Internet, you can use any of the following methods:

- Click a hyperlink
- Type the address of the Internet site into the Address bar
- Select a site from History
- Select a Favorite from the Favorites menu
- Use the Links toolbar
- Use the Search Assistant

Using Hyperlinks

Web documents often include **hyperlinks** which link you to another location on the same Web page, another Web page located on the same server, or another Web page located on a server in another part of the world. Text hyperlinks are generally bright blue and underlined. When you click a text hyperlink, the color changes (usually to purple) to show that you have followed the link.

> **TIP** The best way to find out whether text or a graphic is a hyperlink is to point to the item with the mouse pointer. If the pointer changes to a hand with a pointing finger, the text is a hyperlink.

TASK 2: To Use a Hyperlink

1 Point to text or a graphic that you think is a hyperlink.

2 If the pointer changes to a hand with a pointing finger 🖑, click the text or graphic.

Typing an Address

To get to any site on the Internet, you can enter the site **address** in the text box on the Address bar. Internet addresses are also referred to as **URLs**, which stands for Uniform Resource Locator.

> **TIP** Internet sites may close or move to a different location. The addresses used in the following task may be invalid when you try to use them. If so, visit the SELECT Web site at http://www.prenhall.com/select for the updated address, or ask your instructor for an alternate address.

TASK 3: To Type an Internet Address

1 Click in the Address text box on the Address bar. The insertion point is positioned in the text box and the address is highlighted, as shown in Figure I.2.

FIGURE 1.2

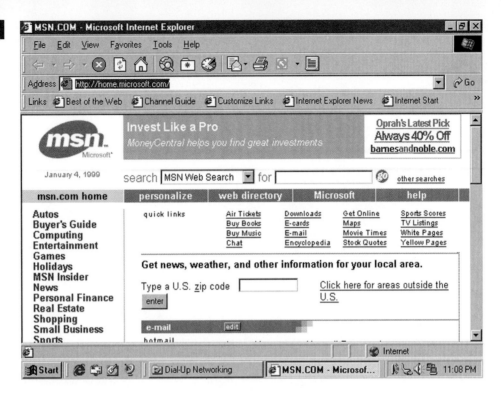

2 Type **espnet.sportszone.com** and press (ENTER). The ESPN SportsZone page appears. Note that you don't have to type **http://**. This is understood.

> **TIP**   If the URL begins with "www" and ends with "com," as in www.yahoo.com, the only part of the address you have to type is "yahoo."

3 Type **gopher.tc.umn.edu** in the Address text box and press (ENTER). The University of Minnesota Gopher site displays. The University of Minnesota named this protocol for the school mascot, the Golden Gophers.

4 Click the Home 🏠 button. The start page appears.

> **TIP**   Web pages with large graphic files (or other types of multimedia files) may take a long time to appear on the screen. You can turn off the downloading of multimedia by choosing Tools, Internet Options, and clicking the Advanced tab. Scroll down to the Multimedia section, deselect all options, and click OK. Check with your lab instructor before making changes such as these to the computers in the lab.

Selecting a Site from History

Internet Explorer 5 maintains a *history* of the sites you visit each day so that you can return to them easily.

TASK 4: To Return to a Page by Using History

1 Click the History 🕔 button. The Explorer bar opens, as shown in Figure I.3.

FIGURE I.3

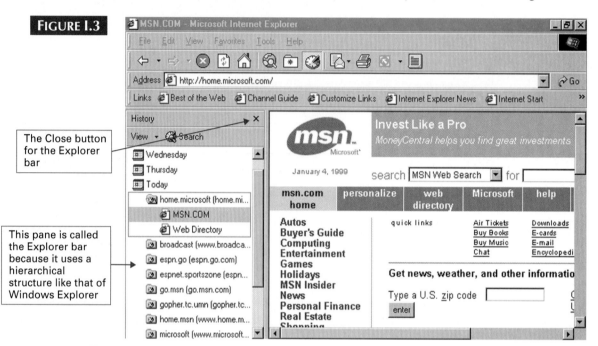

The Close button for the Explorer bar

This pane is called the Explorer bar because it uses a hierarchical structure like that of Windows Explorer

2 Click Today's entry for ESPN's SportsZone. The entry expands to show the pages visited at that site.

3 Click the hyperlink espn.com. The Web page appears in the right pane.

4 Click any hyperlink on the page in the right pane. A new entry is added under the main entry for SportsZone.

5 Click ❌ in the Explorer bar. The Explorer bar closes.

TIP To print what you see on the screen, click the Print 🖨 button.

Selecting a Favorite

Internet Explorer 5 calls shortcuts to Internet sites **Favorites** and lists them on the Favorites menu or in the Explorer bar. You can create shortcuts for your favorite sites if you can't remember the addresses or you don't want to type them every time.

TASK 5: To Add a Favorite

1 Ensure that you are on the SportsZone site and then choose Favorites, Add to Favorites. The Add Favorite dialog box appears, as shown in Figure I.4.

FIGURE I.4

Add Favorite   [?][X]

Internet Explorer will add this page to your Favorites list.   [OK]

[ ] Make available offline   [Customize...]   [Cancel]

Name: [ESPN.com Green Bay-San Francisco recap]   [Create in >>]

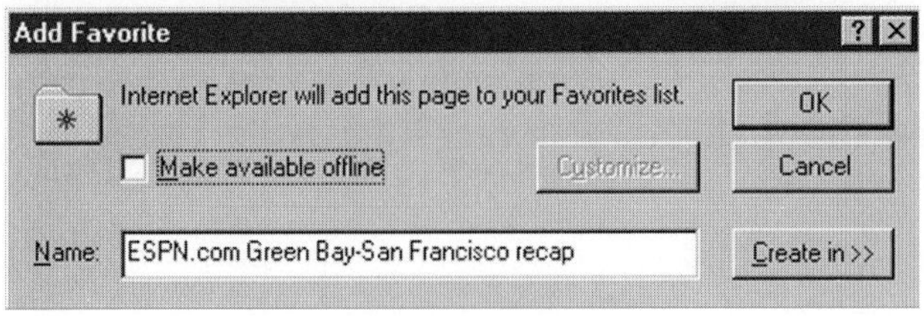

2 Click OK. The dialog box closes, and the page is added to the Favorites menu.

3 Click 🏠. The start page appears.

Using a Favorite

You can select a favorite from the Favorites menu or from the Explorer bar.

TASK 6: To Go to a Favorite

1 Choose Favorites from the menu bar. The Favorites menu appears.

> **TIP** Clicking the Favorites button displays Favorites in the Explorer bar.

2 Scroll, if necessary, and click the shortcut to the ESPN page. The Web page appears.

3 Click 🏠 and then click ⊡. The Explorer bar opens.

4 Click the ESPN entry. The Web page appears.

> **TIP** It is very important to organize Favorites in folders so you don't have too many URLs to scroll through. To create a folder, simply choose Favorites, Organize Favorites, and choose Create New Folder. Type the name of the folder, and press (ENTER).

Searching the Internet

The Internet is so vast that finding information can be a challenge. To meet that challenge, several organizations and companies contain created **search engines**, programs that search the Internet for sites that contain specified text. Internet Explorer 5 uses a feature called the **Search Assistant** to provide access to several popular search engines.

The Search Assistant appears in the Explorer bar. When you find a page you want to read, close the Explorer bar so the page can occupy the complete screen. When you're ready to go to another one of the hyperlinks in the search results, click 🔍 to redisplay the Explorer bar and the previous search results.

TASK 7: To Search for Information Using a Search Engine

1 Click the Search 🔍 button. The Explorer bar opens and displays the Search Assistant, as shown in Figure I.5.

FIGURE I.5

2 In the Find a web page containing text box, type **ski equipment** and click 🔍.

FIGURE I.6

3 Scroll down in the left pane to see the results.

4 Click any hyperlink. The Web page appears.

> **TROUBLESHOOTING** When you look at a Web page that has been identified as having the specified text, the text is not emphasized in any way. To find specific text on a Web page, use the Find command in the Edit menu.

5 Click the drop-down arrow on the Next button and select a different search engine.

6 Scroll down in the left pane and click any hyperlink. The page appears in the right pane.

7 In the left pane, scroll as necessary and click another hyperlink. A new page appears in the right pane.

8 Click the Back ⇦ button. The previous page appears in the right pane.

9 Click the Forward ⇨ button. The next page appears in the right pane.

10 Scroll to the bottom of the left pane and click the hyperlink that displays the next set of hyperlinks found by the search.

11 Click ☒ in the Explorer bar. The Explorer bar closes.

12 Click ☒ again. The same search hyperlinks appear in the Explorer bar.

13 Click ☒ again. The Explorer bar closes.

Using Channels

The Internet feature called **channels** uses **push technology** to send content from a Web page directly to your local hard drive. If you have Web content downloaded, you can browse the Web content **offline** (when you are not connected to the Internet) at your convenience.

> **TIP** To receive Web data automatically, you must first designate the Web site as one that you want to use for offline viewing. In the previous version of Internet Explorer, selecting a Web page for offline viewing was called subscribing.

TASK 8: To Select a Page for Offline Viewing

1 Choose Favorites, Channels, Lifestyle and Travel, as shown in Figure I.7.

FIGURE I.7

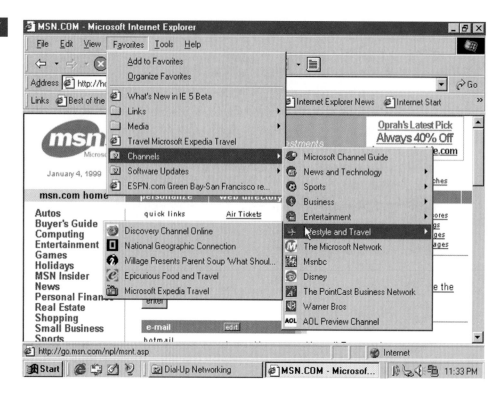

2 Choose Epicurious Food and Travel. The Epicurious page appears, as shown in Figure I.8. Your screen may not look exactly like this one because Web pages are constantly changing.

FIGURE I.8

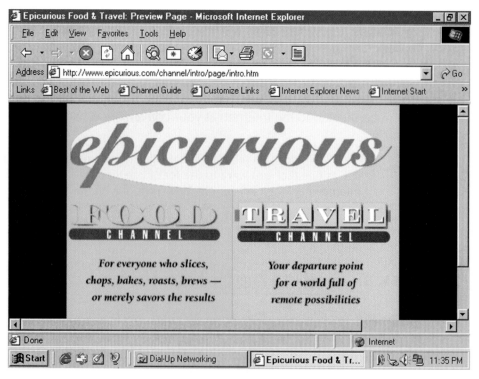

3 Scroll if necessary and click the Add Active Channel hyperlink in the food section. The Offline Favorite Wizard opens.

4 Select Next. The wizard asks whether you would like to view additional linked pages offline, as shown in Figure I.9.

FIGURE I.9

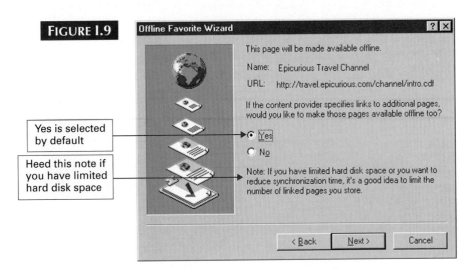

Yes is selected by default

Heed this note if you have limited hard disk space

5 Select Next.

FIGURE I.10

This option downloads files only when you manually choose the Synchronize menu option

This option allows you to create a schedule for automatic down-loading

This option uses the automatic downloading schedule recommended by the Web page

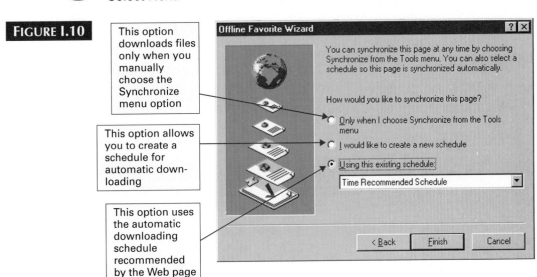

6 Select the option for synchronizing the page (when you synchronize a page, Internet Explorer downloads the page).

7 Select Finish. The dialog box closes and files begin to download.

TASK 9: To Synchronize and Work Offline

1 Choose Tools, Synchronize. The Items to Synchronize dialog box appears, as shown in Figure I.11.

FIGURE I.11

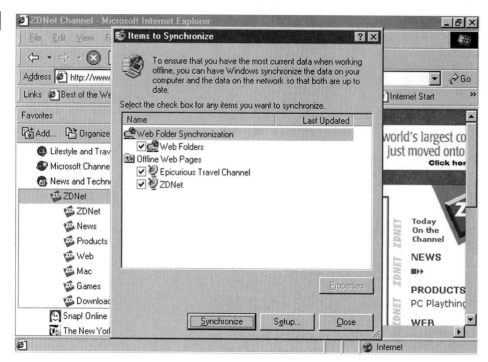

2 Select the items to synchronize and select Synchronize. Internet Explorer downloads pages for the selected channels to the hard drive.

3 Choose File, Work Offline. Internet Explorer will not connect to the Internet when you are viewing the pages that have been downloaded.

4 Choose Favorites, Channels, Lifestyle and Travel, Epicurious Travel.

5 Click the page you want to view.

> **TIP** Clicking a page that is dimmed indicates to Internet Explorer that you want to go online. Only pages that have been downloaded are not dimmed.

Downloading a File

Many Web sites contain files that you can download to your local computer. When downloading files, be careful. There are two basic rules you should follow:

1. Don't download files from sites with which you are unfamiliar.

2. Never download files if you do not have a virus protection program installed.

You could download a file that has a virus, and the next thing you know, your hard disk is corrupted.

> **TIP** Electronic mail or *e-mail*, is a service that allows you to send messages, data files, and software programs to another person electronically. You cannot get a virus from an e-mail message that you have received, only from an e-mail attachment.

In the next task, you will download a file from the Select Web site, a site you can trust.

TASK 10: To Download a File

1 Type **http://www.prenhall.com/divisions/bp/app/select/** in the Address text box and press (ENTER). Select the file *Selections.gif*.

2 When you have located the file, choose File, Save as File, if necessary, or simple click the hyperlink.

3 Select the desired Save in folder and click Save. The file is downloaded to the specified folder.

Accessing Newsgroups

Newsgroups are worldwide electronic discussion groups that allow users to exchange ideas, opinions, and information. To participate in one of the many thousands of newsgroups available, you must have access to a *news server* and have a *newsreader* program, such as the one in Internet Explorer.

Most news servers have the seven major Usenet categories listed below on the left. Other categories which may or may not be carried by a news server include those listed below on the right.

comp	computer-related topics	**alt**	alternative subjects
news	newsgroup information	**bionet**	biological topics
rec	recreational topics	**bit**	miscellaneous topics
sci	scientific research topics	**biz**	business-related topics and advertisements
soc	social issues		
talk	controversial debates	**gnu**	Free Software Foundation topics
misc	everything else	**k12**	educational topics for kindergarten through 12th grade

> **TIP** Usenet is the oldest organization of newsgroups on the Internet.

Launching the Internet Explorer Newsreader

The Internet Explorer 5 newsreader program is part of Outlook Express. You can start Outlook Express from the desktop with the Outlook Express icon or from within Internet Explorer 5.

> **TIP** Internet Explorer 5 also includes an e-mail program called Outlook Express. To launch the program, use the icon on the desktop or choose Start, Programs, Outlook Express. To compose an e-mail message, click the New Mail button, address and type the message, and then click the Send button. If you are using an Internet service provider to get online, you may have to click the Send/Receive button and log on to the Internet. E-mail messages that you receive appear in the Inbox. To read an e-mail message, double-click the message.

TASK 11: <u>To Launch the Newsreader from Internet Explorer 5</u>

1 Click the drop-down list arrow on the Mail button. The Mail menu appears.

2 Click Read News. Outlook Express starts and the news folder is selected in the left pane.

> **TROUBLESHOOTING** In the lab, the Newsreader program should already be set up for you. If you are setting up the Newsreader on your own computer, you must set up a news account. After setting up an account with your name, e-mail address, name of the news server, and so on, Internet Explorer asks if you want to download a list of the newsgroups. Choose Yes. You only have to do this once.

Reading a Message in a Newsgroup

Individual contributions to a newsgroup are called ***articles*** or ***messages***. Submitting a message is called ***posting***. Your reply to a posted message becomes part of a discussion ***thread***. Posting a new message starts a new thread. Threads that have replies are marked with a plus sign (+).

TASK 12: <u>To Read a Message</u>

1 Click the Newsgroups button in the Outlook Express toolbar, if necessary. The Newsgroup Subscriptions dialog box appears.

FIGURE 1.12

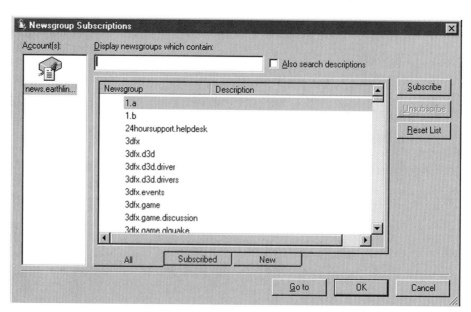

2 Type **skiing** in the Display newsgroups which contain text box. A list of newsgroups containing the word *skiing* appears. Select rec.skiing.marketplace and select Go to.

3 In the upper pane on the right, click an article you want to read. The text appears in the lower pane.

> **TIP** If you double-click an article in the upper pane, the article opens in its own window.

Subscribing to Newsgroups

Subscribing to a newsgroup is not like subscribing to a magazine. No money is involved! When you subscribe to a newsgroup, it is simply listed on a Subscription page in a dialog box so you can access it more easily. By subscribing to newsgroups you are interested in, you eliminate the need to scroll through a long list each time you want to participate in a group.

TASK 13: To Subscribe to a Newsgroup

1 Right-click the rec.skiing.marketplace newsgroup in the left pane. A shortcut menu opens.

2 Choose Subscribe to this Newsgroup. The number of articles posted in the group appears beside the name of the group.

3 Click ▣. The Newsgroup dialog box opens.

4 Click the Subscribed tab. The rec.skiing.marketplace newsgroup is listed.

5 Click ✖. Outlook Express closes but Internet Explorer 5 remains open.

> **TIP** Another easy way to subscribe to a newsgroup is to double-click the name of the newsgroup in the Newsgroup dialog box.

> **TIP** There are informal rules that govern each newsgroup called "netiquette," or Internet etiquette. Look for the rules in a FAQ (frequently asked questions) list posted on the newsgroup. Also check the newsgroup news.announce.newusers for rules of netiquette. If you can't find a FAQ, visit the newsgroup frequently and try to get a feel for how the group works by reading the postings before you participate. This is referred to as "lurking."

Exiting Internet Explorer 5

When you are finished using the Internet, exit Internet Explorer 5 and terminate your connection, if necessary.

TASK 14: To Exit Internet Explorer 5

1 Click ✖.

2 Choose the option to disconnect if you are prompted to disconnect from your Internet service provider's network.

Summary and Exercises

Summary

- The Internet is a network of networks all communicating using Internet Protocol (IP).
- If you have a modem in your computer, you can connect to the Internet via an Internet service provider.
- Services on the Internet include the World Wide Web, e-mail, newsgroups, Internet chat, FTP, Gopher, Internet meetings, and telephone conferences.
- Internet Explorer 5 provides many ways to navigate the Internet, including the Links toolbar, History, Favorites, and the Search Assistant.
- You can create shortcuts, called Favorites, to sites on the Internet that you visit often.
- Channels use push technology to send content from a Web page directly to your local hard drive.
- You can download files from the Internet to your local computer.
- Newsgroups are worldwide electronic discussion groups that allow users to exchange ideas, opinions, and information.

Key Terms and Operations

Key Terms

address	hyperlink	posting
Address bar	Internet Protocol (IP)	push technology
article	Internet service provider	Quick Launch toolbar
channel	(ISP)	Search Assistant
client	InterNIC	search engine
e-mail	message	server
Favorite	network	start page
FTP	news server	thread
gopher	newsgroups	URL
history	newsreader	World Wide Web
host computer	offline	

Operations

download a file	post a message
exit Internet Explorer 5	print a Web page
exit Outlook Express	read a newsgroup message
follow a link	search the Internet
launch Internet Explorer 5	subscribe to a newsgroup
launch Outlook Express	synchronize

Study Questions

Multiple Choice

1. *URL* is
   a. a protocol used on the World Wide Web.
   b. an acronym for Unspecified Resource Link.
   c. an acronym for Uniform Resource Locator.
   d. the organization that regulates the Internet.

2. The gopher protocol was originated at the
   a. University of Illinois
   b. University of Minnesota
   c. University of Wisconsin
   d. National Science Foundation

3. A Web browser is a
   a. user who browses the Web without actively participating.
   b. user who browses the Web and actively participates.
   c. program that accesses Web sites on the Internet.
   d. search engine on a gopher site.

4. The oldest organization of newsgroups is
   a. the Internet.
   b. Usenet.
   c. BITNET.
   d. Clarinet.

5. Submitting a message to a newsgroup is called
   a. submitting.
   b. posting.
   c. lurking.
   d. subscribing.

6. The Find command searches
   a. all Web sites for specified text.
   b. all FTP sites for specified text.
   c. only the current page for specified text.
   d. all gopher sites for specified text.

7. When you click a hyperlink,
   a. a pop-up box appears with a description of the hyperlink.
   b. the name of the hyperlinked file appears.
   c. another location on the Internet is accessed.
   d. you are automatically logged off the Internet.

8. The History folder stores
   a. a log of the dates and times you log on to the Internet.
   b. a list of Favorites.
   c. links to the Internet addresses you have accessed each day.
   d. a list of user names that log on to the Internet.

9. When the mouse pointer hovers over a hyperlink,
   a. the link changes color.
   b. the link blinks.
   c. the pointer changes to a hand with a pointing finger.
   d. the pointer changes color.

10. Adding a channel for offline viewing
    a. entails a fee.
    b. is called subscribing in the previous version of Internet Explorer.
    c. both a and b
    d. none of the above

Short Answer

1. What was the name of the first network on the Internet?

2. What protocol does the World Wide Web use?

3. What does FTP stand for?

4. What are newsgroups?

5. What is a thread?

6. What is a channel?

7. What is a hyperlink?

8. What is the Search Assistant?

9. What is an Internet service provider?

10. What Internet service is named for a school mascot?

Fill in the Blank

1. The Internet began with a network set up by the Department of _____.

2. Use the _____ feature to quickly return to a Web site that you visited last week.

3. To return to the same Web site over and over again, add the site to _____.

4. When displayed, Favorites, History, and the Search Assistant appear in the _____ bar.

5. _____ issues unique server identifiers to companies that want to add their networks to the Internet.

6. When using Internet Explorer 5, you do not have to type _____:// before the address.

7. When you point to a _____, the mouse pointer changes to a hand with a pointing finger.

8. The Home button and the _____ button both take you to the start page.

9. Channels use _____ technology to send data directly to your computer.

10. If you want to download pages from a channel manually, use the _____ command.

For Discussion

1. Discuss the advantages and disadvantages of using channels.

2. Discuss the value of newsgroups.

3. In what ways can you benefit from the Internet personally?

4. Why do you think that e-mail is one of the most popular services on the Internet?

5. Discuss some of the ways you think the Internet will be used in the 21st century.

Hands-On Exercises

1. Finding Out More about InterNIC

Using the Search Assistant, search for "InterNIC" or go to http://www.internic.com or http://www.internic.net and answer the following questions.

1. What connection does Network Solutions, Inc. have with InterNIC?

2. What is a domain name?

3. How much does it cost to register a domain name directly with InterNIC?

4. How much does it cost yearly to renew a domain name?

2. Exploring Links on the Links Toolbar

The Links toolbar has links for many Web sites that Microsoft considers exceptionally good or useful. Use the links to help you explore these sites.

1. Launch Internet Explorer, if necessary.

2. Display the Links toolbar, if necessary.

3. Click the Best of the Web link.

4. Go to several different sites by using the hyperlinks on the site.

5. Print the Web page for each site that you like or think you might use.

On Your Own Exercises

1. Exploring Newsgroups

Explore the newsgroups more thoroughly and visit newsgroups that might be interesting or helpful in running a business. Make a list of the newsgroups that you find.

2. Guessing Addresses of Web Sites

Make a list of addresses for Web sites that you think might exist on the Internet and then try them. Indicate which addresses were correct. Hint: Web addresses generally begin with *www.* and end with a suffix that indicates the type of site (e.g. *.com* for commercial sites, *.edu* for educational sites, *.gov* for government sites, and *.org* for organizations.)

3. Exploring Channels

Choose Favorites, Channels, Microsoft Channel Guide and explore the channels that are available. List the channels that you would want to view offline.

4. Exploring Newsgroup Netiquette

Find a newsgroup that discusses topics you are interested in. Does the newsgroup have a FAQ? If so, print the FAQ. If you cannot find a FAQ, read several of the discussion threads and list three to five topics that are currently under discussion.

Outlook

Introducing Outlook 2000

Microsoft Outlook 2000, a personal desktop organizer similar to Daytimers and Franklin Planners, is installed as an integral part of Microsoft Office 2000. The features in Outlook 2000 help you track appointments, send and receive messages, maintain a list of "to do" tasks, monitor computer activities, and update business and personal contacts in an instant.

Objectives

After completing this project, you will be able to:

➤ Identify Outlook features

➤ Launch Outlook

➤ Use the Outlook Bar

➤ Use Outlook Help

➤ Customize toolbars and menus

➤ Set views

➤ Schedule appointments in the Calendar

➤ Record tasks in the TaskPad

➤ Store contacts in the Contacts List

➤ Work with e-mail

➤ Manage Outlook files

➤ Create Notes

➤ Print from Outlook

➤ Exit Outlook

Identifying Outlook Features

Outlook comes with a number of features designed to keep you organized. You can keep Outlook open as you work in other applications and use it as a reference more easily. Table O.1 lists the features available in Outlook.

Table O.1

Use this feature	to:
Outlook Bar	Access features by clicking the feature icon located in the Outlook window.
Outlook Today	Preview a summary of your appointments, a list of tasks to be accomplished, and the number of new e-mail messages you have received on the same screen.
Inbox	Store messages you receive.
Calendar	Schedule appointments and meetings.
Contacts	Record business and personal contacts on a Rolodex-type file for easy access.
Task List	Record things to do, prioritize the list, and check tasks off as they are completed.
Journal	Monitor computer activities as they happen and create a timeline of events for projects.
Notes	Store notes during phone conversations and meetings on electronic Post-It notes.
Deleted Items	Retrieve "thrown out" items from the wastebasket as long as it hasn't been emptied.

 Web Tip

Have you discovered chat rooms yet? If not, bone up on your chat room acronyms before going online live so you'll look like a pro to others in the chat room. A chat list can be found at http://www.chatlist.com/newcfdocs/searchacro.cfm. TTFN (that's the Internet acronym for "Ta-Ta for now").

Launching Outlook

The techniques you use to launch Outlook are similar to those used to launch other applications. In addition, the typical installation of Microsoft Outlook 2000 creates a desktop shortcut to Outlook for easy access. Use one of the following techniques to launch Outlook:

• Double-click the Microsoft Outlook ⊞ shortcut icon on the Desktop

- Click the Launch Microsoft Outlook  icon on the Quick Launch toolbar

- Choose Start, Programs, Microsoft Outlook.

FIGURE O.1

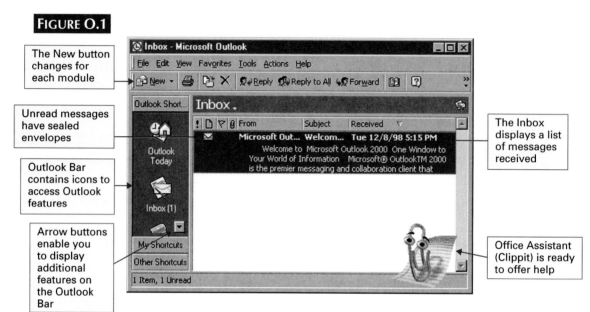

The New button changes for each module

Unread messages have sealed envelopes

Outlook Bar contains icons to access Outlook features

Arrow buttons enable you to display additional features on the Outlook Bar

The Inbox displays a list of messages received

Office Assistant (Clippit) is ready to offer help

TIP The Outlook window on your computer may vary from the one pictured here. Because of installation and customization differences, the group names, folder names, toolbar buttons, and active features may be different thoughout this module.

Using the Outlook Bar

The Outlook Bar groups Outlook features into three different shortcut categories: Outlook Shortcuts, My Shortcuts, and Other Shortcuts. Category names appear on Outlook Bar buttons. When you click a category button, icons representing shortcuts to different features within the category appear. When you click the shortcut icons on the Outlook Bar, the Outlook window changes, sometimes dividing into multiple window panes.

TASK 1: To Access Outlook Features

1 Click the Outlook Shortcuts group button at the top of the Outlook Bar. Outlook default shortcut icons appear.

2 Click the My Shortcuts group button at the bottom of the Outlook Bar.

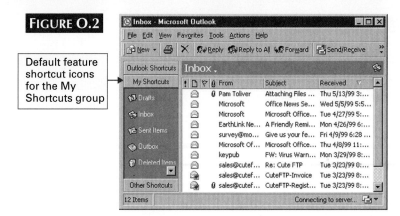

FIGURE O.2

Default feature shortcut icons for the My Shortcuts group

3 Click the Other Shortcuts group button at the bottom of the Outlook Bar.

> **TIP** If your group button is named *Other* rather than *Other Shortcuts* and you would like to change the group name, point to the group name and right-click to display the shortcut menu. Then click Rename Group, type the new group name, and press (ENTER).

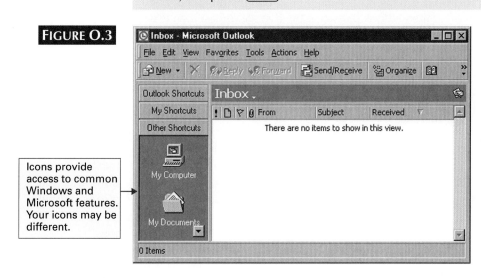

FIGURE O.3

Icons provide access to common Windows and Microsoft features. Your icons may be different.

4 Click the Outlook Shortcuts group button on the Outlook Bar. The Outlook Bar displays the buttons for accessing Outlook features.

5 Click the Scroll Down ▼ button at the bottom of the Outlook Bar. Additional shortcut icons appear and the Scroll Up button ▲ appears at the top of the Outlook Bar, as shown in Figure O.4.

FIGURE O.4

> **TROUBLESHOOTING** Scroll buttons disappear from the top and/or bottom of the Outlook Bar when the first and/or last icon is displayed.

6 Click the Scroll Up ▲ button until the Calendar shortcut appears.

Using the Office Assistant to Get Help

The Office Assistant is available in Outlook and provides assistance as you work by displaying a focused list of help topics related to questions you "ask" the Assistant. Depending on how the person using your computer left the Assistant, it may appear on-screen when you launch applications. When closed, the Assistant waits on the Standard toolbar and appears when you call it to look up information about topics for which you need help.

TASK 2: <u>To Use the Office Assistant</u>

1 Maximize Outlook and click the Microsoft Help ⸮ button on the Standard toolbar.

FIGURE O.5

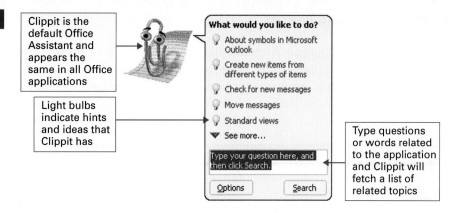

Clippit is the default Office Assistant and appears the same in all Office applications

Light bulbs indicate hints and ideas that Clippit has

What would you like to do?

- About symbols in Microsoft Outlook
- Create new items from different types of items
- Check for new messages
- Move messages
- Standard views
- ▼ See more...

Type your question here, and then click Search.

Options   Search

Type questions or words related to the application and Clippit will fetch a list of related topics

TIP The Office Assistant dialog box appears in different shapes and sizes, depending on how it was last used. Different topics may also appear.

2 Type **How do I sort mail items by category?** The Office Assistant takes notes as you type.

3 Click Search. A list of related topics appears.

4 Click See more to display additional topics.

5 Click About finding e-mail messages. The Help window opens, as shown in Figure O.6. Notice that the Outlook window resizes to accommodate the Help window.

FIGURE O.6

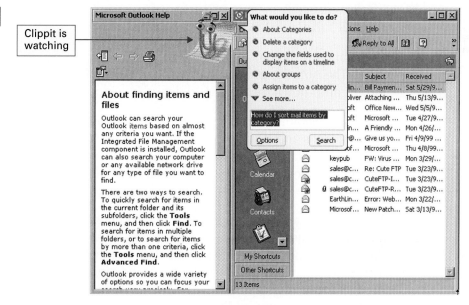

Clippit is watching

6 Review the information and then close the Help window. The Outlook window resizes to its original size.

TIP As you work with Help, you'll discover that the format of information displayed after you select a topic varies. In some cases a list of step-by-step instructions appears in the Help window, while at other times another list of topics related to the topic you select will appear.

Turning Off and On the Office Assistant

When the Office Assistant feature is active, it often offers unsolicited help that can become quite annoying. You can disable the feature in Office 2000 applications. After you turn off the Office Assistant, a Help window automatically opens when you click the Microsoft Help button.

TASK 3: To Turn Off and On the Office Assistant

1 Display the Office Assistant, if necessary, and right-click to display the shortcut menu.

2 Choose Options.

3 Clear the Use the Office Assistant option box. All other boxes are dimmed.

4 Choose OK. The Office Assistant closes.

5 Choose Help, Show the Office Assistant. The Office Assistant feature is reactivated so that clicking the Microsoft Help button will now call the Assistant.

6 Right-click the Office Assistant and choose Hide Assistant. The Office Assistant disappears and waits to be called again.

Customizing Toolbars and Menus

The Standard toolbar and menu bar are displayed by default in Outlook 2000. The AutoCustomize features found in all Office 2000 applications customize drop-down menus and toolbars as you use the program.

Unless you change the default settings, drop-down menus display a short list of commands and display additional commands only when the basic menu has been displayed for a few seconds. When you access a menu command that appears on an extended menu, that command appears in the short set of commands the next time you use the drop-down menu.

The Standard toolbar displays the most frequently used buttons and places additional buttons on a drop-down palette. Each time you use a button on a drop-down toolbar palette, Outlook assumes that the button is one you will use again and automatically customizes the toolbar by placing the button on the toolbar so that it is easier to access. When the space allocated for the toolbar is full, using additional buttons causes existing buttons to be removed to make room for the new button.

You can change settings to enable and disable the AutoCustomize feature in Outlook. In addition, you can customize toolbars manually. Changing the settings in one Outlook component affects the settings in other Outlook components. The procedures for customizing menus and toolbars are the same in all Outlook 2000 components.

TASK 4:   To Change AutoCustomizing Settings and Manually Customize Toolbars

1 Choose Tools, Customize and then click the Options tab. The Customize dialog box opens.

2 Deselect Menus Show Recently Used Commands First if it is selected. Clearing the checkmark for this item turns it off so that all menu commands for each specific menu appear each time you display it.

3 Click the Commands tab. A list of menu items appears at the top of the Categories list and existing toolbars appear at the bottom of the Categories list.

4 Click the Edit category. A list of commands and corresponding buttons appears in the Commands list.

5 Click Copy in the Commands list, drag it to position the I bar between any two buttons on the Standard toolbar, and drop the button.

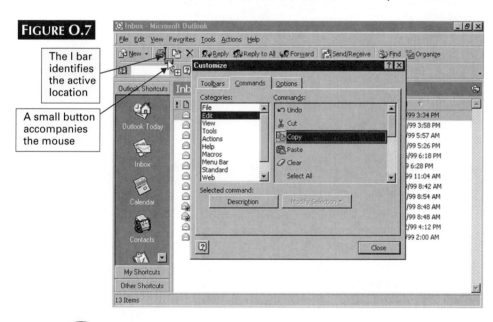

FIGURE O.7

The I bar identifies the active location

A small button accompanies the mouse

6 Click the Toolbars tab and then click the Standard toolbar, if necessary.

7 Click Reset and then click Yes to respond to the message. The Copy button is removed from the toolbar, and the default buttons remain.

8 Click Close.

Working with Outlook Views

Standard views in each Outlook component help you organize and format information. You can change the way information appears on-screen, change the view to display different information on-screen, and customize an existing view to better meet your needs.

TASK 5: To Set View Options and Change Views

1 Click the Inbox [Inbox] button on the Outlook Bar.

2 Choose View, Preview Pane. Choosing Preview Pane turns off the preview pane if it was active or turns it on if it was off.

3 Choose View, Current View and review the available Inbox views.

FIGURE O.8

Available current views

View options change information that displays on-screen

TIP Because you have few messages displayed in the Inbox, changing the view would display little difference. As your list of messages grows, however, you may want to change the arrangement of messages. To change the arrangement of messages, display the Current View listing and select the field or other view arrangement you want to use to arrange messages.

You can customize the fields of information that appear in each view. When you have become more comfortable with Outlook's basic features, you may want to try customizing your views. Display the view you want to customize and then choose View, Current View, Customize. That will get you started and you can explore features contained in the Customize dialog box for the view you are editing.

4 Choose View, Folder List. A list of available folders appears in a separate pane between the Outlook Bar and the Inbox message list.

TROUBLESHOOTING If your folder list was already active, it closes.

5 Click the Folder List Close button, if necessary. The Folder List pane closes.

6 Click the Calendar [Calendar] button on the Outlook Bar.

7 Choose View, Current View, Active Appointments. The Calendar window appears in a table format that lists appointments when you schedule them.

8 Choose View, Current View, Day/Week/Month. The View menu contains different commands when the Active Appointments view is active. Both the View menu and the original view reappear.

Scheduling Appointments in the Calendar

Whether you use the Calendar to keep track of appointments or assignments, recording entries in the Calendar is easy. You can enter appointments directly in the Calendar window or use the Appointment dialog box to enter the appointment and set options.

TASK 6: <u>To Schedule Appointments in the Calendar</u>

1 Click the Outlook Bar Calendar shortcut icon.

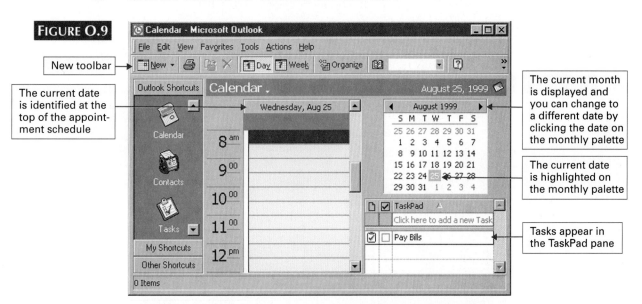

FIGURE O.9

New toolbar →

The current date is identified at the top of the appointment schedule

The current month is displayed and you can change to a different date by clicking the date on the monthly palette

The current date is highlighted on the monthly palette

Tasks appear in the TaskPad pane

TIP The appearance of the Calendar window can be changed using different techniques:

- Drag a pane border to adjust the size.
- Choose Tools, Options, Preferences, Calendar Options, and select appropriate settings.

You can also customize menus and toolbars by choosing Tools, Customize, and select menu and toolbar features.

2 Double-click the 11:00 time slot on the Calendar appointment list. The Untitled Appointment dialog box opens. A completed appointment window appears in Figure O.10. Table O.2 describes fields in the Appointment dialog box.

FIGURE O.10

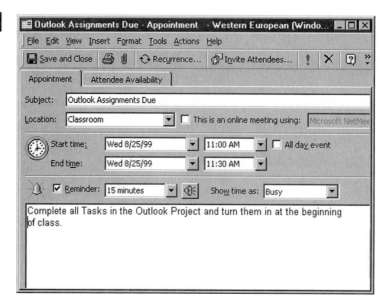

TIP You can also click the New button on the Outlook toolbar to open the Appointment dialog box. The dialog box that opens when you click the New button depends on which Outlook feature is active.

3 Enter the data shown in Figure O.10, changing the date in the Start time and End time boxes to a week from Wednesday.

FIGURE O.11

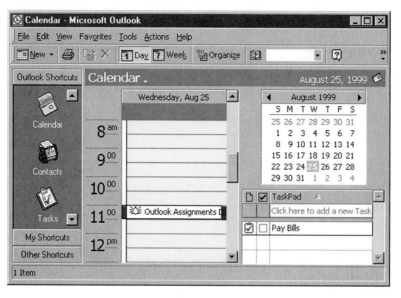

4 Click the Save and Close button.

5 Click monthly calendar palette date for next Wednesday.

Table O.2

Feature	Description
Subject	The topic or purpose of the appointment. Click the text box and type the subject.
Location	The place where the appointment is to take place. Click the text box and type the location.
Online meeting option	Identifies the appointment as an online meeting to which other participants have been invited for online collaboration and participation on a network. Click the option box and then select the program to be used for the meeting from the drop-down list.
Start time	Identifies the date and time the appointment will start. Click the date drop-down list arrow to display a calendar palette from which to choose the start date; click the time drop-down list arrow to display a list of times from which to select the time the meeting or appointment is to start.
End time	Identifies the date and time the appointment will end. Click the date drop-down list arrow to display a calendar palette from which to choose the end date; click the time drop-down list arrow to display a list of times from which to select the time the appointment is to end.
All day event	Marks the appointment as spanning the complete day. When this option is checked, the time fields are removed from the dialog box. All day events appear as a bar at the top of the calendar day just below the date.
Reminder	When checked, a reminder will pop up on-screen to notify you that it is almost time for the appointment. You can set the reminder to notify you several minutes, hours, or days before the appointment. By default, when the reminder is set, a sound accompanies the reminder. You can deactivate the sound feature by clicking the sound button and clearing the option box. When reminders are set, a bell appears beside the appointment in the calendar. To set a reminder, click the Reminder option box and then select a reminder time setting from the reminder drop-down list.
Show time as	Identifies how Outlook should mark the time—free, tentative, busy, or out of office. Select the appropriate setting from the drop-down list. Free appointments appear with a clear border in the calendar; tentative appointments are bordered in light blue; busy time appointments are bordered in dark blue; and out-of-office appointments are bordered in maroon.
Notes	Provides an area for recording important information about the appointment. Click the text box and type notes appropriate to the appointment.

Scheduling Multi-Day Events

Many appointments you schedule will last only a day or part of a day. Events such as trade shows, conferences, and, of course, vacations, can extend over several days. Other appointments, known as recurring appointments, occur at regular intervals—once a week, once a month, and so on. Features in Outlook make scheduling appointments that last several days as well as recurring appointments quick and easy. Recurring appointments can even be identified as recurring appointments!

TASK 7: **To Schedule Multi-Day Events and Recurring Appointments**

1 Click the Calendar [Calendar] button on the Outlook Bar, if necessary.

2 Select the date and time on which one of your classes met for the first time and type the name of the class and the location in a New Appointment window.

3 Click the Recurrence ↻ Recurrence... button to display the Appointment Recurrence dialog box and set the following options:

- Set the Duration of the class.
- Select Weekly.
- Place a checkmark in the check boxes for each day of the week the class meets.
- Verify the Start date and set the End by date.

4 Click OK and then click 🔲 Save and Close.

FIGURE O.12

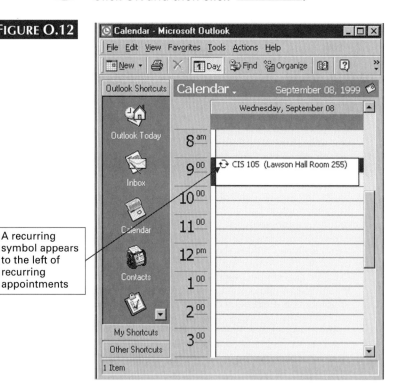

A recurring symbol appears to the left of recurring appointments

5 Display the calendar for the first Saturday in September and double-click the date bar at the top of the appointment calendar. Double-clicking the date bar automatically tells Outlook that this is an all-day event.

6 Type **Holiday Weekend** in the Subject field, type **The Beach** in the Location field, and click Monday's date from the End time drop-down calendar palette.

7 Click 🔲 Save and Close.

FIGURE O.13

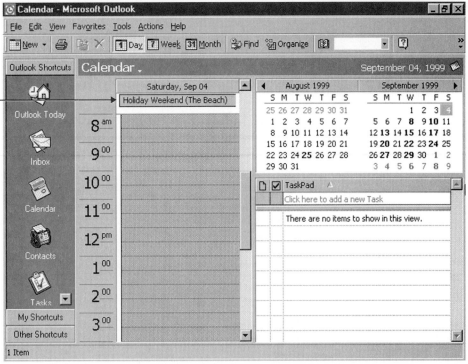

Full-day appointments appear as bars below the date bar

Recording Tasks in the TaskPad

The TaskPad appears in a pane of the Calendar window for easy access. You can, however, display tasks in a full window. An added benefit to the TaskPad in Office 2000 is that it enables you to create tasks for yourself as well as to assign tasks to others—a real bonus!

Entering Basic Tasks

The procedures used to record tasks are the same regardless of whether you enter the task from the Calendar window or display the TaskPad window.

TASK 8: <u>To Record Tasks in the TaskPad</u>

1 Choose Click here to add a new task in the task entry bar. Instruction text disappears and the insertion point appears in the task entry bar.

2 Type **Pick up forms from career center.** and press (ENTER). The task appears in the list.

3 Double-click the task entry bar. The Task dialog box opens. It resembles the Appointment dialog box.

FIGURE O.14

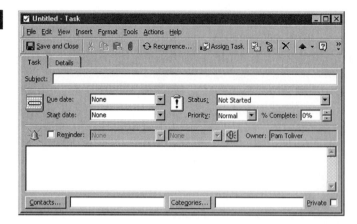

④ Type the data shown in Figure O.15 in the appropriate fields.

FIGURE O.15

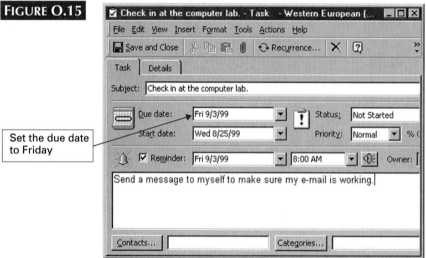

Set the due date to Friday

⑤ Click 🖫 Save and Close . The Outlook window displays the new task.

> **TIP** Text for overdue tasks appears in red. To quickly sort by different columns in the TaskPad, click Tasks on the Outlook Bar and then click the gray column heading button. To change the appearance of the tasks, choose Tools, Options, Task Options, and select the appropriate colors.

⑥ Double-click the line *Welcome to Tasks!* Information about the task appears in the notes area.

⑦ Close the Welcome to Tasks! window.

⑧ Click the checkbox for the *Pick up forms from career center.* task. The task is assumed to be completed and a line is drawn through the task.

⑨ Click the Tasks icon on the Outlook Bar. A complete list of tasks appears.

Storing Contacts in the Contacts List

Contacts stores information—such as names, addresses, phone numbers, and company names—about your personal and/or business contacts. You can use information stored in Contacts in letters and databases. Sending e-mail messages directly to those people whose e-mail addresses you have stored in Contacts, assigning tasks to contacts, and recording new activities directly in the Journal are just a few of the activities you can perform from Contacts. In addition, storing the contacts electronically makes editing information about contacts more efficient.

> **TIP** The Journal automatically tracks activities performed using Microsoft Office applications. When you want to record activities performed in software applications other than Microsoft Office or without a computer and relate the activity to a contact listing, you can display the appropriate contact listing and choose Actions, New Journal Entry for Contract. An Untitled Journal Entry dialog box opens and you can enter the information you want to record. You'll get more practice using the Journal by completing On Your Own Exercise 5 at the end of this project.

TASK 9:   To Add and Edit Contacts Entries

1 Click the Outlook Bar Contacts icon.

FIGURE O.16

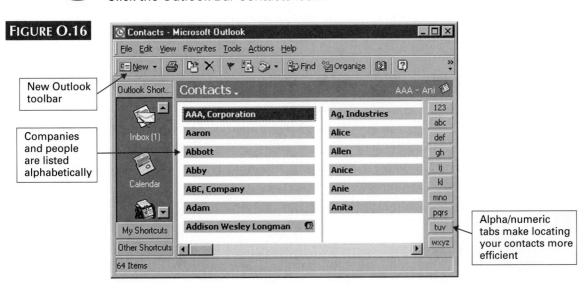

2 Double-click a blank area of the Contacts window. The Contact dialog box opens.

3 Type your own personal data in the fields of the Contact sheet, pressing (TAB) to move from field to field.

4 Click ☒. Your personal information appears alphabetically in the Contacts list, as shown in Figure O.17.

FIGURE O.17

5 Double-click your Contacts listing, position the insertion point in the Address field, and replace your personal address with your school address; move to the Business Phone field and type your school phone number.

6 Click 💾 Save and Close.

Check Point

Add Contact listings for a close friend, your instructor, and two classmates, saving each listing as you complete it. Click 💾 Save and Close after completing the last listing. Click the title bar of the listing for one of your classmates and press (DEL) to remove the listing.

Assigning Tasks to Others

When a task you record is to be completed by someone else, you can enter the task in your TaskPad and assign the task to the other person. When you assign tasks to others, they have the option to accept or reject the task.

TASK 10: To Assign Tasks to Others

1 Display the Tasks window and create a new task. A new Task window opens.

2 Type **Review computer project outline.** in the Subject text box and set the due date to a week from Friday.

3 Click the Assign Task button on the toolbar. A To field appears at the top of the Task window.

4 Click the To button, double-click a classmate's listing from the Contacts list, and click OK. The name appears in the To text box.

5 Choose Send. A message window advises you that you are no longer the task owner, so the reminder about the due date has been turned off.

6 Click OK to acknowledge the message.

Check Point

When you receive a task assigned to you by your classmate, you can accept or decline the task and type notes explaining your reason for declining the task or questions you have about the task. Take the appropriate action on the task assignment you receive. Just click the Accept button to accept the task or click the Decline button to decline the task. Your response is automatically sent to the person who assigned the task.

Break Point

If necessary, you can save your file, exit Outlook, and continue this project later.

Working with E-Mail

Outlook comes equipped with an e-mail feature you can use to communicate with people on a *local area network (LAN)* as well as with people on the Internet, the worldwide computer structure for sharing information. To use the e-mail feature, you must have a valid e-mail account that connects you to the Internet or to a LAN.

The Outlook Inbox stores messages you receive from others and automatically appears each time you launch Outlook to remind you to sign on or log on to the network and check for new messages. The Outbox displayed in the My Shortcuts group stores messages you create until you log on to the network and send the messages.

Web Tip

Looking for a free e-mail program to use outside the classroom or school? There are a number available. Juno (http://www.juno.com), HotMail (http://www.hotmail.com), and Xoom (http://www.xoom.com) are just a few. Each of these services also has a fee-based Internet access program as well, so be careful when you contact the sites to ensure that you're getting the free stuff!

Creating, Sending, and Receiving E-Mail

The Inbox displays e-mail messages you receive from others. It's also the feature from which you create and send e-mail messages. Outlook features enable you to create plain messages or messages formatted using a template. In addition, you can create a signature file so that all messages you send will contain your name and other information you want to transmit.

> **TIP** If you normally connect to your e-mail program via a modem that ties up your phone line, try working offline to create your e-mail messages and then connect when you're ready to send them.

TASK 11: ## To Create, Send, and Receive E-Mail

1 Launch Outlook, if necessary, and click the Outlook Bar Inbox [Inbox] shortcut icon. The Inbox window opens.

> **TROUBLESHOOTING** By default, the Inbox automatically appears each time you launch Outlook. If your settings are different and display another Outlook feature, you will need to click the Outlook Bar Inbox shortcut icon each time you launch Outlook.

2 Choose Actions, New Mail Message Using, More Stationery. The Select a Stationery dialog box opens and displays a list of stationery at the top and a preview of the selected stationery at the bottom.

> **TIP** You can also click the New [New] button on the Outlook toolbar to create a plain e-mail message.

3 Select Ivy and choose OK.

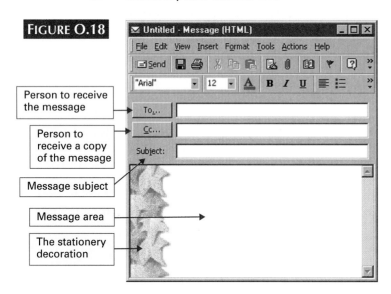

FIGURE O.18

Person to receive the message

Person to receive a copy of the message

Message subject

Message area

The stationery decoration

TROUBLESHOOTING If your system requires that you log on to the network to display a list of valid e-mail users, log on now—you'll need to be connected to continue.

4 Click the To button.

FIGURE O.19

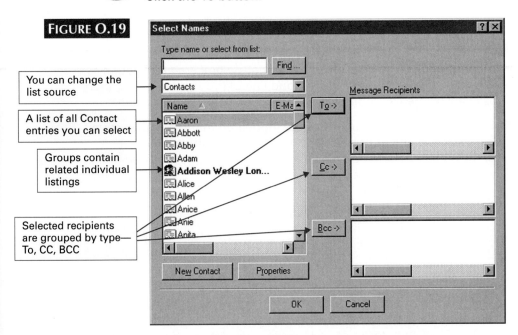

You can change the list source

A list of all Contact entries you can select

Groups contain related individual listings

Selected recipients are grouped by type— To, CC, BCC

5 Double-click your own personal e-mail address in the list on the left and then click OK. The name appears in the To field. If the recipient has a valid e-mail address, the name is underlined.

6 Press ⟨TAB⟩ and type the e-mail address of one of your classmates in the CC field.

7 Press ⟨TAB⟩ until the insertion point appears in the Subject field, and type **My First E-Mail Message Using Outlook**.

8 Press ⟨TAB⟩ and type **This is my first message typed using the Outlook Mail feature that came with Microsoft Office 2000. If I receive this message, I will know that I am actively connected to the campus e-mail system and am able to send and receive messages.** in the message area.

TIP Choosing a stationery to use for your e-mail message automatically formatted the font, font style, font size, paragraph alignment, and other format characteristics for the message text. To change the settings, choose Format, Font, and select appropriate font settings. Then choose Format, Paragraph, and select the appropriate paragraph alignment setting. Changes you make apply to the active message only.

9 Choose Insert, Signature, More. A message box advises you that there are no HTML signatures to insert into the message and asks if you want to create one.

10 Choose Yes. The Create New Signature dialog box opens.

TROUBLESHOOTING If a signature has already been created, choose Tools, Options, Mail Format, and then click Signature Picker. A list of signatures available is displayed at the top of the Signature Picker dialog box and you can choose New to create your own personal signature, Edit to change an existing signature, or Remove to delete an existing signature.

11 Type your name in the Enter a name for your new signature text box and choose Next. The Edit Signature dialog box opens.

12 Type your name on the first line of the signature box area and your class name and section number on the second line of the signature box; then choose Finish. The signature appears at the bottom of the message.

13 Click the Send ⬛Send button. If you are logged on to the e-mail system when you click Send, your message is sent immediately. If you aren't currently logged on to the e-mail system, your message is stored in the Outbox and will be sent the next time you log on.

TIP The only reason to send an e-mail message to yourself is to test your e-mail delivery system, to have mail to read, or to determine approximately when other recipients receive your messages.

14 Double-click the new message in the Inbox window to open it and read it.

TIP When you have multiple messages in the Inbox, you can click the Previous Item ⬆ button to display the previous message or click the Next Item ⬇ button to display the next message in the Inbox.

15 Close the message window.

TIP You can control how e-mail looks and works on your system by changing the e-mail options. Display the main Outlook window and choose Tools, Options. Then click the Preferences tab, if necessary, and click the E-mail Options button. Review the options displayed and decide which settings you prefer. Be sure to check with your instructor before changing any of the settings to ensure that your changes will affect Outlook for your login only.

Web Tip

Did you know that there is a strict etiquette associated with e-mail? It's called *netiquette* and you'll find great netiquette tips on the Web. Check out the Web site http://www.imaginarylandscape.com/helpweb/mail/polite.html for a list of netiquette resources.

Check Point

You need to send your instructor the Contact listing containing your personal information. Rather than retyping the information in a separate e-mail message, you can initiate the e-mail from Contacts (the source Outlook feature) in a format so that it can be added to the instructor's Contact list. Simply right-click on the Contact listing and select Forward as vCard. A new mail message opens and all you have to do is type your instructor's e-mail address in the To field. Add whatever text you want to include and send the listing on its way.

Replying to and Forwarding Messages

Two Outlook features enable you to respond to messages you receive or forward the message on to others when the information may be important to them. You can choose to reply only to the sender of the original message or to reply to all message recipients as well as the sender. When you reply to or forward messages, Outlook provides space in the e-mail message box for you to include additional comments or information.

TASK 12: To Reply to and Forward Messages

1 Open the message you received from your classmate.

2 Click 🔁 Reply . A new message window opens with the sender's e-mail address listed in the To field and space provided above the original message for your response. *RE:* appears in the Subject field.

> **TIP** Always check your To field to ensure that you are sending your message to the person you want to receive it. Messages that have been forwarded to you or to someone else before landing in your Inbox may redirect your reply to the wrong person—and that can be embarrassing!

> **TIP** To reply to all recipients as well as the sender, click 🔁 Reply to All .

3 Type an appropriate response message above the sender's message.

4 Click 📧 Send .

5 Open the response to your original message that you received from your classmate.

6 Click 🔁 Forward . A new message window opens with the To field blank and space provided above the original message for your response. *FW:* appears in the Subject field.

7 Type your instructor's e-mail address in the To field.

8 Type **This message is being forwarded to you from class.**

9 Click ⌧Send .

10 Close all open message windows.

Working with Mail Attachments

As you become more familiar with e-mail, you'll discover that not only can you create new e-mail messages, but you can attach files created in other applications to e-mail messages and send them electronically. In addition, you can receive files attached to e-mail messages. Files you receive attached to e-mail messages can be opened, saved, edited, and printed using techniques similar to the techniques you use to accomplish these tasks in other software programs.

TASK 13: To Attach, Open, and Save Files Using E-Mail

1 Click the Inbox Inbox button on the Outlook Bar and create a new mail message using Ivy stationery, addressing it to your classmate.

2 Create the mail message shown in Figure O.20.

FIGURE O.20

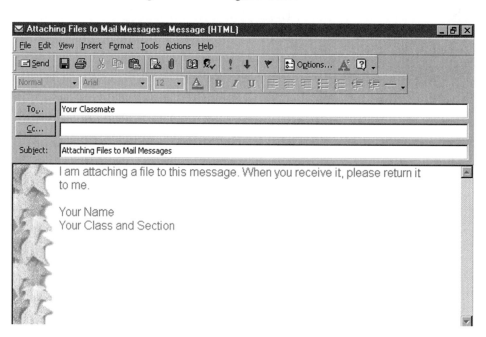

3 Choose Insert, File, open the folder containing your student files, and click *Selections.doc.*

> **TROUBLESHOOTING** If you do not have a copy of this file on your student disk, ask your instructor what file to attach.

4 Click Insert. The message window splits and the file, identified by a Word icon, appears below the split.

5 Click [Send]. The time required to send the message depends on the size of the file you have attached. Because the file you used is small, you should receive your e-mail attachment quickly.

6 Open the message containing the attachment that you receive from your classmate. The procedure for opening messages containing attachments is the same as the procedure used to open regular mail messages.

> **TROUBLESHOOTING** If your computer is equipped with a virus checking program that works automatically, the attachment will be checked for viruses. If your virus checker is initiated manually, it's a good idea to check attachments for viruses before opening them.

7 Double-click the attachment. The application used to create the attachment launches, if necessary, and the file opens.

8 Type your name at the bottom of the file and then choose File, Save As; open the folder containing your student files; and save the document using the file name *E-Mail Selections.doc*.

> **TROUBLESHOOTING** If you open a document, edit it, and then save it by choosing File, Save, edits are saved to the attachment, but you have no copy of the file to use later or to attach to an e-mail response. Depending on how Outlook is set up on your computer, clicking the Reply button may not automatically attach the edited file to the response. As a result, it is safer to save the attachment as a separate file and then attach it to your reply.

Creating Address Book Entries

When the name and e-mail address of someone you want to send messages to does not appear in your Address Book list, you can add the name to the Address Book "on the fly." In addition, you can group related e-mail addresses and send messages to everyone in the group.

TASK 14: To Create Address Book Entries

1 Display the Outlook 2000 Inbox, if necessary.

2 Click [icon]. The Address Book window opens.

3 Click the New [New] button and select New Contact.

FIGURE O.21

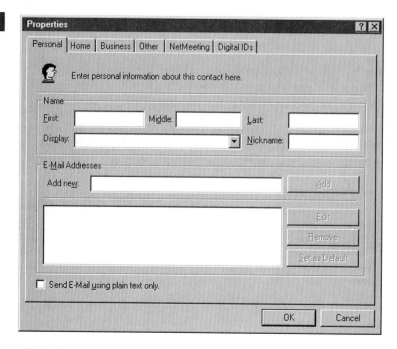

> **TROUBLESHOOTING** Depending on how Outlook is installed on your computer, you may see a new Contact window instead of the Properties dialog box.

4 Complete the name fields of a close friend and enter the e-mail address in the Add new field.

5 Choose OK. The name appears alphabetically among the Contacts listed.

6 Click the New button and select New Group.

> **TROUBLESHOOTING** Depending on how Outlook is installed on your computer, you may see Personal Distribution List or New Distribution List.

FIGURE O.22

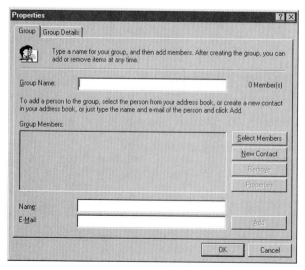

7 Type **Classmates** in the Group Name field.

8 Click Select Members. The Select Group Members dialog box displays the list of contacts.

9 Select the name of a classmate to add to the group and click Select. The selected name appears in the Member list.

> **TIP** To select multiple contiguous entries, select the first member and then hold down the (SHIFT) key and select the last member. To select multiple non-contiguous entries, hold down the (CTRL) key as you select each member.

10 Repeat step 9 to add two additional members to the group and then choose OK. The Classmates Properties dialog box displays group member names in the list box.

11 Choose OK again. The group name appears in bold characters alphabetically in the Contacts list in the Address Book window.

12 Close the Address Book window.

Managing Outlook Files

Features built into Outlook 2000 enable you to manage your messages, appointments, and other files that are stored in Outlook. You can, for example, sort, locate, archive, move, and delete messages. In addition, you can create categories and store Outlook information (tasks, contacts, messages, and so forth) using these categories.

Managing E-Mail

The easiest way to manage e-mail messages is to create e-mail folders for different topics and place messages related to each topic in the appropriate folder. Because messages automatically arrive in your Inbox, you will need to manually place messages in the appropriate folder. Changing Inbox viewing options will make locating messages easier.

TASK 15: To Create Outlook Folders and Sort Messages by Setting Viewing Options

1 Display the My Shortcuts group in Outlook and choose File, Folder, New Folder. The Create New Folder dialog box opens.

2 Type your name in the Name text box and select Inbox from the Select where to place the folder list; then choose OK. The Add Shortcut to Outlook Bar message window asks if you want to place the new folder on the Outlook Bar.

3 Choose Yes. The new folder appears on the Outlook Bar at the bottom of the My Shortcuts group.

4 Click the From column heading at the top of the Inbox messages. The messages are sorted alphabetically by sender name.

> **TIP** Each of the column headings on the Inbox, Outbox, Sent Items, and Deleted Items lists can be used to sort messages by simply clicking on the column heading you want to sort. As a result, you can sort by date received, message subjects, priorities, and so forth. You can also sort messages by choosing View, Current View, and selecting the option for the message arrangement you want to view.

5 Select the message you received from your classmate, drag the message envelope to the Outlook Bar, and drop the message on the folder containing your name.

6 Repeat the procedure to place additional personal messages in your personal folder.

Archiving Files

When a folder contains too many items, you can archive the folder contents and remove older messages from the folder. Archiving messages enables you to move items older than the date you specify to an archive folder so they no longer appear in your folder. Archived files are stored in an archive file in the folder path C:\windows\Local Settings\Application Data\Microsoft\Outlook\archive.pst. This archive file is replaced each time you archive items unless you change the file name.

TASK 16: To Archive Files

1 Click the Your Name folder on the Outlook Bar and choose View, Current View, Last Seven Days. Only the messages received during the last seven days will be displayed.

> **TIP** When you receive messages on which action is required, you can flag the message as a reminder to review message contents again later. Select the message, choose Actions, Flag for Follow Up, and set the follow-up action and due date in the Flag for Follow Up dialog box.

2 Choose File, Archive. The Archive dialog box opens.

3 Select last Friday's date from the Archive items older than drop-down list calendar and choose OK.

> **TIP** To retrieve archived items, choose File, Import and Export, select Import from another program or file, and then open your .pst file. The Import and Export Wizard walks you through the process. All items can be restored to their original folders or to a folder you specify.

Linking and Sorting Outlook Items

Linking and sorting are two Outlook features that will enable you to manage your files more efficiently.

Linking creates an invisible line between items in Outlook so that you can easily locate related items. For example, you might want to link e-mail messages to contacts in your Contacts list or link appointments to the contacts who will be participating in the meeting. By creating a link between the items, you can access one of the items (the contact or appointment, for example) and locate all activities and items associated with the contact. Links must be attached manually to individual items in Outlook.

Sorting enables you to rearrange lists and items—mail messages, contacts, appointments, and so forth—by selecting fields on which Outlook should order the items. You can select a primary field (the field you want Outlook to look at first as it sorts) as well as three additional sort fields, which serve as "tie breakers" when two items with the same information in the primary field are found. By specifying additional sort fields, you can arrange items more precisely in the proper order.

> **TIP** You can also sort items by attaching items to categories. When you display items by category, they automatically sort alphabetically by category, and each item within the category is sorted alphabetically or numerically.

TASK 17: To Link and Sort Outlook Items

1 Click the Inbox icon on the Outlook Bar and choose View, Current View, Customize Current View. The View Summary dialog box opens.

2 Click the Sort button. The Sort dialog box opens.

3 Select the From field from the Sort items by drop-down list and then select the Received field from the Then by drop-down list. The From field automatically sets the Ascending option and the Received field sets the Descending option as the sort order.

4 Click OK twice.

> **TIP** The Filter feature enables you to limit the items displayed to those that meet specific criteria. For example, you could filter your e-mail messages to those that contain specific words in the subject or message fields or filter to display only those messages from a specific contact. After you display the filtered list, you can then sort the items so that they appear in the required order.

5 Click the Contacts button on the Outlook Bar and select the contact listing for your classmate.

6 Choose Actions, Link, Items.

FIGURE O.23

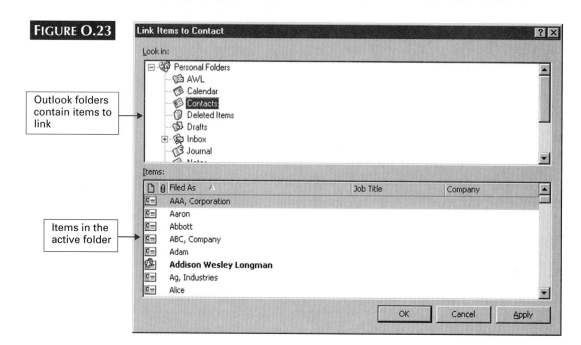

Outlook folders contain items to link

Items in the active folder

7 Click the Inbox folder in the Look in list, if necessary, and then select the messages that you have received from your classmate.

> **TIP** To select multiple messages, press (CTRL) as you click each message. To select multiple continuous messages, select the first message and then press (SHIFT) and click the last message.

8 Click OK. Linked items appear on the Activities page of the Contact dialog box.

9 Open the contact listing, if necessary, and click the Activities tab. Outlook searches for linked activities and displays a list of items linked to the contact.

10 Double-click one of the messages you linked to the contact to open the message.

11 Close all message windows and/or dialog boxes.

 Check Point

You can link tasks recorded in the TaskPad to contacts, Calendar events, notes, and items stored in any of the folders listed in the Look in list. Link assignments for class listed in the TaskPad and e-mail messages sent to your instructor to your instructor's contact listing. Then use the techniques described in this task to sort your contacts by state.

Using Categories to Manage Files

Outlook comes with a default set of categories that enable you to sort related Outlook files—contacts, tasks, appointments, messages, and so on—for sorting and easy retrieval. By categorizing items, you can store them in their original folders and search for them using the category. When the categories contained in the Outlook Master Category list don't include the categories you need, you can create additional categories. Categories you create become part of your Master Category list.

TASK 18: To Create Categories, Assign Items to Categories, and Sort Items by Category

1 Click Contacts on the Outlook Bar and then click the Organize ⚙Organize button on the Standard toolbar. The Ways to Organize Conacts pane opens, as shown in Figure O.24.

FIGURE O.24

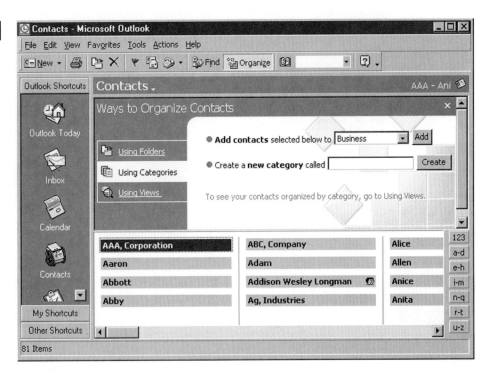

2 Type **Class Files** in the Create a new category called text box and click Create.

> **TIP** To view the list of default categories, choose Edit, Categories from any Outlook feature.

3 Double-click the contact you created for your classmate. The Contact information window opens.

4 Click the Categories button, check the Class Files category check box, and then click Add to List; click OK. Class Files appears in the Categories text box for the Contact.

5 Click 🔲 Save and Close.

6 Choose View, Current View, By Category. Viewing items by category automatically sorts and arranges items within the component alphabetically within each category. Items not assigned to a category appear in the (None) category at the top of the window, as shown in Figure O.25. To view the contacts in the category, click the + beside the category.

FIGURE O.25

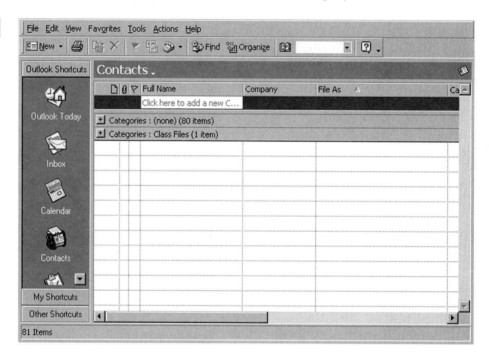

7 Click the (+) on the Class Files category bar and on the (None) category bar. A list of component items (in this case Contacts) contained in each category appears below the category bar.

 Check Point

You can add other items to the Class List category. Try these:

- Display the Tasks list, right-click the Check in at the computer lab task, and choose Categories. Click the Class Files checkbox and Add to List. Then click OK.

- Display the Calendar and select the Outlook assignments appointment you scheduled for a week from Wednesday. Use the method you prefer (clicking the Organize button or right-clicking and choosing Categories) to add the appointment to your Class Files category.

Creating Notes

One of the most fun features in Outlook is the Notes feature. You can create Notes in Outlook and "stick" them on your Outlook window just as you place "sticky notes" on just about everything around you. You can edit notes and organize notes just as your edit and organize tasks, messages, and other files.

TASK 19: <u>To Create, Edit, and Organize Notes</u>

1 Click the Notes icon on the Outlook Bar. The Notes window displays a sample note.

2 Click the New [New] button. A new note appears, as shown in Figure O.26. Notes have title bars but have the appearance of sticky notes. The current date and time are automatically recorded.

FIGURE O.26

4/11/99 2:29 PM

3 Type **Don't forget to complete the Hands-On assignments at the end of Outlook.** Text wraps in the note window as you type.

4 Click ⊠. The note appears in the Notes window of Outlook with the note text below it.

5 Double-click the note icon to open it, double-click *assignments* to select it, and type **exercises**; then close the note.

6 Click [Organize]. The Ways to Organize Notes pane opens in the Notes window.

7 Click the Move Note drop-down list arrow and select Other folder. The Select Folder dialog box opens.

8 Click Tasks, click OK, and then click Move. A new Task window opens and the note appears in the Comments area at the bottom of the window.

9 Click 🖫 Save and Close . The note is removed from the Notes folder and placed in the Tasks folder.

10 Click and ensure that the Note text appears in the Task list.

> **TIP** You can change the note color, size, and font characteristics by choosing Tools, Options, Preferences, and then clicking the Notes Options button and selecting the appropriate options. To change the way Notes appear in the Notes window, choose View, Current View, and then select the view you want to use.

Printing from Outlook

You can print information contained in any of the Outlook features using a variety of different formats. Regardless of which Outlook module you are using, the procedures to print are basically the same. Features and styles displayed in the Print dialog box vary according to the feature you have active when you print.

TASK 20: To Print from Outlook

1 Display the Outlook Calendar and then click the Print 🖨 button.

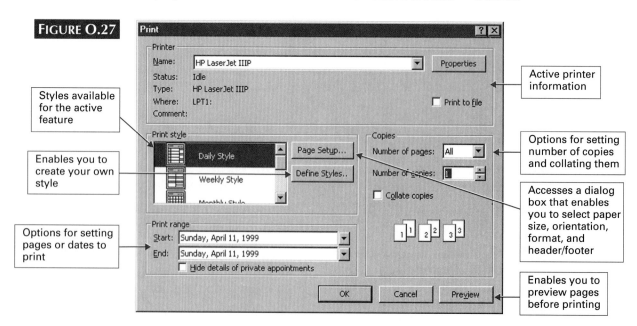

FIGURE O.27

2 Select Weekly Style from the Print style list and then click OK. The weekly calendar prints appointments for seven days beginning with the active date.

3 Open the Inbox and click your personal folder. A list of messages in the folder appears.

4 Open any message in the folder and choose File, Print.

5 Click the Print all linked documents option and then click OK. The active document and all documents related to the active document print.

Exiting Outlook

Because Outlook is an application, you exit Outlook using the same techniques used to exit other applications. Use one of the following techniques to exit Outlook:

- Click the application Close ❌ button.
- Choose File, Exit.
- Double-click the application control menu icon.
- Press (ALT) + (F4).
- Right-click the Outlook feature button on the Windows taskbar and choose Close.

If you have messages in the Outbox when you close Outlook, a message window appears. Read the message carefully and take the appropriate action:

- Choose Yes to log on and deliver the messages.
- Choose No to close Outlook without delivering messages.
- Wait until the counter completes the countdown and closes Outlook automatically.

Summary and Exercises

Summary

- Outlook 2000 helps you track appointments, send and receive messages, maintain a list of to do tasks, monitor computer activities, and update business and personal contacts in an instant.

- You can keep Outlook open as you work in other applications and use it as a reference more easily.

- The techniques you use to launch Outlook are similar to those used to launch other applications.

- The Outlook Bar groups Outlook features into three shortcut categories: Outlook Shortcuts, My Shortcuts, and Other Shortcuts.

- You can enter appointments directly into the Calendar window or use the Appointment dialog box to enter the appointment and set options.

- Contacts stores information such as names, addresses, phone numbers, and company names.

- E-mail can be sent to people on a local area network (LAN) as well as people on the Internet.

- The Notes feature enables you to add electronic "sticky note" reminders to your Outlook screen.

- Each Outlook feature can be customized for the way you work. In addition, files from Outlook features can be categorized to group items from different folders together and make them easier to locate.

- You can print from Outlook using a variety of different formats.

Key Terms and Operations

Key Terms

archive	link
Calendar	local area network (LAN)
categories	notes
Contacts	Outlook Bar
Deleted Items	Outlook Today
e-mail	sort
Inbox	Task List
Journal	

Operations

assign tasks to others	identify Outlook features
create address book entries	launch Outlook
create notes	manage Outlook files
create, send, and receive e-mail	organize messages
exit Outlook	print from Outlook

record tasks in the TaskPad
reply to and forward messages
schedule appointments in the
   Calendar

store contacts in the Contacts List
use categories to manage files
use the Outlook Bar

Study Questions

Multiple Choice

1. To change from one Outlook feature to another,
   a. click the feature icon on the Outlook Bar.
   b. press (CTRL) + (F6).
   c. double-click the feature on the Outlook Bar.
   d. press (ENTER).

2. The Outlook feature designed to keep track of the things you need to do is the
   a. Calendar.
   b. Task Pad.
   c. Schedule.
   d. Journal.

3. The Outlook feature that stores messages you want to send is the
   a. E-mail.
   b. Inbox.
   c. Outbox.
   d. Trash Can.

4. To exit Outlook,
   a. click the application Close button.
   b. press (ALT) + (F6).
   c. choose File, Close.
   d. press (ENTER).

5. To be reminded of an appointment in the Calendar,
   a. Outlook must be running.
   b. select the Calendar date and type the appointment.
   c. copy the appointment from the Journal.
   d. press (ENTER).

Short Answer

1. When viewing messages in the Inbox, how can you tell if a message has been read?

2. In which Outlook Bar group does Outbox appear?

3. Which Outlook features can you use to record notes during a telephone conversation?

4. How do you access a different month in the Calendar?

5. How do you access a blank form for adding contacts to the Contact List?

Fill in the Blank

1. The Outlook feature designed to keep track of meetings is the _____.

2. The Outlook feature designed to store names and addresses of business associates is _____.

3. Features are arranged on the _____ in three different shortcut categories.

4. To read mail, click Inbox on the Outlook Bar, then select _____.

5. Regardless of what module of Outlook you are using, the procedures to _____ are basically the same.

For Discussion

1. List and describe the features contained in Microsoft Outlook.

2. Describe the Outlook feature you believe you would use most.

Hands-On Exercises

1. Integrating Outlook Components with the Calendar

Now that you are familiar with most of the Outlook components, it's time to learn how to integrate items from Outlook components with the Calendar. By displaying items such as tasks and notes on the Calendar, you can print the Calendar and have information and reminders without printing individual listings and items. To add items to your calendar, display the Calendar for the last Friday in November of the current year in Day/Week/Month view. Type **Finish all out-of-class assignments.** as a new task in the TaskPad. Press and hold (CTRL) and drag and drop the task to the daily calendar. As you drag the task, a plus (+) accompanies the mouse and document icons to the calendar pad. When you drop the task, a New Appointment dialog box opens. Save and close the item.

> **TIP** Click the clipboard icon beside the task to drag the task. While you can drag directly from the task text, dragging from the clipboard icon assures that you have the mouse selection pointer rather than the I-beam.

Now, switch to Contacts and select the listing for your instructor. Drag the contact listing to the Calendar icon on the Outlook Bar. A New meeting dialog box addressed to your instructor opens. Type **Final Exam** in the Subject field. Type the location of your exam in the Location field. Set the exam start and end date and times. Send the appointment message to your instructor.

2. Using Outlook to Plan and Schedule Meetings

Outlook also contains features that enable you to schedule meetings, invite others to attend, and automatically enable those invited to respond. What's more, the meeting is automatically added to the attendees' calendars when they accept an invitation to a meeting, and they are automatically reminded 15 minutes (or whatever reminder setting they use) before the meeting!

Complete the following activities to become acquainted with the procedures for accomplishing these tasks. Display the Calendar for the 15th of next month and click the New Appointment button. Complete the event window shown in Figure O.28. When you click the Add day event option, the title bar changes to Event.

FIGURE O.28

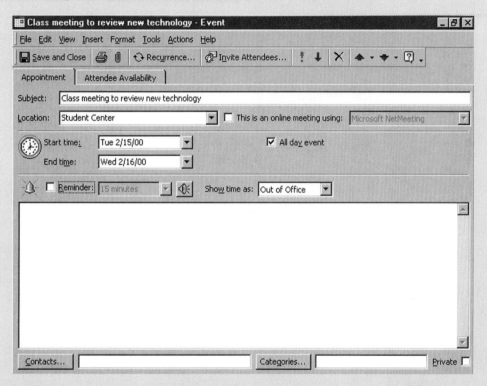

Click the Invite Attendees [Invite Attendees...] button. A To field appears on the event. Click To. The Select Attendees and Resources dialog box displays a list of your contacts.

> **TIP** You can also use the meeting scheduler to reserve resources such as conference rooms if they are listed among your contacts with a contact person assigned. Select the resource you want to reserve and then click Resource.

Select your instructor's listing and then click Required; select the listing of at least one classmate and then click Optional; click OK. Click Send.

> **TIP** If you select the wrong listing from your Contacts list, select the person's name in the Required or Optional list and press (DEL).

FIGURE O.29

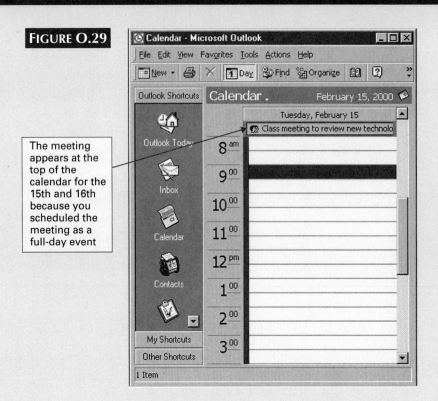

The meeting appears at the top of the calendar for the 15th and 16th because you scheduled the meeting as a full-day event

TIP When you receive a meeting request from your instructor or another classmate, buttons on the message toolbar will enable you to accept or decline the invitation. Click the appropriate response to automatically send your reply. If you are using an e-mail program other than Outlook, these automatic features may not be available.

 Check Point

To facilitate meeting planning, it's nice to have your Calendar posted on the Web where others can identify the best times to plan a meeting. You can get your Calendar ready for posting by saving it as a Web page. Display your Calendar and choose File, Save as Web Page. Set the start date as the first day of the semester and the end date as the last day of final exams for the semester. Type **My Web Calendar** in the File name field and choose Save.

FIGURE O.30

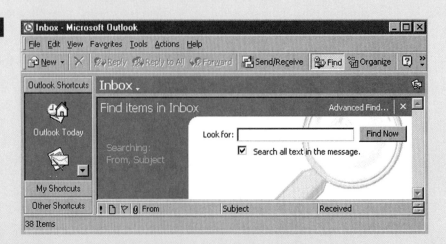

Your default Web browser opens and displays your Calendar. It looks really cool!

> **TROUBLESHOOTING** If the feature required to save the Calendar as a Web page is not installed on your computer, you may be asked if you want to install it. Ask your instructor for the action to take.

3. Finding Messages and Copying Text to the Office Clipboard

The Find feature in Outlook makes locating messages quick and easy—even if you don't know the subject, the sender, or the date on which the message was sent or received! You can actually search the complete text of mail messages to locate specific messages or at least to narrow down the list of messages you need to review. To explore Outlook Find features, follow these instructions.

1. Click the Inbox icon on the Outlook Bar.
2. Click the Find 🔍Find button on the toolbar.
3. Type your instructor's e-mail address in the Look for text box, ensure that the Search all text in the message option box is checked, and then click Find Now.
4. Open each of the messages you find (up to the first 12), select all message text, and copy it to the Office Clipboard.
5. Point to the toolbar, right-click, and select Clipboard. The Office Clipboard appears with an icon representing each snippet of information you copied.

4. Creating Office 2000 Files from Outlook

Outlook contains features that enable you to create new Outlook files as well as files in other Office 2000 applications. To explore this feature, you can use the text you placed on the Office Clipboard to create a new Word document.

1. Display the main Outlook window and choose File, New, Office Document. The New Office Document dialog box opens and displays a program icon for Excel Worksheet, Excel Chart, Word Document, and PowerPoint Presentation.
2. Double-click Microsoft Word Document. A Microsoft Outlook message window presents options to enable you to send the document to someone or post the document in the active folder.
3. Choose Post the document in this folder and then click OK. Word launches, if it is not already running. Display the Clipboard toolbar in the Word window, if necessary. A few different buttons appear on the Word Standard toolbar: Post, Previous Item, and Next Item.
4. Click one of the items on the Clipboard. The text appears in the document.
5. Click Paste All on the Clipboard. All snippets of information on the Office Clipboard are added to the document.

6. Click the Post [Post] button on the Standard toolbar. The document appears in the folder that was active when you started the document. The icon identifies the file as a Word document.

5. Using the Journal

The Journal feature in Outlook automatically records activities performed using Microsoft Office applications. Activities are grouped and listed in the Journal according to the program used to create the item or perform the activity and the date on which the activity occurred. You can open the Journal and display a list of activities you performed using Word, Excel, Outlook, or any other Office product. After you display the items, you can go directly to a file and open it by simply double-clicking the item in the Journal listing.

There will be times when you want to record activities you performed that did not necessarily involve using Microsoft Office programs. You can record these activities manually. Complete the following activity to record items in the Journal:

1. Click the Journal [Journal] button on the Outlook Bar. A list of activities grouped by application appears.

2. Click the New [New] button on the Standard toolbar. The Untitled Journal Entry dialog box opens.

3. Type **Study for Final Exams** in the Subject field.

4. Select Task from the Entry type drop-down list.

5. Select the Saturday before finals as the start date and 8:00 A.M. as the start time.

6. Select 2 days from the Duration drop-down list.

7. Click [Save and Close].

8. Click the drop-down list arrow at the top of the Journal window and display the monthly palette for the task you just recorded. The task you recorded will appear for the Saturday before finals.

9. Scroll, if necessary, to display the Saturday before finals are to start.

Function Reference Guide

WORD 2000

Function	Mouse Action or Button	Menu	Keyboard Shortcut
Bold	Select text and click **B**	Select text, choose format, Font, and select Bold	Select text and press (CTRL) + B
Border, create	Click [icon] to display toolbar. Select object, click down-arrow in Line style button, and select style	Select object and then choose Format, Borders and Shading, Borders tab	
Bulleted list, create	Select paragraph and click [icon]	Select paragraph and choose Format, Bullets and Numbering, Bulleted tab	
Clip Art, insert	Click [icon] to display Drawing toolbar. Position insertion point and click [icon]	Position insertion point and choose Insert, Picture, Clip Art	
Columns, create	Click [icon] and click number of columns	Choose Format, Columns	
Copy	Select text and click [icon]	Select text and choose Edit, Copy	Select text and press (CTRL) + C
Cut	Select text and click [icon]	Select text and choose Edit, Cut	Select text and press (CTRL) + X
Document, close	Click [icon]	Choose File, Close	
Document, create new	Click [icon]	Choose file, New, and select the template	Press (CTRL) + N
Document, preview	Click [icon]	Choose File, Print Preview	
Document, print	Click [icon]	Choose File, Print	Press (CTRL) + P
Document, save	Click [icon]	Choose File, Save	Press (CTRL) + S
Document, select entire		Choose Edit, Select All	Press (CTRL) + A
Envelope, create		Choose Tools, Envelopes and Labels, Envelopes tab	
Find		Choose Edit, Find	Press (CTRL) + F
Go To	Double-click the page number in the Status bar	Choose Edit, Go To	Press (CTRL) + G
Grammar check	Click [icon]	Choose Tools, Spelling and Grammar	Press (F7)
Graphic, insert	N/A	Choose Insert, Picture	

Function	Mouse Action or Button	Menu	Keyboard Shortcut
Header/Footer, create or edit	In Print Layout View, double-click text in the header or footer	Choose View, Header and Footer	
Help	Click [?]	Choose Help, Microsoft Word Help	Press (F1)
Italicize	Select text and click *I*	Select text, choose format, Font, and select Italic	Select text and press (CTRL) + I
Numbered list, create	Select paragraph and click [≣]	Select paragraph and choose Format, Bullets and Numbering, Numbered tab	
Paragraph, align	Select paragraph(s) and click [≣], [≣], [≣], or [≣]	Select paragraph(s) and choose Format, Paragraph, Indents and Spacing, Alignment	Press (CTRL) + L for left, (CTRL) + R for right, (CTRL) + E for center, and (CTRL) + J for justified
Paragraph, format		Select paragraph and choose Format, Paragraph	
Paragraph, decrease indent	Select paragraph(s) and click [≣]	Select paragraph(s) and choose Format, Paragraph, Indents and Spacing tab	Press (CTRL) + (SHIFT) + M
Paragraph, increase indent	Select paragraph(s) and click [≣]	Select paragraph(s) and choose Format, Paragraph, Indents and Spacing tab	Press (CTRL) + M
Paste	Position insertion point and click [📋]	Position insertion point and choose Edit, Paste	Position insertion point and press (CTRL) + V
Redo	Click [↻]	Choose Edit, Redo	
Replace text		Choose Edit, Replace	Press (CTRL)+ H
Section break, delete		Select the section break and choose Edit, Clear	Select the section break and press (DEL)
Section break, insert		Position the insertion point and choose Insert, Break, and select the type of break	
Shading, apply		Select text, paragraph(s), or parts of a table, and choose Format, Borders and Shading, Shading tab	
Select text	Drag insertion point through text	Choose Insert, Symbol, Special Characters	Position insertion point and press (SHIFT) + any cursor movement key, such as (END).
Special characters, insert		Choose Tools, Spelling and Grammar	Press the assigned shortcut keys (e.g., press (CTRL) + (SHIFT) + (SPACE) to insert a non-breaking space)

Function	Mouse Action or Button	Menu	Keyboard Shortcut
Spell check	Click [ABC]	Select text or paragraph(s), choose Format, Style	Press (F7)
Style, apply	Select text or paragraph(s), click the Style drop-down arrow, and click style	Position insertion point in text and choose Format, Tabs	Select text or paragraph(s), press the assigned shortcut keys
Tab, change	Position insertion point in text and drag tab indicator to new location	Position the insertion point and choose Format, Tabs	
Tab, set	Click tab indicator on ruler to select tab type and click ruler where you want the tab stop		
Table, create	Click [table] and select number of columns and rows	Choose Table, Insert Table	
Toolbars, display/hide		Choose View, Toolbars and select toolbar	
Underline	Select the text and click [U]	Select the text and choose Format, Font	Select the text and press (CTRL) + U
Undo	Click [↰]	Choose Edit, Undo	Press (CTRL) + Z
View, change	Click [≡], [▣], [▤], or [▥]	Choose View and select desired view	
Zoom	Click [🔍] in Print Preview	Choose View, Zoom	

EXCEL 2000

Function	Mouse Action or Button	Menu	Keyboard Shortcut
AutoFormat		Select the cells and choose Format, AutoFormat	Press (ALT) + O, A
Border, add	Select the cell(s), click the down arrow on [▦▾], and click on the desired border	Select the cell(s) and choose Format, Cells, Border	
Cell, align	Select the cell(s) and click [≡], [≡], or [≡]	Select the cell(s) and choose Format, Cells, Alignment	
Cell, copy	Select the cell(s) and click [📋]	Select the cell(s) and choose Edit, Copy	Select the cell(s) and press (CTRL) + C
Cell, cut	Select the cell(s) and click [✂]	Select the cell(s) and choose Edit, Cut	Select the cell(s) and press (CTRL) + X
Cell, delete		Select the cell(s) and choose Edit, Delete	
Cell, delete data in		Select the cell(s) and choose Edit, Clear	Select the cell(s) and press (DEL)

Function	Mouse Action or Button	Menu	Keyboard Shortcut
Cell, format	Select the cell(s) and click the appropriate formatting button (**B** , *I* , and so on)	Select the cell(s), choose Format, Cells, and click the desired tab	Press (CTRL) + 1 (one)
Cell, insert		Select the cell(s) and choose Insert, Cells	
Cell, paste	Select the cell(s) and click	Select the cell(s) and choose Edit, Paste	Select the cell(s) and press (CTRL) + V
Cell, select	Drag the mouse pointer through the desired cells		Press (SHIFT) + any navigation key
Chart, create	Click	Choose Chart from the Insert menu	Press (ALT) + I, H
Chart, move	Select the chart and drag		
Chart, size	Select a handle and drag		
Column, change the width	Drag the vertical border of the column in the column indicator row	Select the column and choose Format, Column, Width	Press (ALT) + O, C
Column, delete		Select the column(s) and choose Edit, Delete	Press (ALT) + E, D
Column, insert		Select the column(s) and choose Insert, Columns	Press (ALT) + I, C
Comments, add		Select the cell and choose Insert, Comment	Press (ALT) + I, M
Data, edit	Select the cell, click in the formula bar, and edit as desired; double-click the cell		Select the cell, press (F2), and edit as desired
Data, enter			Select the cell, type the data, and press (ENTER) or any navigation key
Data, find		Choose Edit, Find	Press (CTRL) + F
Data, sort	Select the cell(s) and click or	Select the cell(s) and choose Data, Sort	Press (ALT) + D, F
Exit Excel 2000	Click in the application window	Choose File, Exit	Press (ALT) + (F4)
Fill, add	Select the cell(s), click the down arrow on the , and select a color	Select the cell(s) and choose Format, Cells, Patterns	Press (ALT) + O, C
Font, color	Click	Select the cell(s) and choose Format, Cells, Font	Press (ALT) + O, C

Function	Mouse Action or Button	Menu	Keyboard Shortcut
Footer, create		Choose View, Header and Footer	Press (ALT) + V, H
Format dates		Select the cell(s) and choose Format, Cells, Number	Press (ALT) + O, C
Format numbers	Select the cell(s) and click ▣ , ▣ , ▣ , ▣ ,	Select the cell(s) and choose Format, Cells, or ▣	Press (ALT) + O, C Number
Function, create	Click *fx*	Select Function from the Insert menu	Press (ALT) + I, F
Go to a cell		Edit, Goto	Press (CTRL) + G or (F5)
Header, create		Choose View, Header and Footer	Press (ALT) + V, H
Help	Click ▣	Choose Help, Microsoft Excel Help	Press (F1)
Page break, change		Choose View, Page Break Preview, and drag the page break line	Press (ALT) + V, P and drag the page break line
Page break, view		Choose View, Page Break Preview	Press (ALT) + V, P
Preview	Click ▣	Choose File, Print Preview	Press (ALT) + F, V
Print	Click ▣	Choose File, Print	Press (CTRL) + P
Row, change the height	Drag the horizontal border of the row indicator	Select the row(s) and choose Format, Row, Height	Press (ALT) + O, R, E
Row, delete		Select the row(s) and choose Edit, Delete	Press (ALT) + E, D
Row, insert		Select the number of rows you want to insert and choose Insert, Rows	Press (ALT) + I, R
Spell check	Click ▣	Choose Tools, Spelling	Press (F7)
Start Excel 2000		Choose Start, Programs, Microsoft Excel 2000	
Workbook, close	Click ✕ in the workbook window	Choose File, Close	Press (CTRL) + (F4) or (CTRL) + W
Workbook, create	Click ▣	Choose File, New	Press (CTRL) + N
Workbook, open	Click ▣	Choose File, Open	Press (CTRL) + O
Workbook, save	Click ▣	Choose, File, Save	Press (CTRL) + S

Function	Mouse Action or Button	Menu	Keyboard Shortcut
Worksheet, delete		Click the worksheet tab and choose Edit, Delete Sheet	Press (ALT) + E, L
Worksheet, insert		Click the worksheet tab that should follow the new worksheet and choose Insert, Worksheet	Press (ALT) + I, W
Worksheet, move	Drag the worksheet tab to a new location	Select the worksheet tab and choose Edit, Move or Copy Sheet	Press (ALT) + E, M
Worksheet, name	Double-click the work-sheet name and type new name	Right-click the worksheet tab and choose Rename	

ACCESS 2000

Function	Mouse Action or Button	Menu	Keyboard Shortcut
Database, close	Click X	Choose File, Close	
Database, create new	Click	Choose File, New Database	Press (CTRL) + N
Database, open existing	Click	Choose File, Open	Press (CTRL) + O
Display page of database window	Click the appropriate button	Choose View, Database Objects, and then choose desired data-base window page	Press (CTRL) + (TAB) until the database window page appears
Exit Access 2000	Click X in the application window	Choose File, Exit	Press (ALT) + F, X
Field, delete	Display table in Design view, click field row, and click	Display table in Design view, click field row, and choose Edit,	Display table in Design view, click field row, and press (DEL) Delete Rows
Field, insert	Display table in Design view, click field row where new field is desired, and click	Display table in Design view, click field row where new field is desired, and choose Edit, Insert Row	
Field, sort	Select field in data sheet view and click	Select field in data sheet view (or Form) and Sort Ascending or Sort Descending	choose Records, Sort,
Form, create new	Click the Forms button and click New	Choose Insert, Form	Press (ALT) + I, F
Form, design	Select form name in the database window and click Design OR open form and click	Open form and choose View, Design View	

Function	Mouse Action or Button	Menu	Keyboard Shortcut
Form, open	Select form name in the database window and click ⊞ Open	Select form name in Forms page of database window and press (ENTER)	
Forms, display	Click ⊞ Forms		
Help	Click [?]	Choose Help, Microsoft Access Help	Press (F1)
Open, (Table, Query, Form, Page)	Select the object name in the database window and click ⊞ Open		
Page, display	Click ⊞ Pages		
Page, create new	Click the Pages ⊞ Pages button and click ⊞ New	Choose Insert, Page	Press (ALT) + I, P
Preview	Click ▣	Choose File, Print Preview	Press (ALT) + F, V
Primary key, assign	Display table in Design view, click field, and click ⑨	Display table in Design view, select field, and choose Edit, Primary Key	
Print	Click ⊟	Choose File, Print	Press (CTRL) + P
Query, add fields	Double-click field name		
Query, add table	Click ⊞	Choose Query, Show Table	Press (ALT) + Q, T
Query, create new	Click the Queries ⊞ Queries button and click ⊞ New	Choose Insert, Query	Press (ALT) + I, Q
Query, design	Select query name in the database window and click Design OR open query and click ✎ ▾	Open query and choose View, Design View	
Query, delete		Select the query and choose Edit, Delete	Select the query and press (DEL)
Query, open	Select query name in the database window and click open ⊞ Open		Select query in Forms page of database window and press (ENTER)
Query, run	In Query Design, click ❗	In Query Design, choose Query, Run	
Query, set criteria			Select Criteria row and type operator and symbol
Record, add data		Display Datasheet or Form view and type data into fields	

Function	Mouse Action or Button	Menu	Keyboard Shortcut
Record, delete	Click record selection bar or button, and click ✖	Select record and choose Edit, Delete Record	Select record and press (DEL)
Record, insert	Display table to contain record and click ▶✱	Open table to contain record and choose Insert, New Record	
Report, create new	Click the Reports [Reports] button and click [New]	Choose Insert, Report	
Reports, display	Click [Reports]		
Report, design	Select report name in database window and click Design OR open report and click 📝▾	Open report and choose View, Design View	
Report, open	Select report name in reports page of database window and click [Open]		Select report name in Reports page of database window and press (ENTER)
Save	Click 💾	Choose File, Save	Press (CTRL) + S
Send		Choose File, Send to	Press (ALT) + F, D
Spelling check	Click ✓	Choose Tools, Spelling	Press (F7)
Table, copy structure	Click table name in database window, click 📋, click 📋 and type new table name and select structure only	Click table name in database window, choose Edit, Copy, choose Edit, Paste and type new table name; select structure only	Click table name in database window, press (CTRL) + C, press (CTRL) + V and type new table name; select structure only
Table, create new	Click the Tables [Tables] button and click [New]	Select Table from the Insert menu	Press (ALT) + I, T
Table, design	Select table name in database window and click Design OR Open table and click 📝▾	Open table and choose View, Design View	Open table and press (ALT) + V, D
Tables, display	Click [Tables]		
Table, open	Select table name in Tables page of database window and click [Open]		Select table name in Tables page of database window and press (ENTER)
Text, copy	Select the text and click 📋	Select the text and choose Edit, Copy	Press (CTRL) + C
Text, cut	Select the text and click ✂	Select the text and choose Edit, Cut	Press (CTRL) + X

Function	Mouse Action or Button	Menu	Keyboard Shortcut
Text, find	Click 🔍	Choose Edit, Find	Press (CTRL) + F
Text, paste	Select the text and click 📋	Choose Edit, Paste	Press (CTRL) + V
Text, replace		Choose Edit, Replace	Press (CTRL) + H
Text, select	Drag through text		Press (SHIFT) + any cursor movement key, such as (→) or (END)
Toolbars, display or hide	Right-click toolbar and select the toolbar	Choose View, Toolbars and select the toolbar	Press (ALT) + V, T
Undo	Click ↺	Choose Edit, Undo	Press (CTRL) + Z
View, change	Click 📈 or 🖩	Choose View, Type View	

POWERPOINT 2000

Function	Mouse Action or Button	Menu	Keyboard Shortcut
Add Clip Art	Click 📷, click the category needed, and double-click the image	Choose Insert, Picture, Clip Art, click the category needed, click the image, and choose Insert Clip	
Add New Slide	Click 🗔	Choose Insert, New Slide	Press (CTRL) + M
Add Object		Choose Insert, Object, choose the object type, and choose OK	Press (ALT) + I, O
Add Slide Auto-Layout object	Double-click the object placeholder		
Add Table	Click 🖽 OR double-click the table placeholder on Table AutoLayout	Choose Insert, Table	Press (ALT) + I, B
Align Left	Click 📄	Choose Format, Alignment, Align Left	Press (CTRL) + L
Align Center	Click 📄	Choose Format, Alignment, Center	Press (CTRL) + E
Align Right	Click 📄	Choose Format, Alignment, Align Right	Press (CTRL) + R
Align Justify	Click 📄	Choose Format, Alignment, Justify	Press (CTRL) + J
AutoLayout, Change	Click 🗔 and select the AutoLayout	Choose Format, Slide Layout, and select AutoLayout	Press (ALT) + O, L
Bold	Select text and click **B**	Select text and choose Format, Font, Bold	Select text and press (CTRL) + B
Bulleted List, Format		Choose Format, Bullets and Numbering	

Function	Mouse Action or Button	Menu	Keyboard Shortcut
Clip Art, Insert	Click ▣, click the category needed, click the image, and click Insert Clip	Select Insert, Picture, Clip Art, click the category needed, click the image, and click Insert Clip	
Copy	Select text or object and click ▣	Select text or object and choose Edit, Copy	Select text or object and press (CTRL) + C
Create New Slide	Click ▣	Choose File, New Slide	Press (CTRL) + M
Create New Presentation	Click ▣	Choose File, New	Press (CTRL) + N
Cut	Select text or object and click ✄	Select text or object and choose Edit, Cut	Select text or object and press (CTRL) + X
Delete Slide	In Slide Sorter view, select slide(s) and press (DELETE)	Select or display slide and choose Edit, Delete Slide	In Slide Sorter view, select slide(s) and press (DELETE)
Delete Object	Select the object and press (DELETE)	Select the object and choose Edit, Cut	Select the object and press (DELETE)
Demote Outline Level	Select the bullet level and click ➡ OR right-click on item and choose Insert Tab		Position insertion point at beginning of item and press (TAB)
Exit PowerPoint	Click ✖	Choose File, Exit	Press (ALT) + (F4)
Find	Click ▣ Find	Choose Edit, Find	Press (CTRL) + F
Font, Format	Click [Helvetica ▾] and choose font	Choose Format, Font	
Font, Replace		Choose Format, Replace Fonts	
Help	Click ▣	Choose Help	Press (F1)
Italicize	Select text or object and click *I*	Select text or object, choose Format, Font,	Select text or object and press (CTRL) + I and select Italics
Launch PowerPoint	Double-click program shortcut	Choose Start, Programs, Microsoft PowerPoint	(CTRL) + (ESC), P, Arrows, (ENTER)
Masters, Display		Choose View, Masters and select the appropriate Master	Press (ALT) + V, M
Object Flip		Select the object, choose Draw, Rotate or Flip, Flip Horizontal or Flip Vertical	
Object, Format	Double-click the object	Select the object and choose Edit, Object	Press (ALT) + 2, O
Object Group		Select multiple objects and choose Draw, Group	
Object Insert	Double-click the object placeholder	Choose Insert, Object, choose the object type, and choose OK	Press (ALT) + I, O
Object Move	Select the object and drag it to a new place	Select object, choose Edit, Cut, reposition the insertion point, and choose Edit, Paste choose Edit, Paste	Select the object and press (CTRL) + X, reposition the insertion point, and press (CTRL) + V OR select the object and press the arrow keys to position

Function	Mouse Action or Button	Menu	Keyboard Shortcut
Object Rotate	Select the object and position the mouse pointer on the yellow rotate handle; drag the handle to rotate the object	Select object, choose Draw, Rotate or Flip, and choose the appropriate Rotate action	
Object Size	Select the object and drag the handle		
Object Ungroup		Select the grouped object, and choose Draw, Ungroup	
Pack and Go		Choose File, Pack and Go	Press ⌨ALT + F, K
Page Setup		Choose File, Page Setup	Press ⌨ALT + F, K
Paste	Position the insertion point and click 📋	Position the insertion point and choose Edit, Paste	Position the insertion point and press ⌨CTRL + V
Placeholder, Select	Click the placeholder border		Press ⌨CTRL + ⌨ENTER
Placeholder, Format	Double-click the placeholder border OR right-click the placeholder border and choose Format Placeholder	Select the placeholder and choose Format, Colors and Lines	Press ⌨ALT + O, N
Presentation, Apply Template	Double-click template name	Choose Format, Apply Design Template	Press ⌨ALT + O, Y
Presentation, Close	Click ✖	Choose File, Close	Press ⌨CTRL + ⌨F4
Presentation, Create New	Click 🗋	Choose File, New	Press ⌨CTRL + N
Presentation, Open	Click 📂	Choose File, Open Database	Press ⌨CTRL + O
Presentation, Save	Click 💾	Choose File, Save	Press ⌨CTRL + S
Presentation, Save As		Choose File, Save As	Press ⌨ALT + F, A
Presentation, Show	Click 🖥	Choose View, Slide Show	Press ⌨F5
Preview	Click 🖥	Choose View, Slide Show	Press ⌨F5
Print	Click 🖨	Choose File, Print	Press ⌨CTRL + P
Promote Outline Level Text	Select the bullet level and click ⬅		Position insertion point at beginning of item and press ⌨SHIFT + ⌨TAB
Replace Text		Choose Edit, Replace	Press ⌨CTRL + H
Ruler		Choose View, Ruler	Press ⌨ALT + V, R
Save Presentation	Click 💾	Choose File, Save	Press ⌨CTRL + S
Select Word	Double-click the word		Press ⌨SHIFT + ⌨CTRL + ⌨→
Select Bullet Level	Click the bullet		

Function	Mouse Action or Button	Menu	Keyboard Shortcut
Slide, Add Slide	Click ▣	Choose Insert, New Slide	Press (CTRL) + M
Slide, Delete Slide	In Slide Sorter view, select the slide(s) and press (DELETE)	Select or display the slide and choose Edit, Delete Slide	In Slide Sorter view, select the slide(s) and press (DELETE)
Slide, Display Next	Click ▼		Press (PGDN)
Slide, Display Previous	Click ▲		Press (PGUP)
Slide, Hide	In Slide Sorter view, select the slide(s) and click ▣	Select or display the slide and choose Hide Slide	
Slide, Format Background		Select or display the slide and choose Format, Background	Press (ALT) + O, K
Slide, Move	In Slide Sorter View, drag the slide to a new location	Select or display the slide, choose Edit, Cut, reposition insertion point, and choose Edit, Paste	Select or display the slide and press (CTRL) + X, reposition insertion point, and press (CTRL) + V OR select the object and press the arrow keys to position
Spell Check	Click ▣	Choose Tools, Spelling	Press (F7)
Table, Insert	Click ▣	Choose Insert, Table	Press (ALT) + I, B
Template, Apply	Click ▣ and select design	Choose Format, Apply Design	Press (ALT) + O, Y
Template, Save As	Choose File, Save As, select Design Template from Save as type drop-down list		Press (ALT) + F, A
Toolbar, Display	Right-click on toolbar and choose toolbar	Choose View, Toolbars and choose toolbar	Press (ALT) + V, T
Transitions, Add	In Slide Sorter view, select the slide and select a transition effect from the Effect drop-down list	Choose Slide Show, Slide Transition, and select a transition from the Effect drop-down list	Press (ALT) + O, T
Underline	Select text and click ▣	Select text, choose Format, Font, and select Underline	Select text and press (CTRL) + U
Undo	Click ▣	Choose Edit, Undo	Press (CTRL) + Z
View	Click ▣	Choose View, type of view	
Web		Choose Help, Office on the Web	Press (ALT) + H, W
WordArt, Insert	Click ▣	Choose Insert, Picture, WordArt	Press (ALT) + I, P, W
Zoom	Click 41% ▼ and select zoom percentage	Choose View, Zoom, select the percentage, and choose OK	Press (ALT) + V, Z

Glossary

3-D workbook A workbook comprising of one or more worksheets that contain linking formulas for sharing information among worksheets.

Absolute cell reference A reference to a cell in a formula where both the column and the row reference are preceded by a dollar sign ($). The reference to the cell will never change, regardless of where the formula is copied.

Access menu bar The menu appearing at the top of the screen when Access is launched.

Action button A button you create on a slide that enables you to control the action PowerPoint takes when you click the button during a slide show. You can set the action button to display a specific slide, to open an Office 2000 file, or start a different presentation.

Active cell The specific cell in a worksheet that has the focus. In a selection, the active cell is the cell from which the selection originated.

Active sheet The specific worksheet in a workbook that has the focus. In a selection, the active worksheet is the sheet from which the selection originated.

Address The row and column designation identifying a specific cell, such as A1 (column A, row 1).

Adjacent cells A selection of cells that compose a continuous range.

Alignment The position of text within a placeholder: left, center, or right.

Amortization The process of spreading loan or other obligations (payments) over time.

Amortization schedule A listing of the payments required for paying back a loan or other obligation. A loan amortization schedule often specifies the portion of a loan payment that applies to the principal.

AND condition A query expression using different criteria in the same criteria row of the query design grid. When Access uses the AND operator, only the records that meet the criteria in all the cells will be returned.

Animation Special visual or sound effects added to text and other slide objects.

Annuity functions Excel functions calculating a series of constant cash payments made over a continuous period. In annuity functions, cash you pay out, such as a deposit to savings, is represented by a negative number; cash you receive, such as a dividend check, is represented by a positive number.

Application title bar The title bar for a Microsoft application that contains the window for an open document, and the window controls to minimize, maximize, restore, and close the application.

Argument The values a function uses to perform operations or calculations. The type of argument a function uses is specific to the function. Common arguments used within functions include numeric values, text values, cell references, ranges of cells, names, labels, and nested functions.

Ascending order A sort order in which you arrange records alphabetically from A to Z or numerically from smallest to largest.

AutoComplete A feature that automatically completes many common words and phrases as you type.

AutoContent Wizard A PowerPoint feature that helps you build an outline for specific types of presentations by presenting options for you to choose and enabling you to fill in specific pieces of information about the presentation.

AutoCorrect A feature that automatically corrects many common typographical errors.

AutoForm A feature that you use to create forms using the fields and information stored as part of the table or query.

AutoLayout A PowerPoint slide format that contains object placeholders.

AutoNumber field A field that is set to automatically enter a sequential number as each record is added to the table.

AutoReport A feature you use to create simple report formats using the fields contained in a table or query.

AutoSum In Microsoft Excel, adds numbers automatically with the SUM function. Microsoft Excel suggests the range of cells to be added. If the suggested range is incorrect, drag through the range you want, and then press W.

Bar chart A chart type that represents a data series as horizontal bars.

Black screen A black image displayed on-screen during a slide show to shift the focus of the audience to the presenter.

Body text In an outline, text that has no outline level applied to it.

Bold A font attribute that makes the text appear darker so it stands out.

Border The top, bottom, left, and right lines you add to a table, a table cell, a paragraph, text, or a page.

Borders button The button on the formatting toolbar for applying the specified border to a cell or range of cells.

Bound control A control that is tied to a field in an underlying table or query.

Bullet The character, such as a filled circle, that precedes the text in a bulleted paragraph.

Bullet format The shape of bullets that appear before bulleted list items.

Bulleted list A list set off with bullets.

Calculated control A control that uses an expression as its source of data.

Calculated field A field in a query that contains an expression. When you display the results of a calculation in a field, the results aren't actually stored in the underlying table. Instead, Microsoft Access reruns the calculation each time you run the query so that the results are always based on the most current data in the database.

Case The capitalization of text.

Cell In a table, the intersection of a column and a row. In a worksheet, the intersection of a row and column. All worksheet data is contained in cells.

Cell alignment A setting for cell data that specifies whether data in the cell appears left, center, or right aligned.

Cell border A format applied to one or more cells specifying the format of a line surrounding a cell or range of cells.

Cell reference The reference to a specific cell using its address. Cell references are used in most formulas.

Cell shading A format applied to one or more cells specifying the format of a color or pattern in a cell or range of cells.

Cell tip A descriptive label that appears when you hover over a button on a toolbar or complete a procedure in Excel.

Center To change the alignment of a paragraph so that an equal amount of white space appears on both sides of the text.

Center tab A type of tab that causes data to be centered on the tab stop.

Chart options Options you can set for a chart to change one or more of its features.

Chart sub-type A specific chart type within a category, such as a 3-D exploded pie chart versus a simple two-dimensional pie chart.

Chart type The type of chart you use to communicate numeric data graphically. The type you select depends upon the structure of the data series. Common chart types include bar, column, line, pie, and X-Y scatter.

Chart Wizard An Excel wizard that walks you through the process of creating a chart.

Class A category of objects used in an Access database. A specific table is an instance of an object from the Table class.

Click-n-Type The feature that allows you type in an area that was previously considered a "non-typing" area.

Clip art A graphic provided in a file format such as tif, wpg, bmp, wmf, and so on. Office 2000 provides many clip art files and stores them in the Clip Art Gallery.

Clip Gallery A set of graphic images supplied by Microsoft that you can use to enhance your presentations.

Collapse an outline heading To hide the level(s) under an outline heading.

Color scheme A set of complementary colors used for the background, text, and other components in a presentation or template.

Column A vertical group of cells in a table or the vertical areas of a worksheet, which are identified with a letter (A, B, C, and so on).

Column break A non-printing character that causes the text in a column to go to the next column.

Column chart A chart representing data series as one or more vertical columns.

Control A specific object such as a text box that is added to a form or report to display data, perform actions, or decorate the form or report.

ControlTip A helpful tip that pops up over a control when you move the mouse pointer over it.

Criteria Conditions you set in a query to limit the information displayed in the datasheet.

Currency A data type that is useful for calculations involving money and for fixed-point calculations in which accuracy is particularly important.

Currency style A number format applied to one or more cells that displays a currency symbol, thousands separator, and two decimal places.

Custom animation Special effects added to animation settings using the Custom Animation dialog box.

Data access page A database object for creating a special type of Web page for viewing and working with data stored in a Microsoft Access database or Mi-

crosoft SQL Server database from the Internet or an intranet.

Data integrity A theoretical construct emphasizing the accuracy of data in a worksheet by minimizing redundant instances of data in multiple worksheets. You can use 3-D linking and consolidation formulas to minimize data redundancy, and thereby improve data integrity.

Data Source document A document that contains the variable information that will be used to "fill in the blanks" in a mail merge document.

Data type The characteristic of a field or a variable that determines what kind of data it holds.

Data validation Methods for controlling how data is entered into your database. Validation rules and input masks are two useful methods for data validation.

Database A collection of information related to a particular subject or purpose.

Database Management System (DBMS) A computer application that you use to create and maintain databases.

Database object The tables, queries, forms, pages, reports, macros, or modules that compose an Access database.

Datasheet view The view for a table, query, or form in which you can see multiple records on-screen at the same time; this view makes data entry more efficient.

Date/Time A data type that contains date and time values for the years 100 through 9999.

Decimal tab A type of tab that aligns text on a decimal.

Demote an outline level To convert an outline level to the next lower lever.

Descending order A sort order in which you arrange records alphabetically from Z to A or numerically from largest to smallest.

Design modifications Any enhancements you make to your database objects.

Design view A view of a table, query, form, or report object in which you can modify the object's properties.

Detail section The part of a form or report that holds the field data controls and pulls information from database tables.

Document Map A tool that lists all the document headings, similar to an outline, in a pane on the left. The headings are linked to the document so that you can click a heading and go directly to the text in the document.

Document title bar The bar at the top of the document window that displays the document title and the Minimize, Maximize/Restore, and Close buttons.

Edit To change the field information contained in a record.

Effects Settings applied to text and other slide objects to control the way they appear on-screen during a slide show.

Endnotes The notes (comments or references) grouped together at the end of the document. The reference in the text to which the endnote applies is generally numbered, and the endnote displays the same number

Enter The key you press to end short lines and paragraphs and crate blank lines.

Enter Formula button A button on the formula bar for accepting a formula you have entered or edited. The button appears as a green checkmark.

Expand an outline heading To display the level(s) under an outline level.

Expression A combination of symbols—identifiers, operators, and values—that produces a result.

Expression Builder A graphical workspace for designing expressions for a specific control object or control.

Field A field object represents a column of data with a common data type and a common set of properties. Also, the variable information for each record in a Data Source document. Also, a code that inserts information automatically, such as the Date field.

Field property An attribute of a field that defines one of its characteristics. An example is the size property of a text field.

Fill handle The black square in the lower-right corner of the active cell or selection. When the pointer is on the fill handle, the pointer changes from an arrow to a crosshair. Drag the fill handle down or to the right to fill cells with data based on the current selection.

Filter To select only those records in a table that contain the same value in the selected field.

Filter by Form A technique for filtering data that uses a version of the current form or datasheet with empty fields in which you can type the values you want the filtered records to contain.

Filter by Selection A technique for filtering data that's based on data you select in a form, datasheet, or data access page. In a form or datasheet, you can filter for all or part of a value you select. For example, you can select the first character in a field to find all records that start with that character in the filtered field. In a data access page, you can filter only for the entire value in the field.

Find A feature available using the Find dialog box to locate one or more records displayed in a table or form.

Find and Replace A technique for locating and replacing all instances of a specified value, either all at once or verifying each occurrence one at a time.

First line indent An indentation in the first line of a paragraph.

Flip object Turn a graphic or other object so that it faces the other way.

Font box The box on the Formatting toolbar that lists the available fonts that you can apply to a cell or selection.

Font Size box The box on the Formatting toolbar that you can use to specify the size of a font in a cell or selection.

Footer The bottom of the slide, to which you can add text and other items that you want to appear on each presentation slide. Also, text appearing at the bottom of each page of a printed worksheet. Also, text that prints at the bottom of every page in a section.

Footnotes Comments or references that appear at the bottom of the page. The reference in the text to which the footnote applies is generally numbered, and the footnote displays the same number.

Form An Access database object used to display data from tables or queries in an aesthetically pleasing format.

Form view The view for a form that displays the underlying record set.

Format Painter button A button on the Formatting toolbar that copies the format from a selected object or text and applying it to the object or text you click.

Formatting toolbar The toolbar appearing at the top of the application window that contains buttons and boxes for formatting one or more cells.

Formula Cell data beginning with an equal sign (=) that performs a calculation or returns data.

Formula bar A bar near the top of the window that displays the constant value or formula used in the active cell. To enter or edit

Formula palette When you create a formula that contains a function, the formula palette helps you enter worksheet functions. As you enter a function into the formula, the formula palette displays the name of the function, each of its arguments, a description of the function and each argument, the current result of the function, and the current result of the entire formula.

Function A predefined formula that performs calculations by using specific values, called arguments, in a particular order, or structure.

Graphics Visual pictures and drawings added to Office 2000 files.

Group Combine multiple drawn or graphic objects into one.

Groups bar A button on the Objects bar where you can store the names of

your groups, which can contain shortcuts to database objects of different types.

Handouts PowerPoint presentations printed with multiple slide images on each page and optional lines for note taking.

Hanging indent A paragraph that has the first line extended farther to the left than the subsequent lines in the paragraph.

Hard page break A user-defined page break.

Header Text appearing at the top of each page of a printed worksheet. Also, text that prints at the top of every page in a section.

Hidden slide A slide that contains supplementary information included in a presentation but marked to show only when specifically accessed.

Home cell The uppermost left cell in a worksheet—cell A1.

HTML See Hypertext Markup Language.

Hyperlink The connection that enables you to jump to a specific slide or to open another file when you click an action button during a slide show. Also, a link to another file or page on the World Wide Web. When you click on a hyperlink, the linked file displays on the screen. Also, underlined text or a graphic that you use to jump to a location on the Internet or an intranet, to an object in your database or another database, or to a document on your computer or another computer connected by a network.

HyperText Markup Language The standard language used to create pages for the World Wide Web.

IF function A function that returns one value if a condition you specify evaluates to TRUE and another value if it evaluates to FALSE.

Image control A control that is used to display pictures in an object such as a form or report.

Images Graphical pictures added to slides.

Indent To change the alignment of lines of text. You can indent the first line or indent all the lines of a paragraph on the left or right.

Input mask A field property that displays literal display characters in the field with blanks to fill in.

Insertion point The blinking, vertical line that marks the position where a letter is inserted when you press a key.

Italic The style you apply to text to make the font appear slanted so that it stands out.

Join An association between a field in one table or query and a field of the same data type in another table or query. A join tells Microsoft Access

how data is related. Access allows you to create inner joins, outer joins, and self-joins.

Justify To change the alignment of text so that it is spread evenly between the margins.

Label Text in Excel that defines the structure of a worksheet.

Label control An unbound control used to display descriptive text such as titles, captions, or brief instructions on a form or report.

Landscape Paper orientation that prints with the long side of the paper as the top of the document.

Landscape orientation The page orientation for a worksheet in which the height of the page is smaller than its width.

Leader Characters, such as periods, that appear before the tab. Any type of tab can have a leader.

Left tab A command that causes text to align on the left.

Left-align To change the alignment of paragraphs in your document so that they are aligned at the left margin.

Line chart A chart in which the data series are represented by one or more lines.

Line spacing The setting that controls the amount of space (such as single, double, and so forth) between lines of text. Also, the amount of space between lines of text.

Linking formulas A formula containing a 3-D reference that displays data from a specific cell in a worksheet or workbook. 3-D references are updated automatically whenever the source data changes.

Loan scenario The principal, interest rate, and term of a loan, which determine the monthly payment.

Logical function A category of worksheet functions that make logical comparisons, conduct logical tests, and usually return a value based upon a logical condition.

Lookup field A field that looks up data either from an existing table or query, or from a list that stores a fixed set of values that won't change. You can select a value in the list to store in the field.

Macro A program you write or record that stores a series of commands that you can later use as a single command. Macros can automate complex tasks and reduce the number of steps required to complete tasks that you perform frequently. Macros are recorded in the Visual Basic for Applications programming language.

Mail Merge Helper The dialog box feature that guides you through the process of creating a main document, a data source, and merging the two.

Mail merging A process in which you insert text from a file containing a list of information into a form file, such as a form letter. The process involves three steps: creating the file that contains the list of information, creating the form file and inserting the fields, and merging the two files.

Main document The document, usually a letter, with which you merge the list of names in the Data Source document when you use the mail merge feature.

Margin The white space around the edge of the page.

Master A layout that contains formats for text, bullets, placeholder alignment, headers and footers, and backgrounds.

Memo A data type used to store random entries exceeding 255 characters.

Menu bar The bar at the top of the window that contains menu options.

Merge field code The codes that are inserted in a Main document for the fields contained in the Data Source document.

Mixed cell reference A reference to a cell in a formula where either the column or the row reference is preceded by a dollar sign ($). The reference to the cell or column designated as absolute will never change when the formula is copied.

Module A collection of Visual Basic programming procedures stored together to customize the Access environment.

Name A stored name for a range of cells in a worksheet. Named ranges are viewed and selected using the Name box on the Formatting toolbar.

Navigate To move from one record to another in a table or form.

Newspaper columns The style of columns in which text flows from the bottom of one column flows to the top of the next.

Non-adjacent cells A selection of worksheet cells that are not adjacent to one another.

Normal A paragraph style on which many other styles are based.

Normal view The PowerPoint default tri-pane view that includes a presentation outline, slide image, and slide notes area. Also, a view of a document that does not show margins.

Normalization The process of converting complex data structures into simple data structures. In Access, normalization is accomplished by splitting data into multiple tables that are related.

Null value A value that indicates missing or unknown data in a field.

Number An integer or decimal value entered into a cell. Numbers compose the worksheet data for performing calculations.

Number formats Cell formats that change the appearance of numbers, including dates and times, without changing the number behind the appearance (the actual cell value).

Numbered list A list set off with numbers, often to indicate a sequence of steps.

Numeric (number) Data type used to hold numeric data used in mathematical calculations.

Numeric constants Numbers in an electronic spreadsheet upon which calculations are performed.

Object A table, query, form, page, report, macro, or module in a database. Also, an image, chart, or other data added to an Excel worksheet.

Object shortcuts Shortcuts in the database window for creating new objects using Design view or using a wizard.

Objects bar A vertical toolbar that contains buttons for viewing the specific database objects in the current database.

Office Assistant The interactive Help feature that appears frequently to offer help on the task you're performing. The Office Assistant enables you to ask questions about the task you want to perform, or search the Contents pane for a specific topic.

Office Clipboard A clipboard shared among the Office applications that holds up to 12 entries that can be embedded or linked in Office documents and files.

OLE Object Linking and Embedding, which is a way of automating how information is shared among applications.

Online help The help provided by the software and accessible from the computer.

On-screen presentation A PowerPoint presentation designed for viewing on a computer monitor or projected from a computer onto a screen.

Operands Specific operators that specify the type of calculation that you want to perform on the elements of a formula. Microsoft Excel includes four different types of calculation operators: arithmetic, comparison, text, and reference.

Operator precedence The specific order in which Excel performs calculations when you combine several operators in a single formula.

Orientation The position of information on paper. Portrait orientation is taller than it is wide, and landscape orientation is wider than it is tall. Also, the direction in which text appears in a cell.

Outline Text that is formatted with outline numbering styles.

Outline numbering scheme The complete set of styles applied to each level of an outline.

Outline view The PowerPoint on-screen display that enlarges the outline pane of the Normal view window and reduces the Slide and Slide Notes panes. Also, the view that displays a document in a hierarchical format based on the headings that are applied to the text.

Pack and Go A PowerPoint feature that prepares presentations for showing at another location by compressing them into a format so that they fit on a single disk.

Page break A break that separates pages of text. When a page fills up with text, Word automatically inserts a page break.

Page Break Preview A view of a worksheet that displays the current page breaks.

Page Footer The section of a form that contains any information you want to appear at the bottom of every printed page of a form.

Page Header The section of a form that contains any information you want to appear at the top of every printed page of a form.

Page setup Adjustable options, including the margins, paper size, and orientation, that are preset in Word.

Paper size The size of the paper on which you will print. The default setting is 8.5" by 11".

Parallel columns Columns that do not wrap text from the bottom of one column to the top of the next.

Pie chart An Excel chart type that is used to represent a single data series identifying the parts of a whole.

Placeholder A predefined area outlined on a slide designed to hold specific items such as text, bulleted lists, graphs, tables, and charts.

Portrait Paper orientation that is taller than it is wide.

Portrait orientation The page orientation for a worksheet in which the height of the page is larger than its width.

Primary key A field or set of fields that uniquely identifies each record stored in the table.

Principal The amount of money borrowed for a loan, or the present value of an annuity.

Print areas A specified selection of cells that will print when a worksheet is printed.

Print Layout view A view of a document that displays the document as it will look when it prints.

Print Preview An Excel view of a worksheet or sheet in a workbook as they will appear when printed.

Promote an outline level To convert an outline level to the next higher level.

Property An attribute of an object that defines one of the object's characteristics, such as size, color, screen location, or an aspect of its behavior, such as whether it is enabled or visible. To change the characteristics of an object, you change the values of its properties. Also, specification for a workbook file, such as the author and title of the workbook. Individual controls in Excel such as text boxes, images, and command buttons also have properties that can be set or changed.

Query You use queries to view, change, and analyze data in different ways. You can also use them as the source of records for forms and reports. Query objects contain information that determines how underlying table data is displayed on the screen.

Query datasheet A window that displays the results of a query in a row-and-column format.

Query design grid The lower pane displayed in the query design window containing columns where you define the fields of data the query will display.

Query design view A view for queries where you create or modify a query.

Query option An option that allows you to select or sort records for merging.

Range A selection of cells referenced in a formula or selected when applying formats.

Rate The interest rate for a loan. This is a required element for the PMT function.

Record A collection of related field data stored in a table, such as a person's name and address. Also, all the information, such as a name, address, city, state, zip code, and so on in the fields for one set of data in a Data Source document.

Record source A table or query that contains the records the form displays.

Referential integrity Rules that you follow to preserve the defined relationships between tables when you enter or delete records. If you enforce referential integrity, Microsoft Access prevents you from adding records to a related table when there is no associated record in the primary table, changing values in the primary table that would result in orphan records in a related table, and deleting records from the primary table when there are matching related records in a related table.

Relational Database Management System (RDBMS) A database management system (DBMS) specifically designed to utilize the relational database model.

Relationships window A window containing a graphical workspace for establishing relationships between tables.

Relative cell reference A reference to a cell in a formula where neither the column nor the row reference is preceded by a dollar sign ($). The cell reference will change accordingly when the formula is copied.

Replace An option available in the Find dialog box to replace field values.

Report An organized format for summarizing and grouping database data to provide meaningful information in a printed format.

Report Design window A graphical workspace displaying the report's bound and unbound controls.

Report Footer A report section for specifying the information that you want to appear at the end of an Access report.

Report Header A report section for specifying the information that you want to appear at the beginning of an Access report.

Right tab A command that causes text to align on the right.

Right-align To change the alignment of paragraphs in your document so that they are aligned at the right margin.

Rotate Adjust the tilt or angle of a graphic or other object.

Row A horizontal group of cells in a table. Also, a horizontal storage area in Excel.

Ruler The feature that displays the settings for the margins, tabs, and indents. The ruler also can be used to make these settings.

Run The action of applying query specifications to a table to display specific field and record information. Also, the action of applying the steps stored in an Excel macro.

Scroll bars The shaded bars along the right side and bottom of a window. To scroll to another part of the file, drag the box or click the arrows in the scroll bar.

Section break A nonprinting character that creates a section.

Section A physical division in a document that can be formatted differently.

Select The action of using the mouse or a keyboard shortcut to select one or more cells in a worksheet.

Select All button A button in the upper-left corner of a worksheet that selects all cells in the sheet.

Select Browse Object button A button you use to change the navigation buttons.

Select query A query that returns record information in a query datasheet without changing the underlying data.

Selection A cell or range of cells that have been highlighted.

Shading Various percentages of gray and colors you add to draw attention to important text.

Sheet tabs The tabs appearing in the lower portion of the workbook window that represent the worksheets in a workbook.

Slide Basic units of a presentation. Presentations typically consist of numerous slides. Each slide in a presentation is equivalent to a page of a document, a worksheet in a workbook, or a database record.

Slide show The display of slides in a presentation window without the PowerPoint toolbars, title bar, and status bar so that each slide fills the screen as it is accessed.

Slide Sorter view The PowerPoint view that displays small images (often called thumbnail images) of each slide in a presentation so that you can review the flow of the presentation and easily reorganize the presentation.

Slide view The PowerPoint view that expands the Slide pane of the Normal view and reduces the size of the Outline pane.

Soft page break A break automatically inserted by Word when a page fills with text.

Sort The action of displaying records in ascending or descending order.

Sort criteria Criteria added to a query or report specifying how the records shall be ordered.

Standard toolbar A toolbar displayed in the application window containing buttons to accomplish common tasks such as saving files, opening files, printing, and so on.

Status bar The bar near the bottom of the screen that displays information about a selected command or an operation in progress. The right side of the status bar shows whether keys such as X, Z, or Y are turned on. Choose Status Bar on the View menu to display or hide the status bar.

Style A collection of formats such as font size, patterns, and alignment, that you can define and save as a group.

Syntax Formula syntax is the structure or order of the elements in a formula. Formulas in Microsoft Excel follow a specific syntax that includes an equal sign (=) followed by the elements to be calculated (the operands) and the calculation operators. Each operand can be a value that does not change (a constant value), a cell or range reference, a label, a name, or a worksheet function.

Tab The feature on the ruler or command on the Format menu that aligns text.

Tab stop The location on the ruler where a tab is set.

Table A grouping of columns and rows (like a spreadsheet). Also, the primary object of a database that stores field names, field descriptions, and field data. Tables display multiple records in a row-and-column format similar to a spreadsheet layout.

Table Datasheet view A table view that displays multiple records on the screen in a row and column format.

Table Design view The view used to create or modify a table's structure.

Table design window A window displaying the table design grid.

Table Design Wizard An Access Wizard for creating tables.

Table structure The field names, data types, and properties defining the physical arrangement of a table.

Template A professionally developed slide design that you can apply to presentations to give a consistent look to all slides in a PowerPoint presentation. Also, a pattern for creating a Word document. Also, an Excel workbook you create and then use as the basis for other similar workbooks. You can create templates for workbooks and worksheets.

Term The length of time over which you make a loan or annuity payment. This is a required argument in some financial functions.

Text Letters and numbers added to worksheet cells. Also, text or combinations of text and numbers, as well as numbers that don't require calculations, such as phone numbers. Text fields may contain up to 255 characters of information.

Text box control A bound control that is used primarily on a form to modify or add field data to an underlying field.

Text constants Text data entered into a cell as a descriptive label, title, or heading.

Thesaurus Word's feature that finds and inserts synonyms.

Title Master A special master that contains settings for slides formatted using the Title AutoLayout.

Toolbar A bar that contains buttons for accomplishing commands.

Transitions Special effects that appear as your slides go on and off the screen during a slide show.

Unbound control A control on a form or report that is not bound to a specific field.

Underline The rule added under text so that it stands out.

Ungroup Separate a graphic or drawn object into the individual pieces that, when combined, create the complete image.

Universal Document Viewing In Excel 2000, you can save a workbook in HTML file format and retain the fidelity of your native workbook format. By saving as HTML, you ensure that anyone with a Web browser can view your documents. Editing those documents is not a problem either because Excel 2000 allows you to "round-trip" them back into the original Office program without losing any of the functionality of the workbook file.

Update To change the field data contained in a record.

URL An acronym for Uniform Resource Locator, which is a Web page address.

Validation Rule property A property specifying the requirements for data entered into a record, field, or control.

Validation rule A property used to specify requirements for data entered into a record, field, or control.

Validation Text property A property specifying the message to be displayed to the user when a validationrule property is violated.

Validation text A property used to specify the message to be displayed to the user when a validation rule is violated.

View The four different ways you can display slides on-screen to make working with slides and slide features during development of a presentation more efficient.

Visual Clarity A PowerPoint feature that checks your presentations for font suitability and legibility of slide titles and body text.

Web Page Preview The view of a document that displays the document in Internet Explorer as a Web page.

"What if?" A "what if" analysis is the process of changing certain worksheet values to see the impact these changes have on other values.

Wizard A step-by-step assistant that helps you design specific database objects.

Workbook An Excel file containing one or more worksheets.

Worksheet A two-dimensional grid of data in a row-and-column format in an Excel workbook.

Worksheet area The specific portion of a worksheet in which you enter data, format cells, or enter formulas.

Wrap The feature in word that causes the text that won't fit on a line to automatically be moved to the beginning of the next line.

X-Y scatter chart A chart type used to compare data series for pairs of values.

Yes/No Yes and No values and fields that contain only one of two values (Yes/No, True/False, or On/Off).

Zoom The feature that increases or decreases the size of the text on the screen.

Index

Word 2000

Excel 2000

Access 2000

PowerPoint 2000

Internet Explorer

Outlook